The Dead Sea Scrolls in Ancient Media Culture

Studies on the Texts of the Desert of Judah

Edited by

George J. Brooke
Jutta Jokiranta

Associate Editors

Arjen Bakker
Jonathan Ben-Dov
Charlotte Hempel
Judith Newman
Eibert J. C. Tigchelaar

VOLUME 144

The titles published in this series are listed at *brill.com/stdj*

The Dead Sea Scrolls in Ancient Media Culture

Edited by

Travis B. Williams
Chris Keith
Loren T. Stuckenbruck

BRILL

LEIDEN | BOSTON

Library of Congress Cataloging-in-Publication Data

Names: Williams, Travis B., editor. | Keith, Chris, editor. | Stuckenbruck,
  Loren T., editor.
Title: The Dead Sea scrolls in ancient media culture / edited by Travis B.
  Williams, Chris Keith, Loren T. Stuckenbruck.
Description: Leiden ; Boston : Brill, 2023. | Series: Studies on the texts
  of the desert of Judah, 0169-9962 ; volume 144 | Includes index. |
  Summary: "Media studies is an emerging discipline that is quickly making
  an impact within the wider field of biblical scholarship. This volume is
  designed to evaluate the status quaestionis of the Dead Sea Scrolls as
  products of an ancient media culture, with leading scholars in the Dead
  Sea Scrolls and related disciplines reviewing how scholarship has
  addressed issues of ancient media in the past, assessing the use of
  media criticism in current research, and outlining potential directions
  for future discussions"—Provided by publisher.
Identifiers: LCCN 2022055765 (print) | LCCN 2022055766 (ebook) | ISBN
  9789004529724 (hardback) | ISBN 9789004537804 (ebook)
Subjects: LCSH: Dead Sea scrolls.
Classification: LCC BM487 .D449575 2023 (print) | LCC BM487 (ebook) | DDC
  296.1/55—dc23/eng/20221205
LC record available at https://lccn.loc.gov/2022055765
LC ebook record available at https://lccn.loc.gov/2022055766

Typeface for the Latin, Greek, and Cyrillic scripts: "Brill". See and download: brill.com/brill-typeface.

ISSN 0169-9962
ISBN 978-90-04-52972-4 (hardback)
ISBN 978-90-04-53780-4 (e-book)

Copyright 2023 by Travis B. Williams, Chris Keith and Loren T. Stuckenbruck. Published by Koninklijke
Brill NV, Leiden, The Netherlands.
Koninklijke Brill NV incorporates the imprints Brill, Brill Nijhoff, Brill Hotei, Brill Schöningh, Brill Fink,
Brill mentis, Vandenhoeck & Ruprecht, Böhlau, V&R unipress and Wageningen Academic.
Koninklijke Brill NV reserves the right to protect this publication against unauthorized use. Requests for
re-use and/or translations must be addressed to Koninklijke Brill NV via brill.com or copyright.com.

This book is printed on acid-free paper and produced in a sustainable manner.

Contents

List of Figures   VII
Notes on Contributors   VIII

1   Introduction   1
    Chris Keith

2   Studies in Ancient Media Culture: An Overview   9
    Travis B. Williams

PART 1
Past Perspectives on the Dead Sea Scrolls and Ancient Media

3   Textuality and the Dead Sea Scrolls: An Examination of Modern
    Approaches and Recent Trends   71
    Travis B. Williams

4   Is There a Spoken Voice in This Cave? Orality and the Dead
    Sea Scrolls   135
    Shem Miller

5   Ritual Studies and the Dead Sea Scrolls: A Review   156
    Michael DeVries and Jutta Jokiranta

PART 2
Present Perspectives on the Dead Sea Scrolls and Ancient Media

6   Book Production and Circulation in Ancient Judaea: Evidenced
    by Writing Quality and Skills in the Dead Sea Scrolls Isaiah and
    Serekh Manuscripts   199
    Mladen Popović

7   4Q169 (Pesher Nahum) in Its Ancient Media Context   266
    Pieter B. Hartog

8	The Copper Scroll: The Medium, the Context and the Archaeology 293	
	Joan E. Taylor	

9 Curated Communities: Refracted Realities at Qumran and on Social Media 335
  Charlotte Hempel

10 Orality and Written-ness in the Dead Sea Scrolls: Where Have We Got to and Where Are We Going? 358
  George J. Brooke

11 Rituals as Media: Shared, Embodied, and Extended Knowledge Mediation in Rituals 385
  Jutta Jokiranta

12 Rations, Refreshments, Reading, and Revelation: The Multifunction of the Common Meal in the Qumran Movement 415
  Cecilia Wassén

PART 3
Future Perspectives on the Dead Sea Scrolls and Ancient Media

13 Mediated Textuality: Ambient Orality and the Dead Sea Scrolls 453
  Maxine L. Grossman

14 The Dead Sea Scrolls: A View from New Testament Studies 472
  Chris Keith

15 The Dead Sea Scrolls: A Classicist's View 488
  William A. Johnson

  Index of Modern Authors 507
  Index of Ancient Sources 524

Figures

5.1   Common approaches to ritual: social cohesion, social order, and solidarity; social control, (resolution of) conflict, hierarchy, power; communication, symbolic information, meaning, performance as communication; change, efficacy, experience, performance as action   160

8.1   Jack Ziegler's plan of the Qumran caves area. Detail with marking. Courtesy of the EBAF   294

8.2   Henry de Contenson (top image, left) with three Bedouin workers outside Cave 3Q. Note the position of Cave 3Q is to the left, to the east. In the foreground, to the south, excavation equipment is located, not behind the figures. A large pile of excavated soil and debris lies on the steep slope at the front of the picture, along with boulders. It appears that the original front and south side of the cave collapsed sometime in the past. Black and white photograph. Courtesy of American Schools of Oriental Research   295

8.3   The Copper Scroll at the time of its discovery in March, 1952. Note that there is a small rocky protrusion above the lower scroll, and the upper larger scroll sits unevenly on top of this. Black and white photograph. Courtesy of American Schools of Oriental Research   297

8.4   Unopened rolls of the Copper Scroll on display in the Palestine Archaeological Museum. Note green (oxidised) coloration of the rolls, the damage to the outside edge of the larger scroll (lost top sections of columns III–VIII) and the line of small rivet holes at the bottom inside edge of the smaller scroll (ahead of column IX). Photo: John Allegro. Colour slide held by Manchester Museum: John Allegro. Courtesy of the Allegro estate   298

8.5   Detail of letters pressed into the copper scroll (second roll). Sections 16 to 18 = columns 9–10. Photo: John Allegro. Black and white print and negative held by Manchester Museum. Courtesy of the Allegro estate   299

8.6   Silver scroll amulet (PEF AO2049) found in Samaria, two rolls 31.2 mm and 10 mm high. Courtesy of the Palestine Exploration Fund, London   307

8.7   Plan of Cave 3Q and its surroundings. Drawing by Joan Taylor after Patrich, "Khirbet Qumran," Figure 2, 77   320

Notes on Contributors

George J. Brooke
is Rylands Professor Emeritus of Biblical Criticism and Exegesis, University of Manchester, UK. Amongst his recent publications are *Reading the Dead Sea Scrolls: Essays in Method* (2013) and (co-edited with Charlotte Hempel) the *T&T Clark Companion to the Dead Sea Scrolls* (2019).

Michael DeVries
is a Ph.D. candidate at the University of Birmingham, UK where his research focuses on the Qumran war tradition.

Maxine L. Grossman
is an associate professor of Religious Studies and director of the Meyerhoff Center for Jewish Studies at the University of Maryland. Her research scholarship engages with concepts of religion and identity formation in the sectarian Dead Sea Scrolls, and her publications include *Reading for History in the Damascus Document: A Methodological Study* and the edited volume *Rediscovering the Dead Sea Scrolls: An Assessment of Old and New Approaches and Methods*.

P.B. (Bärry) Hartog
is Assistant Professor of Ancient Judaism at the Protestant Theological University in Groningen. He is the author of *Pesher and Hypomnema: A Comparison of Two Commentary Traditions from the Hellenistic-Roman Period* (2017) and co-editor of *The Dead Sea Scrolls and the Study of the Humanities* (2018); *Jerusalem and Other Holy Places as Foci of Multireligious and Ideological Confrontation* (2021); and *The Dead Sea Scrolls in the Context of Hellenistic Judea* (2023).

Charlotte Hempel
is Professor of Hebrew Bible and Second Temple Judaism at the University of Birmingham, UK and Research Fellow at the University of Pretoria. She has published extensively on the Dead Sea Scrolls, including recently *The Community Rules from Qumran: A Commentary* (2020) and, co-edited with George Brooke, *T&T Clark Companion to the Dead Sea Scrolls* (2019).

William A. Johnson
is Professor of Classical Studies and the Schiff Family Dean of Humanities at Duke University. He works broadly in the cultural history of ancient Greece

and Rome, with particular interest in books, readers, and reading, and with a general interest in how literary pursuits intersect with cultural context and social structure. His publications include *The Oxford Handbook to the Second Sophistic* (2017), *The Essential Herodotus* (2016), *Readers and Reading Culture in the High Empire* (2010), *Ancient Literacies* (2009), *Bookrolls and Scribes in Oxyrhynchus* (2004). See further at profwilliamjohnson.com.

Jutta Jokiranta
is Professor of Hebrew Bible and Cognate Studies, University of Helsinki, Faculty of Theology; President of IOQS; Co-editor of STDJ; Author of *Social Identity and Sectarianism in the Qumran Movement* (Brill) and many articles and co-edited volumes. (Publications may be found at https://researchportal. helsinki.fi/en/persons/jutta-jokiranta/publications/.)

Chris Keith
is Research Professor of New Testament and Early Christianity at MF Norwegian School of Theology, Religion and Society. He serves as the editor of the Library of New Testament Studies and his most recent book is *The Gospel as Manuscript: An Early History of the Jesus Tradition as Material Artifact* (2020).

Shem Miller
is an Instructional Associate Professor for the Department of Philosophy and Religion at the University of Mississippi (Oxford, Mississippi) and a research fellow for the Department of Hebrew at the University of the Free State (Bloemfontein, South Africa). In addition to various articles treating poetry, orality, performance, and tradition in the Dead Sea Scrolls, his publications include *Dead Sea Media: Orality, Textuality, and Memory in the Scrolls from the Judean Desert* (2019).

Mladen Popović
is full professor of Hebrew Bible and Ancient Judaism at the University of Groningen, dean of the Faculty of Religion, Culture and Society, and director of the Qumran Institute.

Loren T. Stuckenbruck
is Professor of New Testament at Ludwig-Maximilian-Universität München. He has acted as editor for a number of journals and monograph series, and has published a number of monographs, edited nearly twenty books, and 160 articles in the areas of New Testament, Second Temple Jewish, early Christian tradition, and Ethiopian studies, including *The Myth of Rebellious Angels* (2017).

Joan E. Taylor

is Professor of Christian Origins and Second Temple Judaism at King's College London and Honorary Professor, in the Institute for Religion and Critical Inquiry at Australian Catholic University, Melbourne. She writes on ancient religious history, culture, archaeology and literature.

Cecilia Wassén

is professor of New Testament Studies at Uppsala University. A scholar of the New Testament and Early Judaism, she has published widely on the historical Jesus and his milieu as well as on socio-historical topics in the Dead Sea Scrolls. Her scholarly core areas include purity laws, gender, apocalypticism, and ancient meals. Her latest book, written together with Tobias Hägerland, is *Jesus the Apocalyptic Prophet* (2021).

Travis B. Williams

is Professor of Religion at Tusculum University. He has published numerous monographs and articles on various topics related to ancient Judaism and early Christianity, including *History and Memory in the Dead Sea Scrolls: Remembering the Teacher of Righteousness* (2019).

CHAPTER 1

Introduction

Chris Keith

The majority of the following essays were first presented at the "Dead Sea Scrolls and Ancient Media Criticism" conference on June 7–8, 2019, hosted by the Centre for the Study of Judaism and Christianity in Antiquity (then named the Centre for the Social-Scientific Study of the Bible) at St Mary's University, Twickenham. The original design of the conference was to bring scholars working on various aspects of ancient media culture (reading, writing, literature, education, textuality, literacy, orality, memory, ritual, etc.) in the Scrolls into direct dialogue with classicist William A. Johnson, and specifically his theory of reading cultures in the Roman Empire.[1] Some Qumran scholars, such as Popović,[2] had made initial applications of Johnson's work in this area, and there were also extant applications in New Testament studies.[3] We were

---

1 See especially William A. Johnson, *Readers and Reading Culture in the High Roman Empire: A Study of Elite Communities*, CCS (New York, NY: Oxford University Press, 2010); idem, "Towards a Sociology of Reading in Classical Antiquity," *AJP* 121 (2000): 593–627.

2 Mladen Popović, "Reading, Writing, and Memorizing Together: Reading Culture in Ancient Judaism and the Dead Sea Scrolls in a Mediterranean Context," *DSD* 24 (2017): 447–70. More broadly on issues of ancient media culture and the Scrolls, see Shem Miller, *Dead Sea Media: Orality, Textuality, and Media in the Scrolls from the Judean Desert*, STDJ 129 (Leiden: Brill, 2019) and Travis B. Williams, *History and Memory in the Dead Sea Scrolls: Remembering the Teacher of Righteousness* (Cambridge: Cambridge University Press, 2019), which were published the same year that we held the conference. See also now Lindsey A. Askin, "Scribal Production and Literacy at Qumran: Considerations of Page Layout and Style," in *Material Aspects of Reading in Ancient and Medieval Cultures: Materiality, Presence and Performance*, eds. Anna Krauß, Jonas Leipziger, and Friederike Schücking-Jungblut, Materiale Textkulturen 26 (Berlin: De Gruyter, 2020), 31; Laura Quick, "Scribal Habits and Scholarly Texts: Codicology at Oxyrhynchus and Qumran," in *Material Aspects*, 44–47; cf. Jonas Leipziger, "Ancient Jewish Greek Practices of Reading and Their Material Aspects," in *Material Aspects*, 149.

3 Larry W. Hurtado, "Manuscripts and the Sociology of Early Christian Reading," in his *Texts and Artefacts: Selected Essays on Textual Criticism and Early Christian Manuscripts*, LNTS 584 (London: T&T Clark, 2018), 99–114 (first published 2012); Larry W. Hurtado and Chris Keith, "Writing and Book Production in the Hellenistic and Roman Periods," in *The New Cambridge History of the Bible: From the Beginning to 600*, ed. James Carleton Paget and Joachim Schaper (Cambridge: Cambridge University Press, 2013), 77–78; Chris Keith, "Early Christian Book Culture and the Emergence of the First Written Gospel," in *Mark, Manuscripts, and Monotheism: Essays in Honor of Larry W. Hurtado*, eds. Chris Keith and Dieter T. Roth, LNTS 528 (London: T&T Clark, 2015), 22–39; John S. Kloppenborg, "Literate Media in Early

---

© CHRIS KEITH, 2023 | DOI:10.1163/9789004537804_002

nevertheless anxious to pour accelerant on the dialogue under the conviction that the community associated with the body of material discovered at Khirbet Qumran was a prime example of what Johnson called "a text-centeredness that is extreme,"[4] and one that attested distinct reading culture practices that could fill out scholarly perspectives of the broader Mediterranean context.

Scrolls scholarship already boasted impressive scholarship on the media culture elements of the texts, of course, and some of those scholars were invited to present. Johnson's model provided a useful heuristic for considering the Scrolls beyond the traditional concerns of Biblical Studies and within the wider book cultures of the Mediterranean. We also included within the scope of the conference an opportunity for a response from a scholar working in New Testament media criticism who was also engaging Johnson's work (Keith). Most important, Johnson himself attended the conference and provided a response from his position as a classicist.

These essays are the published proceedings from those discussions. It experienced some delays due to unforeseen issues, including the Covid-19 quarantine(s) of 2020 and 2021. We also took time to commission several chapters on additional topics, though we are conscious that this collection is in no way comprehensive. As editors, we express our gratitude to the patient contributors who had to wait longer than they should have to see their essays published.

1   Overview of Chapters

The Dead Sea Scrolls in Ancient Media Culture divides into three parts. After Travis B. Williams provides an overview of recent developments in ancient media culture in general as it relates to Biblical Studies (Chapter 2), Part 1 provides up-to-date and in-depth essays on the *status quaestionis* of three topics related to the Scrolls and ancient media criticism. In Chapter 3, Williams focuses more intently on trends associated with textuality in Scrolls scholarship. Topics covered range from work dedicated to the material characteristics of the Scrolls, such as their size, material, or the ink used on them, to work dedicated to broader topics such as the identity of the scribal community or the

---

Christ Groups: The Creation of a Christian Book Cultures," *JECS* 22 (2014): 25, 40–58. Cf. now Larry W. Hurtado, *Destroyer of the gods: Early Christian Distinctiveness in the Roman World* (Waco, TX: Baylor University Press, 2016), 249 n. 95, 250 n. 102; Chris Keith, *The Gospel as Manuscript: An Early History of the Jesus Tradition as Material Artifact* (New York, NY: Oxford University Press, 2020), 17–26.

4   Johnson, *Readers*, 112.

INTRODUCTION

Scrolls' status as a particular "collection." Williams finishes by focusing upon questions of education and literacy, where he underscores the distinction between reading and writing. This comprehensive essay on textuality paints the portrait of a history of scholarship that vacillates between the minutiae of the *realia* and the connections between that *realia* and the social and historical worlds in which they had currency.

In Chapter 4, Shem Miller provides an overview of orality and the Dead Sea Scrolls. He addresses specifically how scholars have understood three issues: oral performance; oral tradition; and oral authority. With regard to the first issue, Miller demonstrates that Scrolls scholarship was, from its outset, aware of at least some effects of oral performance, notably in scholars' categorizations of certain textual variants as related to oral reading of manuscripts. Miller thus rightly insists that the Scrolls should be considered "oral-textual" media since their production and reception inherently depended upon both orality and textuality. With regard to the Scrolls as "oral tradition," Miller argues for understanding this term not as a singular entity, or even as a particular state of tradition per se, but as a reference to a wide network of associations in which the passing and receiving of tradition is actualized. Because the contexts in which such tradition was transmitted orally, aurally, and textually was, at times, characterized by authoritative legal discussion, Miller argues against Schiffman and Jaffee on the issue of oral authority. Whereas these scholars, while noting the presence of orality and oral transmission, have argued that authority was reserved for written tradition, Miller demonstrates that at least in texts such as 1QS, a process is described where authority stems from oral-based discussion of the law among the community members.

Michael DeVries and Jutta Jokiranta provide a general overview of ritual studies and the Dead Sea Scrolls in Chapter 5. They describe the work of Catherine Bell and other founding figures in ritual studies, then detail how these studies were initially imported into Scrolls scholarship. Their essay not only focuses upon the application of ritual studies to the separate genres of literature within the Qumran corpus, but also holds in tension the different approaches to ritual as a mechanism of fostering community cohesion, challenging extant power structures and replacing them with others, communing with the divine, and providing social structure in the present, whether in reality or idealized. Particularly appropriate for the present volume, they note the important difference between rituals and textualizations of rituals that confront readers and scholars in the Scrolls. DeVries and Jokiranta conclude by gesturing toward the fact that there is more work yet to be done on the intersection of the Scrolls and ritual studies, a call that Jokiranta's single-authored essay will answer later in this volume.

Part 2 of the study represents examples of how scholars are currently addressing issues of ancient media in current research. It begins with Mladen Popović's essay on book publishing in ancient Judaism, which answers a simple question: "For whom was a manuscript copied?" Popović answers this question by interrogating two groups of manuscripts in the Qumran scrolls: the Isaiah manuscripts and the Serekh manuscripts. This essay breaks new ground by applying three categories of handwriting that Johnson developed for Oxyrhynchus material—deluxe/elegant, everyday professional, and substandard—for the first time exhaustively to these two groups of Qumran manuscripts. Also included are thorough considerations of line spacing, letter size, later scribal interjections, and other aspects of the material features of the scrolls. Entirely aware of the subjective nature of his procedure, Popović nevertheless demonstrates the likelihood that many of these manuscripts were copied for the personal usage of the copyist(s).

Following Popović, Pieter B. Hartog provides an analysis of 4Q169 (Pesher Nahum) in its media context. Hartog discusses this pesher's material features, such as handwriting, column size, and practice of writing the divine name in square characters, and then reconstructs a plausible context of usage. Hartog proposes that 4Q169 was a travelling manuscript of a teaching authority, influenced both by other written texts and oral teaching during study sessions.

In Chapter 8, Joan Taylor then offers a "thick description" of the fascinating Copper Scroll (3Q15) that describes geographical locations for hidden treasure, likely temple treasure. She provides a history of discovery, publication, and initial discussion followed by a description of the copper medium itself, including the words that appear on it, the means of their scribal production, the ambiguity of some words, and obvious presence of Mishnaic Hebrew as well as Greek loan words. On the basis of these and other details, Taylor argues that the Copper Scroll was a late deposit in Cave 3Q, placed there after an initial collapse of the cave and prior to another, post-68 CE and possibly in the Bar Kokhba era. It was a secretive text, intending to be read only by specialist readers capable of annealing the metal in order to unroll the scroll.

Charlotte Hempel's essay in Chapter 9, "Curated Communities: Refracted Realities at Qumran and on Social Media," brings an innovative approach to the perennial question of the mixture of textuality and reality in ancient portrayals of the past. Blending classical Humanities and the digital Humanities, she asks what studies on the curation of the self in modern social media can teach us about historiography. The net effect of Hempel's argument is to underscore the fact that ancient portrayals of communities in texts like the Community Rule or Damascus Document are also curations. Thus, contrary to a trend in Scrolls scholarship that has sometimes taken documentary texts as carrying a higher degree of "verisimilitude with the presumed practices of a movement,"

INTRODUCTION

Hempel makes a bid for greater nuance: "These inscribed communities only partially resemble life on the ground. The best way to conceive of the final product is of a blended textuality that draws on social realities which are skilfully curated in texts that also stake a claim in the thriving literary landscape of ancient Judaism."

After Hempel's essay on the mixture of reality and imagination in curated imagery, George Brooke addresses the mixture of orality and textuality in Chapter 10. Brooke offers a panorama of scholarship and clearly articulates the present state of the discussion. Focusing upon different reading and study contexts, scribal practices, and evidence of literacy and education, Brooke suggests throughout that orality undergirded and informed almost all textual activity. A secondary value of this essay is that Brooke frequently enlists the insights of similar discussions in classics or even Anglo-Saxon poetry, connecting Scrolls scholarship with trends in the broader Humanities.

In Chapter 11, Jutta Jokiranta considerably expands our consideration of the Scrolls as socially and historically embedded media by approaching them from the perspective of ritual studies. She convincingly demonstrates how the Scrolls and the rituals in which they are intertwined mediate shared knowledge, embodied knowledge, and extended knowledge, all of which contribute heavily, though in distinct ways, to the construction and management of a collective identity. As Jokiranta notes, ritual is ancient, but ritual studies is still in the beginning stages of contributing to Scrolls scholarship. One of the most innovative contributions of this essay is its focus on the impact of embodiment and bodily states in the transmission and comprehension of tradition.

Fleshing out the socio-historically conditioned nature of media transmission in the Qumran community, Cecilia Wassén argues in Chapter 12 that communal meals were a central component of group activities. "Membership in the association," she observes, "was manifested at the table." Wassén provides a thorough overview of such meals, carefully distinguishing between ordinary meals and special meals. She compares and contrasts the latter especially with the activities known through other Second Temple Jewish sources, such as Philo and Josephus, as well as the evidence of Greco-Roman voluntary associations. Wassén demonstrates the centrality of communal meals also to the reading, interpretation, and discussion of Scripture, and thus the role of such meals in the larger identity of Qumran as a "textual community."

Part 3 features responses from Maxine L. Grossman, Chris Keith, and William A. Johnson, which seek to assess the use of media criticism in current research and to mark out potential directions for future discussions. Grossman responds to the essays as a specialist in Second Temple Judaism and as a fellow Scrolls specialist. She notes the contributions of the essays in three areas—orality and writtenness, ritualization, and materiality—and contextualizes them even more deeply in current research. She closes, however, by focusing helpfully on a topic that is seemingly just waiting for a monograph-length study from the methodological base of this volume: tefillin. Despite all we do not know about tefillin, Grossman emphasizes what we do, which is that they are, in her words, "words as worn," language as material objects. Specifically as these material objects, tefillin were anchored into the ritual practices of the community. Grossman highlights the role of media studies in helping scholars ask questions not just about such ritualized language and practices, but also their social functions.

Keith then responds to the essays from the perspective of a New Testament scholar. He briefly discusses considerations of oral tradition in various streams of New Testament scholarship before suggesting that more serious attention was given to the ancient media context of the earliest followers of Jesus only after the work of Werner Kelber. Noting four important developments since then—performance criticism, integration of orality and textuality, memory, and materiality—he then considers how these developments arise also in the essays in this volume. In some cases, New Testament studies seems to be ahead of Scrolls scholarship while in others it lags behind, but, Keith suggests, the potential for scholars in these fields to benefit from sustained engagement is very high.

Johnson, whose work instigated the conference, closes the volume with a response from the perspective of Classics. Using Pliny the Elder's description of the Essenes as "marvellous beyond all the tribes of the earth" as a touchstone, he discusses simultaneously how the Essene theory affects other questions about the reading community (or communities) associated with the Scrolls as well as how such a community would have appeared to the wider impe-rial bookish cultures. Impressive similarities and differences emerge, includ-ing among the latter the common idea in Scrolls scholarship that Qumran consisted of a scribal community producing literature for themselves rather than wide circulation; Johnson notes that this would have been considered odd by many contemporaries in the Mediterranean. He ends with an appro-priate warning, however, about seeking parallels for reading communities in comparative research—despites similarities there was no single way that all ancient readers and writers went about their business.

2   Conclusion

This collection of essays functions as both a contribution to the ongoing dis-cussion of the scribal culture(s) of Second Temple Judaism and, within that broader construct, the community or communities associated with the Dead Sea Scrolls as well as an invitation and, hopefully, prompt for further work. Readers will undoubtedly have little difficulty in noting other texts or issues that could have been included, and we make no claim to comprehensiveness. They hopefully demonstrate, however, the value of approaching the Scrolls as media culture in and of themselves, and that such an approach to the Scrolls is beneficial for all scholars working on the textual communities of the ancient Mediterranean world.

Bibliography

Askin, Lindsey A. "Scribal Production and Literacy at Qumran: Considerations of Page Layout and Style." Pages 23–36 in *Material Aspects of Reading in Ancient and Medieval Cultures: Materiality, Presence and Performance*. Edited by Anna Krauß, Jonas Leipziger, and Friederike Schücking-Jungblut. Materiale Textkulturen 26. Berlin: De Gruyter, 2020.

Hurtado, Larry W. "Manuscripts and the Sociology of Early Christian Reading." Pages 49–62 in *The Early Text of the New Testament*. Edited by Charles E. Hill and Michael J. Kruger. Oxford: Oxford University Press, 2012.

Hurtado, Larry W. *Destroyer of the gods: Early Christian Distinctiveness in the Roman World*. Waco: Baylor University Press, 2016.

Hurtado, Larry W., and Chris Keith. "Writing and Book Production in the Hellenistic and Roman Periods." Pages 63–80 in *The New Cambridge History of the Bible: From the Beginnings to 600*. Edited by James Carleton Paget and Joachim Schaper. Cambridge: Cambridge University Press, 2013.

Johnson, William A. "Toward a Sociology of Reading in Classical Antiquity." *AJP* 121 (2000): 593–627.

Johnson, William A. *Readers and Reading Culture in the High Roman Empire: A Study of Elite Communities*. Classical Culture and Society. Oxford: Oxford University Press, 2010.

Keith, Chris. "Early Christian Book Culture and the Emergence of the First Written Gospel." Pages 22–39 in *Mark, Manuscripts, and Monotheism: Essays in Honor of Larry W. Hurtado*. Edited by Chris Keith and Dieter T. Roth. LNTS 528. London: Bloomsbury T&T Clark, 2015.

Keith, Chris. *Gospel as Manuscript: An Early History of the Jesus Tradition as Material Artifact*. Oxford: Oxford University Press, 2020.

Kloppenborg, John S. "Literate Media in Early Christ Groups: The Creation of a Christian Book Culture." *JECS* 22 (2014): 21–59.

Leipziger, Jonas. "Ancient Jewish Greek Practices of Reading and Their Material Aspects." Pages 149–76 in *Material Aspects of Reading in Ancient and Medieval Cultures: Materiality, Presence and Performance*. Edited by Anna Krauß, Jonas Leipziger and Friederike Schücking-Jungblut. Materiale Textkulturen 26. Berlin: De Gruyter, 2020.

Miller, Shem. *Dead Sea Media: Orality, Textuality, and Memory in the Scrolls from the Judean Desert*. STDJ 129. Leiden: Brill, 2019.

Popović, Mladen. "Reading, Writing, and Memorizing Together: Reading Culture in Ancient Judaism and the Dead Sea Scrolls in a Mediterranean Context." *DSD* 24 (2017): 447–70.

Quick, Laura. "Scribal Habits and Scholarly Texts: Codicology at Oxyrhynchus and Qumran." Pages 37–54 in *Material Aspects of Reading in Ancient and Medieval Cultures: Materiality, Presence and Performance*. Edited by Anna Krauß, Jonas Leipziger, Friederike Schücking-Jungblut. Materiale Textkulturen 26. Berlin: De Gruyter, 2020.

Williams, Travis B. *History and Memory in the Dead Sea Scrolls: Remembering the Teacher of Righteousness*. Cambridge: Cambridge University Press, 2019.

CHAPTER 2

Studies in Ancient Media Culture: An Overview

Travis B. Williams

1 Introduction

The Dead Sea Scrolls provide a window into the production, distribution, and reception of communicative media (words, texts, rituals, etc.)[1] in the Judean desert. Much of the focus of the first generation of Scrolls scholars was on the different ways that the documents might inform historical perspectives. But following the publication of the entire collection of manuscripts from Cave 4, new questions about ancient media have emerged. A growing awareness of the importance of communications culture in antiquity has begun to contribute significantly toward the study of the Scrolls and the community(-ies) who produced, preserved, and performed them. Scholarly engagement with ancient media criticism is still in its infancy, however. As a result, there is much about this interpretive approach that remains to be defined.

For the past decade, interpreters have worked to understand the Dead Sea Scrolls in/as ancient media. In the process, attention has been devoted to issues such as education, scribal habits, reading practices, literacy, oral tradition, memory, textual pluriformity, and the material characteristics of the manuscripts. Significant strides have been made through these efforts. But it has not always been recognized (or at least acknowledged) that such individual, specialized treatments actually contribute toward a much larger issue—the role of communicative media in the Second Temple period and their impact upon Jewish society. One of the main purposes of this volume, therefore, is to provide an analytical framework through which to organize and assess the study of the Dead Sea Scrolls from the perspective of ancient media criticism. This task involves asking about the availability and use of particular

---

1 Ancient cultures, like the one in which the texts in the Judean desert originated, communicated through a variety of forms. In this volume, we have limited our discussion of communicative media to three forms: oral, textual, and ritual. This is partly due to convenience and partly due to the lack of attention that other forms have received in scholarship. Non-verbal communication, for instance, is a fundamental means by which humans convey information to one another; yet the topic has only just begun to be taken up within biblical scholarship (see, e.g., Catherine Hezser, *Rabbinic Body Language: Non-Verbal Communication in Palestinian Rabbinic Literature of Late Antiquity*, JSJSup 179 [Leiden: Brill, 2017]).

© TRAVIS B. WILLIAMS, 2023 | DOI:10.1163/9789004537804_003

media technologies, the preference for certain media formats in specific socio-cultural contexts, the impact of the shift from one medium to another, and a number of related issues.

As a first step toward understanding how media criticism has shaped and could continue to shape the study of the Dead Sea Scrolls, it is crucial to consider the background out of which this approached developed. In what follows, therefore, we will explore how the study of ancient media has gained a foothold within the wider field of biblical studies, and we will preview some of the important theoretical perspectives that have fueled this media turn.

2 Ancient Media Culture in Biblical Studies

Media studies focuses on the ways that various forms of communication impact culture. Applied to the Bible and other related literature, this interdisciplinary field provides scholars with insights into the communicative contexts of the ancient world and the products that were generated therein. Over the last few decades, biblical scholarship has engaged ancient media culture in a variety of ways (e.g., manuscript production, education, oral tradition, ritualization, memory, etc.). It has only been recently, however, that ancient media studies has become recognized as an important and impactful discipline within the wider field of biblical studies.[2] This section is devoted to highlighting some of the key media-related discussions that have been undertaken by scholars of the Bible—many of which overlap with those that have begun to occur in Scrolls research—in order to properly contextualize the move toward media studies in Scrolls scholarship. It is in no way intended to be a comprehensive survey, but instead seeks merely to illustrate how media studies has begun to reshape and redirect modern approaches to the Bible.[3]

2.1 *Textuality*

The concept of textuality, as used here, refers to the various ways that individuals and groups communicate through written media, as well as any means of

---

2 For a review of the engagement with ancient media in biblical studies, see Raymond F. Person and Chris Keith, "Media Studies and Biblical Studies: An Introduction," in *The Dictionary of the Bible and Ancient Media*, ed. Tom Thatcher, Chris Keith, Raymond F. Person, and Elsie R. Stern (London: Bloomsbury, 2017), esp. 9–14.

3 A fuller review of media criticism within New Testament studies, see Nicholas A. Elder, "New Testament Media Criticism," *CBR* 15 (2017): 315–37 (although he omits issues related to textuality and ritual); cf. also J. A. Loubser, "What is Biblical Media Criticism? A Media-Critical Reading of Luke 9:51–56," *Scriptura* 80 (2002): 206–19.

support that makes such communication possible. Over the last few decades, media studies has exerted a profound influence on the approach that biblical scholars have taken toward textuality, both in terms of the questions that are asked and the evidence that is considered.

2.1.1 Education and Literacy

One way that ancient media culture has informed the study of the Bible is by providing a more nuanced perspective on education and literacy in antiquity. Efforts to properly understand these phenomena have begun by asking whether the necessary conditions for the emergence of a literate society were present in ancient Israel or in the Greco-Roman world of early Christianity. Among these prerequisites is the widespread availability of schools. Some years ago, André Lemaire suggested that schools were pervasive across Iron Age Israel, based primarily on biblical sources (e.g., Deut 6:6–9) and the existence of abecedaries, which were presumed to be the exercises of school children.[4] This view has since been extensively critiqued,[5] eventually leading scholars to adopt a more carefully reasoned position.[6] By way of summary, it has been concluded that "there was a mechanism in ancient Israel (defined broadly) that facilitated and orchestrated formal, standardized *scribal* education," but not necessarily "an educational system serving the non-elite masses."[7]

A similar type of correction has been offered to the discussion of education in ancient Judaism. It was relatively common within a previous generation of scholarship to find interpreters who defended the widespread existence of

---

4 See André Lemaire, "A Schoolboy's Exercise on an Ostracon at Lachish," *TA* 3 (1976): 109–10; idem, "Abécédaires et exercices d'écolier en épigraphie nord-ouest sémitique," *JA* 266 (1978): 221–35; idem, *Les écoles et la formation de la Bible dans l'ancien Israël*, OBO 39 (Fribourg: Éditions Universitaires, 1981); idem, "Sagesse et écoles," *VT* 34 (1984): 270–81. Cf. also Bernhard Lang, "Schule und Unterricht im alten Israel," in *La Sagesse de l'Ancien Testament*, ed. Maurice Gilbert (Louvain: Louvain University Press, 1979), 186–201.

5 E.g., James L. Crenshaw, "Education in Ancient Israel," *JBL* 104 (1985): 601–615; Menahem Haran, "On the Diffusion of Literacy and Schools in Ancient Israel," in *Congress Volume Jerusalem 1986*, ed. J. A. Emerton, VTSup 40 (Leiden: Brill, 1988), 81–95.

6 For a review of this discussion, see Laura Quick, "Recent Research on Ancient Israelite Education: A Bibliographic Essay," *CBR* 13 (2014): 9–33.

7 Christopher A. Rollston, "Scribal Education in Ancient Israel: The Old Testament Hebrew Epigraphic Evidence," *BASOR* 344 (2006): 50 (original emphasis). Others have allowed for the presence of schools in ancient Israel, but on a much smaller scale than proposed by Lemaire (e.g., Graham Davies, "Were There Schools in Ancient Israel?" in *Wisdom in Ancient Israel: Essays in Honor of J. A. Emerton*, ed. John Day, Robert P. Gordon, and Hugh G. M. Williamson [Cambridge: Cambridge University Press, 1995], 199–211).

Jewish schools in Hellenistic and Roman times,[8] a view based largely on literary evidence (e.g., Philo, *Legat*. 16.115–116; 31.210; Josephus, *Ag. Ap*. 1.60; 2.204; m. 'Abot 5.21; y. Kethub. 8.32a; b. B.Bat. 21a)[9] and the perceived need to train members of the community to read their sacred texts. But as this question has been further investigated in light of ancient media culture, biblical scholars have found it difficult to demonstrate that literate education was offered indiscriminately to Jewish children at this time.[10] What is more, through comparative analysis, especially with material drawn from Roman Egypt, scholars have been able to achieve much greater specificity regarding the nature of education in antiquity and how this situation impacted literacy.[11]

The window into literate education that is provided by media studies has been key to defining literacy in ancient Jewish and Christian communities. Most notably, scholars have recognized that the issue is more complex than simply asking whether a person[12] could read and/or write; and in this way, simplistic dichotomies that marked earlier treatments of the subject have given way to a greater appreciation for the diversity of literate activity. In antiquity, a wide range of reading and writing abilities could be subsumed under the large

---

8 So, e.g., Emil Schürer, *A History of the Jewish People in the Time of Jesus*, Second Division: *The Internal Condition of Palestine and of the Jewish People in the Time of Jesus Christ*, trans. Sophia Taylor and Peter Christie (Edinburgh: T&T Clark, 1885), 2:46–52; Shmuel Safrai, "Elementary Education, Its Religious and Social Significance in the Talmudic Period," *Cahiers d'histoire mondiale* 11 (1968): 148–69.

9 For skepticism over these literary traditions, see Shaye J. D. Cohen, *From the Maccabees to the Mishnah*, 3rd ed. (Louisville, KY: Westminster John Knox, 2014), 118–21.

10 On this the issue of Jewish education around the turn of the era, see further Catherine Hezser, "Private and Public Education," in *The Oxford Handbook of Jewish Daily Life in Roman Palestine*, ed. Catherine Hezser (New York, NY: Oxford University Press, 2010), 465–81.

11 The practical realities of literate education in the Greco-Roman world have been helpfully traced out by Raffaella Cribiore, *Writing, Teachers, and Students in Graeco-Roman Egypt*, ASP 36 (Atlanta, GA: Scholars, 1996); idem, *Gymnastics of the Mind: Greek Education in Hellenistic and Roman Egypt* (Princeton, NJ: Princeton University Press, 2001). See also Theresa Morgan, *Literate Education in the Hellenistic and Roman Worlds*, Cambridge Classical Studies (Cambridge: Cambridge University Press, 1998).

12 Most studies of ancient literacy have focused on the abilities of men, which is due in large part to the bias of the ancient source materials. Nevertheless, there is some evidence for the literacy of women in antiquity (see Ross S. Kraemer, "Women's Authorship of Jewish and Christian Literature in the Greco-Roman Period," in *"Women Like This": New Perspectives on Jewish Women in the Greco-Roman World*, ed. Amy-Jill Levine, EJL 1 [Atlanta, GA: Scholars, 1991], 221–42; Kim Haines-Eitzen, *Guardians of Letters: Literacy, Power, and the Transmitters of Early Christian Literature* [Oxford: Oxford University Press, 2000]; idem, *The Gendered Palimpsest: Women, Writing, and Representation of Women in Early Christianity* [Oxford: Oxford University Press, 2012]).

umbrella of literacy. This is why literacy is best conceived as a spectrum on which varying levels of skills could be marked.[13] On one end of the spectrum were those who were unable to read and write and who did not participate in textual culture due to financial limitations. Beyond this level, various gradations of abilities were represented: some might only be able to sign their names ('signature literacy'), while others might possess some facility to read and write but only very slowly at a remedial level ('semi-literate'). For individuals who progressed further, the other end of the literacy spectrum might be reached, namely, the mastery of the necessary skills that would allow one to read quickly and to write eloquently.

Further distinctions in ancient literacy might be drawn according to the language(s) in which reading/writing were undertaken. Scholarship has long been aware that ancient Judaism and early Christianity developed in a multilingual context. Much of the discussion in the 20th century focused on which language—Aramaic, Hebrew, or Greek—was most prominent in ancient Palestine during the time of Jesus.[14] More recently, however, media studies has alerted scholars to the various ways that a multilingual environment shapes social dynamics.[15] As it relates to literacy, the most important consideration involves the distinction between bilingualism and biliteracy. In the

---

13   See David E. Aune, "Literacy," in *The Westminster Dictionary of New Testament and Early Christian Literature and Rhetoric* (Louisville, KY: Westminster John Knox, 2003), 275–76; Harry Y. Gamble, "Literacy and Book Culture," in *The Dictionary of New Testament Background*, ed. Craig A. Evans and Stanley E. Porter (Downers Grove, IL: InterVarsity, 2000), 644. For a review of the various gradations of literate skills, see Chris Keith, *Jesus' Literacy: Scribal Culture and the Teacher from Galilee*, LNTS 413 (London: Bloomsbury, 2011), 89–107.

14   In recent scholarship, this debate has continued, although at a slower pace. While there are some who defend the notion that Greek was the *lingua franca* at the time of Jesus, known and used by Jews from all social and economic ranks (e.g., G. Scott Gleaves, *Did Jesus Speak Greek? The Emerging Evidence of Greek Dominance in First-Century Palestine* [Eugene, OR: Pickwick, 2015]), most have come to identify Aramaic as the principal vernacular in first-century Palestine (John C. Poirier, "The Linguistic Situation in Jewish Palestine in Late Antiquity," *JGRChJ* 4 [2007]: 55–134).

15   There is a growing number of studies that have begun to consider the world of the Bible from a sociolinguistic perspective (e.g., Willem Smelik, "Code-Switching: The Public Reading of the Bible in Hebrew, Aramaic and Greek," in *Was ist ein Text? Alttestamentliche, ägyptologische und altorientalische Perspektiven*, ed. Ludwig Morenz and Stefan Schorch, BZAW 362 [Berlin: De Gruyter, 2007], 123–47; Steven D. Fraade, "Language Mix and Multilingualism in Ancient Palestine: Literary and Inscriptional Evidence," *Jewish Studies* 48 [2012]: 1–40; Sang-Il Lee, *Jesus and Gospel Traditions in Bilingual Context: A Study in the Interdirectionality of Language*, BZNW 186 [Berlin: De Gruyter, 2012]; Hughson T. Ong, *The Multilingual Jesus and the Sociolinguistic World of the New Testament*, Linguistic Biblical Studies 12 [Leiden: Brill, 2016]).

Greco-Roman world, the ability to speak multiple languages was no guarantee that one could also read and write in each of those languages.[16] While some Jews living in and around Palestine would have been able to speak Greek, far fewer would have been literate in it. This is especially true of those lower on the socio-economic scale.[17]

These more nuanced perspectives on literacy have naturally led to debate over what percentage of ancient populations attained the various levels of literate abilities.[18] It should be noted that most scholars are hesitant to attribute widespread literacy to the nation of Israel during the First Temple period; instead, reading and writing seems to have been reserved for scribes and royal officials associated with the temple and military.[19] One recent discovery that illustrates the literate abilities of this latter group is the ostraca inscriptions from Arad, an isolated military fort in the southern kingdom.[20] Using algorithmic handwriting analysis and forensic examination, scholars investigated 18 samples from among the 100+ inscriptions preserved at the site. Within this group, the team were able to identify at least 12 different writers. This

---

16   Cribiore, *Gymnastics of the Mind*, 175.

17   See Scott D. Charlesworth, "Recognizing Greek Literacy in Early Roman Documents from the Judaean Desert," *Bulletin of the American Society of Papyrologists* 51 (2014): 161–89. Cf. Chris Keith, "'In My Own Hand': Grapho-Literacy and the Apostle Paul," *Bib* 89 (2008): 47: "In a primarily agrarian society, it was simply (financially) impractical for parents to send a child through the various levels of pedagogy that would eventually allow him (or, more rarely, her) to cite Homer or compose writing. Not only would this lose a worker for the family, the child's life likely would never present an opportunity for him (or her) to use that skill."

18   Some in classical scholarship have attempted to steer the discussion away from quantifications of literacy, particularly given the difficulties associated with the task (see Rosalind Thomas, *Literacy and Orality in Ancient Greece*, Key Themes in Ancient History [Cambridge: Cambridge University Press, 1992], 12; William A. Johnson, "Introduction," in *Ancient Literacies: The Culture of Reading in Greece and Rome*, ed. William A. Johnson and Holt N. Parker [Oxford: Oxford University Press, 2009], 3). Nonetheless, a case can be made for viewing this question as an appropriate (and necessary) starting point (see Michael O. Wise, *Language and Literacy in Roman Judaea: A Study of the Bar Kokhba Documents*, ABRL [New Haven, CT: Yale University Press, 2015], 23).

19   Representative of this majority position are: Ian M. Young, "Israelite Literacy: Interpreting the Evidence," *VT* 48 (1998): 239–53, 408–22; David M. Carr, *Writing on Tablets of the Heart: Origins of Scripture and Literature* (Oxford: Oxford University Press, 2005), 111–73; Christopher A. Rollston, *Writing and Literacy in the World of Ancient Israel: Epigraphic Evidence from the Iron Age*, ABS 11 (Atlanta, GA: SBL, 2010), 127–35.

20   See Arie Shaus, Yana Gerber, Shira Faigenbaum-Golovin, Barak Sober, Eli Piasetzky, Israel Finkelstein, "Forensic Document Examination and Algorithmic Handwriting Analysis of Judahite Biblical Period Inscriptions Reveal Significant Literacy Level," *PLoS ONE* (2020): 1–15.

number is very high given that the fort only accommodated approximately 20–30 Judahite soldiers, perhaps suggesting the existence of some type of educational system by which military personnel were trained. Some scholars, however, view evidence like this, as well as other discoveries of inscriptional writings from peripheral locations across ancient Israel (e.g., Izbet Sartah ostracon; Khirbet Qeiyafa ostracon; Tel Zayit abecedary) as proof of literacy within society more broadly during the First Temple period.[21]

With considerable methodological overlap, the same divide marks the study of literacy in Second Temple Judaism and early Christianity. It is generally believed that literacy was not widespread in the Hellenistic and Roman periods,[22] and therefore that most engagement with written materials came through the oral recitation of literature at public venues (e.g., synagogue, church). Estimations of this low rate of literacy often range from as low as 3% for ancient Jewish communities to 10–15% for the Roman empire more broadly.[23] Among those who adopt this perspective, it is usually agreed that Jesus, despite engaging in activities that invited an assessment of his

---

21 See, e.g., Michael D. Coogan, "Literacy and the Formation of Biblical Literature," in *Realia Dei: Essays in Archaeology and Biblical Interpretation in Honor of Edward F. Campbell, Jr., at His Retirement*, ed. Prescott H. Williams, Jr. and Theodore Hiebert, Homage Series 23 (Atlanta, GA: Scholars, 1999), 47–49; Richard S. Hess, "Literacy in Iron Age Israel," in *Windows into Old Testament History: Evidence, Argument, and the Crisis of Biblical Israel*, ed. V. Philips Long, David W. Baker, and Gordon J. Wenham (Grand Rapids, MI: Eerdmans, 2002), 82–102; Aaron Demsky, *Literacy in Ancient Israel*, The Biblical Encyclopaedia Library 28 (Jerusalem: Bialik Institute, 2012) (Hebrew); idem, "Researching Literacy in Ancient Israel—New Approaches and Recent Developments," in *'See, I Will Bring a Scroll Recounting What Befell Me' (Ps 40:8): Epigraphy and Daily Life from the Bible to the Talmud, Dedicated to the Memory of Professor Hanan Eshel*, ed. Esther Eshel and Yigal Levin, JAJSup 12 (Göttingen: Vandenhoeck & Ruprecht, 2014), 89–104.

22 Examples of those who have projected low levels of literacy during the Hellenistic and Roman periods include: Catherine Hezser, *Jewish Literacy in Roman Palestine*, TSAJ 81 (Tübingen: Mohr Siebeck, 2001); Meier Bar-Ilan, "Writing in Ancient Israel and Early Judaism: Part Two: Scribes and Books in the Late Second Commonwealth and Rabbinic Period," in *Mikra: Text, Translation, Reading and Interpretation of the Hebrew Bible in Ancient Judaism and Early Christianity*, ed. M. J. Mulder and Harry Sysling (Peabody: Hendrickson, 2004), 21–38; Larry W. Hurtado and Chris Keith, "Writing and Book Production in the Hellenistic and Roman Periods," in *The New Cambridge History of the Bible: From the Beginnings to 600*, ed. James Carleton Paget and Joachim Schaper (Cambridge: Cambridge University Press, 2013), 63–80; Wise, *Language and Literacy*.

23 For an estimate of less than a 3% literacy rate among ancient Jewish communities, see Meier Bar-Ilan, "Illiteracy in the Land of Israel in the First Centuries CE," in *Essays in the Social-Scientific Study of Judaism and Jewish Society*. Vol. 2. ed. Simcha Fishbane, Stuart Schoenfeld, and A. Goldschlaeger (New York, NY: Ktav, 1992), 46–61. For an estimate of a 10–15% literacy rate among the general populace of the empire, see Pieter J. J. Botha, "Greco-Roman Literacy as Setting for New Testament Writings," *Neot* 26 (1992): 199.

scribal-literature status, was also outside of this literate minority.[24] The basis for this view is the fact that the necessary preconditions to support mass literacy were lacking in antiquity. These include an extensive network of subsidized schools to provide literate education, the availability of low-cost reading and writing materials as well as aids to reading (e.g., eyeglasses), the social and economic value in large quantities of the population being able to read and write, and religious motivation to educate large numbers of people.[25]

Nonetheless, there are some scholars who are much more optimistic about literacy rates at the time of Jesus.[26] While most avoid postulating specific percentages,[27] they agree that active participation in reading and writing was not reserved for a small minority of elites within the early Christian communities. Moreover, some even claim that this literate membership is a reflection of the group's founder, with Jesus himself having been educated in a Jewish school and thus capable of reading literature (Luke 4:16–17).[28] Claims like these are commonly supported by an appeal to the prevalence of certain forms of media in the Greco-Roman world. Among them are the numerous

---

24   On the illiteracy of the historical Jesus, see Pieter F. Craffert and Pieter J. J. Botha, "Why Jesus Could Walk on the Sea but He Could Not Read or Write," *Neot* 39 (2005): 5–35; Tom Thatcher, *Jesus the Riddler: The Power of Ambiguity in the Gospels* (Louisville, KY: Westminster John Knox, 2006); Keith, *Jesus' Literacy*. Some would even go so far as to question the literate abilities and training of the apostle Paul (see, e.g., Pieter J. J. Botha, "Letter Writing and Oral Communication in Antiquity: Suggested Implications for the Interpretation of Paul's Letter to the Galatians," *Scriptura* 42 [1992]: 17–34; Ryan S. Schellenberg, *Rethinking Paul's Rhetorical Education: Comparative Rhetoric and 2 Corinthians 10–13*, ECL 10 [Atlanta, GA: SBL, 2013]).

25   See further William V. Harris, *Ancient Literacy* (Cambridge, MA: Harvard University Press, 1989), 13–21.

26   E.g., Alan Millard, *Reading and Writing in the Time of Jesus* (Washington Square, NY: New York University Press, 2000), 154–84; Everett Ferguson, *Backgrounds of Early Christianity*, 3rd ed. [Grand Rapids, MI: Eerdmans, 2009], 109–113; Craig A. Evans, *Jesus and His World: The Archaeological Evidence* (Louisville, KY: Westminster John Knox, 2012), 63–88.

27   One exception is Udo Schnelle ("Das frühe Christentum und die Bildung," *NTS* 61 [2015]: 113–43), who proposes that in urban contexts, as much as 50% of a given Christian congregation may have been literate. Even more specificity is provided by Edward D. Andrews (*The Reading Culture of Early Christianity: The Production, Publication, Circulation, and Use of Books in Early Christian Church* [Cambridge, OH: Christian Publishing House, 2019], 108–109). He suggests the following literacy scale in early Christianity: full illiteracy (20%); fragmentary literacy (40%); fundamental literacy (20%); functional literacy (15%); proficient literacy (3%); full literacy (2%).

28   Recent interpreters who defend the literacy of Jesus include: Tor Vegge, "The Literacy of Jesus the Carpenter's Son: On the Literary Style in the Words of Jesus," *ST* 59 (2005): 19–37; Paul Foster, "Educating Jesus: The Search for a Plausible Context," *JSHJ* 4 (2006): 7–33; Paul Rhodes Eddy and Gregory A. Boyd, *The Jesus Legend: A Case for the Historical Reliability of the Synoptic Tradition* (Grand Rapids, MI: Baker Academic, 2007), 247–49.

public inscriptions (e.g., honorary decrees, gravestones, dedications, etc.) scattered throughout civic communities.[29] The widespread occurrence of this phenomenon is thought to indicate that non-elite members of society possessed some level of literate abilities, otherwise the words merely performed a symbolic function. But aside from vast opportunities to read, scholars also point to the numerous examples of informal writing, many of which were undertaken by those from lower social and economic statuses. Examples include graffiti found at sites like Pompeii, or the large cache of non-literary documents discovered at Oxyrhynchus.[30]

2.1.2 Textual Fluidity

When we turn to the question of what was being read in antiquity, we come upon a whole other set of questions related to manuscripts and the texts that were recorded on them. Throughout much of the time that critical inquiry has been applied to the Bible, scriptural writings have been interpreted against a backdrop that was familiar to scholars, *viz.* modern print culture. Within a print culture, literature exists in a fixed form (e.g., a book), stemming from its close association with a given author. As this textual tradition is transmitted, its content remains stable due to reproduction procedures that help to facilitate identical forms. Informed by this model, earlier analysis of scriptural documents commonly proceeded from the typographic assumption that all works began with an "original" and that variants must be judged as deviations from this norm.

The turn toward media studies, however, has caused scholars to re-examine these texts in light of their origin within an ancient manuscript culture. This environment is marked by the recording of information on handwritten documents that are subsequently transmitted by copyists. Among the chirographic

---

29 See Evans, *Jesus and His World*, 65: "The impression one gains is that everybody was expected to be able to read; otherwise, what was the point of all of these expensive inscriptions, incised on stone?" For a challenge to this line of reasoning, see William V. Harris, "Literacy and Epigraphy I," *ZPE* 52 (1983): 87–111; idem, "Inscriptions, Their Readers, and Literacy," *JRA* 22 (2009): 503–507.

30 Several biblical scholars have proposed more widespread literacy among sub-elite groups in antiquity on the basis of the graffiti evidence (e.g., James R. Harrison, *Paul and the Imperial Authorities at Thessalonica and Rome: A Study in the Conflict of Ideology*, WUNT 273 [Tübingen: Mohr Siebeck, 2011], 20–21; Bruce W. Longenecker, *In Stone and Story: Early Christians in the Roman World* [Grand Rapids, MI: Baker Academic, 2020], 148–50) and on the basis of the non-literary papyri (e.g., Eldon J. Epp, "The Codex and Literacy in Early Christianity and at Oxyrhynchus: Issues Raised by Harry Y. Gamble's *Books and Readers in the Early Church*," *CRBR* 11 [1998]: 26–32; Ferguson, *Backgrounds of Early Christianity*, 111).

traditions that are formed, one fundamental characteristic is fluidity (or variance); that is, "texts are constantly in a process of change, both through scribal reworking and copying, and through the work of active readers taking notes in the margins and otherwise interfering with the text."[31]

The impact of interpreting the biblical evidence against the backdrop of ancient manuscript culture has been especially profound in the field of textual criticism. Not only has the purpose of the discipline been re-evaluated, the nature and relationships of the ancient manuscripts themselves have been reassessed. With regard to the Hebrew Bible, the situation is most clearly reflected in the attempt to produce the first eclectic edition of the Tanak (The Hebrew Bible: A Critical Edition, formerly known as the Oxford Hebrew Bible).[32] This collaborative effort attempts to produce a text consisting of the "best" readings selected from different source materials, rather than the readings from a single manuscript (i.e., a diplomatic edition).[33] But what makes this work unique is how it represents the textual pluriformity that existed in antiquity. Since many of the books that make up the Hebrew Bible circulated in multiple editions, this critical text lists multiple archetypes in parallel columns, thereby preserving (rather than masking) the diversity.[34] To this point, only one volume has been published (Proverbs), but more are expected in the future.

---

31   Hugo Lundhaug and Liv Ingeborg Lied, "Studying Snapshots: On Manuscript Culture, Textual Fluidity, and New Philology," in *Snapshots of Evolving Traditions: Jewish and Christian Manuscript Culture, Textual Fluidity, and New Philology*, ed. Hugo Lundhaug and Liv Ingeborg Lied, TUGAL 175 (Berlin: De Gruyter, 2017), 4. The quality of textual variation within chirographs in a manuscript culture is commonly referred to as "mouvance" (see Paul Zumthor, *Oral Poetry: An Introduction*, trans. Kathryn Murphy-Judy, Theory and History of Literature 70 [Minneapolis, MN: University of Minnesota Press, 1990], 103, 203).

32   Ronald Hendel, "The Oxford Hebrew Bible: Prologue to a New Critical Edition," *VT* 58 (2008): 324–51. For the rationale behind the production of The Hebrew Bible: A Critical Edition, see Ronald Hendel, *Steps to a New Edition of the Hebrew Bible*, TCSt 10 (Atlanta, GA: SBL, 2016). For some questions and reservations about this approach, see Hugh G. M. Williamson, "Do We Need A New Bible? Reflections on the Proposed Oxford Hebrew Bible," *Bib* 90 (2009): 153–75; Eibert J. C. Tigchelaar, "Editing the Hebrew Bible: An Overview of Some Problems," in *Editing the Bible: Assessing the Task Past and Present*, ed. John S. Kloppenborg and Judith Newman, RBS 69 (Atlanta, GA: SBL, 2012), 53–60.

33   Alternatively, the Hebrew University Bible Project is a modern, diplomatic edition. For a defense of this approach toward a textual edition of the Hebrew Bible, see Michael Segal, "Methodological Consideration in the Preparation of an Edition of the Hebrew Bible," in *The Text of the Hebrew Bible and Its Editions: Studies in Celebration of the Fifth Centennial of the Complutensian Polygot*, ed. Andrés Piquer Otero and Pablo A. Torijano Morales, Supplements to the Textual History of the Bible 1 (Leiden: Brill, 2017), 34–55.

34   See Sidnie White Crawford, Jan Joosten, and Eugene Ulrich, "Sample Editions of the Oxford Hebrew Bible: Deuteronomy 32:1–9, 1 Kings 11:1–8, and Jeremiah 27:1–10 (34 G),"

Given the nature of the available evidence, an entirely new approach toward textual criticism has been introduced in New Testament studies. The Coherence-Based Genealogical Method (CBGM), which serves as the basis for the *Editio Critica Maior* and Nestle-Aland 28th edition, was designed to trace the genealogical relationships among extant witnesses, allowing textual variants to be both counted and weighed.[35] In this approach, scholars employ the traditional canons of textual criticism to assess variants and to determine their relationship to one another and, by implication, their witnesses. On the basis of their text critical decisions, scholars can then construct computer-generated representations of the genealogical connections of all witnesses and can thus illustrate the "textual flow" of the tradition.[36] So rather than giving preferential treatment to variants because of their attestation in a particular text-type, the CBGM allows for scholars to consider the place of individual manuscripts within the textual transmission and thereby to make more precise judgments about the relative weight of external evidence.[37] Through this type of assessment, practitioners seek not the "original" text, but the *Ausgangstext* (i.e.,

---

VT 58 (2008): 352–66; cf. also Ronald Hendel, "Plural Texts and Literary Criticism: For Instance, 1 Sam 17," *Textus* 23 (2007): 97–114.

35   See Gerd Mink, "Ein umfassende Genealogie der neutestamentlichen Überlieferung," *NTS* 39 (1993): 481–99; idem, "Problems of a Highly Contaminated Tradition, the New Testament: Stemmata of Variants as a Source of a Genealogy for Witnesses," in *Studies in Stemmatology II*, ed. Pieter van Reenen, August den Hollander, Margot van Mulken (Philadelphia, PA: John Benjamins, 2004), 13–85; idem, "Contamination, Coherence, and Coincidence in Textual Transmission: The Coherence-Based Genealogical Method (CBGM) as a Complement and Corrective to Existing Approaches," in *The Textual History of the Greek New Testament: Changing View in Contemporary Research*, ed. Klaus Wachtel and Michael W. Holmes, SBLTCS 8 (Atlanta, GA: SBL, 2011), 141–216. Cf. also Klaus Wachtel, "The Coherence-Based Genealogical Method: A New Way to Reconstruct the Text of the Greek New Testament," in *Editing the Bible: Assessing the Task Past and Present*, ed. John S. Kloppenborg and Judith Newman, RBS 69 (Atlanta, GA: SBL, 2012), 123–38. For a brief comparison of the CBGM with the grouping approach, see David C. Parker, *Textual Scholarship and the Making of the New Testament* (Oxford: Oxford University Press, 2012), 76–100.

36   For this reason, Yii-Jan Lin notes that "it may be easier to think of CBGM not as a method, but rather as an application that textual critics can utilize to generate results based on whatever philological method they choose" (*The Erotic Life of Manuscripts: New Testament Textual Criticism and the Biological Sciences* [Oxford: Oxford University Press, 2016], 125).

37   Cf. Klaus Wachtel, "Toward a Redefinition of External Criteria: The Role of Coherence in Assessing the Origin of Variants," in *Textual Variation: Theological and Social Tendencies? Papers from the Fifth Birmingham Colloquium on the Textual Criticism of the New Testament*, ed. Hugh A. G. Houghton and David C. Parker, TS 3/6 (Piscataway, NJ: Gorgias, 2008), 126.

the earliest accessible text).[38] Still in its infancy, this genealogical approach to the New Testament text has only been applied—in a comprehensive manner—to the Gospel of John and the Catholic Epistles, but the results thus far have been promising.[39]

2.1.3 Manuscripts as Artifacts

Another way that the focus of biblical scholarship has shifted is through an engagement with material philology (aka new philology). This approach toward written documents originated in medieval studies, initially emerging in response to "the problem of manuscript variation and the contradictory objectives of retrieving the authentic form of a text while taking seriously the available manuscript evidence."[40] Rather than treating manuscripts as witnesses to or as (varying) representatives of an ideal text form, material philology began to focus on manuscripts as material artifacts. Accordingly, manuscripts represent physical embodiments of the text whose production was shaped by a number of complex factors within a specific social setting. Consideration is thus afforded to material characteristics alongside textual features. Through this interpretive lens, attention is given, for instance, to the ways that the size and shape of manuscripts might impact the display of a text, or what marginalia and annotations might reveal about the ways that ancient readers accessed a document.

As scholars have begun to transfer this focus to biblical studies, it has created a renewed interest in the physical characteristics of the manuscripts themselves. In particular, influenced by the work of the French literary critic

---

38   On the complex and diverse senses of the term "original" text, see Eldon Jay Epp, "The Multivalence of the Term 'Original Text' in New Testament Textual Criticism," *HTR* 92 (1999): 245–81; Michael W. Holmes, "From 'Original Text' to 'Initial Text': The Traditional Goal of New Testament Textual Criticism in Contemporary Discussion," in *The Text of the New Testament in Contemporary Research: Essays on the Status Quaestionis*, 2nd ed., ed. Bart D. Ehrman and Michael W. Holmes, NTTSD 42 (Leiden: Brill, 2012), 637–88.

39   For a helpful review and evaluation of this approach, see Tommy Wasserman and Peter J. Gurry, *A New Approach to Textual Criticism: An Introduction to the Coherence-Based Genealogical Method*, RBS 80 (Atlanta, GA: SBL, 2017); cf. also Peter J. Gurry, "How Your Greek NT Is Changing: A Simple Introduction to the Coherence-Based Genealogical Method (CBGM)," *JETS* 59 (2016): 675–89; idem, *A Critical Examination of the Coherence-Based Genealogical Method in New Testament Textual Criticism*, NTTSD 55 (Leiden: Brill, 2017); cf. also Stephen C. Carlson, "A Bias at the Heart of the Coherence-Based Genealogical Method (CBGM)," *JBL* 139 (2020): 319–40.

40   Lundhaug and Lied, "Studying Snapshots," 3. For more on material philology, see Stephen Nichols, "The New Philology. Introduction: Philology in a Manuscript Culture," *Speculum* 65 (1990): 1–10; Bernard Cerquiglini, *In Praise of the Variant: A Critical History of Philology*, trans. Betsy Wing (Baltimore, MD: Johns Hopkins University Press, 1999).

Gérard Genette,[41] it is becoming increasingly popular to explore paratextual elements.[42] The designation "paratext," as used in manuscript studies, refers to the features of a manuscript—both content (e.g., annotations, titles, etc.) and physical characteristics (e.g., dimensions of the writing block, ruling patterns, etc.)[43]—that impact how readers experience a text. Many ancient manuscripts, particularly those of the Greek New Testament, contain aesthetic qualities, whereby scribes might decorate (e.g., a headpiece at the beginning of a book; ornamented letters) or visually represent certain aspects of the text (e.g., author images). It is also common to find paratextual markers designed to facilitate and better inform a reader's understanding of the content in a given document (e.g., prefaces, commentaries, marginal notes).[44] One that has received attention in recent scholarship has been the titles that appear either at the beginning or end of a New Testament text. Through the lens of material philology, scholars have drawn attention to the fact that these titles, which

---

41 See Gérard Genette, *The Architext: An Introduction*, trans. Jane E. Lewin (Berkeley, CA: University of California Press, 1992); idem, *Palimpsests: Literature in the Second Degree*, trans. Channa Newman and Claude Doubinsky, Stages 8 (Lincoln, NE: University of Nebraska Press, 1997); idem, *Paratexts: Thresholds of Interpretation*, trans. Jane E. Lewin, Literature, Culture, Theory 20 (Cambridge: Cambridge University Press, 1997).

42 Recent examples include: August den Hollander, Ulrich Schmid, and Willem Smelik, eds., *Paratext and Megatext as Channels of Jewish and Christian Traditions: The Textual Markers of Contextualization*, Jewish and Christian Perspectives 6 (Leiden: Brill, 2003); Garrick V. Allen, *Manuscripts of the Book of Revelation: New Philology, Paratexts, Reception* (Oxford: Oxford University Press, 2020). Various projects have been or are currently being devoted to the paratextual elements of New Testament manuscripts, see Martin Wallraff and Patrick Andrist, "Paratexts of the Bible: A New Research Project on Greek Textual Transmission," *Early Christianity* 6 (2015): 237–43; Darius Müller and Peter Malik, "Rediscovering Paratexts in the Manuscripts of Revelation," *Early Christianity* 11 (2020): 247–64.

43 Paratext is variously defined within scholarship. Rather than including physical characteristics of a manuscript, some would restrict its meaning to content that is directly dependent upon another text in the same manuscript (i.e., the protext) whose meaning it seeks to illuminate; thus, paratexts would be limited to features such as prefaces, annotations, titles, etc. (see Patrick Andrist, "Toward a Definition of Paratexts and Paratextuality: The Case of Ancient Greek Manuscripts," in *Bible as Notepad: Tracing Annotations and Annotation Practices in Late Antique and Medieval Biblical Manuscripts*, ed. Liv Ingeborg Lied and Marilena Maniaci, Manuscripta Biblica 3 [Berlin: De Gruyter, 2018], 130–49).

44 On the way that such introductory material shapes the transmission of particular interpretations of the content, see Eric Scherbenske, "The Vulgate *Primum Quaeritur*, Codex Fuldensis and the Hermeneutical Role of Early Christian Introductory Materials," in *Papers Presented at the Fifteenth International Conference on Patristic Studies held in Oxford 2007. Archaelogica, Arts, Iconographica, Tools, Historica, Biblica, Theologica, Philosophica, Ethica*, ed. Jane Ralls Baun (Leuven: Peeters, 2010), 139–44; idem, *Canonizing Paul: Ancient Editorial Practice and the Corpus Paulinum* (Oxford: Oxford University Press, 2013).

appear to be a very early addition (although whether they were included on the original autographs—whatever "original" might mean—is debated), include varying content, forms, and aesthetics.[45] Finally, paratextual features sometimes include systems of segmentation that assist in the navigation of a manuscript (e.g., page numbers, table of contents). Among these, scholars have devoted the most attention to the Eusebian canon, particularly focusing on the interpretative implications generated by this system of organization.[46]

2.2 *Orality*

The term 'orality' is used in scholarship with a number of different senses, and sometimes it can be difficult to discern the precise meaning. As it is used here, it simply refers to the various ways that individuals and groups communicate through oral media, including any means of support that makes such communication possible.

2.2.1 Oral Tradition

As far back as Hermann Gunkel's seminal efforts to identify the pre-written traditions of ancient Israel through the application of form criticism (*Formgeschichte*), scholars of the Bible have been interested in oral tradition. In much of early research on this topic, however, very little comparative analysis was undertaken. A seismic shift in the approach toward oral tradition

---

45 E.g., Simon Gathercole, "The Earliest Manuscript Title of Matthew's Gospel (BnF Suppl.gr. 1120 ii 3 / P⁴)," *NovT* 54 (2012): 209–35; idem, "The Titles of the Gospels in the Earliest New Testament Manuscripts," *ZNW* 104 (2013): 33–76; cf. Paolo Buzi, "Titoli e colofoni: Riflessioni sugli elementi paratestuali dei manoscritti copti saidici," in *Colofoni armeni a confronto: le sottoscrizioni dei manoscritti in ambito armeno e nelle altre tradizioni scrittorie del mondo mediterraneo: atti del colloquio internazionale, Bologna, 12–13 ottobre 2012*, ed. Anna Sirinian, Paolo Buzi, and Gaga Shurgaia, OrChrAn 299 (Rome: Pontifical Institute, 2016), 203–17. At the moment, a project is underway to document and investigate the titles found in New Testament manuscripts, see Garrick V. Allen and Kelsie G. Rodenbiker, "Titles of the New Testament (TiNT): A New Approach to Manuscripts and the History of Interpretation," *Early Christianity* 11 (2020): 265–80.

46 On the Eusebian canons in New Testament gospel manuscripts (with a focus on their paratextual function), see Matthew R. Crawford, *The Eusebian Canon Tables: Ordering Textual Knowledge in Late Antiquity*, OECS (Oxford: Oxford University Press, 2019); Garrick V. Allen and Anthony Royle, "Paratexts Seeking Understanding: Manuscripts and Aesthetic Cognitivism," *Religions* 11 (2020): 1–25; Martin Wallraff, *Die Kanontafeln des Euseb von Kaisareia: Untersuchung und kritische Edition*, Manuscripta Biblica 1 (Berlin: De Gruyter, 2021); Jeremiah Coogan, *Eusebius the Evangelist*, Cultures of Reading in the Ancient Mediterranean (Oxford: Oxford University Press, 2022). Cf. also T. J. Lang and Matthew R. Crawford, "The Origins of Pauline Theology: Paratexts and Priscillian Avila's *Canons on the Letters of the Apostle Paul*," *NTS* 63 (2017): 125–45, which considers the Priscillian canons in the Pauline corpus.

occurred in the mid-20th century, impacting both classical studies and biblical studies—even generating an entirely new field of study.[47] It was the ethnographic analysis of oral poetry by Milman Parry and his student Albert Lord.[48] After observing hundreds of performances of oral epics by South Slavic poets/singers (guslari), these scholars noted a significant feature about the composition of the oral texts: due to the formulaic nature of the ambient tradition, poets/singers often composed extemporaneously during the performance, which resulted in an oral text that was both traditional and innovative. This observation became foundational for what is known as the oral-formulaic theory.[49] When applied to written texts such as the epic poetry of Homer, which was the topic of Parry and Lord's interest, the oral-formulaic theory provided an important criterion by which to determine whether a written text had been composed orally. From the visible residue of oral themes and formula within the written materials, scholars could thus posit a text's oral origins. For many decades, this approach provided the methodological direction for evaluating ancient literature—not just of poetry, but of all genres.

A significant feature within the oral poetry observed by Parry and Lord was the illiteracy of the performers. From this, a sharp line of distinction was drawn between orality and textuality, with the two forms of media being considered fundamentally distinct and mutually exclusive. In subsequent scholarship, this oral-written dichotomy was further developed at the cultural level, resulting in what is now known as the Great Divide. According to this perspective, orality was the mark of primitive cultures who had not yet evolved literate media. When literacy finally developed within a society, this media shift marked a significant cultural revolution.[50]

---

47   For a review of the comparative study of oral tradition, see Werner H. Kelber, "The Comparative Study of Oral Tradition," in *The Dictionary of the Bible and Ancient Media*, ed. Tom Thatcher, Chris Keith, Raymond F. Person, and Elsie R. Stern (London: Bloomsbury, 2017), 252–59.

48   Although Parry, a classical scholar, initially laid the foundation for this project through his philological work (see Milman Parry, *The Making of Homeric Verse: The Collected Papers of Milman Parry*, ed. Adam Parry [Oxford: Oxford University Press, 1971]), it was Lord who completed the task after Parry's untimely death. The most important publication that derived from this project was Albert B. Lord, *The Singer of Tales*, Harvard Studies in Comparative Literature 24 (Cambridge, MA: Harvard University Press, 1960).

49   On the origins and development of the oral-formulaic theory, see John Miles Foley, *The Theory of Oral Composition: History and Methodology* (Bloomington, IN: Indiana University Press, 1988).

50   Important voices who contributed to the theoretical development of (what later came to be known as) the Great Divide include: Jack Goody, *The Domestication of the Savage Mind*, Themes in the Social Sciences (Cambridge: Cambridge University Press, 1977); idem, *The Interface between the Written and the Oral*, Studies in Literacy, Family, Culture, and the

In biblical studies, both the oral-formulaic theory and the Great Divide have played important roles in the development of scholarly hypotheses about the relationship between oral tradition and biblical literature. While the latter idea has now been discredited and almost entirely abandoned within scholarship,[51] it has served to clarify the discussion by compelling a more precise portrayal of the relationship between oral and written media. The former, on the other hand, continues to influence scholarship on the Hebrew Bible and the New Testament.[52]

The impact of both views is most clearly represented in the ground-breaking work of Susan Niditch on oral tradition and the Hebrew Bible.[53] Through an examination of the "oral register," Niditch seeks to identify various features of oral influence in the Hebrew scriptures, which include repetition, formulas, epithets, traditional referentiality, and the like. In this way, she places her

---

State (Cambridge: Cambridge University Press, 1987); Walter J. Ong, *Orality and Literacy: The Technologizing of the World* (London: Methuen, 1982); Eric A. Havelock, *The Muse Learns to Write: Reflections on Orality and Literacy from Antiquity to Present* (New Haven, CT: Yale University Press, 1986).

51 For critiques of the Great Divide thesis, see Ruth Finnegan, *Literacy and Orality: Studies in the Technology of Communication* (Oxford: Blackwell, 1988); Thomas, *Literacy and Orality*. The influence of this view within biblical studies has not been completely eliminated, however. Some, even while acknowledging more nuanced positions, continue to work from this framework (see, e.g., William M. Schniedewind, *How the Bible Became a Book: The Textualization of Ancient Israel* [Cambridge: Cambridge University Press, 2004], 91; Joanna Dewey, "The Gospel of Mark as Oral Hermeneutic," in *Jesus, the Voice, and the Text: Beyond* The Oral and the Written Gospel, ed. Tom Thatcher [Waco, TX: Baylor University Press, 2008], 73, 86).

52 For more on oral tradition in Hebrew Bible studies, see Robert D. Miller II, *Oral Tradition in Ancient Israel*, Biblical Performance Criticism 4 (Eugene, OR: Cascade, 2011); Raymond F. Person, Jr., "Orality Studies, Oral Tradition: Hebrew Bible," in *The Encyclopedia of Biblical Interpretation*, ed. Steven L. McKenzie (Oxford: Oxford University Press, 2013), 2:55–63. For more on oral tradition in New Testament studies, see Eric Eve, *Behind the Gospels: Understanding the Oral Tradition* (Minneapolis, MN: Fortress, 2014); Rafael Rodríguez, *Oral Tradition and the New Testament: A Guide for the Perplexed* (London: Bloomsbury, 2014).

53 For the fullest development of her ideas on orality and textuality, see Susan Niditch, *Oral World and Written Word: Ancient Israelite Literature*, LAI (Louisville, KY: Westminster John Knox, 1996). Cf. also idem, "Oral Tradition and Biblical Scholarship," *Oral Tradition* 18 (2003): 43–44; idem, "The Challenge of Israelite Epic," in *A Companion to Ancient Epic*, ed. John Miles Foley (London: Blackwell, 2005), 277–87; idem, "Epic and History in the Hebrew Bible: Definitions, 'Ethnic Genres,' and the Challenges of Cultural Identity in the Biblical Book of Judges," in *Epic and History*, ed. David Konstan and Kurt A. Raaflaub (London: Blackwell, 2010), 86–102; idem, "Hebrew Bible and Oral Literature: Misconceptions and New Directions," in *The Interface of Orality and Writing: Speaking, Seeing, Writing in the Shaping of New Genres*, ed. Annette Weissenrieder and Robert B. Coote, WUNT 260 (Tübingen: Mohr Siebeck, 2010), 3–18.

study firmly in the line of the formulaic approach. At the same time, Niditch is quick to emphasize the complementary relationship that exists between oral and written modes of expression, arguing that each played varying roles in the composition of different parts of the Hebrew Bible. Rather than an oral-written dichotomy, therefore, she describes textual production as a continuum,[54] on which some biblical literature is located near the oral end of the spectrum and other scriptural writings are placed much closer to the literate side.[55]

Important implications arise from this approach. Not only does it undermine the basic tenets of form criticism, which generally posits an evolutionary model of development whereby forms of communication progress from simple (oral tradition) to complex (written material), it also challenges the traditional source critical views of the Torah's composition, which assume a variety of written sources that are engaged by scribes through a strictly cut-and-paste technique. Furthermore, the interaction between orality and literacy proposed by Niditch has led to new and innovative ways of conceptualizing the transmission of the scriptural text.[56]

---

54 As an alternative, Jason M. Silverman suggests the designation "dialectic," indicating "the co-existence of two related, but distinct, entities which are in perpetual tension." In other words, "Oral and literacy are related ... because literacy comes out of and transforms oral modes. They are in tension because oral modes in some form *always remain* and have certain tendencies which contradict literate tendencies" (*Persepolis and Jerusalem: Iranian Influence on the Apocalyptic Hermeneutic*, LHBOT 558 [London: T&T Clark, 2012], 121; original emphasis).

55 For some interpreters, this model still represents an unnecessary polarity in which oral and written text are set up in opposition (e.g., Michael H. Floyd, "'Write the Revelation!' (Hab 2:2): Reimagining the Cultural History of Prophecy," in *Writings and Speech in Israelite and Ancient Near Eastern Prophecy*, ed. Ehud Ben Zvi and Michael H. Floyd, SymS 10 [Atlanta, GA: SBL, 2000], 122 n. 29).

56 Two scholars whose work has propelled scholarship forward on this subject are David M. Carr and Raymond F. Person, Jr. A few of their more important works include: Carr, *Writing on the Tablet of the Heart*; idem, "Torah on the Heart: Literary Jewish Textuality within Its Ancient Near Eastern Context," *Oral Tradition* 25 (2010): 17–39; idem, *The Formation of the Hebrew Bible: A New Reconstruction* (Oxford: Oxford University Press, 2011); Raymond F. Person, Jr., "The Ancient Israelite Scribe as Performer," *JBL* 117 (1998): 601–609; idem, "Text Criticism as a Lens for Understanding the Transmission of Ancient Texts in Their Oral Environments," in *Contextualizing Israel's Sacred Writings: Ancient Literacy, Orality, and Literary Production*, ed. Brian Schmidt, AIL 22 (Atlanta, GA: SBL, 2015), 197–215; idem, "Education and Transmission of Tradition," in *Companion to Ancient Israel*, ed. Susan Niditch (Oxford: Blackwell, 2016), 366–78. Some, however, have claimed that studies like these represent an over-emphasis on the oral environment of ancient Israel (see, e.g., Paul S. Evans, "Creating a New 'Great Divide': The Exoticization of Ancient Culture in Some Recent Applications of Orality Studies to the Bible," *JBL* 136 [2017]: 749–64).

Similar to the way that the work of Niditch provided Hebrew Bible scholarship with a firmer methodological foundation, in New Testament studies the impetus for the shift toward orality was (largely) provided by Werner Kelber.[57] Prior to his work, New Testament discussions of oral tradition were informed by perspectives of two prominent form critics: Martin Dibelius and Rudolf Bultmann. In their explanations of the transmission of the Jesus tradition, these scholars maintained that authentic memories of Jesus were concealed and obscured over time by the tradition that grew out of the contemporary disputes of the early Christian movement. As a result, firm distinctions were drawn between the memory that was hidden *within* the written gospels and the tradition that had accumulated *around* it. But drawing upon studies that illuminated how oral and written forms of communication interacted and mutually influenced one another, Kelber issued a serious challenge to this linear, evolutionary model of development. What he demonstrated, instead, was that the oral environment in which the written Gospels were composed significantly shaped their form and function, and that the shift from an oral medium to a textual medium represented a significant disruption rather than a natural conclusion.[58]

Since the time that Kelber first initiated this new approach toward orality, numerous other New Testament scholars have made important contributions to the discussion,[59] with most operating within the framework of the

---

57   Cf. Kelly R. Iverson, "Orality and the Gospels: A Survey of Recent Research," CBR 8 (2009): 77. This is demonstrated, in part, by the two separate volumes that have been dedicated to Kelber's work. See Richard A. Horsley, Jonathan A. Draper, and John Miles Foley, eds., *Performing the Gospel: Orality, Memory, and Mark: Essays Dedicated to Werner Kelber* (Minneapolis, MN: Fortress, 2006); Tom Thatcher, ed., *Jesus, the Voice, and the Text: Beyond* The Oral and the Written Gospel (Waco, TX: Baylor University Press, 2008). An earlier and very important challenge to the agenda of form criticism was also made by Birger Gerhardsson, *Memory and Manuscript: Oral Tradition and Written Transmission in Rabbinic Judaism and Early Christianity*, trans. Eric J. Sharpe, ASNU 22 (Lund: C. W. K. Gleerup, 1961).

58   Most influential among his many publications is Werner Kelber, *The Oral and the Written Gospel: The Hermeneutics of Speaking and Writing in the Synoptic Tradition, Mark, Paul, and Q* (Philadelphia, PA: Fortress, 1983). Cf. also idem, *Imprints, Voiceprints, and Footprints of Memory: Collected Essays of Werner H. Kelber*, RBS 74 (Atlanta, GA: SBL, 2013).

59   Some have explored the transmission of oral tradition (e.g., Kenneth E. Bailey, "Informal Controlled Oral Tradition and the Synoptic Gospels," *Asia Journal of Theology* 5 [1991]: 34–54; idem, "Middle Eastern Oral Tradition and the Synoptic Gospels," *ExpTim* 106 [1994]: 363–67, with varying responses: Theodore J. Weeden, "Kenneth Bailey's Theory of Oral Tradition: A Theory Contested by Its Evidence," *JSHJ* 7 [2009]: 3–43 and James D. G. Dunn, "Kenneth Bailey's Theory of Oral Tradition: Critiquing Theodore Weeden's Critique," *JSHJ* 7 [2009]: 44–62). Others have explored the social aspects of orality, particularly as it relates to textuality (e.g., Richard A. Horsley with Jonathan A. Draper, *Whoever*

oral-formulaic position. Following the approach of Ong, many have scoured New Testament writings to identify characteristics that mark oral communication (e.g., inclusio, parataxis, etc.).[60] This model, which has recently been described as a "morphological" approach toward oral tradition, has been challenged by Rafael Rodríguez.[61] The validity of the morphological approach, he maintains, is dependent upon two fundamental assumptions: (a) that identifiable, oral features in the gospels derive from prewritten oral tradition and not from written communication; and (b) that such features survive the transfer from one medium to another without alteration and apart from any disturbance of the written format. Since neither assumption has been (or can be?) demonstrated, Rodríguez proposes a "contextual" approach as a more natural alternative. Influenced by the work of John Miles Foley,[62] this contextual model of oral tradition "posits the oral expression of tradition as the context within which the written NT texts developed and were written by authors, recited by lectors (and/or oral performers), and received by audiences (and/or readers)."[63]

2.2.2 Reading and Performance

Reading involves the ability to cognitively decipher written letters and/or symbols with the goal of understanding their meaning. In antiquity, just as today, the ability to undertake this act was the direct result of a literate education (see above). But as straightforward as this practice may seem, questions about how reading was carried out in antiquity have the potential to significantly inform social realities operative in ancient Jewish and Christian communities. As scholars have turned toward ancient media culture to better inform the situation, a number of developments have occurred.

    Hears You Hears Me: Prophets, Performance, and Tradition in Q [Harrisburg, PA: Trinity Press International, 1999]; Richard A. Horsley, *Hearing the Whole Story: The Politics of Plot in Mark's Gospel* [Louisville, KY: Westminster John Knox, 2001]).

60   See, e.g., Joanna Dewey, "Oral Methods of Structuring Narrative in Mark," *Int* 43 (1989): 32–44; Pieter J. J. Botha, "Mark's Story as Oral Traditional Literature: Rethinking the Transmission of Some Traditions about Jesus," *HvTSt* 47 (1991): 304–31.

61   Rodríguez, *Oral Tradition*, 55–85. Cf. also idem, *Structuring Early Christian Memory: Jesus in Tradition, Performance and Text*, LNTS 407 (London: T&T Clark, 2010), 81–113.

62   See, e.g., John Miles Foley, *Immanent Art: From Structure to Meaning in Tradition Oral Epic* (Bloomington, IN: Indiana University Press, 1991); idem, *The Singer of Tales in Performance*, Voices in Performance and Text (Bloomington, IN: Indiana University Press, 1995).

63   Rodríguez, *Oral Tradition*, 72. Along similar lines, Kelber introduced the concept of a "biosphere," which he defined as "an invisible nexus of references and identities from which people draw sustenance, in which they live, and in relation to which they make sense of their lives." (Werner Kelber, "Jesus and Tradition: Words in Time, Words in Space," in *Orality and Textuality in Early Christian Literature*, ed. Joanna Dewey, SemeiaSt 65 [Atlanta, GA: SBL, 1995], 159).

The mechanics of reading has received the most attention. To understand how the act of reading was undertaken, scholars of the Bible have drawn on a long-standing discussion in classical scholarship. A previous generation of classical scholars maintained that the normal (or default) mode of reading literary texts in antiquity was through audible vocalization. In fact, it was argued that silently reading a text to oneself was highly unusual, even in private settings.[64] There is a twofold basis for these claims. The first is a passage found in *The Confessions* of Augustine, which describes the reading habits of Ambrose, bishop of Milan. What seems to intrigue Augustine is that Ambrose read silently with his eyes while "his voice and his tongue were at rest" (*Conf.* 6.3). This has led many scholars to conclude that such a mode of reading was unusual. The second reason why all reading is thought to have been performed audibly is because texts were written in *scriptio continua*, meaning that there was no space between words and no punctuation to distinguish sentences or paragraphs. To understand a text's meaning, therefore, required transferring the symbols to sounds. Only by reading the text aloud and hearing familiar sounds could one begin to work out how the letters should be grouped together.[65]

In recent years, the idea that all reading in the ancient world was carried out audibly has been espoused by numerous biblical interpreters.[66] This claim

---

64   Perhaps most influential in the propagation of this view, although its origins predated him by more than a century, was the study by József Balogh, "'Voces Paginarum': Beiträge zur Geschichte des lauten Lessen und Schreibens," *Philogus* 82 (1927): 85–109, 202–40. Thereafter, this view became widespread (see, e.g., Leo Wohleb, "Ein Beitrag zur Geschichte des lauten Lesens," *Philogus* 85 (1929): 111–12; Eugene S. McCartney, "Notes on Reading and Praying Audibly," *Classical Philology* 43 (1948): 184–87; Francesco di Capua, "Osservazioni sulla lettura e sulla preghiera ad alta voce presso gli antichi," *Rendicoti della Accademia di archeologie lettere e belle arti di Napoli* 28 (1953): 59–99; *et al.*

65   See esp. Paul Saenger, *Spaces between Words: The Origins of Silent Reading*, Figurae: Reading Medieval Culture (Stanford, CA: Stanford University Press, 1997), 1–17. Cf. also W. B. Sedgwick, "Reading and Writing in Classical Antiquity," *Contemporary Review* 135 (1990): 93; Nancy A. Mavrogenes, "Reading in Ancient Greece," *Journal of Reading* (1980): 693; Henri I. Marrou, *A History of Education in Antiquity* (Madison, WI: University of Wisconsin Press, 1982), 134.

66   E.g., Paul J. Achtemeier, "*Omne verbum sonat*: The New Testament and the Oral Environment of Late Western Antiquity," *JBL* 109 (1990): 15–16; Pieter J. J. Botha, "Mute Manuscripts: Analysing a Neglected Aspect of Ancient Communication," *Theologia Evangelica* 23 (1990): 43; Harry Y. Gamble, *Books and Readers in the Early Church: A History of Early Christian Texts* (New Haven, CT: Yale University Press, 1995), 203; H. Gregory Snyder, *Teachers and Texts in the Ancient World: Philosophers, Jews and Christians*, Religion in the First Christian Centuries (London: Routledge, 2000), 271 n. 35; Paul D. Mandel, *The Origins of Midrash: From Teaching to Text*, JSJSup 180 (Leiden: Brill, 2017), 233. In arguing this point, scholars commonly point to *scriptio continua* in the textual tradition (see,

has guided the direction of much of New Testament research on the subject. From this starting point, scholarship has focused primarily on group activities wherein written materials are read aloud for the benefit of the community.[67] But even more importantly, the mechanics of reading has become the foundation for new methodologies. Scholars have not been content to envision reading in these contexts as the mere recitation of words on a page; instead, in connection with a culture that is thought to be shaped largely by orality, these events are described as performative readings. In other words, those who conveyed the text are believed to have done so through a theatric, oratorical delivery. This might have involved reciting a text from memory with little to no interaction or dependence on a written manuscript,[68] and it normally consisted of changing one's voice and using hand gestures.[69] This new interpretive approach toward the biblical text is commonly known as performance criticism.[70]

---

e.g., Allen R. Hilton, *Illiterate Apostles: Uneducated Early Christians and the Literates Who Loved Them*, LNTS 541 [London: T&T Clark, 2018], 68).

67   Representative of this focus on communal reading are the studies by Dan Nässelqvist, *Public Reading in Early Christianity: Lectors, Manuscripts, and Sound in the Oral Delivery of John 1–4*, NovTSup 163 (Leiden: Brill, 2016) and Brian J. Wright, *Communal Reading in the Time of Jesus: A Window into Early Christian Reading Practices* (Minneapolis, MN: Fortress, 2017).

68   See William D. Shiell, *Reading Acts: The Lector and the Early Christian Audience*, BIS 70 (Leiden: Brill, 2004); idem, *Delivering from Memory: The Effect of Performance on the Early Christian Audience* (Eugene, OR: Pickwick Publications, 2011).

69   See Whitney T. Shiner, *Proclaiming the Gospel: First-Century Performance in Mark* (Harrisburg, PA: Trinity Press International, 2003). Similar ideas about the performance (rather than the simple recitation) of poetry can be found in classical scholarship as well. For a description and critique this view, see Holt N. Parker, "Books and Reading Latin Poetry," in *Ancient Literacies: The Culture of Reading in Greece and Rome*, ed. William A. Johnson and Holt N. Parker (Oxford: Oxford University Press, 2009), 186–229.

70   For a description of performance criticism, see David Rhoads, "Performance Criticism: An Emerging Methodology in Second Temple Studies," BTB 36 (2006): 118–33, 164–84; Peter S. Perry, "Biblical Performance Criticism: Survey and Prospects," *Religions* 10 (2019): 1–15. A few recent works that are guided by performance criticism include: Antoinette Clark Wire, *The Case for Mark Composed in Performance*, Biblical Performance Criticism 3 (Eugene, OR: Cascade, 2011); Pieter J. J. Botha, *Orality and Literacy in Early Christianity*, Biblical Performance Criticism 5 (Eugene, OR: Cascade, 2012); Joanna Dewey, *The Oral Ethos of the Early Church: Speaking, Writing, and the Gospel of Mark*, Biblical Performance Criticism 8 (Eugene, OR: Cascade, 2013); Richard A. Horsley, *Text and Tradition in Performance and Writing*, Biblical Performance Criticism 9 (Eugene, OR: Cascade, 2013); Bernard Oestreich, *Performance Criticism of the Pauline Letters*, Biblical Performance Criticism 14 (Eugene, OR: Cascade, 2016).

Despite the interesting prospects held out by this approach, there are many who would question its evidential basis.[71] The notion that all, or even most, reading in antiquity was performed audibly runs counter to a large amount of classical evidence. In a comprehensive survey of the conditions and practices of reading in the Greek and Roman worlds, Jan Heilmann has significantly undermined this thesis by producing a wide variety of texts that indicate that direct, non-vocalized reading was a common mode of literary consumption.[72] Evidence like this has caused classical scholars to revisit the question of reading mechanics, with most now abandoning the idea that silent reading was unknown in antiquity.[73] A more nuanced perspective has begun to replace the earlier view, one that takes into account a variety of factors impacting the nature of reading, including the method (e.g., voice, volume, speed), situation (e.g., location, time, duration, attitude, reading medium), and purpose (e.g., study, recording, evaluation, entertainment, meditation).[74] What is more, the other basic tenet undergirding the audible reading position (*viz.* the use of *scriptio continua* necessitates vocalization) seems just as prone to critique. As has recently been pointed out, *scriptio continua* does not present difficulties from the perspective of the cognitive processes of reading, nor was it described as difficult by ancient readers.[75]

---

71   For a critique of performance criticism, see Larry W. Hurtado, "Oral Fixation and New Testament Studies? 'Orality', 'Performance' and Reading Texts in Early Christianity," *NTS* 60 (2014): 321–40, with a response by Kelly R. Iverson, "Oral Fixation or Oral Corrective? A Response to Larry Hurtado," *NTS* 62 (2016): 183–200.

72   Jan Heilmann, *Lesen in Antike und frühem Christentum: Kulturgeschichtliche, philologische sowie kognitionswissenschaftliche Perspektiven und deren Bedeutung für die neutestamentliche Exegese*, TANZ 66 (Tübingen: Narr Francke Attempto, 2021). Others have similarly pointed out that silent reading was not an uncommon occurrence in antiquity, see Emmanuelle Valette-Cagnac, *La lecture à Rome: rites et pratiques*, Antiquité au present (Paris: Belin, 1997), 26–27; R. W. McCutcheon, "Silent Reading in Antiquity and the Future History of the Book," *Book History* 18 (2015): 1–32.

73   Within classical scholarship, there have been numerous challenges to the long-standing view that all reading was performed audibly. Some of the more important treatments are: W. P. Clark, "Ancient Reading," *CJ* 26 (1931): 698–700; B. M. Knox, "Silent Reading in Antiquity," *GRBS* 9 (1968): 421–35; A. K. Gavrilov, "Techniques of Reading in Classical Antiquity," *ClQ* 47 (1997): 56–73; M. F. Burnyeat, "Postscript on Silent Reading," *ClQ* 47 (1997): 74–76; Within biblical studies, see Frank D. Gilliard, "More on Silent Reading in Antiquity: *non omne verbum sonabat*," *JBL* 112 (1993): 689–96.

74   See further Heilmann, *Lesen in Antike*.

75   A helpful critique of this view is provided by Jan Heilmann, "Reading Early New Testament Manuscripts: *Scriptio continua*, 'Reading Aids', and Other Characteristic Features," in *Material Aspects of Reading in Ancient and Medieval Cultures: Materiality, Presence and Performance*, ed. Anna Krauß, Jonas Leipziger, and Friederike Schücking-Jungblut, Materiale Textkulturen 26 (Berlin: De Gruyter, 2020), 178–83.

The direction of scholarship on ancient reading practices has now shifted, moving away from questions of mechanics to the function of various reading practices. Here, scholars have taken a cue from classicist William A. Johnson, who focuses on the sociological dimensions of reading. His primary point of departure is the bookroll as a material artifact. What Johnson points out is that "the physical literary roll not only contained high culture, but was itself an expression of high culture."[76] In other words, the fact that books containing literary works were copied by scribes of the highest quality, with large margins that emphasized aesthetics over functionality, indicates that reading often involved more than the accumulation of knowledge. In many cases, reading was an activity through which elite Greeks and Romans constructed a particular social identity, with bookrolls displaying an owner's wealth and high status as well as his (or her?) education and refined culture. Based on this consideration, Johnson suggests that focus be given to the overall system of reading, including the way that specific "reading events" and the "reading culture" more broadly shaped the negotiation of social status.

Within New Testaments studies, some have begun to follow the direction proposed by Johnson, and to this point it has proven to be fruitful. In contrast to the exclusivity claims generated by the bookrolls of elite Greek and Roman readers, Larry W. Hurtado has suggested that Christian manuscripts were designed for a very different social setting. Against the background of the social display of status, Hurtado has argued that certain reading "aids" in Christian codices (which are much less frequent non-Christian manuscripts) were intended to make the scriptural text more easily accessible to a wider demographic. That is, the assistance provided by punctuation, sense breaks, and diacritical marks allowed readers of varying literate abilities to participate in the consumption of Christian literature.[77] Taking the concepts of

---

76 William A. Johnson, "Toward a Sociology of Reading in Classical Antiquity," *AJP* 121 (2000): 612. His ideas on this subject are further developed in subsequent works: idem, "Constructing Elite Reading Communities in the High Empire," in *Ancient Literacies: The Culture of Reading in Greece and Rome*, ed. William A. Johnson and Holt N. Parker (Oxford: Oxford University Press, 2009), 320–30; idem, *Readers and Reading Culture in the High Roman Empire: A Study of Elite Communities* (Oxford: Oxford University Press, 2010).

77 Larry W. Hurtado, "What Do the Earliest Christian Manuscripts Tell Us About Their Readers?," in *The World of Jesus and the Early Church: Identity and Interpretation in Early Communities of Faith*, ed. Craig A. Evans (Peabody, MA: Hendrickson, 2011), 179–92; idem, "Manuscripts and the Sociology of Early Christian Reading," in *The Early Text of the New Testament*, ed. Charles E. Hill and Michael J. Kruger (Oxford: Oxford University Press, 2012), 49–62; cf. also John S. Kloppenborg, "Literate Media in Early Christ Groups: The Creation of a Christian Book Culture," *JECS* 22 (2014): 44–58. Some have challenged the idea that the layout and paralinguistic marks in Christian manuscripts allow for the

ancient Roman "reading communities" in a different direction, Chris Keith has explored the implications behind the textualization of the gospel.[78] He demonstrates that the transition from an oral to a written medium was significant. The book, as a material artifact, played a key role in the formation of social identity in that the public reading of the gospels became a defining feature of Christian communities. Moreover, the book format was influential in the reception history of the Jesus tradition, leading to competitive textualization and the eventual adoption of a fourfold gospel canon.

2.2.3 Memory

With the turn toward media studies, scholars have also studied different dimensions of memory: cognitive, social, and cultural. Applying insights from the study of the cognitive dimensions of memory has been a particular focus within Jesus studies.[79] Some who have moved in this direction have hypothesized that eyewitnesses played a formative role in the transmission and preservation of the Jesus tradition.[80] Much of their attention has thus been devoted to psychological aspects of autobiographical (or more specifically, episodic) memory, including topics such as flashbulb memories, gist versus details,

---

diagnosis of the social situation in which they were used (see Heilmann, "Reading Early New Testament Manuscripts," 183–90, who notes that similar features are found in non-Christian inscriptions and papyri from a range of genres).

78　Chris Keith, "Early Christian Book Culture and the Emergence of the First Written Gospel," in *Mark, Manuscripts, and Monotheism: Essays in Honor of Larry W. Hurtado*, ed. Chris Keith and Dieter T. Roth, LNTS 528 (London: Bloomsbury T&T Clark, 2015), 22–39; idem, *Gospel as Manuscript: An Early History of the Jesus Tradition as Material Artifact* (Oxford: Oxford University Press, 2020).

79　A few interpreters have considered this question more broadly, however (see, e.g., István Czachesz, "Rethinking Biblical Transmission: Insights from the Cognitive Neuroscience of Memory," in *Mind, Morality and Magic: Cognitive Science Approaches in Biblical Studies*, ed. István Czachesz and Risto Uro [London: Routledge, 2014], 43–61). Not always acknowledged in these approaches is that while individual memory is an important starting point for understanding how the past is mediated in the present, issues of cognition alone are insufficient to explain either the oral tradition or the textualization of the tradition. The reason is because the cognitive processes of memory are interrelated to and even impacted by numerous social and cultural factors.

80　E.g., Samuel Byrskog, *Story as History—History as Story: The Gospel Tradition in the Context of Ancient Oral History*, WUNT 123 (Tübingen: Mohr Siebeck, 2001), 145–76; Robert K. McIver, *Memory, Jesus, and the Synoptic Gospels*, RBS 59 (Atlanta, GA: SBL, 2011); Richard J. Bauckham, *Jesus and the Eyewitnesses: The Gospels as Eyewitness Testimony*, 2nd ed. (Grand Rapids, MI: Eerdmans, 2017), esp. 319–57; idem, "The Psychology of Memory and the Study of the Gospels," *JSHJ* 16 (2018): 136–55; Craig Keener, *Christobiography: Memory, History, and the Reliability of the Gospels* (Grand Rapids, MI: Eerdmans, 2019), 369–400.

emotional involvement, etc.[81] Based on approaches like these, memory theory has occasionally been characterized as the latest methodological avenue through which to affirm the (general) historical reliability of the gospel accounts.[82] Yet, accusations like this reflect a lack of understanding of the full depth of memory studies and a failure to appreciate the wide spectrum of conclusions that have been reached through the application of memory theory.[83] Memory—and especially eyewitness memory[84]—can provide accurate and inaccurate representations of the past. The primary task of memory theorists is not to diagnose the historical accuracy of a given memory—although the mnemonic evidence has become an important tool with new forms of historiography.[85] Memory theory merely seeks to explain the processes by which the past is conceptualized and commemorated by individuals/groups in the present.

Scholarly interest in the social dimensions of memory is normally traced back to the work of the French sociologist, Maurice Halbwachs, who challenged the traditional store-and-retrieval view of memory in favor of a form of remembrance that involved the (re)construction of the past using the

---

81   In response to these approaches, some have emphasized the fallibility of eyewitness memory, see Judith C. S. Redman, "How Accurate Are Eyewitnesses? Bauckham and the Eyewitnesses in the Light of Psychological Research," *JBL* 129 (2010): 177–97. Cf. also the response by Robert K. McIver, "Eyewitnesses as Guarantors of the Accuracy of the Gospel Traditions in the Light of Psychological Research," *JBL* 131 (2012): 529–46.

82   This is the conclusion reached by Paul Foster, "Memory, Orality, and the Fourth Gospel: Three Dead-Ends in Historical Jesus Research," *JSHJ* 10 (2012): 191, 193, 198, 202; see also Zeba A. Crook, "Collective Memory Distortion and the Quest for the Historical Jesus," *JSHS* 11 (2013): 53–76, although the latter has since retracted the claim about there being an "emerging consensus" among those who employ memory theory that the Gospels are reliable witnesses to the historical Jesus. This correction was offered in light of the response by Anthony Le Donne, "The Problems of Selectivity in Memory Research: A Response to Zeba Crook," *JSHJ* 11 (2013): 77–97.

83   See further Chris Keith, "Social Memory Theory and Gospels Research: The First Decade (Part Two)," *Early Christianity* 6 (2015): 536–41.

84   For a recent overview on the (un)reliability of eyewitness memory and the various factors involved therein, see Timothy J. Perfect and D. Stephen Lindsay, eds., *The SAGE Handbook of Applied Memory* (Thousand Oaks, CA: SAGE Publications, 2014), 539–694; cf. also Michael P. Toglia et al., eds., *Handbook of Eyewitness Psychology*, vol. 1: *Memory for Events* (Mahwah, NJ: Lawrence Erlbaum, 2007); R. C. L. Lindsay et al., eds., *The Handbook of Eyewitness Psychology*, vol. 2: *Memory for People* (Mahwah, NJ: Lawrence Erlbaum, 2007).

85   Among those who have employed memory theory for the purpose of historiography, one of the most noteworthy theoreticians is Jens Schröter, *From Jesus to the New Testament: Early Christian Theology and the Origin of the New Testament Canon*, trans. Wayne Coppins, BMSEC (Waco, TX: Baylor University Press, 2013), 9–132.

resources that society provides in the present.[86] Since it was first proposed, the idea that the present exerts a formative influence on memory has been foundational for modern understandings of the way individuals and groups remember. There are many who have built upon this notion over the years, but one memory theorist who has contributed to the discussion in significant ways is sociologist Barry Schwartz. In Halbwachs' construal of social memory, present needs and interests are the primary determinant of how the past is remembered (hence, it is known as a "presentist" perspective). But through his numerous publications on memory, Schwartz has sought to strike a more appropriate balance between past and present influences. He argues that the past is not completely swallowed up by the present, nor is the present completely bound by the past. Both work in different ways and to varying degrees under different circumstances in the fashioning of social memory.

Working from the notion that the conceptualization and articulation of the past is facilitated through the social frameworks of the present, social memory theory (as applied in biblical studies) explores how and why groups remember the past with special emphasis placed on the mnemonic processes by which the past is represented in the present. The study of social memory in the Hebrew Bible has been championed by Ehud Ben Zvi, who has published extensively on this issue.[87] In much of his work, Ben Zvi traces the memory of characters, events, and geographic sites that have played a prominent role in the history of Israel and Judah with the goal of discerning how these persons, places and proceedings have been construed by later mnemonic communities—in particular, the Yehudite literati—and why such memories have been preserved. Much of this focus relates to ways that social memory has shaped the construction of collective identity in the late Persian and early Hellenistic periods. The contributions of Ben Zvi have been foundational for the use of social memory

---

86   See Maurice Halbwachs, *Les cadres sociaux de la mémoire* (Paris: Librairie Félix Alcan, 1925); idem, *La topographie légendaire des Évangiles en Terre Saint: étude de mémoire collective* (Paris: Presses Universitaires de France, 1941); idem, *La mémoire collective* (Paris: Presses Universitaires de France, 1950).

87   A large number of the Ben Zvi's publications on social memory have now been collected in Ehud Ben Zvi, *Social Memory among the Literati of Yehud*, BZAW 509 (Berlin: De Gruyter, 2019). Some of his other works on the topic that are not included in this volume are listed on p. 3 n. 3. Cf. also Ehud Ben Zvi and Christoph Levin, eds., *Remembering and Forgetting in Early Second Temple Period*, FAT 85 (Tübingen: Mohr Siebeck, 2012); Diana V. Edelman and Ehud Ben Zvi, eds., *Remembering Biblical Figures in the Late Persian and Early Hellenistic Periods: Social Memory and Imagination* (Oxford: Oxford University Press, 2013); Diana V. Edelman and Ehud Ben Zvi, eds., *Leadership, Social Memory and Judean Discourse in the Fifth–Second Centuries BCE*, Worlds of the Ancient Near East and Mediterranean (Sheffield: Equinox, 2016).

theory in Hebrew Bible studies in that it has provided a strong methodological grounding as well as direction and motivation for subsequent research.[88]

In New Testament studies, social memory theory has experienced a much wider dispersion within the field.[89] While the topics to which it has been applied are fairly broad,[90] much of its application has focused on Jesus and the gospels.[91] Scholars have addressed a number of specific issues related to the historical Jesus, including whether he possessed scribal literacy[92] and whether he made claims about destroying the temple.[93] But perhaps most important of all, this approach has helped refine the methods by which scholars seek to understand the formation of the gospels. In particular, social memory theory helps to clarify the transmission of the oral Jesus tradition, acting as a corrective against the misconceptions of earlier form critics. Rather than viewing the Jesus tradition as taking shape solely through the controversies and changing

---

88   Many have followed Ben Zvi's methodological approach toward social memory theory in the study of the Hebrew Bible. Note the collection of essays represented in his Festschrift: Ian D. Wilson and Diana Edelman, eds., *History, Memory, Hebrew Scriptures: A Festschrift for Ehud Ben Zvi* (Winona Lake, IN: Eisenbrauns, 2015).

89   The seminal work in this area is Alan Kirk and Tom Thatcher, eds., *Memory, Tradition, and Text: Uses of the Past in Early Christianity*, SemeiaSt 52 (Atlanta, GA: SBL, 2005).

90   See, e.g., Philip F. Esler, "Collective Memory and Hebrews 11: Outlining a New Investigative Framework," in *Memory, Tradition, and Text: Uses of the Past in Early Christianity*, ed. Alan Kirk and Tom Thatcher, SemeiaSt 52 (Atlanta, GA: SBL, 2005), 151–71; Stephen C. Barton, "Memory and Remembrance in Paul," in *Memory in the Bible and Antiquity*, ed. Loren Stuckenbruck, Stephen C. Barton, and Benjamin G. Wold, WUNT 212 (Tübingen: Mohr Siebeck, 2007), 321–38; Markus N. A. Bockmuehl, *The Remembered Peter: Peter in Ancient Reception and Modern Debate*, WUNT 262 (Tübingen: Mohr Siebeck, 2010); Benjamin L. White, *Remembering Paul: Ancient and Modern Contests over the Image of the Apostle* (Oxford: Oxford University Press, 2014). Cf. also Simon Butticaz and Enrico Norelli, eds., *Memory and Memories in Early Christianity: Proceedings of the International Conference Held at the Universities of Geneva and Lausanne (June 2–3, 2016)*, WUNT 398 (Tübingen: Mohr Siebeck, 2018).

91   For a review of the scholarly engagement with social memory theory in Gospels research, see Alan Kirk, "Memory Theory and Jesus Research," in *Handbook for the Study of the Historical Jesus*, vol. 1: *How to Study the Historical Jesus*, ed. Tom Holmén and Stanley E. Porter (Leiden: Brill, 2011), 809–842; Keith, "Social Memory Theory," 354–76, 517–42.

92   See Chris Keith, "The Claim of John 7.15 and the Memory of Jesus' Literacy," *NTS* 56 (2010): 44–63; idem, *Jesus' Literacy*.

93   See Anthony Le Donne, *Historiographical Jesus: Memory, Typology, and the Son of David* (Waco, TX: Baylor University Press, 2009); idem, *Historical Jesus: What Can We Know and How Can We Know It?* (Grand Rapids, MI: Eerdmans, 2011), 120–32; idem, "Memory, Commemoration and History in John 2:19–22: A Critique and Application of Social Memory," in *The Fourth Gospel in First-Century Media Culture*, ed. Anthony Le Donne and Tom Thatcher, LNTS 426 (London: Bloomsbury, 2011), 186–204.

social situations of later communities,[94] memory theorists have stressed the need to account for various ways that the past constrains social memory. This approach has led to a much more complex and nuanced description of the process of transmission. At the same time, social memory theory also contributes toward a new historiography by challenging the foundational assumption that underlies the criteria of authenticity (*viz.* that scholars are able to separate authentic Jesus tradition from inauthentic).[95] Through a recognition that all representations of the past are influenced by the social frameworks of the present, memory theorists maintain that the interpretive categories of the source materials must inform (rather than negate) historical investigation.[96]

The final dimension of memory that is addressed in modern memory studies is the influence of culture on the conceptualization and commemoration of the past. Building on the collective view of memory proposed by Halbwachs, Egyptologist Jan Assmann sought to extend the discussion beyond the impact of group dynamics by considering memory at a cultural level.[97] More specifically, his focus has been on how traditions are transmitted and preserved over time through diverse forms of media. To explore this question, he divides

---

94 Interpreted through the lens of social memory, the traditional views of form criticism represent a clearly presentist perspective (see Barry Schwartz, "Christian Origins: Historical Truth and Social Memory," in *Memory, Tradition, and Text: Uses of the Past in Early Christianity*, ed. Alan Kirk and Tom Thatcher, SemeiaSt 52 [Atlanta, GA: SBL, 2005], 47–50; Chris Keith, "Memory and Authenticity: Jesus Tradition and What Really Happened," *ZNW* 102 [2011]: 170).

95 On the rejection of the criteria of authenticity by memory theorists, see Chris Keith and Anthony Le Donne, eds., *Jesus, Criteria, and the Demise of Authenticity* (London: T&T Clark, 2012). Cf. also Rafael Rodríguez, "Authenticating Criteria: The Use and Misuse of a Critical Method," *JSHJ* 7 (2009): 152–67.

96 See Reuben Zimmermann, "Geschichtstheorien und Neues Testament: Gedächtnis, Diskurs, Kultur und Narration in der historiographischen Diskussion," *Early Christianity* 2 (2011): 440; Jens Schröter, "The Criteria of Authenticity in Jesus Research and Historiographical Method," in *Jesus, Criteria, and the Demise of Authenticity*, ed. Chris Keith and Anthony Le Donne (London: T&T Clark, 2012), 59 n. 35.

97 For the fullest expression of Assmann's views on cultural memory, see esp. idem, *Religion and Cultural Memory: Ten Studies*, Cultural Memory in the Present (Stanford, CA: Stanford University Press, 2006); idem, *Cultural Memory and Early Civilization: Writing, Remembrance, and Political Imagination* (Cambridge: Cambridge University Press, 2011). In some cases, Assmann has applied his views on cultural memory directly to the biblical evidence, with special focus being placed on the story of Moses and the Israelite exodus from Egypt. See, e.g., idem, *Moses the Egyptian: The Memory of Egypt in Western Monotheism* (Cambridge, MA: Harvard University Press, 1997); idem, "Exodus and Memory," in *Israel's Exodus in Transdisciplinary Perspective: Text, Archaeology, Culture, and Geoscience*, ed. Thomas E. Levy, Thomas Schneider, and William H. C. Propp, Quantitative Methods in the Humanities and Social Sciences (Cham: Springer, 2015), 3–15.

collective memory into two subsets: communicative memory and cultural memory. The former represents recent tradition stretching back only a few generations, while the latter refers to an institutionalized mode of remembering that involves the commemorative practices of a group across generations. According to Assmann, prior to the breach of a temporal horizon (ca. 40 years after the occurrence of an event), groups experience a crisis of memory (*Traditionsbruch*) wherein alternative media are required for transmitting and preserving memory. This results in a codification of tradition in the form of texts, monuments, rituals, and other forms of durable media.

In studies on the Hebrew Bible, the natural point of entry into the memory discussion for most scholars has been the cultural memory theory of Assmann. The strong lines of separation that he draws between history and memory have been especially appealing to scholars of the Hebrew Bible. This approach intersects with a larger debate on the historical value of the biblical accounts and the purpose of historiography. For many interpreters, the redeeming quality of this disconnect is that it helps to transition the discussion away from questions about whether the Bible records "what actually happened" in the past and focuses it instead on how and why the ancient Israelites remembered the past in the way(s) it is represented.[98] However, not all scholars have treated cultural memory theory as a replacement for historical inquiry. Moving against the general trend in scholarship, Daniel D. Pioske has proposed that it might be possible to determine whether cultural memory has any meaningful connection to the actual past.[99] What he suggests is a process of "triangulation"

---

98   See, e.g., Joseph Blenkinsopp, "Memory, Tradition, and the Construction of the Past in Ancient Israel," *BTB* 27 (1997): 76–82; Marc Brettler, "Memory in Ancient Israel," in *Memory and History in Christianity and Judaism*, ed. Michael A. Signer (Notre Dame, IN: University of Notre Dame Press, 2001), 1–17; Ronald S. Hendel, "The Exodus in Biblical Memory," *JBL* 120 (2001): 601–22; Mark S. Smith, "Remembering God: Collective Memory in Israelite Religion," *CBQ* 64 (2002): 631–51; Philip R. Davies, *Memories of Ancient Israel: An Introduction to Biblical History—Ancient and Modern* (Louisville, KY: Westminster John Knox, 2008), 105–23; Barat Ellman, *Memory and Covenant: The Role of Israel's and God's Memory in Sustaining the Deuteronomic and Priestly Covenants*, Emerging Scholars (Minneapolis, MN: Fortress, 2013), 18. For more on the tendency to view cultural memory theory as a replacement for historical inquiry, see Hans M. Barstad, "History and Memory," in *The Historian and the Bible: Essays in Honour of Lester L. Grabbe*, ed. Philip R. Davies and Diana V. Edelman, LHBOTS 530 (London: T&T Clark, 2010), 1–2; Jens Bruun Kofoed, "The Old Testament as Cultural Memory," in *Do Historical Matters Matter to Faith? A Critical Appraisal of Modern and Postmodern Approaches to Scripture*, ed. James K. Hoffmeier and Dennis R. Magary (Wheaton, IL: Crossway, 2012), 303–23.

99   Daniel D. Pioske, "Retracing a Remembered Past: Methodological Remarks on Memory, History, and the Hebrew Bible," *BibInt* 23 (2015): 291–315; idem, *David's Jerusalem: Between Memory and History*, Routledge Studies in Religion 45 (London: Routledge, 2015). Others

whereby the textual and material evidence related to the time and place in question are examined in light of cultural memory. The level of continuity between these various data sets is viewed as a way to measure the plausibility of memory claims.

2.3 Ritual

A ritual is an action whose performance is attributed special significance in accordance with existing cultural guidelines. Rituals have long been studied in the social sciences, but it has only been in the last couple of decades that ritual studies has emerged as a recognizable and distinct field of study.[100] In a similar way, many of the topics that are discussed under the heading 'ritual' are familiar to (and have been the focus of) biblical scholars, including sacrifice, prayer, sacred meals, etc. Nevertheless, the application of ritual theory as an analytical tool for interpreting these topics in biblical literature has only just begun in earnest over the past few decades.[101] This theoretical turn toward the social sciences also coincides with the focus that has been placed on comparative ritual practices in other ancient Near Eastern and Greco-Roman societies.[102]

---

have advocated similar approaches, see Ian D. Wilson, *Kingship and Memory in Ancient Judah* (Oxford: Oxford University Press, 2017); idem, "History and the Hebrew Bible: Culture, Narrative, and Memory," *RPBI* 3 (2018): 1–69; Mark Leuchter, *The Levites and the Boundaries of Israelite Identity* (Oxford: Oxford University Press, 2017), 16–20.

100 The emergence of ritual studies is due in large part to the efforts of scholars like Ronald Grimes and Catherine Bell. See Ronald L. Grimes, *Beginnings in Ritual Studies*, 2nd ed. (Columbia, SC: University of South Carolina Press, 1995); idem, *The Craft of Ritual Studies* (Oxford: Oxford University Press, 2014); Catherine Bell, *Ritual Theory, Ritual Practice* (Oxford: Oxford University Press, 1992); idem, *Ritual: Perspectives and Dimensions* (Oxford: Oxford University Press, 1997). For a review of ritual from a historical and theoretical perspective, see Barry Stephenson, *Ritual: A Very Short Introduction* (Oxford: Oxford University Press, 2015).

101 For a review of research on ritual theory in biblical studies, see Frank H. Gorman, Jr., "Ritual Studies and Biblical Studies: Assessment of the Past, Prospects for the Future," in *Transformation, Passages and Processes: Ritual Approaches to Biblical Texts*, Semeia 67 (Atlanta, GA: SBL, 1995), 13–36; Jason T. Lamoreaux, "BTB Readers Guide: Ritual Studies," *BTB* 39 (2009): 153–65; cf. also Gerald A. Klingbeil, *Bridging the Gap: Ritual and Ritual Texts in the Bible*, BBRSup 1 (Winona Lake, IN: Eisenbrauns, 2007), esp. 45–69 (although it primarily covers ritual in Hebrew Bible studies). For one of the fullest methodological engagements with ritual theory, see Ithamar Gruenwald, *Rituals and Ritual Theory in Ancient Israel*, BRLA 10 (Leiden: Brill, 2003), 1–39; idem, "Rituals and Ritual Theory: A Methodological Essay," in *The Oxford Handbook of Ritual and Worship in the Hebrew Bible*, ed. Samuel E. Balentine (Oxford: Oxford University Press, 2020), 109–23.

102 This comparative approach is most clearly evident within Hebrew Bible studies due to the recent archaeological and textual discoveries made from ancient Near Eastern societies (e.g., Hittite, Akkadian, Ugaritic, etc.). See, e.g., David P. Wright, *The Disposal*

2.3.1 Communication and Production

One of the theoretical lenses through which ritual activity has often been interpreted is communication.[103] In the early stages of research, it was common for scholars to approach ritual through semiotics. Among those who adopted this paradigm, the work of Edmund Leach was most prominent. From his perspective, rituals are comparable to language in that they operate according to certain patterns or rules of communication. Just as linguistic signs perform a specific function or express a given meaning in relation to other signs in a sentence, so also rituals work through their own unique syntax to transmit meaning.[104] Eventually, this paradigm of linguistic signs proved difficult to sustain, particularly when describing the universality of ritual practice. As such, scholars began to focus on the symbolic function of rituals. One of the most influential theoreticians in this regard was Clifford Geertz, who situated the observance of rituals within the context of culture.[105] According to Geertz, rituals encode meaning through symbols, as a visual means of expressing ideas.

In recent scholarship, this semiotic approach has faced serious challenges, with many scholars denying that rituals convey propositional ideas and concepts in the same way as language. Some, in fact, have even maintained that rituals are meaningless.[106] This discussion has impacted biblical scholars in an

---

of Impurity: Elimination Rites in the Bible and in Hittite and Mesopotamian Literature, SBLDS 101 (Atlanta, GA: Scholars, 1987); idem, *Ritual in Narrative: The Dynamics of Feasting, Mourning, and Retaliation Rites in the Ugaritic Tale of Aqhat* (Winona Lake, IN: Eisenbrauns, 2001); Gerald A. Klingbeil, *A Comparative Study of the Ritual of Ordination as Found in Leviticus 8 and Emar 369* (Lewiston: Edwin Mellen, 1998); Yitzhaq Feder, *Blood Expiation in Hittite and Biblical Ritual: Origins, Context, and Meaning*, WAWSup 2 (Atlanta, GA: SBL, 2011); Bryan C. Babcock, *Sacred Ritual: A Study of the West Semitic Ritual Calendars in Leviticus 23 and the Akkadian Text Emar 446*, BBRSup 9 (Winona Lake, IN: Eisenbraus, 2014).

103   For a fuller review of how communication has served as a theoretical lens through which to interpret ritual, see Eric W. Rothenbuhler, *Ritual Communication: From Everyday Conversation to Mediated Ceremony* (Thousand Oaks, CA: SAGE Publications, 1998); Günter Thomas, "Communication," in *Theorizing Rituals: Issues, Topics, Approaches, Concepts*, ed. Jens Kreinath, Jan Snoek, and Michael Stausberg, Studies in the History of Religions 114–1 (Leiden: Brill, 2006), 321–43.

104   See Edmund Leach, "Ritual," in *International Encyclopedia of the Social Sciences*, ed. David L. Shils, vol. 13 (New York, NY: Macmillan, 1968), 520–24; idem, *Culture and Communication: The Logic by which Symbols are Connected* (Cambridge: Cambridge University Press, 1976).

105   See Clifford Geertz, "Religion as a Cultural System," in *Anthropological Approaches to the Study of Religion*, ed. Michael Banton (London: Tavistock, 1966), 1–46; idem, *The Interpretation of Cultures: Selected Essays* (New York, NY: Basic Books, 1973).

106   E.g., Frits Staal, "The Meaninglessness of Ritual," *Numen* 26 (1979): 2–22; idem, "The Search for Meaning: Mathematics, Music, and Ritual," *American Journal of Semiotics*

important way, as there has been a growing awareness that a single meaning cannot be facilely applied to all rituals, if rituals convey any symbolism at all.[107] First, rituals are not static. Many have recognized that rituals can and do change over time,[108] making it difficult to establish a consistent diachronic interpretation. Second, even with regard to a particular ritual performed within a specific temporal and geographic context, there is still some hesitancy among scholars to assign a singular meaning. This flows out of the realization that rituals are often interpreted in a variety of ways due to the differentiated experience of practitioners and observers.[109]

One example of how this theoretical consideration has provided new interpretive direction is found in the treatment of sacrifice. Within biblical studies, sacrificial rituals have been a common topic of discussion for many years,[110] and over that time, scholars have proposed a number of meanings underlying the ritual. These various interpretations of sacrifice have been grouped into six categories by Klingbeil: (a) sacrifice provides food for the deity; (b) sacrifice serves as a substitution for wrongdoing; (c) sacrifice effects unity with the deity; (d) sacrifice is gift to the deity; (e) sacrifice is means of substitution for human victims of aggression; and (f) sacrifice functions as a means of removing guilt for killing animal.[111] After surveying the exegetical basis, potential validity, and problematic nature of many of these sociological explanations, David P. Wright draws attention to the potential ambiguity of sacrifice as ritual.

---

2 (1984): 1–57; idem, *Rules Without Meaning: Ritual, Mantras, and the Human Sciences*, Toronto Studies in Religion 4 (New York, NY: Peter Lang, 1989).

107   For a theoretical critique of the semiotic approach toward ritual which finds in it some symbolic meaning, see Dan Sperber, *Rethinking Symbolism* (Cambridge: Cambridge University Press, 1975).

108   See Nathan MacDonald, ed., *Ritual Innovation in the Hebrew Bible and Early Judaism*, BZAW 468 (Berlin: De Gruyter, 2018). Cf. also Eftychia Stavrianopoulou, "Introduction," in *Ritual and Communication in the Graeco-Roman World*, ed. Eftychia Stavrianopoulou, Kernos Supplement 16 (Liége: Centre international d'étude de la religion grecque antique, 2006), 7.

109   On this point, see esp. William K. Gilders, *Blood Ritual in the Hebrew Bible: Meaning and Power* (Baltimore, MD: Johns Hopkins University Press, 2004), 3–6; Wesley J. Bergen, *Reading Ritual: Leviticus in Postmodern Culture*, JSOTSup 417 (London: T&T Clark, 2005), 1–3.

110   For a recent review of the ritual of sacrifice, see Roy E. Gane, "Ritual and Religious Practices," in *The Oxford Handbook of Ritual and Worship in the Hebrew Bible*, ed. Samuel E. Balentine (Oxford: Oxford University Press, 2020), 225–31, and Christian A. Eberhart, "Sacrificial Practice and Language," in *The Oxford Handbook of Early Christian Ritual*, ed. Risto Uro, Juliette Day, Richard E. DeMaris, and Rikard Roitto (Oxford: Oxford University Press, 2019), 462–76. For further bibliography, see Klingbeil, *Comparative Study*, 247–55, with a supplement provided in idem, *Bridging the Gap*, 56 n. 41.

111   Klingbeil, *Bridging the Gap*, 57.

He not only points out that sacrifice could have been interpreted in a variety of ways, he also notes how such multiplicity actually contributes to a ritual's persistence. "The vitality of ritual," he explains, "actually depends on its ability to bear multiple interpretations."[112]

2.3.2 The Negotiation of Power

Rather than focusing on ritual as a symbol or an avenue to communicate information, some ritual theorists have begun to consider the important role of ritual in the production of relationships. In this way, ritual is considered to be generative more than symbolic, with *action* (what do rituals do?) receiving more attention than *meaning* (what do rituals represent?). A significant contribution to this discussion was made by anthropologist Victor Turner, who considered the role of ritual in generating social change. Turner suggested that during rites of passage participants operate in a state of liminality (i.e. in-between), such that traditional social structures break down. This creates an equality among those who partake of the rite, and it opens the possibility of new social relations.[113]

A functionalist approach like the one proposed by Turner invites new ways to think about how ritual relates to the display and exercise of power structures,[114] and this has been one of the more productive interpretive avenues in the study of rituals in the Hebrew Bible. An example of this approach is Saul Olyan's study on the binary categories associated with cultic space in the Hebrew Bible (e.g., holy/common, Israelite/alien, clean/unclean, whole/blemished). Olyan demonstrates that these dyadic pairings create a social hierarchy "by bounding or restricting access to ritual contexts such as the temple,

---

112 David Wright, "The Study of Ritual in the Hebrew Bible," in *The Hebrew Bible: New Insights and Scholarship*, ed. Frederick E. Greenspahn, Jewish Studies in the Twenty-First Century 4 (New York, NY: New York University Press, 2008), 134. Taking this idea even further, William K. Gilders claims that "the Israelite tradents who composed the ritual texts we now possess did not have a strong interest in symbolic interpretation of sacrifice" ("Ancient Israelite Sacrifice as Symbolic Action: Theoretical Reflections," *SEÅ* 78 [2013]: 10).

113 Victor Turner, *The Ritual Process: Structure and Anti-Structure* (London: Routledge, 1969). Turner's work built upon an earlier study by Arnold van Gennep, *The Rites of Passage*, trans. Monika B. Vizedom and Gabrielle L. Caffee (Chicago: University of Chicago Press, 1960).

114 For more on ways that ritual relates to power structures, see, e.g., David I. Kertzer, *Ritual, Politics and Power* (New Haven, CT: Yale University Press, 1989); Catherine Bell, "The Ritual Body and the Dynamics of Ritual Power," *Journal of Ritual Studies* 4 (1990): 299–313.

the Passover table, and the war camp feast."[115] This two-part division privileges certain groups, while excluding others. In this way, sacred spaces in ancient Israel become the primary settings in which social distinction is generated.

Rituals of violence played a similar role in the production of social relationships in ancient Israel.[116] At times, rites were used to transition from a time of warfare to a time of peace. This was the case with the sacrifice of Jephthah's daughter. As a final act of violence, a time of new social relations were thought to begin thereafter.[117] Other rituals symbolically marked a separation from one's previous social and ethnic relations. This was the case with foreign women who were captured as the spoils of war. Because the enemies of Israel were viewed as "others," it was necessary to first transform these women prior to taking them in marriage. Consequently, ritual acts such as hair removal were physical alterations intended to represent a change of status, indicating a new and acceptable form in the eyes of the captors.[118]

One of the first New Testament scholars to approach ritual from a functionalist perspective was Wayne A. Meeks in the groundbreaking work, *The First Urban Christians*.[119] However, scholarship on rituals in early Christianity have undergone changes since the time of Meeks' groundbreaking study, to a large degree reflecting the theoretical developments that have taken place in

---

115 Saul M. Olyan, *Rites and Rank: Hierarchy in Biblical Representations of Cult* (Princeton, NJ: Princeton University Press, 2000), 4. For other examples of ways that ritual was used to establish and confirm power in ancient Israel, see James W. Watts, *Ritual and Rhetoric in Leviticus: From Sacrifice to Scripture* (Cambridge: Cambridge University Press, 2007).

116 For more on rituals of violence, see esp. Saul M. Olyan, *Ritual Violence in the Hebrew Bible: New Perspectives* (Oxford: Oxford University Press, 2015); idem, *Violent Rituals of the Hebrew Bible* (Oxford: Oxford University Press, 2019).

117 Susan Niditch, "A Messy Business: Ritual Violence after the War," in *Warfare, Ritual, and Symbol in Biblical and Modern Contexts*, ed. Brad E. Kelle, Frank R. Ames, and Jacob L. Wright, AIL 18 (Atlanta, GA: SBL, 2014), 187–204. For more on these post-war rituals, see Brad E. Kelle, "Postwar Rituals of Return and Reintegration," in *Warfare, Ritual, and Symbol in Biblical and Modern Contexts*, ed. Brad E. Kelle, Frank R. Ames, and Jacob L. Wright, AIL 18 (Atlanta, GA: SBL, 2014), 205–42.

118 E.g., Saul M. Olyan, "What Do Shaving Rites Accomplish and What Do They Signal in Biblical Ritual Contexts," *JBL* 117 (1998): 611–22; Susan Niditch, *"My Brother Esau is a Hairy Man": Hair and Identity in Ancient Israel* (Oxford: Oxford University Press, 2008), 95–120.

119 Wayne A. Meeks, *The First Urban Christians: The Social World of the Apostle Paul*, 2nd ed. (New Haven, CT: Yale University Press, 2003), 140–63. Until the time of Meeks, ritual was a particular focus of the History of Religions school (see, e.g., Hans Lietzmann, *Messe und Herrenmahl. Eine Studie zur Geschichte der Liturgie*, 3rd ed., Arbeiten zur Kirchengeschichte 8 [Berlin: De Gruyter, 1955]). The goal of these interpreters was to trace the historical roots of a given ritual back to its earliest form. For many, this search for origins was grounded in the desire to uncover an authentic form of the tradition.

the study of ritual more generally.[120] With a view towards the role of ritual in the life of the Christian community, one of the important emphases in this approach has been social negotiation.[121] Rather than simply confirming or imitating present existing structures, rituals might also challenge or disrupt social or political dynamics. This is one place where ritual theory intersects with certain trajectories in the study of early Christianity more broadly. It has become common for scholars to read the New Testament through the lens of resistance, with the literature communicating an implicit (or sometimes, an explicit) critique of empire.[122]

Meals were one ritual by which early Christians negotiated power and status.[123] Early Christian meal tradition allowed for members of varying socio-economic statuses to dine together in spaces marked by equality, which differed dramatically from the dining practices of the wider Greco-Roman world. As the barriers created by gender, ethnicity, and family were dissolved, new relational patterns could be forged, and a distinct Christian identity could

---

120   For some of the developments sparked by Meek's work on ritual, see Louis J. Lawrence, "Ritual and the First Urban Christians: Boundary Crossings of Life and Death," in *After the First Urban Christians: The Social-Scientific Study of Pauline Christianity Twenty-Five Years Later*, ed. Todd D. Still and David G. Horrell (London: T&T Clark, 2009), 99–115. For a review of recent developments on the study of ritual more generally within New Testament studies, see Risto Uro, "Ritual and Christian Origins," in *Understanding the Social World of the New Testament*, ed. Dietmar Neufeld and Richard E. DeMaris (New York, NY: Routledge, 2010), 220–32. Cf. also Richard E. DeMaris, *The New Testament and Its Ritual World* (New York, NY: Routledge, 2008); idem, "Ritualforschung: Eine Bereicherung für die neutestamentliche Wissenschaft," *ZNT* 18 (2015): 31–42; Richard E. DeMaris, Jason T. Lamoreaux, and Steven C. Muir, eds., *Early Christian Ritual* (New York, NY: Routledge, 2018); Risto Uro, Juliette Day, Richard E. DeMaris, and Rikard Roitto, eds., *The Oxford Handbook of Early Christian Ritual* (Oxford: Oxford University Press, 2019).

121   It is common to find ritual being treated as a stable phenomenon that simply confirms traditional ideas and practices. On the various ways that ritual serves to dispute or resist tradition, see Ute Hüsken and Frank Neubert, eds., *Negotiating Rites* (Oxford: Oxford University Press, 2012).

122   See Judy Diehl, "Anti-Imperial Rhetoric in the New Testament," *CBR* 10 (2011): 9–52; idem, "Empire and Epistles: Anti-Roman Rhetoric in the New Testament Epistles," *CBR* 10 (2012): 217–63; idem, "'Babylon': Then, Now, and 'Not Yet': Anti-Roman Rhetoric in the Book of Revelation," *CBR* 11 (2013): 168–95.

123   Hal Taussig, *In the Beginning was the Meal: Social Experimentation and Early Christian Identity* (Minneapolis, MN: Fortress, 2009). Others have similarly studied the ritual function of early Christian meals (e.g., J. L. P. Wolmarans, "The Semiotics of the Ritual Meal in the *Didache*," *Acta Patristica et Byzantina* 16 [2005]: 308–24; Jonathan Schwiebert, *Knowledge and the Coming Kingdom: The Didache's Meal Ritual and its Place in Early Christianity*, LNTS 373 [London: T&T Clark, 2008]; Vojtěch Kaše, "Meal Practices," in *The Oxford Handbook of Early Christian Ritual*, ed. Risto Uro, Juliette Day, Richard E. DeMaris, and Rikard Roitto [Oxford: Oxford University Press, 2019], 409–25).

be established. This egalitarian meal tradition, marked by social inclusion, stood in stark contrast to the hierarchy of imperial Rome. Such an ideal was not always reflected, however. Even within this unified collective, distinctions could still be made through the placement of diners around the table, with those of higher ranks being afforded seats of honor. In fact, over time, the ritualization of meals would require a special agent who was thought to possess unique authority to preside over the rite, and in this way, meal rituals became a means by which to establish hierarchical power structures within the church.[124] Another place where the emphasis on social negotiation has been explored is the practice of kissing among Christians. According to Michael P. Penn, early Christians invested this common cultural practice, which was often associated with eroticism, with a new meaning. As such, the ritualized gesture created social cohesion among the Christian community and reinforced the boundaries that separated them from outsiders.[125]

2.3.3 Cognition and Memory

An extremely important shift in ritual theory over the past couple of decades has been the move away from theoretical attempts to provide universal explanations for rituals.[126] In place of such "grand theories," scholars have begun to take an interdisciplinary approach toward theorizing rituals, drawing eclectically from fields such as cultural anthropology, sociology, performance theory, among others. There are some, however, who continue to explore ways in which ritual practices are part of the shared human experience. Drawing upon the cognitive sciences, these scholars tend to focus on various forms of memory, human evolutionary development, and the physiology of the human mind.[127]

---

124 See further Susan E. Hylen, "Ritual and Emerging Church Hierarchy," in *The Oxford Handbook of Early Christian Ritual*, ed. Risto Uro, Juliette Day, Richard E. DeMaris, and Rikard Roitto (Oxford: Oxford University Press, 2019), 491–502.

125 See Michael P. Penn, "Performing Family: Ritual Kissing and the Construction of Early Christian Kinship," *JECS* 10 (2002): 151–74; idem, *Kissing Christians: Ritual and Community in the Late Ancient Church* (Philadelphia, PA: University of Pennsylvania Press, 2005); idem, "Kissing, Purity, and Early Christian Social Order," in *Studia Patristica*, vol. 40: *Papers Presented at the Fourteenth International Conference on Patristic Studies held in Oxford 2003*, ed. Frances M. Young, Morgan J. Edwards, and Paul M. Parvis (Leuven: Peeters, 2006), 87–92.

126 Cf. Jens Kreinath, Jan Snoek, and Michael Stausberg, "Ritual Studies, Ritual Theory, Theorizing Rituals," in *Theorizing Rituals: Issues, Topics, Approaches, Concepts*, ed. Jens Kreinath, Jan Snoek, and Michael Stausberg, Studies in the History of Religions 114–1 (Leiden: Brill, 2006), xxi.

127 Some are skeptical that these cognitive approaches can provide a complete understanding of ritual behavior (see Gerald A. Klingbeil, "When Action Collides with Meaning: Ritual Biblical Theology, and the New Testament Lord's Supper," *Neot* 50 [2016]: 428–29).

One of the few scholars of the Hebrew Bible to address rituals from the perspective of the cognitive science of religion is Brett E. Maiden. Among the rituals that he explores, the most noteworthy is the Day of Atonement.[128] Maiden approaches the subject using a variety of cognitive theories. Drawing from the work of Boyer and Liénard,[129] he considers certain rites associated with the Day of Atonement (e.g., blood manipulation, washings, etc.) from the perspective a hazard-precaution system in which rituals represent inferred threats to human survival. These elements, he claims, made the ritual more compelling and thus increased the chances that it would be successfully transmitted to future generations. Additionally, using the ritual competence theory (or ritual form theory) developed by Lawson and McCauley,[130] Maiden argues that the Day of Atonement represents a hybrid between a special agent ritual and a special patient ritual, thus creating a rite that was both highly ceremonial while at the same time repeatable.

Within the study of early Christianity, cognitive approaches toward ritual have been slightly more popular due to the efforts of Risto Uro and István Czachesz, both of whom have published widely on the subject.[131] One of

---

128   Brett E. Maiden, *Cognitive Science and Ancient Israelite Religion* (Cambridge: Cambridge University Press, 2020), 211–56. The Day of Atonement ritual has been the focus of a considerable amount of research in Hebrew Bible studies. See, e.g., Benedikt Jürgens, *Heiligkeit und Versöhnung. Levitikus 16 in seinem literarischen Kontext*, HBS 28 (Freiburg: Herder, 2001); Roy E. Gane, *Cult and Character: Purification Offerings, Day of Atonement, and Theodicy* (Winona Lake, IN: Eisenbrauns, 2005).

129   Pascal Boyer and Pierre Liénard, "Why Ritualized Behavior? Precaution Systems and Action Parsing in Development, Pathological and Cultural Rituals," *Behavioral and Brain Sciences* 29 (2006): 595–613; Pierre Liénard and Pascal Boyer, "Whence Collective Rituals? A Cultural Selection Model of Ritualized Behavior," *American Anthropologist* 108 (2006): 814–27.

130   E. Thomas Lawson and Robert N. McCauley, *Rethinking Religion: Connecting Cognition and Culture* (Cambridge: Cambridge University Press, 1990); Robert N. McCauley and E. Thomas Lawson, *Bringing Ritual to Mind: Psychological Foundations of Cultural Forms* (Cambridge: Cambridge University Press, 2002).

131   See, e.g., Risto Uro, "Towards a Cognitive History of Early Christian Rituals," in *Changing Minds: Religion and Cognition through Ages*, ed. István Czachesz and Tamas Bíró, Groningen Studies in Cultural Change 42 (Leuven: Peeters, 2011), 223–35; idem, "Kognitive Ritualtheorien: Neue Modelle für Analyse urchristliche Sakramente," *EvT* 71 (2011): 272–88; idem, "Cognitive and Evolutionary Approaches to Ancient Rituals: Reflections on Recent Theories and Their Relevance for the Historian of Religion," in *Mystery and Secrecy in the Nag Hammadi Collection and Other Ancient Literature: Ideas and Practices*, ed. John D. Turner, Christian H. Bull, and Liv Ingeborg Lied, Nag Hammadi and Manichaean Studies 76 (Leiden: Brill, 2011), 487–510; idem, *Ritual and Christian Beginnings: A Socio-Cognitive Analysis* (Oxford: Oxford University Press, 2016); idem, "Ritual and the Rise of Early Christian Movement," in *Early Christian World*, ed. Philip F. Esler, 2nd ed. (New York,

the ways that early Christian rituals have been informed by this perspective is through a focus on the "modes of religiosity," as introduced by Harvey Whitehouse.[132] According to this cognitive theory of ritual, religions often involve two types of rituals: imagistic, which relates to dramatic rituals that are not frequently observed, and doctrinal, which relates to rituals that generate less dramatic arousal but which are performed more frequently. While the experiential nature of the former engages the episodic memory of participants, the latter relates more to semantic memory in which ideas and concepts are learned. The ritual practices of early Christian groups, it has been shown, likely involved both imagistic and doctrinal rituals.[133] To take but one example, baptism would be considered an imagistic ritual because it was a one-time, initiation experience often accompanied by fasting and prayer;[134] at the same time, preparation for this rite might require an extended period of training, making it a doctrinal ritual as well.

NY: Routledge, 2017), 427–41; István Czachesz, *Cognitive Science and the New Testament: A New Approach to early Christian Research* (Oxford: Oxford University Press 2017); idem, "Ritual and Transmission," in *The Oxford Handbook of Early Christian Ritual*, ed. Risto Uro, Juliette Day, Richard E. DeMaris, and Rikard Roitto (Oxford: Oxford University Press, 2019), 115–33. Cf. also Risto Uro and István Czachesz, eds., *Mind, Morality and Magic: Cognitive Science Approaches in Biblical Studies* (Durham: Acumen, 2013).

132   See Harvey Whitehouse, *Arguments and Icons: Divergent Modes of Religiosity* (Oxford: Oxford University Press, 2000); idem, *Modes of Religiosity: A Cognitive Theory of Religious Transmission* (Walnut Creek, CA: AltaMira, 2004).

133   On this issue, see Risto Uro, "Gnostic Rituals from a Cognitive Perspective," in *Explaining Christian Origins and Early Judaism: Contributions from Cognitive and Social Science*, ed. Petri Luomanen, Ilkka Pyysiäinen, and Risto Uro, BIS 89 (Leiden: Brill, 2007), 115–37; idem, "The Bridal Chamber and Other Mysteries: Ritual System and Ritual Transmission in the Valentinian Movement," in *Sacred Marriages: The Divine-Human Sexual Metaphor from Sumer to Early Christianity*, ed. Martti Nissinen and Risto Uro (Winona Lake, IN: Eisenbrauns, 2008), 457–86.

134   On baptism as an early Christian ritual, see Mark McVann, "Reading Mark Ritually: Honor-Shame and the Ritual of Baptism," in *Transformation, Passages and Processes: Ritual Approaches to Biblical Texts*, SemeiaSt 67 (Atlanta, GA: SBL, 1995), 179–98; Richard DeMaris, "Baptisms and Funerals, Ordinary and Otherwise: Ritual Criticism and Corinthian Rites," *BTB* 29 (1999): 23–34; idem, "Backing Away from Baptism: Early Christian Ambivalence about Its Ritual," *Journal of Ritual Studies* 27 (2013): 11–19; Stephen R. Turley, *The Ritualized Revelation of the Messianic Age: Washings and Meals in Galatians and 1 Corinthians*, LNTS 544 (London: Bloomsbury, 2015), 29–101; Jason N. Yuh, "Analysing Paul's Reference to Baptism in Galatians 3.27 through Studies of Memory, Embodiment and Ritual," *JSNT* 41 (2019): 478–500.

3 Conclusion

The application of media studies in Dead Sea Scrolls scholarship is part of a larger effort to situate early Jewish and Christian literature in their ancient communicative contexts. By exploring some of the key methods and trends that have shaped the discussion in biblical studies, we are now in a better position to consider how the topics of textuality, orality, and ritual have been treated within Dead Sea Scrolls scholarship. The three subsequent chapters provide more specific overviews of this discussion.

Bibliography

Achtemeier, Paul J. "*Omne verbum sonat*: The New Testament and the Oral Environment of Late Western Antiquity." *JBL* 109 (1990): 3–27.

Allen, Garrick V. *Manuscripts of the Book of Revelation: New Philology, Paratexts, Reception*. Oxford: Oxford University Press, 2020.

Allen, Garrick V., and Kelsie G. Rodenbiker. "Titles of the New Testament (TiNT): A New Approach to Manuscripts and the History of Interpretation." *Early Christianity* 11 (2020): 265–80.

Allen, Garrick V., and Anthony Royle. "Paratexts Seeking Understanding: Manuscripts and Aesthetic Cognitivism." *Religions* 11 (2020): 1–25.

Andrews, Edward D. *The Reading Culture of Early Christianity: The Production, Publication, Circulation, and Use of Books in Early Christian Church*. Cambridge, OH: Christian Publishing House, 2019.

Andrist, Patrick. "Toward a Definition of Paratexts and Paratextuality: The Case of Ancient Greek Manuscripts." Pages 130–49 in *Bible as Notepad: Tracing Annotations and Annotation Practices in Late Antique and Medieval Biblical Manuscripts*. Editeed by Liv Ingeborg Lied and Marilena Maniaci. Manuscripta Biblica 3. Berlin: De Gruyter, 2018.

Assmann, Jan. *Moses the Egyptian: The Memory of Egypt in Western Monotheism*. Cambridge, MA: Harvard University Press, 1997.

Assmann, Jan. *Religion and Cultural Memory: Ten Studies*. Translated by Rodney Livingstone. Cultural Memory in the Present. Stanford, CA: Stanford University Press, 2006.

Assmann, Jan. *Cultural Memory and Early Civilization: Writing, Remembrance, and Political Imagination*. Cambridge: Cambridge University Press, 2011.

Assmann, Jan. "Exodus and Memory." Pages 3–15 in *Israel's Exodus in Transdisciplinary Perspective: Text, Archaeology, Culture, and Geoscience*. Edited by Thomas E. Levy,

Thomas Schneider, and William H. C. Propp. Quantitative Methods in the Humanities and Social Sciences. Cham: Springer, 2015.

Aune, David E. "Literacy." Page 275–76 in *The Westminster Dictionary of New Testament and Early Christian Literature and Rhetoric*. Louisville, KY: Westminster John Knox, 2003.

Babcock, Bryan C. *Sacred Ritual: A Study of the West Semitic Ritual Calendars in Leviticus 23 and the Akkadian Text Emar 446*. BBRSup 9. Winona Lake, IN: IN: Eisenbraus, 2014.

Bailey, Kenneth E. "Informal Controlled Oral Tradition and the Synoptic Gospels." *Asia Journal of Theology* 5 (1991): 34–54.

Bailey, Kenneth E. "Middle Eastern Oral Tradition and the Synoptic Gospels." *ExpTim* 106 (1994): 363–67.

Balogh, József. "'Voces Paginarum': Beiträge zur Geschichte des lauten Lessen und Schreibens." *Philogus* 82 (1927): 85–109, 202–40.

Bar-Ilan, Meir. "Illiteracy in the Land of Israel in the First Centuries CE." Pages 2:46–61 in *Essays in the Social Scientific Study of Judaism and Jewish Society*. Edited by Simcha Fishbane and Jack N. Lightstone. Hoboken, NJ: Ktav, 1992.

Bar-Ilan, Meir. "Writing in Ancient Israel and Early Judaism: Part Two: Scribes and Books in the Late Second Commonwealth and Rabbinic Period." Pages 21–38 in *Mikra: Text, Translation, Reading and Interpretation of the Hebrew Bible in Ancient Judaism and Early Christianity*. Edited by M. J. Mulder and Harry Sysling. Peabody: Hendrickson, 2004.

Barstad, Hans M. "History and Memory." Pages 1–10 in *The Historian and the Bible: Essays in Honour of Lester L. Grabbe*. Edited by Philip R. Davies and Diana V. Edelman. LHBOTS 530. London: T&T Clark, 2010.

Barton, Stephen C. "Memory and Remembrance in Paul." Pages 321–38 in *Memory in the Bible and Antiquity*. Edited by Loren Stuckenbruck, Stephen C. Barton, and Benjamin G. Wold. WUNT 212. Tübingen: Mohr Siebeck, 2007.

Bauckham, Richard J. *Jesus and the Eyewitnesses: The Gospels as Eyewitness Testimony*. 2nd ed. Grand Rapids, MI: Eerdmans, 2017.

Bauckham, Richard J. "The Psychology of Memory and the Study of the Gospels." *JSHJ* 16 (2018): 136–55.

Bell, Catherine. "The Ritual Body and the Dynamics of Ritual Power." *Journal of Ritual Studies* 4 (1990): 299–313.

Bell, Catherine. *Ritual Theory, Ritual Practice*. Oxford: Oxford University Press, 1992.

Bell, Catherine. *Ritual: Perspectives and Dimensions*. Oxford: Oxford University Press, 1997.

Ben Zvi, Ehud. *Social Memory among the Literati of Yehud*. BZAW 509. Berlin: De Gruyter, 2019.

Ben Zvi, Ehud, and Christoph Levin, eds. *Remembering and Forgetting in Early Second Temple Period*. FAT 85. Tübingen: Mohr Siebeck, 2012.

Bergen, Wesley J. *Reading Ritual: Leviticus in Postmodern Culture*. JSOTSup 417. London: T&T Clark, 2005.

Blenkinsopp, Joseph. "Memory, Tradition, and the Construction of the Past in Ancient Israel." *BTB* 27 (1997): 76–82.

Bockmuehl, Markus N. A. *The Remembered Peter: Peter in Ancient Reception and Modern Debate*. WUNT 262. Tübingen: Mohr Siebeck, 2010.

Botha, Pieter J. J. "Mute Manuscripts: Analysing a Neglected Aspect of Ancient Communication." *Theologia Evangelica* 23 (1990): 35–47.

Botha, Pieter J. J. "Mark's Story as Oral Traditional Literature: Rethinking the Transmission of Some Traditions about Jesus." *HvTSt* 47 (1991): 304–31.

Botha, Pieter J. J. "Greco-Roman Literacy as Setting for New Testament Writings." *Neot* 26 (1992): 195–215.

Botha, Pieter J. J. "Letter Writing and Oral Communication in Antiquity: Suggested Implications for the Interpretation of Paul's Letter to the Galatians." *Scriptura* 42 (1992): 17–34.

Botha, Pieter J. J. *Orality and Literacy in Early Christianity*. Biblical Performance Criticism 5. Eugene, OR: Cascade, 2012.

Boyer, Pascal, and Pierre Liénard. "Why Ritualized Behavior? Precaution Systems and Action Parsing in Development, Pathological and Cultural Rituals." *Behavioral and Brain Sciences* 29 (2006): 595–613.

Brettler, Marc. "Memory in Ancient Israel." Pages 1–17 in *Memory and History in Christianity and Judaism*. Edited by Michael A. Signer. Notre Dame, IN: University of Notre Dame Press, 2001.

Burnyeat, M. F. "Postscript on Silent Reading." *ClQ* 47 (1997): 74–76.

Butticaz, Simon, and Enrico Norelli, eds. *Memory and Memories in Early Christianity: Proceedings of the International Conference Held at the Universities of Geneva and Lausanne (June 2–3, 2016)*. WUNT 398. Tübingen: Mohr Siebeck, 2018.

Buzi, Paolo. "Titoli e colofoni: Riflessioni sugli elementi paratestuali dei manoscritti copti saidici." Pages 203–17 in *Colofoni armeni a confronto: le sottoscrizioni dei manoscritti in ambito armeno e nelle altre tradizioni scrittorie del mondo mediterraneo: atti del colloquio internazionale, Bologna, 12–13 ottobre 2012*. Edited by Anna Sirinian, Paolo Buzi, and Gaga Shurgaia. OrChrAn 299. Rome: Pontifical Institute, 2016.

Byrskog, Samuel. *Story as History—History as Story: The Gospel Tradition in the Context of Ancient Oral History*. WUNT 123. Tübingen: Mohr Siebeck, 2001.

Capua, Francesco di. "Osservazioni sulla lettura e sulla preghiera ad alta voce presso gli antichi." *Rendicoti della Accademia di archeologie lettere e belle arti di Napoli* 28 (1953): 59–99.

Carlson, Stephen C. "A Bias at the Heart of the Coherence-Based Genealogical Method (CBGM)." *JBL* 139 (2020): 319–40.

Carr, David M. *Writing on Tablets of the Heart: Origins of Scripture and Literature.* Oxford: Oxford University Press, 2005.

Carr, David M. "Torah on the Heart: Literary Jewish Textuality within Its Ancient Near Eastern Context." *Oral Tradition* 25 (2010): 17–39.

Carr, David M. *The Formation of the Hebrew Bible: A New Reconstruction.* Oxford: Oxford University Press, 2011.

Cerquiglini, Bernard. *In Praise of the Variant: A Critical History of Philology.* Translated by Betsy Wing. Baltimore, MD: Johns Hopkins University Press, 1999.

Charlesworth, Scott D. "Recognizing Greek Literacy in Early Roman Documents from the Judaean Desert." *BASP* 51 (2014): 161–89.

Clark, W. P. "Ancient Reading." *CJ* 26 (1931): 698–700.

Clark Wire, Antoinette. *The Case for Mark Composed in Performance.* Biblical Performance Criticism 3. Eugene, OR: Cascade, 2011.

Cohen, Shaye J. D. *From the Maccabees to the Mishnah.* 3rd ed. Louisville, KY: Westminster John Knox, 2014.

Coogan, Jeremiah. *Eusebius the Evangelist.* Cultures of Reading in the Ancient Mediterranean. Oxford: Oxford University Press, 2022.

Coogan, Michael D. "Literacy and the Formation of Biblical Literature." Pages 47–61 in *Realia Dei: Essays in Archaeology and Biblical Interpretation in Honor of Edward F. Campbell, Jr., at His Retirement.* Edited by Prescott H. Williams, Jr. and Theodore Hiebert. Homage Series 23. Atlanta, GA: Scholars, 1999.

Craffert, Pieter F., and Pieter J. J. Botha. "Why Jesus Could Walk on the Sea but He Could Not Read or Write." *Neot* 39 (2005): 5–35.

Crawford, Matthew R. *The Eusebian Canon Tables: Ordering Textual Knowledge in Late Antiquity.* OECS. Oxford: Oxford University Press, 2019.

Crenshaw, James L. "Education in Ancient Israel." *JBL* 104 (1985): 601–15.

Cribiore, Raffaella. *Writing, Teachers, and Students in Graeco-Roman Egypt.* ASP 36. Atlanta, GA: Scholars, 1996.

Cribiore, Raffaella. *Gymnastics of the Mind: Greek Education in Hellenistic and Roman Egypt.* Princeton, NJ: Princeton University Press, 2001.

Crook, Zeba A. "Collective Memory Distortion and the Quest for the Historical Jesus." *JSHS* 11 (2013): 53–76.

Czachesz, István. "Rethinking Biblical Transmission: Insights from the Cognitive Neuroscience of Memory." Pages 43–61 in *Mind, Morality and Magic: Cognitive Science Approaches in Biblical Studies.* Edited by István Czachesz and Risto Uro. London: Routledge, 2014.

Czachesz, István. *Cognitive Science and the New Testament: A New Approach to early Christian Research.* Oxford: Oxford University Press 2017.

Czachesz, István. "Ritual and Transmission." Pages 115–33 in *The Oxford Handbook of Early Christian Ritual*. Edited by Risto Uro, Juliette Day, Richard E. DeMaris, and Rikard Roitto. Oxford: Oxford University Press, 2019.

Davies, Graham. "Were There Schools in Ancient Israel?" Pages 199–211 in *Wisdom in Ancient Israel: Essays in Honour of J. A. Emerton*. Edited by John Day, Robert P. Gordon, and Hugh G. M. Williamson. Cambridge: Cambridge University Press, 1995.

Davies, Philip R. *Memories of Ancient Israel: An Introduction to Biblical History—Ancient and Modern*. Louisville, KY: Westminster John Knox, 2008.

DeMaris, Richard E. "Baptisms and Funerals, Ordinary and Otherwise: Ritual Criticism and Corinthian Rites." *BTB* 29 (1999): 23–34.

DeMaris, Richard E. *The New Testament and Its Ritual World*. New York, NY: Routledge, 2008.

DeMaris, Richard E. "Backing Away from Baptism: Early Christian Ambivalence about Its Ritual." *Journal of Ritual Studies* 27 (2013): 11–19.

DeMaris, Richard E. "Ritualforschung: Eine Bereicherung für die neutestamentliche Wissenschaft." *ZNT* 18 (2015): 31–42.

DeMaris, Richard E., Jason T. Lamoreaux, and Steven C. Muir, eds. *Early Christian Ritual*. New York, NY: Routledge, 2018.

Demsky, Aaron. *Literacy in Ancient Israel*. The Biblical Encyclopaedia Library 28. Jerusalem: Bialik Institute, 2012 (Hebrew).

Demsky, Aaron. "Researching Literacy in Ancient Israel—New Approaches and Recent Developments." Pages 89–104 in *'See, I Will Bring a Scroll Recounting What Befell Me' (Ps 40:8): Epigraphy and Daily Life from the Bible to the Talmud, Dedicated to the Memory of Professor Hanan Eshel*. Edited by Esther Eshel and Yigal Levin. JAJSup 12. Göttingen: Vandenhoeck & Ruprecht, 2014.

Dewey, Joanna. "Oral Methods of Structuring Narrative in Mark." *Int* 43 (1989): 32–44.

Dewey, Joanna. "The Gospel of Mark as Oral Hermeneutic." Pages 71–87 in *Jesus, the Voice, and the Text: Beyond* The Oral and the Written Gospel. Edited by Tom Thatcher. Waco, TX: Baylor University Press, 2008.

Dewey, Joanna. *The Oral Ethos of the Early Church: Speaking, Writing, and the Gospel of Mark*. Biblical Performance Criticism 8. Eugene, OR: Cascade, 2013.

Diehl, Judy. "Anti-Imperial Rhetoric in the New Testament." *CBR* 10 (2011): 9–52.

Diehl, Judy. "Empire and Epistles: Anti-Roman Rhetoric in the New Testament Epistles." *CBR* 10 (2012): 217–63.

Diehl, Judy. "'Babylon': Then, Now, and 'Not Yet': Anti-Roman Rhetoric in the Book of Revelation." *CBR* 11 (2013): 168–95.

Dunn, James D. G. "Kenneth Bailey's Theory of Oral Tradition: Critiquing Theodore Weeden's Critique." *JSHJ* 7 (2009): 44–62.

Eberhart, Christian A. "Sacrificial Practice and Language." Page 462–76 in *The Oxford Handbook of Early Christian Ritual*. Edited by Risto Uro, Juliette Day, Richard E. DeMaris, and Rikard Roitto. Oxford: Oxford University Press, 2019.

Eddy, Paul Rhodes, and Gregory A. Boyd. *The Jesus Legend: A Case for the Historical Reliability of the Synoptic Tradition*. Grand Rapids, MI: Baker Academic, 2007.

Edelman, Diana V., and Ehud Ben Zvi. *Remembering Biblical Figures in the Late Persian and Early Hellenistic Periods: Social Memory and Imagination*. Oxford: Oxford University Press, 2013.

Edelman, Diana V., and Ehud Ben Zvi, eds. *Leadership, Social Memory and Judean Discourse in the Fifth–Second Centuries BCE*. Worlds of the Ancient Near East and Mediterranean. Sheffield: Equinox, 2016.

Elder, Nicholas A. "New Testament Media Criticism." *CBR* 15 (2017): 315–37.

Ellman, Barat. *Memory and Covenant: The Role of Israel's and God's Memory in Sustaining the Deuteronomic and Priestly Covenants*. Emerging Scholars. Minneapolis, MN: Fortress, 2013.

Epp, Eldon J. "The Codex and Literacy in Early Christianity and at Oxyrhynchus: Issues Raised by Harry Y. Gamble's *Books and Readers in the Early Church*." *CRBR* 11 (1998): 15–37.

Epp, Eldon J. "The Multivalence of the Term 'Original Text' in New Testament Textual Criticism." *HTR* 92 (1999): 245–81.

Esler, Philip F. "Collective Memory and Hebrews 11: Outlining a New Investigative Framework." Pages 151–71 in *Memory, Tradition, and Text: Uses of the Past in Early Christianity*. Edited by Alan Kirk and Tom Thatcher. SemeiaSt 52. Atlanta, GA: SBL, 2005.

Evans, Craig A. *Jesus and His World: The Archaeological Evidence*. Louisville, KY: Westminster John Knox, 2012.

Evans, Paul S. "Creating a New 'Great Divide': The Exoticization of Ancient Culture in Some Recent Applications of Orality Studies to the Bible." *JBL* 136 (2017): 749–64.

Eve, Eric. *Behind the Gospels: Understanding the Oral Tradition*. Minneapolis, MN: Fortress, 2014.

Feder, Yitzhaq. *Blood Expiation in Hittite and Biblical Ritual: Origins, Context, and Meaning*. WAWSup 2. Atlanta, GA: SBL, 2011.

Ferguson, Everett. *Backgrounds of Early Christianity*. 3rd ed. Grand Rapids, MI: Eerdmans, 2009.

Finnegan, Ruth. *Literacy and Orality: Studies in the Technology of Communication*. Oxford: Blackwell, 1988.

Floyd, Michael H. "'Write the Revelation!' (Hab 2:2): Reimagining the Cultural History of Prophecy." Pages 103–43 in *Writings and Speech in Israelite and Ancient Near Eastern Prophecy*. Edited by Ehud Ben Zvi and Michael H. Floyd. SymS 10. Atlanta, GA: SBL, 2000.

Foley, John Miles. *The Theory of Oral Composition: History and Methodology*. Bloomington, IN: Indiana University Press, 1988.

Foley, John Miles. *Immanent Art: From Structure to Meaning in Tradition Oral Epic.* Bloomington, IN: Indiana University Press, 1991.

Foley, John Miles. *The Singer of Tales in Performance*, Voices in Performance and Text. Bloomington, IN: Indiana University Press, 1995.

Foster, Paul. "Educating Jesus: The Search for a Plausible Context." *JSHJ* 4 (2006): 7–33.

Foster, Paul. "Memory, Orality, and the Fourth Gospel: Three Dead-Ends in Historical Jesus Research." *JSHJ* 10 (2012): 191–227.

Fraade, Steven D. "Language Mix and Multilingualism in Ancient Palestine: Literary and Inscriptional Evidence." *Jewish Studies* 48 (2012): 1–40.

Gamble, Harry Y. *Books and Readers in the Early Church: A History of Early Christian Texts.* New Haven, CT: Yale University Press, 1995.

Gamble, Harry Y. "Literacy and Book Culture." Pages 644–48 in *The Dictionary of New Testament Background.* Edited by Craig A. Evans and Stanley E. Porter. Downers Grove, IL: InterVarsity, 2000.

Gane, Roy E. *Cult and Character: Purification Offerings, Day of Atonement, and Theodicy.* Winona Lake, IN: Eisenbrauns, 2005.

Gane, Roy E. "Ritual and Religious Practices." Pages 225–31 in *The Oxford Handbook of Ritual and Worship in the Hebrew Bible.* Edited by Samuel E. Balentine. Oxford: Oxford University Press, 2020.

Gathercole, Simon. "The Earliest Manuscript Title of Matthew's Gospel (BnF Suppl.gr. 1120 ii 3 / P⁴)." *NovT* 54 (2012): 209–35.

Gathercole, Simon. "The Titles of the Gospels in the Earliest New Testament Manuscripts." *ZNW* 104 (2013): 33–76.

Gavrilov, A. K. "Techniques of Reading in Classical Antiquity." *ClQ* 47 (1997): 56–73.

Geertz, Clifford. "Religion as a Cultural System." Pages 1–46 in *Anthropological Approaches to the Study of Religion.* Edited by Michael Banton. London: Tavistock, 1966.

Geertz, Clifford. *The Interpretation of Cultures: Selected Essays.* New York, NY: Basic Books, 1973.

Genette, Gérard. *The Architext: An Introduction.* Translated by Jane E. Lewin. Berkeley, CA: University of California Press, 1992.

Genette, Gérard. *Palimpsests: Literature in the Second Degree.* Translated by Channa Newman and Claude Doubinsky. Stages 8. Lincoln, NE: University of Nebraska Press, 1997.

Genette, Gérard. *Paratexts: Thresholds of Interpretation.* Translated by Jane E. Lewin. Literature, Culture, Theory 20. Cambridge: Cambridge University Press, 1997.

Gennep, Arnold van. *The Rites of Passage.* Translated by Monika B. Vizedom and Gabrielle L. Caffee. Chicago: University of Chicago Press, 1960.

Gerhardsson, Birger. *Memory and Manuscript: Oral Tradition and Written Transmission in Rabbinic Judaism and Early Christianity*. Translated by Eric J. Sharpe. ASNU 22. Lund: C. W. K. Gleerup, 1961.

Gilders, William K. *Blood Ritual in the Hebrew Bible: Meaning and Power*. Baltimore, MD: Johns Hopkins University Press, 2004.

Gilders, William K. "Ancient Israelite Sacrifice as Symbolic Action: Theoretical Reflections." *SEÅ* 78 (2013): 1–22.

Gilliard, Frank D. "More on Silent Reading in Antiquity: *non omne verbum sonabat*." *JBL* 112 (1993): 689–96.

Gleaves, G. Scott. *Did Jesus Speak Greek? The Emerging Evidence of Greek Dominance in First-Century Palestine*. Eugene, OR: Pickwick, 2015.

Goody, Jack. *The Domestication of the Savage Mind*. Themes in the Social Sciences. Cambridge: Cambridge University Press, 1977.

Goody, Jack. *The Interface between the Written and the Oral*. Studies in Literacy, Family, Culture, and the State. Cambridge: Cambridge University Press, 1987.

Gorman, Jr., Frank H. "Ritual Studies and Biblical Studies: Assessment of the Past, Prospects for the Future." Pages 13–36 in *Transformation, Passages and Processes: Ritual Approaches to Biblical Texts*. Semeia 67. Atlanta, GA: SBL, 1995.

Grimes, Ronald L. *Beginnings in Ritual Studies*. 2nd ed. Columbia, SC: University of South Carolina Press, 1995.

Grimes, Ronald L. *The Craft of Ritual Studies*. Oxford: Oxford University Press, 2014.

Gruenwald, Ithamar. *Rituals and Ritual Theory in Ancient Israel*. BRLA 10. Leiden: Brill, 2003.

Gruenwald, Ithamar. "Rituals and Ritual Theory: A Methodological Essay." Pages 109–23 in *The Oxford Handbook of Ritual and Worship in the Hebrew Bible*. Edited by Samuel E. Balentine. Oxford: Oxford University Press, 2020.

Gurry, Peter J. "How Your Greek NT Is Changing: A Simple Introduction to the Coherence-Based Genealogical Method (CBGM)." *JETS* 59 (2016): 675–89.

Gurry, Peter J. *A Critical Examination of the Coherence-Based Genealogical Method in New Testament Textual Criticism*. NTTSD 55. Leiden: Brill, 2017.

Haines-Eitzen, Kim. *Guardians of Letters: Literacy, Power, and the Transmitters of Early Christian Literature*. Oxford: Oxford University Press, 2000.

Haines-Eitzen, Kim. *The Gendered Palimpsest: Women, Writing, and Representation of Women in Early Christianity*. Oxford: Oxford University Press, 2012.

Halbwachs, Maurice. *Les cadres sociaux de la mémoire*. Paris: Librairie Félix Alcan, 1925.

Halbwachs, Maurice. *La topographie légendaire des Évangiles en Terre Saint: étude de mémoire collective*. Paris: Presses Universitaires de France, 1941.

Halbwachs, Maurice. *La mémoire collective*. Paris: Presses Universitaires de France, 1950.

Harris, William V. "Literacy and Epigraphy I." *ZPE* 52 (1983): 87–111.

Harris, William V. *Ancient Literacy*. Cambridge, MA: Harvard University Press, 1989.

Harris, William V. "Inscriptions, Their Readers, and Literacy." *JRA* 22 (2009): 503–507.

Harrison, James R. *Paul and the Imperial Authorities at Thessalonica and Rome: A Study in the Conflict of Ideology*. WUNT 273. Tübingen: Mohr Siebeck, 2011.

Havelock, Eric A. *The Muse Learns to Write: Reflections on Orality and Literacy from Antiquity to Present*. New Haven, CT: Yale University Press, 1986.

Heilmann, Jan. "Reading Early New Testament Manuscripts: *Scriptio continua*, 'Reading Aids', and Other Characteristic Features." Pages 177–96 in *Material Aspects of Reading in Ancient and Medieval Cultures: Materiality, Presence and Performance*. Edited by Anna Krauß, Jonas Leipziger, and Friederike Schücking-Jungblut. Materiale Textkulturen 26. Berlin: De Gruyter, 2020.

Heilmann, Jan. *Lesen in Antike und frühem Christentum: Kulturgeschichtliche, philologische sowie kognitionswissenschaftliche Perspektiven und deren Bedeutung für die neutestamentliche Exegese*. TANZ 66. Tübingen: Narr Francke Attempto, 2021.

Hendel, Ronald. "The Exodus in Biblical Memory." *JBL* 120 (2001): 601–22.

Hendel, Ronald. "Plural Texts and Literary Criticism: For Instance, 1 Sam 17." *Textus* 23 (2007): 97–114.

Hendel, Ronald. "The Oxford Hebrew Bible: Prologue to a New Critical Edition." *VT* 58 (2008): 324–51.

Hendel, Ronald. *Steps to a New Edition of the Hebrew Bible*. TCSt 10. Atlanta, GA: SBL, 2016.

Hess, Richard S. "Literacy in Iron Age Israel." Pages 82–102 in *Windows into Old Testament History: Evidence, Argument, and the Crisis of Biblical Israel*. Edited by V. Philips Long, David W. Baker, and Gordon J. Wenham. Grand Rapids, MI: Eerdmans, 2002.

Hezser, Catherine. *Jewish Literacy in Roman Palestine*. TSAJ 81. Tübingen: Mohr Siebeck, 2001.

Hezser, Catherine. "Private and Public Education." Pages 465–81 in *The Oxford Handbook of Jewish Daily Life in Roman Palestine*. Edited by Catherine Hezser. Oxford: Oxford University Press, 2010.

Hezser, Catherine. *Rabbinic Body Language: Non-Verbal Communication in Palestinian Rabbinic Literature of Late Antiquity*. JSJSup 179. Leiden: Brill, 2017.

Hilton, Allen R. *Illiterate Apostles: Uneducated Early Christians and the Literates Who Loved Them*. LNTS 541. London: T&T Clark, 2018.

Hollander, August den, Ulrich Schmid, and Willem Smelik, eds. *Paratext and Megatext as Channels of Jewish and Christian Traditions: The Textual Markers of Contextualization*. Jewish and Christian Perspectives 6. Leiden: Brill, 2003.

Holmes, Michael W. "From 'Original Text' to 'Initial Text': The Traditional Goal of New Testament Textual Criticism in Contemporary Discussion." Pages 637–88 in *The Text of the New Testament in Contemporary Research: Essays on the Status Quaestionis.* 2nd ed. Edited by Bart D. Ehrman and Michael W. Holmes. NTTSD 42. Leiden: Brill, 2012.

Horsley, Richard A. *Hearing the Whole Story: The Politics of Plot in Mark's Gospel.* Louisville, KY: Westminster John Knox, 2001.

Horsley, Richard A. *Text and Tradition in Performance and Writing.* Biblical Performance Criticism 9. Eugene, OR: Cascade, 2013.

Horsley, Richard A., with Jonathan A. Draper. *Whoever Hears You Hears Me: Prophets, Performance, and Tradition in Q.* Harrisburg, PA: Trinity Press International, 1999.

Horsley, Richard A., Jonathan A. Draper, and John Miles Foley, eds. *Performing the Gospel: Orality, Memory, and Mark: Essays Dedicated to Werner Kelber.* Minneapolis, MN: Fortress, 2006.

Hurtado, Larry W. "What Do the Earliest Christian Manuscripts Tell Us About Their Readers?" Pages 179–92 in *The World of Jesus and the Early Church: Identity and Interpretation in Early Communities of Faith.* Edited by Craig A. Evans. Peabody, MA: Hendrickson, 2011.

Hurtado, Larry W. "Manuscripts and the Sociology of Early Christian Reading." Pages 49–62 in *The Early Text of the New Testament.* Edited by Charles E. Hill and Michael J. Kruger. Oxford: Oxford University Press, 2012.

Hurtado, Larry W., and Chris Keith. "Writing and Book Production in the Hellenistic and Roman Periods." Pages 63–80 in *The New Cambridge History of the Bible: From the Beginnings to 600.* Edited by James Carleton Paget and Joachim Schaper. Cambridge: Cambridge University Press, 2013.

Hurtado, Larry W. "Oral Fixation and New Testament Studies? 'Orality', 'Performance' and Reading Texts in Early Christianity." *NTS* 60 (2014): 321–40.

Hüsken, Ute, and Frank Neubert, eds. *Negotiating Rites.* Oxford: Oxford University Press, 2012.

Hylen, Susan E. "Ritual and Emerging Church Hierarchy." Pages 491–502 in *The Oxford Handbook of Early Christian Ritual.* Edited by Risto Uro, Juliette Day, Richard E. DeMaris, and Rikard Roitto. Oxford: Oxford University Press, 2019.

Iverson, Kelly R. "Orality and the Gospels: A Survey of Recent Research." *CBR* 8 (2009): 71–106.

Iverson, Kelly R. "Oral Fixation or Oral Corrective? A Response to Larry Hurtado." *NTS* 62 (2016): 183–200.

Johnson, William A. "Toward a Sociology of Reading in Classical Antiquity." *AJP* 121 (2000): 593–627.

Johnson, William A. "Constructing Elite Reading Communities in the High Empire." Pages 320–30 in *Ancient Literacies: The Culture of Reading in Greece and Rome.* Edited by William A. Johnson and Holt N. Parker. Oxford: Oxford University Press, 2009.

Johnson, William A. "Introduction." Pages 3–10 in *Ancient Literacies: The Culture of Reading in Greece and Rome*. Edited by William A. Johnson and Holt N. Parker. Oxford: Oxford University Press, 2009.

Johnson, William A. *Readers and Reading Culture in the High Roman Empire: A Study of Elite Communities*. Classical Culture and Society. Oxford: Oxford University Press, 2010.

Jürgens, Benedikt. *Heiligkeit und Versöhnung. Levitikus 16 in seinem literarischen Kontext*. HBS 28. Freiburg: Herder, 2001.

Kaše, Vojtěch. "Meal Practices." Pages 409–25 in *The Oxford Handbook of Early Christian Ritual*. Edited by Risto Uro, Juliette Day, Richard E. DeMaris, and Rikard Roitto. Oxford: Oxford University Press, 2019.

Keener, Craig. *Christobiography: Memory, History, and the Reliability of the Gospels*. Grand Rapids, MI: Eerdmans, 2019.

Keith, Chris. "'In My Own Hand': Grapho-Literacy and the Apostle Paul." *Bib* 89 (2008): 39–58.

Keith, Chris. "The Claim of John 7.15 and the Memory of Jesus' Literacy." *NTS* 56 (2010): 44–63.

Keith, Chris. "Memory and Authenticity: Jesus Tradition and What Really Happened." *ZNW* 102 (2011): 155–77.

Keith, Chris. *Jesus' Literacy: Scribal Culture and the Teacher from Galilee*. LNTS 413. London: Bloomsbury, 2011.

Keith, Chris. "Early Christian Book Culture and the Emergence of the First Written Gospel." Pages 22–39 in *Mark, Manuscripts, and Monotheism: Essays in Honor of Larry W. Hurtado*. Edited by Chris Keith and Dieter T. Roth. LNTS 528. London: Bloomsbury T&T Clark, 2015.

Keith, Chris. "Social Memory Theory and Gospels Research: The First Decade." *Early Christianity* 6 (2015): 354–76 (Part One), 517–42 (Part Two).

Keith, Chris. *Gospel as Manuscript: An Early History of the Jesus Tradition as Material Artifact*. Oxford: Oxford University Press, 2020.

Keith, Chris, and Anthony Le Donne, eds. *Jesus, Criteria, and the Demise of Authenticity*. London: T&T Clark, 2012.

Kelber, Werner H. *The Oral and the Written Gospel: The Hermeneutics of Speaking and Writing in the Synoptic Tradition, Mark, Paul, and Q*. Philadelphia, PA: Fortress, 1983.

Kelber, Werner H. "Jesus and Tradition: Words in Time, Words in Space." Pages 139–68 in *Orality and Textuality in Early Christian Literature*. Edited by Joanna Dewey. SemeiaSt 65. Atlanta, GA: SBL, 1995.

Kelber, Werner H. *Imprints, Voiceprints, and Footprints of Memory: Collected Essays of Werner H. Kelber*. RBS 74. Atlanta, GA: SBL, 2013.

Kelber, Werner H. "The Comparative Study of Oral Tradition." Pages 252–59 in *The Dictionary of the Bible and Ancient Media*. Edited by Tom Thatcher, Chris Keith, Raymond F. Person, and Elsie R. Stern. London: Bloomsbury, 2017.

Kelle, Brad E. "Postwar Rituals of Return and Reintegration." Pages 205–42 in *Warfare, Ritual, and Symbol in Biblical and Modern Contexts*. Edited by Brad E. Kelle, Frank R. Ames, and Jacob L. Wright. AIL 18. Atlanta, GA: SBL, 2014.

Kertzer, David I. *Ritual, Politics and Power*. New Haven, CT: Yale University Press, 1989.

Kirk, Alan. "Memory Theory and Jesus Research." Pages 809–842 in *Handbook for the Study of the Historical Jesus*, vol. 1: *How to Study the Historical Jesus*. Edited by Tom Holmén and Stanley E. Porter. Leiden: Brill, 2011.

Kirk, Alan, and Tom Thatcher, eds. *Memory, Tradition, and Text: Uses of the Past in Early Christianity*. SemeiaSt 52. Atlanta, GA: SBL, 2005.

Klingbeil, Gerald A. *A Comparative Study of the Ritual of Ordination as Found in Leviticus 8 and Emar 369*. Lewiston: Edwin Mellen, 1998.

Klingbeil, Gerald A. *Bridging the Gap: Ritual and Ritual Texts in the Bible*. BBRSup 1. Winona Lake, IN: Eisenbrauns, 2007.

Klingbeil, Gerald A. "When Action Collides with Meaning: Ritual Biblical Theology, and the New Testament Lord's Supper." *Neot* 50 (2016): 423–39.

Kloppenborg, John S. "Literate Media in Early Christ Groups: The Creation of a Christian Book Culture." *JECS* 22 (2014): 21–59.

Knox, B. M. "Silent Reading in Antiquity." *GRBS* 9 (1968): 421–35.

Kofoed, Jens Bruun. "The Old Testament as Cultural Memory." Pages 303–23 in *Do Historical Matters Matter to Faith? A Critical Appraisal of Modern and Postmodern Approaches to Scripture*. Edited by James K. Hoffmeier and Dennis R. Magary. Wheaton, IL: Crossway, 2012.

Kraemer, Ross S. "Women's Authorship of Jewish and Christian Literature in the Greco-Roman Period." Pages 221–42 in *"Women Like This": New Perspectives on Jewish Women in the Greco-Roman World*. Edited by Amy-Jill Levine. EJL 1. Atlanta, GA: Scholars, 1991.

Kreinath, Jens, Jan Snoek, and Michael Stausberg. "Ritual Studies, Ritual Theory, Theorizing Rituals." Pages xiii–xxv in *Theorizing Rituals: Issues, Topics, Approaches, Concepts*. Edited by Jens Kreinath, Jan Snoek, and Michael Stausberg. Studies in the History of Religions 114–1. Leiden: Brill, 2006.

Lamoreaux, Jason T. "BTB Readers Guide: Ritual Studies." *BTB* 39 (2009): 153–65.

Lang, Bernhard. "Schule und Unterricht im alten Israel." Pages 186–201 in *La Sagesse de l'Ancien Testament*. Edited by Maurice Gilbert. Louvain: Louvain University Press, 1979.

Lang, T. J., and Matthew R. Crawford. "The Origins of Pauline Theology: Paratexts and Priscillian Avila's *Canons on the Letters of the Apostle Paul*." *NTS* 63 (2017): 125–45.

Lawrence, Louis J. "Ritual and the First Urban Christians: Boundary Crossings of Life and Death." Pages 99–115 in *After the First Urban Christians: The Social-Scientific Study of Pauline Christianity Twenty-Five Years Later.* Edited by Todd D. Still and David G. Horrell. London: T&T Clark, 2009.

Lawson, E. Thomas, and Robert N. McCauley. *Rethinking Religion: Connecting Cognition and Culture.* Cambridge: Cambridge University Press, 1990.

Leach, Edmund. "Ritual." Pages 520–24 in *International Encyclopedia of the Social Sciences.* Edited by David L. Shils. vol. 13. New York, NY: Macmillan, 1968.

Leach, Edmund. *Culture and Communication: The Logic by which Symbols are Connected.* Cambridge: Cambridge University Press, 1976.

Le Donne, Anthony. *Historiographical Jesus: Memory, Typology, and the Son of David.* Waco, TX: Baylor University Press, 2009.

Le Donne, Anthony. *Historical Jesus: What Can We Know and How Can We Know It?* Grand Rapids, MI: Eerdmans, 2011.

Le Donne, Anthony. "Memory, Commemoration and History in John 2:19–22: A Critique and Application of Social Memory." Pages 186–204 in *The Fourth Gospel in First-Century Media Culture.* Edited by Anthony Le Donne and Tom Thatcher. LNTS 426. London: Bloomsbury, 2011.

Le Donne, Anthony. "The Problems of Selectivity in Memory Research: A Response to Zeba Crook." *JSHJ* 11 (2013): 77–97.

Lee, Sang-Il. *Jesus and Gospel Traditions in Bilingual Context: A Study in the Interdirectionality of Language.* BZNW 186. Berlin: De Gruyter, 2012.

Lemaire, André. "A Schoolboy's Exercise on an Ostracon at Lachish." *TA* 3 (1976): 109–10.

Lemaire, André. "Abécédaires et exercices d'écolier en épigraphie nord-ouest sémitique." *JA* 266 (1978): 221–35.

Lemaire, André. *Les écoles et la formation de la Bible dans l'ancien Israël.* OBO 39. Fribourg: Éditions Universitaires, 1981.

Lemaire, André. "Sagesse et écoles." *VT* 34 (1984): 270–81.

Leuchter, Mark. *The Levites and the Boundaries of Israelite Identity.* Oxford: Oxford University Press, 2017.

Liénard, Pierre, and Pascal Boyer. "Whence Collective Rituals? A Cultural Selection Model of Ritualized Behavior." *American Anthropologist* 108 (2006): 814–27.

Lietzmann, Hans. *Messe und Herrenmahl. Eine Studie zur Geschichte der Liturgie.* 3rd ed. Arbeiten zur Kirchengeschichte 8. Berlin: De Gruyter, 1955.

Lin, Yii-Jan. *The Erotic Life of Manuscripts: New Testament Textual Criticism and the Biological Sciences.* Oxford: Oxford University Press, 2016.

Lindsay, R. C. L., David F. Ross, J. Don Read, and Michael P. Toglia, eds. *The Handbook of Eyewitness Psychology*, vol. 2: *Memory for People.* Mahwah, NJ: Lawrence Erlbaum, 2007.

Longenecker, Bruce W. *In Stone and Story: Early Christians in the Roman World*. Grand Rapids, MI: Baker Academic, 2020.

Lord, Albert B. *The Singer of Tales*. Harvard Studies in Comparative Literature 24. Cambridge, MA: Harvard University Press, 1960.

Lundhaug, Hugo, and Liv Ingeborg Lied. "Studying Snapshots: On Manuscript Culture, Textual Fluidity, and New Philology." Pages 1–19 in *Snapshots of Evolving Traditions: Jewish and Christian Manuscript Culture, Textual Fluidity, and New Philology*. Edited by Hugo Lundhaug and Liv Ingeborg Lied. TUGAL 175. Berlin: De Gruyter, 2017.

Loubser, J. A. "What is Biblical Media Criticism? A Media-Critical Reading of Luke 9:51–56." *Scriptura* 80 (2002): 206–19.

MacDonald, Nathan, ed. *Ritual Innovation in the Hebrew Bible and Early Judaism*. BZAW 468. Berlin: De Gruyter, 2018.

Maiden, Brett E. *Cognitive Science and Ancient Israelite Religion*. Cambridge: Cambridge University Press, 2020.

Mandel, Paul D. *The Origins of Midrash: From Teaching to Text*. JSJSup 180. Leiden: Brill, 2017.

Marrou, Henri I. *A History of Education in Antiquity*. Madison, WI: University of Wisconsin Press, 1982.

Mavrogenes, Nancy A. "Reading in Ancient Greece." *Journal of Reading* (1980): 691–97.

McCartney, Eugene S. "Notes on Reading and Praying Audibly." *CP* 43 (1948): 184–87.

McCauley, Robert N., and E. Thomas Lawson. *Bringing Ritual to Mind: Psychological Foundations of Cultural Forms*. Cambridge: Cambridge University Press, 2002.

McCutcheon, R. W. "Silent Reading in Antiquity and the Future History of the Book." *Book History* 18 (2015): 1–32.

McIver, Robert K. *Memory, Jesus, and the Synoptic Gospels*. RBS 59. Atlanta, GA: SBL, 2011.

McIver, Robert K. "Eyewitnesses as Guarantors of the Accuracy of the Gospel Traditions in the Light of Psychological Research." *JBL* 131 (2012): 529–46.

McVann, Mark. "Reading Mark Ritually: Honor-Shame and the Ritual of Baptism." Pages 179–98 in *Transformation, Passages and Processes: Ritual Approaches to Biblical Texts*. SemeiaSt 67 Atlanta, GA: SBL, 1995.

Meeks, Wayne A. *The First Urban Christians: The Social World of the Apostle Paul*. 2nd ed. New Haven, CT: Yale University Press, 2003.

Millard, Alan. *Reading and Writing in the Time of Jesus*. New York, NY: New York University Press, 2000.

Miller II, Robert D. *Oral Tradition in Ancient Israel*. Biblical Performance Criticism 4. Eugene, OR: Cascade, 2011.

Mink, Gerd. "Ein umfassende Genealogie der neutestamentlichen Überlieferung." *NTS* 39 (1993): 481–99.

Mink, Gerd. "Problems of a Highly Contaminated Tradition, the New Testament: Stemmata of Variants as a Source of a Genealogy for Witnesses." Pages 13–85 in

Studies in Stemmatology 11. Edited by Pieter van Reenen, August den Hollander, Margot van Mulken. Philadelphia, PA: John Benjamins, 2004.

Mink, Gerd. "Contamination, Coherence, and Coincidence in Textual Transmission: The Coherence-Based Genealogical Method (CBGM) as a Complement and Corrective to Existing Approaches." Pages 141–216 in *The Textual History of the Greek New Testament: Changing View in Contemporary Research.* Edited by Klaus Wachtel and Michael W. Holmes. SBLTCS 8. Atlanta, GA: SBL, 2011.

Morgan, Theresa. *Literate Education in the Hellenistic and Roman Worlds.* Cambridge Classical Studies. Cambridge: Cambridge University Press, 1998.

Müller, Darius, and Peter Malik. "Rediscovering Paratexts in the Manuscripts of Revelation." *Early Christianity* 11 (2020): 247–64.

Nässelqvist, Dan. *Public Reading in Early Christianity: Lectors, Manuscripts, and Sound in the Oral Delivery of John 1–4.* NovTSup 163. Leiden: Brill, 2016.

Nichols, Stephen. "The New Philology. Introduction: Philology in a Manuscript Culture." *Speculum* 65 (1990): 1–10.

Niditch, Susan. *Oral World and Written Word: Ancient Israelite Literature.* LAI. Louisville, KY: Westminster John Knox, 1996.

Niditch, Susan. "Oral Tradition and Biblical Scholarship." *Oral Tradition* 18 (2003): 43–44.

Niditch, Susan. "The Challenge of Israelite Epic." Pages 277–87 in *A Companion to Ancient Epic.* Edited by John Miles Foley. London: Blackwell, 2005.

Niditch, Susan. *"My Brother Esau is a Hairy Man": Hair and Identity in Ancient Israel.* Oxford: Oxford University Press, 2008.

Niditch, Susan. "Epic and History in the Hebrew Bible: Definitions, 'Ethnic Genres,' and the Challenges of Cultural Identity in the Biblical Book of Judges." Pages 86–102 in *Epic and History.* Edited by David Konstan and Kurt A. Raaflaub. London: Blackwell, 2010.

Niditch, Susan. "Hebrew Bible and Oral Literature: Misconceptions and New Directions." Pages 3–18 in *The Interface of Orality and Writing: Speaking, Seeing, Writing in the Shaping of New Genres.* Edited by Annette Weisenrieder and Robert B. Coote. WUNT 260. Tübingen: Mohr Siebeck, 2010.

Niditch, Susan. "A Messy Business: Ritual Violence after the War." Pages 187–204 in *Warfare, Ritual, and Symbol in Biblical and Modern Contexts.* Edited by Brad E. Kelle, Frank R. Ames, and Jacob L. Wright. AIL 18. Atlanta, GA: SBL, 2014.

Oestreich, Bernard. *Performance Criticism of the Pauline Letters.* Biblical Performance Criticism 14. Eugene, OR: Cascade, 2016.

Olyan, Saul M. "What Do Shaving Rites Accomplish and What Do They Signal in Biblical Ritual Contexts." *JBL* 117 (1998): 611–22.

Olyan, Saul M. *Rites and Rank: Hierarchy in Biblical Representations of Cult.* Princeton, NJ: Princeton University Press, 2000.

Olyan, Saul M. *Ritual Violence in the Hebrew Bible: New Perspectives*. Oxford: Oxford University Press, 2015.

Olyan, Saul M. *Violent Rituals of the Hebrew Bible*. Oxford: Oxford University Press, 2019.

Ong, Hughson T. *The Multilingual Jesus and the Sociolinguistic World of the New Testament*. Linguistic Biblical Studies 12. Leiden: Brill, 2016.

Ong, Walter J. *Orality and Literacy: The Technologizing of the World*. 2nd ed. London: Routledge, 2002.

Parker, David C. *Textual Scholarship and the Making of the New Testament*. Oxford: Oxford University Press, 2012.

Parker, Holt N. "Books and Reading Latin Poetry." Pages 186–229 in *Ancient Literacies: The Culture of Reading in Greece and Rome*. Edited William A. Johnson and Holt N. Parker. Oxford: Oxford University Press, 2009.

Parry, Milman. *The Making of Homeric Verse: The Collected Papers of Milman Parry*. Edited by Adam Parry. Oxford: Oxford University Press, 1971.

Penn, Michael P. "Performing Family: Ritual Kissing and the Construction of Early Christian Kinship." *JECS* 10 (2002): 151–74.

Penn, Michael P. *Kissing Christians: Ritual and Community in the Late Ancient Church*. Philadelphia, PA: University of Pennsylvania Press, 2005.

Penn, Michael P. "Kissing, Purity, and Early Christian Social Order." Pages 87–92 in *Studia Patristica*, vol. 40: *Papers Presented at the Fourteenth International Conference on Patristic Studies held in Oxford 2003*. Edited by Frances M. Young, Morgan J. Edwards, and Paul M. Parvis. Leuven: Peeters, 2006.

Perfect, Timothy J., and D. Stephen Lindsay, eds. *The SAGE Handbook of Applied Memory*. Thousand Oaks, CA: SAGE Publications, 2014.

Perry, Peter S. "Biblical Performance Criticism: Survey and Prospects." *Religions* 10 (2019): 1–15.

Person, Jr., Raymond F. "The Ancient Israelite Scribe as Performer." *JBL* 117 (1998): 601–609.

Person, Jr., Raymond F. "Orality Studies, Oral Tradition: Hebrew Bible." Pages 2:55–63 in *The Encyclopedia of Biblical Interpretation*. Edited by Steven L. McKenzie. Oxford: Oxford University Press, 2013.

Person, Jr., Raymond F. "Text Criticism as a Lens for Understanding the Transmission of Ancient Texts in Their Oral Environments." Pages 197–215 in *Contextualizing Israel's Sacred Writings: Ancient Literacy, Orality, and Literary Production*. Edited by Brian Schmidt. AIL 22. Atlanta, GA: SBL, 2015.

Person, Jr., Raymond F. "Education and Transmission of Tradition." Pages 366–78 in *Companion to Ancient Israel*. Edited by Susan Niditch. Oxford: Blackwell, 2016.

Person, Jr., Raymond F., and Chris Keith. "Media Studies and Biblical Studies: An Introduction." Pages 1–15 in *The Dictionary of the Bible and Ancient Media*. Edited by Tom Thatcher, Chris Keith, Raymond F. Person, Jr., and Elsie R. Stern. London: Bloomsbury, 2017.

Pioske, Daniel D. "Retracing a Remembered Past: Methodological Remarks on Memory, History, and the Hebrew Bible." *BibInt* 23 (2015): 291–315.

Pioske, Daniel D. *David's Jerusalem: Between Memory and History*. Routledge Studies in Religion 45. London: Routledge, 2015.

Poirier, John C. "The Linguistic Situation in Jewish Palestine in Late Antiquity." *JGRChJ* 4 (2007): 55–134.

Quick, Laura. "Recent Research on Ancient Israelite Education: A Bibliographic Essay." *CBR* 13 (2014): 9–33.

Redman, Judith C. S. "How Accurate Are Eyewitnesses? Bauckham and the Eyewitnesses in the Light of Psychological Research." *JBL* 129 (2010): 177–97.

Rhoads, David. "Performance Criticism: An Emerging Methodology in Second Temple Studies." *BTB* 36 (2006): 118–33, 164–84.

Rodríguez, Rafael. "Authenticating Criteria: The Use and Misuse of a Critical Method." *JSHJ* 7 (2009): 152–67.

Rodríguez, Rafael. *Structuring Early Christian Memory: Jesus in Tradition, Performance and Text.* LNTS 407. London: T&T Clark, 2010.

Rodríguez, Rafael. *Oral Tradition and the New Testament: A Guide for the Perplexed.* London: Bloomsbury, 2014.

Rollston, Christopher A. "Scribal Education in Ancient Israel: The Old Testament Hebrew Epigraphic Evidence." *BASOR* 344 (2006): 47–74.

Rollston, Christopher A. *Writing and Literacy in the World of Ancient Israel: Epigraphic Evidence from the Iron Age.* ABS 11. Atlanta, GA: SBL 2010.

Rothenbuhler, Eric W. *Ritual Communication: From Everyday Conversation to Mediated Ceremony.* Thousand Oaks, CA: SAGE Publications, 1998.

Safrai, Shmuel. "Elementary Education, Its Religious and Social Significance in the Talmudic Period." *Cahiers d'histoire mondiale* 11 (1968): 148–69.

Saenger, Paul. *Spaces between Words: The Origins of Silent Reading.* Figurae: Reading Medieval Culture. Stanford, CA: Stanford University Press, 1997.

Schellenberg, Ryan S. *Rethinking Paul's Rhetorical Education: Comparative Rhetoric and 2 Corinthians 10–13.* ECL 10. Atlanta, GA: SBL, 2013.

Scherbenske, Eric. "The Vulgate *Primum Quaeritur*, Codex Fuldensis and the Hermeneutical Role of Early Christian Introductory Materials." Pages 139–44 in *Papers Presented at the Fifteenth International Conference on Patristic Studies held in Oxford 2007. Archaelogica, Arts, Iconographica, Tools, Historica, Biblica, Theologica, Philosophica, Ethica.* Edited by Jane Ralls Baun. Leuven: Peeters, 2010.

Scherbenske, Eric. *Canonizing Paul: Ancient Editorial Practice and the Corpus Paulinum.* Oxford: Oxford University Press, 2013.

Schnelle, Udo. "Das frühe Christentum und die Bildung." *NTS* 61 (2015): 113–43.

Schniedewind, William M. *How the Bible Became a Book: The Textualization of Ancient Israel.* Cambridge: Cambridge University Press, 2004.

Schröter, Jens. "The Criteria of Authenticity in Jesus Research and Historiographical Method." Pages 59–65 in *Jesus, Criteria, and the Demise of Authenticity*. Edited by Chris Keith and Anthony Le Donne. London: T&T Clark, 2012.

Schröter, Jens. *From Jesus to the New Testament: Early Christian Theology and the Origin of the New Testament Canon*. Translated by Wayne Coppins. BMSEC. Waco, TX: Baylor University Press, 2013.

Schürer, Emil. *A History of the Jewish People in the Time of Jesus*, Second Division: *The Internal Condition of Palestine and of the Jewish People in the Time of Jesus Christ*. Translated by Sophia Taylor and Peter Christie. Edinburgh: T&T Clark, 1885.

Schwartz, Barry. "Christian Origins: Historical Truth and Social Memory." Pages 43–56 in *Memory, Tradition, and Text: Uses of the Past in Early Christianity*. Edited by Alan Kirk and Tom Thatcher. SemeiaSt 52. Atlanta, GA: SBL, 2005.

Schwiebert, Jonathan. *Knowledge and the Coming Kingdom: The Didache's Meal Ritual and its Place in Early Christianity*. LNTS 373. London: T&T Clark, 2008.

Sedgwick, W. B. "Reading and Writing in Classical Antiquity." *Contemporary Review* 135 (1990): 90–94.

Segal, Michael. "Methodological Considerations in the Preparation of an Edition of the Hebrew Bible." Pages 34–55 in *The Text of the Hebrew Bible and Its Editions: Studies in Celebration of the Fifth Centennial of the Complutensian Polygot*. Edited by Andrés Piquer Otero and Pablo Torijano Morales. Supplements to the Textual History of the Bible 1. Leiden: Brill, 2017.

Shaus, Arie, Yana Gerber, Shira Faigenbaum-Golovin, Barak Sober, Eli Piasetzky, and Israel Finkelstein. "Forensic Document Examination and Algorithmic Handwriting Analysis of Judahite Biblical Period Inscriptions Reveal Significant Literacy Level." *PLoS ONE* (2020): 1–15.

Shiell, William D. *Reading Acts: The Lector and the Early Christian Audience*. BIS 70. Leiden: Brill, 2004.

Shiell, William D. *Delivering from Memory: The Effect of Performance on the Early Christian Audience*. Eugene, OR: Pickwick Publications, 2011.

Shiner, Whitney T. *Proclaiming the Gospel: First-Century Performance in Mark*. Harrisburg, PA: Trinity Press International, 2003.

Silverman, Jason M. *Persepolis and Jerusalem: Iranian Influence on the Apocalyptic Hermeneutic*. LHBOT 558. London: T&T Clark, 2012.

Smelik, Willem. "Code-Switching: The Public Reading of the Bible in Hebrew, Aramaic and Greek." Pages 123–47 in *Was ist ein Text? Alttestamentliche, ägyptologische und altorientalische Perspektiven*. Edited by Ludwig Morenz and Stefan Schorch. BZAW 362. Berlin: De Gruyter, 2007.

Smith, Mark S. "Remembering God: Collective Memory in Israelite Religion." *CBQ* 64 (2002): 631–51.

Snyder, H. Gregory. *Teachers and Texts in the Ancient World: Philosophers, Jews, and Christians*. Religion in the First Christian Centuries. London: Routledge, 2000.

Sperber, Dan. *Rethinking Symbolism*. Cambridge: Cambridge University Press, 1975.

Staal, Frits. "The Meaninglessness of Ritual." *Numen* 26 (1979): 2–22.

Staal, Frits. "The Search for Meaning: Mathematics, Music, and Ritual." *American Journal of Semiotics* 2 (1984): 1–57.

Staal, Frits. *Rules Without Meaning: Ritual, Mantras, and the Human Sciences*. Toronto Studies in Religion 4. New York, NY: Peter Lang, 1989.

Stavrianopoulou, Eftychia. "Introduction." Pages 7–22 in *Ritual and Communication in the Graeco-Roman World*. Edited by Eftychia Stavrianopoulou. Kernos Supplement 16. Liége: Centre international d'étude de la religion grecque antique, 2006.

Stephenson, Barry. *Ritual: A Very Short Introduction*. Oxford: Oxford University Press, 2015.

Taussig, Hal. *In the Beginning was the Meal: Social Experimentation and Early Christian Identity*. Minneapolis, MN: Fortress, 2009.

Thatcher, Tom. *Jesus the Riddler: The Power of Ambiguity in the Gospels*. Louisville, KY: Westminster John Knox, 2006.

Thatcher, Tom, ed. *Jesus, the Voice, and the Text: Beyond* The Oral and the Written Gospel. Waco, TX: Baylor University Press, 2008.

Thomas, Günter. "Communication." Pages 321–43 in *Theorizing Rituals: Issues, Topics, Approaches, Concepts*. Edited by Jens Kreinath, Jan Snoek, and Michael Stausberg. Studies in the History of Religions 114–1. Leiden: Brill, 2006.

Thomas, Rosalind. *Literacy and Orality in Ancient Greece*. Key Themes in Ancient History. Cambridge: Cambridge University Press, 1992.

Tigchelaar, Eibert J. C. "Editing the Hebrew Bible: An Overview of Some Problems." Pages 41–65 in *Editing the Bible: Assessing the Task Past and Present*. Edited by John S. Kloppenborg and Judith Newman. RBS 69. Atlanta, GA: SBL, 2012.

Toglia, Michael P., J. Don Read, David F. Ross, and R. C. L. Lindsay, eds. *Handbook of Eyewitness Psychology*, vol. 1: *Memory for Events*. Mahwah, NJ: Lawrence Erlbaum, 2007.

Turley, Stephen R. *The Ritualized Revelation of the Messianic Age: Washings and Meals in Galatians and 1 Corinthians*. LNTS 544. London: Bloomsbury, 2015.

Turner, Victor. *The Ritual Process: Structure and Anti-Structure*. London: Routledge, 1969.

Uro, Risto. "Gnostic Rituals from a Cognitive Perspective." Pages 115–37 in *Explaining Christian Origins and Early Judaism: Contributions from Cognitive and Social Science*. Edited by Petri Luomanen, Ilkka Pyysiäinen, and Risto Uro. BIS 89. Leiden: Brill, 2007.

Uro, Risto. "The Bridal Chamber and Other Mysteries: Ritual System and Ritual Transmission in the Valentinian Movement." Pages 457–86 in *Sacred Marriages: The Divine-Human Sexual Metaphor from Sumer to Early Christianity*. Edited by Martti Nissinen and Risto Uro. Winona Lake, IN: Eisenbrauns, 2008.

Uro, Risto. "Ritual and Christian Origins." Pages 220–32 in *Understanding the Social World of the New Testament*. Edited by Dietmar Neufeld and Richard E. DeMaris. New York, NY: Routledge, 2010.

Uro, Risto. "Kognitive Ritualtheorien: Neue Modelle für Analyse urchristliche Sakramente." *EvT* 71 (2011): 272–88.

Uro, Risto. "Cognitive and Evolutionary Approaches to Ancient Rituals: Reflections on Recent Theories and Their Relevance for the Historian of Religion." Pages 487–510 in *Mystery and Secrecy in the Nag Hammadi Collection and Other Ancient Literature: Ideas and Practices*. Edited by John D. Turner, Christian H. Bull, and Liv Ingeborg Lied. Nag Hammadi and Manichaean Studies 76. Leiden: Brill, 2011.

Uro, Risto. "Towards a Cognitive History of Early Christian Rituals." Pages 223–35 in *Changing Minds: Religion and Cognition through Ages*. Edited by István Czachesz and Tamas Bíró. Groningen Studies in Cultural Change 42. Leuven: Peeters, 2011.

Uro, Risto. *Ritual and Christian Beginnings: A Socio-Cognitive Analysis*. Oxford: Oxford University Press, 2016.

Uro, Risto. "Ritual and the Rise of Early Christian Movement." Pages 427–41 in *Early Christian World*. Edited by Philip F. Esler. 2nd ed. New York, NY: Routledge, 2017.

Uro, Risto, and István Czachesz, eds. *Mind, Morality and Magic: Cognitive Science Approaches in Biblical Studies*. Durham: Acumen, 2013.

Uro, Risto, Juliette Day, Richard E. DeMaris, and Rikard Roitto, eds. *The Oxford Handbook of Early Christian Ritual*. Oxford: Oxford University Press, 2019.

Valette-Cagnac, Emmanuelle. *La lecture à Rome: rites et pratiques*. Antiquité au present. Paris: Belin, 1997.

Vegge, Tor. "The Literacy of Jesus the Carpenter's Son: On the Literary Style in the Words of Jesus." *ST* 59 (2005): 19–37.

Wachtel, Klaus. "Toward a Redefinition of External Criteria: The Role of Coherence in Assessing the Origin of Variants." Pages 109–28 in *Textual Variation: Theological and Social Tendencies? Papers from the Fifth Birmingham Colloquium on the Textual Criticism of the New Testament*. Edited by Hugh A. G. Houghton and David C. Parker. TS 3/6. Piscataway, NJ: Gorgias, 2008.

Wachtel, Klaus. "The Coherence-Based Genealogical Method: A New Way to Reconstruct the Text of the Greek New Testament." Pages 123–38 in *Editing the Bible: Assessing the Task Past and Present*. Edited by John S. Kloppenborg and Judith Newman. RBS 69. Atlanta, GA: SBL, 2012.

Wallraff, Martin. *Die Kanontafeln des Euseb von Kaisareia: Untersuchung und kritische Edition*. Manuscripta Biblica 1. Berlin: De Gruyter, 2021.

Wallraff, Martin, and Patrick Andrist. "Paratexts of the Bible: A New Research Project on Greek Textual Transmission." *Early Christianity* 6 (2015): 237–43.

Wasserman, Tommy, and Peter J. Gurry. *A New Approach to Textual Criticism: An Introduction to the Coherence-Based Genealogical Method*. RBS 80. Atlanta, GA: SBL, 2017.

Watts, James W. *Ritual and Rhetoric in Leviticus: From Sacrifice to Scripture*. Cambridge: Cambridge University Press, 2007.

Weeden, Theodore J. "Kenneth Bailey's Theory of Oral Tradition: A Theory Contested by Its Evidence." *JSHJ* 7 (2009): 3–43.

White, Benjamin L. *Remembering Paul: Ancient and Modern Contests over the Image of the Apostle*. Oxford: Oxford University Press, 2014.

White Crawford, Sidnie, Jan Joosten, and Eugene Ulrich. "Sample Editions of the Oxford Hebrew Bible: Deuteronomy 32:1–9, 1 Kings 11:1–8, and Jeremiah 27:1–10 (34 G)." *VT* 58 (2008): 352–66.

Whitehouse, Harvey. *Arguments and Icons: Divergent Modes of Religiosity*. Oxford: Oxford University Press, 2000.

Whitehouse, Harvey. *Modes of Religiosity: A Cognitive Theory of Religious Transmission*. Walnut Creek, CA: AltaMira, 2004.

Williamson, Hugh G. M. "Do We Need A New Bible? Reflections on the Proposed Oxford Hebrew Bible." *Bib* 90 (2009): 153–75.

Wilson, Ian D. *Kingship and Memory in Ancient Judah*. Oxford: Oxford University Press, 2017.

Wilson, Ian D. "History and the Hebrew Bible: Culture, Narrative, and Memory." *RPBI* 3 (2018): 1–69.

Wilson, Ian D., and Diana Edelman, eds. *History, Memory, Hebrew Scriptures: A Festschrift for Ehud Ben Zvi*. Winona Lake, IN: Eisenbrauns, 2015.

Wise, Michael O. *Language and Literacy in Roman Judaea: A Study of the Bar Kokhba Documents*. AYBRL. New Haven, CT: Yale University Press, 2015.

Wohleb, Leo. "Ein Beitrag zur Geschichte des lauten Lesens." *Philologus* 85 (1929): 111–12.

Wolmarans, J. L. P. "The Semiotics of the Ritual Meal in the *Didache*." *Acta Patristica et Byzantina* 16 (2005): 308–24.

Wright, Brian J. *Communal Reading in the Time of Jesus: A Window into Early Christian Reading Practices*. Minneapolis, MN: Fortress, 2017.

Wright, David P. *The Disposal of Impurity: Elimination Rites in the Bible and in Hittite and Mesopotamian Literature*. SBLDS 101. Atlanta, GA: Scholars, 1987.

Wright, David P. *Ritual in Narrative: The Dynamics of Feasting, Mourning, and Retaliation Rites in the Ugaritic Tale of Aqhat*. Winona Lake, IN: Eisenbrauns, 2001.

Wright, David P. "The Study of Ritual in the Hebrew Bible." Pages 120–38 in *The Hebrew Bible: New Insights and Scholarship*. Edited by Frederick E. Greenspahn. Jewish Studies in the Twenty-First Century 4. New York, NY: New York University Press, 2008.

Young, Ian M. "Israelite Literacy: Interpreting the Evidence." *VT* 48 (1998): 239–53, 408–22.

Yuh, Jason N. "Analysing Paul's Reference to Baptism in Galatians 3.27 through Studies of Memory, Embodiment and Ritual." *JSNT* 41 (2019): 478–500.

Zimmermann, Reuben. "Geschichtstheorien und Neues Testament: Gedächtnis, Diskurs, Kultur und Narration in der historiographischen Diskussion." *Early Christianity* 2 (2011): 417–44.

Zumthor, Paul. *Oral Poetry: An Introduction*. Translated by Kathryn Murphy-Judy. Theory and History of Literature 70. Minneapolis, MN: University of Minnesota Press, 1990.

PART 1

Past Perspectives on the Dead Sea Scrolls and Ancient Media

∵

CHAPTER 3

Textuality and the Dead Sea Scrolls: An Examination of Modern Approaches and Recent Trends

Travis B. Williams

1   Introduction

A growing awareness of the importance of ancient communications culture has begun to contribute significantly to the study of the Dead Sea Scrolls and the community(-ies) who produced and preserved them. While historical inquiry fueled much of the earliest research on these documents,[1] their value as a window into ancient media culture has not gone unrecognized. From the very beginning, paleographic analysis was performed on the writings to better understand their various scripts,[2] and throughout the years, scholars have worked to painstakingly assess scribal habits. Further, scientific investigation has been conducted into the material character of the manuscripts as well as the ink that was used during the process of writing. All of this represents a natural first step toward properly understanding the Qumran discoveries.

Within more recent scholarship, new questions about ancient media have emerged. Fueling these developments are advances in technology, the full publication of the textual and archaeological evidence from Qumran, and the methodological shifts that have taken place in the field. In an effort to gain perspective on these issues, scholars are attempting to both broaden and sharpen their research focus. Inquiry has extended beyond the material nature of the

---

1   Throughout this essay, I will be distinguishing between 'text' (= 'writing'), by which I mean a series of words on a page, 'work' (= 'composition'), by which I refer to an identifiable textual unit that circulates in a relatively consistent form, and 'manuscript' (= 'document'), by which I describe a material artefact that preserves writing. Cf. Matthew James Driscoll, "The Words on a Page: Thoughts on Philology Old and New," in *Creating the Medieval Saga: Versions, Variability, and Editorial Interpretations of Old Norse Saga Literature*, ed. Judy Quinn and Emily Lethbridge (Odense: Syddansk Universitetsforlag, 2010), 93.

2   For a review of this discussion, see Eibert J. C. Tigchelaar, "Seventy Years of Palaeographic Dating of the Dead Sea Scrolls," in *Sacred Texts and Disparate Interpretations: Qumran Manuscripts Seventy Years Later: Proceedings of the International Conference Held at the John Paul II Catholic University of Lublin, 24–26 October 2017*, ed. Henryk Drawnel, STDJ 133 (Leiden: Brill, 2020), 258–78.

© TRAVIS B. WILLIAMS, 2023 | DOI:10.1163/9789004537804_004

textual resources to include topics such as literacy, performance, and memory. What is more, many are working to contextualize the finds through comparisons with other manuscript discoveries from the Judean desert as well as broader media trends from the classical world. Yet, since these efforts are only in their infancy, there is still much to be learned about ancient media culture and how the Scrolls fit into this setting.

In light of this situation, it is an ideal time to evaluate the current state of media research on the Scrolls and to cast a vision for the future. This paper will contribute to that end by reviewing recent treatments of the Scrolls in the context of ancient textuality. Given the potential breadth of this topic, however, we will not attempt to provide a full history of research. Instead, our focus will be on current trends that are reshaping the field.

2 The Characteristics of the Scrolls

Research into the physical characteristics of the Scrolls is just one area where new questions and fresh approaches have led to important shifts in scholarship. Earlier investigations considered issues such as the composition of the ink as well as the size and material make-up of the manuscripts. These studies represent a natural first step toward understanding the Scrolls as ancient artefacts.[3] As the methods of these investigations continue to be refined, a

---

3 Although not always considered, developments in modern media could also potentially impact the study of the Scrolls as ancient artefacts. To take just one example, we might note the tremendously important and painstaking efforts to digitize the Dead Sea Scrolls undertaken by The Israel Antiquities Authority. This collection of high-resolution images, known as the Leon Levy Dead Sea Scrolls Digital Library, is a profound achievement that has provided universal access to the Scrolls in format that expands the potential for future study (see Pnina Shor, "The Leon Levy Dead Sea Scrolls Digital Library: The Digitization Project of the Dead Sea Scrolls," in *Digital Humanities in Biblical, Early Jewish and Early Christian Studies*, ed. Claire Clivaz, Andrew Gregory, and David Hamidović, Scholarly Communication 2 [Leiden: Brill, 2013], 11–20). But such merits notwithstanding, a media approach forces us to consider how this change in media technology could affect the experience of documents and (potentially) modern understandings of them (see Claire Clivaz, "Digitization and Manuscripts as Visual Objects: Reflections from a Media Studies Perspective," in *Ancient Manuscripts in Digital Culture: Visualisation, Data Mining, Communication*, ed. David Hamidović, Claire Clivaz, and Sarah Bowen Savant, Digital Biblical Studies 3 [Leiden: Brill, 2019], 15–29). In other words, as scholarly access to the Scrolls transitions from handling the physical objects to viewing content on a screen, might anything be lost? In what ways could this media shift create similar limitations to those generated by accessing texts through print editions (see above)? While the benefits of this digitization process will undoubtedly outweigh any potential drawbacks, questions like these must still be considered. And with a view toward the

common trend in recent scholarship has been to consider what this evidence might reveal about the groups or individuals who used them.

2.1   *Ink from the Scrolls*

In antiquity, two types of ink were used for writing. Carbon-based ink was made from lampblack or soot, which tended to rest on the surface of the parchment. Iron-gall-based ink, on the other hand, was made from copperas, which tended to penetrate the parchment.[4] Given its bearing on the dating of manuscripts,[5] the earliest investigations into the ink used to compose the Dead Sea Scrolls focused on their chemical composition. The black ink used on the scrolls from Cave 1 was first analyzed by spectroscopic methods in the 1950s, and it was determined to be carbon-based.[6] This finding was later confirmed on manuscripts from Caves 1 and 4 using Energy-Dispersive X-Ray Fluorescence (EDXRF).[7] While the deterioration of some manuscripts has led to speculation about the presence of iron in the ink,[8] subsequent studies have concluded that the degradation was accelerated either by the use of a bronze inkwell or by the binding agent that was employed.[9]

---

impact of media technology on knowledge and practice, it might perhaps benefit scholars to think about constructing facsimiles of the manuscripts in an effort to gain a better appreciation and further insights into how the documents may have been constructed or employed in antiquity. Some classical scholars have begun moving in this direction, at least for teaching purposes (see Raymond Starr, "Ancient Bookrolls in Modern Classrooms," *New England Classical Journal* 45 [2018]: 39–43).

4   See Charles A. Mitchell and Thomas C. Hepworth, *Inks: Their Composition and Manufacture*, 3rd ed. (London: C. Griffin & Co., 1924), 3–10, 33–34; David Diringer, *The Book before Printing: Ancient, Medieval, and Oriental* (New York, NY: Dover Publications, 1982) 548–52.

5   It is generally agreed that iron-gall ink became popular from the third century CE onward (see Adam Bülow-Jacobsen, "Writing Materials in the Ancient World," in *The Oxford Handbook of Papyrology*, ed. Roger S. Bagnall [Oxford: Oxford University Press, 2009], 18).

6   Harold J. Plenderleith, "Technical Note on Unwrapping of Dead Sea Scrolls Fragments," in *Qumran Cave 1*, ed. Dominique Barthélemy and Józef T. Milik, DJD 1 (Oxford: Clarendon Press, 1955), 39. Cf. also Solomon H. Steckoll, "Investigations of the Inks used in Writing the Dead Sea Scrolls," *Nature* 220 (1968): 91–92, who examined the ink from funeral texts written on stones and concluded that it was carbon-based.

7   Yoram Nir-El and Magen Broshi, "The Black Ink of the Qumran Scrolls," *DSD* 3 (1996): 157–67.

8   The editors of 4QpaleoGenesis-Exodus[l] claim that iron ink was used in the manuscript's composition (see Patrick W. Skehan et al., "4QpaleoGenesis-Exodus[l]," in *Qumran Cave 4.IV: Palaeo-Hebrew and Greek Biblical Manuscripts*, ed. Patrick W. Skehan et al., DJD 9 [Oxford: Clarendon Press, 1992], 18).

9   On the latter, see Bridget Murphy et al., "Degradation Of Parchment And Ink Of The Dead Sea Scrolls Investigated Using Synchrotron-Based X-Ray And Infrared Microscopy," in *Holistic Qumran: Trans-Disciplinary Research of Qumran and the Dead Sea Scrolls*, ed. Jan Gunneweg et al., STDJ 87 (Leiden: Brill, 2010), 77–98.

As technology has developed, new methods of examining the ink have been introduced. Some of these have the potential to contribute significantly toward modern understandings of the Scrolls. One issue is whether the ink might help determine the provenance of composition. Scholars have noted that carbon-based ink is treated twice with water during production. In the initial stage, water is used as a solvent to create ink pellets or bar, and then later when writing is about to commence, water is mixed with the dry ink to create a fluid. This means that the level of trace elements in the ink should reflect the same ones in the water. By determining unique water signatures from around the region, some researchers are confident that they can identify the location at which the ink was employed. Since the water in and around the Dead Sea exhibits extremely high levels of bromine, investigations have searched for similar levels in the ink from the Scrolls.[10] Recently, 1QH[a] was submitted as a test case. Scientists discovered that the ink did, in fact, display high levels of bromine, leading the group to conclude that it was composed at Qumran.[11]

While this evidence could go a long way toward answering the question of where the Scrolls were composed, not everyone has been convinced by this approach. According to one group of researchers, the elevated bromine levels in the samples that were tested could be explained through other means. They contend that the bromine "could have come to the scrolls via sea spray, provided the manuscripts were stored near to the Dead Sea for a prolonged time."[12] What is more, they point to the lack of comparative data on bromine levels from other sites (e.g., Jerusalem, Jericho) as an indication that any conclusions about the provenance of an ink sample would be premature. The approach they pursue, instead, is to analyze the ink for "distinct, recognizable

---

10   Ira Rabin et al., "Characterization of the Writing Media of the Dead Sea Scrolls," in *Holistic Qumran: Trans-Disciplinary Research of Qumran and the Dead Sea Scrolls*, ed. Jan Gunneweg et al., STDJ 87 (Leiden: Brill, 2010), 123–34; Ira Rabin, "Archaeometry of the Dead Sea Scrolls," *DSD* 20 (2013): 139–40. The same assumption informs recent provenance work performed on the parchment as well (see Ioanna Mantouvalou et al., "3D Micro-XRF for Cultural Heritage Objects: New Analysis Strategies for the Investigation of the Dead Sea Scrolls," *Analytical Chemistry* 83 [2011]: 6308–15; Timo Wolff et al., "Provenance Studies on Dead Sea Scrolls Parchment by Means of Quantitative Micro-XRF," *Analytical and Bioanalytical Chemistry* 402 [2012]: 1493–503).

11   Ira Rabin, et al., "On the Origin of the Ink of the Thanksgiving Scroll (1QHodayot[a])," *DSD* 16 (2009): 97–106.

12   Kaare Lund Rasmussen et al., "The Constituents of the Ink from a Qumran Inkwell: New Prospects for Provenancing the Ink on the Dead Sea Scrolls," *Journal of Archaeological Science* 39 (2012): 2957. Another possibility is raised by Joan E. Taylor (*The Essenes, the Scrolls, and the Dead Sea* [Oxford: Oxford University Press, 2014], 285), who proposes that the high bromine to chlorine ratio can be attributed to the fact that the scrolls were treated with local salts prior to their burial in the caves.

and diagnostic parameters" by which to match specimens to other samples. When the alignment of specific parameters occurs, they suggest that its primary contribution is to distinguish particular copyists by the uniqueness of the ink recipes, rather than indicating the provenance of the composition.

The conclusion of this debate awaits subsequent research, but regardless of the how it is resolved, it will have a significant impact on the interpretation of the Scrolls.

2.2 Materiality of the Scrolls

Scientific investigation into the Scrolls also extends to their materiality. Much like with studies of the ink, researchers have spent a great deal of time analyzing the parchment on which the Scrolls were written in an effort to determine their provenance.[13] Rather than reviewing this discussion again, we will consider the materiality of the Scrolls from another angle. Recently, the physical composition of the manuscripts has been studied with a view toward what it might reveal about the Scrolls community. In antiquity writing was performed on a number of different materials (e.g., wax tablets, papyrus, leather, pottery, wood, metal, stone). Among Greek and Roman writers, papyrus was overwhelmingly preferred to parchment as a surface for composing both literary and documentary texts.[14] In the case of the Scrolls, however, the situation is

---

13 Recent studies on the parchment of the Scrolls include: Scott R. Woodward et al., "Analysis of Parchment Fragments from the Judean Desert Using DNA Techniques," in *Current Research and Technological Developments on the Dead Sea Scrolls: Conference on the Texts from the Judean Desert, Jerusalem, 30 April 1995*, ed. Donald W. Parry and Stephen D. Ricks, STDJ 20 (Leiden: Brill, 1996), 215–38; Gila Kahila Bar-Gal et al., "The Genetic Signature of the Dead Sea Scrolls," in *Historical Perspectives: From the Hasmoneans to Bar Kokhba in Light of the Dead Sea Scrolls. Proceedings of the Fourth International Symposium of the Orion Center for the Study of the Dead Sea Scrolls and Associated Literature, 27–31 January 1999*, ed. David M. Goodblatt et al., STDJ 37 (Leiden: Brill, 2001), 165–71; Gila Kahila Bar-Gal, "Principles of the Recovery of Ancient Data: What it Tells us of Plant and Animal Domestication and the Origin of the Scroll Parchment," in *Bio- and Material Cultures at Qumran: Papers from a COST Action G8 Working Group Meeting Held in Jerusalem, Israel on 22–23 May 2005*, ed. Jan Gunneweg et al. (Stuttgart: Fraunhofer IRB, 2006), 41–50; Jan Gunneweg, "The Dead Sea, the Nearest Neighbor of Qumran and the Dead Sea Manuscripts: What SEM, XRD and Instrumental Neutron Activation May Show about Dead Sea Mud," in *Holistic Qumran: Trans-Disciplinary Research of Qumran and the Dead Sea Scrolls*, ed. Jan Gunneweg et al., STDJ 87 (Leiden: Brill, 2010), 175–82; Mantouvalou et al., "3D Micro-XRF for Cultural Heritage Objects," 6308–15; Wolff et al., "Provenance Studies on Dead Sea Scrolls," 1493–503; Ira Rabin and Oliver Hahn, "Characterization of the Dead Sea Scrolls by Advanced Analytical Techniques," *Analytical Methods* 5 (2013): 4648–54.

14 See Daniel K. Falk, "Material Aspects of Prayer Manuscripts at Qumran," in *Literature or Liturgy? Early Christian Hymns and Prayers in their Literary and Liturgical Context*

reversed. The number of works written on parchment far outnumbers those written on papyrus.[15] Various discussions have, therefore, focused on why the authors of the Scrolls selected one material over another.

The use of parchment is sometimes connected to later halakhic decisions.[16] In rabbinic literature, animal skins are the prescribed medium for scriptural texts (m. Meg. 2:2; y. Meg. 1:71d; Sof. 1:1–4). As such, the situation may reflect a general preference among Jews in the Second Temple period and beyond. This theory is consistent with other manuscript finds from the Judaean desert, where documentary texts are generally written on papyrus, while the few literary works that have been discovered are mostly on parchment.[17] Nevertheless, it should be noted that a number of non-documentary texts from the Qumran caves were written on papyrus, including authoritative works such as Isaiah (4Q69) and Jubilees (4Q223–224). This is also true of some "sectarian" writings, such as the Community Rule (4Q255; 4Q257), the Damascus Document (4Q273), and MMT (4Q398).[18]

---

in Antiquity, ed. Clemens Leonhard and Hermut Löhr, WUNT 2/363 (Tübingen: Mohr Siebeck, 2014), 42. A search of the Leuven Database of Ancient Books (www.trismegis tos.org/ldab) turned up over 37,000 records of works written on papyrus over the period of 300 BCE–300 CE, but less than 1,000 on parchment.

15   According to the estimate of Emanuel Tov (*Scribal Practices and Approaches Reflected in the Texts Found in the Judean Desert*, STDJ 54 [Leiden: Brill, 2004] 44–45), papyrus makes up on about 14% (or 131 scrolls) of the written materials. But Falk believes this list requires some revision. He suggests that a better estimate might be around 10% of the total corpus (see Falk, "Material Aspects of Prayer Manuscripts at Qumran," 42 n. 41).

16   See, e.g., Meir Bar-Ilan, "Writing Materials," in *Encyclopedia of the Dead Sea Scrolls*, ed. Lawrence H. Schiffman and James C. VanderKam (Oxford: Oxford University Press, 2000), 2:996–97; James C. VanderKam and Peter W. Flint, *The Meaning of the Dead Sea Scrolls: Their Significance for Understanding the Bible, Judaism, Jesus, and Christianity* (San Francisco: HarperSanFrancisco, 2002), 152–53; cf. Jeffrey S. Siker, *Liquid Scripture: The Bible in a Digital World* (Minneapolis, MN: Fortress, 2017), 23. A related view has been proposed by Stephen J. Pfann, "Reassessing the Judean Desert Caves: Libraries, Archives, Genizas and Hiding Places," *Bulletin of the Anglo-Israel Archaeological Society* 25 (2007): 156–59, who suggests that the ratio is representative of a division among users: papyrus was used by lay members of the group while priests preferred leather.

17   See Armin Lange and Ulrike Mittmann-Richert, "Annotated List of the Texts from the Judaean Desert Classified by Content and Genre," in *The Texts from the Judaean Desert: Indices and and Introduction to the Discoveries in the Judaean Desert Series*, ed. Emanuel Tov, DJD 39 (Oxford: Clarendon, 2002), 149–64.

18   Cf. Ingo Kottsieper, "Physicality of Manuscripts and Material Culture," in *T&T Clark Companion to the Dead Sea Scrolls*, ed. George J. Brooke and Charlotte Hempel, with the assistance of Michael DeVries and Drew Longacre (London: T&T Clark, 2019), 173. On the distinctiveness of Qumran's non-documentary papyri among the Judaean finds, see Emanuel Tov, "The Corpus of the Qumran Papyri," in *Semitic Papyrology in Context: A*

Some scholars think that the choice of parchment represents a pragmatic decision based on functionality. Parchment offered a number of practical advantages over papyrus.[19] It provided a "smooth and strong surface," and it allowed for "the easy correction of mistakes,"[20] which was not always the case with thin, fragile sheets of papyrus. Further, it was more durable than papyrus. As Ingo Kottsieper notes, "literary texts were written to be read and used repeatedly for as long as possible. Thus, parchment, a much more solid material, would be preferable."[21]

It is possible that economics also played a role in the decision, particularly in those cases where papyrus was used. While there has been debate over whether papyrus was a luxury,[22] most agree that papyrus was generally less expensive than parchment.[23] For this reason, scholars often surmise that the papyrus manuscripts may represent personal copies.[24] Support for this hypothesis may be added by the presence of opisthographs among the Scrolls collection.[25] Since this practice posed some difficulties (*viz.* the rubbing of

---

Climate of Creativity: Papers from a New York University Conference Marking the Retirement of Baruch A. Levine, ed. Lawrence H. Schiffman, CHANE 14 (Leiden: Brill, 2003), 86.

19 See Frederic G. Kenyon, *Books and Readers in Ancient Greece and Rome*, 2nd ed. (Oxford: Clarendon, 1951), 86–119; Ronald Reed, *The Nature and Making of Parchment* (Leeds: Elmete, 1975), 47.

20 Catherine Hezser, *Jewish Literacy in Roman Palestine*, TSAJ 81 (Tübingen: Mohr Siebeck, 2001), 140.

21 Kottsieper, "Physicality of Manuscripts and Material Culture," 173.

22 See T. C. Skeat, "Was Papyrus Regarded as 'Cheap' or 'Expensive' in the Ancient World?," *Aegyptus* 75 (1995): 75–93.

23 See, e.g., Karel van der Toorn, *Scribal Culture and the Making of the Hebrew Bible* (Cambridge, MA: Harvard University Press, 2009), 19–20; Kottsieper, "Physicality of Manuscripts and Material Culture," 173. Cf. Michael L. Ryder, "The Biology and History of Parchment," in *Pergament: Geschichte, Struktur, Restaurierung, Herstellung*, ed. Peter Rück, Historische Hilfsweissenschaften 2 (Simarigen: Thorbecke, 1991), 25.

24 As suggested, e.g., by Michael O. Wise, "Accidents and Accidence: A Scribal View of Linguistic Dating of the Aramaic Scrolls from Qumran," in *Thunder in Gemini Thunder in Gemini, and other Essays on the History, Language and Literature of Second Temple Palestine*, JSPSup 15 (Sheffield: Sheffield Academic Press, 1994), 129–30; Tov, "The Corpus of the Qumran Papyri," 99; Falk, "Material Aspects of Prayer Manuscripts at Qumran," 43–45.

25 For a discussion of the opisthographs from among the Dead Sea Scrolls corpus, see Emanuel Tov, "Opisthographs from the Judean Desert," in *A Multiform Heritage: Studies on Early Judaism and Christianity in Honor of Robert A. Kraft*, ed. Benjamin G. Wright, Homage Series 24 (Atlanta, GA: Scholars, 1999), 11–18; George J. Brooke, "Between Scroll and Codex? Reconsidering the Qumran Opisthographs," in *On Stone and Scroll: Studies in Honour of Graham I. Davies*, ed. James K. Aitken et al., BZAW 420 (Berlin: De Gruyter, 2011), 123–38; Antony Perrot, "Reading an Opisthograph at Qumran," in *Material Aspects of Reading in Ancient and Medieval Cultures: Materiality, Presence and Performance*, ed. Anna

one's hands—and thus the possible erasure of text—during use), it is commonly understood as an economical measure intended to save money on additional writing materials.[26] As to be expected, the majority of the opisthographs from Qumran were written on papyrus.

It is important to recognize that the different suggestions relating to the selection of writing materials are not exclusionary. This point has recently been stressed by George J. Brooke when discussing the choice of papyrus over parchment. He notes that such a decision is "the reflection of a complicated set of motives" which are "the result of individual agency in a wider social context."[27] The price of papyrus, for instance, would have varied based on the quality or grade. Consequently, sociological considerations also factor into the equation: if high quality papyrus is selected, it may represent elite cultural values.[28] As a rare and valuable material resource, high quality papyrus would stand in contrast to animal skins, a resource to which the community had much easier access.[29] Instead of working from broad generalizations about the potential of ancient writing materials, then, more attention needs to be devoted to the individual manuscripts themselves.

A significant step in this direction was recently suggested by Eibert J. C. Tigchelaar, who specified how interpreters might refine this investigation. One aspect on which he focuses is the script. In the case of 4Q217 (a fragmentary text of Jubilees written on papyrus), the letters are relatively large, and it is composed in a semi-cursive script (cf. 4Q223–4Q224, which are papyrus manuscripts with smaller script). Since the size of the letters seems to rule

---

Krauß, Jonas Leipziger, and Friederike Schücking-Jungblut, Materiale Textkulturen 26 [Berlin: De Gruyter, 2020], 101–14.

26   This economic explanation does not hold true in every instance, however. Although elegant copies written on the back of a documentary papyri—which is technically not the true definition of an opisthograph (see Manfredo Manfredi, "Opistografo," *La parola del passato* 38 [1983]: 44–54)—are rare, some examples are known (Mariachiara Lama, "Aspetti di tecnica libraria ad Ossirinco: Copie letterarie su rotoli documentari," *Aegyptus* 71 [1991]: 94–99).

27   George J. Brooke, "Choosing Between Papyrus and Skin: Cultural Complexity and Multiple Identities in the Qumran Library," in *Jewish Cultural Encounters in the Ancient Mediterranean and Near Eastern World*, ed. Mladen Popović et al., JSJSup 178 (Leiden: Brill, 2017), 135.

28   See Brooke, "Choosing Between Papyrus and Skin," 132.

29   Cf. Philip S. Alexander, "Literacy Among Jews in Second Temple Palestine: Reflections on the Evidence from Qumran," in *Hamlet on a Hill: Semitic and Greek Studies Presented to Professor T. Muraoka on the Occasion of his Sixty-Fifth Birthday*, ed. Martin F. J. Baasten and Wido T. van Peursen, OLA 118 (Leuven: Peeters, 2003), 7: "The small community at the Dead Sea could only have acquired such rolls through the outlay of precious cash or good. Skins, however, were all around them on the backs of their animals."

out the possibility that the manuscript contained the entire book of Jubilees, Tigchelaar has proposed that the papyrus manuscript provided a medium on which the scribe could compose portions of an early draft.[30] Another point which he emphasizes is the need to better understand the nature of scrolls' materiality. Tigchelaar points out that "no-one has hitherto systematically analysed the quality of either parchment or papyrus Dead Sea Scrolls manuscripts, nor their provenance, nor, for that matter, other correlations such as text density in comparison to quality of material."[31] Issues like these—and potentially more (e.g., the cave in which a manuscript was discovered)—must be addressed before the selection of materials can be properly addressed.

2.3 *Size of the Scrolls*

The scrolls discovered at Qumran were originally of varying shapes and sizes. Scholars have concluded when assessing their physical dimensions that "size matters."[32] A prime example is what Emanuel Tov has labelled "*de luxe* editions."[33] These manuscripts, which were prepared with extreme care, are marked primarily by their large margins at the top and bottom. They also regularly display "a large writing block, fine calligraphy, the proto-rabbinic text form of Scripture, and only a limited amount of scribal intervention."[34] This type of deluxe format is most commonly represented among manuscripts containing scriptural works. Scholars have naturally focused on what these physical characteristics reveal about the texts that are inscribed on them. One possibility that Tov considers is that "the large format was used mainly or only for authoritative texts, since this distinctive format gave the scroll prestige."[35]

While the display character of a given manuscript does seem to reflect the authoritative status of its text, one must be careful not to assume the opposite, *viz.* that the non-display character of a given manuscript reflects the text's lack of authoritative status.[36] For many of the same compositions that are

---

30 Eibert J. C. Tigchelaar, "The Qumran Jubilees Manuscripts as Evidence for the Literary Growth of the Book," *RevQ* 26 (2014): 579–94.

31 Idem, "The Material Variance of the Dead Sea Scrolls: On Texts and Artefacts," *HTS Teologiese Studies/Theological Studies* 72 (2016): 4.

32 George J. Brooke, "Scripture and Scriptural Tradition in Transmission: Light from the Dead Sea Scrolls," in *The Scrolls and Biblical Traditions: Proceedings of the Seventh Meeting of the IOQS in Helsinki*, ed. George J. Brooke et al., STDJ 103 (Leiden: Brill, 2012), 5.

33 Tov, *Scribal Practices*, 125–30.

34 Ibid., 126.

35 Ibid., 91.

36 A statement by George J. Brooke seems to come very close to drawing this conclusion. Contrasting the production of *pesharim* manuscripts with other types of display copies, he notes, "The sectarian commentary literature does not seem to have been reproduced

formatted in deluxe editions also appear in manuscripts of other sizes and shapes. Equally influential in the construction of a scroll was the function it was intended to perform. This is a point that has recently been emphasized by Pieter B. Hartog in his assessment of the physical characteristics of pesharim. After noting the similarities between the preparation of the commentaries and of scriptural texts, he suggests that "the physicality of Pesharim manuscripts" are better understood as a "reflect[ion of] their intended purpose rather than their status."[37] In terms of their functionality, Hartog locates the pesher manuscripts "in scholarly-educational settings, where the study and teaching of Jewish prophetic Scriptures occupied a central place."[38] Here, the size of the manuscript would be dictated by utilitarian, rather than display, purposes.

This functional approach is also thought to account for other formats of documents discovered at Qumran. Most notable are the miniature scrolls often described as "pocket editions."[39] These are manuscripts whose height allows for a very small writing block (usually 7–10 lines per column). Since these miniatures were first discovered, a variety of proposals have been offered to explain the specific reading contexts in which they were employed and the purpose(s) they served.[40] One context that has been frequently posited is a

---

with ideas of its distinctive status and authority in mind, as was the case with many of the scriptural books and even the Hodayot which are extant in 'de luxe' copies" ("Aspects of the Physical and Scribal Features of Some Cave 4 'Continuous' Pesharim," in *The Dead Sea Scrolls: Transmission of Traditions and Production of Texts*, ed. Sarianna Metso et al., STDJ 92 [Leiden: Brill, 2010], 139). For this reason, the statement was challenged by Pieter B. Hartog, *Pesher and Hypomnema: A Comparison of Two Commentary Collections from the Hellenistic-Roman Period*, STDJ 121 (Leiden: Brill, 2017), 85. Elsewhere, however, Brooke clearly emphasizes that the size of a manuscript was dictated in large part by its function (see idem, "La « bibliothèque » une collection sans cesse revisitée," *Le Monde de la Bible* 220 [2017]: 46–53).

37 Hartog, *Pesher and Hypomnema*, 85.
38 Hartog, *Pesher and Hypomnema*, 85.
39 For a list of manuscripts considered to be "pocket editions," see Józef T. Milik, "Les modèles araméens du livre d'Esther dans la grotte 4 de Qumrân," *RevQ* 15 (1992): 363–64; Stephen J. Pfann, "4Q298: The Maskîl's Address to All Sons of Dawn," *JQR* 85 (1994): 213 n. 14. Cf. also Tov, *Scribal Practices*, 84–86.
40 On occasion, scholars have associated this small format with a particular literary genre. This is the case with the study of Jewish novels by Lawrence M. Wills. Drawing on J. T. Milik's study of the 'prototypes' of the book of Esther discovered at Qumran, Wills makes note of Milik's reference to a group of miniature scrolls that were unknown to scholarship at the time. He points out that "the fragments of some of the novelistic works from Qumran ... are printed on scrolls in a small-page format." But where Wills presses Milik's study to the point of inaccurate representation is when he claims that these miniatures typify "a format not used for other genres" (*The Jewish Novel in the Ancient World*, Myth and Poetics [Ithaca, NY: Cornell University Press, 1995], 27 n. 51; cf. also Laura

liturgical setting, a view that is based on the likelihood that smaller dimensions would have aided recitation during times of communal worship.[41] In particular, most manuscripts of the five books that would eventually come to make up the *Meghillot* generally fall into this category.[42] The size of these scrolls has led some to conclude that they were used "for public liturgical reading at festivals."[43] This liturgical hypothesis is common in scholarship today, and in the case of scrolls containing poetry and prayers, it may be correct. Where it is not entirely satisfactory is when function becomes determinative in explaining the size of scrolls, for there are many texts written on larger scrolls that were probably used for liturgical purposes (e.g., 4QShirShabb[d]; 4QTest; 4QPs[a,c,e,q]; 11QPs[a]). Furthermore, miniature size was not reserved for one particular kind of text. A variety of compositions appear in this format, including works focused on the community, parabiblical texts, excerpted scriptural texts.[44] What is more, certain texts appear in both larger and smaller sizes. This is the case with the Community Rule,[45] and even works later included among the *Meghillot*.[46]

Quick, "Scribal Habits and Scholarly Texts: Codicology at Oxyrhynchus and Qumran," in *Material Aspects of Reading in Ancient and Medieval Cultures: Materiality, Presence and Performance*, ed. Anna Krauß, Jonas Leipziger, and Friederike Schücking-Jungblut, Materiale Textkulturen 26 [Berlin: De Gruyter, 2020], 42, 47–49, whose otherwise excellent study connects the views of Milik with Wills). While such a consideration, if accurate, would be an important point on which to build a theory about the function of Jewish novels, as it turns out, Milik actually stated the very opposite. After beginning with a discussion of such narrative texts, he acknowledges, "Il ne manque pas, cependant, des rouleaux tres petits ou minuscules pour d'autres genres littéraires: commentaires, recueils de preières, règles" ("Les modèles araméens," 364).

41   See, e.g., Emanuel Tov, "Excerpted and Abbreviated Biblical Texts from Qumran," *RevQ* 16 (1995): 596; idem, "Three Manuscripts (Abbreviated Texts?) of Canticles from Qumran Cave 4," *JJS* 46 (1995): 91; idem, "Canticles," in *Qumran Cave 4.XI: Psalms to Chronicles*, ed. Eugene Ulrich, et al., DJD 16 (Oxford: Clarendon Press, 2000), 198.

42   See Emanuel Tov, "The Dimensions of the Qumran Scrolls," *DSD* 5 (1998): 74.

43   E.g., Brooke, "Scripture and Scriptural Tradition," 6; Daniel K. Falk, "Liturgical Texts," in *T&T Clark Companion to the Dead Sea Scrolls*, ed. George J. Brooke and Charlotte Hempel, with the assistance of Michael DeVries and Drew Longacre (London: T&T Clark, 2019), 431.

44   Community texts: 4QS[b,d,f,j]; 4QHalakha B; 4QList of False Prophets; 4QWords of the Maskil; 4QMMT[c,f]; 4QCal Doc/Mish B. Parabiblical texts: 4QprEsther[a,b,d] ar; 4QDanSuz? ar; 4QapocrLam B; 4QapocrMos[a]; 4QapocrDan ar; 4QApocr Psalm and Prayer. Excerpted scriptural texts: 4QDeut[n,q]; 4QExod[e]; 4QPs[g].

45   That is, to the extent that the Community Rule can be categorized as a single composition (see below).

46   The books of Ruth, Esther, Qohelet, Lamentations, and Canticles are often written on smaller scrolls, and as a result, they are commonly understood as portable books used in connection with Jewish festivals (see Tov, *Scribal Practices*, 90; idem, "Canticles," 197–98).

Miniature scrolls have also been explained as an aid to portability. For travelers, these manuscripts are said to have served as copies that could be easily transported from one location to another.[47] Some have even envisioned more specific contexts in which these scrolls might have been used. According to Torleif Elgvin, "small-sized scrolls also were made for itinerant use by wandering teachers, *Yahad* officials, or travelers."[48] Like the liturgical hypothesis, this theory also has a great deal of merit. The use of small books to ease portability does find support in the literary evidence, where miniature books were later used during travel.[49] Nevertheless, this explanation still leaves many questions unanswered. The most notable relates to the comparative size of other ancient media whose primary purpose was to be transported from one location to another: ancient letters. In a recent study of the material aspects

---

Among the many unanswered questions surrounding this view, the most important is whether these books were actually used as festival readings at this point in Jewish history (cf. Torleif Elgvin, *The Literary Growth of the Song of Songs during the Hasmonean and Early-Herodian Periods*, CBET 89 [Leuven: Peeters, 2018], 192). Regardless of the answer to this question, the important point is that some copies of the *Meghillot* are larger (e.g., 4QQoh^a). In the case of 4Q(?)Ruth (= MS 5441), we have a fragmentary copy of Ruth whose bottom margin has been estimated to 3.6 cm (Tofleif Elgvin, "MS5441. 4Q(?)Ruth (Ruth 2.1–2)," in *Gleanings from the Caves: Dead Sea Scrolls and Artefacts from The Schøyen Collection*, ed. Torleif Elgvin, et al., LSTS 71 [London: Bloomsbury, 2016], 243), which would be consistent with Tov's criteria for defining a deluxe edition; nevertheless, this fragment has been judged to be a forgery (see Torleif Elgvin and Michael Langlois, "Looking Back: (More) Dead Sea Scrolls Forgeries in The Schøyen Collection," *RevQ* 113 [2019]: 122).

47 Those who have stressed the portability created by the size of the miniature scrolls include: Stephen J. Pfann, "The Writings in Esoteric Script from Qumran," in *The Dead Sea Scrolls Fifty Years after Their Discovery: Proceedings of the Jerusalem Congress, July 20–25, 1997*, ed. Lawrence H. Schiffman, et al. (Jerusalem: Israel Exploration Society in cooperation with The Shrine of the Book, 2000), 181; H. Gregory Snyder, *Teachers and Texts in the Ancient World: Philosophers, Jews, and Christians*, Religion in the First Christian Centuries (London: Routledge, 2000), 149; Alexander, "Literacy Among Jews," 12; Brent A. Strawn, "Excerpted Manuscripts at Qumran: Their Significance for the Textual History of the Hebrew Bible and the Socio-Religious History of the Qumran Community and Its Literature," in *The Bible and the Dead Sea Scrolls*, vol. 2: *The Dead Sea Scrolls and the Qumran Community*, ed. James H. Charlesworth (Waco, TX: Baylor University Press, 2006) 116; Hartog, *Pesher and Hypomnema*, 85–86.

48 Torleif Elgvin, "How to Reconstruct a Fragmented Scroll: The Puzzle of 4Q422," in *Northern Lights on the Dead Sea Scrolls: Proceedings of the Nordic Qumran Network 2003–2006*, ed. Anders Klostergaard Peterson, et al., STDJ 80 (Leiden: Brill, 2009), 231–32; cf. idem, *Literary Growth of the Song of Songs*, 69, who suggests, "The deliberately small format [of 6QCant] makes it an exemplar of first-century CE portable scrolls."

49 For instance, later Christian monks were known for carrying around small codices during their travels (see, e.g., *Regular Magistri* 57.4; John Moschus, *Pratum spiritual* 31 [PG 87.3:2880]).

of letter writing in antiquity, Antonia Sarri collects a number of completely preserved letters from the Greco-Roman world. Although some would qualify as miniature in size, most are much larger. In fact, Sarri notes that many of these examples "correspond to the height of a [book] roll."[50] When the average height of these documents is calculated, it turns out to be 22.9 cm.[51] So while a miniature format would have certainly aided portability, the standard size of book rolls in antiquity would apparently have been sufficient to facilitate transportation.[52] This raises the question of whether other factors may have been involved in the choice of a diminutive-sized roll.

A more practical explanation has recently been posed by Brian P. Gault, who argues that what determines the size of a scroll is not simply its function, but, more pragmatically, the length of the text that is contains. This proposal is based partly on logic: "If longer texts were copied on larger scrolls with bigger writing blocks and taller columns, one can assume that shorter texts would be copied on small scrolls with smaller writing blocks and shorter columns."[53] Further support for this thesis is drawn from the quality of material chosen for *tefillin* and *mezuzot*, which were generally composed on materials that had been leftover or discarded. According to Gault, then, the connection between size and liturgy "should be regarded as a secondary phenomenon resulting from the fact that liturgical texts are shorter in nature, so less parchment or leather was needed."[54] While this suggestion, like the others that have been discussed, has a great deal of explanatory power, it cannot account for the miniature format more generally. The problem is that some miniature book rolls were relatively long, such as P.Lond.Lit. 96, which measures 12.4 cm high and 4.45 meters long, despite the manuscript being incomplete.[55] In the end, it

---

50 Antonia Sarri, *Material Aspects of Letter Writing in the Graeco-Roman World: 500 BC–AD 300*, Materiale Textkulturen 12 (Berlin: De Gruyter, 2018), 77.

51 Ibid., 337–45.

52 In the Hellenistic period, the average height of a literary book roll seems to have been ca. 19–25 cm, while this size increased slightly in the Roman period to ca. 25–33 cm (see William A. Johnson, *Bookrolls and Scribes in Oxyrhynchus*, Studies in Book and Print Culture [Toronto: University of Toronto Press, 2004], 141–43).

53 Brian P. Gault, "The Fragments of 'Canticles' from Qumran: Implications and Limitations for Interpretation," *RevQ* 24 (2010): 366.

54 Ibid.

55 For comparison sake, the Mani Codex is also a miniature (3.5 × 4.5 cm), but contains 192 pages (see A. Henrich and L. Koenen, "Ein griechischer Mani-Codex (P. Colon. inv. nr. 4780)," *ZPE* 5 [1970]: 97–216). Similarly, P.Oxy. VI 849 is a fragmentary copy of a miniature codex containing the *Acts of Peter*. On the top margin, it contains the page numbers 167 and 168.

is difficult to say too much about the length of the miniatures from Qumran because most are fragmentary copies.

Rather than focusing on what the aesthetic qualities of manuscripts indicate about the how books were used, others have turned their attention to the social status that the physical characteristics may have afforded those who produced them. It is from this perspective that Charlotte Hempel has considered Rule Texts such as 1QS, 1QSa, and 1QSb. Imagining that the manuscripts would have been used in what William A. Johnson refers to as "a display setting,"[56] Hempel draws the following observation: "The physicality of the Rule scrolls—mostly valuable leather scrolls—implies a desire to promote the significance of this literature and the self-presentation of those responsible for it."[57] To support this claim, she notes the time and effort that went into their preparation as well as the educational abilities that would have facilitated the task.[58] Regardless of whether 1QS, 1QSa, 1QSb technically qualify as deluxe editions, she points out that their physical characteristics "nevertheless send a powerful message."[59] They communicate that those who prepared the manuscripts possess an authoritative status as text brokers. It is through them that important information is mediated to the community.

3 Writing the Dead Sea Scrolls

There have been different avenues through which scholars have explored the compositional activity involved in producing the Dead Sea Scrolls. We will limit

---

56 William A. Johnson, *Readers and Reading Culture in the High Roman Empire: A Study of Elite Communities*, Classical Culture and Society (Oxford: Oxford University Press, 2010), 22.

57 Charlotte Hempel, "Reflections on Literacy, Textuality, and Community in the Qumran Dead Sea Scrolls," in *Is There a Text in this Cave? Studies in the Textuality of the Dead Sea Scrolls in Honour of George J. Brooke*, ed. Ariel Feldman et al., STDJ 119 (Leiden: Brill, 2017), 77.

58 An alternative assessment of the literary abilities of the scribe who copied 1QS is provided by Alexander. While he concedes that "[t]he hand looks professional," he contends that "the scribe has clearly made a bit of a mess of it." As proof, he points to the central columns of the manuscript, which "is full of scratchings-out, corrections and illogical gaps" ("Literacy Among Jews in Second Temple Palestine," 17). Based on these and other issues, Alexander concludes that "1QS may not have been copied by a real scholar." Instead, he suggests, "1QS is the work of the less educated copyist detailed to write out the fair copy of the scholar's text" (18).

59 Hempel, "Reflections on Literacy," 79.

TEXTUALITY AND THE DEAD SEA SCROLLS

our discussion to scribal practices and the identification of individual copyists, focusing on the important advances that have been made in each area.

3.1 Scribal Practices

Over the years, considerable attention has been devoted to the scribal practices employed by those who produced the Scrolls.[60] Perhaps the most substantive, and consequently, the most lasting, contribution to this discussion has been made by Emanuel Tov. In his numerous publications on the subject, Tov has described both the compositional techniques used to create new texts as well as the editorial practices involved in transmitting existing ones.[61] But it has been his transition from descriptive analysis to theory that has generated the most controversy.

The foundation of Tov's theoretical approach is the identification of a distinct set of scribal practices within the Scrolls corpus. They consist of unique orthographic, morphological, and scribal characteristics present only in certain manuscripts.[62] From an orthographic perspective, the most notable feature of

---

60 Earlier discussions of these issues include: Malachi Martin, *The Scribal Character of the Dead Sea Scrolls*, Bibliothèque du Muséon 44–45 (Louvain: Publications universitaires, 1958); Jonathan P. Siegel, "The Scribes of Qumran: Studies in the Early History of Jewish Scribal Customs, with Special Reference to the Qumran Biblical Scrolls and to the Tannaitic Traditions of *Massekheth Soferim*," (Ph.D. dissertation, Brandies University, 1972); J. C. Lübee, "Certain Implications of the Scribal Process of 4QSam^c," *RevQ* 14 (1989): 255–65.

61 Among the large list of his publications on the subject, one should consult Emanuel Tov, "Scribal Practices Reflected in the Paleo-Hebrew Texts from the Judean Desert," *Scripta Classica Israelica* 15 (1996): 268–73; idem, "Scribal Markings in the Texts from the Judean Desert," in *Current Research and Technological Developments on the Dead Sea Scrolls*, ed. Donald W. Parry and Stephen D. Ricks, STDJ 20 (Leiden: Brill, 1996), 41–77; idem, "The Scribes of the Texts Found in the Judean Desert," in *The Quest for Context and Meaning: Studies in Biblical Intertextuality in Honor of James A. Sanders*, ed. Craig A. Evans and Shemaryahu Talmon, BIS 28 (Leiden: Brill, 1997), 131–52; idem, "Scribal Practices Reflected in the Texts from the Judaean Desert," in *The Dead Sea Scrolls after Fifty Years: A Comprehensive Assessment*, ed. Peter W. Flint and James C. VanderKam (Leiden: Brill, 1998), 1:403–29; idem, "Correction Procedures in the Texts from the Judean Desert," in *The Provo International Conference on the Dead Sea Scrolls: Technological Innovations, New Texts, and Reformulated Issues*, ed. Donald W. Parry and Eugene C. Ulrich, STDJ 30 (Leiden: Brill, 1999), 232–63. Many of these insights have been collected in idem, *Scribal Practices*. Subsequent works are listed below.

62 This view has been explained and defended in a number of publications, e.g., Emanuel Tov, "The Orthography and Language of the Hebrew Scrolls Found at Qumran and the Origin of These Scrolls," *Text* 13 (1986): 31–57; idem, "Hebrew Biblical Manuscripts from the Judaean Desert: Their Contribution to Textual Criticism," *JJS* 39 (1988): 10–16; idem, "Further Evidence for the Existence of a Qumran Scribal School," in *The Dead Sea Scrolls Fifty Years after Their Discovery: Proceedings of the Jerusalem Congress, July 20–25, 1997*,

this Qumran scribal practice is full (*plene*) phonetic spelling. Morphologically, other characteristics include lengthened independent pronouns, lengthened pronominal suffixes for 2nd and 3rd persons plural, free usage of pausal verbal forms, lengthened future forms, verbal forms with pronominal suffix constructed as *yqwṭlnw*, the form (*w*)*qṭltmh* for the 2nd person plural, and the forms מאודה/מואדה/מודה.[63] Scribal practices are also considered alongside orthography and morphology, with the most noteworthy being the use of cancellation dots. While it is rare to find all of these features used together in a single composition, the combined presence of some features is widespread across a variety of manuscripts. What is most significant is that "sectarian" works are almost all written in accordance with these unique orthographic, linguistic, and scribal practices. This observation has led Tov to conclude that manuscripts which contained these features were composed by a scribal school at Qumran, while those which lack such features were brought to the site from other locations.

Although Tov's proposal has been accepted by many,[64] and even used as a means of discerning the "sectarian" character of given compositions, it has also been criticized on a number of fronts.[65] Some have pointed out that a variety of the orthographic and morphological features that Tov identifies cannot be attributed to any sectarian community since they are attested (however rarely)

---

    ed. Lawrence H. Schiffman et al. (Jerusalem: Israel Exploration Society & The Shrine of the Book, 2000), 199–216; idem, "The Qumran Scribal Practice: The Evidence from Orthography and Morphology," *Studia Orientalia Electronica* 99 (2004): 353–68.

63   The initial list of morphological and orthographical features representative of texts written according to Qumran scribal practice can be found in Tov, "Orthography and Language of the Hebrew Scrolls," 36. For a more recent list, see idem, *Scribal Practices*, 227–88, 337–43. Cf. also Martin G. Abegg, "Scribal Practice and the Pony in the Manure Pile," in *Reading the Bible in Ancient Traditions and Modern Editions: Studies in Memory of Peter W. Flint*, ed. Andrew B. Perrin et al., EJL 47 (Atlanta, GA: SBL, 2017), 65–88.

64   See, e.g., Martin G. Abegg, "The Linguistic Analysis of the Dead Sea Scrolls: More Than (Initially) Meets the Eye," in *Rediscovering the Dead Sea Scrolls: An Assessment of Old and New Approaches and Methods*, ed. Maxine L. Grossman (Grand Rapids, MI: Eerdmans, 2010), 48–68; idem, "Qumran Scribal Practice: Won Moor Thyme," in *Scribal Practice, Text and Canon in the Dead Sea Scrolls: Essays in Memory of Peter W. Flint*, ed. John J. Collins and Ananda Geyser-Fouché, STDJ 130 (Leiden: Brill, 2019), 175–204, which affirm and build upon the thesis of Tov.

65   A few of the discussions devoted to critically evaluating Tov's proposal include: Johann Cook, "Orthographical Peculiarities in the Dead Sea Scrolls Biblical Scrolls," *RevQ* 14 (1989): 293–305; Dong-Hyuk Kim, "Free Orthography in a Strict Society: Reconsidering Tov's 'Qumran Orthography,'" *DSD* 11 (2004): 72–81. The most substantive engagement with Tov's proposal can be found in Eibert J. C. Tigchelaar, "Assessing Emanuel Tov's 'Qumran Scribal Practice,'" in *The Dead Sea Scrolls: Transmission of Traditions and Production of Texts*, ed. Sarianna Metso et al., STDJ 92 (Leiden: Brill, 2010), 173–207.

in other Hebrew writings.[66] Others have argued that the palaeographic dates assigned to some of the texts which reflect this Qumran practice (e.g., 4QPs[a]; 4QQoh[a]; 4QDibHam[a]) predate the time when the settlement of Qumran is thought to have been occupied by the sectarian community.[67] Nevertheless, as the position of Tov has evolved over the years (partly in response to objections like these), he has adequately addressed most of these challenges.[68]

Where, then, does that leave the discussion? Most scholars recognize that some manuscripts contain *plene* spelling while others are marked by defective orthography characteristic of the later Masoretic tradition, and it is commonly agreed that those writings associated with the "sectarian" movement generally contain varying amounts of orthographic, morphological, and scribal features that sets them apart from other manuscripts. But agreement has been difficult to achieve over how best to explain variations among the manuscripts with regard to the prevalence and consistency of the features that Tov identifies with a Qumran scribal practice. Tov attributes this evidence to the unique proclivities of individual copyists who were often copying from manuscripts that employed an alternative scribal practice.[69] Others interpret this situation as requiring a broader analytical framework. Rather than accounting for the differences with binary categories, they have proposed locating manuscripts along a spectrum or continuum.[70] This is the impasse at which scholarship currently finds itself. As scholars continue to work toward some type of

---

66 Cf. David Noel Freedman, "The Evolution of Hebrew Orthography," in *Studies in Hebrew and Aramaic Orthography*, ed. David N. Freedman et al., BJSUCSD 2 (Winona Lake, IN: Eisenbrauns, 1992), 14; Jonathan G. Campbell, "Hebrew and its Study at Qumran," in *Hebrew Study from Ezra to Ben-Yehuda*, ed. William Horbury (Edinburgh: T&T Clark, 1999), 41.

67 Cf. Esther G. Chazon, "Is *Divrei ha-me'orot* a Sectarian Prayer?," in *The Dead Sea Scrolls: Forty Years of Research*, ed. Devorah Dimant and Uriel Rappaport, STDJ 10 (Leiden: Brill, 1992), 6; Armin Lange, "Kriterien essenischer Texte," in *Qumran kontrovers: Beiträge zu den Textfunden vom Toten Meer*, ed. Jörg Frey and Hartmut Stegemann, Einblicke 6 (Paderborn: Bonifatius, 2003), 68.

68 For a recent response to criticisms levelled against his theory, see Emanuel Tov, "*Scribal Practices and Approaches* Revisited," *HBAI* 3/4 (2014): 363–74.

69 See, e.g., Emauel Tov, "Some Reflections on Consistency in the Activity of Scribes and Translators," in *Juda und Jerusalem in der Seleukidenzeit: Herrschaft—Widerstand—Identität*, ed. Ulrich Dahmen and Johannes Schnocks, BBB 159 (Göttingen: Vandenhoeck & Ruprecht, 2010), 325–37; idem, "The Coincidental Textual Nature of the Collections of Ancient Scriptures," in *Congress Volume Ljubljana 2007*, ed. Andre Lemaire, VTSup 133 (Leiden: Brill, 2010), 153–69; idem, "Scribal Features of Two Qumran Scrolls," in *Hebrew in the Second Temple Period: The Hebrew of the Dead Sea Scrolls and of Other Contemporary Sources*, ed. Steven E. Fassberg et al., STDJ 108 (Leiden: Brill, 2013), 241–58.

70 See Martin G. Abegg, "The Hebrew of the Dead Sea Scrolls," in *The Dead Sea Scrolls after Fifty Years: A Comprehensive Assessment*, ed. Peter W. Flint and James C. VanderKam

resolution, the discussion will likely draw from the ongoing investigation into the ink and parchment of the Scrolls (see above) as well as the new theoretical formulations that have emerged to account for the pluriformity of scriptural works at Qumran (see below).

3.2 Writer Identification

Within the broader dialogue on scribal activity, one particular question of interest has been the detection and identification of individual scribal hands. Using various features related to handwriting styles, the goal has been to connect the writing of an individual scribal hand across multiple documents. Because of the fragmentary nature of the evidence and due to the formal character of the various writing styles, this task has proven difficult. Nonetheless, various connections have been proposed.[71] These are usually restricted to an individual writer composing two separate manuscripts. In a few cases, however, the production output is thought to be somewhat more substantial. One writer is believed to have been responsible for composing 1QS, 1QSa, 1QSb, 4QTestimonia, and 4QSam^c,[72] and there may also be evidence that this same individual made several corrections to 1QIsa^a.[73] The most prolific writer to be identified so far is a scribe active during the late-first century BCE who, according to Ada Yardeni, was responsible for over 50 different manuscripts.[74]

(Leiden: Brill, 1998), 328; Tigchelaar, "Assessing Emanuel Tov's 'Qumran Scribal Practice,'" 195–96, 202–203.

71 For a full list of writer identifications, see Tov, *Scribal Practices*, 23. To this list, one could add the recent suggestion by Eugene C. Ulrich, "Identification of a Scribe Active at Qumran: 1QPs^b–4QIsa^c–11QM," in *Meghillot: Studies in the Dead Sea Scrolls v–vi. A Festschrift for Devorah Dimant*, ed. Moshe Bar-Asher and Emanuel Tov (Jerusalem: Bialik Institute, 2007), 201–10 (Hebrew), who claims that the same individual was responsible for 4QIsa^c, 1QPs^b, and 11QM.

72 See further Eugene C. Ulrich, "4QSam^c: A Fragmentary Manuscript of 2 Samuel 14–15 from the Scribe of the Serek Hay-yahad (1QS)," *BASOR* 235 (1979): 1–25; Eibert J. C. Tigchelaar, "In Search of the Scribe of 1QS," in *Emanuel: Studies in Hebrew Bible, Septuagint, and Dead Sea Scrolls in Honor of Emanuel Tov*, ed. Shalom M. Paul et al., VTSup 94 (Leiden: Brill, 2003), 439–52.

73 This suggestion was first made by John C. Trever, "A Paleographic Study of the Jerusalem Scrolls," *BASOR* 113 (1949): 15, and then subsequently repeated by others (e.g., Frank Moore Cross, "Introduction," in *Scrolls from Qumrân Cave 1: The Great Isaiah Scroll, the Order of the Community, the Pesher to Habakkuk*, ed. Frank Moore Cross et al. [Jerusalem: Albright Institute of Archaeological Research, 1972] 3–4). Recently, the validity of this hypothesis has been challenged by Årstein Justnes, "The Hand of the Corrector in 1QIsaa XXXIII 7 (Isa 40,7–8). Some Observations," *Sem* 57 (2015): 205–10.

74 Ada Yardeni, "A Note on a Qumran Scribe," in *New Seals and Inscriptions: Hebrew Idumean, and Cuneiform*, ed. Meir Lubetski, Hebrew Bible Monographs 8 (Sheffield: Sheffield Phoenix, 2007), 287–98.

By identifying individual writers through the process of palaeographic analysis, scholars have reached an important preliminary conclusion: the Scrolls reflect a large variety of scribal hands. While some have estimated as many as 500 different writers,[75] most place the number of handwriting styles around 150.[76] Interpreted in light of the number of inhabitants who lived at Qumran (ca. 150–200 inhabitants) and the duration over which the settlement was occupied (ca. 120–170 years),[77] this fact casts significant doubt on the possibility that the collection was produced by "a small scribbling sect" of Jewish scribes.[78]

Due to the challenges involved, however, identifying individual writers has proven to be a slow and laborious task. What is more, "such identifications are subjective given the present lack of a theoretical framework and methodological approach which assesses the significance of both graphic correspondences and graphic differences for the identification of individual scribes."[79] Recently, the search for scribal hands has taken exciting new directions, due in large

---

75 See, e.g., Wise, "Accidents and Accidence," 123–25; Philip R. Davies, "Was There Really a Qumran Community?," *CurBS* 3 (1995): 15.

76 Norman Golb, "Khirbet Qumran and the Manuscript Finds of the Judaean Wilderness," in *Methods of Investigation of the Dead Sea Scrolls and the Khirbet Qumran Site: Present Realities and Future Prospects*, ed. Michael O. Wise et al., Annals of the New York Academy of Sciences 722 (New York, NY: New York Academy of Sciences, 1994), 65, who claims that there is "over five hundred scribal handwritings preserved in the scrolls discovered in the caves near Qumran." Cf. idem, *Who Wrote the Dead Sea Scrolls? The Search for the Secret of Qumran* (New York, NY: Scribner, 1995), 97–98, 151–52.

77 For an estimate of the number of inhabitants at Qumran, see Magen Broshi, "The Archaeology of Qumran: A Reconsideration," in *The Dead Sea Scrolls: Forty Years of Research*, ed. Devorah Dimant and Uriel Rappaport, STDJ 10 (Leiden: Brill, 1992), 113–14. For an estimate of the occupation of Qumran, see Jodi Magness, *The Archaeology of Qumran and the Dead Sea Scrolls*, Studies in the Dead Sea Scrolls and Related Literature (Grand Rapids, MI: Eerdmans, 2002), 63–69.

78 Philip R. Davies, "Reflections on DJD XVIII," in *The Dead Sea Scrolls at Fifty: Proceedings of the 1997 Society of Biblical Literature Qumran Section Meetings*, ed. Robert A. Kugler and Eileen M. Schuller, EJL 15 (Atlanta, GA: Scholars, 1999), 156. Along with the palaeographic evidence, some have also brought sociological models to bear on the question, arguing for the unlikelihood that a single community produced the Scrolls (see Steve Delamarter, "Sociological Models for Understanding the Scribal Practices in the Biblical Dead Sea Scrolls," in *Rediscovering the Dead Sea Scrolls: An Assessment of Old and New Approaches and Methods*, ed. Maxine L. Grossman [Grand Rapids, MI: Eerdmans, 2010], 182–97). Others have argued that there is very little evidence of writing at Qumran (see Juhana M. Saukkonen, "A Few Inkwells, Many Hands: Were There Scribes at Qumran?," in *Houses Full of All Good Things: Essays in Memory of Timo Veijola*, ed. Juha Pakkala and Martti Nissinen [Helsinki: Finnish Exegetical Society, 2008], 538–53).

79 Eibert J. C. Tigchelaar, "The Scribes of the Scrolls," in *T&T Clark Companion to the Dead Sea Scrolls*, ed. George J. Brooke and Charlotte Hempel, with the assistance of Michael DeVries and Drew Longacre (London: T&T Clark, 2019), 530.

part to technological advances. Most promising among them is the digital palaeographic approach led by Mladen Popović. "This multidisciplinary project brings together the natural sciences, artificial intelligence, and the humanities in order to shed new light on ancient Jewish scribal culture by investigating two aspects of the scrolls' palaeography: handwriting recognition (the typological development of writing styles) and writer identification."[80] In this way, it holds out the possibility of a more scientific (and thus more definitive) assessment of the material evidence. Since the project is still in the process of being completed, however, we must eagerly await the results.

4   The Function of the Dead Sea Scrolls

Moving from the composition of the Scrolls to their collective and individual function provides further evidence of the shifts that have recently taken place in scholarship. Not only have long-standing views about the manuscripts' lived context been re-evaluated, even the nature of individual "books" has been reimagined.

4.1   *The Scrolls as a "Collection" of Texts*
Scholars have long believed that the Scrolls were in some way related to the group who inhabited the ancient settlement at Qumran. A view that gained an early stronghold within the field was that the manuscripts represented the library of a single group, who had chosen to retreat to the desert because of conflict with Jewish leadership in Jerusalem. While some allowance was made for the possibility that Scrolls were brought to the site, the inhabitants were commonly envisioned as scribes who devoted themselves to the creation and copying of documents.[81] Interpreters reached this conclusion not only from the

---

80   Maruf A. Dhali et al., "A Digital Palaeographic Approach towards Writer Identification in the Dead Sea Scrolls," in *Proceedings of the 6th International Conference on Pattern Recognition Applications and Methods, ICPRAM 2017, Porto, Portugal, February 24–26, 2017*, ed. Maria De Marsico et al. (Setúbal: SciTePress, 2017), 693. A similar type of approach was proposed some years earlier by David Hamidović, "Dead Sea Scrolls inside Digital Humanities. A Sample," in *Digital Humanities in Biblical, Early Jewish and Early Christian Studies*, ed. Claire Clivaz, Andrew Gregory, and David Hamidović, Scholarly Communication 2 (Leiden: Brill, 2013), 21–30.

81   Hartmut Stegemann even went so far as to claim that the scrolls were manufactured and stored at the site and then sold for profit (see *The Library of Qumran: On the Essenes, Qumran, John the Baptist, and Jesus* [Grand Rapids, MI: Eerdmans, 1998] 51–55. For a critical response to Stegemann's view, see Ferdinand Rohrhirsch, *Wissenschaftstheorie und Qumran: Die Geltungsbegrüdungen von Aussagen in der biblischen Archäologie am Beispiel*

large cache of writings that were discovered, but also from what many interpreted as a "scriptorium" within the settlement. This is where many of these manuscripts were thought to have been produced. Advocates of this approach maintained that the deposit of the collection was an emergency decision: the group was forced to quickly hide the scrolls in nearby caves before the Romans destroyed the site in approximately 68 CE.[82]

Many continue to defend the broad contours of this early consensus. But with the publication of the textual and archaeological evidence now completed, interpreters have been forced to account for a variety of new considerations, including the large number of scribal hands represented in the collection, divergences in theological content of the writings, the varying storage techniques used in the different caves, etc. As a result, the major tenets of this view have all been challenged.[83]

The first tenet that has undergone critique is the collection's function as the library of a single community.[84] Pushback on this point has been fueled in large part by the recent efforts to avoid confining the Essenes (or even more specifically, the *yaḥad*) to the settlement at Qumran. Rather than being a small, isolated entity, many have concluded that the movement exhibited much wider geographical distribution.[85] It is from this perspective that Alison Schofield has explored the *Serekh* manuscripts from Qumran to determine how they might

---

von Chirbet Qumran und En Feschcha, NTOA 32 (Göttingen: Vandenhoeck & Ruprecht, 1996), and idem, "Die Geltungsbegründungen der Industrie-Rollen-Theorie zu Chirbet Qumran und En Feschcha auf dem methodolo-gischen Prüfstand: Relativierung und Widerlegung," *DSD* 6 (1999): 267–81.

82　This was the consensus view within an earlier generation of Scrolls scholarship. It is perhaps most closely associated with the work of Roland de Vaux, *Archaeology and the Dead Sea Scrolls* (London: Oxford University Press, 1973), 105.

83　See Albert I. Baumgarten, "Crisis in the Scrollery: A Dying Consensus," *Judaism* 44 (1995): 399–413.

84　While some have become more hesitant to affirm the scrolls functioned as a singular library, many continue to maintain that they should be categorized as such (e.g., Sidnie White Crawford, "The Qumran Collection as a Scribal Library," in *The Dead Sea Scrolls at Qumran and the Concept of a Library*, ed. Sidnie White Crawford and Cecilia Wassén, STDJ 116 [Leiden: Brill, 2016], 107–31; Armin Lange, "The Qumran Library in Context: The Canonical History and Textual Standardization of the Hebrew Bible in Light of the Qumran Library," in *The Dead Sea Scrolls at Qumran and the Concept of a Library*, ed. Sidnie White Crawford and Cecilia Wassén, STDJ 116 [Leiden: Brill, 2016], 259–79).

85　See, e.g., Torleif Elgvin, "The *Yaḥad* is More than Qumran," in *Enoch and Qumran Origins: New Light on a Forgotten Connection*, ed. Gabriele Boccaccini (Grand Rapids, MI: Eerdmans, 2005), 273–79; John J. Collins, "The *Yaḥad* and 'The Qumran Community'," in *Biblical Traditions in Transmission: Essays in Honour of Michael A. Knibb*, ed. Charlotte Hempel and Judith M. Lieu, JSJSup 111 (Leiden: Brill, 2006), 81–96.

inform our understanding of the wider collection.[86] Schofield recognizes a fundamental (ideological) unity within the corpus, noting that "[t]he Scrolls were not just a random assortment of Second Temple literature."[87] At the same time, she argues that "some, if not a substantial portion, of the Scrolls originated outside of Qumran proper, either in content or in actual copies," which means that the collection was not "intended to be a comprehensive library in the Hellenistic or modern sense."[88] She suggests that the manuscripts belonged to the same movement, yet they were not originally part of a single collection. They were instead brought to the site by members who were part of smaller cell-groups scattered around the region.[89] This would have occurred either as visitors or newcomers transported their documents to the site over time, or all at once as an emergency procedure during the Jewish revolt. Regardless of how the different collections arrived, though, their original geographical separation plays a key role in the interpretation of the evidence.

Schofield's proposal does not attempt to reconcile how the diversity of the Scrolls relates to the intentionality of their accumulation. This is a question taken up in a broader study by Mladen Popović. After conducting a synchronic analysis of the Qumran collection, he points out that the "sheer number of manuscripts and the predominance of literary texts set it apart from other

---

86   Alison Schofield, *From Qumran to the* Yaḥad: *A New Paradigm of Textual Development for The Community Rule*, STDJ 77 (Leiden: Brill, 2009), esp. 51–59. Others have similarly emphasized geography as a way to explain the differences within the collection, e.g., James R. Davila, "Enochians, Essenes, and Qumran Essenes," in *Enoch and Qumran Origins: New Light on a Forgotten Connection*, ed. Gabriele Boccaccini (Grand Rapids, MI: Eerdmans, 2005), 358; John J. Collins, *Beyond the Qumran Community: The Sectarian Movement of the Dead Sea Scrolls* (Grand Rapids, MI: Eerdmans, 2010), 3.

87   Schofield, *From Qumran to the* Yaḥad, 58.

88   Schofield, *From Qumran to the* Yaḥad, 58.

89   Schofield is not the only scholar who has argued that the Scrolls represent multiple collections that have been brought together, e.g., Jonathan D. H. Norton, "The Qumran Library and the Shadow it Casts on the Wall of the Cave," in *Ancient Readers and Their Scriptures: Engaging the Hebrew Bible in Early Judaism and Christianity*, ed. Garrick V. Allen and John Anthony Dunne, AJEC 107 (Leiden: Brill, 2018), 40–74; Lindsey A. Askin, "Scribal Production and Literacy at Qumran: Considerations of Page Layout and Style," in *Material Aspects of Reading in Ancient and Medieval Cultures: Materiality, Presence and Performance*, ed. Anna Krauß, Jonas Leipziger, and Friederike Schücking-Jungblut, Materiale Textkulturen 26 (Berlin: De Gruyter, 2020), 26–28. One of the strongest points that Norton raises against viewing the collection as the library single community is the existence of multiple, pluriform copies of many works, which stands at odds with most ancient libraries, where the tendency was the possess a single, corrected copy of a given work (see Norton, "The Qumran Library," 66–72).

manuscript collections that have been found in the Judaean Desert."[90] This consideration leads Popović to conclude that the corpus is best interpreted within a Jewish intellectual milieu. He thus identifies the group associated with the Scrolls as a textual community consisting of members who were engaged in the study of written documents.[91] The nature of this community, according to Popović, has an important bearing on how the Scrolls are understood. Within a scholarly setting, literary collections would naturally be diverse, having been accumulated over time and perhaps even containing works with slightly different ideological perspectives.[92] So even though he is hesitant to label the collection a 'library,' particularly in light of the inconclusive nature of the physical evidence from Qumran,[93] he does emphasize the unifying

---

90   Mladen Popović, "Qumran as Scroll Storehouse in Times of Crisis? A Comparative Perspective on Judaean Desert Manuscript Collections," *JSJ* 43 (2012): 590. Cf. also idem, "The Ancient 'Library' of Qumran between Urban and Rural Culture," in *The Dead Sea Scrolls at Qumran and the Concept of a Library*, ed. Sidnie White Crawford and Cecilia Wassén, STDJ 116 (Leiden: Brill, 2016), 155–67.

91   Along similar lines, others have argued that Qumran was a centralized location which functioned as a "house of study" (*beth midrash*) where members of the Essene movement could come to read and study (see André Lemaire, "Qoumrân: sa fonction et ses manuscrits," in *Qoumrân et les Manuscrits de la mer Morte. Un cinquantenaire*, ed. Ernest-Marie Laperrousaz [Paris: Éditions du Cerf, 1997], 117–49; idem, "Réflexions sur la fonction du site de Qumrân," in *Józef Tadeusz Milik et cinquantenaire de la découverte des manuscrits de la mer morte de Qumrân* , ed. Dariusz Długosz and Henryk Ratajczak (Varsovie: PAN, 2000), 37–43; cf. Benedict T. Viviano, "Study and Education," in *Encyclopedia of the Dead Sea Scrolls*, ed. Lawrence H. Schiffman and James C. VanderKam (Oxford: Oxford University Press, 2000), 2:896–98). This view has been denied by others, however (e.g., Yaacov Shavit, "The 'Qumran Library' in the Light of the Attitude towards Books and Libraries in the Second Temple Period," in *Methods of Investigation of the Dead Sea Scrolls and the Khirbet Qumran Site: Present Realities and Future Prospects*, ed. Michael O. Wise et al., Annals of the New York Academy of Sciences 722 [New York, NY: New York Academy of Sciences, 1994], 307).

92   This point is consistent with a recent interpretation of the calendaric texts from Qumran by Helen R. Jacobus. Rather than postulating different groups behind each of the various calendars, she contends that "[t]he Qumran collection … suggests an integrated interest in intra-calendar plurality and the preservation of historical knowledge in a library of interlocking texts" ("Calendars in the Qumran Collection," in *The Dead Sea Scrolls at Qumran and the Concept of a Library*, ed. Sidnie White Crawford and Cecilia Wassén, STDJ 116 [Leiden: Brill, 2016], 241).

93   Recent emphasis has been placed on comparative analysis, with the textual and archaeological evidence from Qumran being interpreted in light of libraries in the Hellenistic and Roman worlds (see Monica Berti, "Greek and Roman Libraries in the Hellenistic Age," in *The Dead Sea Scrolls at Qumran and the Concept of a Library*, ed. Sidnie White Crawford and Cecilia Wassén, STDJ 116 [Leiden: Brill, 2016], 31–54; Corrado Martone, "The Qumran 'Library' and Other Ancient Libraries: Elements for a Comparison," in *The Dead Sea Scrolls at Qumran and the Concept of a Library*, ed. Sidnie White Crawford and Cecilia Wassén,

function of the collection. In fact, the texts and the community are said to exist in a type of symbiotic relationship: "The collection of texts attracted people and shaped their thinking, while at the same time people shaped the collection, producing and gathering more texts."[94]

Another tenet of the early consensus that has been challenged in recent scholarship is the close association between the Scrolls and the settlement at Qumran.[95] Some have completely severed the connection between the manuscripts and the settlement, claiming that the entire collection originated elsewhere and was brought to the caves only as a result of the Roman invasion.[96] Others have maintained that a connection exists, but that the ownership of the manuscripts extended beyond the group who inhabited the site. This view has recently been defended by Stephen J. Pfann, who argues that the individual caves represent separate collections of distinct groups.[97] According to Pfann, some caves housed the collections of the Essene movement. This is the case with Caves 1 and 6, which are said to represent the libraries of priests and laity, respectively. It is also true of Caves 4 and 5. These, Pfann argues, functioned

STDJ 116 [Leiden: Brill, 2016], 55–77). There are, it has been argued, some architectural features which are consistent with the use of certain portions of Qumran as a library (see Ian Werrett, "Is Qumran a Library?," in *The Dead Sea Scrolls at Qumran and the Concept of a Library*, ed. Sidnie White Crawford and Cecilia Wassén, STDJ 116 [Leiden: Brill, 2016], esp. 91–96).

94 Popović, "Qumran as Scroll Storehouse," 591.

95 Despite the reservations of some, many scholars still link the collection very closely with the settlement (e.g., Sidnie White Crawford, "Qumran: Caves, Scrolls, and Buildings," in *A Teacher for All Generations: Essays in Honor of James C. VanderKam*, ed. Eric F. Mason et al., JSJSup 153 [Leiden: Brill, 2011], 251–73).

96 This view was first espoused by Karl H. Rengstorf, who claimed that the collection originated from the library of the Jerusalem temple and was transported to the caves shortly before the attack by the Roman army (see *Ḥirbet Qumrân und die Bibliothek vom Toten Meer*, Abhandlungen und Texte aus dem Institutum Judaicum Delitzschianum 5 [Stuttgart: Kohlhammer, 1960]). Similar ideas (with some variations) have also been proposed more recently, see, e.g., Norman Golb, "Khirbet Qumran and the Manuscripts of the Judaean Wilderness: Observations on the Logic of Their Investigation," *JNES* 49 (1990): 103–14; Lena Cansdale, *Qumran and the Essenes: A Re-Evaluation of the Evidence*, TSAJ 60 (Tübingen: Mohr, 1997), 94–97, 189; Yizhar Hirschfeld, *Qumran in Context: Reassessing the Archaeological Evidence* (Peabody, MA: Hendrickson, 2004), 5, 230; Yitzhak Magen and Yuval Peleg, *The Qumran Excavations 1993–2004: Preliminary Report* (Jerusalem: Judea & Samaria Publications, 2007), 63–66; David Stacey and Gregory L. Doudna, *Qumran Revisited: A Reassessment of the Archaeology of the Site and Its Texts*, BARIS 2520 (Oxford: Archaeopress, 2013), 63.

97 Pfann, "Reassessing the Judean Desert Caves," 147–70. For a discussion of the differences between the various caves, see idem, "The Ancient 'Library' or 'Libraries' of Qumran: The Specter of Cave 1Q," in *The Dead Sea Scrolls at Qumran and the Concept of a Library*, ed. Sidnie White Crawford and Cecilia Wassén, STDJ 116 (Leiden: Brill, 2016), 168–213.

TEXTUALITY AND THE DEAD SEA SCROLLS

95

as *genizot* which stored manuscripts that had been retired from usage. The manuscripts found in Caves 3 and 11, however, are assigned to Zealot groups at the end of the First Revolt. The remains from Caves 7–10 are thought to be too meager to determine ownership and function with any certainty, although Pfann does note that "they all appear to have been used at the end of Period IIb (AD 66–68) as residences for the rebels."[98]

Finally, some have stood opposed to the third major tenet of the consensus, namely, that the collection as a whole was quickly hidden away in the caves prior to the Roman invasion.[99] In response to this popular view, Daniel Stökl Ben Ezra has provided a statistical analysis of the collection in which he uses the palaeographic dates customarily assigned to the manuscripts to calculate the average scroll age of each cave. He discovered that the manuscripts from Caves 1 and 4 are generally older than those found in Caves 2, 3, 5, 6, and 11. To determine the significance of this disparity, he has applied a Kruskal-Wallis Test (H-Test) to the evidence. From this statistical calculation, he concluded that "it is highly improbable that the same single book collection was distributed hastily among the Caves 2, 3, 5, 6, and 11 as well as Caves 1 and 4."[100] To explain this situation, Stökl Ben Ezra proposed that the manuscripts were deposited by the same community, but at different times. Those documents in the "old" caves (Caves 1 and 4) represent the library of the community that was stored away prior to the settlement's violent destruction in 9/8 BCE.[101] The scrolls remained in the caves from this point onward—either serving as an additional space where documents could be stored or as a depository for damaged manuscripts.

---

98   Pfann, "Reassessing the Judean Desert Caves," 166.

99   This quick, collective hiding scenario continues to have many defenders (e.g., Mladen Popović, "Roman Book Destruction in Qumran Cave 4 and the Roman Destruction of Khirbet Qumran Revisited," in *Qumran und die Archäologie: Texte und Contexte*, ed. Jörg Frey et al., WUNT 278 [Tübingen: Mohr Siebeck, 2011], 239–91).

100   Daniel Stökl Ben Ezra, "Old Caves and Young Caves: A Statistical Reevaluation of a Qumran Consensus," *DSD* 14 (2007): 321. Cf. also idem, "Wie viele Bibliotheken gab es in Qumran?," in *Qumran und die Archäologie: Texte und Contexte*, ed. Jörg Frey et al., WUNT 278 (Tübingen: Mohr Siebeck, 2011), 327–46. For a critique of the theory of Stökl Ben Ezra, see Florentino García Martínez, "Cave 11 in Context," in *The Dead Sea Scrolls: Texts and Contexts*, ed. Charlotte Hempel, STDJ 90 (Leiden: Brill, 2010), 204–205; idem, "Reconsidering The Cave 1 Texts Sixty Years After Their Discovery: An Overview," in *Qumran Cave 1 Revisited: Texts from Cave 1 Sixty Years after Their Discovery. Proceedings of the Sixth Meeting of the IOQS in Ljubljana*, ed. Daniel K. Falk et al., STDJ 91 (Leiden: Brill, 2010), 8–10. A response to these criticisms can be found in Daniel Stökl Ben Ezra, "Further Reflections On Caves 1 And 11: A Response To Florentino García Martínez," in *The Dead Sea Scrolls: Texts and Contexts*, ed. Charlotte Hempel, STDJ 90 (Leiden: Brill, 2010), 211–23.

101   These dates represent the revised chronology of settlement proposed by Magness, *Archaeology of Qumran*, 63–69.

The "young" caves (Caves 2, 3, 5, 6, and 11), on the other hand, housed the collection that accumulated at Qumran after the site was rebuilt, and thus they represent "the last stage of the library *in* the settlement."[102] This latter group of documents, according to Stökl Ben Ezra, was also hidden away in the caves before the site was destroyed by the Romans in 68 CE.

Another view, which shares a similar chronological emphasis as Stökl Ben Ezra, while also affirming the geographical considerations raised by Schofield, is the '*genizah*' theory set forward by Joan E. Taylor. What distinguishes her approach is an important caveat related to the storage function of the scrolls within the various caves.[103] Taylor argues that the manuscripts originally belonged not to a single library housed at Qumran, but to the wider Essene movement which "had a great many communities all over Judaea which required libraries for the study of their scriptures."[104] More specifically, she suggests that the Essenes had amassed a vast collection of written materials which were spread across "hundreds of small libraries."[105] The manuscripts discovered in the caves surrounding Qumran, while once part of this collection, represent "old, heterodox, redundant or damaged scrolls" which were brought to the site for the purpose of burial.[106] According to Taylor, two different forms of long-term preservation are evidenced at Qumran. Some scrolls were wrapped in (bitumen-impregnated) linen and placed in sealed jars inside natural caves; others were buried in the Qumran cemetery and have since decomposed. This situation leads Taylor to reassess the function of the marl caves, particularly Cave 4 where the largest cache of manuscripts was discovered. Rather than serving as the location where scrolls from the Qumran library were quickly deposited prior to the Roman invasion, these caves are said to have housed scrolls that were no longer in use and which were being prepared for burial. In other words, these documents belonged to a *genizah* whose "processing was interrupted by the destruction or abandonment of the site."[107]

---

102   Stökl Ben Ezra, "Old Caves and Young Caves," 328 (original emphasis).

103   Joan E. Taylor, "Buried Manuscripts and Empty Tombs: The Qumran Genizah Theory Revisited," in '*Go Out and Study the Land*' (*Judges 18:2*): *Archaeological, Historical and Textual Studies in Honor of Hanan Eshel*, ed. Aren M. Maeir et al., JSJSup 148 (Leiden: Brill, 2011), 269–315, reprinted in a modified and updated form in idem, *The Essenes, the Scrolls, and the Dead Sea*, 272–303.

104   Taylor, "Buried Manuscripts and Empty Tombs," 306.

105   Ibid., 304.

106   Ibid., 305.

107   Ibid., 295. The theory of Taylor represents a reconfiguration and thorough revision of an earlier suggestion by Eleazar L. Sukenik, who envisioned Cave 1 as a *genizah* (see *The Dead Sea Scrolls of the Hebrew University* [Jerusalem: Magnes, 1955], 17). Others have similarly proposed that the manuscripts in certain caves may represent a *genizah*. This has

TEXTUALITY AND THE DEAD SEA SCROLLS

Exactly how this large collection of manuscripts should be interpreted—and whether and to what extent these challenges require the consensus to be reassessed—is a question that is currently being worked out within scholarship.

4.2 *The Scrolls as a Collection of "Texts"*

Not only has the collective function of the Scrolls been open to debate, even more fundamental questions, such as the nature of the texts themselves, have been re-evaluated. When the Scrolls were discovered, they were naturally interpreted against the background of modern print culture. But recently there has been a move away from a typographic model, which has been informed by new interpretive approaches that challenge scholars to think differently about the material evidence. One avenue through which these differences have been explored is digital textuality.[108] This is the direction taken by Eva Mroczek, who borrows concepts commonly associated with digital information to provide a new lens for viewing the ancient evidence. She points to the "fluid, collective processes of rewriting and updating" which mark electronic texts and notes how these characteristics destabilize "coherent textual identity and authorial property."[109] This relativization of authorship, which is precipitated by textual instability and unboundedness, is also said to occur in the Scrolls, but for different reasons. Mroczek contends that the ancient Jewish scribe, motivated by concepts of divine revelation, became "an inspired performer, as renewer and updater." The texts that were produced, in turn, were "expanding collections of

---

been suggested of the texts from Cave 1 (see George J. Brooke, *Qumran and the Jewish Jesus: Reading the New Testament in the Light of the Scrolls* [Cambridge: Grove Books, 2005], 9, 68) as well as Caves 4a–b and 5 (Pfann, "Reassessing the Judean Desert Caves," 152–54). Cf. also David Stacey, "Seasonal Industries at Qumran," *Bulletin of the Anglo-Israel Archaeological Society* 26 (2008): 24.

108   For an introduction to digital textuality, see Roger Chartier, *Forms and Meanings: Texts, Performances and Audiences from Codex to Computer* (Philadelphia, PA: University of Pennsylvania Press, 1995); idem, "Languages, Books, and Reading from the Printed Word to the Digital Text," *Critical Inquiry* 31 (2004): 133–51; Kathryn Sutherland, ed., *Electronic Text: Investigations in Method and Theory* (Oxford: Oxford University Press, 1997); Jerome J. McGann, *Radiant Textuality: Literature After the World Wide Web* (New York, NY: Palgrave, 2001); Christian Vandendorpe, *From Papyrus to Hypertext: Toward the Universal Digital Library*, trans. Phyllis Aronoff and Howard Scott (Urbana: University of Illinois Press, 2009).

109   Eva Mroczek, "Thinking Digitally about the Dead Sea Scrolls: Book History Before and Beyond the Book," *Book History* 14 (2011): 248. This approach has also been applied more broadly with regard to the literature of the ancient Near East (see Scott B. Noegel, "Text, Script, and Media: New Observations on Scribal Activity in the Ancient Near East," in *Voice, Text, Hypertext: Emerging Practices in Textual Studies*, ed. Raimonda Modiano et al. [Seattle: University of Washington Press, 2004], 133–43).

discourse that all claim to participate in a larger, undefined body of revelatory traditions."[110] To substantiate this claim, she references the different order and arrangements of Psalms during the Second Temple period: while the form and content of these works eventually reached a fixed state, during the time prior to the turn of the century Psalms existed as "an indeterminate collection without a stable order, inventory, or boundaries."[111]

Another evaluative lens through which the Scrolls have recently been explored is material philology (aka new philology). This approach has grown increasingly popular and has begun to make a tremendous impact on scholarship.[112] Some have employed this interpretive lens as a way to direct their focus toward the social environment that gave rise to individual manuscripts and way(s) they functioned as unique cultural artefacts.[113] Others have considered the implications for editing both scriptural and non-scriptural

---

110   Mroczek, "Thinking Digitally," 252 and 253, respectively.

111   Eva Mroczek, *The Literary Imagination in Jewish Antiquity* (Oxford: Oxford University Press, 2016), 26; cf. idem, "The End of the Psalms in the Dead Sea Scrolls, Greek Codices, and Syriac Manuscripts," in *Snapshots of Evolving Traditions: Jewish and Christian Manuscript Culture, Textual Fluidity, and New Philology*, ed. Hugo Lundhaug and Liv Ingeborg Lied, TUGAL 175 (Berlin: De Gruyter, 2017), 297–322. See also Mika S. Pajunen, "Perspectives on the Existence of a Particular Authoritative Book of Psalms in the Late Second Temple Period," *JSOT* 39 (2014): 139–63; Eva Jain, *Psalmen oder Psalter? Materielle Rekonstruktion und inhaltliche Untersuchung der Psalmenhandschriften aus der Wüste Juda*, STDJ 109 (Leiden: Brill, 2014).

112   The influence of material philology is evident from the fact that some have begun to employ insights from this interpretive perspective without interacting directly with or directly acknowledging it. This is the case with Ian Young who attempts to read the idiosyncrasies of certain Psalms manuscripts as reflecting their performance within specific community traditions (see idem, "Manuscripts and Authors of the Psalms," *Studia Biblica Slovaka* 8 [2016]: 123–36). In another instance, Gregory P. Fewster has sought to further refine the study of ancient pseudepigraphy by prioritizing individual manuscripts from the Scrolls over idealized literary forms (see idem, "Manuscript, Voice, and the Construction of Pseudepigraphal Identities: Composing a Mutable David in Some Qumran Psalms Scrolls," *JBL* 137 [2018]: 893–914).

113   See, e.g., Kipp Davis, "'There and Back Again': Reconstruction and Reconciliation of the War Text 4QMilḥamaᵃ (4Q491ᵃ⁻ᶜ)," in *The War Scroll, Violence, War and Peace in the Dead Sea Scrolls and Related Literature: Essays in Honour of Martin G. Abegg on the Occasion of His 65th Birthday*, ed. Kipp Davis et al., STDJ 115 (Leiden: Brill, 2015), 125–46; idem, "The Social Milieu of 4QJerᵃ (4Q70) in a Second Temple Jewish Manuscript Culture: Fragments, Manuscripts, Variance, and Meaning," in *The Dead Sea Scrolls and the Study of the Humanities: Method, Theory, Meaning: Proceedings of the Eighth Meeting of the International Organization for Qumran Studies (Munich, 4–7 August, 2013)*, ed. Pieter B. Hartog et al., STDJ 125 (Leiden: Brill, 2018), 53–76.

TEXTUALITY AND THE DEAD SEA SCROLLS

texts in printed editions.[114] Insights from material philology have also helped to mediate debates that arose due to the pluriformity in works found in multiple copies at Qumran, and it is this contribution that we will consider in further detail.

Much has been written on the pluriform state of scriptural works during the Second Temple period.[115] But, an increasing amount of attention has recently been devoted to the pluriformity that exists in other compositions. The Rule texts have been a particular focus since multiple copies of various works have proven to represent very different textual forms. It is natural, therefore, that the early discussion revolved around textual history. What impacted this discussion the most was the process by which the Rule texts were discovered. Scholars were first introduced to works like the Community Rule, the War Scroll, and the Damascus Document through relatively complete copies. As a result, these came to be viewed prescriptively; that is, the manuscripts from Cave 1 (1QS; 1QM) and the Cairo genizah (CD) came to define the form and content expected from similar works. When more copies were uncovered in other caves, variations were analyzed with a view toward determining the "original" form and perhaps even the basis for the deviation. Further, in cases where portions of one copy were missing due to the manuscript's deterioration, "parallel" sections from better preserved copies were used to reconstruct the fragmentary portions.

---

114 For an overview of this discussion, see Michael Segal, "Methodological Considerations in the Preparation of an Edition of the Hebrew Bible," in *The Text of the Hebrew Bible and Its Editions: Studies in Celebration of the Fifth Centennial of the Complutensian Polygot*, ed. Andrés Piquer Otero and Pablo Torijano Morales, Supplements to the Textual History of the Bible 1 (Leiden: Brill, 2017), 34–55; Sarianna Metso and James M. Tucker, "The Changing Landscape of Editing Ancient Jewish Texts," in *Reading the Bible in Ancient Traditions and Modern Editions: Studies in Memory of Peter W. Flint*, ed. Andrew B. Perrin et al., EJL 47 (Atlanta, GA: SBL, 2017), 269–87.

115 While textual pluriformity is an important issue which directly relates to the use of the Dead Sea Scrolls as ancient media, space will not permit us to rehearse this long and detailed discussion. For a review of research on the pluriformity of scriptural texts, see Eugene C. Ulrich, "Biblical Scrolls Scholarship in North America," in *The Dead Sea Scrolls in Scholarly Perspective: A History of Research*, ed. Devorah Dimant, STDJ 99 (Leiden: Brill, 2012), 49–74; Emanuel Tov, "Israeli Scholarship on the Biblical Texts from the Judean Desert," in *The Dead Sea Scrolls in Scholarly Perspective: A History of Research*, ed. Devorah Dimant, STDJ 99 (Leiden: Brill, 2012), 297–313. For a review of research on "rewritten scripture," which has become its own subfield within the discipline, see Sidnie White Crawford, "'Rewritten Bible' in North American Scholarship," in *The Dead Sea Scrolls in Scholarly Perspective: A History of Research*, ed. Devorah Dimant, STDJ 99 (Leiden: Brill, 2012), 75–78; Michael Segal, "Qumran Research in Israel: Rewritten Bible and Biblical Interpretation," in *The Dead Sea Scrolls in Scholarly Perspective: A History of Research*, ed. Devorah Dimant, STDJ 99 (Leiden: Brill, 2012), 315–33.

Work on the textual history of the Community Rule has been particularly divisive. This debate has been fueled by the fact that copies from Cave 4 (4QS[b,d]) represent a shorter form than the one found in Cave 1. Philip S. Alexander has claimed that the paleographic dates of individual manuscripts reveal the order in which the various forms of the Community Rule originated.[116] As such, he views the longer form preserved in 1QS (early-first century BCE) to be antecedent to the shorter form represented in copies from Cave 4 (late-first century BCE). Over time, he maintains, certain portions of the compositions (e.g., references to the Zadokites) were intentionally omitted to reflect the changing situation of the community. The opposite conclusion was reached by Sarianna Metso, who argues that the shorter form represents the earlier version.[117] According to her interpretation, 1QS brings together two streams of the S tradition: the traditions underlying 4QS[e] and 4QS[b,d]. At the same time, she suggests that these earlier traditions are modified to provide scriptural legitimization for the community's legal regulations and to reflect their updated structural organization. If she is correct, it would mean that "the community had continued copying older versions even when newer, expanded versions were available."[118]

While this dispute has played an important role in helping to reconstruct the textual history of the Community Rule manuscripts, others have claimed that it provides only a partial glimpse into the situation that lies behind the pluriformity. This is the argument recently made in a valuable contribution by Jutta Jokiranta. Drawing insights from both material philology and digital textuality, she contends that the conceptual categories used to investigate the Community Rule are insufficient. At issue is the fact that, within a manuscript culture, variation is the essence of textual transmission; it is the product of communities adapting existing information to address new situations. When this occurs, Jokiranta notes, "such processes result in variant versions, used simultaneously, and often with no linear evolution."[119] This implies that the

---

116   Philip S. Alexander, "The Redaction-History of *Serekh Ha-Yaḥad*: A Proposal," *RevQ* 17 (1996): 437–56. Cf. also Markus N. A. Bockmuehl, "Redaction and Ideology in the Rule of the Community (1QS/4QS)," *RevQ* 18 (1998): 541–60; Devorah Dimant, "The Composite Character of the Qumran Sectarian Literature as an Indication of Its Date and Provenance," *RevQ* 22 (2006): 615–30.

117   Sarianna Metso, *The Textual Development of the Qumran Community Rule*, STDJ 21 (Leiden: Brill, 1997). Cf. also Géza Vermès, "Preliminary Remarks on Unpublished Fragments of the Community Rule from Qumran Cave 4," *JJS* 42 (1991): 250–55.

118   Sarianna Metso, *The Serekh Texts*, LSTS 62 (London: T&T Clark, 2007), 18.

119   Jutta Jokiranta, "What is 'Serekh ha-Yahad (S)'? Thinking About Ancient Manuscripts as Information Processing," in *Sibyls, Scriptures, and Scrolls: John Collins at Seventy*, ed. Joel S. Baden et al., JSJSup 175 (Leiden: Brill, 2016), 621. Cf. Jutta Jokiranta and Hanna

textual history of the Community Rule would have likely been much more complicated than initially imagined.[120]

What is needed, according to Jokiranta, is to ask another set of questions beyond those of textual history. These include questions about "what scrolls and manuscripts and rules are for their users, and how each individual product is both unique and a carrier of traditions or knowledge."[121] When these aspects are considered, interpreters can begin to appreciate the various copies of the Community Rule in new ways. From this perspective, "[A]ll the extant S and related manuscripts are exemplars of the kind of information that persisted, was being used, and affected the perception of existing information."[122] This moves the discussion away from simply thinking about textual variation "as different editions of the same literary work," and it allows the fluidity to also be understood "as representing the rule traditions in multiple ways and organizing the existing information in each case uniquely."[123]

5 Education and the Dead Sea Scrolls

Scholars have also focused on what the Scrolls reveal about the educational practices of the sectarian movement—both in terms of their content and as material artefacts. Much of this attention has been devoted to the question of whether the movement trained its members in grapho-literacy, and if so, what types of pedagogical practices were employed.

5.1 *Evidence of Educational Practices from the Scrolls*
When considering the recipients of educational instruction, scholars often begin by asking about the training received by children. The Rule of the

---

Vanonen, "Multiple Copies of Rule Texts or Multiple Rule Texts? Boundaries of the S and M Documents," in *Crossing Imaginary Boundaries: The Dead Sea Scrolls in the Context of Second Temple Judaism*, ed. Mika S. Pajunen and Hanna Tervanotko, Publications of the Finnish Exegetical Society 108 (Helsinki: Finnish Exegetical Society, 2015), 17.

120 Others have argued for a more complex situation as well, e.g., Charlotte Hempel, "The Literary Development of the S Tradition—A New Paradigm," *RevQ* 22 (2006): 389–401; Alison Schofield, "Rereading S: A New Model of Textual Development in Light of the Cave 4 *Serekh* Copies," *DSD* 15 (2008): 96–120; Maxine L. Grossman, "Community Rule or Community Rules: Examining a Supplementary Approach in Light of the Sectarian Dead Sea Scrolls," in *Empirical Models Challenging Biblical Criticism*, ed. Raymond F. Person and Robert Rezetko, AIL 25 (Atlanta, GA: SBL, 2016), 303–30.

121 Jokiranta, "What is 'Serekh ha-Yahad (S)'?," 622.

122 Ibid., 634–35.

123 Ibid., 635.

Congregation has factored most prominently into this discussion. This work is thought to indicate that participants in the educational process included not only men but also women and children. Some type of training is described as taking place at the community's covenant renewal ceremony. It states, "When they come, they shall assemble all those who enter, (including) children (טף) along with women; and they shall read in [their] h[earing al]l the statutes of the covenant, and instruct them in all [th]eir judg[ments] lest they err g[reatly]" (1QSa 1:4–5).[124] Elsewhere, the document refers to the instruction that children were expected to receive in the book of Hagu. This training, which a child is said to undertake "from [his you]th" (1:6), is marked by progressive levels of education in the "statutes of the covenant" and the "precepts" of the group (1:7–8).

The problem is that the Rule of the Congregation is not entirely clear about when this training took place. Some claim that the educational practices described in 1QSa reflect the contemporary circumstances of the movement, while others believe that they represent ideal conditions in a future utopian environment. It is possible to assume that the group would have maintained some level of consistency in the type of training that was offered, with the result that the pedagogical practices of the future should mirror those from earlier periods.[125] Many, however, are cautious about drawing any firm conclusions about the educational practices of the group from these statements alone.[126]

An even more significant obstacle is that the Rule of the Congregation, like most Jewish writings from the Second Temple period,[127] lacks any specific

---

124 Translation by James H. Charlesworth and Loren T. Stuckenbruck, "Rule of the Congregation (1QSa)," in *The Dead Sea Scrolls: Hebrew, Aramaic, and Greek Texts with English Translations*, vol. 1: *Rule of the Community and Related Documents*, ed. James H. Charlesworth, PTSDSSP (Tübigen: Mohr Siebeck; Louisville, KY: Westminster John Knox Press, 1994), 111.

125 Many have maintained this position, e.g., Steven D. Fraade, "Interpretive Authority in the Studying Community at Qumran," *JJS* 44 (1993): 55–56; Bilhah Nitzan, "Education and Wisdom in the Dead Sea Scrolls in Light of their Background in Antiquity," in *New Perspectives on Old Texts: Proceedings of the Tenth International Symposium of the Orion Center for the Study of the Dead Sea Scrolls and Associated Literature, 9–11 January, 2005*, ed. Esther G. Chazon et al., STDJ 88 (Leiden: Brill, 2010), 106; Cecilia Wassén, "On the Education of Children in the Dead Sea Scrolls," *Studies in Religion/Sciences Religieuses* 41 (2012): 351. Those who adopt this position generally follow the assessment by Lawrence H. Schiffman, *The Eschatological Community of the Dead Sea Scrolls: A Study of the Rule of the Congregation*, SBLMS 38 (Atlanta, GA: Scholars, 1989), 9.

126 Note, e.g., Matthew J. Goff, "Students of God in the House of Torah: Education in the Dead Sea Scrolls," in *Second Temple Jewish 'Paideia' in Context*, ed. Jason M. Zurawski and Gabriele Boccaccini, BZNW 228 (Berlin: De Gruyter, 2017), 83–85.

127 For a discussion of exceptions, see Patrick Pouchelle, "Discipline, Transmission, and Writing: Notes on Education in the Testament of the Twelve Patriarchs," in *Second Temple*

indications that the education of children involved reading and writing skills. Therefore, whether grapho-literacy was part of the sectarian curriculum must be deduced from other considerations. Affirming that such training did take place, Cecilia Wassén points to the emphasis on education in collective memory and its role in community standing. What weighs heaviest on her decision, however, is the literary production of the group, which is thought to have involved composing and transmitting many of the manuscripts within the Qumran collection.[128] According to Wassén, the performance of these tasks "testifies to the need for the sectarians not only to memorize and read sacred texts, but also to be able to write and compose new works." It was these "skills that were passed on to the children."[129]

Wassén also argues that the movement departed from contemporary educational trends by making literacy the responsibility of the community rather than the family. She notes that "the Dead Sea Scrolls are the earliest references to what appears to be mandatory, communal elementary education for Jewish children."[130] If Wassén is correct about the obligatory, communal nature of this training, it would hold out important implications for the literacy rates within the movement: the vast majority of the membership would be literate in no less than a generation. The basic premise of this position has not gone unchallenged, however. Based on a reading found in a Cave 4 manuscript of the Damascus Document, Matthew Goff advocates continuing to locate education within the family. The document he cites in this regard is 4Q266 9 iii 5–7, which specifies that the Overseer has the responsibility of instructing the children of those who are divorced. According to Goff, the fact that the Overseer inherited this task indicates that it was normally the responsibility of the father.[131] Further work is necessary if this question is to be resolved.

Aside from the education of children, consideration has also been given to the training received by adults. Those who have recently addressed this topic have avoided representing Qumran as a facility where adults received their elementary education. According to Philip S. Alexander, members joined the movement having already completed their literacy training elsewhere. This situation is thought to explain the diversity of scripts found in the manuscript record. Alexander does not deny that some type of educational activities took place within the community. He acknowledges that "Qumran did

---

 Jewish 'Paideia' in Context, ed. Jason M. Zurawski and Gabriele Boccaccini, BZNW 228 (Berlin: De Gruyter, 2017), 138–39.

128 Wassén, "On the Education of Children," 354–55.
129 Ibid., 358.
130 Ibid., 355. Cf. also Fraade, "Interpretive Authority," 56.
131 Goff, "Students of God," 85.

function as a kind of school in which a body of knowledge was studied and passed on, but from an educational standpoint it must be classified as a tertiary institution."[132] The specialized training that some received at Qumran has been briefly addressed by George J. Brooke. He notes the possibility that scribes might have received instruction in both preparing specialized writing surfaces (e.g., deluxe manuscripts; *tefillin*) as well as composing distinct scripts (e.g., cryptic alphabet; paleo-Hebrew).[133]

5.2 *The Scrolls as Evidence of Educational Practices*

Not only is the content of the Scrolls thought to attest to educational pursuits, many are convinced that the Scrolls themselves, as material artefacts, reveal something about the didactic practices of the group. Part of this discussion has focused on the archaeological evidence from the settlement of Qumran. One of the most noteworthy discoveries was the presence of abecedaries.[134] These alphabetic inscriptions are commonly interpreted as exercises composed by novices who were in the early stages of literacy training. The most notable proponent of this view is André Lemaire. Within his numerous publications on the subject, he has suggested that abecedaries should be viewed as indicators of schools providing instruction in writing. Much of the evidence that he has discussed pertains to the First Temple period;[135] but he has applied this same line of reasoning to the evidence from Qumran.[136] This interpretation seems to fit well in the case of KhQ 161, an ostracon discovered just outside the settlement which contains the complete alphabet. The rudimentary quality of its

---

132 Alexander, "Literacy Among Jews," 14.

133 George J. Brooke, "Aspects of Education in the Sectarian Scrolls from the Qumran Caves," in *Jewish Education from Antiquity to the Middle Ages: Studies in Honour of Philip S. Alexander*, ed. George J. Brooke and Renate Smithuis, AJEC 100 (Leiden: Brill, 2017), 32–35.

134 On the abecedaries discovered at Qumran, see G. Wilhelm Nebe, "Alphabets," in *Encyclopedia of the Dead Sea Scrolls*, ed. Lawrence H. Schiffman and James C. VanderKam (Oxford: Oxford University Press, 2000), 1:18–20.

135 See, e.g., André Lemaire, "A Schoolboy's Exercise on an Ostracon at Lachish," *TA* 3 (1976): 109–10; idem, "Abécédaires et exercices d'écolier en épigraphie nord-ouest sémitique," *JA* 266 (1978): 221–35; idem, *Les écoles et la formation de la Bible dans l'ancien Israël*, OBO 39 (Fribourg: Éditions Universitaires, 1981), esp. 7–33.

136 See, e.g., André Lemaire, "L'enseignement essénien et l'école de Qumrân," in *Hellenica et Judaica: Hommage à Valentin Nikiprowetzky*, ed. André Caquot et al. (Leuven: Peeters, 1986), 201–202; idem, "Lire, écrire, étudier à Qoumrân et ailleurs," in *Qoumrân et la judaïsme du tournant de notre ère: Actes de la Table Ronde, Collège de France, 16 novembre 2004*, eds. André Lemaire and Simon C. Mimouni, Collection de la Revue des études juives 40 (Leuven: Peeters, 2006) 69. Others have likewise connected abecedaries with training in writing (e.g., Tov, "The Scribes of the Texts," 140; Nitzan, "Education and Wisdom," 103–104).

TEXTUALITY AND THE DEAD SEA SCROLLS

letter formations as well as the duplication of some letters appears to point in this direction.[137] What is more, the partition of the letters conforms to a pattern thought to reflect a standardized mnemonic technique in which the letters of the alphabet were learned in two divisions: *aleph–kaf* and *lamed–taw*.[138]

But, with the recognition that alphabet inscriptions were also employed in magical or apotropaic settings, some have wondered whether all of these abecedaries must necessarily be given a pedagogical interpretation. In the broader discussion of abecedaries found in and around ancient Palestine, it has become common for scholars to assign an apotropaic function to inscriptions discovered on ossuaries and the walls of desert caves.[139] It is even assumed that a cheap and easily-accessible surface like ostraca could have potentially been used for magical purposes.[140] In the case of KhQ 2289, the alphabet appears on a polished limestone plaque. The nature of this surface has led some to understand the inscription as an apotropaic abecedary.[141]

Most acknowledge that some type of instruction was carried out at Qumran and that abecedaries may connect to these efforts. But recently scholars have

---

137　The inscription was also published as KhQOstracon 3 within the DJD series: Esther Eshel, "Khirbet Qumran Ostracon," in *Qumran Cave 4.XXVI: Cryptic Texts and Miscellanea, Part 1*, ed. Stephen J. Pfann and Philip S. Alexander, DJD 36 (Oxford: Clarendon, 2000), 509–12. The rudimentary nature of this inscription has led to its interpretation as an elementary exercise (e.g., Roland de Vaux, "Fouilles au Khirbet Qumrân: Rapport préliminaire sur la deuxième campagne," *RB* 61 [1954] 214, 229; André Lemaire, "Inscriptions du Khirbeh, des grottes et de 'Aïn Feshkha," in *Fouilles de Khirbet Qumrân et de Aïn Feshkha. II, Études d'anthropologie, de physique et de chimie*, eds. Jean-Baptiste Humbert and Jan Gunneweg, NTOA.SA 3 [Göttingen: Vandenhoeck & Ruprecht, 2003] 341–42; Émile Puech, "L'épigraphie de Qumrân: Son apport à l'identification du site," *RevQ* 24 [2010]: 438 n. 16).

138　On this pattern, see Michael D. Coogan, "Alphabets and Elements," *BASOR* 216 (1974): 61–63.

139　For alphabet inscriptions on graves, see Rachel Hachlili, "Did the Use of the Alphabet Already Have a Magical Significance in the First Century C.E.?," *Cathedra* 31 (1984): 27–30 (Hebrew); Alice Bij de Vaate, "Alphabet-Inscriptions from Jewish Graves," in *Studies in Early Jewish Epigraphy*, eds. Jan Willem van Henten and Pieter W. van der Horst, AGJU 21 (Leiden: Brill, 1994), 148–61. For alphabet inscriptions on cave walls, see Rechav Rubin and Joseph Patrich, "Wadi Suweinit," *Excavations and Surveys in Israel* 2 (1983): 107–109.

140　It is generally assumed that broken pieces of pottery signify a writing exercise (cf. Haggai Misgav, "The Ostraca," in *Back to Qumran: Final Report (1993–2004)*, ed. Yitzhak Magen and Yuval Peleg, Judea and Samaria Publications 18 [Jerusalem: Israel Antiquities Authority, 2018], 433). But Bij de Vaate points out that "the use of ostraca in magic is attested and even recommended in several recipes" ("Alphabet-Inscriptions from Jewish Graves," 160; cf. Hezser, *Jewish Literacy in Roman Palestine*, 87).

141　See, e.g., Juhana M. Saukkonen, "Dwellers at Qumran: Reflections on Their Literacy, Social Status, and Identity," in *Scripture in Transition: Essays on Septuagint, Hebrew Bible, and Dead Sea Scrolls in Honour of Raija Sollamo*, ed. Anssi Voitila and Jutta Jokiranta, JSJSup 126 (Leiden: Brill, 2008), 620–21.

cautioned against drawing too much from this evidence. As Goff has noted, the alphabet inscriptions at Qumran must first be interpreted within their regional context. Particularly noteworthy is that "[t]he writings found at Masada and Murabba'at, both sizable but much smaller corpora when compared with that of Qumran, include more abecedaries than the Dead Sea Scrolls."[142] The presence of alphabetic artefacts at Qumran should, therefore, not be understood as incontrovertible proof of organized efforts to provide rudimentary education in writing. Their bearing on the question of whether training was carried out at a communal level must also be answered with care, since grapho-literacy would have involved the same types of learning exercises at both the individual and group level.[143] Conclusions like these serve to reign in some of the sweeping claims about abecedaries and what they reveal about the educational practices undertaken at Qumran.

Along with the archaeological evidence, several documents from the caves around Qumran are thought to provide insight into communal education.[144] Early palaeographic assessments claimed to have uncovered evidence of copies that were made by scribes in training. In one instance, J. T. Milik described 4QEn^a ar (4Q201) as a "school-exercise copied by a young scribe from the master's dictation."[145] Elsewhere, 4QPs^x (4Q98g, formerly classified as 4Q236) was said to represent a "practice page from memory," composed by a scribe who made several mistakes.[146] More recently, the focus has shifted to three specific

---

142   Goff, "Students of God," 88.

143   Cf. John C. Poirier, "Education/Literacy in Jewish Galilee: Was There Any and at What Level?," in *Galilee in the Late Second Temple and Mishnaic Periods*, vol. 1: *Life, Culture, and Society*, ed. David A. Fiensy and James R. Strange (Minneapolis, MN: Augsburg Fortress, 2014), 257.

144   Another artefact cited in connection with this discussion is an ostracon (KhQ 2207) which contains numerous Hebrew letters written in a sequence that does not appear to form any logical combinations of words. This inscription is often referred to as a school or scribal exercise (see, e.g., Daniel Stökl Ben Ezra, *Qumran: Die Texte vom Toten Meer und das antike Judentum*, Jüdische Studien 3 [Tübingen: Mohr Siebeck, 2016], 117; Sidnie White Crawford, "The Inscriptional Evidence from Qumran and its Relationship to the Cave 4Q Documents," in *The Caves of Qumran: Proceedings of the International Conference, Lugano 2014*, ed. Marcello Fidanzio, STDJ 118 [Leiden: Brill, 2017], 210–11).

145   Józef T. Milik, *The Books of Enoch: Aramaic fragments of Qumrân Cave 4* (Oxford: Clarendon, 1976), 141. Cf. idem, "Daniel et Susanne à Qumrân?," in *De la Tôrah au Messie: Études d'exégèse et d'herméneutique bibliques offertes à Henri Cazelles pour ses 25 années d'enseignement a l'Institut catholique de Paris, octobre 1979*, ed. Maurice Carrez, et al. (Paris: Desclée, 1981), 355, where he proposes that 4QDanSuz (?) ar (4Q551) may have been written by an apprentice scribe.

146   See Patrick W. Skehan, "Gleanings from Psalm Texts from Qumran," in *Mélanges bibliques et orientaux en l'honneur de M. Henri Cazelles*, ed. André Caquot and Mathias Delcor, AOAT 212 (Neukirchen/Vluyn: Neukirchener Verlag, 1981), 439. Similarly, 4QGen^f (4Q6),

TEXTUALITY AND THE DEAD SEA SCROLLS

documents thought to represent writing exercises. 4Q234 is a parchment that may have contained Gen 27:19–21, although its fragmentary nature makes identification difficult. What is striking is that the text is written in multiple directions: horizontal, sideways, and upside-down. The same holds true for 4Q360, which preserves traces of letters and what appears to be the name Menaḥem written three separate times. The text is written vertically (on the right side) and horizontally in two different places (left side and bottom).

Some have interpreted these manuscripts within the context of educational instruction. In particular, they have been connected to the training received by scribes. As Emanuel Tov explains, "[S]cribes were introduced to their trade during the course of a training period, in which they learned writing and the various scribal procedures connected with it." Further, he notes, "Scribes had to master various technical skills relating to the material on which they wrote, the use of writing implements, and the preparation of ink." Based on these considerations, he suggests that documents such as 4Q234, 4Q360, and 4Q341 are "scribal exercises" that reflect "a learning process."[147] The recent attention devoted to 4Q341, however, has led to a slightly more nuanced interpretation.

Initially, 4Q341 was interpreted as a medicinal or pharmacological composition by John M. Allegro (and thus dubbed 4QTherapeia). It was thought to contain "a clinical report on some aspects of Essene therapy as practiced at Qumran."[148] Reading the work in an altogether different manner, Joseph Naveh suggested that the fragment represents "a small left-over piece of leather" that was used by the writer to compose "some meaningless words and letters and thus to accustom his hand to the pen and ink and to the writing material before beginning to write in earnest."[149] Against those who would read the text

---

which appears to have been a single sheet containing Gen 48:1–11, has been described as a scribal exercise that was poorly executed (Tov, "The Scribes of the Texts," 141).

147 Tov, *Scribal Practices*, 14. Cf. White Crawford, "Qumran Collection as a Scribal Library," 129, who describes these texts (and possibly 4Q338) as "evidence of scribal training."

148 John M. Allegro, *The Dead Sea Scrolls and the Christian Myth*, 2nd ed. (Amherst, NY: Prometheus, 1992), 3, 235–40. This interpretation was followed by James H. Charlesworth, *The Discovery of a Dead Sea Scroll (4Q Therapeia): Its Importance in the History of Medicine and Jesus Research*, ICASALS Publication 85–1 (Lubbock, TX: Texas Tech University, 1985), although he later retracted this view; see idem, "A Misunderstood Recently Published Dead Sea Scroll," *Explorations* 1.2 (1987): 2. Some continue to espouse this theory (e.g., Andrew Daunton-Fear, *Healing in the Early Church: The Church's Ministry of Healing and Exorcism from the First to the Fifth Century*, Studies in Christian History and Thought [Eugene, OR: Wipf & Stock, 2009], 15).

149 Joseph Naveh, "A Medical Document or a Writing Exercise? The So-Called 4QTherapeia," *IEJ* 36 (1986): 53. Cf. also idem, "Exercitium Calami C," in *Qumran Cave 4.XXVI: Cryptic Texts and Miscellanea, Part 1*, ed. Stephen J. Pfann and Philip S. Alexander, DJD 36 (Oxford: Clarendon, 2000), 291–94.

as the work of one seeking to improve his writing skills,[150] Naveh argued that the style reflects "a fairly skilled person, perhaps a scribe,"[151] a conclusion he reached by comparing the handwriting with a similar writing exercise published by Puech.[152] This text, which was written on an ostracon, contains many of the same names, often written in the same order; nevertheless, it was composed in a hand which had not yet mastered all of the letters.

Subsequent scholars have taken exception to Naveh's claim that the writer merely composed a list of "meaningless words and letters" and have begun to explore what this composition might reveal about the purposes of the author and the educational processes reflected therein. Moving beyond the preparatory nature of the text, George J. Brooke has inquired further into authorial aims. His interest, more specifically, lies in discerning the type of situation that would have led a writer to inscribe both the alphabet and a list of (alphabetic) names. After considering the various contexts in which such preparation might be necessary, Brooke points out that "scribes concerned with the production of the realia of what may be broadly termed 'magic' might have been distinctively interested in both."[153] For support, he points to the First Book of Cyranides, a magical writing which similarly uses the alphabet and alphabetized terms as part of its organization. Understood from this perspective, 4Q341 would not simply be an exercise intended to prepare the scribe for writing. This combination would indicate that "the scribe of 4Q341 was being trained or was training himself so as to be able to provide 'magical' texts."[154]

A different approach to the question of authorial aims has recently been taken by Joan E. Taylor. By situating 4Q341 more firmly within the context of ancient educational exercises, she attributes this particular list of letters and names to the prior training of the writer. But despite the connection with elementary instruction, Taylor is careful not to describe the text as a pedagogical exercise. The accomplished hand of the scribe and the fact that the writing occurs on leather (rather than an ostracon) leads her away from this conclusion. Like Naveh, she believes that "4Q341 was indeed a 'warm-up' for a scribe

---

150 See, e.g., White Crawford, "Inscriptional Evidence from Qumran," 217: "[T]he most likely explanation for the list of names is that they are the names of individuals known to the scribe, who practiced his craft by writing the names of his friends."

151 Naveh, "A Medical Document or a Writing Exercise?," 53.

152 Émile Puech, "Abécédaire et liste alphabétique de noms hébreux du début du IIe s. A.D.," RB 87 (1980): 118–26.

153 George J. Brooke, "4Q341: An Exercise for Spelling and for Spells?," in Writing and Ancient Near Eastern Society: Papers in Honour of Alan R. Millard, ed. Piotr Bienkowski et al., LHBOTS 426 (London: T&T Clark International, 2005), 276.

154 Ibid., 278 and 279, respectively.

TEXTUALITY AND THE DEAD SEA SCROLLS

for the purpose of familiarization with the available writing instrument and ink."[155] Consequently, she regards the management of ink-flow as the primary object of the writer's concern. Noteworthy is that this utilitarian focus is thought to reveal something important about the writer's educational training. Since the scribe is focused more on his writing utensils than any specific content, the material likely reflects an exercise that could have been produced without any effort, one that had been internalized through years of practice. In other words, Taylor contends that 4Q341 provides a rare glimpse into "the kind of writing exercises he would have learnt when he was a beginner."[156] As such, it informs our understanding of the processes by which grapho-literacy was achieved,[157] although it does not indicate that formal instruction was taking place at Qumran.

6   Literacy and the Dead Sea Scrolls

Literacy among the Scrolls community is another topic that has been taken in new directions. In particular, interpreters have begun to situate the evidence within the wider discussion of education in antiquity. This, in turn, has provided further insight into the social dynamics of the group.

6.1   *Distinguishing the Languages of Literacy*
To this point, the discussion of literacy at Qumran has largely been conducted without much consideration given to the language(s) involved. One of the few who has explicitly addressed this issue is Lemaire. The sheer number of documents that were preserved in Hebrew and Aramaic has led him to believe that most of the members could read at least two languages.[158] He even surmises that a large number of members were proficient in Greek and paleo-Hebrew

---

155   Joan E. Taylor, "4Q341: A Writing Exercise Remembered," in *Is There a Text in this Cave? Studies in the Textuality of the Dead Sea Scrolls in Honour of George J. Brooke*, ed. Ariel Feldman et al., STDJ 119 (Leiden: Brill, 2017), 150.

156   Ibid., 151. Cf. Goff, "Students of God," 87: "This little known Qumran text may provide evidence of a mnemonic used at the time to learn the alphabet, even if the fragment is not necessarily the product of a beginner scribe."

157   In particular, it would illustrate that one important elementary exercise was "executing similar and therefore potentially confusing sound combinations" (Phillip R. Callaway, "Some Thoughts on Writing Exercise (4Q341)," *QC* 13 [2006]: 149).

158   Lemaire, "Lire, écrire, étudier à Qoumrân et ailleurs," 66.

as well.[159] This position is consistent with some earlier assessments of the diverse linguistic situation in Roman Palestine.[160]

More recently, important questions have been raised about the prevalence of multi-language literacy in the ancient world. In light of studies which suggest that tri- and even bi-literacy was a rare phenomenon in antiquity, Stephen Reed notes that if widespread literacy in a variety of languages is to be posed at Qumran, it would be imperative to explain how such proficiency developed.[161] He argues that "[w]hile the different languages (Hebrew, Aramaic, Greek) found in the Dead Sea Scrolls were used by some people at that time this does not mean that everyone could speak and write all three languages."[162] Issues like these will require further exploration in the future.

6.2 Distinguishing Types of Literacy at Qumran

The sheer amount of literary evidence discovered at Qumran has, at times, been viewed as representative of Jewish society more generally. Some have even concluded that Jewish literacy levels during this period exceeded those in other ancient cultures.[163] More often, however, the educational achievements represented among the Scrolls community have been contrasted with trends found in Second Temple Judaism.[164] With many estimating the literacy rates in

---

159   Ibid., 67.

160   See, e.g., Chaim Rabin, "Hebrew and Aramaic in the First Century," in *The Jewish People in the First Century*, ed. Shmuel Safrai and Menahem Stern (Philadephia: Fortress, 1976), 1007–39; Bernard Spolsky, "Triglossia and Literacy in Jewish Palestine of the First Century," *IJSL* 42 (1983): 95–109.

161   Stephen Reed, "The Linguistic Diversity of the Texts Found at Qumran," in *The Dead Sea Scrolls at Qumran and the Concept of a Library*, ed. Sidnie White Crawford and Cecilia Wassén, STDJ 116 (Leiden: Brill, 2016), 135–36. He cites the work of Jonathan J. Price and Shlomo Naeh ("On the Margins of Culture: The Practice of Transcription in the Ancient World," in *From Hellenism to Islam: Cultural and Linguistic Change in the Roman Near East*, ed. Hannah M. Cotton et al. [Cambridge: Cambridge University Press, 2009]), who note: "Although bilingualism was common in antiquity, biliteracy was rarer" (260).

162   Reed, "The Linguistic Diversity," 135.

163   Eric M. Meyers and Mark A. Chancey, *Archaeology of the Land of the Bible*, vol. 3: *Alexander to Constantine*, ABRL (New Haven, CT: Yale University Press, 2012), 112: "The amazing variety and number of compositions associated with both the Qumran and Jerusalem communities point to an unprecedented and unique moment in Jewish history and to a literacy rate that probably exceeds many other cultures in antiquity." Others would contest this conclusion, however (e.g., Luke Timothy Johnson, *Among the Gentiles: Greco-Roman Religion and Christianity*, ABRL [New Haven, CT: Yale University Press, 2010], 115).

164   See, e.g., Robert A. Kugler, "Hearing 4Q225: A Case Study in Reconstructing the Religious Imagination of the Qumran Community," *DSD* 10 (2003): 83, who claims that "the people of Qumran" were "probably highly literate by comparison with other Jews of the era."

TEXTUALITY AND THE DEAD SEA SCROLLS

Roman Palestine at somewhere around 3–10% of the population,[165] the situation at Qumran is striking due to the fact that the sectarians are commonly identified as a highly literate group.[166]

Further specificity has recently been added to this description as scholars have insisted on separating the requisite skills for reading and writing. The former, many contend, was a skill possessed by a large majority of the community. According to Alexander, "Qumran appears to have been a highly literate community, which laid great store by the written word." As a result, he notes, "It is possible that most, if not all, of its members could read."[167]

Various considerations have led scholars to posit high reading literacy at Qumran. Perhaps none has been more influential than the reference to a nightly group study session involving members of the community reading from the Torah (1QS 6:6–8). With such emphasis on the study of written documents, some interpreters have proposed that the ability to read was essential for membership in the group.[168] Another consideration thought to support

165 Some years ago, William V. Harris (*Ancient Literacy* [Cambridge, MA: Harvard University Press, 1989]) argued that the ancient Greek and Roman worlds lacked the necessary institutional mechanisms essential for mass literacy. His 'high level' approach, based on comparative social history, indicated that no more than 10 percent of the Roman citizenry would have been literate at the start of the Principate. In the land of Palestine, the numbers are thought to be even lower due to various social and historical factors (see, e.g., Meir Bar-Ilan, "Illiteracy in the Land of Israel in the First Centuries CE," in *Essays in the Social Scientific Study of Judaism and Jewish Society*, ed. Simcha Fishbane and Jack N. Lightstone [Hoboken, NJ: Ktav, 1992], 2:46–61; Hezser, *Jewish Literacy in Roman Palestine*). Through a recent investigation of signature literacy in the Bar Kokhba texts, Michael O. Wise (*Language & Literacy in Roman Judaea: A Study of the Bar Kokhba Documents*, AYBRL [New Haven, CT: Yale University Press, 2015]) has estimated that 'between 5 and 10 percent of Judaean men in the years dividing Pompey from Hadrian were able to read books' (349–50; emphasis removed).

166 This is a conclusion which is regularly repeated in scholarship, see, e.g., John J. Collins, "Qumran, Apocalypticism and the New Testament," in *The Dead Sea Scrolls Fifty Years after Their Discovery 1947–1997: Proceedings of the Jerusalem Congress, July 20–25, 1997*, ed. Lawrence H. Schiffman et al. (Jerusalem: Israel Exploration Society & The Shrine of the Book, 2000), 135: "the Qumran sect has a scribal, literate character"; Alexander, "Literacy Among Jews," 5: "That the Community at Qumran was literate on any definition of that term seems beyond doubt"; Alex P. Jassen, "The Dead Sea Scrolls and Violence: Sectarian Formation and Eschatological Imagination," *BibInt* 17 (2009): 20: "Though scholars continue to debate the extent of literacy in Second Temple Judaism, the Qumran community and its interlocutors seem to be among the literate members of society."

167 Alexander, "The Redaction-History of *Serekh Ha-Yaḥad*," 449. Cf. also idem, "Literacy Among Jews," 16; Lemaire, "Lire, écrire, étudier à Qoumrân et ailleurs," 67–69.

168 See, e.g., Brooke, "Aspects of Education in the Sectarian Scrolls," 23: "While writing might have been a common skill, at least for a sub-group within the sectarian movement, with some scribes having specialist expertise, reading seems to have been a sectarian

high literacy rates is the cryptic (or esoteric) script found in some manuscripts. The purpose of this mysterious type of writing, according to some, was to conceal the content from other members of the group.[169] When understood in this light, the cryptic script reveals a great deal about the literacy of the group. "If these cryptic alphabets were directed internally toward members of the Community, then they offer some proof that we are dealing with a literate group, where many members could have read anything not in code."[170]

Yet, whereas the ability to read is thought to have been pervasive among the inhabitants at Qumran, written literacy is a different story. According to Lemaire, individuals who joined the group would have already mastered the skills necessary to study and recite written works. What many would have lacked, he insists, is the ability to write. He points out that this skill was far more rare in the educational environment of ancient Palestine, where orality served as the primary pedagogical method.[171] For this reason, he interprets the discovery of abecedaries and writing exercises as indications that members were learning to write (see above). Others have, likewise, argued that

---

requirement, at least for men." Others have similarly argued for high reading literacy among the community based on 1QS 6.6–8 (e.g., Albert I. Baumgarten, "The Rule of the Martian as Applied to Qumran," *IOS* 14 (1994): 128 n. 36; idem, *The Flourishing of Jewish Sects in the Maccabean Era: An Interpretation*, JSJSup 55 [Leiden: Brill, 1997], 48; Fraade, "Interpretive Authority," 58 n. 35). An alternative interpretation of this evidence is offered by Hezser. She notes that "one could also hypothesize that [the ability to read] was required of those who wanted to advance to higher positions within the sect but not absolutely necessary for everyone." For, as she points out, "[a]t communal gatherings the texts would be read aloud and the esoteric knowledge and sectarian rules could also be taught orally to the new members" (*Jewish Literacy in Roman Palestine*, 199 n. 67).

169 In the case of 4Q298, specifically, Pfann has claimed that the cryptic script was meant to conceal the content from outsiders ("The Maskîl's Address to All Sons of Dawn," 224–25; idem, "The Writings in Esoteric Script," 178, 182). However, he acknowledges that more broadly, cryptic script could serve as a way for community elites to hide material from other group members (see idem, "The Use of Cryptographic and Esoteric Scripts in Second Temple Judaism and the Surrounding Cultures," in *Interpreting 4 Ezra and 2 Baruch: International Studies*, ed. Gabriele Boccaccini and Jason M. Zurawski, LSTS 87 [London: Bloomsbury, 2014], 193–95).

170 Alexander, "Literacy Among Jews," 19. The same conclusion has been reached by Daniel Stökl Ben Ezra ("Bücherlesen im Jachad Qumrans Himmlische Bücher zwischen Katechese, kollektivem Studium und esoterischer Geheimschrift," in *Metatexte: Erzählungen von schrifttragenden Artefakten in der alttestamentlichen und mittelalterlichen Literatur*, ed. Friedrich-Emanuel Focken and Michael R. Ott, Materiale Textkulturen 15 [Berlin: De Gruyter, 2016]), who claims, "Die Entwicklung einer derartigen Geheimschrift ist … nur dann notwendig, wenn einerseits viele Gruppenmitglieder lesen konnten und andererseits der Zugang zu besonders esoterischen Traditionen begrenzt werden sollte" (83).

171 Lemaire, "Lire, écrire, étudier à Qoumrân et ailleurs," 67–69.

TEXTUALITY AND THE DEAD SEA SCROLLS

facility in writing was not an ability that was common among the membership at Qumran.[172]

This interpretation is a movement away from earlier reconstructions that envisioned the community as a group of scribes whose efforts were primarily devoted to copying and composing documents in the scriptorium. Part of the reason for this shift relates to the recent efforts to understand the sociology of writing in antiquity. What has been discovered is that there was no one-to-one correlation between written literacy and social status. Many of the elite members of society were illiterate, while some with low social status could have been highly literate. Even scribal abilities did not guarantee prestige, for they did not necessarily place the bearer within the scholarly elite.[173]

Another factor contributing to this shift has been the reassessment of writing and copying at Qumran. While few would deny that writing took place within the community,[174] the amount of writing seems to have been somewhat more restricted than originally assumed. Not only are many of the scrolls now thought to have been composed elsewhere (see above), in terms of the duties of individual members, only the Overseer had the responsibility of recording information in written form (cf. 4Q477).[175] Further, scholars have noted the lack of references to and representations of scribes in the sectarian literature. As Samuel L. Adams points out, "it is noteworthy that the sectarians who were part of the *yahad* do not refer to themselves as scribes in their preservation and composition of texts, despite the high literacy rate among some members of

---

172 After claiming that reading was widespread among the Qumran community, he qualifies his statement by noting the limited number who would have possessed written literacy: "It should not, however, be too readily assumed that all, or most of, its members would have had equal facility with writing" (Alexander, "The Redaction-History of *Serekh Ha-Yaḥad*," 449).

173 Cf. Kipp Davis, "Paleographical and Physical Features of the Dead Sea Scrolls in the Museum of the Bible Collection: A Synopsis," in *Dead Sea Scrolls Fragments in the Museum Collection*, ed. Emanuel Tov et al., Publications of Museum of the Bible 1 (Leiden: Brill, 2016), 30: "it is possible that most scribes were actually not highly trained scholars; rather, as members of a professional guild, they would have been commissioned to write and copy any number of texts from simple documents to expensive and exquisite literary works. While these professional scribes could also have been scholars, this was not necessarily the case." See also Alexander, "Literacy Among Jews," 17.

174 As proof, most point to the inkwells that were discovered at Qumran, see Stephen Goranson, "An Inkwell from Qumran," *Michmanim* 6 (1992): 37–40; idem, "Qumran: The Evidence of the Inkwells," *BAR* 19 (1993): 67; idem, "Qumran—A Hub of Scribal Activity," *BAR* 20 (1994): 36–39. Some have also claimed that locus 30 at the settlement also functioned as a scriptorium.

175 See Tigchelaar, "The Scribes of the Scrolls," 526–27.

this community and their intensive work in composing and editing complex manuscripts."[176]

6.3 Distinguishing Literacy Rates at Qumran

While many continue to advocate for a high rate of (reading) literacy at Qumran, there has been some resistance to this interpretation. From a pragmatic perspective, Juhana M. Saukkonen has observed that a portion of the inhabitants would have had to carry out the daily responsibilities which allowed the community to continue its existence. "To keep the everyday life going," he notes, "there were people who took care of agriculture, pottery production, food processing, building, and other mundane tasks. Many of these responsibilities required specific skills and training."[177] Although it is possible to suppose that some of the highly educated members of the community acquired additional training to perform these (mundane) tasks, Saukkonen stresses that the situation could just as easily imply that literacy was not an indispensable part of group membership.

This conclusion is consistent with the comparative reading of the Qumran community recently proposed by Charlotte Hempel. Even though Hempel affirms "the determinative leadership of a stratum of elite scholars and scribes," she also seeks to expose "the inevitable though largely unrecognized presence of a significant proportion of the membership who were illiterate or semi-literate."[178] For this latter group, elevated social status was not achieved through an ability to read or write, but simply through their connection with scribal elites who were engaged in scholarly pursuits.

Two considerations lead Hempel to this conclusion. The first is the social value attached to written works in the ancient world. Aside from serving merely as a medium on which to preserve information, manuscripts were also used as a means of displaying prestige and status by those who owned them—regardless of whether the owners could access the content for themselves.[179] This means that the mere possession of written documents should not be taken as an

---

176 Samuel L. Adams, "The Social Location of the Scribe in the Second Temple Period," in *Sibyls, Scriptures, and Scrolls: John Collins at Seventy*, ed. Joel S. Baden et al., JSJSup 175 (Leiden: Brill, 2016), 35. Cf. Armin Lange, "Sages and Scribes in the Qumran Literature," in *Scribes, Sages and Seers: The Sage in the Eastern Mediterranean World*, ed. Leo G. Perdue, FRLANT 219 (Göttingen: Vandenhoeck & Ruprecht, 2008), 292.
177 Saukkonen, "Dwellers at Qumran," 627.
178 Hempel, "Reflections on Literacy," 82.
179 Cf. Popović, "Qumran as Scroll Storehouse," 573–75.

indication that the majority of the group was capable of reading them.[180] A second consideration is the social dynamics involved in communal study. Drawing from the work of Brian Stock on the social organization connected to authoritative writings, Hempel argues that Qumran represented an ancient "textual community" where non-literates were dependent on literates for their understanding of the text. As such, the group would have been structured according to a defined social hierarchy, with the various levels reflecting each person's literary proficiencies.

7 Conclusion

From this survey, it is clear that Dead Sea Scrolls scholarship has begun to approach the textual evidence in new and important directions. Informed by theoretical insights gleaned from media studies, and with a focus that has been sharpened through comparative analysis with other manuscript cultures, the current interpretive trajectory has the potential to reshape modern understandings of the Qumran discoveries in significant ways. But exactly how this turn toward ancient media culture will impact the field remains to be seen.

Bibliography

Abegg, Martin G. "The Linguistic Analysis of the Dead Sea Scrolls: More Than (Initially) Meets the Eye." Pages 48–68 in *Rediscovering the Dead Sea Scrolls: An Assessment of Old and New Approaches and Methods*. Edited by Maxine L. Grossman. Grand Rapids, MI: Eerdmans, 2010.

Abegg, Martin G. "Scribal Practice and the Pony in the Manure Pile." Pages 65–88 in *Reading the Bible in Ancient Traditions and Modern Editions: Studies in Memory of Peter W. Flint*. Edited by Andrew B. Perrin, Kyung S. Baek, and Daniel K. Falk. EJL 47. Atlanta, GA: SBL, 2017.

Abegg, Martin G. "Qumran Scribal Practice: Won Moor Thyme." Pages 175–204 in *Scribal Practice, Text and Canon in the Dead Sea Scrolls: Essays in Memory of Peter W. Flint*. Edited by John J. Collins and Ananda Geyser-Fouché. STDJ 130. Leiden: Brill, 2019.

---

180   On the problem of confusing literacy with textuality by using the presence of texts to argue for wide-spread literacy, see Chris Keith, *Jesus' Literacy: Scribal Culture and the Teacher from Galilee*, LNTS 413 (London: Bloomsbury, 2011), 87–88; cf. also Sean Freyne, "Could Jesus Really Read? Literacy in Roman Galilee," in *Jewish Education from Antiquity to the Middle Ages: Studies in Honour of Philip S. Alexander*, ed. George J. Brooke and Renate Smithuis, AJEC 100 (Leiden: Brill, 2017), 45.

Adams, Samuel L. "The Social Location of the Scribe in the Second Temple Period." Pages 22–37 in *Sibyls, Scriptures, and Scrolls: John Collins at Seventy*. Edited by Joel S. Baden, Hindy Najman, Eibert J. C. Tigchelaar. JSJSup 175. Leiden: Brill, 2016.

Alexander, Philip S. "The Redaction-History of *Serekh Ha-Yaḥad*: A Proposal." *RevQ* 17 (1996): 437–56.

Alexander, Philip S. "Literacy Among Jews in Second Temple Palestine: Reflections on the Evidence from Qumran." Pages 3–24 in *Hamlet on a Hill: Semitic and Greek Studies Presented to Professor T. Muraoka on the Occasion of his Sixty-Fifth Birthday*. Edited by Martin F. J. Baasten and Wido T. van Peursen. OLA 118. Leuven: Peeters, 2003.

Allegro, John M. *The Dead Sea Scrolls and the Christian Myth*. 2nd ed. Amherst, NY: Prometheus, 1992.

Askin, Lindsey A. "Scribal Production and Literacy at Qumran: Considerations of Page Layout and Style." Pages 23–36 in *Material Aspects of Reading in Ancient and Medieval Cultures: Materiality, Presence and Performance*. Edited by Anna Krauß, Jonas Leipziger, and Friederike Schücking-Jungblut. Materiale Textkulturen 26. Berlin: De Gruyter, 2020.

Bar-Gal, Gila Kahila. "Principles of the Recovery of Ancient Data: What it Tells us of Plant and Animal Domestication and the Origin of the Scroll Parchment." Pages 41–50 in *Bio- and Material Cultures at Qumran: Papers from a COST Action G8 Working Group Meeting Held in Jerusalem, Israel on 22–23 May 2005*. Edited by Jan Gunneweg, Charles Greenblatt, and Annemie Adriaens. Stuttgart: Fraunhofer IRB, 2006.

Bar-Gal, Gila Kahila, Charles Greenblatt, Scott R. Woodward, Magen Broshi, and Patricia Smith. "The Genetic Signature of the Dead Sea Scrolls." Pages 165–71 in *Historical Perspectives: From the Hasmoneans to Bar Kokhba in Light of the Dead Sea Scrolls. Proceedings of the Fourth International Symposium of the Orion Center for the Study of the Dead Sea Scrolls and Associated Literature, 27–31 January 1999*. Edited by David M. Goodblatt, Avital Pinnick, and Daniel R. Schwartz. STDJ 37. Leiden: Brill, 2001.

Bar-Ilan, Meir. "Illiteracy in the Land of Israel in the First Centuries CE." Pages 2:46–61 in *Essays in the Social Scientific Study of Judaism and Jewish Society*. Edited by Simcha Fishbane and Jack N. Lightstone. Hoboken, NJ: Ktav, 1992.

Bar-Ilan, Meir. "Writing Materials." Pages 2:996–97 in *Encyclopedia of the Dead Sea Scrolls*. Edited by Lawrence H. Schiffman and James C. VanderKam. 2 vols. Oxford: Oxford University Press, 2000.

Baumgarten, Albert I. "The Rule of the Martian as Applied to Qumran." *IOS* 14 (1994): 179–200.

TEXTUALITY AND THE DEAD SEA SCROLLS

Baumgarten, Albert I. "Crisis in the Scrollery: A Dying Consensus." *Judaism* 44 (1995): 399–413.

Baumgarten, Albert I. *The Flourishing of Jewish Sects in the Maccabean Era: An Interpretation*. JSJSup 55. Leiden: Brill, 1997.

Berti, Monica. "Greek and Roman Libraries in the Hellenistic Age." Pages 31–54 in *The Dead Sea Scrolls at Qumran and the Concept of a Library*. Edited by Sidnie White Crawford and Cecilia Wassén. STDJ 116. Leiden: Brill, 2016.

Bij de Vaate, Alice. "Alphabet-Inscriptions from Jewish Graves." Pages 148–61 in *Studies in Early Jewish Epigraphy*. Edited by Jan Willem van Henten and Pieter W. van der Horst. AGJU 21. Leiden: Brill, 1994.

Bockmuehl, Markus N. A. "Redaction and Ideology in the Rule of the Community (1QS/4QS)." *RevQ* 18 (1998): 541–60.

Brooke, George J. "4Q341: An Exercise for Spelling and for Spells?" Pages 271–82 in *Writing and Ancient Near Eastern Society: Papers in Honour of Alan R. Millard*. Edited by Piotr Bienkowski, Christopher Mee, and Elizabeth Slater. LHBOTS 426. London: T&T Clark International, 2005.

Brooke, George J. *Qumran and the Jewish Jesus: Reading the New Testament in the Light of the Scrolls*. Cambridge: Grove Books, 2005.

Brooke, George J. "Aspects of the Physical and Scribal Features of Some Cave 4 'Continuous' Pesharim." Pages 133–50 in *The Dead Sea Scrolls: Transmission of Traditions and Production of Texts*. Edited by Sarianna Metso, Hindy Najman, and Eileen Schuller. STDJ 92. Leiden: Brill, 2010.

Brooke, George J. "Between Scroll and Codex? Reconsidering the Qumran Opisthographs." Pages 123–38 in *On Stone and Scroll: Studies in Honour of Graham I. Davies*. Edited by James K. Aitken, Katharine J. Dell, and Brian A. Mastin. BZAW 420. Berlin: De Gruyter, 2011.

Brooke, George J. "Scripture and Scriptural Tradition in Transmission: Light from the Dead Sea Scrolls." Pages 1–17 in *The Scrolls and Biblical Traditions: Proceedings of the Seventh Meeting of the IOQS in Helsinki*. Edited by George J. Brooke, Daniel K. Falk, Eibert J. C. Tigchelaar, and Molly M. Zahn. STDJ 103. Leiden: Brill, 2012.

Brooke, George J. "Aspects of Education in the Sectarian Scrolls from the Qumran Caves." Pages 11–42 in *Jewish Education from Antiquity to the Middle Ages: Studies in Honour of Philip S. Alexander*. Edited by George J. Brooke and Renate Smithuis. AJEC 100. Leiden: Brill, 2017.

Brooke, George J. "La « bibliothèque » une collection sans cesse revisitée." *Le Monde de la Bible* 220 (2017): 46–53.

Brooke, George J. "Choosing Between Papyrus and Skin: Cultural Complexity and Multiple Identities in the Qumran Library." Pages 119–35 in *Jewish Cultural Encounters in the Ancient Mediterranean and Near Eastern World*. Edited by Mladen Popović, Myles Schoonover, and Marijn Vandenberghe. JSJSup 178. Leiden: Brill, 2017.

Broshi, Magen. "The Archaeology of Qumran: A Reconsideration." Pages 103–15 in *The Dead Sea Scrolls: Forty Years of Research*. Edited by Devorah Dimant and Uriel Rappaport. STDJ 10. Leiden: Brill, 1992.

Bülow-Jacobsen, Adam. "Writing Materials in the Ancient World." Pages 3–29 in *The Oxford Handbook of Papyrology*. Edited by Roger S. Bagnall. Oxford: Oxford University Press, 2009.

Callaway, Phillip R. "Some Thoughts on Writing Exercise (4Q341)." *QC* 13 (2006) 147–51.

Campbell, Jonathan G. "Hebrew and its Study at Qumran." Pages 38–52 in *Hebrew Study from Ezra to Ben-Yehuda*. Edited by William Horbury. Edinburgh: T&T Clark, 1999.

Cansdale, Lena. *Qumran and the Essenes: A Re-Evaluation of the Evidence*. TSAJ 60. Tübingen: Mohr, 1997.

Charlesworth, James H. *The Discovery of a Dead Sea Scroll (4Q Therapeia): Its Importance in the History of Medicine and Jesus Research*. ICASALS Publication 85–1. Lubbock, TX: Texas Tech University, 1985.

Charlesworth, James H. "A Misunderstood Recently Published Dead Sea Scroll." *Explorations* 1.2 (1987): 2.

Charlesworth, James H., and Loren T. Stuckenbruck. "Rule of the Congregation (1QSa)." Pages 108–18 in *The Dead Sea Scrolls: Hebrew, Aramaic, and Greek Texts with English Translations*, vol. 1: *Rule of the Community and Related Documents*. Edited by James H. Charlesworth. PTSDSSP. Tübingen: Mohr Siebeck; Louisville, KY: Westminster John Knox Press, 1994.

Chartier, Roger. *Forms and Meanings: Texts, Performances and Audiences from Codex to Computer*. Philadelphia, PA: University of Pennsylvania Press, 1995.

Chartier, Roger. "Languages, Books, and Reading from the Printed Word to the Digital Text." *Critical Inquiry* 31 (2004): 133–51.

Chazon, Esther G. "Is *Divrei ha-me'orot* a Sectarian Prayer?" Pages 3–17 in *The Dead Sea Scrolls: Forty Years of Research*. Edited by Devorah Dimant and Uriel Rappaport. STDJ 10. Leiden: Brill, 1992.

Clivaz, Claire. "Digitization and Manuscripts as Visual Objects: Reflections from a Media Studies Perspective." Pages 15–29 in *Ancient Manuscripts in Digital Culture: Visualisation, Data Mining, Communication*. Edited by David Hamidović, Claire Clivaz, and Sarah Bowen Savant. Digital Biblical Studies 3. Leiden: Brill, 2019.

Collins, John J. "Qumran, Apocalypticism and the New Testament." Pages 133–38 in *The Dead Sea Scrolls Fifty Years after Their Discovery 1947–1997: Proceedings of the Jerusalem Congress, July 20–25, 1997*. Edited by Lawrence H. Schiffman, Emanuel Tov, James C. VanderKam, and Galen Marquis. Jerusalem: Israel Exploration Society & The Shrine of the Book, 2000.

Collins, John J. "The *Yaḥad* and 'The Qumran Community'." Pages 81–96 in *Biblical Traditions in Transmission: Essays in Honour of Michael A. Knibb*. Edited by Charlotte Hempel and Judith M. Lieu. JSJSup 111. Leiden: Brill, 2006.

Collins, John J. *Beyond the Qumran Community: The Sectarian Movement of the Dead Sea Scrolls*. Grand Rapids, MI: Eerdmans, 2010.

Coogan, Michael D. "Alphabets and Elements." *BASOR* 216 (1974): 61–63.

Cook, Johann. "Orthographical Peculiarities in the Dead Sea Scrolls Biblical Scrolls." *RevQ* 14 (1989): 293–305.

Cross, Frank Moore. "Introduction." Pages 1–5 in *Scrolls from Qumrân Cave 1: The Great Isaiah Scroll, the Order of the Community, the Pesher to Habakkuk*. Edited by Frank Moore Cross, David Noel Freedman, and James A. Sanders. Jerusalem: Albright Institute of Archaeological Research, 1972.

Daunton-Fear, Andrew. *Healing in the Early Church: The Church's Ministry of Healing and Exorcism from the First to the Fifth Century*. Studies in Christian History and Thought. Eugene, OR: Wipf & Stock, 2009.

Davies, Philip R. "Was There Really a Qumran Community?" *CurBS* 3 (1995): 9–35.

Davies, Philip R. "Reflections on DJD XVIII." Pages 151–65 in *The Dead Sea Scrolls at Fifty: Proceedings of the 1997 Society of Biblical Literature Qumran Section Meetings*. Edited by Robert A. Kugler and Eileen M. Schuller. EJL 15. Atlanta, GA: Scholars, 1999.

Davila, James R. "Enochians, Essenes, and Qumran Essenes." Pages 356–59 in *Enoch and Qumran Origins: New Light on a Forgotten Connection*. Edited by Gabriele Boccaccini. Grand Rapids, MI: Eerdmans, 2005.

Davis, Kipp. "'There and Back Again': Reconstruction and Reconciliation of the War Text 4QMilḥama^a (4Q491^{a-c})." Pages 125–46 in *The War Scroll, Violence, War and Peace in the Dead Sea Scrolls and Related Literature: Essays in Honour of Martin G. Abegg on the Occasion of His 65th Birthday*. Edited by Kipp Davis, Kyung S. Baek, Peter W. Flint, and Dorothy Peters. STDJ 115. Leiden: Brill, 2015.

Davis, Kipp. "Paleographical and Physical Features of the Dead Sea Scrolls in the Museum of the Bible Collection: A Synopsis." Pages 19–35 in *Dead Sea Scrolls Fragments in the Museum Collection*. Edited by Emanuel Tov, Kipp Davis, and Robert Duke. Publications of Museum of the Bible 1. Leiden: Brill, 2016.

Davis, Kipp. "The Social Milieu of 4QJer^a (4Q70) in a Second Temple Jewish Manuscript Culture: Fragments, Manuscripts, Variance, and Meaning." Pages 53–76 in *The Dead Sea Scrolls and the Study of the Humanities: Method, Theory, Meaning: Proceedings of the Eighth Meeting of the International Organization for Qumran Studies (Munich, 4–7 August, 2013)*. Edited by Pieter B. Hartog, Alison Schofield, and Samuel I. Thomas. STDJ 125. Leiden: Brill, 2018.

Delamarter, Steve. "Sociological Models for Understanding the Scribal Practices in the Biblical Dead Sea Scrolls." Pages 182–97 in *Rediscovering the Dead Sea Scrolls: An Assessment of Old and New Approaches and Methods*. Edited by Maxine L. Grossman. Grand Rapids, MI: Eerdmans, 2010.

Dhali, Maruf A., Sheng He, Mladen Popović, Eibert J. C. Tigchelaar, and Lambert Schomaker. "A Digital Palaeographic Approach towards Writer Identification in the Dead Sea Scrolls." Pages 693–702 in *Proceedings of the 6th International Conference on Pattern Recognition Applications and Methods, ICPRAM 2017, Porto, Portugal, February 24–26, 2017*. Edited by Maria De Marsico et al. Setúbal: SciTePress, 2017.

Dimant, Devorah. "The Composite Character of the Qumran Sectarian Literature as an Indication of Its Date and Provenance." *RevQ* 22 (2006): 615–30.

Diringer, David. *The Book before Printing: Ancient, Medieval, and Oriental*. New York, NY: Dover Publications, 1982.

Driscoll, Matthew James. "The Words on a Page: Thoughts on Philology Old and New." Pages 85–102 in *Creating the Medieval Saga: Versions, Variability, and Editorial Interpretations of Old Norse Saga Literature*. Edited by Judy Quinn and Emily Lethbridge. Odense: Syddansk Universitetsforlag, 2010.

Elgvin, Torleif. "The *Yaḥad* is More than Qumran." Pages 273–79 in *Enoch and Qumran Origins: New Light on a Forgotten Connection*. Edited by Gabriele Boccaccini. Grand Rapids, MI: Eerdmans, 2005.

Elgvin, Torleif. "How to Reconstruct a Fragmented Scroll: The Puzzle of 4Q422." Pages 223–36 in *Northern Lights on the Dead Sea Scrolls: Proceedings of the Nordic Qumran Network 2003–2006*. Edited by Anders Klostergaard Peterson, Torleif Elgvin, Cecilia Wassén, Hanne von Weissenberg, and Mikael Winninge. STDJ 80. Leiden: Brill, 2009.

Elgvin, Torleif. "MS5441. 4Q(?)Ruth (Ruth 2.1–2)." Pages 243–46 in *Gleanings from the Caves: Dead Sea Scrolls and Artefacts from The Schøyen Collection*. Edited by Torleif Elgvin, Michael Langlois, and Kipp Davis. LSTS 71. London: Bloomsbury, 2016.

Elgvin, Torleif. *The Literary Growth of the Song of Songs during the Hasmonean and Early-Herodian Periods*. CBET 89. Leuven: Peeters, 2018.

Elgvin, Torleif, and Michael Langlois. "Looking Back: (More) Dead Sea Scrolls Forgeries in The Schøyen Collection." *RevQ* 113 (2019): 111–13.

Eshel, Esther. "Khirbet Qumran Ostracon." Pages 509–512 in *Qumran Cave 4.XXVI: Cryptic Texts and Miscellanea, Part 1*. Edited by Stephen J. Pfann and Philip S. Alexander. DJD 36. Oxford: Clarendon, 2000.

Falk, Daniel K. "Material Aspects of Prayer Manuscripts at Qumran." Pages 33–88 in *Literature or Liturgy? Early Christian Hymns and Prayers in their Literary and Liturgical Context in Antiquity*. Edited by Clemens Leonhard and Hermut Löhr. WUNT 2/363. Tübingen: Mohr Siebeck, 2014.

Falk, Daniel K. "Liturgical Texts." Pages 423–34 in *T&T Clark Companion to the Dead Sea Scrolls*. Edited by George J. Brooke and Charlotte Hempel, with the assistance of Michael DeVries and Drew Longacre. London: T&T Clark, 2019.

Fewster, Gregory P. "Manuscript, Voice, and the Construction of Pseudepigraphal Identities: Composing a Mutable David in Some Qumran Psalms Scrolls." *JBL* 137 (2018): 893–914.

Fraade, Steven D. "Interpretive Authority in the Studying Community at Qumran." *JJS* 44 (1993): 46–69.

Freedman, David Noel. "The Evolution of Hebrew Orthography." Pages 3–15 in *Studies in Hebrew and Aramaic Orthography*. David Noel Freedman, A. Dean Forbes, and Francis I. Anderson. BJSUCSD 2. Winona Lake, IN: Eisenbrauns, 1992.

Freyne, Sean. "Could Jesus Really Read? Literacy in Roman Galilee." Page 43–62 in *Jewish Education from Antiquity to the Middle Ages: Studies in Honour of Philip S. Alexander*. Edited by George J. Brooke and Renate Smithuis. AJEC 100. Leiden: Brill, 2017.

García Martínez, Florentino. "Cave 11 in Context." Pages 199–209 in *The Dead Sea Scrolls: Texts and Contexts*. Edited by Charlotte Hempel. STDJ 90. Leiden: Brill, 2010.

García Martínez, Florentino. "Reconsidering the Cave 1 Texts Sixty Years After Their Discovery: An Overview." Pages 1–13 in *Qumran Cave 1 Revisited: Texts from Cave 1 Sixty Years after Their Discovery. Proceedings of the Sixth Meeting of the IOQS in Ljubljana*. Daniel K. Falk, Sarianna Metso, Donald W. Parry, and Eibert J. C. Tigchelaar. STDJ 91. Leiden: Brill, 2010.

Gault, Brian P. "The Fragments of 'Canticles' from Qumran: Implications and Limitations for Interpretation." *RevQ* 24 (2010): 351–71.

Goff, Matthew J. "Students of God in the House of Torah: Education in the Dead Sea Scrolls." Pages 71–89 in *Second Temple Jewish 'Paideia' in Context*. Edited by Jason M. Zurawski and Gabriele Boccaccini. BZNW 228. Berlin: De Gruyter, 2017.

Golb, Norman. "Khirbet Qumran and the Manuscripts of the Judaean Wilderness: Observations on the Logic of Their Investigation." *JNES* 49 (1990): 103–14.

Golb, Norman. "Khirbet Qumran and the Manuscript Finds of the Judaean Wilderness." Pages 51–72 in *Methods of Investigation of the Dead Sea Scrolls and the Khirbet Qumran Site: Present Realities and Future Prospects*. Edited by Michael O. Wise, Norman Golb, John J. Collins, and Dennis G. Pardee. Annals of the New York Academy of Sciences 722. New York, NY: New York Academy of Sciences, 1994.

Golb, Norman. *Who Wrote the Dead Sea Scrolls? The Search for the Secret of Qumran*. New York, NY: Scribner, 1995.

Goranson, Stephen. "An Inkwell from Qumran." *Michmanim* 6 (1992): 37–40.

Goranson, Stephen. "Qumran: The Evidence of the Inkwells." *BAR* 19 (1993): 67.

Goranson, Stephen. "Qumran—A Hub of Scribal Activity." *BAR* 20 (1994): 36–39.

Grossman, Maxine L. "Community Rule or Community Rules: Examining a Supplementary Approach in Light of the Sectarian Dead Sea Scrolls." Pages 303–30 in *Empirical Models Challenging Biblical Criticism*. Edited by Raymond F. Person and Robert Rezetko. AIL 25. Atlanta, GA: SBL, 2016.

Gunneweg, Jan. "The Dead Sea, the Nearest Neighbor of Qumran and the Dead Sea Manuscripts: What SEM, XRD and Instrumental Neutron Activation May Show about Dead Sea Mud." Pages 175–82 in *Holistic Qumran: Trans-Disciplinary Research of Qumran and the Dead Sea Scrolls*. Edited by Jan Gunneweg, Annemie Adriaens, and Joris Dik. STDJ 87. Leiden: Brill, 2010.

Hachlili, Rachel. "Did the Use of the Alphabet Already Have a Magical Significance in the First Century C.E.?" *Cathedra* 31 (1984): 27–30 (Hebrew).

Hamidović, David. "Dead Sea Scrolls inside Digital Humanities. A Sample." Pages 21–30 in *Digital Humanities in Biblical, Early Jewish and Early Christian Studies*. Edited by Claire Clivaz, Andrew Gregory, and David Hamidović. Scholarly Communication 2. Leiden: Brill, 2013.

Harris, William V. *Ancient Literacy*. Cambridge, MA: Harvard University Press, 1989.

Hartog, Pieter B. *Pesher and Hypomnema: A Comparison of Two Commentary Collections from the Hellenistic-Roman Period*. STDJ 121. Leiden: Brill, 2017.

Hempel, Charlotte. "The Literary Development of the S Tradition—A New Paradigm." *RevQ* 22 (2006): 389–401.

Hempel, Charlotte. "Reflections on Literacy, Textuality, and Community in the Qumran Dead Sea Scrolls." Pages 69–82 in *Is There a Text in this Cave? Studies in the Textuality of the Dead Sea Scrolls in Honour of George J. Brooke*. Edited by Ariel Feldman, Maria Cioată, and Charlotte Hempel. STDJ 119. Leiden: Brill, 2017.

Henrich, A., and L. Koenen. "Ein griechischer Mani-Codex (P. Colon. inv. nr. 4780)." *ZPE* 5 (1970): 97–216.

Hezser, Catherine. *Jewish Literacy in Roman Palestine*. TSAJ 81. Tübingen: Mohr Siebeck, 2001.

Hirschfeld, Yizhar. *Qumran in Context: Reassessing the Archaeological Evidence*. Peabody, MA: Hendrickson, 2004.

Jacobus, Helen R. "Calendars in the Qumran Collection." Pages 215–43 in *The Dead Sea Scrolls at Qumran and the Concept of a Library*. Edited by Sidnie White Crawford and Cecilia Wassén. STDJ 116. Leiden: Brill, 2016.

Jain, Eva. *Psalmen oder Psalter? Materielle Rekonstruktion und inhaltliche Untersuchung der Psalmenhandschriften aus der Wüste Juda*. STDJ 109. Leiden: Brill, 2014.

Jassen, Alex P. "The Dead Sea Scrolls and Violence: Sectarian Formation and Eschatological Imagination." *BibInt* 17 (2009): 12–44.

Johnson, Luke Timothy. *Among the Gentiles: Greco-Roman Religion and Christianity*. ABRL. New Haven, CT: Yale University Press, 2010.

Johnson, William A. *Bookrolls and Scribes in Oxyrhynchus*. Studies in Book and Print Culture. Toronto: University of Toronto Press, 2004.

Johnson, William A. *Readers and Reading Culture in the High Roman Empire: A Study of Elite Communities*. Classical Culture and Society. Oxford: Oxford University Press, 2010.

Jokiranta, Jutta. "What is '*Serekh ha-Yahad* (S)'? Thinking About Ancient Manuscripts as Information Processing." Pages 611–35 in *Sibyls, Scriptures, and Scrolls: John Collins at Seventy*. Joel S. Baden, Hindy Najman, and Eibert J. C. Tigchelaar. JSJSup 175. Leiden: Brill, 2016.

Jokiranta, Jutta, and Hanna Vanonen. "Multiple Copies of Rule Texts or Multiple Rule Texts? Boundaries of the S and M Documents." Pages 11–60 in *Crossing Imaginary Boundaries: The Dead Sea Scrolls in the Context of Second Temple Judaism*. Edited by Mika S. Pajunen and Hanna Tervanotko. Publications of the Finnish Exegetical Society 108. Helsinki: Finnish Exegetical Society, 2015.

Justnes, Årstein. "The Hand of the Corrector in 1QIsaa XXXIII 7 (Isa 40,7–8). Some Observations." *Sem* 57 (2015): 205–10.

Keith, Chris. *Jesus' Literacy: Scribal Culture and the Teacher from Galilee*. LNTS 413. London: Bloomsbury, 2011.

Kenyon, Frederic G. *Books and Readers in Ancient Greece and Rome*. 2nd ed. Oxford: Clarendon, 1951.

Kim, Dong-Hyuk. "Free Orthography in a Strict Society: Reconsidering Tov's 'Qumran Orthography'." *DSD* 11 (2004): 72–81.

Kottsieper, Ingo. "Physicality of Manuscripts and Material Culture." Pages 167–77 in *T&T Clark Companion to the Dead Sea Scrolls*. Edited by George J. Brooke and Charlotte Hempel, with the assistance of Michael DeVries and Drew Longacre. London: T&T Clark, 2019.

Kugler, Robert A. "Hearing 4Q225: A Case Study in Reconstructing the Religious Imagination of the Qumran Community." *DSD* 10 (2003): 81–103.

Lama, Mariachiara. "Aspetti di tecnica libraria ad Ossirinco: Copie letterarie su rotoli documentari." *Aegyptus* 71 (1991): 55–120.

Lange, Armin. "Kriterien essenischer Texte." Pages 59–69 in *Qumran kontrovers: Beiträge zu den Textfunden vom Toten Meer*. Edited by Jörg Frey and Hartmut Stegemann. Einblicke 6. Paderborn: Bonifatius, 2003.

Lange, Armin. "Sages and Scribes in the Qumran Literature." Pages 271–93 in *Scribes, Sages and Seers: The Sage in the Eastern Mediterranean World*. Edited by Leo G. Perdue. FRLANT 219. Göttingen: Vandenhoeck & Ruprecht, 2008.

Lange, Armin. "The Qumran Library in Context: The Canonical History and Textual Standardization of the Hebrew Bible in Light of the Qumran Library." Pages 259–79 in *The Dead Sea Scrolls at Qumran and the Concept of a Library*. Edited by Sidnie White Crawford and Cecilia Wassén. STDJ 116. Leiden: Brill, 2016.

Lange, Armin, and Ulrike Mittmann-Richert. "Annotated List of the Texts from the Judaean Desert Classified by Content and Genre." Pages 115–64 in *The Texts from the Judaean Desert: Indices and and Introduction to the Discoveries in the Judaean Desert Series*. Edited by Emanuel Tov. DJD 39. Oxford: Clarendon, 2002.

Lemaire, André. "A Schoolboy's Exercise on an Ostracon at Lachish." *TA* 3 (1976): 109–10.

Lemaire, André. "Abécédaires et exercices d'écolier en épigraphie nord-ouest sémitique." *JA* 266 (1978): 221–35.

Lemaire, André. *Les écoles et la formation de la Bible dans l'ancien Israël.* OBO 39. Fribourg: Éditions Universitaires, 1981.

Lemaire, André. "L'enseignement essénien et l'école de Qumrân." Pages 191–203 in *Hellenica et Judaica: Hommage à Valentin Nikiprowetzky.* Edited by André Caquot, Mireille Hadas-Lebel, and Jean Riaud. Leuven: Peeters, 1986.

Lemaire, André. "Qoumrân: sa fonction et ses manuscrits." Pages 117–49 in *Qoumrân et les Manuscrits de la mer Morte. Un cinquantenaire.* Edited by Ernest-Marie Laperrousaz. Paris: Éditions du Cerf, 1997.

Lemaire, André. "Réflexions sur la fonction du site de Qumrân." Pages 37–43 in *Józef Tadeusz Milik et cinquantenaire de la découverte des manuscrits de la mer morte de Qumrân.* Dariusz Długosz and Henryk Ratajczak. Varsovie: PAN, 2000.

Lemaire, André. "Inscriptions du Khirbeh, des grottes et de ʿAïn Feshkha." Pages 341–88 in *Fouilles de Khirbet Qumrân et de Aïn Feshkha.* II, *Études d'anthropologie, de physique et de chimie.* Edited by Jean-Baptiste Humbert and Jan Gunneweg. NTOA.SA 3. Göttingen: Vandenhoeck & Ruprecht, 2003.

Lemaire, André. "Lire, écrire, étudier à Qoumrân et ailleurs." Pages 63–79 in *Qoumrân et la judaïsme du tournant de notre ère: Actes de la Table Ronde, Collège de France, 16 novembre 2004.* Edited by André Lemaire and Simon C. Mimouni. Collection de la Revue des études juives 40. Leuven: Peeters, 2006.

Lübee, J. C. "Certain Implications of the Scribal Process of 4QSamᶜ." *RevQ* 14 (1989): 255–65.

Magen, Yitzhak, and Yuval Peleg. *The Qumran Excavations 1993–2004: Preliminary Report.* Jerusalem: Judea & Samaria Publications, 2007.

Magness, Jodi. *The Archaeology of Qumran and the Dead Sea Scrolls.* Studies in the Dead Sea Scrolls and Related Literature. Grand Rapids, MI: Eerdmans, 2002.

Manfredi, Manfredo. "Opistografo." *La parola del passato* 38 (1983): 44–54.

Mantouvalou, Ioanna, Timo Wolff, Oliver Hahn, Ira Rabin, Lars Lühl, Marcel Pagels, Wolfgang Malzer, and Birgit Kanngießer. "3D Micro-XRF for Cultural Heritage Objects: New Analysis Strategies for the Investigation of the Dead Sea Scrolls." *Analytical Chemistry* 83 (2011): 6308–15.

Martin, Malachi. *The Scribal Character of the Dead Sea Scrolls.* Bibliothèque du Muséon 44–45. Louvain: Publications universitaires, 1958.

Martone, Corrado. "The Qumran 'Library' and Other Ancient Libraries: Elements for a Comparison." Pages 55–77 in *The Dead Sea Scrolls at Qumran and the Concept of a Library.* Edited by Sidnie White Crawford and Cecilia Wassén. STDJ 116. Leiden: Brill, 2016.

McGann, Jerome J. *Radiant Textuality: Literature After the World Wide Web.* New York, NY: Palgrave, 2001.

Metso, Sarianna. *The Textual Development of the Qumran Community Rule.* STDJ 21. Leiden: Brill, 1997.

Metso, Sarianna. *The Serekh Texts*. LSTS 62. London: T&T Clark, 2007.

Metso, Sarianna, and James M. Tucker. "The Changing Landscape of Editing Ancient Jewish Texts." Pages 269–87 in *Reading the Bible in Ancient Traditions and Modern Editions: Studies in Memory of Peter W. Flint*. Edited by Andrew B. Perrin, Kyung S. Baek, and Daniel K. Falk. EJL 47. Atlanta, GA: SBL, 2017.

Meyers, Eric M., and Mark A. Chancey. *Archaeology of the Land of the Bible*, vol. 3: *Alexander to Constantine*. ABRL. New Haven, CT: Yale University Press, 2012.

Milik, Józef T. *The Books of Enoch: Aramaic fragments of Qumrân Cave 4*. Oxford: Clarendon, 1976.

Milik, Józef T. "Daniel et Susanne à Qumrân?" Pages 337–59 in *De la Tôrah au Messie: Études d'exégèse et d'herméneutique bibliques offertes à Henri Cazelles pour ses 25 années d'enseignement a l'Institut catholique de Paris, octobre 1979*. Edited by Maurice Carrez, Joseph Doré, and Pierre Grelot. Paris: Desclée, 1981.

Milik, Józef T. "Les modèles araméens du livre d'Esther dans la grotte 4 de Qumrân." *RevQ* 15 (1992): 321–406.

Misgav, Haggai. "The Ostraca." Pages 431–41 in *Back to Qumran: Final Report (1993–2004)*. Edited by Yitzhak Magen and Yuval Peleg. Judea and Samaria Publications 18. Jerusalem: Israel Antiquities Authority, 2018.

Mitchell, Charles A., and Thomas C. Hepworth. *Inks: Their Composition and Manufacture*. 3rd ed. London: C. Griffin & Co., 1924.

Mroczek, Eva. "Thinking Digitally about the Dead Sea Scrolls: Book History Before and Beyond the Book." *Book History* 14 (2011): 241–69.

Mroczek, Eva. *The Literary Imagination in Jewish Antiquity*. Oxford: Oxford University Press, 2016.

Mroczek, Eva. "The End of the Psalms in the Dead Sea Scrolls, Greek Codices, and Syriac Manuscripts." Pages 297–322 in *Snapshots of Evolving Traditions: Jewish and Christian Manuscript Culture, Textual Fluidity, and New Philology*. Edited by Hugo Lundhaug and Liv Ingeborg Lied. TUGAL 175. Berlin: De Gruyter, 2017.

Murphy, Bridget, Marine Cotte, Martin Mueller, Marta Balla, and Jan Gunnneweg. "Degradation of Parchment and Ink of the Dead Sea Scrolls Investigated Using Synchrotron-Based X-Ray and Infrared Microscopy." Pages 77–98 in *Holistic Qumran: Trans-Disciplinary Research of Qumran and the Dead Sea Scrolls*. Edited by Jan Gunneweg, Annemie Adriaens, and Joris Dik. STDJ 87. Leiden: Brill, 2010.

Naveh, Joseph. "A Medical Document or a Writing Exercise? The So-Called 4QTherapeia." *IEJ* 36 (1986): 53.

Naveh, Joseph. "Exercitium Calami C." Pages 291–94 in *Qumran Cave 4.XXVI: Cryptic Texts and Miscellanea, Part 1*. Edited by Stephen J. Pfann and Philip S. Alexander. DJD 36. Oxford: Clarendon, 2000.

Nebe, G. Wilhelm. "Alphabets." Pages 1:18–20 in *Encyclopedia of the Dead Sea Scrolls*. Edited by Lawrence H. Schiffman and James C. VanderKam. 2 vols. Oxford: Oxford University Press, 2000.

Nir-El, Yoram, and Magen Broshi. "The Black Ink of the Qumran Scrolls." *DSD* 3 (1996): 157–67.

Nitzan, Bilhah. "Education and Wisdom in the Dead Sea Scrolls in Light of their Background in Antiquity." Pages 95–116 in *New Perspectives on Old Texts: Proceedings of the Tenth International Symposium of the Orion Center for the Study of the Dead Sea Scrolls and Associated Literature, 9–11 January, 2005*. Edited by Esther G. Chazon, Betsy Halpern-Amaru, and Ruth Clements. STDJ 88. Leiden: Brill, 2010.

Noegel, Scott B. "Text, Script, and Media: New Observations on Scribal Activity in the Ancient Near East." Pages 133–43 in *Voice, Text, Hypertext: Emerging Practices in Textual Studies*. Edited by Raimonda Modiano, Leroy F. Searle, and Peter L. Shillingsburg. Seattle: University of Washington Press, 2004.

Norton, Jonathan D. H. "The Qumran Library and the Shadow it Casts on the Wall of the Cave." Pages 40–74 in *Ancient Readers and Their Scriptures: Engaging the Hebrew Bible in Early Judaism and Christianity*. Edited by Garrick V. Allen and John Anthony Dunne. AJEC 107. Leiden: Brill, 2018.

Pajunen, Mika S. "Perspectives on the Existence of a Particular Authoritative Book of Psalms in the Late Second Temple Period." *JSOT* 39 (2014): 139–63.

Perrot, Antony. "Reading an Opisthograph at Qumran." Pages 101–14 in *Material Aspects of Reading in Ancient and Medieval Cultures: Materiality, Presence and Performance*. Edited by Anna Krauß, Jonas Leipziger, and Friederike Schücking-Jungblut. Materiale Textkulturen 26. Berlin: De Gruyter, 2020.

Pfann, Stephen J. "4Q298: The Maskîl's Address to All Sons of Dawn." *JQR* 85 (1994): 203–35.

Pfann, Stephen J. "The Writings in Esoteric Script from Qumran." Pages 177–90 in *The Dead Sea Scrolls Fifty Years after Their Discovery 1947–1997: Proceedings of the Jerusalem Congress, July 20–25, 1997*. Edited by Lawrence H. Schiffman, Emanuel Tov, James C. Vanderkam. Jerusalem: Israel Exploration Society & The Shrine of the Book, 2000.

Pfann, Stephen J. "Reassessing the Judean Desert Caves: Libraries, Archives, Genizas and Hiding Places." *Bulletin of the Anglo-Israel Archaeological Society* 25 (2007): 147–70.

Pfann, Stephen J. "The Use of Cryptographic and Esoteric Scripts in Second Temple Judaism and the Surrounding Cultures." Pages 173–96 in *Interpreting 4 Ezra and 2 Baruch: International Studies*. Edited by Gabriele Boccaccini and Jason M. Zurawski. LSTS 87. London: Bloomsbury, 2014.

Pfann, Stephen J. "The Ancient 'Library' or 'Libraries' of Qumran: The Specter of Cave 1Q." Pages 168–213 in *The Dead Sea Scrolls at Qumran and the Concept of a Library*. Edited by Sidnie White Crawford and Cecilia Wassén. STDJ 116. Leiden: Brill, 2016.

Plenderleith, Harold J. "Technical Note on Unwrapping of Dead Sea Scrolls Fragments." Pages 39–40 in *Qumran Cave 1*. Edited by Dominique Barthélemy and Józef T. Milik. DJD 1. Oxford: Clarendon Press, 1955.

Poirier, John C. "Education/Literacy in Jewish Galilee: Was There Any and at What Level?" Pages 253–60 in *Galilee in the Late Second Temple and Mishnaic Periods*, vol. 1: *Life, Culture, and Society*. Edited by David A. Fiensy and James R. Strange. Minneapolis, MN: Augsburg Fortress, 2014.

Popović, Mladen. "Roman Book Destruction in Qumran Cave 4 and the Roman Destruction of Khirbet Qumran Revisited." Pages 239–91 in *Qumran und die Archäologie: Texte und Contexte*. Edited by Jörg Frey, Carsten Claußen, and Nadine Kessler. WUNT 278. Tübingen: Mohr Siebeck, 2011.

Popović, Mladen. "Qumran as Scroll Storehouse in Times of Crisis? A Comparative Perspective on Judaean Desert Manuscript Collections." *JSJ* 43 (2012): 551–94.

Popović, Mladen. "The Ancient 'Library' of Qumran between Urban and Rural Culture." Pages 155–67 in *The Dead Sea Scrolls at Qumran and the Concept of a Library*. Edited by Sidnie White Crawford and Cecilia Wassén. STDJ 116. Leiden: Brill, 2016.

Popović, Mladen. "Reading, Writing, and Memorizing Together: Reading Culture in Ancient Judaism and the Dead Sea Scrolls in a Mediterranean Context." *DSD* 24 (2017): 447–70.

Pouchelle, Patrick. "Discipline, Transmission, and Writing: Notes on Education in the Testament of the Twelve Patriarchs." Pages 131–40 in *Second Temple Jewish 'Paideia' in Context*. Edited by Jason M. Zurawski and Gabriele Boccaccini. BZNW 228. Berlin: De Gruyter, 2017.

Price, Jonathan J., and Shlomo Naeh. "On the Margins of Culture: The Practice of Transcription in the Ancient World." Pages 257–88 in *From Hellenism to Islam: Cultural and Linguistic Change in the Roman Near East*. Edited by Hannah M. Cotton, Robert G. Hoyland, Jonathan J. Price, and David J. Wasserstein. Cambridge: Cambridge University Press, 2009.

Puech, Émile. "Abécédaire et liste alphabétique de noms hébreux du début du IIe s. A.D." *RB* 87 (1980): 118–26.

Puech, Émile. "L'épigraphie de Qumrân: Son apport à l'identification du site." *RevQ* 24 (2010): 433–40.

Quick, Laura. "Scribal Habits and Scholarly Texts: Codicology at Oxyrhynchus and Qumran." Pages 37–54 in *Material Aspects of Reading in Ancient and Medieval Cultures: Materiality, Presence and Performance*. Edited by Anna Krauß, Jonas Leipziger, Friederike Schücking-Jungblut. Materiale Textkulturen 26. Berlin: De Gruyter, 2020.

Rabin, Chaim. "Hebrew and Aramaic in the First Century." Pages 1007–39 in *The Jewish People in the First Century*. Edited by Shmuel Safrai and Menahem Stern. Philadelphia: Fortress, 1976.

Rabin, Ira. "Archaeometry of the Dead Sea Scrolls." *DSD* 20 (2013): 124–42.

Rabin, Ira, and Oliver Hahn. "Characterization of the Dead Sea Scrolls by Advanced Analytical Techniques." *Analytical Methods* 5 (2013): 4648–54.

Rabin, Ira, Oliver Hahn, Timo Wolff, Emanuel Kindzorra, Admir Masic, Ulrich Schade, and Gisela Weinberg. "Characterization of the Writing Media of the Dead Sea Scrolls." Pages 123–34 in *Holistic Qumran: Trans-Disciplinary Research of Qumran and the Dead Sea Scrolls*. Edited by Jan Gunneweg, Annemie Adriaens, and Joris Dik. STDJ 87. Leiden: Brill, 2010.

Rabin, Ira, Oliver Hahn, Timo Wolff, Admir Masic, and Gisela Weinberg. "On the Origin of the Ink of the Thanksgiving Scroll (1QHodayot^a)." *DSD* 16 (2009): 97–106.

Rasmussen, Kaare Lund, Anna Lluveras Tenorio, Ilaria Bonaduce, Maria Perla Colombini, Leila Birolo, Eugenio Galano, Angela Amoresano, Greg Doudna, Andrew D. Bond, Vincenzo Palleschi, Giulia Lorenzetti, Stefano Legnaioli, Johannes van der Plicht, and Jan Gunneweg. "The Constituents of the Ink from a Qumran Inkwell: New Prospects for Provenancing the Ink on the Dead Sea Scrolls." *Journal of Archaeological Science* 39 (2012): 2956–68.

Reed, Ronald. *The Nature and Making of Parchment*. Leeds: Elmete, 1975.

Reed, Stephen. "The Linguistic Diversity of the Texts Found at Qumran." Pages 132–54 in *The Dead Sea Scrolls at Qumran and the Concept of a Library*. Edited by Sidnie White Crawford and Cecilia Wassén. STDJ 116. Leiden: Brill, 2016.

Rengstorf, Karl H. *Ḥirbet Qumrân und die Bibliothek vom Toten Meer*. Abhandlungen und Texte aus dem Institutum Judaicum Delitzschianum 5. Stuttgart: Kohlhammer, 1960.

Rohrhirsch, Ferdinand. *Wissenschaftstheorie und Qumran: Die Geltungsbegrüdungen von Aussagen in der biblischen Archäologie am Beispiel von Chirbet Qumran und En Feschcha*. NTOA 32. Göttingen: Vandenhoeck & Ruprecht, 1996.

Rohrhirsch, Ferdinand. "Die Geltungsbegründungen der Industrie-Rollen-Theorie zu Chirbet Qumran und En Feschcha auf dem methodologischen Prüfstand: Relativierung und Widerlegung." *DSD* 6 (1999): 267–81.

Rubin, Rechav, and Joseph Patrich. "Wadi Suweinit." *Excavations and Surveys in Israel* 2 (1983): 107–109.

Ryder, Michael L. "The Biology and History of Parchment." Pages 25–33 in *Pergament: Geschichte, Struktur, Restaurierung, Herstellung*. Edited by Peter Rück. Historische Hilfsweissenschaften 2. Simarigen: Thorbecke, 1991.

Sarri, Antonia. *Material Aspects of Letter Writing in the Graeco-Roman World: 500 BC–AD 300*. Materiale Textkulturen 12. Berlin: De Gruyter, 2018.

Saukkonen, Juhana M. "A Few Inkwells, Many Hands: Were There Scribes at Qumran?" Pages 538–53 in *Houses Full of All Good Things: Essays in Memory of Timo Veijola*. Edited by Juha Pakkala and Martti Nissinen. Helsinki: Finnish Exegetical Society, 2008.

Saukkonen, Juhana M. "Dwellers at Qumran: Reflections on Their Literacy, Social Status, and Identity." Pages 621–34 in *Scripture in Transition: Essays on Septuagint,*

Hebrew Bible, and Dead Sea Scrolls in Honour of Raija Sollamo. Edited by Anssi Voitila and Jutta Jokiranta. JSJSup 126. Leiden: Brill, 2008.

Schiffman, Lawrence H. *The Eschatological Community of the Dead Sea Scrolls: A Study of the Rule of the Congregation*. SBLMS 38. Atlanta, GA: Scholars, 1989.

Schofield, Alison. "Rereading S: A New Model of Textual Development in Light of the Cave 4 *Serekh* Copies." *DSD* 15 (2008): 96–120.

Schofield, Alison. *From Qumran to the* Yaḥad*: A New Paradigm of Textual Development for The Community Rule*. STDJ 77. Leiden: Brill, 2009.

Segal, Michael. "Qumran Research in Israel: Rewritten Bible and Biblical Interpretation." Pages 315–33 in *The Dead Sea Scrolls in Scholarly Perspective: A History of Research*. Edited by Devorah Dimant. STDJ 99. Leiden: Brill, 2012.

Segal, Michael. "Methodological Considerations in the Preparation of an Edition of the Hebrew Bible." Pages 34–55 in *The Text of the Hebrew Bible and Its Editions: Studies in Celebration of the Fifth Centennial of the Complutensian Polygot*. Edited by Andrés Piquer Otero and Pablo Torijano Morales. Supplements to the Textual History of the Bible 1. Leiden: Brill, 2017.

Shavit, Yaacov. "The 'Qumran Library' in the Light of the Attitude towards Books and Libraries in the Second Temple Period." Pages 299–315 in *Methods of Investigation of the Dead Sea Scrolls and the Khirbet Qumran Site: Present Realities and Future Prospects*. Edited by Michael O. Wise, Norman Golb, John J. Collins, and Dennis G. Pardee. Annals of the New York Academy of Sciences 722. New York, NY: New York Academy of Sciences, 1994.

Shor, Pnina. "The Leon Levy Dead Sea Scrolls Digital Library: The Digitization Project of the Dead Sea Scrolls." Pages 11–20 in *Digital Humanities in Biblical, Early Jewish and Early Christian Studies*. Edited by Claire Clivaz, Andrew Gregory, and David Hamidović. Scholarly Communication 2. Leiden: Brill, 2013.

Siegel, Jonathan P. "The Scribes of Qumran: Studies in the Early History of Jewish Scribal Customs, with Special Reference to the Qumran Biblical Scrolls and to the Tannaitic Traditions of *Massekheth Soferim*." Ph.D. dissertation, Brandies University, 1972.

Siker, Jeffrey S. *Liquid Scripture: The Bible in a Digital World*. Minneapolis, MN: Fortress, 2017.

Skeat, T. C. "Was Papyrus Regarded as 'Cheap' or 'Expensive' in the Ancient World?" *Aegyptus* 75 (1995): 75–93.

Skehan, Patrick W. "Gleanings from Psalm Texts from Qumran." Pages 439–45 in *Mélanges bibliques et orientaux en l'honneur de M. Henri Cazelles*. Edited by André Caquot and Mathias Delcor. AOAT 212. Neukirchen/Vluyn: Neukirchener Verlag, 1981.

Skehan, Patrick W., Eugene Ulrich, and Judith E. Sanderson. "4QpaleoGenesis-Exodus[l]." Pages 17–50 in *Qumran Cave 4.IV: Palaeo-Hebrew and Greek Biblical Manuscripts*. Edited by Patrick W. Skehan, Eugene Ulrich, and Judith E. Sanderson. DJD 9. Oxford: Clarendon Press, 1992.

Snyder, H. Gregory. *Teachers and Texts in the Ancient World: Philosophers, Jews, and Christians*. Religion in the First Christian Centuries. London: Routledge, 2000.

Spolsky, Bernard. "Triglossia and Literacy in Jewish Palestine of the First Century." *IJSL* 42 (1983): 95–109.

Stacey, David. "Seasonal Industries at Qumran." *Bulletin of the Anglo-Israel Archaeological Society* 26 (2008): 7–29.

Stacey, David, and Gregory L. Doudna. *Qumran Revisited: A Reassessment of the Archaeology of the Site and Its Texts*. BARIS 2520. Oxford: Archaeopress, 2013.

Starr, Raymond J. "Ancient Bookrolls in Modern Classrooms." *New England Classical Journal* 45 (2018): 39–43.

Steckoll, Solomon H. "Investigations of the Inks used in Writing the Dead Sea Scrolls." *Nature* 220 (1968): 91–92.

Stegemann, Hartmut. *The Library of Qumran: On the Essenes, Qumran, John the Baptist, and Jesus*. Grand Rapids, MI: Eerdmans, 1998.

Stökl Ben Ezra, Daniel. "Old Caves and Young Caves: A Statistical Reevaluation of a Qumran Consensus." *DSD* 14 (2007): 313–33.

Stökl Ben Ezra, Daniel. "Further Reflections On Caves 1 And 11: A Response To Florentino García Martínez." Pages 211–23 in *The Dead Sea Scrolls: Texts and Contexts*. Edited by Charlotte Hempel. STDJ 90. Leiden: Brill, 2010.

Stökl Ben Ezra, Daniel. "Wie viele Bibliotheken gab es in Qumran?" Pages 327–46 in *Qumran und die Archäologie: Texte und Contexte*. Edited by Jörg Frey, Carsten Claußen, and Nadine Kessler. WUNT 278. Tübingen: Mohr Siebeck, 2011.

Stökl Ben Ezra, Daniel. "Bücherlesen im Jachad Qumrans Himmlische Bücher zwischen Katechese, kollektivem Studium und esoterischer Geheimschrift." Pages 75–95 in *Metatexte: Erzählungen von schrifttragenden Artefakten in der alttestamentlichen und mittelalterlichen Literatur*. Edited by Friedrich-Emanuel Focken and Michael R. Ott. Materiale Textkulturen 15. Berlin: De Gruyter, 2016.

Stökl Ben Ezra, Daniel. *Qumran: Die Texte vom Toten Meer und das antike Judentum*. Jüdische Studien 3. Tübingen: Mohr Siebeck, 2016.

Strawn, Brent A. "Excerpted Manuscripts at Qumran: Their Significance for the Textual History of the Hebrew Bible and the Socio-Religious History of the Qumran Community and Its Literature." Pages 107–67 in *The Bible and the Dead Sea Scrolls*, vol. 2: *The Dead Sea Scrolls and the Qumran Community*. Edited by James H. Charlesworth. Waco, TX: Baylor University Press, 2006.

Sukenik, Eleazar L. *The Dead Sea Scrolls of the Hebrew University*. Jerusalem: Magnes, 1955.

Sutherland, Kathryn, ed. *Electronic Text: Investigations in Method and Theory*. Oxford: Oxford University Press, 1997.

Taylor, Joan E. "Buried Manuscripts and Empty Tombs: The Qumran Genizah Theory Revisited." Pages 269–315 in *'Go Out and Study the Land' (Judges 18:2): Archaeological,*

Historical and Textual Studies in Honor of Hanan Eshel. Edited by Aren M. Maeir, Jodi Magness, and Lawrence Schiffman. JSJSup 148. Leiden: Brill, 2011.

Taylor, Joan E. *The Essenes, the Scrolls, and the Dead Sea.* Oxford: Oxford University Press, 2012.

Taylor, Joan E. "4Q341: A Writing Exercise Remembered." Pages 133–51 in *Is There a Text in this Cave? Studies in the Textuality of the Dead Sea Scrolls in Honour of George J. Brooke.* Edited by Ariel Feldman, Maria Cioată, and Charlotte Hempel. STDJ 119. Leiden: Brill, 2017.

Tigchelaar, Eibert J. C. "In Search of the Scribe of 1QS." Pages 439–52 in *Emanuel: Studies in Hebrew Bible, Septuagint, and Dead Sea Scrolls in Honor of Emanuel Tov.* Edited by Shalom M. Paul, Robert A. Kraft, Lawrence H. Schiffman, and Weston W. Fields. VTSup 94. Leiden: Brill, 2003.

Tigchelaar, Eibert J. C. "Assessing Emanuel Tov's 'Qumran Scribal Practice'." Pages 173–207 in *The Dead Sea Scrolls: Transmission of Traditions and Production of Texts.* Edited by Sarianna Metso, Hindy Najman, and Eileen Schuller. STDJ 92. Leiden: Brill, 2010.

Tigchelaar, Eibert J. C. "The Qumran Jubilees Manuscripts as Evidence for the Literary Growth of the Book." *RevQ* 26 (2014): 579–94.

Tigchelaar, Eibert J. C. "The Material Variance of the Dead Sea Scrolls: On Texts and Artefacts," *HTS Teologiese Studies/Theological Studies* 72 (2016): a3281.

Tigchelaar, Eibert J. C. "The Scribes of the Scrolls." Pages 524–32 in *T&T Clark Companion to the Dead Sea Scrolls.* Edited by George J. Brooke and Charlotte Hempel, with the assistance of Michael DeVries and Drew Longacre. London: T&T Clark, 2019.

Tigchelaar, Eibert J. C. "Seventy Years of Palaeographic Dating of the Dead Sea Scrolls." Pages 258–78 in *Sacred Texts and Disparate Interpretations: Qumran Manuscripts Seventy Years Later: Proceedings of the International Conference Held at the John Paul II Catholic University of Lublin, 24–26 October 2017.* Edited by Henryk Drawnel. STDJ 133. Leiden: Brill, 2020.

Toorn, Karel van der. *Scribal Culture and the Making of the Hebrew Bible.* Cambridge, MA: Harvard University Press, 2009.

Tov, Emanuel. "The Orthography and Language of the Hebrew Scrolls Found at Qumran and the Origin of These Scrolls." *Text* 13 (1986): 31–57.

Tov, Emanuel. "Hebrew Biblical Manuscripts from the Judaean Desert: Their Contribution to Textual Criticism." *JJS* 39 (1988): 10–16.

Tov, Emanuel. "Three Manuscripts (Abbreviated Texts?) of Canticles from Qumran Cave 4." *JJS* 46 (1995): 88–111.

Tov, Emanuel. "Excerpted and Abbreviated Biblical Texts from Qumran." *RevQ* 16 (1995): 581–600.

Tov, Emanuel. "Scribal Markings in the Texts from the Judean Desert." Pages 41–77 in *Current Research and Technological Developments on the Dead Sea Scrolls.* Edited by Donald W. Parry and Stephen D. Ricks. STDJ 20. Leiden: Brill, 1996.

Tov, Emanuel. "Scribal Practices Reflected in the Paleo-Hebrew Texts from the Judean Desert." *Scripta Classica Israelica* 15 (1996): 268–73.

Tov, Emanuel. "The Scribes of the Texts Found in the Judean Desert." Pages 131–52 in *The Quest for Context and Meaning: Studies in Biblical Intertextuality in Honor of James A. Sanders*. Edited by Craig A. Evans and Shemaryahu Talmon. BIS 28. Leiden: Brill, 1997.

Tov, Emanuel. "Scribal Practices Reflected in the Texts from the Judaean Desert." Pages 1:403–29 in *The Dead Sea Scrolls after Fifty Years: A Comprehensive Assessment*. Edited by Peter W. Flint and James C. VanderKam. Leiden: Brill, 1998.

Tov, Emanuel. "The Dimensions of the Qumran Scrolls." *DSD* 5 (1998): 69–91.

Tov, Emanuel. "Correction Procedures in the Texts from the Judean Desert." Pages 232–63 in *The Provo International Conference on the Dead Sea Scrolls: Technological Innovations, New Texts, and Reformulated Issues*. Edited by Donald W. Parry and Eugene C. Ulrich. STDJ 30. Leiden: Brill, 1999.

Tov, Emanuel. "Opisthographs from the Judean Desert." Pages 11–18 in *A Multiform Heritage: Studies on Early Judaism and Christianity in Honor of Robert A. Kraft*. Edited by Benjamin G. Wright. Homage Series 24. Atlanta, GA: Scholars, 1999.

Tov, Emanuel. "Canticles." Pages 195–219 in *Qumran Cave 4.XI: Psalms to Chronicles*. Edited by Eugene Ulrich, Frank Moore Cross, Joseph A. Fitzmyer, Peter W. Flint, Sarianna Metso, Catherine M. Murphy, Curt Niccum, Patrick W. Skehan, Emanuel Tov, and Julio Trebolle Barrera. DJD 16. Oxford: Clarendon Press, 2000.

Tov, Emanuel. "Further Evidence for the Existence of a Qumran Scribal School." Pages 199–216 in *The Dead Sea Scrolls Fifty Years after Their Discovery: Proceedings of the Jerusalem Congress, July 20–25, 1997*. Edited by Lawrence H. Schiffman, Emanuel Tov, and James C. VanderKam. Jerusalem: Israel Exploration Society & The Shrine of the Book, 2000.

Tov, Emanuel. "The Corpus of the Qumran Papyri." Pages 85–103 in *Semitic Papyrology in Context: A Climate of Creativity: Papers from a New York University Conference Marking the Retirement of Baruch A. Levine*. Edited by Lawrence H. Schiffman. CHANE 14. Leiden: Brill, 2003.

Tov, Emanuel. "The Qumran Scribal Practice: The Evidence from Orthography and Morphology." *Studia Orientalia Electronica* 99 (2004): 353–68.

Tov, Emanuel. *Scribal Practices and Approaches Reflected in the Texts Found in the Judean Desert*. STDJ 54. Leiden: Brill, 2004.

Tov, Emanuel. "The Coincidental Textual Nature of the Collections of Ancient Scriptures." Pages 153–69 in *Congress Volume Ljubljana 2007*. Edited by Andre Lemaire. VTSup 133. Leiden: Brill, 2010.

Tov, Emanuel. "Some Reflections on Consistency in the Activity of Scribes and Translators." Pages 325–37 in *Juda und Jerusalem in der Seleukidenzeit: Herrschaft—*

Widerstand—Identität. Edited by Ulrich Dahmen and Johannes Schnocks. BBB 159. Göttingen: Vandenhoeck & Ruprecht, 2010.

Tov, Emanuel. "Israeli Scholarship on the Biblical Texts from the Judean Desert." Pages 297–313 in *The Dead Sea Scrolls in Scholarly Perspective: A History of Research*. Edited by Devorah Dimant. STDJ 99. Leiden: Brill, 2012.

Tov, Emanuel. "Scribal Features of Two Qumran Scrolls." Pages 241–58 in *Hebrew in the Second Temple Period: The Hebrew of the Dead Sea Scrolls and of Other Contemporary Sources*. Edited by Steven E. Fassberg, Moshe Bar-Asher, and Ruth Clements. STDJ 108. Leiden: Brill, 2013.

Tov, Emanuel. "*Scribal Practices and Approaches* Revisited." *HBAI* 3/4 (2014): 363–74.

Trever, John C. "A Paleographic Study of the Jerusalem Scrolls." *BASOR* 113 (1949): 6–23.

Ulrich, Eugene C. "4QSamᶜ: A Fragmentary Manuscript of 2 Samuel 14–15 from the Scribe of the Serek Hay-yaḥad (1QS)." *BASOR* 235 (1979): 1–25.

Ulrich, Eugene C. "Identification of a Scribe Active at Qumran: 1QPsᵇ–4QIsaᶜ–11QM." Pages 201–10 in *Meghillot: Studies in the Dead Sea Scrolls V–VI. A Festschrift for Devorah Dimant*. Edited by Moshe Bar-Asher and Emanuel Tov. Jerusalem: Bialik Institute, 2007. (Hebrew)

Ulrich, Eugene C. "Biblical Scrolls Scholarship in North America." Pages 49–74 in *The Dead Sea Scrolls in Scholarly Perspective: A History of Research*. Edited by Devorah Dimant. STDJ 99. Leiden: Brill, 2012.

Vandendorpe, Christian. *From Papyrus to Hypertext: Toward the Universal Digital Library*. Translated by Phyllis Aronoff and Howard Scott. Urbana: University of Illinois Press, 2009.

VanderKam, James C., and Peter W. Flint. *The Meaning of the Dead Sea Scrolls: Their Significance for Understanding the Bible, Judaism, Jesus, and Christianity*. San Francisco: HarperSanFrancisco, 2002.

Vaux, Roland de. "Fouilles au Khirbet Qumrân: Rapport préliminaire sur la deuxième campagne." *RB* 61 (1954): 206–36.

Vaux, Roland de. *Archaeology and the Dead Sea Scrolls*. London: Oxford University Press, 1973.

Vermès, Géza. "Preliminary Remarks on Unpublished Fragments of the Community Rule from Qumran Cave 4." *JJS* 42 (1991): 250–55.

Viviano, Benedict T. "Study and Education." Pages 2:896–98 in *Encyclopedia of the Dead Sea Scrolls*. Edited by Lawrence H. Schiffman and James C. VanderKam. 2 vols. Oxford: Oxford University Press, 2000.

Wassén, Cecilia. "On the Education of Children in the Dead Sea Scrolls." *Studies in Religion/Sciences Religieuses* 41 (2012): 350–63.

Werrett, Ian. "Is Qumran a Library?" Pages 78–105 in *The Dead Sea Scrolls at Qumran and the Concept of a Library*. Edited by Sidnie White Crawford and Cecilia Wassén. STDJ 116. Leiden: Brill, 2016.

White Crawford, Sidnie. "Qumran: Caves, Scrolls, and Buildings." Pages 251–73 in *A Teacher for All Generations: Essays in Honor of James C. VanderKam*. Edited by Eric F. Mason, et al. JSJSup 153. Leiden: Brill, 2011.

White Crawford, Sidnie. "'Rewritten Bible' in North American Scholarship." Pages 75–78 in *The Dead Sea Scrolls in Scholarly Perspective: A History of Research*. Edited by Devorah Dimant. STDJ 99. Leiden: Brill, 2012.

White Crawford, Sidnie. "The Qumran Collection as a Scribal Library." Pages 107–31 in *The Dead Sea Scrolls at Qumran and the Concept of a Library*. Edited by Sidnie White Crawford and Cecilia Wassén. STDJ 116. Leiden: Brill, 2016.

White Crawford, Sidnie. "The Inscriptional Evidence from Qumran and its Relationship to the Cave 4Q Documents." Pages 211–20 in *The Caves of Qumran: Proceedings of the International Conference, Lugano 2014*. Edited by Marcello Fidanzio. STDJ 118. Leiden: Brill, 2017.

Wills, Lawrence M. *The Jewish Novel in the Ancient World*, Myth and Poetics. Ithaca, NY: Cornell University Press, 1995.

Wise, Michael O. "Accidents and Accidence: A Scribal View of Linguistic Dating of the Aramaic Scrolls from Qumran." Pages 103–51 in *Thunder in Gemini, and other Essays on the History, Language and Literature of Second Temple Palestine*. JSPSup 15. Sheffield: Sheffield Academic Press, 1994.

Wise, Michael O. *Language and Literacy in Roman Judaea: A Study of the Bar Kokhba Documents*. AYBRL. New Haven, CT: Yale University Press, 2015.

Wolff, Timo, Ira Rabin, Ioanna Mantouvalou, Birgit Kannießer, Wolfgang Malzer, Emanuel Kindzorra, and Oliver Hahn. "Provenance Studies on Dead Sea Scrolls Parchment by Means of Quantitative Micro-XRF." *Analytical and Bioanalytical Chemistry* 402 (2012): 1493–503.

Woodward, Scott R., Gila Kahila, Patricia Smith, Charles Greenblatt, Joe Zias, and Magen Broshi. "Analysis of Parchment Fragments from the Judean Desert Using DNA Techniques." Pages 215–38 in *Current Research and Technological Developments on the Dead Sea Scrolls: Conference on the Texts from the Judean Desert, Jerusalem, 30 April 1995*. Edited by Donald W. Parry and Stephen D. Ricks. STDJ 20. Leiden: Brill, 1996.

Yardeni, Ada. "A Note on a Qumran Scribe." Pages 287–98 in *New Seals and Inscriptions: Hebrew Idumean, and Cuneiform*. Edited by Meir Lubetski. Hebrew Bible Monographs 8. Sheffield: Sheffield Phoenix, 2007.

Young, Ian M. "Manuscripts and Authors of the Psalms." *Studia Biblica Slovaka* 8 (2016): 123–36.

CHAPTER 4

Is There a Spoken Voice in This Cave?
Orality and the Dead Sea Scrolls

Shem Miller

1   Introduction

The title of my presentation alludes to George Brooke's recent *Festschrift*, *Is There a Text in This Cave?*, which explores the textuality of the Dead Sea Scrolls from a variety of perspectives.[1] In this presentation, I would like to discuss an interrelated topic within media studies—namely, orality. Of course, literally speaking, the answer to the question posed by my title is "no." To be sure, we possess not one spoken syllable, not one iota of one spoken syllable, of any composition from the Dead Sea Scrolls. Written texts are all that remain. But this is *not* how Jews in antiquity would have experienced the Dead Sea Scrolls. For the ancient Jews who used them, the Scrolls were both oral and written mediums. In Shemaryahu Talmon's fitting characterization, "In the milieu which engulfed all varieties of Judaism at the turn of the era, a text was by definition an aural text, a spoken writing, a performed story."[2] In this sense, we can affirm that there was a voice in this cave—that is, the scrolls discovered in the eleven caves above Qumran are records of both written and oral communication. The question, then, is not *if* there was a voice in this cave but *how* do we hear this voice today?

In order to answer this question, I should begin by defining what I intend to convey by the term "orality." Most basically, "oral" and "orality" essentially denote a "spoken" quality. But orality's coloring quickly blends in with its surroundings, altering its shades of meaning and camouflaging any unitary identity. Indeed, as Ruth Finnegan provocatively concludes in her famous essay on orality, orality is impossible to define as *one thing* or perhaps even

---

1   Ariel Feldman, Maria Cioată, and Charlotte Hempel, eds., *Is There a Text in This Cave? Studies in the Textuality of the Dead Sea Scrolls in Honour of George J. Brooke*, STDJ 119 (Leiden: Brill, 2017).

2   Shemaryahu Talmon, "Oral Tradition and Written Transmission, or the Heard and the Seen Word in Judaism of the Second Temple Period," in *Jesus and the Oral Gospel Tradition*, ed. Henry Wansbrough, JSNTSup 64 (Sheffield: Sheffield Academic, 1991), 121–58, esp. 150.

© SHEM MILLER, 2023 | DOI:10.1163/9789004537804_005

as *anything*.[3] On account of this, some media critics avoid using the word orality altogether.[4] In my opinion, however, the chameleonic nature of orality does not annihilate its meaning; rather, orality's striking multivalency demands careful treatment of each specific sense. This is particularly relevant to my current topic, as each nuance of orality can manifest itself differently in written media. As a result, we are able to hear the voice of the scrolls in various manners depending upon what aspect of orality we are attempting to perceive. With this observation in mind, I will consider three specific aspects of orality: oral performance, oral tradition, and oral authority.

2 Oral Performance

A survey of oral performance and the Dead Sea Scrolls should begin during the formative years of Qumran scholarship, when a handful of text critics began to identify certain types of variant readings in biblical texts related to the "oral register" of language. By the term "oral register," I mean a linguistic repertoire (in written texts) associated with spoken communication.[5] For instance, not long after the discovery of the first seven scrolls, Harry Orlinsky and Moshe Greenberg recognized that some variant readings (and perhaps an entire edition of Isaiah) were "oral variations."[6] During the subsequent phases of Scrolls scholarship, too, other scholars such as Shemaryahu Talmon and Edward Greenstein identified readings in the Dead Sea Scrolls that were created by speech (i.e., phonetic similarities) and oral transmission (i.e., "misquotations"

---

3 Ruth Finnegan, "What Is Orality—If Anything?" *Byzantine and Modern Greek Studies* 14 (1990): 130–49, esp. 146. "For my overall conclusion is that in one sense 'orality' is *not* anything: or at any rate not anything in the apparently unitary sense that the term seems to imply."

4 Rafael Rodríguez, *Oral Tradition and the New Testament: A Guide for the Perplexed* (London: Bloomsbury, 2014), 7.

5 Concerning this definition of "oral register," see Susan Niditch, *Oral World and Written Word: Ancient Israelite Literature*, LAI (Louisville, KY: Westminster John Knox, 1996), 10; M. A. K. Halliday, *Language as a Social Semiotic: The Social Interpretation of Language and Meaning* (London: University Park Press, 1978), 111; Dell Hymes, "Ways of Speaking," in *Explorations in the Ethnography of Speaking*, ed. Richard Bauman and Joel Sherzer (Cambridge: Cambridge University Press, 1989), 433–75, esp. 440; Asif Agha, "Register," in *Key Terms in Language and Culture*, ed. Alessandro Duranti (Oxford: Blackwell, 2001), 212–15.

6 Harry M. Orlinsky, "Studies in the St. Mark's Isaiah Scroll," *JBL* 69 (1950): 149–66, esp. 157; Moshe Greenberg, "The Stabilization of the Text of the Hebrew Bible Reviewed in Light of the Biblical Manuscripts from the Judean Desert," *JAOS* 76 (1956): 157–67, esp. 164.

and "synonymous readings").[7] These types of variants eventually became canonized in Emanuel Tov's now classic *Textual Criticism of the Hebrew Bible*, which recognizes that some variant readings in biblical texts were created by "phonological similarity" during the course of textual transmission.[8] As a result, David Carr's recent textual criticism has even advocated for an updated taxonomy that recognizes "aural variants," which "arise when texts are misheard during performance."[9]

Oral performance may be defined as the reading, recitation, or enactment of a text *before an audience*. Although the earliest forays into oral performance and the Dead Sea Scrolls laid a solid foundation for later scholarship, they often lacked sufficient inquiry into the social settings of oral performance. As text critical studies, they naturally focused on analyzing oral performance through the lens of scribal writing practices. In more recent trends, however, the role of oral performance in liturgical, reading, and educational practices has garnered more attention in scholarly imagination. These recent trends suggest three broad points about the social setting of the Dead Sea Scrolls.

First, written texts must be understood in relationship to both the literacy and the orality of the masses.[10] Orality was a pervasive form of communication in ancient cultures, and written texts were usually orally communicated. This is especially true for Jews in Ancient Judea because, as William Harris's study on literacy rates in Roman Palestine has estimated, probably less than ten percent of the total population could read.[11] Consequentially, most ancient Jews did not experience the content of the Scrolls as written documents *per se* but

---

7 Shemaryahu Talmon, "Synonymous Readings in the Textual Traditions of the Old Testament," *ScrHier* 8 (1961): 335–83; Edward L. Greenstein, "Misquotation of Scripture in the Dead Sea Scrolls," in *The Frank Talmage Memorial Volume 1*, ed. Barry Walfish (Haifa: Haifa University Press, 1993), 71–83.

8 Emanuel Tov, *Textual Criticism of the Hebrew Bible*, 3rd ed. (Minneapolis, MN: Fortress, 2012), 233–34, 257–58.

9 David M. Carr, *The Formation of the Hebrew Bible: A New Reconstruction* (Oxford: Oxford University Press, 2011), 165.

10 Raymond F. Person and Chris Keith, "Media Studies and Biblical Studies: An Introduction," in *The Dictionary of the Bible and Ancient Media*, ed. Tom Thatcher, et al. (London: Bloomsbury, 2017), 1–15, esp. 2. "Even in those ancient societies in which reading and writing existed," as Raymond Person and Chris Keith argue, "written texts must be understood in relationship to the orality of the masses."

11 Concerning literacy in Roman Palestine, see William V. Harris, *Ancient Literacy* (Cambridge: Harvard University Press, 1989), 272; Catherine Hezser, *Jewish Literacy in Roman Palestine*, TSAJ 81 (Tübingen: Mohr Siebeck, 2001), 34–36. Concerning reading practices and reading cultures in ancient Roman society, see William A. Johnson, *Readers and Reading Culture in the High Roman Empire: A Study of Elite Communities* (Oxford: Oxford University Press, 2010), 3–16.

by hearing them read aloud or recited from memory.[12] Similar to how we experience audiobooks today, ancient Jews "read" the written text aurally through the oral performance of a reader. Overall, as recently pointed out by Charlotte Hempel, "A significant proportion of members of the sectarian movement … were probably illiterate and experienced texts aurally."[13]

Second, recent trends emphasize that oral performance was an integral component of social life in the communities associated with the Scrolls. This has become increasingly obvious in light of a number of analyses on the broader Greco-Roman context of the Dead Sea Scrolls. Mladen Popović's recent study of reading culture in ancient Judaism, for instance, emphasizes that the sociolinguistic context of the Scrolls primarily points toward reading aloud in "deeply social contexts."[14] Similarly, according to Michael Wise's study of language and literacy in Judea, reading within the Yaḥad would have involved public oral performance, discussion, and interpretation.[15] The importance of public oral performance has also been underscored by close studies of various descriptions of community meetings in Rule Texts, particularly the nightly study session in 1QS 6:7b–8a.[16] According to this well-known passage in the

---

12   Person and Keith, "Media Studies and Biblical Studies," 2. In other words, texts were usually disseminated and transmitted *orally*. Concerning reading practices in the communities associated with the Scrolls, see Mladen Popović, "Reading, Writing, and Memorizing Together: Reading Culture in Ancient Judaism and the Dead Sea Scrolls in a Mediterranean Context," DSD 24 (2017): 447–70, esp. 453–56. As Popović's study of reading culture in ancient Judaism emphasizes, although reading alone or reading silently may have occurred in some cases, the sociolinguistic context of the Scrolls primarily points toward reading aloud in "deeply social contexts" ("Reading, Writing, and Memorizing Together," 448). Concerning silent, individual reading in educational contexts, see André Lemaire, "Liré, écrire, étudier à Qoumrân et ailleurs," in *Qoumrân et le judaïsme du tournant de notre ère: Actes de la Table Ronde, Collège de France, 16 novembre 2004*, ed. André Lemaire and Simon C. Mimouni, CREJ 40 (Louvain: Peeters, 2006), 63–79, esp. 66.

13   Charlotte Hempel, "Reflections on Literacy, Textuality, and Community in the Qumran Dead Sea Scrolls," in *Is There a Text in This Cave? Studies in the Textuality of the Dead Sea Scrolls in Honour of George J. Brooke*, ed. Ariel Feldman, Maria Cioată, and Charlotte Hempel, STDJ 119 (Leiden: Brill, 2017), 69–82, esp. 81–82. As Hempel has argued, "a significant proportion" of "the 'textual community' responsible for the literary riches unearthed at and near Qumran" was "illiterate or semi-literate."

14   Popović, "Reading, Writing, and Memorizing Together," 448.

15   Michael O. Wise, *Language and Literacy in Roman Judaea: A Study of the Bar Kokhba Documents* (New Haven, CT: Yale University Press, 2015), 308. In this quote, Wise is referring to 1QSa 6–8 (not 1QS 6:7b–8a); moreover, he is speaking more broadly about ancient Jewish educational practices in Judea. That being said, his thought equally applies to the education curriculum within the communities associated with the Scrolls.

16   For other meetings that include explicit descriptions of oral performance, see local chapter meetings (1QS 6:1b–7a), general membership meetings (1QS 6:8b–13a; CD 14:3b–12a), covenant renewal ceremonies (1QS 1:24–26; CD 20:27–30), and admission procedures (1QS 5:7c–9a, 6:13b–23; CD 15:5b–10a).

Community Rule, all members must gather together for the first third of every night in order to "read the book," "study the ruling," and "bless together." All three of these activities, as suggested by George Brooke's study of this passage, involved oral performance.[17]

Third, recent trends emphasize that the Yaḥad was an "oral-textual" community. The term "oral-textual" conveys the notion of an interface between orality and textuality when assessing literacy, education, and social practices. On the one hand, the sectarian communities associated with the Scrolls were obviously not cultures of "primary orality." Primary orality, a term coined by Walter Ong, describes the verbal communication within cultures that are "untouched by any knowledge of writing or print."[18] Despite the extremely low literacy rates in Roman Palestine, most ancient Jews were thoroughly aware of writing and used written texts to define themselves.[19] Nor were they, for lack of a better antithetical neologism, cultures of "primary literacy"—that is, untouched by any knowledge of orality. Thus, although the sectarian communities associated with the Scrolls could be accurately described as "textual communities," they are best understood as neither oral nor textual communities but as *oral-textual communities*.

3 Oral Tradition

The term "oral-textual communities" elicits Brian Stock's model of "textual communities," which has become increasingly important for those interested in Christianity and Judaism in antiquity.[20] Similar to the medieval reform movements studied by Stock, ancient Jewish groups used authoritative texts

---

17 According to Brooke, the term reading "seems to be more than recitation from text or memory; it seems to involve comprehension and even some kind of active engagement with the text as it was performed." See George J. Brooke, "Reading, Searching and Blessing: A Functional Approach to Scriptural Interpretation in the יחד," in *The Temple in Text and Tradition: A Festschrift in Honour of Robert Hayward*, ed. R. Timothy McLay, LSTS 83 (London: Bloomsbury, 2015), 140–56, esp. 145.

18 Walter J. Ong, *Orality and Literacy: The Technologizing of the Word*, 2nd ed. (London: Routledge, 2002), 6, 10.

19 For a discussion of textuality in the Greco-Roman world, see Larry W. Hurtado, "Greco-Roman Textuality and the Gospel of Mark: A Critical Assessment of Werner H. Kelber's *The Oral and the Written Gospel*," *BBR* 7 (1997): 91–106, esp. 99–105. Concerning the widespread degree of textuality, as well as the spectrum of literacy in Christianity and Judaism in Roman Palestine, see Chris Keith, *Jesus' Literacy: Scribal Culture and the Teacher from Galilee*, LNTS 413 (London: Bloomsbury, 2011), 85–110.

20 As pointed out by Tom Thatcher, "the society from which he drew his samples—Europe at the turn of the millennium—paralleled the media culture of ancient Israel and Late Second Temple Judaism in important respects" ("Textual Communities," in *The Dictionary*

to define their identity and justify their breach with tradition.[21] Moreover, the sectarian movement associated with the Scrolls formed on the basis of shared reinterpretations of authoritative texts.[22] As Carol Newsom has aptly described, "discerning and practicing the correct interpretation of Torah" was "the *raison d'être* for the entire community."[23] As a consequence, the Yaḥad depended not on mass literacy but on elite exegesis—inspired interpretation of texts that defined the boundary between "us" and "them."[24] In the communities associated with the Scrolls, the Teacher of Righteousness and the Maskil, amongst others, fulfilled this need for a textual exegete *par excellence*.

As indicated by Stock, the "text" of textual communities "need not be written down nor the majority of auditors actually literate."[25] In other words, the oral-textual communities associated with the Dead Sea Scrolls did not just crystallize around the leadership's reinterpretation of *written* texts. Oral traditions, in many cases, were just as indispensable to communal identity. From a pre-critical point of view, oral tradition is information or texts passed on by word of mouth rather than in writing. But we require a more sophisticated definition, since we obviously cannot hear the spoken word in ancient texts—that is, the actual oral communication of ancient people is beyond our reach. Generally speaking, the term "tradition" denotes a multivalent body of established thought, meaning, or interpretation.[26] When this tradition is

---

    of the Bible and Ancient Media, ed. Tom Thatcher, et al. [London: Bloomsbury, 2017], 417–18).

21   By "tradition," I intend to convey both "Great Tradition" and "little traditions." The term "Great Tradition" denotes the total set of values that maintains the distinct identity of ancient Jewish society, whereas "little traditions" describe local variations within subgroups that modify, defy, or subvert these values. Concerning these sociological terms, see Tom Thatcher, "Great Tradition/Little Tradition," in *The Dictionary of the Bible and Ancient Media*, ed. Tom Thatcher, et al. (London: Bloomsbury, 2017), 162–63.

22   Brian Stock, *The Implications of Literacy: Written Language and Models of Interpretation in the Eleventh and Twelfth Centuries* (Princeton, NJ: Princeton University Press, 1983), 88–106, esp. 90–99.

23   Carol A. Newsom, "The Sage in the Literature of Qumran: The Functions of the Maskîl," in *The Sage in Israel and the Ancient Near East*, ed. John G. Gammie and Leo G. Perdue (Winona Lake, IN: Eisenbrauns, 1990), 373–82, esp. 375.

24   Stock, *Implications of Literacy*, 90.

25   Stock, *Implications of Literacy*, 32.

26   According to Rafael Rodríguez, tradition is "a body of established, inherited patterns of speech, behavior, thought, social organization, and so on" (*Oral Tradition and the New Testament*, 30). My definition is also influenced by the work of John Miles Foley, who describes tradition as "a dynamic, multivalent body of meaning that preserves much that a group has invented and transmitted but which also includes as necessary, defining features both an inherent indeterminacy and a predisposition to various kinds of changes or

IS THERE A SPOKEN VOICE IN THIS CAVE? 141

composed, performed, or received orally (in part or in whole), we call this "oral tradition."[27]

That being said, oral tradition—like orality—is impossible to define as one thing. On the one hand, oral tradition may describe oral interpretive traditions. "Oral interpretive traditions" denote not only what Jonathan Norton calls the "sense contours" of texts—the exegetical ideas traditionally associated with specific passages of authoritative texts—but also the traditions about the membership's common descent and fictionalized past that informed sectarian texts.[28] On the other hand, oral tradition may denote what scholars of comparative oral tradition call "oral-traditional texts." According to John Miles Foley, oral-traditional texts (also known as "oral-derived" texts) are texts that "either stem directly from or have roots in oral tradition."[29] I should emphasize, however, that Foley has in mind a broader linguistic definition of "text." An overly narrow definition of "text" as *written media* creates an apparent contradiction between orality and texts. Sounds (by their very nature) may be "un-representable" in written texts, but texts can nonetheless be oral because not all texts comprise written words.[30] Whether spoken or written, a text is a unit of speech that is designed to be stored and transmitted.[31] Even more

---

modifications." See John Miles Foley, *The Singer of Tales in Performance* (Indiana: Indiana University Press, 1995), xii.

27   John Miles Foley, *How to Read an Oral Poem* (Chicago: University of Illinois Press, 2002), 39. This definition is based on Foley's fourfold typology of oral-traditional texts.

28   Jonathan D. H. Norton, *Contours of Text: Textual Variation in the Writings of Paul, Josephus and the Yaḥad*, LNTS 430 (London: Bloomsbury, 2011), 52–53.

29   John Miles Foley, *Immanent Art: From Structure to Meaning in Traditional Oral Epic* (Bloomington: Indiana University Press, 1991), xi. Concerning "oral-traditional texts" (also known as "oral derived texts"), see Foley, *How to Read an Oral Poem*, 38–53. Since some "oral-derived texts" are composed in writing, I prefer to use the synonym "oral-traditional texts."

30   Werner H. Kelber, "Oral Tradition, the Comparative Study of," in *The Dictionary of the Bible and Ancient Media*, ed. Tom Thatcher, et al. (London: Bloomsbury, 2017), 252–59, esp. 253. Kelber's formulation of the problematic relationship between speech and texts is worth repeating. "Today the realization prevails," according to Kelber, "that the notion of detachable speech is problematic because spoken words are sound, so that they are un-representable and therefore irretrievable in textual form. Nonetheless, a very large number of texts in the ancient world are examples of intermediality" ("Oral Tradition," 253).

31   Konrad Ehlich, "Text und sprachliches Handeln: Die Entstehung von Texten aus dem Bedürfnis nach Überlieferung," in *Schrift und Gedächtnis: Beiträge zur Archäologie der literarischen Kommunikation*, ed. Aleida Assmann, Jan Assmann, and Christof Hardmeier (Munich: Wilhelm Fink Verlag, 1983), 24–43, esp. 24–27; Jan Assmann, *Religion and Cultural Memory: Ten Studies*, trans. Rodney Livingstone (Stanford, CA: Stanford University Press, 2006), 101–105.

importantly, written texts can be "intermedial"—that is, they are in some way related to, or derived from, oral communication.[32]

For an example of oral interpretive traditions in the Dead Sea Scrolls, let us briefly consider the coded language of the pesharim. Aside from the references to Demetrius and Antiochus in the Nahum Pesher, all references to leaders and groups in biblical commentaries appear in coded language.[33] Readers must therefore rely on oral-written traditions to decode the full meaning of sobriquets and stereotypes in the pesharim. As John Collins has argued, for example, the Habakkuk Pesher's description of the Man of the Lie and the Teacher of Righteousness assumes a narrative "about the Teacher and his adversaries that is then correlated with the prophetic text, by means of the catchwords 'traitors' and 'believe.'"[34] In other words, as Collins summarizes, the pesharim "have to rely on *tradition*, whether oral or written."[35] As a result, according to Foley's description of individual-oriented phraseology in traditional texts, sobriquets in the pesharim can act as "formulas that represent specific characters" as well as a "broader traditional identity."[36] Or in Jutta Jokiranta's words speaking specifically about the pesharim, stereotypical names can function "as theological evaluations of individuals and groups, rather than as secret code names for them."[37] The term "righteous" in the Habakkuk Pesher, for example, represents both the Teacher of Righteousness and the Teacher's righteous followers.[38]

---

32 According to Kelber, "Intermediality designates written texts that are in some ways related to, or derived from, an oral or oral-scribal performance tradition and that were, therefore, partially or in toto in place prior to their present existence" ("Oral Tradition," 253).

33 Timothy H. Lim, *Pesharim*, CQS (Sheffield: Sheffield Academic, 2002), 65.

34 John J. Collins, "Prophecy and History in the Pesharim," in *Authoritative Scriptures in Ancient Judaism*, ed. Mladen Popović, JSJSup 141 (Leiden: Brill, 2010), 209–26, esp. 218.

35 John J. Collins, "Historiography in the Dead Sea Scrolls," *DSD* 19 (2012): 159–76, esp. 167; emphasis added. In the same vein, Michael A. Knibb states, "Attempts have been made to exploit the commentaries in order to reconstruct the history of the Qumran community. This is, however, more difficult to do than is often assumed because the pieces of interpretation frequently follow traditional lines of interpretation and their language is opaque" (*The Qumran Community*, CCJCW 2 [Cambridge: Cambridge University Press, 1987], 208).

36 John Miles Foley, "Traditional History in South Slavic Epic," in *Epic and History*, ed. David Konstan and Kurt A. Raaflaub (Chichester: Wiley-Blackwell, 2010), 347–61, esp. 353.

37 Jutta Jokiranta, "Pesharim: A Mirror for Self-Understanding," in *Reading the Present in the Qumran Library: The Perception of the Contemporary by Means of Scriptural Interpretations*, eds. Kristin De Troyer and Armin Lange, SBLSymS 30 (Atlanta, GA: SBL, 2005), 23–34, esp. 28.

38 As Collins observes, "הצדיק, 'the righteous,' from Hab 1:13 is interpreted as the Teacher of Righteousness in 1QpHab 5:10, but the צדיק of Hab 2:4b ('the righteous man will live by his faithfulness') is interpreted as everyone who observes the Law and is faithful to the Teacher in 1QpHab 8:1–3" ("Prophecy and History in the Pesharim," 219).

IS THERE A SPOKEN VOICE IN THIS CAVE? 143

For an example of oral-traditional texts in the Dead Sea Scrolls, I turn to two dynamic bodies of tradition called the "mystery of existence" (רז נהיה) and the "wonderful mysteries" (רזי פלא).[39] Despite being partly inscribed in sapiential literature such as Instruction (1Q26, 4Q415–418) and Mysteries (1Q27, 4Q299–300), the "mystery of existence" and "wonderful mysteries" were probably not viewed as written texts. First, as pointed out by John Kampen, their content was far too broad for any single written text.[40] Indeed, mystery language in the Scrolls—like oral tradition—elicits what Foley calls an "untextualizable network of traditional semantic associations."[41] Second, these mysteries are not directly connected with any specific literary text.[42] In Kampen's words, "Texts only provided hints and clues, leaving the reader and/or adherent free to delve further into the revelation of the mystery."[43] Third, and most important, neither the "mystery of existence" nor the "wonderful mysteries" is ever described using nouns for written texts; moreover, they are neither "read" (קרא) nor "written" (כתב).[44] Instead, they are often described as being "revealed

---

39   Because it is nuanced by various genres, compositions, and constructions, mystery language covers a host of connotations in the Dead Sea Scrolls. For a complete survey of "mysteries," see Samuel I. Thomas, *The "Mysteries" of Qumran: Mystery, Secrecy, and Esotericism in the Dead Sea Scrolls*, EJL 25 (Atlanta, GA: SBL, 2009), 127–86. Most broadly speaking, the "wonderful mysteries" pertain to God's acts of judgment and redemption over both his creation and his elect, whereas the "mystery of existence" covers eschatology, history, and creation. We find mystery language primarily in sapiential literature such as Instruction (1Q26, 4Q415–418) and Mysteries (1Q27, 4Q299–300), a composition so-named by the editors of the *editio princeps* because of its repeated references to "mysteries" (רזים). In addition, mysteries are described in various other genres such as poetic and liturgical works (e.g., the Hodayot), legal texts (e.g., 1QS), and apocalyptic texts (e.g., the War Rule).

40   John Kampen, *Wisdom Literature* (Grand Rapids, MI: Eerdmans, 2011), 49–50. According to Kampen, "It seems doubtful that … the entire mystery was contained within any one text" (*Wisdom Literature*, 49).

41   Foley, *The Singer of Tales in Performance*, 54.

42   Kampen, *Wisdom Literature*, 49.

43   Kampen, *Wisdom Literature*, 50.

44   They are never designated as (or compared with) nouns for written texts, such as "scroll" (מגלה), "book" (ספר), "rule" (סרך), or "text" (כתב). And they are never "read" (קרא) or "written" (כתב). Concerning the use of these words to denote written texts, see Lawrence H. Schiffman, "'Memory and Manuscript': Books, Scrolls, and the Tradition of Qumran Texts," in *New Perspectives on Old Texts: Proceedings of the Tenth International Symposium of the Orion Center for the Study of the Dead Sea Scrolls and Associated Literature, 9–11 January, 2005*, ed. Esther G. Chazon, Baruch Halpern-Amaru, and Ruth A. Clements, STDJ 88 (Leiden: Brill, 2010), 133–50, esp. 137–43.

to one's ear."[45] Overall, as Kampen notes, it appears that these mysteries relied on "continuing oral tradition passed on by 'teachers' within the group."[46]

4 Oral Authority

Although there are certainly a few notable exceptions, past Scroll's scholarship has tended to deny oral authority in the communities associated with the Dead Sea Scrolls on the basis of three lines of argumentation. First, and most problematic, some past denials of oral authority are based on Oral Law. At worst, this sort of objection equates Oral Law with oral tradition, as if absence of the former provides evidence for lack of the latter. At best, this type of objection results from an inadequate differentiation of oral tradition from Oral Law. The influential studies of Lawrence Schiffman, an expert in the field of sectarian law in the Dead Sea Scrolls, provide a good illustration of this position.[47] Since the communities did not hold Oral Law, according to Schiffman, the *only source* of sectarian halakhah must be written Law.[48] In short, his argument presumes that Oral Law was the only possible source of oral traditions. As a consequence, as Schiffman states elsewhere, the "Qumranites never attribute any authority to tradition."[49] Overall, in Schiffman's opinion, "Authority is

---

45   I should note that both the "mystery of existence" and the "wonderful mysteries" have many verbal associations. For a detailed list of all the verbs used with these mysteries, see Thomas, *The "Mysteries" of Qumran*, 184–86.

46   John Kampen's full statement is worth repeating: "Since the center of this group's existence is around an unwritten body of knowledge known as the 'mystery of existence,' elements of which are explained within *Instruction* but which rely on a continuing oral tradition passed on by 'teachers' within the group, this is not public knowledge available to anyone. It is rather an exclusive body of knowledge available only to those who make a commitment to join this group, the first step in appropriating the knowledge of the mystery of existence" (*Wisdom Literature*, 59).

47   According to Schiffman's critique of Oral Law, written *not* oral tradition was authoritative, and written *not* oral transmission was the norm in the communities associated with the Scrolls. See Lawrence H. Schiffman, *The Halakhah at Qumran*, SJLA 16 (Leiden: Brill, 1975), 76, 134; idem, *Sectarian Law in the Dead Sea Scrolls: Courts, Testimony and the Penal Code*, BJS 33 (Scholars Press, 1983), 16.

48   According to Schiffman, "Both the Dead Sea sect and the Karaites lack an oral [*sic*] Law concept. Scripture, then, becomes the *sole source* of halakhah" (*Halakhah at Qumran*, 134; emphasis added).

49   Schiffman, *Sectarian Law*, 16. Similarly, Schiffman claims that *nistar*, the hidden teachings derived from sectarian interpretation, "knows no oral authority" (*Halakhah at Qumran*, 134).

placed in written texts, rather than in both written and oral traditions,"[50] and "written not oral transmission was the norm."[51]

Viewing oral tradition and oral transmission through the lens of later rabbinic concepts distorts a proper view traditional authority in Second Temple Judaism. Or, in Steven Fraade's more assertive opinion,

> Biblical Israelite and postbiblical Jewish cultures were undoubtedly suffused with oral traditions that accompanied written scriptures and para-biblical texts of many sorts, as is common in all traditional cultures. But to confuse such oral tradition with the Rabbinic fiction of Oral Torah is not only to produce terminological dilution, but to blur a critical ideological and performative distinction between the Rabbinic culture of Torah study and its antecedents.[52]

In fact, the oral-written textuality of tradition in ancient Judaism is a perfect foil for the later rabbis' artificial dichotomy between Oral Law and written Law.[53] According to the rhetoric of the rabbis, Oral Law originated orally and was transmitted orally, whereas written Law was originally composed and transmitted in written form.[54] The communities associated with the Scrolls, however, viewed orality and textuality as "complementary means for the

---

50 Schiffman, "'Memory and Manuscript'," 134. In Schiffman's words, "Regarding the Qumran corpus, we seem to be dealing with a group that places authority in written texts, rather than both written and oral traditions" (134).

51 Schiffman, *Sectarian Law*, 16; Schiffman, *Halakhah at Qumran*, 76.

52 Steven D. Fraade, "Literary Composition and Oral Performance in Early Midrashim," *Oral Tradition* 14 (1999): 33–51, esp. 42.

53 Oral Law is "Torah that is spoken" (תורה שבעל פה), whereas written Law is "Torah that is written" (תורה שבכתב). As Jaffee and others have correctly argued, this dichotomy was artificial because the rabbinic teachers drew heavily on oral tradition for their textual compositions, which in many cases were themselves subject to reoralization. See Martin S. Jaffee, *Torah in the Mouth: Writing and Oral Tradition in Palestinian Judaism, 200 BCE–400 CE* (Oxford: Oxford University Press, 2001), 100–125. In Jaffee's apposite words, there was a "continuous loop of manuscript and performance" (*Torah in the Mouth*, 124). For more on the interface between orality and writing in rabbinic literature, see Catherine Hezser, "From Oral Conversations to Written Texts: Randomness in the Transmission of Rabbinic Traditions" in *The Interface of Orality and Writing: Speaking, Seeing, Writing in the Shaping of New Genres*, ed. Annette Weissenrieder and Robert B. Coote, WUNT 260 (Tübingen: Mohr Siebeck, 2010), 36–51; eadem, *Jewish Literacy in Roman Palestine*, 190–209; Fraade, "Literary Composition and Oral Performance," 33–51.

54 Schiffman, *Halakhah at Qumran*, 20. According to Schiffman, the rabbis "argued that Jewish tradition was made up of components originally composed or revealed in written form, and also of material that had originated orally and been transmitted by memory and not by manuscript" ("'Memory and Manuscript'," 133).

preservation of revered teachings."[55] Tradition is delineated neither by oral transmission nor by oral content. Oral tradition can contain both written and oral content; moreover, it can be composed, performed, or transmitted in both oral and textual mediums. As argued by Talmon, instead of "oral tradition versus written transmission," written texts and oral traditions were transmitted in both memory and manuscript, by both sound and sight.[56]

Second, some past rejections of oral authority are based upon a denial of progressive revelation as a source of legal traditions and authoritative interpretation. According to Schiffman, for example, sectarian law was not "dependent on revelation as a continuing process."[57] More recent views, however, have recognized that legal traditions were sometimes derived from progressive revelation.[58] Alex Jassen, for example, has persuasively argued that the sectarians viewed ancient prophets as lawgivers, as inspired recipients of the progressive revelation of law; furthermore, "the community viewed itself as the heir to the ancient prophetic lawgivers and saw its own legislative program as the most recent stage in the prophetic revelation of divine law."[59] Jassen's summary is worth repeating:

> The interpretation of the Torah and the formulation of post-biblical law were disclosed to successive generations through a series of later revelations. The community viewed itself as the current beneficiary of

---

55   Talmon, "Oral Tradition and Written Transmission," 148–49. As Schiffman points out, the medium was closely connected to the message in rabbinic thought: "When the rabbis prescribed that what in their view had been revealed in writing was to be passed down in writing, and what had been revealed orally was to be transmitted orally, they essentially asserted that to some extent the medium was closely connected to the message" ("'Memory and Manuscript,'" 133). In contrast to the rabbis, however, the communities associated with the Scrolls did not prescribe an intrinsic link between medium and message. In Shemaryahu Talmon's words, "Memory and manuscript were not conceived as alternatives, but rather as complementary means for the preservation of revered teachings" ("Oral Tradition and Written Transmission," 148–49).

56   Talmon, "Oral Tradition and Written Transmission," 149–50.

57   Contrary to Baumgarten's position that sees "Qumran law as dependent on revelation as a continuing process," Schiffman asserts that "his [i.e., Baumgarten's] conclusion cannot be accepted" (*Halakhah at Qumran*, 76 n. 347). For Schiffman, "exegesis (not revelation)" was the basis of legislation in the communities associated with the Scrolls (*Halakhah at Qumran*, 76 n. 347).

58   Alex P. Jassen, *Mediating the Divine: Prophecy and Revelation in the Dead Sea Scrolls and Second Temple Judaism*, STDJ 68 (Leiden: Brill, 2007), 331–42. See also Joseph M. Baumgarten, *Studies in Qumran Law*, SJLA 24 (Leiden: Brill, 1977), 29–33.

59   Alex P. Jassen, "The Presentation of the Ancient Prophets as Lawgivers at Qumran," *JBL* 127 (2008): 307–37, esp. 311.

IS THERE A SPOKEN VOICE IN THIS CAVE? 147

this revelation. Its leaders, most notably the Teacher of Righteousness, were regarded as inspired individuals who interpreted the Torah and formulated law based on their status as recipients of legislative revelation. The Qumran rule books represent the record of the legislative activity of these inspired individuals during nightly study sessions.[60]

The gap between Sinai and the sect was not bridged by a chain of authoritative oral tradition but rather by progressive revelation of law to members and leaders of the sectarian communities associated with the Scrolls. Authority, as Judith Newman has pointed out, was derived from the inspired status of the leadership's teaching, which was endued with a special, God-given ability to give a "response of the tongue."[61]

Third, some past denials of oral authority are based upon an underappreciation of the authoritative status of oral performance during community meetings, especially for the generation and promulgation of sectarian laws. Even in those cases where Rule Texts clearly portray oral performance of sectarian regulations, such as during nightly study sessions or general membership meetings, Schiffman characterizes oral performance as an essentially text-bound activity:

> To the sectarians of Qumran, there was a written text that transmitted God's revealed word, and it was accompanied by exegetical teachings; but ... these interpretations were closely based on the written word, and they themselves were *always written*, even if they may have emerged from discussion—an oral activity to be sure.[62]

Thus, although Schiffman recognizes that exegesis could have "emerged" from an "oral activity," authority is only generated once it is written.[63] Similarly, elsewhere he states that "many of these laws were probably derived at the sessions of the *mosheb ha-rabbim* [i.e., the general membership meeting], the sect's legislative and judicial assembly."[64] But these "newly derived laws" were not "officially promulgated" until they were arranged in "written lists" called *serakhim*

---

60 Jassen, "Ancient Prophets as Lawgivers," 308.
61 Judith H. Newman, "The Thanksgiving Hymns of 1QHᵃ and the Construction of the Ideal Sage through Liturgical Performance," in *Sibyls, Scriptures, and Scrolls: John Collins at Seventy*, ed. Joel Baden, Hindy Najman, and Eibert J. C. Tigchelaar, JSJSup 175 (Leiden: Brill, 2016), 940–57, esp. 953–54.
62 Schiffman, "'Memory and Manuscript'," 134; emphasis added.
63 Schiffman, "'Memory and Manuscript'," 134.
64 Schiffman, *Halakhah at Qumran*, 76.

148   MILLER

"after each session."[65] Thus, despite the clearly oral activities that took place at these meetings, he concludes that "Qumran legal traditions are derived exclusively though exegesis [of written texts]."[66]

I have chosen to critique Schiffman's views not only because they contrast with my own but also because his suppositions continue to exert influence on scholarly discussion. Indeed, one could say that Schiffman's views are emblematic of past trends in Scrolls scholarship, particularly in regard to oral authority and sectarian law. For example, according to Martin Jaffee, who is undoubtedly well-versed in Schiffman's studies on sectarian law,

> There is no suggestion in any of the Yaḥad-related materials, however, that the group assigned authoritative status to an unwritten body of collective tradition on the specific grounds that it had been orally mediated through ancient tradition. While oral teaching was clearly the norm ... the authority of the teaching appears to have been connected inextricably to that of the writings from which it originated. And the definitive expression of its authority was found not in its oral nature, but rather *in the fact of its having been itself inscribed* on the leaves of scrolls.[67]

In light of Jaffee's clear sensitivity to issues surrounding orality, I find his denial of oral authority surprising. While Jaffee correctly asserts that authority is not based (1) on orality *per se* or (2) on oral transmission (i.e., mediation "through ancient tradition"), he falsely grounds all authority on written texts.[68] Similarly, according to Alison Schofield's brief discussion of oral versus written authority, oral decisions were only binding once they were written down.[69] Authority, in her view, "was primarily derived from inspired scriptural exegesis, a text-bound activity."[70]

5   Conclusion

Over the past fifty years, much excellent work has been done on the oral background of the Hebrew Bible and the New Testament, as well as the oral-written

---

65   Schiffman, *Halakhah at Qumran*, 76.
66   Schiffman, *Halakhah at Qumran*, 19.
67   Jaffee, *Torah in the Mouth*, 37–38; emphasis added.
68   Jaffee, *Torah in the Mouth*, 17–18, 37–38.
69   Alison Schofield, *From Qumran to the Yaḥad: A New Paradigm of Textual Development for the Community Rule*, STDJ 77 (Leiden: Brill, 2008), 186–87.
70   Schofield, *From Qumran to the* Yaḥad, 187.

process of their textualization in ancient Israel and the Greco-Roman world.[71] Although this theory is indispensable for anyone interested in hearing the spoken voice of the Scrolls, scholarship on the Dead Sea Scrolls has only recently begun to make use of some well-established theories of orality in the fields of (HB and NT) media studies. As a result, certain prominent theories within both media studies and orality studies, which are more or less common knowledge among some circles of Hebrew Bible and New Testament scholars, are just now beginning to filter into Qumran scholarship. Take, for example, the relationship between orality and textuality. Although there are certainly notable exceptions, the bulk of past Dead Sea Scrolls' scholarship has presupposed what media critics call the Great Divide. And this misconception has inhibited our ability to properly appreciate the roles of oral performance, oral tradition, and oral authority in the communities associated with the Scrolls.

The Great Divide, according to Rafael Rodríguez's succinct definition, refers to the "widely discredited assumption" that "oral and written media are fundamentally different and distinct."[72] To my mind, Schiffman and others' rejection of oral authority is ultimately a result of their assumption that written laws were distinct from spoken laws. But why, I wonder, presuppose the supremacy of the written word when descriptions of oral performance seem to suggest that verbal and written communication can be equally authoritative in certain performance arenas? The daily life of the community described in the Community Rule centered around the oral communication of leaders who managed affairs and adjudicated disputes by word of mouth (1QS 5:2, 9:3). And in certain performance arenas, such as the general membership meeting (1QS 6:8b–13a), it was *not a written text* but the verbal content of oral performance—the oral text of the meeting—that immediately promulgated sectarian law and juridical decisions. As first suggested by Sarianna Metso, the purpose of the Community Rule "was not to serve as a law-book, but rather as a record of judicial decisions and *an accurate report of oral traditions*."[73]

---

71   For examples in Hebrew Bible scholarship, see the now-classic works of Niditch, *Oral World and Written Word*; William M. Schniedewind, *How the Bible Became a Book: The Textualization of Ancient Israel* (New York, NY: Cambridge University Press, 2004).

72   Rafael Rodríguez, "Great Divide," in *The Dictionary of the Bible and Ancient Media*, ed. Tom Thatcher, et al. (London: Bloomsbury, 2017), 163–64.

73   Sarianna Metso, "In Search of the *Sitz im Leben* of the *Community Rule*," in *The Provo International Conference on the Dead Sea Scrolls: Technological Innovations, New Texts, and Reformulated Issues*, ed. Donald W. Parry and Eugene Ulrich, STDJ 30 (Leiden: Brill, 1998), 86–93, esp. 314; emphasis added. See also Sarianna Metso, *The Serekh Texts*, LSTS 62 (London: T&T Clark, 2007), 70.

150 MILLER

As an illustration of my point, consider a rhetorical question posed in the footnotes of Schofield's study of the Community Rule:

> Can we say that if oral decisions were made, did not the written record of them make them binding? This would be the current author's preferred explanation, as we have some indication that at least some judicial decisions were made by the *rabbim* [i.e., 'the many'].[74]

Schofield is here alluding to the general membership meeting described in 1QS 6:8b–13a, during which members were periodically "questioned about the ruling":

> In that order they shall be questioned about the ruling, and *any deliberation or matter* that may come before the general membership (וכן ישאלו למשפט ולכול עצת ודבר), so that each man may state his opinion to the party of the Yaḥad. None should interrupt the words of his comrade, speaking before his brother finishes what he has to say. Neither should anyone speak before another of a higher rank. Only the man being questioned shall speak in his turn. (1QS 6:9–11a)[75]

According to this passage, each member must undergo an oral examination about the content of the ruling and a number of other legal matters. In other words, sectarian laws were orally transmitted during these convocations. Even more noteworthy, the description of these legal proceedings lacks any explicit reference to a written body of laws as the basis of authority. The general membership and the priestly leadership endow oral performance with comprehensive authority to adjudicate "any deliberation or matter" (כול עצת ודבר) that may arise during this meeting.[76] Sarianna Metso, as well, finds this striking: "What catches my attention in these passages is the total lack of reference to any written text. The authority for decision-making is granted not to any book but rather to the *rabbim* [i.e., general membership] (e.g., 1QS 6:8–13), members

---

74   Schofield, *From Qumran to the* Yaḥad, 186 n. 172.
75   The translation is from Donald W. Parry and Emanuel Tov, eds., *The Dead Sea Scrolls Reader, Part 1: Texts Concerned with Religious Law* (Leiden: Brill, 2004), 27.
76   Alternatively, according to Schofield's interpretation, "It is certainly feasible that Yaḥad members arrived at some decisions via oral consultation. The governing body of the 'Many' did have a type of judicial function, but the texts connect it specifically with deciding whether or not an initiate should be admitted to the community. If other oral decisions were reached jointly, we may never know" (*From Qumran to the* Yaḥad, 187). In light of the above study, this conclusion cannot be accepted. Oral authority was not limited to decisions regarding admission.

of the camps (CD 14:3–6), or to the sons of Aaron (1QS 9:7)."[77] Thus, contrary to Jaffee and Schiffman, authority is not always based on "the fact of it having been itself inscribed."[78] In this particular performance arena, as Metso correctly emphasizes, authority is also based on the oral performance of priests (i.e., "the sons of Aaron") or "the many" (i.e., the general membership).

The overarching point I wish to stress is twofold. On the one hand, the Dead Sea Scrolls were not texts frozen in written media; rather, they were dynamic discourses that represented spoken words (speech) heard in shifting contexts of oral performance (reading). For the Jews who used them, they functioned as reference points for study, reading, and memorization. Moreover, as oral mediums, they stored the oral interpretive traditions and oral traditional texts of the communities associated with the Scrolls. On the other hand, both the social context of the Scrolls and the descriptions of oral performance in the Scrolls demand an influential place for orality in our reconstructions of daily life. For members of the sectarian movement, the Yaḥad was an oral-textual community: *oral* because they lived in a predominately oral culture in which oral performance, oral tradition, and oral authority were all integral to social life and identity; *textual* because they were also a group of people whose social identity centered around the leadership's interpretation of authoritative texts. Overall, a rich interface between orality and texts occurred in the social life of the communities associated with the Scrolls.[79]

Bibliography

Agha, Asif. "Register." Pages 212–15 in *Key Terms in Language and Culture.* Edited by Alessandro Duranti. Oxford: Blackwell, 2001.

Assmann, Jan. *Religion and Cultural Memory: Ten Studies.* Translated by Rodney Livingstone. Cultural Memory in the Present. Stanford, CA: Stanford University Press, 2006.

Baumgarten, Joseph M. *Studies in Qumran Law.* SJLA 24. Leiden: Brill, 1977.

Brooke, George J. "Reading, Searching and Blessing: A Functional Approach to Scriptural Interpretation in the יחד." Pages 140–56 in *The Temple in Text and Tradition: A Festschrift in Honour of Robert Hayward.* Edited by R. Timothy McLay. LSTS 83. London: Bloomsbury, 2015.

---

77 Metso, *Serekh Texts*, 66.

78 Jaffee, *Torah in the Mouth*, 38.

79 Portions of this paper have been previously published in *Dead Sea Media: Orality, Textuality, and Memory in the Scrolls from the Judean Desert.*

Carr, David M. *The Formation of the Hebrew Bible: A New Reconstruction.* Oxford: Oxford University Press, 2011.

Collins, John J. "Prophecy and History in the Pesharim." Pages 209–26 in *Authoritative Scriptures in Ancient Judaism.* Edited by Mladen Popović. JSJSup 141. Leiden: Brill, 2010.

Collins, John J. "Historiography in the Dead Sea Scrolls." *DSD* 19 (2012): 159–76.

Ehlich, Konrad. "Text und sprachliches Handeln: Die Entstehung von Texten aus dem Bedürfnis nach Überlieferung." Pages 24–43 in *Schrift und Gedächtnis: Beiträge zur Archäologie der literarischen Kommunikation.* Edited by Aleida Assmann, Jan Assmann, and Christof Hardmeier. Munich: Wilhelm Fink Verlag, 1983.

Feldman, Ariel, Maria Cioată, and Charlotte Hempel, eds. *Is There a Text in This Cave? Studies in the Textuality of the Dead Sea Scrolls in Honour of George J. Brooke.* STDJ 119. Leiden: Brill, 2017.

Finnegan, Ruth. "What Is Orality—If Anything?" *Byzantine and Modern Greek Studies* 14 (1990): 130–49.

Foley, John Miles. *Immanent Art: From Structure to Meaning in Tradition Oral Epic.* Bloomington, IN: Indiana University Press, 1991.

Foley, John Miles. *The Singer of Tales in Performance*, Voices in Performance and Text. Bloomington, IN: Indiana University Press, 1995.

Foley, John Miles. *How to Read an Oral Poem.* Urbana, IL: University of Illinois Press, 2002.

Foley, John Miles. "Traditional History in South Slavic Epic." Pages 347–61 in *Epic and History.* Edited by David Konstan and Kurt A. Raaflaub. Chichester: Wiley-Blackwell, 2010.

Fraade, Steven D. "Literary Composition and Oral Performance in Early Midrashim." *Oral Tradition* 14 (1999): 33–51.

Greenberg, Moshe. "The Stabilization of the Text of the Hebrew Bible Reviewed in Light of the Biblical Manuscripts from the Judean Desert," *JAOS* 76 (1956): 157–67.

Greenstein, Edward L. "Misquotation of Scripture in the Dead Sea Scrolls." Pages 71–83 in *The Frank Talmage Memorial Volume 1.* Edited by Barry Walfish. Haifa: Haifa University Press, 1993.

Halliday, M. A. K. *Language as a Social Semiotic: The Social Interpretation of Language and Meaning.* London: University Park Press, 1978.

Harris, William V. *Ancient Literacy.* Cambridge, MA: Harvard University Press, 1989.

Hempel, Charlotte. "Reflections on Literacy, Textuality, and Community in the Qumran Dead Sea Scrolls." Pages 69–82 in *Is There a Text in this Cave? Studies in the Textuality of the Dead Sea Scrolls in Honour of George J. Brooke.* Edited by Ariel Feldman, Maria Cioată, and Charlotte Hempel. STDJ 119. Leiden: Brill, 2017.

Hezser, Catherine. *Jewish Literacy in Roman Palestine.* TSAJ 81. Tübingen: Mohr Siebeck, 2001.

Hezser, Catherine. "From Oral Conversations to Written Texts: Randomness in the Transmission of Rabbinic Traditions." Pages 36–51 in *The Interface of Orality and Writing: Speaking, Seeing, Writing in the Shaping of New Genres*. Edited by Annette Weissenrieder and Robert B. Coote. WUNT 260. Tübingen: Mohr Siebeck, 2010.

Hurtado, Larry W. "Greco-Roman Textuality and the Gospel of Mark: A Critical Assessment of Werner H. Kelber's *The Oral and the Written Gospel*." *BBR* 7 (1997): 91–106.

Hymes, Dell. "Ways of Speaking." Pages 433–75 in *Explorations in the Ethnography of Speaking*. Edited by Richard Bauman and Joel Sherzer. Cambridge: Cambridge University Press, 1989.

Jaffee, Martin S. *Torah in the Mouth: Writing and Oral Tradition in Palestinian Judaism, 200 BCE–400 CE*. Oxford: Oxford University Press, 2001.

Jassen, Alex P. *Mediating the Divine: Prophecy and Revelation in the Dead Sea Scrolls and Second Temple Judaism*. STDJ 68. Leiden: Brill, 2007.

Jassen, Alex P. "The Presentation of the Ancient Prophets as Lawgivers at Qumran." *JBL* 127 (2008): 307–37.

Johnson, William A. *Readers and Reading Culture in the High Roman Empire: A Study of Elite Communities*. Classical Culture and Society. Oxford: Oxford University Press, 2010.

Jokiranta, Jutta. "Pesharim: A Mirror for Self-Understanding." Pages 23–34 in *Reading the Present in the Qumran Library: The Perception of the Contemporary by Means of Scriptural Interpretations*. Edited by Kristin De Troyer and Armin Lange. SBLSymS 30. Atlanta, GA: SBL, 2005.

Kampen, John. *Wisdom Literature*. Eerdmans Commentaries on the Dead Sea Scrolls. Grand Rapids, MI: Eerdmans, 2011.

Keith, Chris. *Jesus' Literacy: Scribal Culture and the Teacher from Galilee*. LNTS 413. London: Bloomsbury, 2011.

Kelber, Werner H. "Oral Tradition, the Comparative Study of." Pages 252–59 in *The Dictionary of the Bible and Ancient Media*. Edited by Tom Thatcher, Chris Keith, Raymond F. Person, Jr., and Elsie R. Stern. London: Bloomsbury, 2017.

Knibb, Michael A. *The Qumran Community*. CCJCW 2. Cambridge: Cambridge University Press, 1987.

Lemaire, André. "Lire, écrire, étudier à Qoumrân et ailleurs." Pages 63–79 in *Qoumrân et la judaïsme du tournant de notre ère: Actes de la Table Ronde, Collège de France, 16 novembre 2004*. Edited by André Lemaire and Simon C. Mimouni. Collection de la Revue des études juives 40. Leuven: Peeters, 2006.

Lim, Timothy H. *Pesharim*. CQS. Sheffield: Sheffield Academic, 2002.

Metso, Sarianna. "In Search of the *Sitz im Leben* of the *Community Rule*." Pages 86–93 in *The Provo International Conference on the Dead Sea Scrolls: Technological Innovations, New Texts, and Reformulated Issues*. Edited by Donald W. Parry and Eugene Ulrich. STDJ 30. Leiden: Brill, 1998.

Metso, Sarianna. *The Serekh Texts*. LSTS 62. London: T&T Clark, 2007.

Newman, Judith H. "The Thanksgiving Hymns of 1QH[a] and the Construction of the Ideal Sage through Liturgical Performance." Pages 940–57 in *Sibyls, Scriptures, and Scrolls: John Collins at Seventy*. Edited by Joel Baden, Hindy Najman, and Eibert J. C. Tigchelaar. JSJSup 175. Leiden: Brill, 2016.

Newsom, Carol A. "The Sage in the Literature of Qumran: The Functions of the Maskîl." Pages 373–82 in *The Sage in Israel and the Ancient Near East*. Edited by John G. Gammie and Leo G. Perdue. Winona Lake, IN: Eisenbrauns, 1990.

Niditch, Susan. *Oral World and Written Word: Ancient Israelite Literature*. LAI. Louisville, KY: Westminster John Knox, 1996.

Norton, Jonathan D. H. *Contours of Text: Textual Variation in the Writings of Paul, Josephus and the Yaḥad*. LNTS 430. London: Bloomsbury, 2011.

Ong, Walter J. *Orality and Literacy: The Technologizing of the World*. 2nd ed. London: Routledge, 2002.

Orlinsky, Harry M. "Studies in the St. Mark's Isaiah Scroll." *JBL* 69 (1950): 149–66.

Parry, Donald W. and Emanuel Tov, eds. *The Dead Sea Scrolls Reader*, Part 1: *Texts Concerned with Religious Law*. Leiden: Brill, 2004.

Person, Jr., Raymond F., and Chris Keith. "Media Studies and Biblical Studies: An Introduction." Pages 1–15 in *The Dictionary of the Bible and Ancient Media*. Edited by Tom Thatcher, Chris Keith, Raymond F. Person, Jr., and Elsie R. Stern. London: Bloomsbury, 2017.

Popović, Mladen. "Reading, Writing, and Memorizing Together: Reading Culture in Ancient Judaism and the Dead Sea Scrolls in a Mediterranean Context." *DSD* 24 (2017): 447–70.

Rodríguez, Rafael. *Oral Tradition and the New Testament: A Guide for the Perplexed*. London: Bloomsbury, 2014.

Rodríguez, Rafael. "Great Divide." Pages 163–64 in *The Dictionary of the Bible and Ancient Media*. Edited by Tom Thatcher, Chris Keith, Raymond F. Person, Jr., and Elsie R. Stern. London: Bloomsbury, 2017.

Schiffman, Lawrence H. *The Halakhah at Qumran*. SJLA 16. Leiden: Brill, 1975.

Schiffman, Lawrence H. *Sectarian Law in the Dead Sea Scrolls: Courts, Testimony and the Penal Code*. BJS 33. Scholars Press, 1983.

Schiffman, Lawrence H. "'Memory and Manuscript': Books, Scrolls, and the Tradition of Qumran Texts." Pages 133–50 in *New perspectives on Old Texts: Proceedings of the Tenth International Symposium of the Orion Center for the Study of the Dead Sea Scrolls and Associated Literature, 9–11 January, 2005*. Edited by Esther G. Chazon, Baruch Halpern-Amaru, and Ruth A. Clements. STDJ 88. Leiden: Brill, 2010.

Schniedewind, William M. *How the Bible Became a Book: The Textualization of Ancient Israel*. Cambridge: Cambridge University Press, 2004.

Schofield, Alison. *From Qumran to the Yaḥad: A New Paradigm of Textual Development for The Community Rule*. STDJ 77. Leiden: Brill, 2009.

Stock, Brian. *The Implications of Literacy: Written Language and Models of Interpretation in the Eleventh and Twelfth Centuries*. Princeton, NJ: Princeton University Press, 1983.

Talmon, Shemaryahu. "Synonymous Readings in the Textual Traditions of the Old Testament." *ScrHeir* 8 (1961): 335–83.

Talmon, Shemaryahu. "Oral Tradition and Written Transmission, or the Heard and the Seen Word in Judaism of the Second Temple Period." Pages 121–58 in *Jesus and the Oral Gospel Tradition*. Edited by Henry Wansbrough. JSNTSup 64. Sheffield: Sheffield Academic, 1991.

Thatcher, Tom. "Textual Communities." Pages 417–18 in *The Dictionary of the Bible and Ancient Media*. Edited by Tom Thatcher, Chris Keith, Raymond F. Person, Jr., and Elsie R. Stern. London: Bloomsbury, 2017.

Thatcher, Tom. "Great Tradition/Little Tradition." Pages 162–63 in *The Dictionary of the Bible and Ancient Media*. Edited by Tom Thatcher, Chris Keith, Raymond F. Person, Jr., and Elsie R. Stern. London: Bloomsbury, 2017.

Thomas, Samuel I. *The "Mysteries" of Qumran: Mystery, Secrecy, and Esotericism in the Dead Sea Scrolls*. EJL 25. Atlanta, GA: SBL, 2009.

Tov, Emanuel. *Textual Criticism of the Hebrew Bible*. 3rd ed. Minneapolis, MN: Fortress, 2012.

Wise, Michael O. *Language and Literacy in Roman Judaea: A Study of the Bar Kokhba Documents*. AYBRL. New Haven, CT: Yale University Press, 2015.

CHAPTER 5

Ritual Studies and the Dead Sea Scrolls: A Review

Michael DeVries and Jutta Jokiranta

1 Introduction

Much of ritual studies concerns mapping out different dimensions of rituals, defining how ritual activities are different from other ways of acting, and deciding what their study can reveal of human relations in general. Rituals do not need to be religious in character. Ritual creates a social body, but the social body is always also ambivalent, disharmonious.

Ritual is a form of communication. But ritual is also much more. In ritual studies, the multiplicity of definitions of ritual as well as various perspectives to study ritual makes it difficult to say anything definite about what this "more" is.[1] The field of ritual studies has been rising but also diversifying. We shall first introduce a few theorists and directions that ritual studies have taken[2] before we evaluate how this is relevant for media studies, and then look deeper into the Dead Sea Scrolls and their ritual investigations.

2 Rise of Ritual Studies and Theories

The dichotomy of ritual and myth, practice and belief, colored much of earlier scholarship. Ritual was often perceived to be a practice of primitive societies, superstition without higher theology, redundancy without significance. While some 19th and early 20th century theorists debated whether ritual was the

---

1 For definitions and the art of defining ritual, see, e.g., Jens Kreinath, Jan Snoek, and Michael Stausberg, eds., *Theorizing Rituals: Issues, Topics, Approaches, Concepts*, Studies in the History of Religion 114:1 (Leiden: Brill, 2006), 3–98; Ronald L. Grimes, *The Craft of Ritual Studies* (Oxford: Oxford University Press, 2014), 185–210.

2 Our emphasis is on recent theorists who have contributed to ritual studies and continued to refine the work of the late 19th century–early 20th century classics. For a more comprehensive research history of ritual studies, see the work of Catherine Bell and Ronald Grimes (references below).

© MICHAEL DEVRIES AND JUTTA JOKIRANTA, 2023 | DOI:10.1163/9789004537804_006

RITUAL STUDIES AND THE DEAD SEA SCROLLS 157

expression of myth or the other way around,[3] this dichotomy is now largely abandoned as artificial or false. Ritual is valued as forming the self and its well-being, as a means to understand culture and human relations, embracing both symbolic and non-symbolic aspects of human behavior. This is due to larger changes—the linguistic turn that acknowledged the significance of the human way of conceptualization things for understanding how humans make sense of reality, as well as materiality and cognitive turns that see humans as embodied and embedded beings whose ideas and belief worlds cannot be separated from their expressions and mediation in material form from one setting to another.[4]

A very common perspective on ritual has been the way in which rituals create or advance social cohesion, solidarity, cooperation, social order, feelings of belonging, wellbeing, or common ingroup identity. Starting from Émile Durkheim, society has been seen to create itself around a toteme, a common sacred practice or value.[5] On the other hand, rituals can be arenas of hierarchies, boundary-making, crises, and social conflict. Victor Turner's famous distinction between structure and communitas stressed the underlying contradictions and conflicts and showed that the experience of a communitas was often only temporary, confined to the state of liminality.[6] Catherine Bell notes the ambiguity of symbols employed in rituals: "Ritual does not necessarily cultivate or inculcate shared beliefs for the sake of solidarity and social control."[7] She emphasizes ritualization as a strategy for constructing power relations (see below). There is also a research tradition that identifies a correlation between the type of ritual and the form of society or organization. For example, according to Harvey Whitehouse's modes of religiosity theory, too much dull ritual leads to factions in the religious tradition, and too much infrequent intense

---

3 For these debates, see, e.g., Robert A. Segal, "Myth and Ritual," in *Theorizing Rituals*, 101–21; Catherine Bell, *Ritual: Perspectives and Dimensions* (New York, NY: Oxford University Press, 1997), 3–22. Bell stresses that dichotomies are seldom differentiations of two equal terms.

4 For example, Steve W. Fuller, *The Cognitive Turn: Sociological and Psychological Perspectives on Science* (Dordrecht: Kluwer, 1989).

5 Émile Durkheim, *The Elementary Forms of the Religious Life*, 5th ed. (London: George Allen & Unwin, 1964 [1912]). The COVID-19 pandemic could be seen as a global test to see if social order is risked—and how—when various types of collective rituals, from religious liturgy to family celebrations and rock festivals, are on hold or postponed.

6 Victor Turner, *The Ritual Process: Structure and Anti-Structure* (London: Routledge & Kegan, 1969). For both perspectives, ritual as solidarity and ritual as power, see Ursula Rao, "Ritual in Society," in *Theorizing Rituals*, 143–60.

7 Catherine Bell, *Ritual Theory, Ritual Practice* (New York, NY: Oxford University Press, 2009 [1992]), 187.

experience leads to loss of transmission and continuity.[8] Rituals are never merely places for (re-establishing) social order.[9]

Another common approach to ritual is via its association with communication.[10] Again, Durkheim is often referred to as approaching ritual for its expressive function, as a medium of emotions.[11] Turner too included this aspect in his work and saw rituals as composed of multivocal symbols.[12] Ritual communicates cultural and cosmic information and provides a meaning-making platform. According to Clifford Geertz, ritual is a window into the worldview and an invitation to this worldview, a desired state of affairs.[13] But the communication approach too has been counterbalanced by its challenge: ritual does not need to be understood in order to work. In its extreme, ritual is pure action, without meaning, as Frits Staal argued.[14] For Roy Rappaport, ritual communicates both "self-referential" information (immediate information about the state of a person in the structural system) and culturally specific "canonical" information (general and enduring information not encoded by participants); rituals generate and communicate an unquestioned order of things, sacred reality. Conventional and arbitrary becomes natural and necessary by mere doing.[15] James Laidlaw and Caroline Humphrey emphasize how

---

8   Harvey Whitehouse, *Arguments and Icons: Divergent Modes of Religiosity*, Oxford Studies in Social and Cultural Anthropology (Oxford: Oxford University Press, 2000). Whitehouse's theory is based on the age-old church-sect distinction but grounds it in different encoding systems of human memory. Another example of relating ritual to social organization could be Mary Douglas, *Natural Symbols* (New York, NY: Random House, 1973), with her grid and group model: when grid (rules) and group (identification to community) are strong, there tend to be greater amount of ritual.

9   See further discussion on social control, see Bell, *Ritual Theory, Ritual Practice*, 169–81.

10   For example, Günter Thomas, "Communication," in *Theorizing Rituals*, 321–43.

11   Florian Jeserich, "An Invitation to 'Theorizing' Theorizing Rituals: Some Suggestions for Using the Indexes," in *Theorizing Rituals*, 693.

12   Victor Turner, "Symbols and Social Experience in Religious Ritual," *Studia Missionalia* 23 (1974): 1–21; idem, "Ritual as Communication and Potency: A Ndembu Case Study," in *Symbols and Society: Essays on Belief Systems in Action*, ed. Caroline E. Hill, Southern Anthropological Society Proceedings 9 (Athens, GA: University of Georgia Press, 1975), 58–81.

13   Clifford Geertz, *The Interpretation of Cultures: Selected Essays* (New York, NY: Basic Books, 1973), esp. 112, 126–27.

14   Frits Staal, *Rules without Meaning: Ritual, Mantras, and the Human Sciences* (New York, NY: Peter Lang, 1989), esp. 131.

15   Roy A. Rappaport, *Ecology, Meaning, and Religion* (Richmond, CA: North Atlantic Books, 1979); idem, *Ritual and Religion in the Making of Humanity* (Cambridge: Cambridge University Press, 1999). Rappaport's definition of ritual as "the performance of more or less invariant sequences of formal acts and utterances not entirely encoded by the performers" (*Ritual and Religion*, 24) emphasizes that ritual act does not need to be

ritual participants accept prior prescriptions and stipulations—the ritual act does not rely on their intentions.[16] With a language analogy, Thomas Lawson and Robert McCauley identified a "ritual grammar," intuitive knowledge that ritual practitioners have about the actors, instruments, and objects (patients) of action in rituals, but the emphasis is on participants' intuition concerning why the ritual works, not what it means.[17] Speech acts theorists stress that words accomplish the things that are said, not merely pass on information.[18] Performance-theoretical scholars have viewed rituals as part of a wide array of human activity, comparable to drama or theater.[19] Approaching ritual as performance has not produced a unified theory: some see rituals as a communicative performance, expressing moral values, whereas others stress its alienation to communication and effects on changing people's perceptions.[20]

"encoded", interpreted and defined by the participants. Rappaport draws away from symbolic and functional approaches and promotes formality and non-instrumentality: "Ritual is a unique structure although none of its elements—performance, invariance, formality and so on—belongs to it alone" (*ibid.*, 26). Although elements are not unique, their relations are. Yet, Rappaport does not exclude meaning-making in rituals; rather he distinguishes different levels of meaning-making: low level where we make distinctions between things in the world; middle level where we draw similarities between things, and high level where we experience unity and identity with things most significant (see *ibid.*, 70–74). Rappaport is also known for his ecological interpretation of ritual as management of scarce resources, Roy A. Rappaport, *Pigs for the Ancestors: Ritual in the Ecology of a New Guinea People* (New Haven, NY: Yale University Press, 1967).

16   James A. Laidlaw and Caroline Humphrey, *The Archetypal Actions of Ritual: An Essay on Ritual as Action Illustrated by the Jain Rite of Worship* (Oxford: Clarendon Press, 1994).

17   E. Thomas Lawson and Robert N. McCauley, *Rethinking Religion: Connecting and Culture* (Cambridge: Cambridge University Press, 1990); Robert N. McCauley and E. Thomas Lawson, *Bringing Ritual to Mind: Psychological Foundations of Cultural Forms* (Cambridge: Cambridge University Press, 2002).

18   John R. Searle, *Speech Acts: An Essay in the Philosophy of Language* (Cambridge: Cambridge University Press, 1969); John L. Austin, *How to Do Things with Words: The William James Lectures Delivered at Harvard University in 1955* (Oxford: Oxford University Press, 1976).

19   For example, Victor Turner, *From Ritual to Theatre: The Human Seriousness of Play*, Performance Studies Series 1 (New York, NY: PAJ Publications, 1982).

20   Bell, *Ritual: Perspectives and Dimensions*, 72–76. For a helpful review and evaluation of major performance theorists, Goffman, Turner, Schneider, and also Bell's view on performance, see Ronald L. Grimes, "Performance Theory and the Study of Ritual," *New Approaches to the Study of Religion*, vol. 2: *Textual, Comparative, Sociological, and Cognitive Approaches*, eds. Peter Antes, Armin W. Geertz, and Randi R. Warni (Berlin: De Gruyter, 2008), 109–38.

According to these common themes, we could present this preliminary working model of the most prominent approaches to ritual (Figure 5.1):[21]

FIGURE 5.1
Common approaches to ritual: social cohesion, social order, and solidarity; social control, (resolution of) conflict, hierarchy, power; communication, symbolic information, meaning, performance as communication; change, efficacy, experience, performance as action

Ritual studies emerged as its own discipline from the 1960s onwards.[22] In the two-volume *Theorizing Rituals*, an annotated bibliography starts from 1966, and Jens Kreinath, Jan Snoek, and Michael Stausberg distinguish between "study of rituals," which often includes descriptive, *emic* approaches, from "ritual studies," which seeks a comparative, *etic* approach but which has, in their view, remained undertheorized.[23] The title "theorizing" rituals sends a message that the time of grand theories is over and scholars will do better in explaining *some* aspect of ritual or human behavior.[24] The volume has a section on "Clas-

---

21 This model owes but is not identical to Risto Uro, "Rituaalit, ympäristö ja uskonto—kognitiivinen näkökulma tutkimusalojen vuoropuheluun," *Uskonnontutkija* 10.1 (2021): 1–21 (in Finnish; "Rituals, Environment and Religion—A Cognitive Perspective to Dialogue between Disciplines").
22 *Journal of Ritual Studies* was founded in 1987.
23 Jens Kreinath, Jan Snoek, and Michael Stausberg, eds., *Theorizing Rituals: Annotated Bibliography of Ritual Theory, 1966–2005*, Studies in the History of Religion 114:2 (Leiden: Brill, 2007); Jens Kreinath, Jan Snoek, and Michael Stausberg, eds., *Theorizing Rituals: Issues, Topics, Approaches, Concepts*, Studies in the History of Religion 114:1 (Leiden: Brill, 2006).
24 Jens Kreinath, Jan Snoek, and Michael Stausberg, "Ritual Studies, Ritual Theory, Theorizing Rituals—An Introductory Essay," in *Theorizing Rituals*, xv–xxvii (esp. xxiii, n. 12). Similarly, Ilkka Pyysiäinen, *How Religion Works: Towards a New Cognitive Science of Religion*,

sical Topics Revisited," but also "Theoretical Approaches" and "Paradigmatic Concepts," and theorizing is presented as a reflective, open-ended practice where relevant theories are operationalized for a given task but also critiqued, revised, and placed into competition with each other.

Catherine Bell has been one influential theorist from the 1990s onwards, although her work is not always the easiest to read.[25] In her 1992 *Ritual Theory, Ritual Practice*,[26] Bell first provides a critique of the previous practice of approaching ritual by seeking to identify some sort of fundamental element in human history or universal structure underlying religion. Often, while working with the dichotomy between thought and action (or belief and practice, myth and ritual, individual and society), ritual was, on the one hand, distinguished from thought but, on the other hand, put to the role of integrating and reconciling thought and action (or the theorists provided the "thought" of making sense of the "action"). Theorists furthermore find what they set out to identify, and thus often exercise circular argumentation, according to Bell. When theorists look for contradictions, they find them. "The notion of ritual that resolves a fundamental social contradiction can be seen as a type of myth legitimating the whole apparatus of ritual studies."[27] Similarly, performance theorists and others who look at ritual as communication objectify the action as a text to be read and decoded. Equally unuseful are the attempts to define ritual and distinguish it from other social practices like liturgy, ceremony, or drama, reducing ritual into some ready-made, closed object.

As a cure, Bell introduces the study of "ritualization," that is, of the very processes by which social dynamics becomes differentiated and actions come to be recognized as distinct. Ritualization reveals the strategic ways of acting in a particular context and situation. The ways in which activities are differentiated and privileged are culturally and situationally specific and cannot be generalized, though Bell does mention *potential* ways such as formality, repetition, traditionality. Ritualization involves nuanced differences to other types of acting. In the latter part of her *Ritual Theory, Ritual Practice*, Bell investigates the relationship between ritualization and the construction of power. Rituals

---

Cognition and Culture Book Series 1 (Leiden: Brill, 2001), viii: a theory of ritual is not possible, but theories about ritual are.

25   Cf. Grimes, "Performance Theory and the Study of Ritual," 123: According to Grimes, it is often difficult to know if Bell presents her own views or that of other scholars or ritual participants. Another difficulty lies in the very abstract nature of Bell's work (esp. 1992 book); when examples (referring to other studies) are given, it is presumed that the reader already knows them.

26   Bell, *Ritual Theory, Ritual Practice*. See also Catherine M. Bell, "Ritual (Further Considerations)," *Encyclopedia of Religion*, 2nd ed., ed. Lindsay Jones (Detroit, MI: Macmillan, 2005), 11:7848–56.

27   Bell, *Ritual Theory, Ritual Practice*, 37.

do not *reflect* power relations; they themselves *produce* and *negotiate* them. Influenced by Michel Foucault's conception of power, Bell sees ritualization as a strategy for constituting power relations: participants embody dominance and subordination without realizing it. Ritualization empowers those who control the ritual practice: they derive their authority from external sources. Yet, here is also the limit of ritualization: the power of the dominant can break if the cycle of re-creation is broken. Subordination, on the other hand, relies on an imagined consensus of the participants and their consent to participate. Therefore, the participants also have an opportunity to resist or appropriate their consent. Ritualization may produce a distancing between one's private and social self.[28]

In her *Ritual: Perspectives and Dimensions* from 1997, Bell gives a more systematic review of theories. She also provides a six-class categorization of ritual activities, with examples of each category, as well as characteristics of "ritual-like" activities. This latter section confirms her approach to ritualization as a strategic way of acting, emphasizing that these characteristics—formalism, traditionalism, invariance, rule-governance, sacral symbolism, performance—are only "an initial lexicon" of the possible ways of ritualizing.[29] In the last part of the book, Bell reviews theories that have sought to explain ritual density (and differences in modern and pre-modern societies), ritual change and innovation. As her last chapter "Ritual Reification" exemplifies, Bell's analysis is often at a meta-level about how theorists have approached their subject matter, and how the notion of ritual has emerged and then affected practices we see today.

In Bell's work, ritualization does not need to be restricted to religious practice. Similarly, Ronald Grimes makes use of the concept of ritualization as a tool for seeing *degrees* by which actions may become ritualized, constructed as ritual. "'Ritualizing' is the act of cultivating and inventing rites."[30] However, ritualization has also been used in a more specific sense, of cognitive mechanism that plays a role in relieving anxiety in the face of ambiguous stimuli or sense of threat: according to Pascal Boyer and Pierre Liénard, at least some ritual actions demand focused attention and are thus the opposite of routinization.[31]

---

28 Bell, *Ritual Theory, Ritual Practice*, Chapter 9, "The Power of Ritualization," is the most revealing in this respect.

29 Bell, *Ritual: Perspectives and Dimensions*, 138.

30 Grimes, *The Craft of Ritual Studies*, 189–97 (quotation at 193). Grimes refers to his use of ritualization as a family resemblance or fuzzy set theory.

31 Pascal Boyer and Pierre Liénard, "Why Ritualized Behavior? Precaution Systems and Action Parsing in Developmental, Pathological and Cultural Rituals," *Behavioral and Brain Sciences* 29 (2006): 595–613.

The mechanism also includes the action parsing system, where lower-level actions gain priority (not just 'drinking' but 'stretching hand in order to take the cup, pouring water into the cup, lifting the cup, etc.'); focusing on detailed actions may send relief signals to the brain. This perspective connects ritual to resolving an *individual's* sense of conflict, not a societal conflict as in the Durkheimian tradition.

Cognitive theories have greatly increased in number during recent years. Cognitive science of religion has been launched as a new multidisciplinary field of study, although it often is based on previous traditional dichotomies or classifications.[32] Many theories deal with ritual, too. The emphasis is on efficacy beliefs: why do ritual actions feel good or convincing or uniting (e.g., bodies as media of communication), what is the mechanism of magical thinking, and how is ritual represented in the mind.[33] Other central questions address ritual's role in enhancing prosocial behavior.[34]

Grimes is one of the few to think through what "theorizing" means in ritual studies.[35] Some authors are more easily understood as presenting a theory, with well-defined (technical) terminology and structured diagrams (such as E. Thomas Lawson and Robert McCauley).[36] Other authors may present ethnographies or essays from which it is much harder to distill a clearly articulated theory (such as Pierre Bourdieu).[37] Neither do readers know if they are

---

32   For a recent introduction, see Claire White, *An Introduction to the Cognitive Science of Religion: Connecting Evolution, Brain, Cognition and Culture* (London: Routledge, 2021).

33   Efficacy can be understood as creating concrete changes in the world, or as Rappaport, *Ritual and Religion in the Making of Humanity*, sees it, as creating non-physical effects: "The point of importance here is that if the occult efficacy of ritual rests in whole or in part upon words (both in folk and analytic theory) then the distinction between ritual as communication and ritual as efficacious action breaks down" (50; see also 108–13). See further, William S. Sax, Johannes Quack, and Jan Weinhold, eds., *The Problem of Ritual Efficacy*, Oxford Ritual Studies (Oxford: Oxford University Press, 2010). For other themes, see Jesper Sørensen, *A Cognitive Theory of Magic* (London: AltaMira Press, 2007); Whitehouse, *Arguments and Icons*; McCauley and Lawson, *Bringing Ritual to Mind*.

34   For example, Panagiotis Mitkidis, Pierre Liénard, Kristoffer L. Nielbo, and Jesper Sørensen, "Does Goal-Demotion Enhance Cooperation?," *Journal of Cognition and Culture* 14 (2014): 263–72; Joseph Bulbulia and Richard Sosis, "Signaling Theory and the Evolution of Religious Cooperation," *Religion* 41 (2011): 363–88.

35   Grimes, *The Craft of Ritual Studies*, 165–184.

36   Lawson and McCauley, *Rethinking Religion*; McCauley and Lawson, *Bringing Ritual to Mind*. Cognitive Science of Religion has openly sought to present testable, specific theories, and put these theories into empirical testing, both in (cross-cultural) settings and historically, collecting evidence for a certain question; see e.g., White, *An Introduction to the Cognitive Science of Religion*, 21–23.

37   Bourdieu is associated with the theory of practice but much of his work is presented in case studies, e.g., Pierre Bourdieu, *The Bachelor's Ball* (Cambridge: Polity, 2008); idem,

supposed to "apply" a theory, "test" a theory, or perhaps "use" it heuristically.[38] Grimes ends up preferring the metaphor of theorizing as *craft*, art-like practice where human imagination is strongly and openly employed. He highlights which metaphors of ritual have fallen out of fashion (e.g., "structure," implying something static), and which are more appealing (e.g., "web," implying something interconnected). Being aware of the underlying metaphors, images, and analogies in each theory helps us to see what is included and what is excluded. A good theory should be able to incorporate "static elements (using, e.g., mechanical metaphors), internal dynamics (using, e.g., narrative and dramatic metaphors), interactions with their contexts (using, e.g., complex systems, cybernetic, ecological, or cognitive metaphors)."[39] Grimes does not provide a typology or categorization of rituals but instead offers six "modes of ritual" (ritualization, decorum, ceremony, magic, liturgy, celebration) as layers of ritual, several of which may be present in one rite. These help the investigator to "mine" the rite and go further into comparing that activity to other activities.[40] In the end of his book, Grimes provides a sort of guidebook for students for asking questions of various elements and dynamics of ritual.

3 Ritual Studies and Media Studies

What then does ritual have to do with media? *The Dictionary of the Bible and Ancient Media* from 2017[41] does not include an entry for "ritual." Instead this rich volume includes several entries that can be seen as covering particular ritual practices, such as "Blessings and Curses," "Circumcision," "Exorcism," "Fasting," "Hymns," "Initiation Rituals," "Oaths," "Pilgrimage," "Purification Rituals," "Sabbath," "Song," "Torah Reading," "War Rituals," or entries that illuminate ritual behavior from a certain perspective, such as "Collective Memory/ Social Memory," "Master Commemorative Narrative," "Performance Arena," "Schema," "Synagogue," "Temple," "Worship." Already this list shows that rituals can be approached from multiple perspectives and are relevant for media studies for various purposes. Not very many articles in the volume, however, make explicit the ways in which their subject is related to media or communication.

     Distinction: A Social Critique of the Judgement of Taste, trans. Richard Nice (London: Routledge, 2010).

38   Cf. Grimes, *The Craft of Ritual Studies*, 172.

39   Grimes, *The Craft of Ritual Studies*, 178–83 (183).

40   Grimes, *The Craft of Ritual Studies*, 203–7.

41   Tom Thatcher, Chris Keith, Raymond F. Person Jr., and Elsie R. Stern, eds., *Dictionary of the Bible and Ancient Media* (New York, NY: Bloomsbury, 2017).

The volume is focused on issues of orality and textuality and illuminating how these concepts meet and mingle in different contexts and phenomena.

Using the model of ritual approaches outlined above, we may think of at least three (partly overlapping) ways that ritual and media are interconnected, and a fourth one emerging from media studies.

The first in a general, wide perspective: ritual is one medium, among other human practices, where communication takes place. It is not a strictly defined medium, though, since it may include a variety of other media, such as oral speech, bodily movements, artefacts (with writing or not). But often ritual is considered to have special or unique properties that the other media do not have, which justifies an investigation of its own. This approach may include various sub-questions, such as what information is transmitted via ritual events; to what extent the ritual succeeds in transmitting information; why ritual makes such an effective means of communication; which aspects in the ritual actually create the knowledge that is explicitly or implicitly present; how various communication channels come together, meet, or compete in rituals.

Secondly, it may be relevant to analyze whether the major mode of information offered in the ritual is symbolic or non-symbolic. Symbolic communication has often been of major interest, leading to questions such as "What does this practice mean?" But the non-symbolic may be equally important, leading to questions such as "What effects does this practice have?"

Thirdly, it may be relevant to focus on ritual practices in society as rituals-of-confirmation or rituals-of-resistance. Thus, rituals have a specific function of maintaining social order or offering means to resist prevailing order. They are the "subtext" of the society and its tensions and identities.[42]

Fourthly, rituals themselves are represented, culturally inherited, and socially learned via media such as texts, visual art, and architecture. In modern media studies, rituals are viewed not only as *mediated* via novel or expanding technology, but also as *mediatized*. This concept is variously defined but here it refers to the multifaceted ways in which rituals become modified and reconstructed to adapt to rules and logic of media, or the ways in which media may engage in enacting an event in ritualistic ways and take on functions of rituals, such as creating an imagined community or finding meaning and purpose.[43]

---

42   Simon Cottle, "Mediatized Rituals: Beyond Manufacturing Consent," *Media, Culture & Society* 28 (2006): 411–32.

43   Cottle, "Mediatized Rituals," 415–16. See further, Nick Couldry, *Media Rituals: A Critical Approach* (London: Routledge, 2003); Stig Hjarvard, *The Mediatization of Culture and Society* (London: Routledge, 2012); Nick Couldry and Andreas Hepp, "Conceptualizing Mediatization: Contexts, Traditions, Arguments," *Communication Theory* 23 (2013): 191–202; Johanna Sumiala, "Mediatized Ritual—Expanding the Field in the Study of Media and

Mediatization may also refer to the way in which individuals employ and make use of media as part of their everyday (ritualized) practices, meaning that media is seen as part of their "normal," true, or meaningful reality.[44] Although ancient technologies differ from modern ones, this perspective may lead to asking to what extent rituals are represented in various media and different kinds of media, how detailed or not those representations are, how ritual representation influence ritual practices or new ritual enactments, how people use media (such as texts) in their everyday practices and what role the media play in their lives.

4   Ritual Theory and the Study of the Dead Sea Scrolls

Over the past thirty years, the field of ritual studies has experienced a significant expansion as ritual theories have found inroads into the fields of anthropology, sociology, and religion. During this time, ritual theorists have fruitfully explored various facets of ritual—structural, phenomenological, functional, performative, and, most recently, cognitive—in order to gain insight into the symbolic and non-symbolic meaning of ritual practice within a particular cultural context. Ritual theories have likewise found application in studies engaging both the Hebrew Bible and the New Testament.[45] Of particular significance

---

Ritual," *Sociology Compass* 8 (2014): 939–47. Bell, *Ritual: Perspectives and Dimensions*, 242–51, discusses "Media and Message" largely from a ritual scholar's point of view, e.g., video documentation of Vedic ritual. See also Ronald L. Grimes, *Rite Out of Place: Ritual, Media, and the Arts* (Oxford: Oxford University Press, 2006); Ronald L. Grimes, Ute Hüsken, Udo Simon, and Eric Venbrux, eds., *Ritual, Media, and Conflict* (Oxford: Oxford University Press, 2011).

44   Xi Cui, "Mediatized Rituals: Understanding the Media in the Age of Deep Mediatization," *International Journal of Communication* (Online) (2019): 4155–68. According to Cui (p. 4163), mediatized rituals are "people's ritualistic orientation in their mundane lives that privileges the social reality constructed through ensembles of technologies that collect, process, and act on data and metadata." The use of the terms "ritual," "ritualistic," and "ritualized" in media studies seems vague and ill-defined. They often seem to refer to people's search for something sacred, true, or meaningful, or something that brings people together—we might often replace "ritual" with "religion," or "religious."

45   On application to the Hebrew Bible, see Frank H. Gorman, *Ideology of Ritual: Space, Time and Status in the Priestly Theology*, JSOTSup 91 (Sheffield: JSOT Press, 1990); Ithamar Gruenwald, *Ritual and Ritual Theory in Ancient Israel*, BRLA 10 (Leiden: Brill, 2003); David Janzen, *The Social Meanings of Sacrifice in the Hebrew Bible: A Study of Four Writings*, BZAW 344 (Berlin: De Gruyter, 2004); Gerald A. Klingbeil, *Bridging the Gap: Ritual and Ritual Texts in the Bible*, BBRSup 1 (Winona Lake, IN: Eisenbrauns, 2007); James W. Watts, *Ritual and Rhetoric in Leviticus: From Sacrifice to Scripture* (Cambridge: Cambridge University Press, 2007); Rodney A. Werline, "Prayer, Politics, and Social Vision in Daniel 9,"

has been the pioneering work of Bell and Grimes.[46] Only recently, however, has there been an attempt to apply the insights gained from ritual studies to corpora outside of these collections, including the Qumran corpus.[47]

Regarding the application of ritual theories to the study of the Scrolls, Bell's has been the most influential to date. Foremost has been the application of her proposed six-class typology of ritual actions to the categorization of ritual practices preserved in the Qumran corpus: rites of passage; calendrical and commemorative rites; rites of exchange and communion; rites of affliction;

---

in *Seeking the Favor of God*, vol. 2: *The Development of Penitential Prayer in Second Temple Judaism*, eds. Mark J. Boda, Daniel K. Falk, and Rodney A. Werline, EJL 22 (Atlanta, GA: SBL 2007), 17–32; Bryan D. Bibb, *Ritual Words and Narrative Worlds in the Book of Leviticus*, LHBOTS 480 (New York, NY: T&T Clark, 2009); David P. Wright, "Ritual Theory, Ritual Texts, and the Priestly-Holiness Writings of the Pentateuch," in *Social Theory and the Study of Israelite Religion: Essays in Retrospect and Prospect*, ed. Saul M. Olyan, RBS 71 (Atlanta, GA: SBL 2012), 195–216; Nathan MacDonald, ed., *Ritual Innovation and the Hebrew Bible and Early Judaism*, BZAW 468 (Berlin: De Gruyter, 2018); Cat Quine, *Casting Down the Hosts of Heaven: The Rhetoric of Ritual Failure in the Polemic Against the Host of Heaven*, OtSt 78 (Leiden: Brill, 2020); Samuel E. Balentine, ed., *The Oxford Handbook on Ritual and Worship in the Hebrew Bible* (New York, NY: Oxford University Press, 2020). Regarding the New Testament, see Risto Uro et al., eds., *The Oxford Handbook of Early Christian Ritual* (Oxford: Oxford University Press, 2019); Risto Uro, *Ritual and Christian Beginnings: A Socio-Cognitive Analysis* (Oxford: Oxford University Press, 2016); Richard E. DeMaris, *The New Testament in Its Ritual World* (London: Routledge, 2008).

46   Bell, *Ritual Theory, Ritual Practice*; idem, *Ritual: Perspectives and Dimensions*; Ronald L. Grimes, *Beginnings of Ritual Studies*, Rev. ed., SCR (Columbia: University of South Carolina Press, 1995); and recently idem, *The Craft of Ritual Studies*.

47   For example, see James R. Davila, "Ritual in the Jewish Pseudepigrapha," in *Anthropology and Biblical Studies: Avenues of Approach*, ed. Louise J. Lawrence and Mario I. Aguilar (Leiden: Deo Publishing, 2004), 158–83; Rodney A. Werline, "Reflections on Penitential Prayer: Definition and Form," in *Seeking the Favor of God*, vol. 2: *The Development of Penitential Prayer in Second Temple Judaism*, eds. Mark J. Boda, Daniel K. Falk, and Rodney A. Werline, EJL 22 (Atlanta, GA: SBL 2007), 209–25; idem, "Ritual, Order and the Construction of an Audience in *1 Enoch* 1–36," *DSD* 22 (2015): 325–41; James R. Davila, *Liturgical Works*, ECDSS (Grand Rapids, MI: Eerdmans, 2000); John J. Collins and Robert A. Kugler, eds., *Religion in the Dead Sea Scrolls* (Grand Rapids, MI: Eerdmans, 2000). For an early application of ritual studies to the scrolls, see Steven Weitzman, "Revisiting Myth and Ritual in Early Judaism," *DSD* 4 (1997): 21–54. For an overview of the benefit and impact of ritual studies on the field of the Dead Sea Scrolls, see Russell C. D. Arnold, "The Dead Sea Scrolls, Qumran, and Ritual Studies," in *The Dead Sea Scrolls in Context: Integrating the Dead Sea Scrolls in the Study of Ancient Texts, Languages, and Cultures*, eds. Armin Lange, Emanuel Tov, and Matthias Weigold, VTSup 140 (Leiden: Brill, 2011), 2:547–62; Eileen M. Schuller, "Ritual and Worship at Qumran," in *The Oxford Handbook of Ritual and Worship in the Hebrew Bible*, ed. Samuel E. Balentine (New York, NY: Oxford University Press, 2020), 365–77; Judith H. Newman, "Ritual and Worship in Early Judaism," in *The Oxford Handbook of Ritual and Worship*, 393–409.

rites of feasting, fasting, and festivals; and political rituals.[48] Additionally, Bell's concepts of "ritual density," the amount of ritual activity in a particular culture as a fundamental aspect of context, and "ritual change," the amount of variation and innovation within ritual practice over time, have likewise been brought to bear on the study of the Scrolls.[49] It is with these particular studies that we will begin our survey.

In 2002, in what was one of the first studies to substantively engage ritual theory, Robert Kugler sought to catalogue and interpret ritual practices preserved in the Qumran corpus employing Bell's six-fold typology of ritual practices as a framework.[50] Kugler's conclusion was twofold. First, the evidence overwhelmingly demonstrated a community characterized by what Bell has characterized as "ritual density" noting that "the people of Qumran patterned their actions in 'more or less invariant sequences of formal acts and utterances' aimed at bringing them closer to God."[51] Rituals, according to Kugler, were so pervasive within community life that every facet of experience was imbued with a religious quality. Second, and no less significant, Kugler highlighted the variation and innovation of ritual expressed in the Qumran texts as opposed to the ritual practices of their Jewish contemporaries, most notably in the areas of initiation rites, calendrical rites, and rites of affliction in particular. Kugler suggested that the intensity and variation of ritual at Qumran represented an effort by the Qumran community to establish a new orthodoxy vis-à-vis the rejected orthopraxy of the Jerusalem temple and its priesthood, mediated through a new interpretation of constitutive authoritative texts.[52] Kugler concluded that the ritual practices at Qumran were hegemonic in that they created a new religious reality, one in which community members were inextricably connected to the will of God for the cosmos while simultaneously separated from those who were considered a part of a world profaned and defiled.[53]

---

48 Bell, *Ritual: Perspectives and Dimensions*, 93–137. For application of Bell's typology to liturgical texts, see Daniel K. Falk, "Liturgical Texts," in *T&T Clark Companion to the Dead Sea Scrolls*, eds. George J. Brooke and Charlotte Hempel, with the assistance of Michael DeVries and Drew Longacre (London: Bloomsbury T&T Clark, 2019), 423–34.

49 Bell, *Ritual: Perspectives and Dimensions*, 173–252.

50 Robert A. Kugler, "Making All Experience Religious: The Hegemony of Ritual at Qumran," *JSJ* 33 (2002): 131–52.

51 Kugler, "Making All Experience Religious," 149. Here, Kugler is utilizing a definition of ritual from Roy Rappaport. See Rappaport, *Ecology, Meaning, and Religion*, 175; idem, *Ritual and Religion in the Making of Humanity*, 24.

52 Kugler, "Making All Experience Religious," 151–52. See Bell, *Ritual: Perspectives and Dimensions*, 205–9; Brian Stock, *The Implications of Literacy* (Princeton, NJ: Princeton University Press, 1983).

53 Kugler, "Making All Experience Religious," 152.

In his 2006 monograph, the most extensive study to date, Russell Arnold undertook an extensive analysis of liturgical texts within the Qumran corpus utilizing Bell's typology of ritual.[54] Differing from Kugler, Arnold sought to examine the relationship between ritual and ideology within the context of the extensive liturgical practices of the Qumran community. For Arnold, liturgical prayer, rather than being a replacement for sacrifice, served a larger sociological function. It was instead a way of establishing and reinforcing group boundaries, providing assurance and justification for God's election of the community, and fostering structure and significance to society and the world writ large.[55] Liturgical practices, therefore, functioned as an instrument for the shaping and reinforcement of group identity and ideology within the Qumran community, with the annual initiation and covenant ceremony in 1QS being a main vehicle for shaping the identity of the community and affirming each member's place in it. Additionally, Arnold argued that the inclusion of curses, apotropaic prayers, and incantations within the corpus is suggestive of not only the belief of a perceived threat facing the community in an age of wickedness, but also that liturgy functioned as a weapon against the forces of darkness.[56] In the end, for Arnold, the extensive liturgical tradition at Qumran fulfills a social function, the formation of a community in which all aspects of communal life were directed toward maintaining perfect holiness in obedience to God's commands and the coming day of restoration.

In addition to exploring ways in which ritual practice has shaped social identity and cohesion, matters of ritual purity have likewise garnered significant attention within Scrolls scholarship, much of which has been directed towards the prescribed practices described in the texts. While matters of purity and purification in general are much studied ritual practices, often these studies focus on reconstructing the details of the prescriptions and practices and on their relationship with one another and those found in the Priestly strata of the Hebrew Bible or later Rabbinic literature.[57] Oftentimes assessments are made concerning a coherent system of Qumran ritual purity practices or the

---

54 Russell C. D. Arnold, *The Social Role of Liturgy in the Religion of the Qumran Community*, STDJ 60 (Leiden: Brill, 2006).

55 Arnold, *The Social Role of Liturgy*, 234.

56 Arnold, *The Social Role of Liturgy*, 234–35. On prayer and liturgy as a weapon in the eschatological war, see Daniel K. Falk, "Prayer, Liturgy, and War," in *The War Scroll, Violence, War and Peace in the Dead Sea Scrolls and Related Literature: Essays in Honour of Martin G. Abegg on the Occasion of His 65th Birthday*, ed. Kipp Davis et al., STDJ 115 (Leiden: Brill, 2016), 285–89.

57 For example, see Hannah K. Harrington, *The Purity Texts*, CQS 5 (London: T&T Clark, 2004); Ian C. Werrett, *Ritual Purity and the Dead Sea Scrolls*, STDJ 72 (Leiden: Brill, 2007); and Hannah K. Harrington, "Examining Rabbinic Halakhah Through the Lens of Qumran," in *The Qumran Legal Texts between the Hebrew Bible and the Its Interpretation*, eds. Kristin

ideology implied by such practices. Purity practices have also been fruitfully explored as a way of possibly filling a halakhic lacuna between purity prescriptions in the Priestly strata and those contained in later Rabbinic literature.[58] Additionally, some studies have focused on what light ritual texts might shed on physical practice and archaeological remains, such as the practice of ablution and burial practices.[59] What remains outstanding, however, is a more integrated approach between ritual theories and matters of purity and purification in the texts from Qumran. In this vein, Michael Daise applied Bell's concept of ritual density alongside Jacob Milgrom's systematic reading of ritual practices in Leviticus[60] to understand ritual practice at Qumran in general and the rite of ablution prescribed in the Community Rule in specific.[61] Daise observed that in 1QS ablutions are not systematically connected to the "drink" (משקה, cf. 1QS 6:20–21; 7:18–20) as they are to "the purity" (טהרה, cf. 1QS 5:13). That said, however, he argued that ritual ablutions should be regarded as requisite for access to both טהרה and משקה.[62]

De Troyer and Armin Lange, with the assistance of James Seth Adcock, CBET 61 (Leuven: Peeters, 2011), 137–55.

[58] Vered Noam, "Corpse-Blood Impurity: A Lost Biblical Reading?," *JBL* 128 (2009): 243–51; idem, "Stringency in Qumran: A Reassessment," *JSJ* 40 (2009): 1–14; idem, "Qumran and the Rabbis on Corpse-Impurity: Common Exegesis—Tacit Polemic," in *The Dead Sea Scrolls: Texts and Contexts*, ed. Charlotte Hempel, STDJ 90 (Leiden: Brill, 2010), 397–430.

[59] See Yonatan Adler, "The Decline of Jewish Ritual Purity Observance in Roman Palaestina: An Archaeological Perspective on Chronology and Historical Context," in *Expressions of Cult in the Southern Levant in the Greco-Roman Period: Manifestations in Text and Material Culture*, eds. Oren Tal and Zeev Weiss, Contextualizing the Sacred 6 (Turnhout: Brepols, 2017), 269–84; Hannah K. Harrington, "Accessing Holiness via Ritual Ablutions in the Dead Sea Scrolls and Related Literature," in *Sacrifice, Cult, and Atonement in Early Judaism and Christianity: Constituents and Critique*, eds. Henrietta L. Wiley and Christian A. Eberhart, RBS 85 (Atlanta, GA: SBL 2017), 71–96; Ari Mermelstein, "Emotional Regimes, Ritual Practice, and the Shaping of Sectarian Identity: The Experience of Ablutions in the Dead Sea Scrolls," *BibInt* 24 (2016): 492–513; Ian Werrett, "Walking over the Dead: Burial Practices and the Possibility of Ritual Innovation at Qumran," in *Ritual Innovation in the Hebrew Bible and Early Judaism*, ed. Nathan MacDonald, BZAW 468 (Berlin: De Gruyter, 2016), 151–66.

[60] See Jacob Milgrom, *Leviticus 1–16: A New Translation with Introduction and Commentary*, AB 3 (Garden City, NY: Doubleday, 1991), 667–68, 746, 934–35.

[61] Michael A. Daise, "Ritual Density in Qumran Practice: Ablutions in the *Serekh Ha-Yahad*," in *New Perspectives on Old Texts: Proceedings of the Tenth Annual International Symposium of the Orion Center for the Study of the Dead Sea Scrolls and Associated Literature, 9–11 January, 2005*, eds. Esther G. Chazon and Betsy Halpern-Amaru, STDJ 88 (Leiden: Brill, 2010), 51–66. See also idem, "Processual Modality in Qumran Ritual: Induction into the Counsel of the 'Yachad' in 1QS," *Annali di Storia dell'Esegesi* 30 (2013): 303–15.

[62] Daise, "Ritual Density in Qumran Practice," 56–61.

RITUAL STUDIES AND THE DEAD SEA SCROLLS   171

The work of Kugler and Arnold, as well as Bell for that matter, has not been accepted without refinement. Daniel Stökl Ben Ezra has raised concerns about Bell's typology using her category of "rites of affliction" as a test case.[63] Analyzing both Kugler's and Arnold's application of Bell's typology, Stökl Ben Ezra offered his own understanding of rites of affliction in the Qumran corpus. Noting the polyvalence of rites (e.g., Yom Kippur) and "borderline" cases (e.g., curses and incantations), which seem to defy a singular categorization, Stökl Ben Ezra suggested a new model, introducing both *rituals* of affliction and *rites* of affliction.[64] The former consists of incantations, independent purifications, punishments described in the penal code, Yom Kippur (borderline with calendrical rituals), burials and mourning rites (borderline with rites of passage), and the covenant renewal ceremony. The latter includes apotropaic prayers, minor purifications, confessions, and curses (borderline with political rituals). Importantly, Stökl Ben Ezra correctly noted that caution must be taken in analyzing ritual practices at Qumran as the information we have is largely incomplete, particularly with reference to the actual performance of rituals and an understanding of larger ritual context at Qumran.[65]

Another critique regarding the concepts of "ritual density" and "ritual hegemony" was presented by Jutta Jokiranta, who observed that rituals do not always bring about social cohesion, that frequent practice does not mean automatic acceptance, and that rituals are never equally experienced and adopted by all ritual participants. Rituals are important places for both constructing hierarchies and reflecting and testing one's attitude to those hierarchies.[66] Engaging with the work of Whitehouse on the "tedium effect" and that of Lawson and McCauley on ritual form and balance, Jokiranta examined the most frequent ritual practices—ritual purification, Sabbath rituals and regulations, and communal meals and study—and concluded that while frequency and routinization of ritual practice in the Qumran movement might over time threaten the commitment of members, they created "balancing elements" in the movement to ensure continued motivation and sense of closeness to God.[67]

---

63   Daniel Stökl Ben Ezra, "When the Bell Rings: The Qumran Rituals of Affliction in Context," in *The Dead Sea Scrolls in Context*, 2:533–46.
64   Stökl Ben Ezra, "When the Bell Rings," 542.
65   Stökl Ben Ezra, "When the Bell Rings," 546.
66   Jutta Jokiranta, "Ritual System in the Qumran Movement: Frequency, Boredom, and Balance," in *Mind, Morality and Magic: Cognitive Science Approaches in Biblical Studies*, eds. István Czachesz and Risto Uro (Durham: Acumen, 2013), 144–63.
67   Jokiranta, "Ritual System in the Qumran Movement," 162. For meals as both creating togetherness and hierarchies, see, e.g., Arnold, "The Dead Sea Scrolls, Qumran, and Ritual Studies," 559; Cecilia Wassén, "Common Meals in the Qumran Movement with Special Attention to Purity Regulations," in *The Eucharist—Its Origins and Contexts: Sacred Meal,*

John Collins, in his 2012 study on prayer and the meaning of ritual at Qumran, argued, in contradistinction to Staal's assertion of the meaninglessness of ritual, that ritual practice preserved in the Qumran corpus displays a distinct purpose, meaning, and function for the Qumran movement.[68] Engaging with the work of Bell, Collins noted that not only is ritual practice a way of "creating solidarity and social cohesion," but also functions idealistically drawing contrast between the way things are, how they ought to be, and how the world should be organized.[69] Collins explored the ritual of prayer, the discourse and ritual involved in the covenant ceremony (1QS 1:16–3:12), and rites of confession and ablution concluding that the significance of ritual writ large must be understood within the context of the larger milieu of ritual preserved in the corpus rather than on any individual ritual itself. Citing the work of Kugler and Arnold, Collins further suggested that the ritual density at Qumran reflects a sort of *habitus*,[70] a ritualized life:

> It constituted a *habitus*, an enactment of the world as it ought to be, characterized by obedience to what was believed to be divine law, as interpreted and amplified by the priestly leaders of the community, and by purity, which entailed separation from the outside world. It ensured community cohesion, by requiring that members eat together, bless together and take counsel together. At the same time, it implemented the hierarchical structure of the community.[71]

For Collins, the textualization of prayer as a standardizing and institutionalizing endeavor is a clear demonstration of the *habitus*-creating process. Thus,

---

    Communal Meal, Table Fellowship in Late Antiquity, Early Judaism, and Early Christianity, eds. David Hellholm and Dieter Sänger (Tübingen: Mohr Siebeck, 2017), 1:77–100; See also Cecilia Wassén's contribution in this volume.

68   John J. Collins, "Prayer and the Meaning of Ritual in the Dead Sea Scrolls," in *Prayer and Poetry in the Dead Sea Scrolls and Related Literature: Essays in Honor of Eileen Schuller on the Occasion of Her 65th Birthday*, eds. Jeremy Penner, Ken M. Penner, and Cecilia Wassén, STDJ 98 (Leiden: Brill, 2012), 69–85. See Frits Staal, "The Meaninglessness of Ritual," *Numen* 26 (1979): 2–22.

69   Collins, "Prayer and the Meaning of Ritual," 71–72. See Bell, *Ritual Theory, Ritual Practice*, 171–72, and 206.

70   Here, Collins relies on the work of Pierre Bourdieu and Marcel Mauss on ritual as *habitus*. See Pierre Bourdieu, *Outline of a Theory of Practice*, trans. Richard Nice (Cambridge: Cambridge University Press, 1977), 72–95; Marcel Mauss, "Body Techniques," in *Sociology and Psychology: Essays by Marcel Mauss*, ed. and trans. Ben Brewster (London: Routledge and Kegan Paul, 1979), 122.

71   Collins, "Prayer and the Meaning of Ritual," 84–85.

more than the content of prayer itself, the mere act of performing prayer in a prescribed manner is instrumental in the formation of the sanctified life of the *yaḥad*. Similarly, Carol Newsom's work has been indispensable in showing how the texts like the *serakhim* and Hodayot literally construct a sectarian being by teaching the member a new language and discourse.[72]

Both the work of performance theorists and theorists of ritual practice, particularly as formulated by Bourdieu and Bell, have similarly had influence in the field of Dead Sea Scrolls scholarship, specifically within the study of liturgical texts.[73] The focus here has been on what a ritual *does* as opposed to purely what a ritual is supposed to mean. Particularly in the case of liturgy as ritual, liturgy has been examined as a way of acting, one that effects some kind of change, socially or culturally, and shapes community identity. Angela Kim Harkins has argued for the Hodayot to be seen as "an affective script for the ancient reader to imitate and reenact."[74] Harkins proposes that the Hodayot were read and experienced by the Qumran community through the practice of performative prayer by which the reader sought to reenact the affective experience of the text emotionally leading the participant into a progressively deepening religious experience.[75]

Daniel Falk applied performance and practice theories in assessing the degree to which the diverse prayer collections preserved at Qumran can been envisaged as evidence for "a liturgical progression" engendering a progressive religious experience for participants.[76] Falk concluded that while the Words of the Luminaries (4Q504–506) and the Songs of the Sabbath Sacrifice (4Q400–407, 11Q17, and Masık) offer clear evidence of a deliberately

---

72   Carol A. Newsom, *The Self as Symbolic Space: Constructing Identity and Community at Qumran*, STDJ 52 (Leiden: Brill, 2004).

73   On performance, see Victor Turner, *Dramas, Fields, and Metaphors: Symbolic Action in Human Society* (Ithaca, NY: Cornell University Press, 1974); Maurice Bloch, "Symbols, Song, Dance and Features of Articulation: Is Religion and Extreme Form of Traditional Authority?" *European Journal of Sociology* 15 (1974): 55–81; Austin, *How to Do Things with Words*; Richard Schechner, *Essays in Performance Theory 1970–1976* (New York, NY: Drama Book Specialists, 1977); idem, *The Future of Ritual: Writings on Culture and Performance* (London: Routledge, 1993), among others. On ritual practice, see Geertz, *The Interpretation of Cultures*; Bourdieu, *Outline of a Theory of Practice*; idem, *The Logic of Practice*, trans. Richard Nice (Stanford, CA: Stanford University Press, 1990); Bell, *Ritual: Perspectives and Dimensions*, 72–83.

74   Angela Kim Harkins, *Reading with an "I" to the Heavens: Looking at the Qumran Hodayot Through the Lens of Visionary Traditions*, Ekstasis 3 (Berlin: De Gruyter, 2012), 55–68, quote from 68.

75   Harkins, *Reading with an "I"*, 267–73.

76   Daniel K. Falk, "Liturgical Progression and the Experience of Transformation in Prayers from Qumran," *DSD* 22 (2015): 267–84.

constructed liturgical progression over the course of the cycle, which prepared the worshipper for a deepening weekly religious experience with God, the Daily Prayers (4Q503) and Festival Prayers (1Q34+34bis, 4Q507–509 + 505) are far less certain.[77] These latter collections, Falk tentatively proposed, potentially form an intentional liturgical progression, in this case a daily scripted ritual experience within a larger liturgical cycle. Both studies effectively demonstrate how performance and practice, rituals as ways of acting, can facilitate a progressive religious experience and lend to the construction of what Rappaport has described as "time out of time"—the distinction of sacred over mundane time in which transformation is affected.[78]

Furthermore, the performative function of *words* is important in the application of speech act theory. Jeff Anderson places speech act theory between magical and merely symbolic approaches.[79] Examining covenant renewal traditions, war prayers, and other references to blessings and curses from their performative functions, Anderson has argued that blessings and curses delineate ingroup-outgroup as well as ingroup-innergroup boundaries. "The curses not only made explicit a known division between competing communities but actually enacted that relationship each time the ritual was performed."[80]

The view that curses were means of the powerless to *change* matters also suggests that blessings and curses may have been seen as something more than just enacting group boundaries and channeling political frustrations. The many blessings of God (often translated as praising God), and the abundance of hymn texts from Qumran invites another perspective: the blessing/praising activity was conceived as capable of bringing the divine sphere into the mundane, transferring divine power. To look at blessings and curses as prayers and petitions *or* as spells and invocations produces different results. Following Jesper Sørensen's cognitive theory of magic, questioning the ages-old dichotomy between religion and magic, Jokiranta has explored how the covenant ceremony may be viewed as producing beliefs of efficacy and how the magical agency could have been located in the actors or actions of the ceremony.[81] From the point of view of media studies, efficacy beliefs and symbolic interpretations are not necessarily both present at the same time or at the same

---

77   Falk, "Liturgical Progression," 283–84.

78   Rappaport, *Ritual and Religion*, 117–26, 169–70, 181, 209.

79   Jeff S. Anderson, "Curse and Blessings: Social Control and Self Definition in the Dead Sea Scrolls," in *The Dead Sea Scrolls in Context*, 1:47–60.

80   Anderson, "Curse and Blessings," 52–53.

81   Jutta Jokiranta, "Towards a Cognitive Theory of Blessing: Dead Sea Scrolls as Test Case," in *Functions of Psalms and Prayers in the Late Second Temple Period*, eds. Mika S. Pajunen and Jeremy Penner, BZAW 486 (Berlin: De Gruyter, 2017), 25–47.

level: magical (efficacy) beliefs are intuitive inferences that the ritual "works," whereas symbolic interpretations require reflective thinking to carry messages about what the ritual is about and why it works.[82] Yet, the cognitive theory of magic and the speech-act theory need not be in contradiction: the former may also offer tools to understand the cognitive *mechanism* by which the speech-acts have an impact.

That this performative aspect of ritual can be viewed as communication is stressed, for example, by Arnold: "Looking at Qumran ritual practice we see how ritual and liturgy can communicate through the doing, not just the meaning of the words to be recited."[83] For Arnold, the Qumran prayers and festivals create a complete ritual system that maintained the cosmic order by aligning the worship with the proper calendric times. In like manner, other theories have been drawn upon to illuminate the communicative aspects of ritual. Relying upon the work of Michael Suk-Young Chwe regarding the necessity of common knowledge for coordinated action, Kugler has addressed the potential function of 4QS[e]–4QOtot and its conspicuous absence from the Community Rule.[84] For Kugler, 4QOtot (4Q319) functioned as a practical calendar, which, when read, created "common knowledge" of the application of the 364-day calendar to all phases of life. The absence of 4QOtot from the later literary strata of 1QS, Kugler suggested, denotes that not only was the continued public reading of 4QOtot highly unlikely, but moreover that by the time of the Community Rule, the community had sufficient common knowledge of how to reckon the 364-day calendar as to make the public reading of 4QOtot unnecessary.[85]

Recently, embodied aspects of rituals have received more attention. Employing the work of Rappaport and Bourdieu, Judith Newman has suggested that

---

82 On magic in the Second Temple period and at Qumran, see Gideon Bohak, *Ancient Jewish Magic: A History* (Cambridge: Cambridge University Press, 2008); idem, "Mystical Texts, Magic, and Divination," in *T&T Clark Companion to the Dead Sea Scrolls*, ed. George J. Brooke and Charlotte Hempel, with the assistance of Michael DeVries and Drew Longacre (London: Bloomsbury T&T Clark, 2019), 457–66; Philip S. Alexander, "Magic and Magical Texts," *EDSS* 1:502–4.

83 Arnold, "The Dead Sea Scrolls, Qumran, and Ritual Studies," 551.

84 Robert Kugler, "Of Calendars, Community Rules, and Common Knowledge: Understanding 4QS[e]–4QOtot, with the Help of Ritual Studies," in *Rediscovering the Dead Sea Scrolls: An Assessment of Old and New Methods*, ed. Maxine L. Grossman (Grand Rapids, MI: Eerdmans, 2010), 215–28. See Michael Suk-Young Chwe, *Rational Ritual: Culture, Coordination, and Common Knowledge* (Princeton, NJ: Princeton University Press, 2001). See also Jutta Jokiranta's contribution in this volume.

85 Kugler, "Of Calendars, Community Rules, and Common Knowledge," 223–27. Another possibility is that the calendar had become more of an ideal but not used in practice.

the physical prostration of the *maskil* in 1QH^a 5:12–14 was not only a visual cue, but also constituted a canonical message, linking the practice of humility of the sectarians to that of Moses and his intercession for restoring the covenant.[86] Newman's work has also touched upon the cognitive effects of visual images on the spectators, drawing from Antonio Damasio's work.[87] Other insights from cognitive theorists include the concept of "ritualization," not in the sense that Bell used it (i.e., to denote the ways in which mundane actions are made special and separated from the everyday actions), but in the sense that Boyer and Liénard have studied it, as compelling action, relying on several neuropsychological mechanisms such as the precaution system.[88] Jokiranta has asked if this perspective could explain some of the extensive lists in the scrolls, for example, in 4QBerakhot^a (4Q286) where repetitive actions or actions demanding focused attention may provide a relief signal to the human brain in the face of ambiguous threats.[89]

5   The Qumran Corpus and Ritual Studies

The distinction between a ritual act and a "textualization" of a ritual has long been acknowledged, a distinction James Watts has clearly noted in stating "texts are not rituals and rituals are not texts."[90] In short, whereas ritual acts can themselves be observed, the textualization of ritual provides a different medium by which a ritual is encountered. A textualization of ritual, or what is often described as a "ritual text," while not completely divorced from an embodied act, provides the reader or audience with a description of or a

---

86   Judith H. Newman, "Embodied Techniques: The Communal Formation of the Maskil's Self," *DSD* 22 (2015): 249–66; idem, "The Thanksgiving Hymn of 1QH^a and the Construction of the Ideal Sage through Liturgical Performance," in *Sibyls, Scriptures, and Scrolls: John Collins at Seventy*, eds. Joel Baden, Hindy Najman, and Eibert Tigchelaar, JSJSup 175 (Leiden: Brill, 2016), 2:940–57. See also idem, *Before the Bible: The Liturgical Body and the Formation of Scriptures in Early Judaism* (New York, NY: Oxford University Press, 2018).

87   Antonio Damasio, *Self Comes to Mind: Constructing the Conscious Brain* (New York, NY: Pantheon/Random House, 2010), esp. 102–6.

88   Boyer and Liénard, "Why Ritualized Behavior?," 595–613.

89   Jutta Jokiranta, "Ritualization and Power of Listing in 4QBerakhot^a (4Q286)," in *Is There a Text in This Cave? Studies in the Textuality of the Dead Sea Scrolls in Honour of George J. Brooke*, eds. Ariel Feldman, Maria Cioată, and Charlotte Hempel, STDJ 119 (Leiden: Brill, 2017), 438–58.

90   Watts, *Ritual and Rhetoric in Leviticus*, 29. For warnings to take ritual representations in texts as rituals, see also William K. Gilders, "Social and Cultural Anthropology," in *The Oxford Handbook of Ritual and Worship*, 125–41, esp. 136–37.

prescription for a particular ritual act, which may or not reflect actual ritual praxis, but may have a distinct rhetorical function apart from the codification of ritual instruction. In other words, the textualization of a ritual may have a function different from that of the mere preservation and transmission of a particular ritual practice.[91] As Bell has noted, textualizations themselves are textual objects that structure the social interactions associated with their use and transmission.[92] Textualizations, therefore, have social and performative power: the text itself becomes an actor, an agent of transformative power in the actualized world with the ability to shape meaning and social interactions.[93]

This distinction is instructional from the standpoint that when we deal with ritual practices at Qumran what we are dealing with is the textualization of ritual. Whereas some of the textualizations may have grounding in actual ritual praxis, others may be more reflective of other concerns, such as rhetorically shaping the identity and ideology of the movement. Ritual texts, therefore, should not be read univocally as the preservation and transmission of ritual praxis, but potentially, as Charlotte Hempel has suggested regarding the Community Rules, as "curated" texts by which the movement intentionally shaped texts to present an idealized community.[94] This curative quality is displayed in the War Scroll where ritual and ritualized features are employed within an imagined future eschatological setting. Regarding textualization, it is also important to acknowledge that the relationship between social reality and its depiction in the Scrolls is complex. For example, while there is a distinct connection between the heightened concern for ritual purity expressed in various compositions and the presence of stepped pools at Qumran and elsewhere, we cannot be certain of which textualizations reflect actual ritual practice and which are more idealized in nature. That said, the specific texts and genres of texts which have garnered the most attention is instructive for the how ritual studies have been engaged and to what end. Broadly speaking, attention has been focused on the following: *serekh* texts, liturgical texts (including prayer texts, blessings/curses, apotropaic texts, and calendrical

---

91   Watts, *Ritual and Rhetoric*, 27–29; idem, *Leviticus 1–10*, HCOT (Leuven: Peeters, 2013), 63, where Watts further suggests, "Written texts usually encode rhetorical purposes different from the goals that motivate ritual performances."

92   Catherine Bell, "The Ritualization of Texts and the Textualization of Ritual in the Codification of Taoist Literature," HR 27 (1988): 390. For an application of Bell's idea in Second Temple Judaism, see Judith H. Newman, "Ritualizing the Text in Early Judaism: Two Examples of Innovation," *HeBAI* 7 (2018): 449–65.

93   Bell, "The Ritualization of Texts," 367–69.

94   Charlotte Hempel, *The Community Rules from Qumran: A Commentary*, TSAJ 183 (Tübingen: Mohr Siebeck, 2020), 9–10. See also Hempel's contribution in this volume.

texts), and *halakhic* texts (including purity and Sabbath regulations as well as texts including various other rites).

5.1 Serekh *Texts*

When considering the conception of *serekh* texts, scholarly attention has tended to focus either on those entire compositions containing *serekh* in the heading or those contained in a loosely defined literary genre, of which the Community Rule is typically considered pre-eminent.[95] It is important to note, however, that since the term *serekh* is used in a variety of ways within the Qumran corpus the notion of *serekh* texts should be expanded to include those texts which contain distinct literary components incorporated into larger compositions, such as the Damascus Document and the War Scroll, the latter of which contains the most occurrences of the term *serekh*.[96] It is in this fashion that we will discuss ritual studies' engagement with *serekh* texts.

With reference to the application of ritual studies, the Community Rule has arguably drawn the most engagement, in particular the Covenant Ceremony in 1QS 1:16–3:12.[97] Often described in terms of a rite of passage, the ceremony, which draws from Deuteronomy 27 and 29:17–20, consists of admission rites (1:16–2:18) including a confession of trespasses and a collection of blessings and curses, a communal procession (2:19–25a), and a warning for those who refuse to enter into the covenant or who are recalcitrant (2:25b–3:12).[98] From a ritual theory perspective, the ceremony is often understood as a mechanism of social cohesion or even "social control."[99] The ceremony establishes and reaffirms a specific structural hierarchy while affirming the pre-ordained

---

95   Rather than approaching *serekh* texts as a distinct literary genre, the concept of "family resemblance" has been advanced as a more helpful model. See Carol Newsom, "Pairing Research Questions and Theories of Genre: A Case Study with the Hodayot," DSD 17 (2010): 241–59 (esp. 35–36); Charlotte Hempel, *The Qumran Rule Texts in Context: Collected Essays*, TSAJ 154 (Tübingen: Mohr Siebeck, 2013), 1.

96   See Charlotte Hempel, "Rules," in *T&T Clark Companion to the Dead Sea Scrolls*, ed. George J. Brooke and Charlotte Hempel, with the assistance of Michael DeVries and Drew Longacre (London: Bloomsbury T&T Clark, 2019), 408–10. On the root סרך in the Qumran corpus, see Charlotte Hempel, "סֶרֶךְ særæk," in ThWQ 2:1111–17; Lawrence H. Schiffman, *The Halakhah at Qumran*, SJLA 16 (Leiden: E. J. Brill, 1975), 60–68. On the question of which texts should be considered *serakhim* and their subsequent examination, see Philip S. Alexander, "Rules," EDSS 2:799–803.

97   Cf. 1QS 1:16–3:12 // 4Q255 2:1–9 // 4Q256 2:1–6, 12–13; 3:1–4 // 4Q257 2:1–8; 3:1–14 // 4Q262 1:1–4 // 5Q11 1 i.

98   For sustained commentary on the Covenant Ceremony, see Hempel, *The Community Rules from Qumran*, 67–95.

99   On the strict discipline expressed in the Covenant Ceremony as "social control," see Arnold, "The Dead Sea Scrolls, Qumran, and Ritual Studies," 557.

and assigned position of initiates and members within the covenant and the community writ large. The ceremony itself, therefore, functions as a medium for the mediation of knowledge, enacting particular values and beliefs of the movement. The rites expressed in the ceremony, both in content and performance, play an active role in the shaping of group identity and the reification of the hierarchical structure of the community. Through the ritual and liturgy of the ceremony, therefore, current community members and those seeking initiation are described as participating in the shaping of the shared identity of the community.

Communal meals represent a significant ritualized communal activity and have subsequently drawn significant scholarly attention. More frequently associated with the wider discourse on ritual purity within the Qumran movement, communal meals have also been explored for matters of boundary formation as well as their connection with the pure food and drink of the community within the larger admissions process.[100] Communal meals, being restricted to members of the movement only, function to clearly demarcate those who are inside the movement from those outside, thus functioning to shape and continually reinforce the identity of the movement.[101] Significantly, the shared meal described in 1QS 6:4c–5 (cf. 4Q258 2:9–10a; 4Q261 2a–c: 4b–5) occurs within a larger section of regulations regarding meetings "in every place where there are found ten people" (6:3b). The presence of a priest is required who, with reference to the preparation of the table for the meal, is to stretch out his hand to bless the first fruits of bread and new wine. These details suggest that the shared meal in 1QS 6 can be understood as embodying and reinforcing a hierarchical stratification within the movement by which authority is established and maintained.[102] Similar regulations for priestly involvement and a concern for hierarchy are likewise seen in the eschatological "Messianic meal" in the Rule of the Congregation (cf. 1QSa 2:11–22), which, as in the case of 1QS 6,

---

100 Charlotte Hempel, "Who is Making Dinner at Qumran?," *JTS* 63 (2012): 49–65; Jokiranta, "Ritual System in the Qumran Movement," 159–62; Cecilia Wassén, "The (Im)purity Levels of Communal Meals within the Qumran Movement," *JAJ* 7 (2016): 102–22; idem, "Common Meals in the Qumran Movement," 1:77–100; idem, "Daily Life," in *T&T Clark Companion to the Dead Sea Scrolls*, ed. George J. Brooke and Charlotte Hempel, with the assistance of Michael DeVries and Drew Longacre (London: Bloomsbury T&T Clark, 2019), 554–56. See also Wassén's contribution in this volume.

101 Wassén, "Daily Life," 554.

102 On meals as designed to visualize hierarchies and inscribe them into daily life, see Benedikt Eckhardt, "Meals and Politics in the *Yaḥad*: A Reconsideration," *DSD* 17 (2010): 180–209.

is to take place "[when] at least ten me[n are ga]thered" (2:22).[103] The function that communal meals play within the Qumran movement regarding boundary formation, the establishment and maintenance of hierarchy, as well as their potential performative value all invite further investigation.

Whereas the Community Rule has garnered much attention, the War Scroll (1QM) has remained largely undertheorized from a ritual studies perspective. This is surprising considering the "ritualistic" nature of the War Scroll has long been acknowledged by commentators going all the way back to Yigael Yadin in 1955.[104] Subsequent scholarly engagement with 1QM has continued to acknowledge the "ritualistic" character of the War Scroll, often pointing to matters of ritual purity in the text or the central role of the priesthood in the eschatological battle.[105] Recently, however, the War Scroll has begun to draw more sustained interest from a ritual studies point of view, particularly regarding issues of performativity. Of particular interest have been the prayers contained in 1QM 10–14 and their potential liturgical performance given the number of preserved texts, the presence of prayer formulas commonly found in other liturgical prayers, and evidence of textual re-use.[106] The opisthographic preservation of two war traditions on the verso side of papyri containing prayer texts, which appear to reflect an intentional collection for personal use, is highly suggestive of some degree of performativity.[107] Beyond columns 10–14, the War Scroll

---

103   On the Messianic meal, see Lawrence H. Schiffman, "The Messianic Banquet," in *The Eschatological Community of the Dead Sea Scrolls*, SBLMS 38 (Atlanta, GA: Scholars Press, 1989), 53–67. For a non-eschatological reading of 1QSa, see Jutta Jokiranta, "Competition rather than Conflict: Identity Discourse in the Qumran Rule Scrolls," in *Negotiating Identities: Conflict, Conversion, and Consolidation in Early Judaism and Christianity* (200 *BCE–600 CE*), eds. Karin Hedner Zetterholm, Anders Runesson, Cecilia Wassén, and Magnus Zetterholm, ConB (Lanham, MD: Lexington Books/Fortress Academic, 2022), 35–50.

104   For example, Yadin described 1QM 9:17–14:15 as the "Ritual Serekh Series" consisting of "forms of prayers for the various phases of the war." See Yigael Yadin, *The Scroll of the War of the Sons of Light against the Sons of Darkness*, trans. by Batya and Chaim Rabin (Oxford: Oxford University Press, 1962 [Hebrew, 1955]), 10. Moreover, Yadin committed an entire chapter to what he considers to be "rites of the congregation" (Chapter 8, 198–228).

105   See, for example, John J. Collins, *Apocalypticism in the Dead Sea Scrolls* (London: Routledge, 1997), 96–97; Lester L. Grabbe, "Warfare: Eschatological Warfare," *EDSS* 2:965. More recently, Christophe Batsch, "Priests in Warfare in the Second Temple Judaism: 1QM, or the *Anti-Phinehas*," in *Qumran Cave 1 Revisited: Texts from Cave 1 Sixty Years after Their Discovery: Proceedings of the Sixth Meeting of the IOQS in Ljubljana*, eds. Daniel K. Falk et al., STDJ 91 (Leiden: Brill, 2010), 165–78; Ian Werrett and Stephen Parker, "Purity in War: What is it Good for?," in *The War Scroll, Violence, War and Peace in the Dead Sea Scrolls*, 295–316.

106   See Falk, "Prayer, Liturgy, and War," 275–94.

107   Cf. 4QpapWar Scroll-like Text A (4Q497) on verso with 4QpapHymns/Prayers (4Q499) on recto and 4QpapM^f (4Q496) and 4QpapWords of the Luminaries^c (4Q506) both on verso with 4QpapFestival Prayers (4Q509 + 4Q505) on recto.

RITUAL STUDIES AND THE DEAD SEA SCROLLS 181

bears additional textual indicators of orality and performativity suggesting its potential as a performative spoken text.[108] These avenues are ripe for further exploration. What remains underexplored from a ritual studies perspective, however, is the textualization of rituals connected with cultic service in 1QM 2:1–6 (cf. 4QM^d [4Q494], 4QWar Scroll-like Text B [4Q471], and potentially 4QpapM^f [4Q496]) and its potential rhetorical and performative value.

5.2 Liturgical Texts

The number of texts preserved within the Qumran corpus considered liturgical is numerous. However, what constitutes a "liturgical text" is difficult to delineate and is a matter of some debate.[109] As Falk has suggested, any such endeavor needs to distinguish liturgical texts from accounts of liturgical performances and liturgical elements included in other genres.[110] Additionally, a measured sense of caution is needed in dealing with liturgical material as liturgical texts do not proffer unfettered access to liturgical praxis. While engaging this discussion in depth is beyond our scope here, some attempt to address liturgical texts from a ritual studies perspective is warranted. Broadly speaking, texts considered liturgical have often been classified according to Bell's six-class ritual typology as noted above. Furthermore, and importantly, liturgical texts have been approached predominantly for what they accomplish through performance over and above their content as texts.

The liturgical texts which have drawn the most attention from a ritual perspective are those compositions containing formulaic rubrics for the offering of fixed prayers at set times within the calendar.[111] Of these compositions several are noteworthy. Daily Prayers (4Q503) contains two short blessings for each day of the month, one to be offered at sunrise and another at sunset. Words of the Luminaries (4Q504–506) includes petitionary prayers for each day of the week and a hymn-like doxology for the Sabbath. Songs for the Sabbath Sacrifice (4Q400–407, 11Q17, and Masık) consists of thirteen songs, one each

---

108 Rebekah Haigh, "Oral Aspects: A Performative Approach to 1QM," *DSD* 26 (2019): 189–219. Steven Weitzman has cogently argued for the text of the War Scroll as an effort to mobilize emotion within the reader or audience similar to and perhaps in reaction against Greco-Roman military practices. See Steven Weitzman, "Warring Against Terror: The War Scroll and the Mobilization of Emotion," *JSJ* 40 (2009): 213–41.

109 See Eileen M. Schuller, "Functions of Psalms and Prayers in the Late Second Temple Period," in *Functions of Psalms and Prayers in the Late Second Temple Period*, 5–24 (esp. 18–19). For a recent overview and further literature, see Falk, "Liturgical Texts," 423–34.

110 Falk, "Liturgical Texts," 423.

111 For an overview of fixed prayers, see Daniel K. Falk, *Daily, Sabbath, and Festival Prayers in the Dead Sea Scrolls*, STDJ 27 (Leiden: Brill, 1998). See also Schuller, "Ritual and Worship at Qumran," 370–71; Jeremy Penner, *Patterns of Daily Prayer in Second Temple Period Judaism*, STDJ 104 (Leiden: Brill, 2012).

for the first thirteen Sabbaths of the year, the first quarter of the year according to the 364-day calendar. The recitation of each song envisages a union with the angelic realm in joint worship in the heavenly Temple.[112] Finally, Festival Prayers (1Q34+34bis, 4Q507–509 + 505) consists of a collection of prayers presumably offered for each festival throughout the year. In general terms, these texts offer a window onto a growing tradition of fixed prayers within the late Second Temple period, which undoubtedly extended outside the Qumran movement. More specifically, they provide evidence that in the practice of fixed prayers, the movement embodied a cosmic cycle by which the pre-ordained, divinely established order was maintained.

Certain liturgical texts have been fruitfully explored within the notion of performativity. The thirty-five psalms of the Hodayot, although difficult to place within a particular liturgical setting, have been understood as potentially performative, either personal or communal. In either case, the Hodayot emotively elevates the reader or audience into a greater religious experience fostering a shared and cohesive identity. Apotropaic texts consist of those texts thought to fend off or provide personal protection from the demonic, such as Apocryphal Psalms (11Q11), Magic Booklet (4Q560), and Hymn (8Q5), or those thought to provide communal protection, such as Song of the Sage (4Q510–511), Incantation (4Q444), and Hymn (6Q18). Not only do these texts demonstrate the belief that demonic powers pose a real threat to the community, both individually and corporately, but also the sense of efficacy associated with their ritual performance.[113] For the movement, the ritual performance of these texts had real apotropaic potential giving the ritual specialist authority over the powers of darkness.

---

112 On Songs for the Sabbath Sacrifice, see Judith H. Newman, "Songs for the Sabbath Sacrifice," in *T&T Clark Companion to the Dead Sea Scrolls*, ed. George J. Brooke and Charlotte Hempel, with the assistance of Michael DeVries and Drew Longacre (London: Bloomsbury T&T Clark, 2019), 347–49; Carol A. Newsom, "Shirot 'Olat HaShabbat," in *Qumran Cave 4.VI: Poetical and Liturgical Texts, Part 1*, ed. Esther Eshel et al. in consultation with James VanderKam and Monica Brady, DJD 11 (Oxford: Clarendon, 1998), 173–401.

113 On apotropaic prayer, see Miryam T. Brand, "Apotropaic Prayer and the Views of Demonic Influence," in *Evil Within and Without: The Source of Sin and Its Nature in Second Temple Literature*, JSJSup 9 (Göttingen: Vandenhoeck & Ruprecht, 2013), 198–217; Esther Eshel, "Apotropaic Prayers in the Second Temple Period," in *Liturgical Perspectives: Prayer and Poetry in Light of the Dead Sea Scrolls. Proceedings of the Fifth International Symposium of the Orion Center for the Study of the Dead Sea Scrolls and Associated Literature, 19–23 January, 2000*, eds. Esther G. Chazon with collaboration of Ruth A. Clements and Avital Pinnick, STDJ 48 (Leiden: Brill, 2003), 69–88. See also, Charlotte Hempel, "The Apotropaic Function of the Final Hymn in the Community Rules," in *Petitioners, Penitents, and Poets: On Prayer and Praying in the Second Temple Judaism*, eds. Timothy J. Sandoval and Ariel Feldman, BZAW 524 (Berlin: De Gruyter, 2020), 131–54.

RITUAL STUDIES AND THE DEAD SEA SCROLLS 183

Closely related to apotropaic rites are blessing and cursing texts or those texts in which blessings and curses are incorporated as literary components, which are employed for the protection of the community and the purposes of God against demonic threat. 4QBerakhot (4Q286–290) consists of a series of blessings to God and curses upon Belial and all those under his authority. The fragmentary 4QCurses (4Q280) preserves curses directed toward Melchiresha that are terminologically similar to curses found in 1QS 2.[114] 5QCurses (5Q14) is highly fragmentary and cannot be securely situated in any specific liturgical setting. Noteworthy is the fact that 4QBerakhot[a] (4Q286) 7 ii 1–5 and 1QM 13:4–6 both preserve the same ritual cursing of Belial and the spirits of his lot. This case of textual re-use is significant due to the instruction given prior to the curse in 4Q286 7 ii 1, "of the council of the community, all of them will say together: 'Amen. Amen.'"[115] The clear indication of community performance in 4QBerakhot[a] suggests that a similar performative quality regarding the War Scroll is not out of the question.[116] Broadly speaking, what can be said is that blessings and curses, like apotropaic rites, were envisaged as having performative force and efficacy as weapons against the powers of darkness.

Finally, various texts within the Qumran corpus also provide evidence of ritual innovation, or at least textualized rituals, such as Communal Ceremony (4Q275), Four Lots (4Q279), Communal Confession (4Q393), Purification Liturgy (4Q284), Ritual Purification A (4Q414), Ritual Purification B (4Q512), Rebukes Reported by the Overseer (4Q477), Ritual of Marriage (4Q502).[117] These varied compositions point toward similar trends we see taking place in the halakhic genre, namely expansions and the need to verbalize ritual action.

5.3 Halakhic Texts

Halakhic texts contain legal interpretation on several topics that are themselves often categorized under rituals or ritual practices, such as safeguarding the Temple as sacred space, offering sacrifice and other Temple gifts, keeping the Sabbath and the festivals, purifying from ritual impurity, and following

---

114 See specifically 4Q280 2:2–3 // 1QS 2:5–6 and 4Q280 2:3–4 // 1QS 2:8–9. On the terminological relationship, see Hempel, *The Community Rules from Qumran*, 76, 85.

115 For analysis on 4QBerakhot[a], see Bilhan Nitzan, "4QBerakhot[a]," in *Qumran Cave 4.VI: Poetical and Liturgical Texts, Part 1*, ed. Esther Eshel et al. in consultation with James VanderKam and Monica Brady, DJD 11 (Oxford: Clarendon, 1998), 7–48. Translation here by Nitzan, "4QBerakhot[a]," 28. For 4QBerakhot[a] from the perspective of anxiety-relief, see Jokiranta, "Ritualization and Power of Listing."

116 See Andrew R. Krause, "Performing the Eschaton: Apotropaic Performance in the Liturgy of the War Scroll," *RevQ* 30 (2018): 27–46; idem, "Apotropaic Means and Methods in the Rules of the Trumpets and Banners (1QM 3–4)," *Henoch* 42 (2020): 117–35.

117 For an overview, see Davila, *Liturgical Works*.

kosher and marriage laws.[118] In comparison to Torah laws, certain themes clearly receive growing attention and elaboration in the Qumran evidence: Temple and ritual purity in the Temple Scroll and 4QMMT, and the Sabbath and ritual purity in Jubilees, the Damascus Document, and several halakhic texts: Halakhah A (4Q251), Miscellaneous Rules (4Q265), Tohorot A (4Q274), Harvesting (4Q284a). Much of the scholarly energy has been targeted on reconstructing fragmentary scrolls and on understanding the relation of different laws to each other and to rabbinic evidence, but the practices themselves remain undertheorized from ritual studies point of view. For example, Sabbath and kosher rules invite an investigation along *inaction* and boundary maintenance by *banning*, more akin to *taboo* rules than rules of prescribed action. To know what *not* to do and not to eat requires focused attention, unless this is alleviated by a local community who follows the same practices or produces and oversees food production and trade and so on. If the Qumran movement was scattered in the Land, such local communities may have existed, but there may also have been more interaction with outsiders and need for caution and precision than is often thought.

Moreover, ritual purity and purification are themes central to ritual studies. The underlying theology of ritual purity has probably received more attention than the cognitive and evolutionary basis of such practices.[119] As Thomas Kazen has argued, it is important to recognize the different levels of explanation when purity rules are studied.[120] The cognitive mechanism present in this human practice is one thing, and the socio-political dimensions or gender distinctions of how such practices are prescribed and controlled is another thing. Circumcision is little discussed but often assumed. The fact that it appears in Qumran texts more in a moral, symbolic sense than as a prescribed practice is also telling: besides purity, circumcision too attracted spiritualized interpretations.[121] Furthermore, halakhic texts bring forward the question of

---

118 For a recent overview and further literature, see Vered Noam, "Halakhah," in *T&T Clark Companion to the Dead Sea Scrolls*, ed. George J. Brooke and Charlotte Hempel, with the assistance of Michael DeVries and Drew Longacre (London: Bloomsbury T&T Clark, 2019), 395–404.

119 For theology and ideology, see, e.g., Harrington, *The Purity Texts*; Marcel Poorthuis and Joshua J. Schwartz, eds., *Purity and Holiness: The Heritage of Leviticus*, Jewish and Christian Perspectives Series 2 (Leiden: Brill, 2000); Eyal Regev, "Priestly Dynamic Holiness and Deuteronomic Static Holiness," *VT* 51 (2001): 243–61. For evolutionary basis of biblical laws, including purity rules, see Thomas Kazen, *Emotions in Biblical Law: A Cognitive Science Approach*, HBM 36 (Sheffield: Sheffield Phoenix Press, 2011).

120 Thomas Kazen, "Levels of Explanation for Ideas of Impurity: Why Structuralist and Symbolic Models Often Fail While Evolutionary and Cognitive Models Succeed," *JAJ* 9 (2018): 75–100.

121 Newman, "Ritual and Worship in Early Judaism," 395.

the *scope* of Torah observance: "What did it mean to fulfill the law?"; "How far does the law stretch?" The Qumran calendrical texts and so-called liturgical or prayer texts strongly suggest that their concern went beyond defining sacred space (and traditional priestly space): recognizing and studying sacred *time* and divine cosmic plan, as well as aligning their worship with the heavenly worship became equally significant dimensions of Torah observance.[122] Therefore, halakhic discourse is not about specific isolated ritual practices; it is in a way about ritualization of everyday practice.

As noted above, texts themselves may have functioned as ritual objects by recitation. Qumran finds have uncovered the first *tefillin* and *mezuzot*, minute texts in leather boxes, that follow the rule to inscribe the instructions on arms and forehead (e.g., Exod 13:9).[123] Furthermore, stepped pools are material markings of purity practices that in Leviticus 12–15 did not yet receive detailed instructions on *how* and *where* to purify. These pools did not exist only at Qumran but seem to have been spread all over from the Hasmonean time onwards.[124] Materiality is an important dimension when investigating which impact different halakhic rules may have had or which practices were visually manifest and to whom.

6   Conclusion

In conclusion, there is more room to investigate the Scrolls from ritual studies perspectives. Ritual studies is not a unified field but presents a multidisciplinary area, inviting a focused look at various levels, from cognitive to social

---

122   Jonathan Ben-Dov and Lutz Doering, eds., *The Construction of Time in Antiquity: Ritual, Art, and Identity* (Cambridge: Cambridge University Press, 2017); Yonatan S. Miller, "Sabbath-Temple-Eden: Purity Rituals at the Intersection of Sacred Time and Space," *JAJ* 9 (2018): 46–74.

123   See further Yehudah B. Cohn, "Reading Material Features of Qumran Tefillin and Mezuzot," in *Material Aspects of Reading in Ancient and Medieval Cultures: Materiality, Presence and Performance*, eds. Anna Krauß, Jonas Leipziger, and Friederike Schücking-Jungblut, Materiale Textkulturen 26 (Berlin: De Gruyter, 2020), 89–100; Emanuel Tov, "The Tefillin from the Judean Desert and the Textual Criticism of the Hebrew Bible," in *Is There a Text in this Cave?*, 277–92; Yonatan Adler, "The Distribution of Tefillin Finds among the Judean Desert Caves," in *The Caves of Qumran: Proceedings of the International Conference, Lugano 2014*, ed. Marcello Fidanzio, STDJ 118 (Leiden: Brill, 2016), 161–73.

124   See further Yonatan Adler, "The Hellenistic Origins of Jewish Ritual Immersion," *JJS* 69 (2018): 1–21; Stuart Miller, *At the Intersection of Texts and Material Finds: Stepped Pools, Stone Vessels, and Ritual Purity among the Jews of Roman Galilee* (Göttingen: Vandenhoeck & Ruprecht, 2015).

and cultural. It draws heavily from the Classics from the twentieth century but is also moving in new directions. We suggested that the central emphases in theories of ritual vary from ritual as the basis for social belonging and co-operation, to ritual as structuring society, reinforcing hierarchies, and exposing tensions; and from ritual as a symbolic form of communication to ritual as action that accomplishes changes in the world. These emphases (that is, cohesion, conflict, communication, change) are merely heuristic tools to gather numerous, more specific theories that are growingly emerging, also as part of cognitive science of religion. In Qumran studies, the strongest emphasis has probably been on cohesion: rituals like the covenant renewal create the community as the individuals come together and become to see themselves in terms of a collective corpus, set for a cosmic purpose in the world. In the everyday life, similar function may have been in the purity regulations. Also, the process of individual change to a sectarian has been stressed, not necessarily accomplished by rituals but as it is reflected in the texts. Transformation and change is present also in the ways in which humans participate in the heavenly worship and, according to some, become angelic or god-like, or ward off evil spirits and get access to protection. When it comes to communication, much attention has been dedicated to deciphering scriptural traditions and reinterpretations in the scrolls. Less attention has been paid to which information rituals themselves transmit, how the textual representations relate to actual practices, and to what extent those traditions were likely memorable or not. Open avenues wait for more explorations on rituals as addressing conflicts and anxieties, or the material texts themselves as ritual vehicles.

Bibliography

Adler, Yonatan. "The Distribution of Tefillin Finds among the Judean Desert Caves." Pages 161–73 in *The Caves of Qumran: Proceedings of the International Conference, Lugano 2014.* Edited by Marcello Fidanzio. STDJ 118. Leiden: Brill, 2016.

Adler, Yonatan. "The Decline of Jewish Ritual Purity Observance in Roman Palaestina: An Archaeological Perspective on Chronology and Historical Context." Pages 269–84 in *Expressions of Cult in the Southern Levant in the Greco-Roman Period: Manifestations in Text and Material Culture.* Edited by Oren Tal and Zeev Weiss. Contextualizing the Sacred 6. Turnhout: Brepols, 2017.

Adler, Yonatan. "The Hellenistic Origins of Jewish Ritual Immersion." *JJS* 69 (2018): 1–21.

Alexander, Philip S. "Magic and Magical Texts." *EDSS* 1:502–4.

Alexander, Philip S. "Rules." *EDSS* 2:799–803.

Anderson, Jeff S. "Curse and Blessings: Social Control and Self Definition in the Dead Sea Scrolls." Pages 47–60 in vol. 1 of *The Dead Sea Scrolls in Context: Integrating the Dead Sea Scrolls in the Study of Ancient Texts, Languages, and Cultures.* Edited by Armin Lange, Emanuel Tov, and Matthias Weigold. VTSup 140. Leiden: Brill, 2011.

Arnold, Russell C. D. *The Social Role of Liturgy in the Religion of the Qumran Community.* STDJ 60. Leiden: Brill, 2006.

Arnold, Russell C. D. "The Dead Sea Scrolls, Qumran, and Ritual Studies." Pages 2:547–62 in *The Dead Sea Scrolls in Context: Integrating the Dead Sea Scrolls in the Study of Ancient Texts, Languages, and Cultures.* Edited by Armin Lange, Emanuel Tov, and Matthias Weigold. VTSup 140. Leiden: Brill, 2011.

Austin, John L. *How to Do Things with Words: The William James Lectures Delivered at Harvard University in 1955.* Oxford: Oxford University Press, 1976.

Balentine, Samuel E., ed. *The Oxford Handbook on Ritual and Worship in the Hebrew Bible.* New York, NY: Oxford University Press, 2020.

Batsch, Christophe. "Priests in Warfare in the Second Temple Judaism: 1QM, or the Anti-Phinehas." Pages 165–78 in *Qumran Cave 1 Revisited: Texts from Cave 1 Sixty Years after Their Discovery: Proceedings of the Sixth Meeting of the IOQS in Ljubljana.* Edited by Daniel K. Falk, Sarianna Metso, Donald W. Parry, and Eibert J. C. Tigchelaar. STDJ 91. Leiden: Brill, 2010.

Bell, Catherine. "Ritual (Further Considerations)." Pages 7848–56 in vol. 11 of *Encyclopedia of Religion.* 2nd ed. Edited by Lindsay Jones. Detroit: Macmillan, 2005.

Bell, Catherine. *Ritual: Perspectives and Dimensions.* Oxford: Oxford University Press, 1997.

Bell, Catherine. *Ritual Theory, Ritual Practice.* Oxford: Oxford University Press, 1992.

Bell, Catherine. "The Ritualization of Texts and the Textualization of Ritual in the Codification of Taoist Literature." *HR* 27 (1988): 366–92.

Ben-Dov, Jonathan, and Lutz Doering, eds. *The Construction of Time in Antiquity: Ritual, Art, and Identity.* Cambridge: Cambridge University Press, 2017.

Bibb, Bryan D. *Ritual Words and Narrative Worlds in the Book of Leviticus.* LHBOTS 480. New York, NY: T&T Clark, 2009.

Bloch, Maurice. "Symbols, Song, Dance and Features of Articulation: Is Religion and Extreme Form of Traditional Authority?" *European Journal of Sociology* 15 (1974): 55–81.

Bohak, Gideon. *Ancient Jewish Magic: A History.* Cambridge: Cambridge University Press, 2008.

Bohak, Gideon. "Mystical Texts, Magic, and Divination." Pages 457–66 in *T&T Clark Companion to the Dead Sea Scrolls.* Edited by George J. Brooke and Charlotte Hempel, with the assistance of Michael DeVries and Drew Longacre. London: Bloomsbury T&T Clark, 2019.

Boyer, Pascal, and Pierre Liénard. "Why Ritualized Behavior? Precaution Systems and Action Parsing in Developmental, Pathological and Cultural Rituals." *Behavioral and Brain Sciences* 29 (2006): 595–613.

Bourdieu, Pierre. *Outline of a Theory of Practice*. Translated by Richard Nice. Cambridge: Cambridge University Press, 1977.

Bourdieu, Pierre. *The Logic of Practice*. Translated by Richard Nice. Stanford, CA: Stanford University Press, 1990.

Bourdieu, Pierre. *The Bachelor's Ball*. Cambridge: Polity, 2008.

Bourdieu, Pierre. *Distinction: A Social Critique of the Judgement of Taste*. Translated by Richard Nice. London: Routledge, 2010.

Brand, Miryam T. *Evil Within and Without: The Source of Sin and Its Nature in Second Temple Literature*. JSJSup 9. Göttingen: Vandenhoeck & Ruprecht, 2013.

Bulbulia, Joseph, and Richard Sosis. "Signaling Theory and the Evolution of Religious Cooperation." *Religion* 41 (2011): 363–88.

Chwe, Michael Suk-Young. *Rational Ritual: Culture, Coordination, and Common Knowledge*. Princeton, NJ: Princeton University Press, 2001.

Cohn, Yehudah B. "Reading Material Features of Qumran Tefillin and Mezuzot." Pages 89–100 in *Material Aspects of Reading in Ancient and Medieval Cultures: Materiality, Presence and Performance*. Edited by Anna Krauß, Jonas Leipziger, and Friederike Schücking-Jungblut. Materiale Textkulturen 26. Berlin: De Gruyter, 2020.

Collins, John J. *Apocalypticism in the Dead Sea Scrolls*. London: Routledge, 1997.

Collins, John J. "Prayer and the Meaning of Ritual in the Dead Sea Scrolls." Pages 69–85 in *Prayer and Poetry in the Dead Sea Scrolls and Related Literature: Essays in Honor of Eileen Schuller on the Occasion of Her 65th Birthday*. Edited by Jeremy Penner, Ken M. Penner, and Cecilia Wassén. STDJ 98. Leiden: Brill, 2012.

Collins, John J., and Robert A. Kugler, eds. *Religion in the Dead Sea Scrolls*. Grand Rapids, MI: Eerdmans, 2000.

Cottle, Simon. "Mediatized Rituals: Beyond Manufacturing Consent." *Media, Culture & Society* 28.3 (2006): 411–32.

Couldry, Nick. *Media Rituals: A Critical Approach*. London: Routledge, 2003.

Couldry, Nick, and Andreas Hepp. "Conceptualizing Mediatization: Contexts, Traditions, Arguments." *Communication Theory* 23 (2013): 191–202.

Cui, Xi. "Mediatized Rituals: Understanding the Media in the Age of Deep Mediatization." *International Journal of Communication* (Online) (2019): 4155–68.

Daise, Michael A. "Ritual Density in Qumran Practice: Ablutions in the *Serekh Ha-Yahad*." Pages 51–66 in *New Perspectives on Old Texts: Proceedings of the Tenth Annual International Symposium of the Orion Center for the Study of the Dead Sea Scrolls and Associated Literature, 9–11 January, 2005*. Edited by Esther G. Chazon and Betsy Halpern-Amaru. STDJ 88. Leiden: Brill, 2010.

Daise, Michael A. "Processual Modality in Qumran Ritual: Induction into the Counsel of the 'Yachad' in 1QS." *Annali di Storia dell'Esegesi* 30.2 (2013): 303–15.

Damasio, Antonio. *Self Comes to Mind: Constructing the Conscious Brain*. New York, NY: Pantheon/Random House, 2010.

Davila, James R. *Liturgical Works*. ECDSS. Grand Rapids, MI: Eerdmans, 2000.

Davila, James R. "Ritual in the Jewish Pseudepigrapha." Pages 158–83 in *Anthropology and Biblical Studies: Avenues of Approach*. Edited by Louise J. Lawrence and Mario I. Aguilar. Leiden: Brill, 2004.

DeMaris, Richard E. *The New Testament in Its Ritual World*. London: Routledge, 2008.

Douglas, Mary. *Natural Symbols*. New York, NY: Random House, 1973.

Durkheim, Émile. *The Elementary Forms of the Religious Life*. 5th ed. London: George Allen & Unwin, 1964 (1912).

Eckhardt, Benedikt. "Meals and Politics in the *Yaḥad*: A Reconsideration." DSD 17 (2010): 180–209.

Eshel, Esther. "Apotropaic Prayers in the Second Temple Period." Pages 69–88 in *Liturgical Perspectives: Prayer and Poetry in Light of the Dead Sea Scrolls. Proceedings of the Fifth International Symposium of the Orion Center for the Study of the Dead Sea Scrolls and Associated Literature, 19–23 January, 2000*. Edited by Esther G. Chazon with collaboration of Ruth A. Clements and Avital Pinnick. STDJ 48. Leiden: Brill, 2003.

Falk, Daniel K. *Daily, Sabbath, and Festival Prayers in the Dead Sea Scrolls*. STDJ 27. Leiden: Brill, 1998.

Falk, Daniel K. "Liturgical Progression and the Experience of Transformation in Prayers from Qumran." DSD 22 (2015): 267–84.

Falk, Daniel K. "Prayer, Liturgy, and War." Pages 275–94 in *The War Scroll, Violence, War and Peace in the Dead Sea Scrolls and Related Literature: Essays in Honour of Martin G. Abegg on the Occasion of His 65th Birthday*. Edited by Kipp Davis, Kyung S. Baek, Peter W. Flint, and Dorothy Peters. STDJ 115. Leiden: Brill, 2016.

Falk, Daniel K. "Liturgical Texts." Pages 423–34 in *T&T Clark Companion to the Dead Sea Scrolls*. Edited by George J. Brooke and Charlotte Hempel, with the assistance of Michael DeVries and Drew Longacre. London: T&T Clark, 2019.

Fuller, Steve W. *The Cognitive Turn: Sociological and Psychological Perspectives on Science*. Dordrecht: Kluwer, 1989.

Geertz, Clifford. *The Interpretation of Cultures*. New York, NY: Basic Books, 1973.

Gilders, William K. "Social and Cultural Anthropology." Pages 125–41 in *The Oxford Handbook of Ritual and Worship in the Hebrew Bible*. Edited by Samuel E. Balentine. New York, NY: Oxford University Press, 2020.

Gorman, Frank H. *Ideology of Ritual: Space, Time and Status in the Priestly Theology*. JSOTSup 91. Sheffield: JSOT Press, 1990.

Grabbe, Lester L. "Warfare: Eschatological Warfare." *EDSS* 2:961–65.

Grimes, Ronald L. *Beginnings in Ritual Studies*. 2nd ed. Columbia, SC: University of South Carolina Press, 1995.

Grimes, Ronald L. *Rite Out of Place: Ritual, Media, and the Arts*. Oxford: Oxford University Press, 2006.

Grimes, Ronald L. "Performance Theory and the Study of Ritual." Pages 109–38 in *New Approaches to the Study of Religion, Vol. 2: Textual, Comparative, Sociological, and Cognitive Approaches*. Edited by Peter Antes, Armin W. Geertz, and Randi R. Warni. Berlin: De Gruyter, 2008.

Grimes, Ronald L., Ute Hüsken, Udo Simon, and Eric Venbrux, eds. *Ritual, Media, and Conflict*. Oxford: Oxford University Press, 2011.

Grimes, Ronald L. *The Craft of Ritual Studies*. Oxford: Oxford University Press, 2014.

Gruenwald, Ithamar. *Ritual and Ritual Theory in Ancient Israel*. BRLA 10. Leiden: Brill, 2003.

Haigh, Rebekah. "Oral Aspects: A Performative Approach to 1QM." *DSD* 26 (2019): 189–219.

Harkins, Angela Kim. *Reading with an "I" to the Heavens: Looking at the Qumran Hodayot Through the Lens of Visionary Traditions*. Ekstasis 3. Berlin: De Gruyter, 2012.

Harrington, Hannah K. *The Purity Texts*. CQS 5. London: T&T Clark, 2004.

Harrington, Hannah K. "Examining Rabbinic Halakhah Through the Lens of Qumran." Pages 137–55 in *The Qumran Legal Texts between the Hebrew Bible and the Its Interpretation*. Edited by Kristin De Troyer and Armin Lange, with the Assistance of James Seth Adcock. CBET 61. Leuven: Peeters, 2011.

Harrington, Hannah K. "Accessing Holiness via Ritual Ablutions in the Dead Sea Scrolls and Related Literature." Pages 71–96 in *Sacrifice, Cult, and Atonement in Early Judaism and Christianity: Constituents and Critique*. Edited by Henrietta L. Wiley and Christian A. Eberhart. RBS 85. Atlanta, GA: SBL, 2017.

Hempel, Charlotte. "Who is Making Dinner at Qumran?" *JTS* 63 (2012): 49–65.

Hempel, Charlotte. "סֶרֶךְ særæk," Pages 1111–17 in *Theologisches Wörterbuch zu den Qumrantexten*. Edited by Heinz-Josef Fabry and Ulrich Dahmen. Vol. 2. Stuttgart: Kohlhammer, 2013.

Hempel, Charlotte. *Qumran Rule Texts in Context: Collected Studies*. TSAJ 154. Tübingen: Mohr Siebeck, 2013.

Hempel, Charlotte. "Rules." Pages 405–12 in *T&T Clark Companion to the Dead Sea Scrolls*. George J. Brooke and Charlotte Hempel, with the assistance of Michael DeVries and Drew Longacre. London: Bloomsbury, 2019.

Hempel, Charlotte. "The Apotropaic Function of the Final Hymn in the Community Rules." Pages 131–54 in *Petitioners, Penitents, and Poets: On Prayer and Praying in the Second Temple Judaism*. Edited by Timothy J. Sandoval and Ariel Feldman. BZAW 524. Berlin: De Gruyter, 2020.

Hempel, Charlotte. *The Community Rules from Qumran: A Commentary.* TSAJ 183. Tübingen: Mohr Siebeck, 2020.

Hjarvard, Stig. *The Mediatization of Culture and Society.* London: Routledge, 2012.

Janzen, David. *The Social Meanings of Sacrifice in the Hebrew Bible: A Study of Four Writings.* BZAW 344. Berlin: De Gruyter, 2004.

Jeserich, Florian. "An Invitation to 'Theorizing' Theorizing Rituals: Some Suggestions for Using the Indexes." Pages 687–713 in *Theorizing Rituals: Issues, Topics, Approaches, Concepts.* Edited by Jens Kreinath, Jan Snoek, and Michael Stausberg. Studies in the History of Religion 114–1. Leiden: Brill, 2006.

Jokiranta, Jutta. "Ritual System in the Qumran Movement: Frequency, Boredom, and Balance." Pages 144–63 in *Mind, Morality and Magic: Cognitive Science Approaches in Biblical Studies.* Edited by István Czachesz and Risto Uro. Durham: Acumen, 2013.

Jokiranta, Jutta. "Towards a Cognitive Theory of Blessing: Dead Sea Scrolls as Test Case." Pages 25–47 in *Functions of Psalms and Prayers in the Late Second Temple Period.* Edited by Mika S. Pajunen and Jeremy Penner. BZAW 486. Berlin: De Gruyter, 2017.

Jokiranta, Jutta. "Ritualization and Power of Listing in 4QBerakhot[a] (4Q286)." Pages 438–58 in *Is There a Text in this Cave? Studies in the Textuality of the Dead Sea Scrolls in Honour of George J. Brooke.* Edited by Ariel Feldman, Maria Cioată and Charlotte Hempel. STDJ 119. Leiden: Brill, 2017.

Jokiranta, Jutta. "Competition rather than Conflict: Identity Discourse in the Qumran Rule Scrolls." Forthcoming in *Negotiating Identities: Conflict, Conversion, and Consolidation in Early Judaism and Christianity (200 BCE–400 CE).* Edited by Karin Hedner Zetterholm, Anders Runesson, Magnus Zetterholm, and Cecilia Wassén. JSJ Supplement Series. Leiden: Brill.

Kazen, Thomas. *Emotions in Biblical Law: A Cognitive Science Approach.* HBM 36. Sheffield: Sheffield Phoenix Press, 2011.

Kazen, Thomas. "Levels of Explanation for Ideas of Impurity: Why Structuralist and Symbolic Models Often Fail While Evolutionary and Cognitive Models Succeed." *JAJ* 9 (2018): 75–100.

Klingbeil, Gerald A. *Bridging the Gap: Ritual and Ritual Texts in the Bible.* BBRSup 1. Winona Lake, IN: Eisenbrauns, 2007.

Krause, Andrew R. "Performing the Eschaton: Apotropaic Performance in the Liturgy of the War Scroll." *RevQ* 30 (2018): 27–46.

Krause, Andrew R. "Apotropaic Means and Methods in the Rules of the Trumpets and Banners (1QM 3–4)." *Henoch* 42 (2020): 117–35.

Kreinath, Jens, Jan Snoek, and Michael Stausberg. "Ritual Studies, Ritual Theory, Theorizing Rituals—An Introductory Essay." Pages xv–xxvii in in *Theorizing Rituals: Issues, Topics, Approaches, Concepts.* Edited by Jens Kreinath, Jan Snoek, and Michael Stausberg. Studies in the History of Religion 114–1. Leiden: Brill, 2006.

Kreinath, Jens, Jan Snoek, and Michael Stausberg. *Theorizing Rituals: Issues, Topics, Approaches, Concepts.* Studies in the History of Religion 114–1. Leiden: Brill, 2006.

Kreinath, Jens, Jan Snoek, and Michael Stausberg, eds. *Theorizing Rituals: Annotated Bibliography of Ritual Theory, 1966–2005*. Studies in the History of Religion 114–2. Leiden: Brill, 2007.

Kugler, Robert A. "Making All Experience Religious: The Hegemony of Ritual at Qumran." *JSJ* 33 (2002): 131–52.

Kugler, Robert A. "Of Calendars, Community Rules, and Common Knowledge: Understanding 4QS^e–4QOtot, with the Help of Ritual Studies." Pages 215–28 in *Rediscovering the Dead Sea Scrolls: An Assessment of Old and New Methods*. Edited by Maxine L. Grossman. Grand Rapids, MI: Eerdmans, 2010.

Laidlaw, James Alexander, and Caroline Humphrey. *The Archetypal Actions of Ritual: An Essay on Ritual as Action Illustrated by the Jain Rite of Worship*. Oxford: Clarendon Press, 1994.

Lawson, E. Thomas, and Robert N. McCauley. *Rethinking Religion: Connecting Cognition and Culture*. Cambridge: Cambridge University Press, 1990.

MacDonald, Nathan, ed. *Ritual Innovation and the Hebrew Bible and Early Judaism*. BZAW 468. Berlin: De Gruyter, 2018.

Mauss, Marcel. *Sociology and Psychology: Essays by Marcel Mauss*. Edited and translated by Ben Brewster. London: Routledge and Kegan Paul, 1979.

McCauley, Robert N., and E. Thomas Lawson. *Bringing Ritual to Mind: Psychological Foundations of Cultural Forms*. Cambridge: Cambridge University Press, 2002.

Mermelstein, Ari. "Emotional Regimes, Ritual Practice, and the Shaping of Sectarian Identity: The Experience of Ablutions in the Dead Sea Scrolls." *BibInt* 24 (2016): 492–513.

Milgrom, Jacob. *Leviticus 1–16: A New Translation with Introduction and Commentary*. AB 3. Garden City, NY: Doubleday, 1991.

Miller, Stuart. *At the Intersection of Texts and Material Finds: Stepped Pools, Stone Vessels, and Ritual Purity among the Jews of Roman Galilee*. Göttingen: Vandenhoeck & Ruprecht, 2015.

Miller, Yonatan S. "Sabbath-Temple-Eden: Purity Rituals at the Intersection of Sacred Time and Space." *JAJ* 9 (2018): 46–74.

Mitkidis, Panagiotis, Pierre Liénard, Kristoffer L. Nielbo, and Jesper Sørensen. "Does Goal-Demotion Enhance Cooperation?" *Journal of Cognition and Culture* 14 (2014): 263–72.

Newman, Judith H. "Embodied Techniques: The Communal Formation of the *Maskil's* Self." *DSD* 22 (2015): 249–66.

Newman, Judith H. "The Thanksgiving Hymns of 1QH^a and the Construction of the Ideal Sage through Liturgical Performance." Pages 940–57 in *Sibyls, Scriptures, and Scrolls: John Collins at Seventy*. Edited by Joel Baden, Hindy Najman, and Eibert J. C. Tigchelaar. JSJSup 175. Leiden: Brill, 2016.

Newman, Judith H. *Before the Bible: The Liturgical Body and the Formation of Scriptures in Early Judaism*. New York, NY: Oxford University Press, 2018.

Newman, Judith H. "Ritualizing the Text in Early Judaism: Two Examples of Innovation." *HeBAI* 7 (2018): 449–65.

Newman, Judith H. "Songs for the Sabbath Sacrifice." Pages 347–9 in *T&T Clark Companion to the Dead Sea Scrolls*. Edited by George J. Brooke and Charlotte Hempel, with the assistance of Michael DeVries and Drew Longacre. London: Bloomsbury T&T Clark, 2019.

Newman, Judith H. "Ritual and Worship in Early Judaism." Pages 393–409 in *The Oxford Handbook of Ritual and Worship in the Hebrew Bible*. Edited by Samuel E. Balentine. New York, NY: Oxford University Press, 2020.

Newsom, Carol A. "Shirot ʿOlat HaShabbat." Pages 173–401 in *Qumran Cave 4.VI: Poetical and Liturgical Texts, Part 1*. Edited by Esther Eshel et al. in consultation with James VanderKam and Monica Brady. DJD 11. Oxford: Clarendon, 1998.

Newsom, Carol A. *The Self as Symbolic Space: Constructing Identity and Community at Qumran*. STDJ 52. Leiden: Brill, 2004.

Newsom, Carol A. "Pairing Research Questions and Theories of Genre: A Case Study with the Hodayot." *DSD* 17 (2010): 241–59.

Nitzan, Bilhan. "4QBerakhotᵃ." Pages 7–48 in *Qumran Cave 4.VI: Poetical and Liturgical Texts, Part 1*. Edited by Esther Eshel et al. in consultation with James VanderKam and Monica Brady. Oxford: Clarendon, 1998.

Noam, Vered. "Corpse-Blood Impurity: A Lost Biblical Reading?" *JBL* 128 (2009): 243–51.

Noam, Vered. "Stringency in Qumran: A Reassessment." *JSJ* 40 (2009): 342–55.

Noam, Vered. "Qumran and the Rabbis on Corpse-Impurity: Common Exegesis—Tacit Polemic." Pages 397–430 in *The Dead Sea Scrolls: Texts and Contexts*. Edited by Charlotte Hempel. STDJ 90. Leiden: Brill, 2010.

Noam, Vered. "Halakhah." Pages 395–404 in *T&T Clark Companion to the Dead Sea Scrolls*. Edited by George J. Brooke and Charlotte Hempel, with the assistance of Michael DeVries and Drew Longacre. London: Bloomsbury T&T Clark, 2019.

Penner, Jeremy. *Patterns of Daily Prayer in Second Temple Period Judaism*. STDJ 104. Leiden: Brill, 2012.

Poorthuis, Marcel, and Joshua J. Schwartz, eds. *Purity and Holiness: The Heritage of Leviticus*. Jewish and Christian Perspectives Series 2. Leiden: Brill, 2000.

Pyysiäinen, Ilkka. *How Religion Works: Towards a New Cognitive Science of Religion*. Cognition and Culture Book Series 1. Leiden: Brill, 2001.

Quine, Cat. *Casting Down the Hosts of Heaven: The Rhetoric of Ritual Failure in the Polemic Against the Host of Heaven*. OtSt 78. Leiden: Brill, 2020.

Rappaport, Roy A. *Pigs for the Ancestors: Ritual in the Ecology of a New Guinea People*. New Haven, NY: Yale University Press, 1967.

Rappaport, Roy A. *Ecology, Meaning, and Religion*. Richmond, CA: North Atlantic Books, 1979.

Rappaport, Roy A. *Ritual and Religion in the Making of Humanity*. Cambridge: Cambridge University Press, 1999.

Regev, Eyal. "Priestly Dynamic Holiness and Deuteronomic Static Holiness." *VT* 51 (2001): 243–61.

Sax, William S., Johannes Quack, and Jan Weinhold, eds. *The Problem of Ritual Efficacy*. Oxford Ritual Studies. Oxford: Oxford University Press, 2010.

Schechner, Richard. *Essays in Performance Theory 1970–1976*. New York, NY: Drama Book Specialists, 1977.

Schechner, Richard. *The Future of Ritual: Writings on Culture and Performance*. London: Routledge, 1993.

Schiffman, Lawrence H. *The Halakhah at Qumran*. SJLA 16. Leiden: Brill, 1975.

Schiffman, Lawrence H. *The Eschatological Community of the Dead Sea Scrolls: A Study of the Rule of the Congregation*. SBLMS 38. Atlanta, GA: Scholars, 1989.

Schuller, Eileen M. "Functions of Psalms and Prayers in the Late Second Temple Period." Pages 5–24 in *Functions of Psalms and Prayers in the Late Second Temple Period*. Edited by Mika S. Pajunen and Jeremy Penner. BZAW 486. Berlin: De Gruyter, 2017.

Schuller, Eileen M. "Ritual and Worship at Qumran." Pages 365–77 in *The Oxford Handbook of Ritual and Worship in the Hebrew Bible*. Edited by Samuel E. Balentine. New York, NY: Oxford University Press, 2020.

Searle, John R. *Speech Acts: An Essay in the Philosophy of Language*. Cambridge: Cambridge University Press, 1969.

Segal, Robert A. "Myth and Ritual." Pages 101–21 in *Theorizing Rituals: Issues, Topics, Approaches, Concepts*. Edited by Jens Kreinath, Jan Snoek, and Michael Stausberg. Studies in the History of Religion 114–1. Leiden: Brill, 2006.

Sørensen, Jesper. *A Cognitive Theory of Magic*. London: AltaMira Press, 2007.

Staal, Frits. "The Meaninglessness of Ritual." *Numen* 26 (1979): 2–22.

Staal, Frits. *Rules Without Meaning: Ritual, Mantras, and the Human Sciences*. Toronto Studies in Religion 4. New York, NY: Peter Lang, 1989.

Stock, Brian. *The Implications of Literacy: Written Language and Models of Interpretation in the Eleventh and Twelfth Centuries*. Princeton, NJ: Princeton University Press, 1983.

Stökl Ben Ezra, Daniel. "When the Bell Rings: The Qumran Rituals of Affliction in Context." Pages 2:533–46 in *The Dead Sea Scrolls in Context: Integrating the Dead Sea Scrolls in the Study of Ancient Texts, Languages, and Cultures*. Edited by Armin Lange, Emanuel Tov, and Matthias Weigold. VTSup 140. Leiden: Brill, 2011.

Sumiala, Johanna. "Mediatized Ritual—Expanding the Field in the Study of Media and Ritual." *Sociology Compass* 8.7 (2014): 939–47.

Thatcher, Tom, Chris Keith, Raymond F. Person, Jr., and Elise R. Stern, eds. *The Dictionary of the Bible and Ancient Media*. London: Bloomsbury T&T Clark, 2017.

Thomas, Günter. "Communication." Pages 321–43 in *Theorizing Rituals: Issues, Topics, Approaches, Concepts*. Edited by Jens Kreinath, Jan Snoek, and Michael Stausberg. Studies in the History of Religion 114–1. Leiden: Brill, 2006.

Tov, Emanuel. "The Tefillin from the Judean Desert and the Textual Criticism of the Hebrew Bible." Pages 277–92 in *Is There a Text in this Cave? Studies in the Textuality of the Dead Sea Scrolls in Honour of George J. Brooke*. Edited by Ariel Feldman, Maria Cioată, and Charlotte Hempel. STDJ 119. Leiden: Brill, 2017.

Turner, Victor. *The Ritual Process: Structure and Anti-Structure*. London: Routledge, 1969.

Turner, Victor. *Dramas, Fields, and Metaphors: Symbolic Action in Human Society*. Ithaca, NY: Cornell University Press, 1974.

Turner, Victor. "Symbols and Social Experience in Religious Ritual." *Studia Missionalia* 23 (1974): 1–21.

Turner, Victor. "Ritual as Communication and Potency: A Ndembu Case Study." Pages 58–81 in *Symbols and Society: Essays on Belief Systems in Action*, ed. Caroline E. Hill, Southern Anthropological Society Proceedings 9. Athens, GA: University of Georgia Press, 1975.

Turner, Victor. *From Ritual to Theatre: The Human Seriousness of Play*. Performance Studies Series 1. New York, NY: PAJ Publications, 1982.

Uro, Risto. *Ritual and Christian Beginnings: A Socio-Cognitive Analysis*. Oxford: Oxford University Press, 2016.

Uro, Risto. "Rituaalit, ympäristö ja uskonto—kognitiivinen näkökulma tutkimusalojen vuoropuheluun." *Uskonnontutkija* 10 (2021): 1–21.

Uro, Risto, Juliette Day, Richard E. DeMaris, and Rikard Roitto, eds. *The Oxford Handbook of Early Christian Ritual*. Oxford: Oxford University Press, 2019.

Wassén, Cecilia. "The (Im)purity Levels of Communal Meals within the Qumran Movement." *JAJ* 7 (2016): 102–22.

Wassén, Cecilia. "Common Meals in the Qumran Movement with Special Attention to Purity Regulations." Pages 77–100 in vol. 1 of *The Eucharist—Its Origins and Contexts: Sacred Meal, Communal Meal, Table Fellowship in Late Antiquity, Early Judaism, and Early Christianity*. Edited by David Hellholm and Dieter Sänger. Tübingen: Mohr Siebeck, 2017.

Wassén, Cecilia. "Daily Life." Pages 547–58 in *T&T Clark Companion to the Dead Sea Scrolls*. Edited by George J. Brooke and Charlotte Hempel, with the assistance of Michael DeVries and Drew Longacre. London: Bloomsbury T&T Clark, 2019.

Watts, James W. *Ritual and Rhetoric in Leviticus: From Sacrifice to Scripture*. Cambridge: Cambridge University Press, 2007.

Watts, James W. *Leviticus 1–10*. HCOT. Leuven: Peeters, 2013.

Weitzman, Steven. "Revisiting Myth and Ritual in Early Judaism." *DSD* 4 (1997): 21–54.

Weitzman, Steven. "Warring Against Terror: The War Scroll and the Mobilization of Emotion." *JSJ* 40 (2009): 213–41.

Werline, Rodney A. "Prayer, Politics, and Social Vision in Daniel 9." Pages 17–32 in *Seeking the Favor of God*, vol. 2: *The Development of Penitential Prayer in Second*

Temple Judaism. Edited by Mark J. Boda, Daniel K. Falk, and Rodney A. Werline. EJL 22. Atlanta, GA: SBL 2007.

Werline, Rodney A. "Reflections on Penitential Prayer: Definition and Form." Pages 209–25 in *Seeking the Favor of God*, vol. 2: *The Development of Penitential Prayer in Second Temple Judaism*. Edited by Mark J. Boda, Daniel K. Falk, and Rodney A. Werline. EJL 22. Atlanta, GA: SBL 2007.

Werrett, Ian. *Ritual Purity and the Dead Sea Scrolls.* STDJ 72. Leiden: Brill, 2007.

Werrett, Ian. "Walking over the Dead: Burial Practices and the Possibility of Ritual Innovation at Qumran." Pages 151–66 in *Ritual Innovation in the Hebrew Bible and Early Judaism*. Edited by Nathan MacDonald. BZAW 468. Berlin: De Gruyter, 2016.

Werrett, Ian, and Stephen Parker. "Purity in War: What is it Good for?" Pages 295–316 in *The War Scroll, Violence, War and Peace in the Dead Sea Scrolls and Related Literature: Essays in Honour of Martin G. Abegg on the Occasion of His 65th Birthday*. Edited by Kipp Davis, Kyung S. Baek, Peter W. Flint, and Dorothy Peters. STDJ 115. Leiden: Brill, 2016.

White, Claire. *An Introduction to the Cognitive Science of Religion: Connecting Evolution, Brain, Cognition and Culture.* London: Routledge, 2021.

Whitehouse, Harvey. *Arguments and Icons: Divergent Modes of Religiosity*. Oxford Studies in Social and Cultural Anthropology. Oxford: Oxford University Press, 2000.

Wright, David P. "Ritual Theory, Ritual Texts, and the Priestly-Holiness Writings of the Pentateuch." Pages 195–216 in *Social Theory and the Study of Israelite Religion: Essays in Retrospect and Prospect*. Edited by Saul M. Olyan. RBS 71. Atlanta, GA: SBL, 2012.

Yadin, Yigael. *The Scroll of the War of the Sons of Light against the Sons of Darkness.* Translated by Batya and Chaim Rabin. Oxford: Oxford University Press, 1962.

PART 2

*Present Perspectives on the Dead Sea Scrolls
and Ancient Media*

∵

CHAPTER 6

Book Production and Circulation in Ancient Judaea: Evidenced by Writing Quality and Skills in the Dead Sea Scrolls Isaiah and Serekh Manuscripts

Mladen Popović

1 Introduction*

When thinking about the Dead Sea Scrolls and ancient media, scribes play a central role, not only as the perceived faithful transmitters of a text, but also as taking part in the production, elaboration, transmission and circulation of texts—orally, aurally, and textually.[1] An important aspect in all of this, but one that is largely neglected,[2] is the question of how texts were published in ancient Judaea. How exactly should we envisage the spread of texts beyond the

---

* The research for this article was carried out within the ERC Starting Grant project of the European Research Council (EU Horizon 2020): *The Hands that Wrote the Bible: Digital Palaeography and Scribal Culture of the Dead Sea Scrolls* (HandsandBible #640497). Preliminary versions of this paper benefitted from the feedback of colleagues at conferences in Tbilisi—organised by the Cluster of Excellence in 'Changes in Sacred Texts and Traditions of the University of Helsinki (funded by the Academy of Finland) at Tbilisi Javakhishvili State University, Georgia, May 2018—and London at St Mary's University, United Kingdom, June 2019. In addition, I am also grateful for the feedback on the version published in this volume from the editors, Chris Keith and Travis Williams, and from the project team member's Gemma Hayes, Drew Longacre, and Ayhan Aksu, and also Eibert Tigchelaar.

1 For a recent entry, see Eibert J. C. Tigchelaar, "The Scribes of the Scrolls," in *T&T Clark Companion to the Dead Sea Scrolls*, ed. George J. Brooke and Charlotte Hempel, with the assistance of Michael DeVries and Drew Longacre (London: T&T Clark, 2019), 524–32. Following the work of William Johnson, I have argued that in the intellectual reading culture in Hellenistic and early Roman Judaea as reflected by the scrolls, the activities of reading, writing, and memorizing should also be understood as intertwined aspects—part of the procedure of reading as a multi-dimensional activity—that occurred in deeply social contexts of group reading and study of texts; Mladen Popović, "Reading, Writing, and Memorizing Together: Reading Culture in Ancient Judaism and the Dead Sea Scrolls in a Mediterranean Context," *DSD* 24 (2017): 447–70.

2 See, however, Michael O. Wise, "Accidents and Accidence: A Scribal View of Linguistic Dating of the Aramaic Scrolls from Qumran," in *Thunder in Gemini, and Other Essays on the History, Language and Literature of Second Temple Palestine*, JSPSup 15 (Sheffield: Sheffield Academic Press, 1994), 103–51, esp. 119–46.

© MLADEN POPOVIĆ, 2023 | DOI:10.1163/9789004537804_007

first author or authors? What do we mean by publication? Does some other term capture the production and circulation of texts better?

This neglect in research is to a large part due to the dearth of evidence. If texts were central to the social life of the people behind the Dead Sea Scrolls, it may strike as somewhat remarkable that in their self-presentation they do not say much about the different activities involved in making and collecting texts. For comparative purposes, we might turn to Greco-Roman reading cultures, where researchers have carefully deconstructed anachronistic notions about publishing in the ancient world.

While studying ancient Jewish reading culture, I was intrigued by William Johnson's discussion of the relationship between recitation and publication. Discussing the recitation of literary texts as presented in Pliny the Younger, Johnson examined "the ways in which recitation intersected, generally, with the social mechanics surrounding the literary practices that Pliny recommends, and, specifically, with the need to make public—to 'publish'—creative literary endeavor."[3] Similar to, for example, Raymond Starr and Jon Iddeng,[4] Johnson took as point of departure that, "In Roman society, there was no publisher or other agent who acted as a gatekeeper for publications."[5] Important is Johnson's argument that "the gatekeeper function was the product of a complex social interaction, and the various circles of the literarily interested—such as the circle around Pliny—played an essential role in promoting or rejecting new authors."[6] Could we imagine the movement or group behind the Dead Sea Scrolls performing such a gatekeeper function? The Dead Sea Scrolls may provide the possibility to approach the issue of "publishing" in Judaea in the Hellenistic and early Roman periods from both conceptual and material perspectives.

Yet, instead of approaching the issues of "publishing" as text production and circulation at large, in this article I limit the research focus to the scrolls in relation to the perceived group or movement behind them and wish to draw attention to one important yet neglected aspect in scrolls studies: For whom was a manuscript copied? This question has not been raised much in Dead Sea Scrolls studies, if at all. Of course, scholars have asked after the function of certain manuscripts, but that is not precisely the same, even though the question

---

3 William A. Johnson, *Readers and Reading Culture in the High Roman Empire: A Study of Elite Reading Communities* (Oxford: Oxford University Press, 2010), 52.

4 Raymond J. Starr, "The Circulation of Literary Texts in the Roman World," *ClQ* 37 (1987): 213–223; Jon W. Iddeng, "Publica aut peri! The Releasing and Distribution of Roman Books," *SO* 81 (2006): 58–84.

5 Johnson, *Readers and Reading Culture*, 53.

6 Johnson, *Readers and Reading Culture*, 53.

of a manuscript's function can intersect with the question for whom it was copied. Scholars have also looked at the material evidence of multiple copies of a single composition, but mainly for studying textual transmission and compositional history. Asking for whom a manuscript was copied invites looking anew at the material evidence and to study, for example, the variance in script styles, the quality of writing, and the level of writing skills.[7] These allow us to better understand what kind of manuscript a specific specimen may have represented and what that may mean in terms of production and circulation in the context of the perceived group or movement behind the Dead Sea Scrolls.

In this article, I will first briefly discuss how scholars approach the relationship between the manuscripts, the people living in the settlement at Qumran, and a broader movement, at various places. The range of possible users of and markets for the scrolls puts the topic of "publishing" in terms of production and circulation on the table.

Second, I will give a brief, inexhaustive, overview of some recent research on "publishing" in the Roman Mediterranean and ancient Judaea. This will redirect and limit the focus to the central role of scribes and to the distinction between trained and untrained copyists in relation to the level of writing skills they have achieved. This will allow us to focus on the question for whom a manuscript was copied, and in what context.

Third, as a way of probing the data, I will give a preliminary consideration of a number of manuscripts of two compositions, namely those of Isaiah and those of the Serekh (Community Rule). The concrete evidence of these two groups of manuscripts enables interaction with various scholarly scenarios of text production and circulation in connection with different models of communities or movements behind the scrolls. The Isaiah manuscripts are interesting as "biblical" manuscripts for our purposes because they, or manuscripts like them, were broadly circulated in ancient Judaism. Furthermore, despite the numerous textual variants, which can be classified as individual variants, the text of Isaiah was remarkably stable with the extant textual evidence pointing to a single main edition of the work circulating in ancient Judaism.[8]

---

7 Often, when palaeographers speak of the "quality" of the hand, they mean something like the ability of the writer to produce text in the desired script style consistently and accurately. While there can be overlap between "quality" and "level of writing skills" in relation to script style, "quality" can also be understood distinct from "level of writing skills" in order to differentiate, for example, evidence where a skilled scribe, say one who had attained a high level of writing skills, shows a lower-level quality execution of writing in a specific copy, see the discussion below, e.g., 4Q62a (4QIsa^i).

8 George J. Brooke, "Isaiah in the Qumran Scrolls," in *The Oxford Handbook of Isaiah*, ed. Lena-Sofia Tiemeyer (Oxford: Oxford University Press, 2021), 433–35; Eugene Ulrich and

The Serekh manuscripts are interesting because they have been understood in scholarship to be sectarian manuscripts *par excellence*, while their scholarly understanding of a Qumran-only context has evolved to also include multiple, related groups, understood as Essene, Yaḥad or otherwise, at different locations in ancient Judaea. Furthermore, far from pointing to a stable text, the extant manuscript evidence demonstrates that there was not a single moment of "publication," no finalised text, but rather textual fluidity. Scholars have drawn different conclusions for what this means for our understanding of what each manuscript copy represented, calling into question too what constituted the work "Community Rule/Rules" in the minds of the scribes.[9] Here, I show how a focus on the scribes' writing style, quality of writing, and level of writing skills can sharpen and improve our understanding of what the manuscript evidence as a distinct physical object may have represented for the one copying it as well as for those for whom it was copied.

2 The Scrolls, Qumran, and the Yaḥad Community or Movement

Ever since the discovery of the Dead Sea Scrolls between 1947 and 1956, the relationship between the manuscripts and the people living in the settlement at Qumran has been debated. The debate has focused mainly on the question of material connections between the archaeology of the settlement and of the

---

Peter W. Flint, with a contribution by Martin G. Abegg, Jr., *Qumran Cave 1.11: The Isaiah Scrolls*, DJD 32 (Oxford: Clarendon, 2010), 2:91; Eugene Ulrich, "Isaiah, Book of," in *Encyclopedia of the Dead Sea Scrolls*, Lawrence H. Schiffman and James C. VanderKam (Oxford: Oxford University Press, 2000), 386.

9   See, e.g., David Hamidović, "Editing a Cluster of Texts: The Digital Solution," in *Ancient Worlds in Digital Culture*, ed. Claire Clivaz, Paul Dilley, and David Hamidović, Digital Biblical Studies 1 (Leiden: Brill, 2016), 196–213; idem, "Living *Serakhim*: Process of Authority in the *Community Rule*," in *The Process of Authority: The Dynamics in Transmission and Reception of Canonical Texts*, ed. Jan Dušek and Jan Roskovec, DCLS 27 (Berlin: De Gruyter, 2016), 61–90; Jutta Jokiranta, "Thinking About Ancient Manuscripts as Information Processing," in *Sibyls, Scriptures, and Scrolls: John Collins at Seventy*, ed. Joel Baden, Hindy Najman, and Eibert J.C. Tigchelaar, JSJSup 175 (2 vols.; Leiden: Brill, 2017), 1:611–35; Sarianna Metso and James M. Tucker, "The Changing Landscape of Editing Ancient Jewish Texts," in *Reading the Bible in Ancient Traditions and Modern Editions: Studies in Memory of Peter W. Flint*, ed. Andrew B. Perrin, Kyung S. Baek, and Daniel K. Falk, EJL 47 (Atlanta, GA: SBL, 2017), 269–87; Sarianna Metso, *The Community Rule: A Critical Edition with Translation*, EJL 51 (Atlanta, GA: SBL, 2019), 6; Charlotte Hempel, *The Community Rules from Qumran: A Commentary*, TSAJ 183 (Tübingen: Mohr Siebeck, 2020), 2, 34; James Nati, *Textual Criticism and the Ontology of Literature in Early Judaism: An Analysis of the* Serekh ha-Yaḥad, JSJSup 198 (Leiden: Brill, 2022).

caves.[10] Early on, statements were also made as to the inscriptional evidence from the site and the scrolls showing the same writing, though, to my knowledge, this has never really been assessed otherwise.[11] Scholars reiterate that no scrolls were found in the site itself, arguing against a connection or explaining that such is to be expected after the site's destruction but that this does not speak against a connection.[12]

Linking the site and the scrolls, scholars have suggested various scenarios for understanding how the manuscripts may have belonged to the people living at Qumran.[13] In addition to archaeological interpretations of the tangible evidence at the site, in the caves near Qumran, and from the immediate surroundings, these scenarios also depend in part on various literary and historical interpretations of the textual evidence, in the Dead Sea Scrolls as well as from other ancient sources.

For example, for Roland de Vaux and other scholars, it was clear that manuscripts were copied in what he identified as the scriptorium of Qumran (locus 30) and also that certain works were composed on site. In addition to practising agriculture and certain industries, as well as living under a community regime with special rules and rituals, the people living at Qumran, de Vaux argued, owned and read the manuscripts that were found, in modern times, in the surrounding caves. These manuscripts were copied on the spot or had come from elsewhere.[14] While de Vaux did not exclude the possibility that those at Qumran could have sold the manuscripts which they copied for gain,

---

10   For convenient overviews of the state of the art, see, e.g., Roland de Vaux, *Archaeology and the Dead Sea Scrolls* (London: Oxford University Press, 1973); Jodi Magness, *The Archaeology of Qumran and the Dead Sea Scrolls*, Studies in the Dead Sea Scrolls and Related Literature (Grand Rapids, MI: Eerdmans, 2002); Dennis Mizzi, "Archaeology of Qumran," in *T&T Companion to the Dead Sea Scrolls*, ed. George J. Brooke and Charlotte Hempel, with the assistance of Michael DeVries and Drew Longacre (London: Bloomsbury, 2019), 17–36.

11   See de Vaux, *Archaeology and the Dead Sea Scrolls*, 103. Claiming an absolute dating peg for his palaeographic typology, Frank Moore Cross also linked the two, see "The Development of the Jewish Scripts," in *The Bible and the Ancient Near East: Essays in Honor of William Foxwell Albright*, ed. G. Ernest Wright (Garden City, NY: Doubleday, 1961), 134 n. 9, updated in *Leaves from an Epigrapher's Notebook: Collected Papers in Hebrew and West Semitic Palaeography and Epigraphy*, HSS 51 (Winona Lake, IN: Eisenbrauns, 2003), 4 n. 9.

12   See, however, Wise, "Accidents and Accidence," 120 n. 56.

13   For our purposes here, I focus only on those scenarios of a more sustained connection, not those that limit a possible connection only to the moment of depositing the manuscripts in the caves in the context of the Jewish revolt against Rome in 66–70/73 CE.

14   De Vaux, *Archaeology and the Dead Sea Scrolls*, 104–105. See also, e.g., Józef T. Milik, *Ten Years of Discovery in the Wilderness of Judaea*, trans. John Strugnell (London: SCM, 1959), 103; Frank Moore Cross, *The Ancient Library of Qumran*, 3rd ed. (Sheffield: Sheffield Academic Press, 1995), 64.

Hartmut Stegemann went further and argued that the whole reason for the settlement of Qumran, and Ein Feshkha, was to be a scrolls production centre for the many Essene settlements throughout the country.[15] But when Qumran would have been unoccupied after the earthquake of 31 BCE, according to de Vaux's interpretation,[16] Stegemann allowed for scrolls to have also been produced elsewhere while production continued, on a smaller scale, at Qumran.[17]

More recently, Sidnie White Crawford continued this line of thought and argued that Qumran was a scribal centre and library for a wider Essene movement.[18] Differently from Stegemann, she assumed that the scroll collections in the individual caves came from different local Essene communities before being processed for long-term storage at Qumran.[19]

Attributing the origin of manuscripts also to sites other than Qumran, albeit unknown ones, White Crawford is in agreement with a number of researchers that have argued for a more diverse movement of authors, scribes, or owners behind the scrolls, a movement that would have extended beyond the site of Qumran itself.[20] This reorientation in research is due in part to the full publication of the scrolls in the 1990s and 2000s, which enabled scholars to engage with all the extant texts. Acknowledging, for example, that a text like 1QS 6:1–2/4Q258 2:6 ("In this way they shall behave in all their places of residence") is written with more than one community in mind, or that the multiple copies in different versions of the Damascus Document and the Rule of the Community, regarded by scholars to be foundational community compositions, point to a more complex and dynamic development than of just one community, scholars have argued for the existence of multiple, related communities—at different sites than just Qumran.[21]

---

15 Hartmut Stegemann, *Die Essener, Qumran, Johannes der Täufer und Jesus: Ein Sachbuch* (Freiburg: Herder, 1993), 77–82.

16 See, however, Dennis Mizzi and Jodi Magness, "Was Qumran Abandoned at the End of the First Century BCE?" *JBL* 135 (2016): 301–20.

17 Stegemann, *Die Essener*, 83–84.

18 Sidnie White Crawford, *Scribes and Scrolls at Qumran* (Grand Rapids, Eerdmans, 2019).

19 White Crawford, *Scribes and Scrolls at Qumran*, 315–20.

20 This differentiation of related groups across the country is sometimes similar but sometimes not exactly the same as the differentiation researchers made between different Essene groups, e.g., celibate at Qumran and non-celibate elsewhere, and used as a model in earlier phases of Dead Sea Scrolls research.

21 See, e.g., Philip R. Davies, "The Judaism(s) of the Damascus Document," in *The Damascus Document: A Centennial of Discovery*, ed. Joseph M. Baumgarten, STDJ 34 (Leiden: Brill, 2000), 27–43; idem, "Sects from Texts: On the Problems of Doing a Sociology of the Qumran Literature," in *New Directions in Qumran Studies: Proceedings of the Bristol*

BOOK PRODUCTION AND CIRCULATION IN ANCIENT JUDAEA   205

Focusing on writing or scribal activities for which we have material evidence, the presence of many ostraca, inscribed jars and at least six, but maybe eight, inkwells indicates that various writing activities took place on site at Qumran.[22] André Lemaire argued for sectarian education at Qumran, referring also to one inscribed jar in particular (KhQ 1313) to argue that its fine and regular writing, being of unusual good quality for a jar inscription, pointed to a scribe that was accustomed to writing on manuscripts.[23] Although the find sites of the ostraca give no indication of a concentration of writing anywhere at Qumran specifically, the presence of abecedaries or student exercises such as KhQ 161 and KhQ 2207 can be taken to indicate that scribes were present at Qumran and also that some elementary exercises or training in writing may have taken place there.[24] As to the manuscripts from the caves near Qumran, it is evident that those who composed and copied them must have received some form of education, but, as Eibert Tigchelaar has cautioned, the concrete evidence for this education is limited. (And we have no idea what it was like for "non-Qumran" Jews either.) This scribal training or education may have happened at Qumran or elsewhere.[25]

    Colloquium on the Dead Sea Scrolls, 8–10 September 2003, ed. Jonathan G. Campbell, William J. Lyons, and Lloyd K. Pietersen (London: T&T Clark, 2005), 26–42; Eyal Regev, *Sectarianism in Qumran: A Cross-Cultural Perspective*, Religion and Society 45 (Berlin: De Gruyter, 2007); Alison Schofield, *From Qumran to the Yaḥad: A New Paradigm of Textual Development for The Community Rule*, STDJ 77 (Leiden: Brill, 2009); John J. Collins, *Beyond the Qumran Community: The Sectarian Movement of the Dead Sea Scrolls* (Grand Rapids, MI: Eerdmans, 2010); Charlotte Hempel, *The Qumran Rule Texts in Context*, TSAJ 154 (Tübingen: Mohr Siebeck, 2013); Alison Schofield, "Forms of Community," in *T&T Companion to the Dead Sea Scrolls*, ed. George J. Brooke and Charlotte Hempel, with the assistance of Michael DeVries and Drew Longacre. London: Bloomsbury, 2019), 533–46; Hempel, *The Community Rules from Qumran*.

22   André Lemaire, "Inscriptions du khirbeh, des grottes et de 'Aïn Feshkha," in *Khirbet Qumrân et 'Aïn Feshkha II: Études d'anthropologie, de physique et de chimie, Studies of Anthropology, Physics and Chemistry*, ed. Jean-Baptiste Humbert and Jan Gunneweg, NTOA.SA 3 (Fribourg: Academic Press Fribourg, 2003), 341–88; Mladen Popović, "The Ancient 'Library' of Qumran between Urban and Rural Culture," in *The Scrolls from Qumran and the Concept of a Library*, ed. Sidnie White Crawford and Cecilia Wassén, STDJ 116 (Leiden: Brill, 2016), 155–67; White Crawford, *Scribes and Scrolls at Qumran*, 195.

23   André Lemaire, "Lire, écrire, étudier à Qoumrân et ailleurs," in *Qoumrân et le Judaïsme du tournant de notre ère: Actes de la Table Ronde, Collège de France, 16 novembre 2004*, ed. André Lemaire and Simon C. Mimouni, Collection de la Revue des Études Juives 40 (Leuven: Peeters, 2006), 64; Lemaire, "Inscriptions du khirbeh," 354.

24   White Crawford, *Scribes and Scrolls at Qumran*, 189–92; Émile Puech, "Exercises de deux scribes à Khirbet Qumrân: KhQ 161 et KhQ 2207," *RevQ* 32 (2020): 43–56.

25   Tigchelaar, "The Scribes of the Scrolls," 530–31.

It is clear that a significant number of manuscripts predates the period that the site of Qumran was settled, whether according to the traditional chronology proposed by de Vaux beginning in the second century BCE, sometime prior to the rule of John Hyrcanus (135–104 BCE), or according to Jodi Magness's interpretation of the archaeological evidence that suggests a beginning in the first half of the first century BCE.[26] White Crawford has suggested that we must assume the group was already in existence prior to the settlement at Qumran and owned those manuscripts, and also that Qumran was only one of the places where they were located.[27] In addition to the possibility that scrolls were brought to Qumran for safekeeping from various Essene settlements, John Collins allowed for the possibility that scrolls copied at various locations were brought to Qumran by sectarians who moved there at various times, adding the cautious note that much remains uncertain about the provenance and use of the scrolls found in the caves.[28]

Magness's redating has especially challenged scholarly interpretations of the Serekh manuscripts as reflecting a group directly connected with the site of Qumran.[29] A further complicating factor is the literary nature of most of the manuscript evidence. Charlotte Hempel, for example, has cautioned against reading the Serekh texts as "reality literature," as if text and social reality directly converged without the involvement of any ideology or interest to present matters in a certain way, as can be expected from literary texts with a complex development history. Hempel's comments as to the dating of Serekh manuscripts in relation to Magness's revised chronology for the communal occupation call into question a neat alignment between text and historical reality as it is unlikely, she said, that 1QS can be associated with life at Qumran from the beginning, since the document allows for a considerable time to have elapsed in the movement's life.[30]

---

26 De Vaux, *Archaeology and the Dead Sea Scrolls*, 5; Magness, *The Archaeology of Qumran*, 63–66.

27 White Crawford, *Scribes and Scrolls at Qumran*, 141. See also Esther G. Chazon, "Is *Divrei Ha-Me'orot* a Sectarian Prayer?" in *The Dead Sea Scrolls: Forty Years of Research*, ed. Devorah Dimant and Uriel Rappaport, STDJ 10 (Leiden: Brill, 1992), 6–7.

28 Collins, *Beyond the Qumran Community*, 210, and see further below. See also Mladen Popović, "Qumran as Scroll Storehouse in Times of Crisis? A Comparative Perspective on Judaean Desert Manuscript Collections," *JSJ* 43 (2012): 578.

29 See, e.g., Schofield, *From Qumran to the* Yaḥad, 268; Hempel, *The Community Rules from Qumran*, 8–9.

30 Hempel, *The Qumran Rule Texts in Context*, 8; eadem, "The Theatre of the Written Word: Reading the Community Rule with Steven Fraade," in *The Faces of Torah: Studies in the Texts and Contexts of Ancient Judaism in Honor of Steven Fraade*, ed. Michal Bar-Asher

BOOK PRODUCTION AND CIRCULATION IN ANCIENT JUDAEA 207

Yet, Hempel rightly cautioned about assuming too stark an opposition between the ideal and the real when she said that parts of the penal code and 4Q477 do indicate hints of reality.[31] Another, and different, kind of "reality literature" are the writing exercises referred to by Tigchelaar (4Q6, 4Q201, 4Q234, 4Q341, and 4Q360), which should be taken into account when hypothesising about the nature of the collections in the caves.[32] In addition to 4Q477, White Crawford also referred to 4Q339 and 4Q340 to suggest that it is unlikely that such notes were transported to Qumran from elsewhere; they must have been written at Qumran, and, what is more, indicate the local nature of the collection. She also argued that if a particular rule was being followed in the Qumran settlement, that rule would have most likely been some form of the Serekh, again also referring to 4Q477.[33]

The relationship between manuscripts, site, and community has to be considered before asking for whom a particular manuscript was copied because of an assumption in the field that seems to be operative in the background when studying the textual and manuscript variation evidenced by the scrolls. The assumption seems to be that many (most?) of the manuscripts were produced and copied for the internal consumption of the presumed community, whether at Qumran or also elsewhere, catering to their specific needs, whether, for example, literary, liturgical, scholarly, or educational. This comes most clearly to the fore with regard to the extant Serekh manuscripts.[34]

Thus, Collins argued, for example, that different versions of the Serekh were not copied side by side in the same community, but in different communities,

---

Siegal, Tzvi Novick, and Christine Hayes, JAJSup 22 (Göttingen: Vandenhoeck & Ruprecht, 2017), 124–27; eadem, *The Community Rules from Qumran*, 9.

It is interesting to note that Cross seems to have let his palaeographic dating of Serekh manuscripts be determined by his understanding of the site's dating and the connection between manuscripts, site and community. Referring to 1QS and two other, early Serekh manuscripts (the papyrus copy being referred to is 4Q255; cf. Philip S. Alexander and Geza Vermes, *Qumran Cave 4.XIX: Serekh ha-Yaḥad and Two Related Texts*, DJD 26 [Oxford: Clarendon, 1998], 21, 24), Cross said, "Obviously none of these was copied before the founding of the community" (*The Ancient Library of Qumran*, 95); see also, with regard to 4Q53, Eugene C. Ulrich, "4QSam^c: A Fragmentary Manuscript of 2 Samuel 14–15 from the Scribe of *Serek Hay-yaḥad* (1QS)," *BASOR* 235 (1979): 2–3. This, however, may not seem so obvious anymore since a strict, exclusive, connection between scrolls and site, and in particular the so-called sectarian manuscripts and the site of Qumran, has been reconsidered in recent scholarship.

31   Hempel, *The Qumran Rule Texts in Context*, 9, 44–45.
32   Tigchelaar, "The Scribes of the Scrolls," 531.
33   White Crawford, *Scribes and Scrolls at Qumran*, 144, 275–76.
34   Cf., e.g., Schofield, *From Qumran to the* Yaḥad, 128 n. 179.

and were serving those different communities at the same time.[35] Collins was cautious about connecting 1QS or any of the other Serekh manuscripts directly with Qumran. Alison Schofield was cautious too when she seemed to connect 1QS more directly with Qumran as she tentatively suggested that 1QS may have been the official Qumran copy.[36] But she also argued for the manuscript variance (e.g., regarding orthography) to be explained in terms of different scribal circles in the Yaḥad movement having distinct localized training,[37] with Qumran as a hierarchical centre of the larger movement.[38] In terms of a "sectarian scribe," Eugene Ulrich argued that the scribe who copied 1Q11, 4Q57, and 11Q14 (see section 3.1.1 below) and the scribe of 1QS did their work at Qumran because they copied sectarian literature.[39] But if sectarian literature could also have been copied within the context of related communities outside of Qumran, then the copying of sectarian texts cannot be used as evidence for a direct connection of a scribe with the site of Qumran.

A closer look at the details of scribal practices evident from the manuscript evidence is important for understanding connections, commonalities, clusters of texts and differences across the totality of manuscripts available. As Tigchelaar has argued, on the one hand, shared scribal practices evident from the manuscript evidence may indicate a shared scribal culture; on the other hand, the collection as a whole also exhibits a large variety of scribal practices that cannot be taken to indicate a common provenance or a specific scribal school.[40]

Instead of assuming that many of the manuscripts were produced for the internal consumption of the presumed community, Michael Wise has argued that at least some of the scrolls are the products of the broader book culture in Judaea and also that the great majority of the scrolls constitute a cross-section of that trade.[41] Following Wise, Daniel Falk, focusing on the physical realia of writing and handling prayer texts (liturgical prose prayers, sectarian religious poetry, and apotropaic prayers and poems, and in comparison with scriptural scrolls and rule and legal scrolls), has suggested a commercial market for some

---

35 Collins, *Beyond the Qumran Community*, 3, 68–69.

36 Schofield, *From Qumran to the* Yaḥad, 130. See also Eibert J. C. Tigchelaar, "In Search of the Scribe of 1QS," in *Emanuel: Studies in Hebrew Bible, Septuagint, and Dead Sea Scrolls in Honor of Emanuel Tov*, ed. Shalom M. Paul et al., VTSup 94 (Leiden: Brill, 2003), 451.

37 Schofield, *From Qumran to the* Yaḥad, 129.

38 Schofield, *From Qumran to the* Yaḥad, 271.

39 Eugene C. Ulrich, "Identification of a Scribe Active at Qumran: 1QPs[b]–4QIsa[c]–11QM," *Meghillot* 5–6 (2008): 208–9.

40 Tigchelaar, "The Scribes of the Scrolls," 531.

41 Wise, "Accidents and Accidence," 120.

of the small scriptural books, extracted scriptural texts and apotropaic prayers and poems type of scrolls. He suggested a wide range of uses and market, possibly including personal copies, scholar's study editions, and official and master copies, for sectarian poetic texts and rule texts that show a diversity in format: both elegant and rustic, and both larger and small format copies of the same text. For the liturgical prose prayers, on the basis of their compact format, more rustic appearance, commonplace and varied quality of writing, Falk suggested that these are to be regarded as personal copies, for the recording and aiding of what was an oral performance.[42]

This range of possible users and markets puts the topic of publishing in terms of production and circulation on the table.

3 Recent Research on "Publishing" in the Roman Mediterranean and Ancient Judaea

For more recent scholarly understandings of publishing in the ancient Mediterranean world, Starr was instrumental. He set out to clarify how publishing in late Republican and early Imperial Rome was very different from modern notions informed by commercial publishing as a large-scale and professional industry. Over against such a modern conception, Starr argued, "Romans circulated texts in a series of widening concentric circles determined primarily by friendship, which might, of course, be influenced by literary interests, and by the forces of social status that regulated friendship. Bookstores and 'public' libraries, which made a text available to individuals personally unknown to the author and his friends, were comparatively late developments."[43]

The whole process was thus deeply social in terms of network. First came the inner circle of the author's friends. Only later, Starr argued, came the outermost circles of strangers.[44] The first phase, for the inner circle of friends, had three stages:[45] (1) a draft copy was made, in the author's home at his own

---

42 Daniel K. Falk, "Material Aspects of Prayer Texts at Qumran," in *Literature or Liturgy? Early Christian Hymns and Prayers in their Literary and Liturgical Context in Antiquity*, ed. Clemens Leonhard and Hermut Löhr, WUNT 2/363 (Tübingen: Mohr Siebeck, 2014), 74–75, 81–83. The implied meaning of "rustic appearance" seems to be defined as a manuscript or fragment with narrow line spacing relative to letter size, and uneven line spacing (66).

43 Starr, "The Circulation of Literary Texts," 213.

44 Starr, "The Circulation of Literary Texts," 213–16.

45 See also Myles McDonnel, "Writing, Copying, and Autograph Manuscripts in Ancient Rome," *ClQ* 46 (1996): 486; Dan Nässelqvist, "Publication," in *The Dictionary of the Bible and Ancient Media*, ed. Tom Thatcher, Chris Keith, Raymond F. Person, and Elsie R. Stern (London: Bloomsbury T&T Clark, 2017), 319–20.

expense by his slaves, and shared with friends, asking for comments and advice upon which (2) an author revised the draft and shared it with a slightly wider group of friends. This could be done by sending draft copies or inviting friends to attend a recital of the composition. These recitals had small audiences with whom the author was already in social contact, including patrons and clients. These first readings were closed and the work remained in the control of the author. In the final stage, (3) multiple copies were made of the final, polished version by the author's own scribes or by a friend's *librarii*, though the testing and revision of a work continued. Gift copies were presented to friends.

After these three stages of the author's inner circle—with the gift copies of a finished text—came the phase of the outermost circle of strangers. According to Starr, it then was possible for people unknown to the author to acquire a text by making a copy from a friend's copy. Only at this stage, Starr argues, was a text made public or intended for release. Starr and others prefer the term "release" over "publish" because the latter may imply modern connotations. Starr stresses how the connections are almost always through friends and connecting networks,[46] and no commercial transaction was involved. Of course, there are examples where things went differently, and Starr also acknowledged these.[47] When Atticus circulated a preliminary draft text of Cicero without his approval, he received an angry letter from Cicero. This shows that a draft text could be circulated more broadly without the author's approval and also that this may have posed a problem for the author.[48]

Starr listed five ways in which an author could make a text available for copying by others: (1) sending a gift copy to a friend without placing any restrictions on its being copied; (2) recitation of the work to friends and allowing copies to be made; (3) depositing a copy in one of the public libraries, placing it in the public domain as it were; (4) encouraging friends to make the book known; (5) depositing a copy with a book dealer.[49]

Starr's work has been influential, also with regard to thinking about publishing in ancient Judaism.[50] It makes sense, as Steve Mason has argued,[51] for

---

46   Starr, "The Circulation of Literary Texts," 215: "Most readers depended largely if not entirely on privately made copies."

47   Starr, "The Circulation of Literary Texts," 218–19.

48   See also Sander M. Goldberg, *Constructing Literature in the Roman Republic: Poetry and Its Reception* (Cambridge: Cambridge University Press, 2005), 47–48. I thank Ayhan Aksu for this reference.

49   Starr, "The Circulation of Literary Texts," 217.

50   I do not deal here with the Prologue to Ben Sira where in prol. 30 the verb *ekdidōmi*, "to publish," is used: "with the aim of bringing the book to completion and to publish it also for those living abroad if they wish to become learned."

51   Steve Mason, "Of Audience and Meaning: Reading Josephus' *Bellum Judaicum* in the Context of a Flavian Audience," in *Josephus and Jewish History in Flavian Rome and*

Josephus, working and writing in Rome, to have participated in the custom of literary production and dissemination. Mason emphasised that also for Josephus the production and release of his texts was a local and social project.[52] He discussed how Josephus circulated pieces of the *War* to others, including Agrippa, in Rome while he was writing and that this exchange involved some personal contact. Mason suggested that Josephus's use of *synergoi*—co-workers or literary friends—reflects the social nature of writing a book and not the work of an isolated individual.[53] Josephus and his contemporaries probably knew each other's work in progress, quite possibly through recitation or seeing advance copies or extracts via friends:[54] "They normally wrote in community, sharing their work with friends and acquaintances who lived, ate, and slept in—or were visiting—the same location. Wider dissemination was possible, if supportive others were willing, but that came later."[55]

Wise discussed publication as an aspect of ancient Judaean book culture, including also reproduction and circulation. Wise posited that an author in the first century CE might publish his work by any of three methods: (1) he could deposit the work in the temple at Jerusalem (this being probably the most frequent method used for publication); (2) an author could also deposit his principal copy, if not with a group, then with a wealthy and influential friend, who would then have copies made and distributed (Wise here refers to the Aramaic version of Josephus's *War*); (3) an author might provide an authorial copy to one or more *librarii* to copy and sell.[56]

Wise understood book production to have been largely a private matter, but he also saw a role for booksellers (*librarii*), employing one or more professional scribes to produce copies in multiples by dictation if there was a large demand or just one copy to meet the demand of a single order.[57]

With regard to book circulation, Wise considered literacy rates, the cost of books, the breadth of circulation (evidence from Judaean sites other than Qumran), and the availability of libraries. Considering these factors, he argued that fair numbers of Aramaic, Hebrew, and Greek literary works circulated in the outlying villages of Judaea. Wise also referred to P.Oxy. XVIII 2192 from

---

Beyond, ed. Joseph Sievers and Gaia Lembi (Leiden: Brill, 2005), 71–100; idem, "Josephus, Publication, and Audiences: A Response," *Zutot* 8 (2011): 81–94.

52   Mason, "Of Audience and Meaning," 78, 80, 82, 84.

53   Mason, "Of Audience and Meaning," 85–86.

54   Mason, "Of Audience and Meaning," 88, 90.

55   Mason, "Josephus, Publication, and Audiences," 88.

56   Wise, "Accidents and Accidence," 137–138.

57   Wise, "Accidents and Accidence," 139–140.

173 CE.[58] This is a letter from learned individuals, showing at least three different scribal hands,[59] requesting from friends/acquaintances elsewhere copies of books to be made that they do not have themselves, in addition to asking some of their own books to be sent to them. If a bookseller or library was not an option, then books would have been copied and passed around among educated readers, which must have been a common way to obtain books unavailable locally, or to expand a private library at minimal cost, and it would have been in this context that personal copies were produced.[60] Wise also looked specifically at personal copies in the Dead Sea Scrolls as distinct from manuscripts that would have circulated in the regular book trade, signalling out literary works on papyrus, especially if written in a cursive or semicursive script, and especially also opisthographs.[61] Wise concluded that the Dead Sea Scrolls had a far wider circulation than exclusively within the confines of a small and insular group and that some of the manuscripts were probably authored or copied in rural villages.[62]

Starr's proposal has by and large met with broad consensus, but there are some aspects in which other scholars have taken a different stance.[63] Johnson was "inclined to agree that much book circulation in antiquity was informed by 'a series of widening concentric circles determined primarily by friendship,'" but the important question he put emphasis on was: who is doing the copying?[64]

---

58   Wise, "Accidents and Accidence," 145. See also Johnson, *Readers and Reading Culture*, 181–84; Popović, "Reading, Writing, and Memorizing Together," 468.

59   A high-resolution image can be found on www.papyrology.ox.ac.uk/POxy/.

60   Wise, "Accidents and Accidence," 145–46.

61   Wise, "Accidents and Accidence," 125–36.

62   Wise, "Accidents and Accidence," 145–49.

63   Thus, Iddeng, "Publica aut peri," followed, on the one hand, the argumentation of Starr's article but, on the other hand, and just like Johnson, also went in a different direction with regard to the aspect of recitation and releasing. First, with regard to recitation, Iddeng argued that "the *recitatio* institution was developed along with an expanding book culture and an increasing demand for written texts" (61, see also 60). He is not convinced that these recitations were attended only by friends with a special invitation (61) and rather compares them to present-day art vernissages (62). Second, with regard to releasing and large-scale distribution, Iddeng agrees with Starr for the Republican period but suggests that in the Imperial period, around the turn of the first century, we can detect, alongside private copying and exchange, a more large-scale system of book releasing, consisting of low-status craftsmen and traders editing and reproducing books for a commercial market (68–69).

64   William A. Johnson, *Bookrolls and Scribes in Oxyrhynchus* (Toronto: University of Toronto Press, 2004), 158.

Johnson suggested that examples like that of Cicero and Atticus are rather the exception than the rule, and that we should not presuppose that "most culturally inclined Greeks and Romans as a matter of course had on staff someone trained to make copies consistent with the rather exacting standards" for manuscript production, which he had detailed in his study. Johnson saw a much closer affinity between booksellers and copyists or scribes, as implied by the Latin term *librarius*.[65]

With regard to book circulation, Johnson understood the source of the master copy as essential and he distinguished conceptually between "circulation stemming from the author and his friends, and circulation stemming from 'public' sources such as a *librarius* or a public library."[66] But the production of a book may well have involved a *librarius* regardless of the source of the master copy. Indeed, "The financial feasibility of a 'book trade' in fact makes much more sense if we try to re-imagine a *librarius* not as a 'bookseller' but as a scribe or scribal shop that performs multiple functions."[67] With regard to book production, Johnson argued, the opposition was not between individual and trade or between private and public but rather between private and professional.

A better distinction still is that between trained and untrained copyists in relation to the level of attainment they have achieved. Most of the bookrolls that Johnson studied from Oxyrhynchus for his research show a remarkable uniformity and slight individual variation and stylistic changes over time, with only a few significantly aberrant examples. Thus, one of the most salient features of the bookrolls from Oxyrhynchus is this very professionalism and especially its sheer dominance and near uniformity. In other words, the copyist or scribe takes centre stage.[68]

Therefore, with a focus on the central role of scribes, I will look anew at the manuscript evidence for Isaiah and the Serekh, not with an eye to what they show us about textual transmission or compositional history, but with a focus on the variance in script styles, quality of writing, and level of writing skills. These allow us to better understand what kind of manuscript a specific specimen may have represented in terms of, for example, a professional or untrained copy, a trade or private copy. A copy of a text made by an author for circulation in a close circle of friends would presumably have looked different from an everyday professional or display copy made by a scribe on order for a client.

---

65   Johnson, *Bookrolls and Scribes*, 159.
66   Johnson, *Bookrolls and Scribes*, 159.
67   Johnson, *Bookrolls and Scribes*, 159.
68   Johnson, *Bookrolls and Scribes*, 160.

4 Variance in Script Styles, Quality of Writing, and Level of Writing Skills in Isaiah and Serekh Manuscripts

As noted earlier, absent in scrolls studies when considering manuscripts as evidence for variant editions, or the like, is the simple but crucial question "For whom a specific manuscript was copied?" This is a crucial question because it challenges us to consider whether a specific manuscript was produced for broader use or circulation beyond the particular context of the scribe copying it. Script styles, quality of writing, and level of writing skills should be studied because these can provide further indications of the social context of copying and thus also for whom a manuscript was copied.[69]

When asking for whom a manuscript was copied, we should consider making certain distinctions. Such distinctions may be between, for example, large scrolls, deluxe scrolls, and smaller scrolls, finely written scrolls and crudely written ones. Another important distinction is that between carefully produced scrolls and those produced with less care. For example, Emanuel Tov reserved the category of "deluxe" editions, in scrolls from 50 BCE onwards, for manuscript having large top and bottom margins, having large or very large writing blocks, reflecting the medieval text of MT, and showing a limited amount of scribal intervention.[70] While Tov briefly mentioned fine calligraphy, the feature of script was not put into operation and the four aforementioned features were taken as the indicative criteria for the category of "deluxe" editions. This is also how scholars in the field have usually adopted Tov's deluxe category, with a perspective limited to the codicological dimensions but foregoing analysis of the quality of the handwriting. This is strikingly different from Greco-Roman manuscript cultures, as evidenced by the slightly later Oxyrhynchus papyri for which, Johnson argued, the typical "deluxe" manuscript often did not show characteristics different from those of an everyday production, except for the fine execution of the script.[71] Thus, attention to the quality and level of writing,

---

69 See for comparative purposes, from a different cultural and historical context, e.g., Johnathan Yogev and Shamir Yona, "A Trainee and a Skilled Ugaritic Scribe—KTU 1.12 and KTU 1.4," *ANES* 50 (2013): 237–42; Alice Mandell, "When Form Is Function: A Reassessment of the *Marziḥu* Contract (*KTU* 3.9) as a Scribal Exercise," *Maarav* 23 (2019): 39–67. I thank Eibert Tigchelaar for these references.

70 Emanuel Tov, *Scribal Practices and Approaches Reflected in the Texts Found in the Judean Desert*, STDJ 54 (Leiden: Brill, 2004), 125–29. Cf. also Falk, "Material Aspects of Prayer Texts," 58.

71 Johnson, *Bookrolls and Scribes*, 156. Cf. also 4: "Analysis of finely written rolls overturns the prejudicial assumption (taken from codex culture, but firmly implanted in the papyrological literature) that a tall roll or column was considered more elegant than a short roll or column."

the calligraphy, can call into question assessments of specific Dead Sea Scrolls manuscripts to have been deluxe copies.[72]

Regarding variance in script styles evident in the scrolls, one should be aware that in general the distinctions made between formal, semiformal, and semicursive are often arbitrary, applying "at best to origin or destiny of a tradition."[73] Frank Moore Cross was not able to provide exemplary specimens for each style across the continuum of the chronological range covered by the scrolls.[74] Furthermore, often manuscripts exhibit a mixture of these presumed styles, for example, mixing in some letters that are deemed semicursive in what are otherwise deemed semiformal written manuscripts. This calls further into question some of the distinctions made. These caveats should be borne in mind when I use script styles to characterise Serekh and Isaiah manuscripts for heuristic purposes.

Whereas scholars have commented before on the script styles used in specific manuscripts, mostly for purposes of dating and labelling, not much attention has been devoted to the level of writing skills demonstrated by the manuscripts. Notable exceptions have been Józef Milik, John Strugnell, Ada Yardeni, Émile Puech, Philip Alexander, and Michael Wise, but mostly these have been aside remarks, not sustained analyses.[75] Wise has discussed the use

---

72 See, e.g., Charlotte Hempel, "Reflections of Literacy, Textuality, and Community in the Qumran Dead Sea Scrolls," in *Is There a Texts in This Cave? Studies in the Textuality of the Dead Sea Scrolls in Honour of George J. Brooke*, ed. Ariel Feldman, Maria Cioată, and Charlotte Hempel, STDJ 119 (Leiden: Brill, 2017), 78–79, regarding 1QS-1QSa-1QSb (see section 3.2.1 below for the handwriting of 1QS, which is not finely executed or calligraphic); Laura Quick, "Scribal Habits and Scholarly Texts: Codicology at Oxyrhynchus and Qumran," in *Material Aspects of Reading in Ancient and Medieval Cultures: Materiality, Presence and Performance*, ed. Anna Krauß, Jonas Leipziger, and Friederike Schücking-Jungblut, Materiale Textkulturen 26 (Berlin: De Gruyter, 2020), 37–54, regarding 4Q242 and 4Q550, but the handwriting of 4Q242 is not calligraphic, and the letter and inking variance in 4Q550 is not the hallmark of neat handwriting, nor—with an average letter size of ~3 mm—is the handwriting particularly small.

73 Cross, "The Development of the Jewish Scripts," 144 (1961), 12 (2003); although he said this explicitly for the distinction between formal and cursive, this also applies to semiformal and semicursive.

74 See also Drew Longacre, "Disambiguating the Concept of Formality in Palaeographic Descriptions: Stylistic Classification and the Ancient Jewish Hebrew/Aramaic Scripts," *COMSt Bulletin* 5 (2019): 101–28; Eibert J. C. Tigchelaar, "Seventy Years of Palaeographic Dating of the Dead Sea Scrolls," in *Sacred Texts and Disparate Interpretations: Qumran Manuscripts Seventy Years Later: Proceedings of the International Conference Held at the John Paul II Catholic University of Lublin, 24–26 October 2017*, ed. Henryk Drawnel, STDJ 133 (Leiden: Brill, 2020), 258–78.

75 E.g., Philip S. Alexander, "Literacy among Jews in Second Temple Palestine: Reflections on the Evidence from Qumran," in *Hamlet on a Hill: Semitic and Greek Studies Presented*

of semicursive and cursive script styles with respect to manuscripts deemed personal copies.[76] Falk also gave some attention to varying writing skills of multiple copies of the same composition, using qualifications such as commonplace, rustic, and elegant,[77] although some of his assessments can be disputed.[78]

Recently, Drew Longacre has argued that the notion of formality in handwriting can be understood as an overall impression of the level of handwriting based on the type of model script chosen to reproduce (morphology), the skill and care with which it was written (execution), and the purpose for which the manuscript was created (function).[79] For script styles in Dead Sea Psalm Scrolls, Longacre suggested different usage registers in relation to a manuscript's form and function.[80] Tigchelaar especially has raised the issue of judging calligraphy and levels of skilled writing and care among Dead Sea Scrolls' scribes by paying attention to how the basic forms of the letters were executed, to how letters relate to each other (regularity) in size, ductus, height, and inking, and to how letters, words and lines of words are vertically and horizontally arranged (proportion and arrangement).[81]

---

to Professor T. Muraoka on the Occasion of this Sixty-Fifth Birthday, ed. Martin F. J. Baasten and Wido Th. van Peursen, OLA 118 (Leuven: Peeters, 2003), 16–18; Michael O. Wise, *Language and Literacy in Roman Judaea: A Study of the Bar Kokhba Documents*, AYBRL (New Haven, CT: Yale University Press, 2015), focused specifically on the Judaean Desert evidence, not Qumran.

76   See Wise, "Accidents and Accidence," 126–27, 130–36.

77   Falk, "Material Aspects of Prayer Texts."

78   For example, regarding 11Q11 which Falk, "Material Aspects of Prayer Texts," 73, assessed as expertly made, but looking, e.g., at the irregular letter proportioning, the range of letter variance, and the uneven beginning of the lines from the right margin, not flush, may indicate that the scribe is not so skilled or expert. Furthermore, regarding 4Q400 (Falk, "Material Aspects of Prayer Texts," 70), the letter size is irregular between frg. 1 and frg. 2, there is more variance in frg. 2 in how the basic forms of the letters were executed, and there is also more inking variation especially in frg. 2. It seems possible to me that we have here two different scribes at work in 4Q400 1 and 2. See the images of frg. 1 and frg. 2 at the Leon Levy Dead Sea Scrolls Digital Library: https://www.deadseascrolls.org.il/explore -the-archive/image/B-295361 and https://www.deadseascrolls.org.il/explore-the-archive /image/B-295360.

79   Longacre, "Disambiguating the Concept of Formality."

80   Drew Longacre, "Paleographic Style and the Forms and Functions of the Dead Sea Psalm Scrolls: A Hand Fitting for the Occasion?" *VT* 72 (2021): 67–92.

81   See, on YouTube, Eibert J. C. Tigchelaar, "Beautiful Bookhands and Careless Characters: An Alternative Approach to the Dead Sea Scrolls," (paper presented as the 8th Annual Rabbi Tann Memorial Lecture, University of Birmingham, 2018), https://www.youtube.com /watch?v=thB2tH1kwtU; idem, "Elementary and Unskilled Hands," (paper presented at the Groningen conference on Digital Palaeography and Hebrew/Aramaic Scribal

Tigchelaar has also been the first to systematically address the issue of writing skills in multiple copies of the same composition.[82] However, we must not only gain insight into how one copy compares to another copy of the same composition. Taking this approach further, we would also need to compare each of the multiple copies of the same composition with multiple copies of other compositions that can be attributed to the same style and period. This will allow us to gain a better overall understanding of the level of writing skills at a certain time and place.

The aspect of chronology is important to take into account when assessing writing skills. Over the course of the few centuries that are covered by the manuscript evidence from the Judaean Desert, developments in writing took place that were caused, for example, by a greater demand for texts and thus an increased need of trained scribes,[83] or by shared developments in the ancient Mediterranean.[84] These developments affected not only how the writing looked but also determined the standards of skilled and careful writing so that what may seem skilled writing in one period was not so in another period.[85] An increase in demand and in circulation of texts in ancient Judaea and thus an increased production of books must be factored in when examining the extant manuscript evidence as snapshots of developments over time. We should not assume one model to have been in operation throughout Hellenistic and early Roman Judaea.

Having said that, it is not straightforward to determine what the standards were in different periods. For ancient Judaea we do not have, for example, something akin to a school-book papyrus that demonstrates what was likely to have been the standard script taught in schools,[86] or an edict setting out

---

Culture, University of Groningen, 6–8 April 2021), https://www.youtube.com/watch?v =F8pskj7jSKc.

82   Tigchelaar, "Beautiful Bookhands and Careless Characters."

83   See, e.g., Albert I. Baumgarten, *The Flourishing of Jewish Sects in the Maccabean Era: An Interpretation*, JSJSup 55 (Leiden: Brill, 1997). Ptolemaic Egypt witnessed an increase in book production (literary texts copied on papyrus rolls) that generated intense copying activity which caused scribes to develop ways of accelerated writing as well as graphically standardized and refined letter forms and editorial conventions, see Guglielmo Cavallo and Herwig Maehler, *Hellenistic Bookhands* (Berlin: De Gruyter, 2008), 9.

84   Tigchelaar, "Beautiful Bookhands and Careless Characters," see at 59 minutes; Drew Longacre, "Comparative Hellenistic and Roman Manuscript Studies (CHRoMS): Scripts Interactions and Hebrew/Aramaic Writing Culture," *COMSt Bulletin* 7 (2021): 7–50.

85   Tigchelaar, "Beautiful Bookhands and Careless Characters," see at 57:20 minutes, asks whether we should reckon with an increase in neat and skilled writing.

86   Cf. Cavallo and Maehler, *Hellenistic Bookhands*, 10.

the payment of scribes according to the quality of their writing.[87] For the Oxyrhynchus papyri, admittedly from a slightly later period with regard to the development of the Greek script and book production, Johnson was able to divide the scripts into three categories: deluxe or elegant; everyday professional; and substandard.[88] Most papyri fall in the first two categories. Only a minority is of substandard quality.[89]

> The overwhelming bulk of bookrolls ... show ... the mix of general uniformity and slight individual variation, with stylistic changes over time .... For bookrolls ... the evidence for untrained copying is slim: for most ancient readers, the professional look and feel of the bookroll was an essential aspect of its utility, since the bookroll's sociological function as a cultural icon was as important as its contents.[90]

For the Herodian-period evidence, it seems easier to determine a quality standard, but this seems more difficult to do for the Hasmonaean period material. Cross singled out only 4Q30 (4QDeut^c) as typical formal Hasmonaean, also including 1QIsa^a, but he did not explain why this was so.[91] Scholars have simply followed suit and assumed that especially 4Q30 represents the typical Hasmonaean formal. This unclarity regarding standards means that the comments regarding writing quality and skills, sometimes in agreement with previous assessments, sometimes in disagreement, that follow below are a first and preliminary attempt at clarifying some of the outstanding issues and challenges.

4.1 Isaiah Manuscripts
Let us turn to the evidence for variance in script styles, quality of writing, and level of writing skills in the Isaiah manuscripts from the Judaean Desert. Scholars have identified twenty-two manuscript remains as Isaiah manuscripts: 1QIsa^a, 1Q8 (1QIsa^b), 4Q55 (4QIsa^a), 4Q56 (4QIsa^b), 4Q57 (4QIsa^c), 4Q58 (4QIsa^d), 4Q59 (4QIsa^e), 4Q60 (4QIsa^f), 4Q61 (4QIsa^g), 4Q62 (4QIsa^h),

---

87   Johnson, *Bookrolls and Scribes*, 102.
88   Johnson, *Bookrolls and Scribes*, 7, 102–103, 122–23, 155–56.
89   See also Alan Mugridge, "Writing and Writers in Antiquity: Two 'Spectra' in Greek Handwriting," in *Proceedings of the 25th International Congress of Papyrology*, ed. Traianos Gagos (Ann Arbor: Scholarly Publishing Office, The University of Michigan Library, 2010), 573–80; idem, *Copying Early Christian Texts: A Study of Scribal Practice*, WUNT 362 (Tübingen: Mohr Siebeck, 2016), 20–25.
90   Johnson, *Bookrolls and Scribes*, 160.
91   Cross, "The Development of the Jewish Scripts," 138, 166–67 (1961), 9, 27 (2003).

BOOK PRODUCTION AND CIRCULATION IN ANCIENT JUDAEA 219

4Q62a (4QIsa[i]), 4Q63 (4QIsa[j]), 4Q64 (4QIsa[k]), 4Q65 (4QIsa[l]), 4Q66 (4QIsa[m]), 4Q67 (4QIsa[n]), 4Q68 (4QIsa[o]), 4Q69 (4QpapIsa[p]), 4Q69a (4QIsa[q]), 4Q69b (4QIsa[r]), 5Q3 (5QIsa), and Mur3 (MurIsa).[92] All these need not be considered fragments of once full copies, as they can also include excerpts.

Regarding material aspects of the manuscript evidence, scholars have considered, for example, scribal marks and layout of the text in order to understand how a scribe may have understood the prophetic book, which by that time had a largely stable text tradition and a single main edition.[93] Probing the data, I will present here preliminary considerations that show how attention to the quality and level of writing skills can shed fresh light on the social context of copying Isaiah manuscripts.

For heuristic purposes, I have divided, as Johnson did for the Oxyrhynchus papyri, the scripts of the Isaiah manuscripts into three categories of writing skills or quality (deluxe or elegant, everyday professional, or substandard).[94] Furthermore, I have also correlated these script categorizations with the size of letters according to their average heights because this has not been systematically done before[95] and also because, for the Oxyrhynchus evidence,

---

92   Images of the smaller fragments of 1Q8 (1QIsa[b]) and all the fragments of the Cave 4 Isaiah manuscripts are available online on the website of the Leon Levy Dead Sea Scrolls Digital Library: www.deadseascrolls.org.il/. Images of 1QIsa[a] are available online on the website of the Shrine of the Book (Israel Museum): dss.collections.imj.org.il/shrine. Images of all the fragments of 1Q8 (1QIsa[b]), including the larger fragments, can be seen in Ulrich and Flint, DJD 32/1, plates LV–LXXIV. The two fragments of 5Q3 can be seen in Maurice Baillet, Józef T. Milik, and Roland de Vaux, with a contribution from H. Wright Baker, *Les 'petites grottes' de Qumrân*, DJD 3 (Oxford: Clarendon, 1962), plate XXXVI.

93   Brooke, "Isaiah in the Qumran Scrolls," 435.

94   Of course, the distinctions from the Greek manuscript evidence cannot be easily transferred to the Hebrew and Aramaic script evidence in the scrolls. Johnson, *Bookrolls and Scribes*, 102, divided his sample set of elegant, everyday professional, and substandard as follows: the first class of script contains formal, semiformal, or pretentious; the second contains informal and unexceptional (but for the most part probably professional); the third class contains substandard or cursive. Since for the scrolls the stylistic categories of formal, semiformal, and semicursive are often arbitrary (see above) and we have no literary manuscripts in cursive, there is no straightforward analogy to be made with Johnson's underlying categorizations for Greek bookrolls.

95   Cf. the observations regarding letter size to distinguish between individual scribes in Tov, *Scribal Practices and Approaches*, 17. For Dead Sea Psalm manuscripts, see Mika S. Pajunen, "Reading Psalm and Prayer Manuscripts from Qumran," in *Material Aspects of Reading in Ancient and Medieval Cultures: Materiality, Presence and Performance*, ed. Anna Krauß, Jonas Leipziger, and Friederike Schücking-Jungblut, Materiale Textkulturen 26 (Berlin: De Gruyter, 2020), 55–70.

Johnson argued for the majority of very large scripts to be elegant.[96] I readily issue two caveats regarding my procedure. First, unlike the Oxyrhynchus evidence, we cannot be sure that the Isaiah manuscript evidence are all originally from bookrolls.[97] While for a bookroll one may expect certain quality standards of writing, this may not apply to other types of text such as excerpts or writing exercises. Second, my qualifications as to a script being elegant, everyday professional, or substandard are inherently subjective because there is no state of the art for this in our field yet.[98] By explicating some of the reasons why I put one manuscript in one category and not in the other, I aim to generate further discussion as to its appropriateness and thus to a certain degree of intersubjectivity of assessing such scripts.[99] The differentiation based on these correlations is not meant as an absolute classification. It is meant, nevertheless, to contribute heuristically what we can learn by ordering according to writing quality and script size, and therefore to contribute also what we can

---

96 Cf. chart 3.9a in Johnson, *Bookrolls and Scribes*, 155. The average letter sizes or heights for the Cave 4 Isaiah manuscripts are not provided in DJD 15, except for a remark once or twice that letter size varies noticeably, but I was able to easily measure them, as well as for 1Q8 (1QIsa^b) and Mur3, using the scale bar in the images on the Leon Levy Dead Sea Scrolls Digital Library. For 1QIsa^a, I based myself on the images in DJD 32/1, see Ulrich and Flint, DJD 32/2:21. The small fragments of 4Q69a (4QIsa^q), 4Q69b (4QIsa^r), and 5Q3 (5QIsa) are only available on PAM images, but I was not able to easily measure their average letter sizes. My letter size measurements are averages based on letters such as *aleph, bet, gimel, he, khet, kaph, mem, pe, resh, shin*, and I acknowledge that some letters may be smaller or larger, not least because of their basic morphology, such as *yod* or *lamed*. Nonetheless, the estimations give a fair illustration of the general trend of average letter size by height in a manuscript, and the distinctions are not meant as an absolute classification.

97 Cf., e.g., Eugene Ulrich et al., *Qumran Cave 4.X: The Prophets*, DJD 15 (Oxford: Clarendon, 1997), 139, regarding 4Q69 (4QpapIsa^p): "Because of the small amount preserved, one cannot be certain that this was a manuscript of the complete biblical Book of Isaiah." This may also apply to other Isaiah manuscripts that are only preserved in one or more smaller fragments.

98 Tigchelaar, "Beautiful Bookhands and Careless Characters," see at 55:35 minutes, suggested to distinguish between skilled (often on larger scrolls, entire works, probably copied for the use by others) and unskilled (often on smaller scrolls, perhaps only sections of texts, for private use, and in the process of learning by copying).

99 This attempt to distinguish between manuscripts according to quality of writing and the level of writing skills demonstrated by them, whether that is according to skilled or unskilled or elegant, everyday professional, or substandard distinctions, or a combination thereof or otherwise invites further research questions such as: Is a skilled copied manuscript the same as a carefully copied one?; Is an unskilled copied manuscript different from an uncarefully copied one, or can a very skilled scribe have uncarefully copied a manuscript, and if so, how can we recognize that and differentiate between those?; How exactly do we differentiate between trained and professional scribes, assuming they are not exactly the same thing?; and Is an untrained scribe the same as a scribe in training?

BOOK PRODUCTION AND CIRCULATION IN ANCIENT JUDAEA 221

reveal about a manuscript's purpose or character, together with other scribal and content features.

Bearing the above considerations in mind, the data for the Isaiah manuscripts is as follows:

	~2–2.5 mm	~2.5–3 mm	~3–3.5 mm	~3.5–4 mm	~4–4.5 mm	~4.5–5 mm
Elegant		4Q57?		4Q69?		
Professional	1Q8, 4Q55, 4Q56, 4Q58	1QIsaᵃ, 4Q59, 4Q60, 4Q61, Mur3		4Q62a?		
Substandard	4Q64		4Q63, 4Q68	4Q65, 4Q66	4Q62	4Q67

Let us zoom in on the manuscripts and categorizations. First of all, regarding script size, the Isaiah scrolls do not demonstrate a correlation between elegant scripts and very large letter size such as is demonstrated by the Oxyrhynchus evidence. The script of most of the everyday professional copies falls within the range of 2–3 mm, which may be an indicator for what was deemed a regular size for bookrolls of the entire book of Isaiah, since 1QIsaᵃ, 1Q8 (1QIsaᵇ), 4Q56 (4QIsaᵇ), and 4Q57 (4QIsaᶜ) fall within this range.[100]

4.1.1 Elegant and Everyday Professional Isaiah Copies

It is difficult to classify manuscripts in the highest quality category of elegant script. Only two seem to qualify. Regarding 4Q57 (4QIsaᶜ), the quality of its formal Herodian script can be regarded as elegant and that of a skilled scribe. But the interlinear spacing is inconsistent, varying from 4.5–8 mm.[101] The tetragrammaton is written in palaeo-Hebrew, including prefixes and suffixes, as are also אלוהים, צבאות, and אדוני, though they also appear in Aramaic or square characters. There are a number of corrections and insertions.[102] The manuscript is estimated to have had 40 lines per column and the original scroll would have

---

100 All manuscript evidence should be examined on script size so as to quantify and qualify categorizations such as petite, small, normal, regular, large, etc. This is not available at the moment and there are different estimations in the field about what constitutes, for example, normal-sized script; cf., e.g., Alexander and Vermes, DJD 26:66; Tov, *Scribal Practices and Approaches*, 17.

101 Ulrich, DJD 15:45.

102 Ulrich, DJD 15:49.

contained the entire prophetic book.[103] Tov listed this manuscript as a possible deluxe edition.[104] While the script is finely executed, the inconsistency in interlinear spacing casts doubt on this manuscript being a deluxe edition.

Regarding 4Q69 (4QpapIsa[p]), the quality of its writing is clearly professional, maybe even elegant writing. From what little material is left, the impression is that of a skilled scribe whose handwriting shows fine and regular lettering and who can keep straight horizontal lines. This is the only Isaiah manuscript extant on papyrus, but too little material is left to be even sure whether the original manuscript may have been more than an excerpt. So, it is doubtful whether the two small fragments of 4Q69 were once an elegant bookroll of the entire book of Isaiah. The script size of 4Q69 is also larger than that of 4Q57, but perhaps the difference in writing material (leather, papyrus) between the two specimens may account for that.

It is sometimes hard to decide on whether certain manuscripts could still be regarded as professional or should rather be qualified as substandard. Consider, for example, 4Q56 (4QIsa[b]). Tov listed this manuscript as a possible deluxe edition.[105] It is estimated to have had 45 lines per column and would have contained the entire prophetic book.[106] The script style can be categorized as formal early Herodian. While the manuscript may have been meticulously ruled,[107] the scribe, for one reason or another, was often not able to write his letters horizontally straight, or keep the interlinear space consistent, showing irregularity in this regard, although his writing seems more consistent in some fragments than in others. There is also irregularity in inking in a number of the fragments. The scribe's ability to write the basic letter forms is clear, though certainly not elegant. There is also rather much variance in writing individual letters (see, e.g., *aleph* and *shin* in frg. 26). The spacing of individual letters within words often gives the impression that his flow of writing was somehow less skilled. These aspects of irregularity, inconsistency, and spacing raise doubts about whether 4Q56 should be considered as a professional copy, let alone a deluxe edition. On the other hand, classifying it as a substandard copy would seem unwarranted since the scribe evidently had attained a certain level of training. We might, therefore, qualify this scribe as one with intermediate skills. Also, we should reckon with a certain bandwidth or range of attained skills within a category. Thus, perhaps a manuscript such as 4Q56 should be

---

103   Ulrich, DJD 15:45.
104   Tov, *Scribal Practices and Approaches*, 129.
105   Tov, *Scribal Practices and Approaches*, 129.
106   Ulrich, DJD 15:19–20.
107   Ulrich, DJD 15:19.

regarded as one at the lower end of the professional spectrum. Tigchelaar has suggested that some of the manuscript evidence of the scrolls, especially small scrolls with short sections of biblical books, can be regarded to have been writing exercises.[108] But the explanation for 4Q56 to have been a writing exercise is unsatisfactory, since the manuscript would not have contained one section or a few sections but probably the entire prophetic book.

If we consider two other manuscript remains that originally would have contained the entire book of Isaiah and come from the same Herodian period, broadly speaking, then the idea of a certain bandwidth of attained skills within a category makes sense. (For 1QIsaᵃ, see below.) Comparing 4Q56 with 1Q8 and 4Q57 shows that 4Q57, also probably at the later range of the period, stands out because of the fine execution of the script, which may be regarded as elegant.[109] The comparison also illustrates that the script in 1Q8 is more consistent and regular than in 4Q56 so that 1Q8 can be regarded a copy of better quality than 4Q56.[110]

This range in writing quality is also demonstrated by the other manuscripts that I have categorized as professional. 4Q55 (4QIsaᵃ) contains material from various chapters of the first part of Isaiah up until Isa 23:12 and perhaps also Isa 33:16–17. The remaining fragments show a consistent and skilled execution of the letter forms in a formal script. Although there is variance in interlinear spacing, the lines are horizontally straight, demonstrating this to be a professional copy, possibly from the higher end of the spectrum.

4Q61 (4QIsaᵍ), preserving text from Isa 42:14–25 and Isa 43:1–4, 16–24, likewise demonstrates a nicely executed script with care, regularity, and consistency from the higher end of the professional spectrum.

The same may apply to the professionally and carefully copied 4Q58 (4QIsaᵈ), preserving various parts of the text from Isa 45:20 until 58:7, as well as to the nicely copied 4Q60 (4QIsaᶠ), preserving various parts of the text from Isa 1:10 until possibly Isa 28:22 or 29:8, although some fragments show more consistent interlinear spacing than others (cf. frg. 12 and frg. 17).

---

108 Eibert Tigchelaar, "The Scribes of the Dead Sea Scrolls: The Case of 4Q10," theo.kuleu ven.be/apps/press/theologyresearchnews/2022/01/03/the-scribes-of-the-dead-sea-scrolls -the-case-of-4q10/.

109 Ulrich, "Identification of a Scribe Active at Qumran," suggested that the scribe of 4Q57 also copied 1Q11 (1QPsᵇ) and 11Q14 (Sefer ha-Milhamah). However, contrary to what Ulrich claimed, the size of the script of 4Q57 (~3 mm) and 11Q14 (~4 mm) is not the same, but the identification of this scribe is not under discussion here.

110 Cf. DJD 32/2:199, comparing 1Q8 with 4Q51 (4QSamᵃ) and 1QM, but less stylish and graceful than the latter. Tov, *Scribal Practices and Approaches*, 129, lists 1Q8 as a possible deluxe edition based on the number of lines per column being 35. See, however, DJD 32/2:199, for the average being 51 lines per column.

4Q59 (4QIsa^e), however, may not be from the higher end of the professional spectrum but be the work of a fairly skilled scribe, as the remaining material, preserving part of the text from Isa 2:1 until 14:24,[111] shows evidence of uneven lettering, inconsistent vertical lining, and sometimes little space between words.

Finally, 4Q62a (4QIsa^i), preserving only part of Isa 56:7–57:8, is to my mind a wonderful example of a very experienced, skilled scribe who, however, did not apply himself here fully by demonstrating an elegant script. The fragments rather give the impression of a skilled but quickly written text (cf. variance in letters, see, e.g., *ayin*, *mem* and *he* in the two fragments). The writing skill may be that of a professional scribe, yet the copy seems originally not to have been a professional bookroll but rather an excerpt, possibly also indicated by the rather large size of the script (~3.5–4 mm). On the other hand, the clear evidence for stitching in frg. 2 (the thread of the stitching and some of the leather of the previous sheet are preserved) may indicate this either to have originally been a bookroll, with the full text of Isaiah or only the second half, or to have been a series of excerpts from Isaiah or also other texts.

4.1.2 Substandard Isaiah Copies

Some of the substandard specimens are relatively easy to qualify, yet at the same time these examples are more difficult to assess as to what kind of copies they originally may have represented. Regarding 4Q64 (4QIsa^k), the five small fragments of a single column preserve text from Isa 28:26–29:9. The script can be qualified as rather crude writing: the letters are unevenly arranged, the lining is not regular, and there is much variability in letter execution. This does not give the impression of a skilled scribe, let alone a carefully copied bookroll. The remains may attest to textual variance and the editors wondered whether these fragments "hold clues either for a sound text or at least as a further witness to one form of the text as it circulated in the first century BCE."[112] Instead of treating these remains as signifying what was once an Isaiah bookroll, 4Q64 should instead be treated as a substandard specimen copied by an unskilled or inexperienced scribe. I am not sure 4Q64 illustrates a copy by a scribe in training, one who is still developing his writing skills. But, then again, how are we to distinguish between a copy made by a scribe who has had a basic training but did not turn into a professional scribe (and so remained a trained

---

111   It is not certain that frg. 25 (Isa 59:15–16) belongs together with the other fragments, Ulrich, DJD 15:97.

112   Ulrich, DJD 15:125.

BOOK PRODUCTION AND CIRCULATION IN ANCIENT JUDAEA 225

but inexperienced scribe developing his own particular way of writing) from a copy made by a scribe who is still learning to write?

Regarding another unskilled, substandard specimen, 4Q68 (4QIsa°) shows a somewhat consistent and regular execution of individual letters (using final *mem* in all positions), with cursive tendencies, but the interlinear spacing and especially the inter-word spacing and arrangement of letters, giving the impression of careful but slow letter-by-letter writing, indicate a scribe that was not very skilled. One might perhaps think of a training exercise, but I am not sure because of the possible evidence for stitching between skins, assuming that training exercises were not made on multiple sheets. Another possibility is that of a collection of excerpts, not meant for trade but for private circulation. If that were the case, then 4Q68, containing part of Isa 14:28–15:2, may be evidence of copies made of parts of the book of Isaiah for private consumption, and perhaps this may also apply to 4Q64.

Evidence of a training exercise may be clearer for 4Q63 (4QIsa^j). The fragment is tiny, but what little that remains shows irregular inking, letter variance, and irregular interlinear spacing, giving the impression of an unskilled, substandard execution. Given that this fragment contains the beginning of Isaiah, and also given its script size being slightly larger than what was perhaps the regular size, perhaps 4Q63 represents a training exercise by a scribe developing his writing skills.

We should also consider a range of writing quality and skills for the substandard category, not least in correlation with the possible type of text they originally represented. 4Q65 (4QIsa^l) shows a skilled scribe in individual letter execution, but also demonstrates irregular letter variance (consider, e.g., *he*) and irregular horizontal lining.

Yet, the scribe of 4Q65 seems to demonstrate a better grip of his pen than the scribe of 4Q66 (4QIsa^m). The irregularity in letter variance, arrangement of letters, and horizontal lining in 4Q66 shows a somewhat adequate but not very skilled scribe. Whereas the scribe of 4Q66 clearly demonstrates a substandard specimen, perhaps the scribe of 4Q65 may have been in the higher end of the substandard or even in the lower end of the professional category.

As another substandard example, 4Q62 (4QIsa^h) illustrates distinctive but not careful handwriting. The letter proportioning and arrangement are uneven. The script seems to show trained handwriting but not that of a professional scribe. 4Q62 gives the impression of a particular manner of writing, considering, for example, the positioning and execution of the *lamed*.

My final example of a substandard specimen is 4Q67 (4QIsa^n). With an average of 4.5–5 mm, its letter size is the largest to be encountered in the extant Isaiah manuscripts. Although in some instances, the ductus of letter strokes

226   POPOVIĆ

seems that of a skilled scribe, the variance in inking, letter size and execution, and the little amount of space left between words and between lines demonstrates this to be a substandard copy, containing Isa 58:13–14.

Like 4Q64 and 4Q68, 4Q66 (containing Isa 61:3–6),[113] 4Q62 (containing Isa 42:4–11), and 4Q67 may be considered to have been excerpts by non-professional scribes. 4Q65 preserves two columns, containing text from Isa 7:14–15 and 8:11–14, and may originally have been a series of excerpts or perhaps a copy of a larger part of the book by a non-professional scribe. If all of these five manuscripts originally were excerpts, the considerable variation in letter size between them is perhaps a further indicator for the non-professional character of their scribes.

4.1.3   Implications of Writing Quality and Skills for the Question for
         Whom Isaiah Manuscripts Were Copied
Based on the above, a preliminary consideration of the quality of writing and the level of writing skills in Isaiah manuscripts makes it possible to differentiate between the evidence and to assess it in new ways. This differentiation demonstrates a diversity and pluriformity in the production of Isaiah manuscripts so that we should no longer treat all manuscript evidence as representing editions of the biblical book of Isaiah.

Also, this differentiation can improve our understanding of the social context of the production of these Isaiah manuscripts. In general, those fragments that demonstrate a lower level of writing quality and skills seem to be best regarded not as editions or bookrolls of the book of Isaiah, but rather as excerpts or some even as training exercises. In answering the question for whom such manuscripts were produced, the most obvious answer seems to be that it was for the individual himself who had copied it. However, we cannot exclude that some of these were copied for the benefit of others. Thus, a copy such as 4Q65 may have been copied on order for someone other than the scribe who made it. In any case, we should not simply equate our modern assessment of low-quality writing or level of writing skills with individual or private use of the original copies.

The manuscripts of everyday professional and elegant quality, in general, originally covered the whole book or the first or second half of the book,[114]

---

113   I am not sure that fragments 1–3 and 4–5 belong to the same manuscript as argued for in
       Ulrich, DJD 15:131, as the handwriting seems that of a different scribe, so I leave fragments
       1–3 out of consideration here.
114   On the bisection of Isaiah manuscripts, see, e.g., Brooke, "Isaiah in the Qumran Scrolls,"
       432, 438–41.

although 4Q62a may be an exception. For whom were these manuscripts copied? I have not yet included Mur3 (MurIsa) in the discussion because so little material is left. Yet, the following considerations raised by this manuscript help to differentiate between different aspects that help to think about for whom the Isaiah manuscripts from Qumran of everyday professional and elegant quality were copied. These aspects relate to how we think of book market contexts in terms of quality in relation to supply and demand as well as to how we understand the circumstances of trade and private.

Given the very wide right margin that has been preserved it seems reasonable to assume that Mur3 was the beginning of a scroll containing the entire book of Isaiah. Mur3 shows fairly straight horizontal lining, very little to no space between words, and Milik noted the badly formed *tet* in line 5.[115] The writing is skilled but does not give the impression of the best professional scribe; the letter spacing within words is irregular resulting in spaces within words. Based on the quality of writing this manuscript would not come to mind as a deluxe edition, although that is exactly what has been suggested on the basis of other criteria than the quality of its handwriting.[116] Mur3 was found not at Qumran but at Murabba'at. I have argued previously that copies such as Mur3 were owned by individual families from local elite background.[117] However, I would now qualify at least one of my earlier considerations. I do not think that most literary copies found at sites in the Judaean Desert other than Qumran were deluxe editions. Mur3 is a case in point to consider such qualifications anew. This also applies to most of the other Isaiah manuscripts that have previously been regarded as deluxe editions but erroneously so in light of their writing quality, as demonstrated above.

But if Mur3 is a candidate for a book produced on order for an educated Judaean from the local elite stratum, and therefore an example of book trade and market in ancient Judaea, then this indicates that different categories of

---

115 Pierre Benoit, Józef T. Milik, and Roland de Vaux, with contributions from Grace M. Crowfoot and Elizabeth Crowfoot, Adolf Grohmann, eds., *Les grottes de Murabba'ât*, DJD 2 (Oxford: Clarendon, 1961), 80.

116 Tov, *Scribal Practices and Approaches*, 126, classified Mur3 as a deluxe edition, only according to the bottom margin, and then again (129) as a possible deluxe edition, on the basis of bottom margin as well as the number of lines per column. For the number of lines per column, see Milik, DJD 2:79.

117 Popović, "Qumran as Scroll Storehouse," 566–70, 573–76. Cf. also Wise, "Accidents and Accidence," 142–43; Mladen Popović, "Multilingualism, Multiscripturalism, and Knowledge Transfer in the Dead Sea Scrolls and Graeco-Roman Judaea," in *Sharing and Hiding Religious Knowledge in Early Judaism, Christianity, and Islam*, ed. Mladen Popović, Lautaro Roig Lanzillotta, and Clare Wilde, Judaism, Christianity, and Islam—Tension, Transmission, Transformation 10 (Berlin: De Gruyter, 2018), 54–57.

production quality were part of that market, and not only the highest one of elegant, deluxe copies. Such a differentiation of the book products on offer in terms of production quality adds to previous references to book trade and market (Wise, Falk; see above) by allowing for further distinctions and nuances. We do not know much of what book market circumstances looked like in ancient Judaea. Perhaps we should allow for various standards in different parts of the region. Thus, quality standards for bookroll or excerpt production were perhaps higher in some areas, such as cities, and lower in others, such as rural areas, but this may be a biased assumption.[118] Another possibility is that the quality was determined by various other factors, or a combination thereof, such as the availability of trained scribes or the amount of money people were able to spend.

In any case, the considerations raised here about lower and higher quality text production stimulate us to further qualify what we mean by book production and circulation in terms of market, trade, private, professional, and untrained. Here, the distinction between book production and book circulation, which Johnson emphasized (see above), is important to keep in mind. In terms of book production, we need to distinguish between private and professional or, even better, between trained and untrained copyists. Regarding book circulation, the source of the master copy is essential, differentiating between circulation originating from an author and his friends and circulation originating from sources other than the author such as a public library or a scribe or a scribal shop that performed multiple functions.

In this regard, the Isaiah manuscripts that I have studied here are especially interesting because the extant copies certainly do not originate from the author. Should we then assume that the Isaiah manuscripts from Qumran of everyday professional and elegant quality were copied for the general book trade? Perhaps some were, such as Mur3, but for a manuscript of low handwriting quality like 4Q56 this does not make sense. It makes better sense to understand 4Q56 and Mur3 as different products in different settings. Therefore, in addition to a scribe or scribal shop producing copies on order within the

---

118 Chris Keith, "Urbanization and Literate Status in Early Christian Rome: Hermas and Justin Martyr as Examples," in *The Urban World and the First Christians*, ed. Steve Walton, Paul R. Trebilco, and David W. J. Gill (Grand Rapids, MI: Eerdmans, 2017), 187–204, discussed a similar phenomenon for second-century CE Rome. He argued that though literacy rates and literacy acquisition were also, statistically, tied to whether an individual was in a rural or urban area that does not mean we can use rural or urban environments as predictors or as decisive evidence because there were exceptions all over the place. Stated otherwise, urban and rural contexts were a factor, but not the only factor. Keith argued that social class was the more determinative factor in the acquisition of a literate education.

context of a general book trade, we should allow for the possibility that some were produced in a more private setting.[119]

Here, private need not be restricted to a sense of individual or personal, but could also encompass a broader sense that includes a group of people, whether friends, acquaintances or otherwise like-minded people.[120] Such a broader sense of private book production and circulation can be connected with various scholarly models of the presumed community behind the scrolls because these models are determined by the communal aspect that defines them.

This sense of a private, communal environment enables differentiating between manuscripts copied within such a context from manuscripts copied within a commercial book market environment. Regarding the Dead Sea Scrolls, this does not mean that every professional or elegant manuscript that was not copied in a commercial market context must automatically be regarded as one copied within the presumed community behind the scrolls.

The specific identification of a manuscript written within this or that context is not straightforward. The writing quality can be an important criterion, such as the low quality of 4Q56, to argue persuasively against a commercial market context. But writing quality is not the only or decisive factor in each and every case. Other factors need also to be considered. For example, was 4Q57 copied for the general market? One might argue that it was not because of the writing of the divine names in palaeo-Hebrew characters, though not consistently so. Yet, one might question whether a special link between the writing of the divine names in palaeo-Hebrew characters and the Qumran community has been proven.[121] If apart from writing quality there are no other clear factors, such as for 1Q8, 4Q55, 4Q58, or 4Q61, how then to decide between communal or commercial market context? This is not possible in each and every case.

---

119 Starr, "The Circulation of Literary Texts," 216, argued, "Private circulation was not restricted to new works. Non-current works, ranging from the very old to the relatively recent, also circulated privately, without the substantial intervention of any commercial system of distribution. The channels of circulation ran from one friend to another, never between strangers." Johnson, *Bookrolls and Scribes*, 158 n. 81, observed that this does not adequately account for the fact that texts from the classical canon (and not 'new' texts) form the bulk of the literary texts recovered in Egypt, implying that also professional scribes produced such classical copies on order. If for ancient Judaea we consider "biblical" texts to have been classical texts, I suggest that there too both options may have been in operation.

120 On public and private contexts with regard to ancient reading practices, see Chris Keith, *The Gospel as Manuscript: An Early History of the Jesus Tradition as Material Artifact* (Oxford: Oxford University Press, 2020), 171–73.

121 For a convenient overview, see Tov, *Scribal Practices and Approaches*, 238–46.

4.1.4 The Great Isaiah Scroll (1QIsaᵃ) as a Communal, Scholarly Copy

The one copy of Isaiah that I have not yet discussed, 1QIsaᵃ, illustrates what a broader sense of private or, rather, communal book production and circulation, including trained and untrained scribes, may have looked like, covering also a longer period of time. The Great Isaiah Scroll, or 1QIsaᵃ, from Qumran Cave 1 preserves a complete copy, with an average scroll height of ~26.2 cm and length of 7.34 m.[122] It is also the oldest known manuscript of the book. The general style of writing is formal.[123] In a recent publication, Maruf Dhali, Lambert Schomaker, and I have demonstrated that two scribes originally produced the two halves of this complete bookroll, one copying columns 1–27 and the other copying columns 28–54. We suggested that the mimetic ability of one scribe to mirror another scribe's handwriting testifies to their professionalism, although our tests also showed that the range of variance increases with the second scribe, which is indicative of more variable writing patterns with this scribe.[124] Although the script of both scribes is clearly professional and the horizontal lining is quite consistent, other features such as the variance in column widths, the variance in inking, the prominent scribal marks,[125] and the many corrections and insertions argue against classifying this copy as an elegant edition but rather as an everyday professional copy. However, 1QIsaᵃ is not just any everyday professional copy, but, I suggest, a scholarly copy. This is indicated by the many scribal marks throughout the copy and by the various other scribes that added their handwriting to the copy.

Here, I focus on the intervention of those subsequent scribes. Although scholars may not agree on all the specifics of what text exactly should count as an insertion or to whom or to what period such text should be attributed, it

---

122 Millar Burrows, John C. Trever, and William H. Brownlee, *The Dead Sea Scrolls of St. Mark's Monastery, Volume 1: The Isaiah Manuscript and the Habakkuk Commentary* (New Haven, CT: American Schools of Oriental Research, 1950), xvii–xviii.

123 Cross qualified 1QIsaᵃ as a characteristic, Hasmonaean formal hand, together with 4Q30, also an example of a typical Hasmonaean script, see Cross, "The Development of the Jewish Scripts," 138, 167 (1961), 9, 27 (2003); idem, "Introduction," in *Scrolls from Qumrân Cave 1: The Great Isaiah Scroll, the Order of the Community, the Pesher to Habakkuk*, ed. John C. Trever, Frank Moore Cross, David Noel Freedman, and James A. Sanders (Jerusalem: The Albright Institute of Archaeological Research and the Shrine of the Book, 1972), 3; see also Ulrich and Flint, DJD 32/2:61.

124 Mladen Popović, Maruf A. Dhali, and Lambert Schomaker, "Artificial Intelligence Based Writer Identification Generates New Evidence for the Unknown Scribes of the Dead Sea Scrolls Exemplified by the Great Isaiah Scroll (1QIsaᵃ)," *PLoS ONE* 16/4 (2021): 1–28, doi.org/10.1371/journal.pone.0249769.

125 See Ulrich and Flint, DJD 32/2:86–88.

is generally agreed that not long after the original production of 1QIsa[a] other scribes worked on the bookroll, scribes from decades to perhaps as much as a century later. John Trever was the first to suggest, already in 1948 and 1949, that insertions were made, not only by the original scribe (assuming there was only one), such as in 1QIsa[a] 30:10–12 (in two and a half lines left blank), crossing over to the next sheet and continuing vertically in the intercolumn space, but also by other scribes from the Hasmonaean and later Herodian period: 1QIsa[a] 28:18–19 (in two lines in a line left blank by the original scribe); 32:14 and vertical margin; 33:14–16 (in two and a half lines left blank by the original scribe); the supralinear insertion of שלחני in 49:26 from the Hasmonaean period. Trever was also the first to suggest the scribe of another scroll from Qumran Cave 1, 1QS, as one of the scribes who after the production of the scroll had made an insertion in the copy, specifically in column 33, starting in the interlinear space above line 7 and continuing vertically along the edge of the sheet. Trever argued for this identity on the basis of what he saw as almost identical forms of *aleph, bet, dalet, he, kaph* (medial), *lamed, mem, ayin,* and *tsade.*[126] Cross distinguished between late Hasmonaean and early Herodian scribal insertions and also suggested, although without further clarification, identifying more insertions as having been made by the scribe of 1QS in his Hasmonaean semiformal script: 1QS scribe (28:25[?], 33:7, 54:15, 16 [one letter, *tav*]), a late Hasmonaean hand, ca. 50–25 BCE (32:14 and left margin; 33:14–16, 19), and an early Herodian hand, ca. 30–1 BCE (28:19f.).[127] In the official DJD edition of 1QIsa[a], Ulrich and Peter Flint distinguished between the insertions as follows:[128]

> Original scribe, ca. 125–100 BCE:
> – Heavy overwriting in the final column, and other such heavy letters throughout, such as in 40:13, 21, and 29
> – Original or not original scribe: large insertion 30:10–11b and the last four words in 44:15

---

126 John C. Trever, "Preliminary Observations on the Jerusalem Scrolls," *BASOR* 111 (1948): 6 plate I, 8 (especially 8 n. 16); idem, "A Paleographic Study of the Jerusalem Scrolls," *BASOR* 113 (1949): 6, 15–16. As an aside, Trever's suggestion that the insertion in 1QIsa[a] 32:14 was made by the scribe who copied 1QH[a] has not received the same traction as his suggestion for the insertion made by the scribe of 1QS.

127 Cross, "Introduction," 3–4.

128 Ulrich and Flint, DJD 32/2:64–65, 110, and in the section on notes on the manuscript and readings.

Similar Hasmonaean hand, but another scribe:
- Large insertion at 32:12–14 and the supralinear correction of שלחני at 49:26[129]

A generation later, ca. 100–75 BCE, the scribe of 1QS:
- Inserted 33:7, using the series of four dots for the tetragrammaton

About a century after the original production, ca. 30–1 BCE, one or as many as three Herodian-period scribes:
- Same hand in 32:14 and 33:14–16
- The tiny script of the long insertion at 28:19a–19b and the two-word insertion at 33:19 are possibly the same hand
- Cursive *tav* at 10:15 shows no signs of connection with any of the other hands

What does the fact that subsequent scribes over time intervened in 1QIsa[a] say about for whom the copy was made? This evidence demonstrates at least the prolonged engagement with this manuscript by multiple scribes. Furthermore, the quality of writing and perhaps also the writing skills of the scribes that intervened varies greatly as comparison of the various insertions shows. This may indicate that, different from the original scribes, who were professionals, and also different from the other professional scribes that intervened later, there were less well trained or less professional scribes that left their writing contributions on this copy.

If the original copy can be regarded as at least a good quality professional copy, would that be what one expects from a trade copy? Or should we see this as a private copy? Private, not in the sense of personal, being of one individual, but private in terms of not for trade, or, rather, private in the sense of copied for the benefit of a group of people, whether friends, acquaintances or otherwise like-minded people. If we are to regard the study of such texts as a learned and scholarly endeavour—and the presence of the many scribal marks throughout the copy may indicate just that—then perhaps a social context for 1QIsa[a] not wholly dissimilar to P.Oxy. XVIII 18.2192 (see section 2 above) may apply, where learned people could ask for copies of books to be made for them. Such copies could be made on order by professional scribes, or perhaps there were scribes within the group of sufficient professional training that could see the

---

129   I disagree that these two are the same handwriting. Letters such as *khet, nun,* and *shin* in 49:26 seem too different from those in 32:12–14. The insertion in 49:26 is likewise different from the one in 33:7; see also Trever, "A Paleographic Study of the Jerusalem Scrolls," 15.

BOOK PRODUCTION AND CIRCULATION IN ANCIENT JUDAEA 233

job through. The latter option seems very well possible given that a number of the later insertions clearly show a level of writing skills that can be judged to have been that of a professional scribe. And if such a group existed for a longer period of time (cf. perhaps Herculaneum), then a prolonged scholarly engagement of study and research, also including textual additions, may be exactly what we now see in the copy of 1QIsaᵃ as it came to be over time.

In addition to scribes directly intervening in this copy, there is other evidence, I suggest, for a scribal or learned engagement with 1QIsaᵃ by at least one scribe from another scroll from Qumran Cave 1,[130] the well-known commentary, or pesher, on Habakkuk. Bärry Hartog has argued that the quotation of Isa 13:18 in 1QpHab 6:11–12 comes from that verse, as it is also attested in 1QIsaᵃ 11:25–26, but not in the Masoretic text.[131] Together, 1QIsaᵃ and 1QpHab can illustrate in different ways how the manuscript copies from the Dead Sea Scrolls can be studied to understand part of the learned, scholarly context in which people in ancient Judaea worked with texts.

We have to be careful when reasoning back from the archaeological deposition context to a lived context in which these copies were actively used, but the fact that both these copies were found together by the Bedouin in the first cave, presumably well-enclosed wrapped in linen and put in a jar, and possibly also together with 1QS,[132] is suggestive of these two scrolls, that were produced in different time periods perhaps a century apart, having been used in tandem for at least some period of time, as may be indicated by some of the Herodian-period insertions in 1QIsaᵃ being more or less contemporary with the style of writing in 1QpHab. If such a scenario is correct, then for some

---

130   Cf. perhaps also Menahem Kister, "Wisdom Literature and Its Relation to Other Genres: From Ben Sira to Mysteries," in *Sapiential Perspectives: Wisdom Literature in Light of the Dead Sea Scrolls*, ed. John J. Collins, Gregory E. Sterling, and Ruth A. Clements, STDJ 51 (Leiden: Brill, 2004), 26. I thank Eibert Tigchelaar for this reference.

131   Pieter B. Hartog, *Pesher and Hypomnema: A Comparison of Two Commentary Traditions from the Hellenistic-Roman Period*, STDJ 121 (Leiden: Brill: 2017), 153 n. 59, 158, 253–54. Perhaps also evidence from Qumran Cave 4 indicates the use of 1QIsaᵃ. Peter W. Flint, "The Interpretation of Scriptural Isaiah in the Qumran Scrolls: Quotations, Citations, Allusions, and the Form of the Scriptural Source Text," in *A Teacher for All Generations: Essays in Honor of James C. VanderKam*, ed. Eric F. Mason, Samuel I. Thomas, Alison Schofield, and Eugene Ulrich, JSJSup 153 (Leiden: Brill, 2012), 1:402, 404–405, suggested that several readings in 4Q162 (4QpIsaᵃ) were based on 1QIsaᵃ or a text very like it; see also Brooke, "Isaiah in the Qumran Scrolls," 437.

132   Gerald Lankester Harding, "Introductory: The Discovery, the Excavation, Minor Finds," in *Qumran Cave I*, DJD 1 (Oxford: Clarendon, 1955), 5; Joan E. Taylor, Dennis Mizzi, and Marcello Fidanzio, "Revisiting Qumran Cave 1Q and Its Archaeological Assemblage," *PEQ* 149 (2017): 299, 301; Hempel, *The Community Rules from Qumran*, 18.

period before their deposition, at the least, they were kept together and then put together in the cave.

No Scribe of 1QS in 1QIsa^a. Finally, I will review the insertion attributed to the scribe of 1QS in 1QIsa^a 33:7. (I ignore the other suggestions by Cross for insertions by the scribe of 1QS because they are too unclear.) As I will also look at the Serekh manuscripts, the suggestion that the scribe of 1QS was one of the scribes that also handled the copy of 1QIsa^a warrants this further attention, also because past scholarship has assumed the scribe of 1QS to have been active at the site of Qumran.[133]

Methodologically, any palaeographic comparison between 1QS and the few inserted words in 1QIsa^a 33:7 will be unbalanced. Whereas particular instances of the letters in the insertion only amount to one (*dalet, ayin*), two (*aleph, shin*), or up to four (*he*), five (*bet*) or six (*yod*), the instances in 1QS run in the hundreds (e.g., *aleph*: 875; *bet*: 951; *dalet*: 577; *he*: 1008; *yod*: 662; *ayin*: 634; *shin*: 678). Also, many of the letters run vertically, cramped against the edge of the sheet. Finally, 1QS shows a range of variance in the execution of letters that could be turned into heatmaps representing the aggregated visualizations of the shape of each letter, but this cannot be done for the few instances in 1QIsa^a 33:7 so that it is questionable what any similarity or difference between them might indicate.[134]

Despite these limitations that hinder palaeographic comparison, the following observations may cast doubt on the assumption that it was the scribe of 1QS who was at work in 1QIsa^a 33:7.[135] A closer examination of individual letters, of the arrangement of a combination of letters, such as *shin* following

---

133 See, e.g., Frank Moore Cross, Donald W. Parry, Richard J. Saley, and Eugene Ulrich, *Qumran Cave 4.XII: 1–2 Samuel*, DJD 17 (Oxford: Clarendon, 2005), 247. Regarding 1QIsa^a, Ulrich and Flint, DJD 32/2:98, mention it being a common but unproven assumption that, since 1QIsa^a was found at Qumran, it was copied at the site, but the early date of the copy reduces the likelihood that it was copied at Qumran; Brooke, "Isaiah in the Qumran Scrolls," 433 states that 1QIsa^a was almost certainly not copied at Qumran. In both cases these authors argue so presumably because of the palaeographic date of 125–100 BCE being incongruent with the date of the Qumran settlement having been established in the first half of the first century BCE (see section 2 above).

134 Cf. Popović, Dhali, and Schomaker, "Artificial Intelligence Based Writer Identification," 9, 18–20.

135 For another approach that also casts doubt on the identification, see Årstein Justnes, "The Hand of the Correction in 1QIsa^a XXXIII 7 (Isa 40,7–8): Some Observations," *Sem* 57 (2015): 205–10.

BOOK PRODUCTION AND CIRCULATION IN ANCIENT JUDAEA 235

nun,[136] or *bet* following *shin*,[137] or *shin* following *bet*,[138] or of whole words that occur in both manuscripts, such as העם,[139] or בי/כיא,[140] do not demonstrate a striking similarity or them being nearly identical beyond sharing a similar style. On the contrary, the letter forms in their individual execution as well as the letter arrangement and proportioning look rather different in 1QS than in the insertion in 1QIsaᵃ 33:7. One might assume a range of letter variance. Since creating heatmaps is not possible, however, as explained above, this must remain a general, and unproven, assumption. There is not enough evidence to make a robust analysis that can show the concrete range of variance.

Orthography is not a clear indication for identity either, or against it for that matter. The scribe that made the insertion in 1QIsaᵃ 33:7 started with כי, as it is in the Masoretic text of Isaiah. In general, the scribe of 1QS is said to have used the fuller form of spelling.[141] In 1QS, the scribe overwhelmingly used the fuller form כיא (33 times), but only once כי, in 5:14 (perhaps the *aleph* dropped out there because of אם following directly afterward; see also 1QSa 1:10, though damaged). One might argue that the scribe of 1QS in his insertion in 1QIsaᵃ 33:7 simply followed a text akin to the Masoretic one. Such an argument may find support in referring to 4Q175 (4QTest) 17, if indeed this was copied by the scribe of 1QS. Here the scribe, quoting from Deut 33:9, followed the defective spelling כי. However, with biblical texts or quotations the evidence is not that clear-cut. If we assume that this scribe also copied 4Q53 (4QSamᶜ) and if indeed frg. 5 ii line 2 would attest to the fuller form כיא,[142] then that may demonstrate that the scribe of 1QS had no problem using the fuller form contrary to the defective form of a biblical text known from the Masoretic tradition. To add to the confusion, whereas the scribe of the insertion in 1QIsaᵃ 33:7 followed the defective

---

136 Cf. 1QS 5:17, נשמה, *nun* connects with *shin*, and also *nun* and *shin* look different from the 1QIsaᵃ 33:7 insertion; 1QS 6:25, ונענשו, *nun* does not connect with *shin*, but both letters look different from the 1QIsaᵃ 33:7 insertion; 1QS 7:2, 3, 4, 5, 6, 8, 12, 13, 14, 15, 16, 18, 19, ונענש, *nun* seems somewhat similar but mostly not and *shin* is not similar.

137 Cf., e.g., 1QS 2:24, ומחשבת, different *shin*, *bet* also small, but the arrangement of both letters is different from the 1QIsaᵃ 33:7 insertion: in 1QS 2:24, *bet* does not touch baseline as *shin* does; 1QS 3:1, 4, יתחשב, different; 1QS 3:15, מחשבתם, and 1QS 3:16, כמחשבת, different manner of writing the letters *bet* and *shin* than in the 1QIsaᵃ 33:7 insertion; 1QS 6:4, 8, 9, ישבו, different from the 1QIsaᵃ 33:7 insertion.

138 Cf. the instances of בשר in 1QS 3:9; 4:21; 9:4; 11:7, 9, 12; these are different from the 1QIsaᵃ 33:7 insertion.

139 העם occurs also in 1QS 2:21 and 6:9. The occurrence in 1QS 2:21 is not exactly the same: all three letters are written differently. 1QS 6:9 is also not exactly the same: *ayin* is broader and curves more to the left, touching the final *mem*.

140 Cf. e.g., 1QS 2:14, 24, 26; 3:2, 6; 5:11 (twice), 14; 6:4; 9:1; 10:2, 16; 11:17.

141 See, e.g., Tigchelaar, "In Search of the Scribe of 1QS," 447–450.

142 See Ulrich, DJD 17:261.

spelling with כי, a few words further down the line he departed from the usual spelling by writing בוא instead of בו, which is something that the scribe of 1QS did not do, as far as the extant material shows.

In addition to palaeography and orthography, there is the occurrence of writing four dots for the tetragrammaton, which is taken as indicative for the scribe of 1QS.[143] However, this particular practice for writing the divine name also occurs in other manuscripts, mostly in copies from the Hasmonaean period.[144] This indicates that this manner of writing the tetragrammaton was not limited to the scribe of 1QS but was a scribal practice shared by other scribes as well, extending over a longer period. To argue that the scribe of 1QS was the only one to employ this practice in biblical manuscripts[145] depends on whether the insertion in 1QIsaᵃ 33:7 is indeed from that scribe, but the four dots alone cannot be evidence for that.

Perhaps that further comparison with more of the other manuscripts attributed to the scribe of 1QS will turn up evidence to support a positive identification with the insertion in 1QIsaᵃ 33:7. Thus far, however, the comparison does not provide sufficient reasons for a positive identification between the handwriting in 1QIsaᵃ 33:7 and in 1QS. Therefore, the idea that the scribe of 1QS intervened in the copy of 1QIsaᵃ should be abandoned.

4.2 *Serekh Manuscripts*

Let us turn to the evidence for variance in script styles, quality of writing, and level of writing skills in the Serekh manuscripts.[146] Scholars have identified twelve manuscript remains as Serekh manuscripts: 1QS, 4Q255 (4QpapSᵃ), 4Q256 (4QSᵇ), 4Q257 (4QpapSᶜ), 4Q258 (4QSᵈ), 4Q259 (4QSᵉ), 4Q260 (4QSᶠ), 4Q261 (4QSᵍ), 4Q262 (4QSʰ), 4Q263 (4QSⁱ), 4Q264 (4QSʲ), and 5Q11 (5QS).[147] Recent overviews of the Serekh manuscripts include material considerations

---

143　The possible occurrence in 35:15 I leave out of consideration here; see Ulrich and Flint, DJD 32/2:111.

144　See, e.g., Tov, *Scribal Practices and Approaches*, 218–219.

145　Tigchelaar, "In Search of the Scribe of 1QS," 441–442.

146　Tigchelaar, "Beautiful Bookhands and Careless Characters," also comments on 1QS and the Cave 4 Serekh manuscripts, see at 49:45 minutes.

147　1Q29a and 11Q29 I leave out of consideration here because the first is possibly a shorter and alternative form of the Two Spirits Treatise but there is nothing else to indicate other parts of the Serekh that warrant qualifying it as a second Serekh manuscript from Cave 1, and the latter contains so little legible text that one cannot conclude whether it is part of a Serekh copy or from a different composition which relates or refers to it; see Eibert J. C. Tigchelaar, "'These Are the Names of the Spirits of …': A Preliminary Edition of *4QCatalogue of Spirits (4Q230)* and New Manuscript Evidence for the *Two Spirits Treatise (4Q257 and 1Q29a),*" *RevQ* 21 (2004): 545; Florentino García Martínez, Eibert J. C.

BOOK PRODUCTION AND CIRCULATION IN ANCIENT JUDAEA 237

but they do not provide analyses of the script styles, except for general considerations of palaeographic dating, or writing skills evident in the Serekh manuscripts.[148]

Bearing in mind the same caveats as for the Isaiah copies (see section 3.1 above), the data for the Serekh manuscripts is as follows:[149]

	~1.5– 2 mm	~2– 2.5 mm	~2.5– 3 mm	~3– 3.5 mm	~3.5– 4 mm	~4– 4.5 mm	~4.5– 5 mm
Elegant							
Professional	4Q258, 4Q264	4Q256, 4Q260		1QS	4Q257		
Substandard		5Q11	4Q263		4Q259	4Q261, 4Q262	4Q255

Let us zoom in on the manuscripts and categorizations. First of all, regarding script size, the Serekh copies, like the Isaiah copies, do not demonstrate a correlation between elegant scripts and very large letter size. On the contrary, if a

Tigchelaar, and Adam S. van der Woude, ed., *Qumran Cave 11.11: 11Q2–18, 11Q20–31*, DJD 23 (Oxford: Clarendon, 1998), 433.

    Images of all the fragments of the Cave 4 Serekh manuscripts and 5Q11 are available online on the website of the Leon Levy Dead Sea Scrolls Digital Library: www.deadsea scrolls.org.il/. Images of 1QS are available online on the website of the Shrine of the Book (Israel Museum): dss.collections.imj.org.il/shrine.

148   Metso, *The Community Rule*, 2–6; Hempel, *The Community Rules from Qumran*, 15–51; Nati, *Textual Criticism and the Ontology of Literature*, 45–59. And see also the overview of the Cave 4 materials in the official publication, Alexander and Vermes, DJD 26, 4–12, 18–21, who in discussing the particular manuscripts in some cases do make brief observations as to the quality of writing.

149   Cf. also the measurements in Alexander and Vermes, DJD 6:18–19, table 4, and see also Alexander and Vermes, DJD 26:8 n. 18, 22–23, reproducing some of the traced letter forms according to actual size. In some cases, my measurements differ slightly, possibly because I use smaller ranges of 0.5 mm. For 1QS, Alexander and Vermes, DJD 26:18 noted 3 mm, but on p. 23 1QS looks slightly larger than 4Q263 which Alexander and Vermes, also put down as 3 mm. Unlike at the Leon Levy Dead Sea Scrolls Digital Library, the online image of 1QS at the Shrine of the Book has no scale bar. However, since I was able to measure 4Q263 at ~2.5–3 mm and 1QS is slightly larger than 4Q263 in the representation in DJD 26:23 it is reasonable to put 1QS in the average range of 3–3.5 mm. Moreover, if this same scribe also copied 4Q53 (4QSam^c) and if we assume he wrote in both copies with the similar average letter height, which is ~3–3.5 mm (sometimes 4mm) in 4Q53, then this is further support for the measurements given here for 1QS.

correlation between size and quality were to exist, then with the Serekh manuscripts it seems that the copies with the smallest average letter size, between the range of 1.5–2.5 mm, show, relatively, the best quality of handwriting: 4Q256 (4QS^b), 4Q258 (4QS^d), 4Q260 (4QS^f), and 4Q264 (4QS^j); and, conversely, the larger the letter size, the lower the quality of writing: 4Q255 (4QpapS^a), 4Q259 (4QS^e), 4Q261 (4QS^g), 4Q262 (4QS^h), and 1QS and 4Q257 (4QpapS^c) in between.

4.2.1 Everyday Professional Serekh Copies

Here too, we have to reckon with a range in writing quality for the manuscripts that I have categorized as professional. It is difficult to decide which copy represents the best professional one for the Serekh, 4Q256 (4QS^b) or 4Q258 (4QS^d).[150] In the execution of the basic letter forms, 4Q258 shows a bit more regularity than 4Q256, but the spacing between letters in words is slightly better in 4Q256 than in 4Q258. Regarding interlinear spacing, with an average of ~5 mm 4Q256 shows even more distance between the lines than 4Q258 (average of ~4 mm), but the letter size is also slightly larger in 4Q256 than in 4Q258.

For heuristic purposes, we can compare these two Serekh copies with professional copies of Isaiah of similar size, although that is not exactly possible for the small size of 4Q258, as the smallest letter size Isaiah copies are a bit larger: 1Q8, 4Q55, 4Q56, and 4Q58. The quality of writing in 4Q258 clearly is better than in 4Q56, which I qualify as a copy at the lower end of the professional

---

150   Frank Moore Cross, "Palaeographic Dates of the Manuscripts," in *The Dead Sea Scrolls: Hebrew, Aramaic, and Greek Texts with English Translations*, vol. 1: *Rule of the Community and Related Documents*, ed. James H. Charlesworth, PTSDSSP 1 (Tübingen and Louisville, KY: Mohr Siebeck and Westminster John Knox, 1994), 57 characterized 4Q256 as written in a typical early Herodian formal script, 30–1 BCE, but Józef T. Milik, "Numérotation des feuilles des rouleaux dans le scriptorium de Qumrân (Planches X et XI)," *Sem* 27 (1977): 78, thought the script was transitional between Hasmonaean and Herodian, 50–25 BCE. Alexander and Vermes, DJD 26:45 only mentioned Cross, while Metso, *The Community Rule*, 4; Hempel, *The Community Rules from Qumran*, 35; Nati, *Textual Criticism and the Ontology of Literature*, 49, mentioned both Cross and Milik without deciding between the two. I think 4Q256 could also be late Hasmonaean but this depends on how exactly one defines the defining features to distinguish between late Hasmonaean and early Herodian. For example, if "full uniformity of letter size" (Cross, "The Development of the Jewish Scripts," 136, n. 27, 173 [1961], 6 n. 28, 32 [2003]) is such a distinguishing feature then 4Q256 does not show that. Cross, "Palaeographic Dates of the Manuscripts," 57, characterized 4Q258 also as early Herodian formal (see also Metso, *The Community Rule*, 4; Hempel, *The Community Rules from Qumran*, 37; Nati, *Textual Criticism and the Ontology of Literature*, 51). In addition, Alexander and Vermes, DJD 26:89, noted that despite the similarities in script, date of writing, and in recension, the differences in orthography between 4Q256 and 4Q258 were all the more striking, with 4Q256 showing predominantly full spelling and 4Q258 demonstrating predominantly defective spelling but also in two instances the scribal practice of writing the divine name in palaeo-Hebrew script (8:9 and 9:8).

spectrum. When it comes to spacing between letters in words, the level of writing skills in 4Q55 is better. In terms of being a copy by a professional scribe, 4Q258 can be reckoned as such but not one of the highest professional quality; it is similar perhaps to 1Q8 and 4Q58.

4Q256 shows a general resemblance in style with 4Q55, but the latter seems to be the work of a slightly more skilled scribe. Regarding the spacing between letters in words, the scribe of 4Q256 seems to have done a better job than the one in 4Q58. Again, these are not absolute distinctions. And no decision is needed on which one is the best professional copy. To discuss the difficulty of which one represents the better Serekh copy means to highlight different aspects of writing skills, such as basic letter form execution or spacing of letters, that can inform our impression of the overall quality of writing.

4Q264 (4QS^j) is an interesting example because of the mixed impression it gives of skilled and somewhat careless handwriting. Philip Alexander and Geza Vermes described the handwriting as neat and very regular.[151] But the execution of the basic letter forms is irregular (cf., e.g., *aleph, he, lamed, ayin, pe*), showing more variance perhaps than 4Q258 with similar-sized letters. The spacing between letters within words is better here than in 4Q258. Also, sometimes the letter strokes give a sense of talent or skill (see, e.g., line 8: במעשי פלאך;[152] yet, this is also a good example for not leaving any space between the two words, but that is a practice that can occur in high quality manuscripts, as in 4Q57, for example). It is this combination of irregularity and skill that may indicate this to have been a skilled scribe that did not produce his most careful copy with 4Q264. With an average of ~1.5 mm interlinear spacing, 4Q264 has far less spacing between the lines than 4Q258. The small fragment preserves an upper and left margin, and perhaps also a bottom margin and would then measure only ~4.4 cm in height. The ten preserved lines of writing parallel the final lines of 1QS (11:14–22), with variants of course. Stitching on the left edge of the fragment indicates another sheet followed; whether that was a blank handle sheet or another sheet with writing cannot be determined. Scholars have considered whether this fragment was the end of the manuscript[153] or more text followed that may have corresponded to 4Q256 23:2 or something else.[154] Scholars have also wondered whether 4Q264 was a miniature scroll containing the whole of the Serekh text, but the length of such a scroll being disproportionate to its height of only ~4.4 cm would seem to argue against

---

151 Alexander and Vermes, DJD 26:202.

152 The *mem* is damaged in the fragment.

153 Metso, *The Community Rule*, 5.

154 Alexander and Vermes, DJD 26:201; Hempel, *The Community Rules from Qumran*, 47.

that. Another possibility, suggested by Alexander and Vermes, is that 4Q264 contained only a short liturgical miscellany, including the Maskil's Hymn from the Serekh,[155] and should therefore better be called 4QS-Hymn, as suggested by Jutta Jokiranta.[156]

Given the mixed quality of handwriting, and especially the very small interlinear spacing, it is doubtful whether 4Q264 would have been a scroll instead of an excerpt copy of some sort. Although 4Q258 is similar in its small letter size, the average height of that copy is surmised to have been ~8.4 cm,[157] which is still quite miniature and easily portable. In any case, there is no need to label 4Q264 a Serekh manuscript in the sense of it being a version or edition of the Serekh or containing rule material similar to other copies such as 1QS, 4Q256, or 4Q258.

In this sense, as with some of the Isaiah manuscripts discussed earlier such as 4Q62a (4QIsa^i), 4Q264 not being a bookroll complicates efforts to categorize it as a professional copy. The level of writing skills is professional, but this is not a professional copy of a bookroll. At the same time, the level of writing skills that 4Q264 shows argues against seeing it as a writing exercise of some sort; for that, the handwriting is too skilled.

4Q260 (4QS^f) consists of the remains of five columns that preserve text such as in 1QS 9–10, with variants of course. Although the manuscript was clearly ruled, the scribe was not consistent in keeping his lines of writing horizontal; frg 5 looks a bit better than frgs. 4a and 4b, but, overall, the horizontal arrangement is inconsistent. The basic letter forms are not regular and expertly formed,[158] but often irregular: compare, e.g., in frg. 5 *ayin* in line 1 with *ayin*, twice, in line 2, or in frg. 4a *aleph* in lines 1, 2, 4, 5, and 9. In frg. 1 i line 2 letters are cramped in really small to make them fit. The scribe has certainly attained a more than basic level of writing skills but he also shows flaws in the quality of his writing. 4Q260 is perhaps not yet a substandard copy but if its handwriting can be characterized as professional then 4Q260 was a lower quality professional copy.

4Q260 has been aligned with 4Q264 in terms of its format as small and portable,[159] but in terms of scroll height 4Q260 is with an estimated height of

---

155   Alexander and Vermes, DJD 26:201. See also Falk, "Material Aspects of Prayer Texts," 64.

156   Jokiranta, "Thinking About Ancient Manuscripts," 620; Hempel, *The Community Rules from Qumran*, 47.

157   Alexander and Vermes, DJD 26:85. See also Sarianna Metso, *The Textual Development of the Community Rule*, STDJ 21 (Leiden: Brill, 1997), 36.

158   Cf. Alexander and Vermes, DJD 26:157.

159   Alexander and Vermes, DJD 26:154; Falk, "Material Aspects of Prayer Texts," 64; Hempel, *The Community Rules from Qumran*, 44.

BOOK PRODUCTION AND CIRCULATION IN ANCIENT JUDAEA 241

~8.3 cm rather more akin to 4Q258 (~8.4 cm).[160] Also, 4Q260 clearly preserves material from consecutive columns, 4Q264 does not and what more preceding text in addition to what is preserved it originally may have had is unknown. In terms of letter size, 4Q260 is only slightly larger than 4Q258, and 4Q260 too has a wide interlinear space; its average of interlinear space of ~4.5–5 mm is a bit more than in 4Q258 (~4 mm), but it is also more irregular and sometimes even has an interlinear space of more than 5 mm. In terms of level of writing skills, 4Q260 was from a less skilled scribe than 4Q256 and 4Q258, but in terms of format 4Q260 and 4Q258 are more alike than 4Q256.

4Q257 (4QpapS[c]) is on papyrus and the fragments preserve text that parallels 1QS 1–4.[161] It has the largest average letter size of the Serekh copies that can be characterized as professional, albeit of a lower skill level than the other professional copies. If for Serekh copies large letter size is indicative for lower writing quality (see above), then 4Q257 may be a good example of the spectrum across the dividing line between professional and substandard. Cross described the script as somewhat unusual, but nonetheless a Hasmonaean semiformal, close to the script of 4Q502 (4QpapRitMar), and he compared it to 1QS, dating it also to 100–75 BCE.[162] Alexander and Vermes have described 4Q257 as carefully and expertly written, its writing bold and firm, and the letters well shaped.[163] But the quality of writing is less than expert. The scribe shows inconsistent arrangement of his horizontal lines. The execution of basic letter forms as well as his spacing of letters within words show that the scribe had attained a practiced level of writing skill but there is much irregularity in writing the individual letters that indicate he was not very skilled.

4Q257 may have had one of the highest scroll sizes of professional Serekh copies, with an estimated scroll height of possibly ~20.1 cm.[164] Only 1QS has a higher scroll size, with an average height of ~24.1 cm.[165] This height is significantly more than the next copy in height, 4Q256 (~12.5 cm), not to mention 4Q258 (~8.4 cm) and 4Q260 (~8.3 cm), and illustrates the different formats used, over time, for Serekh copies of considerable length.

The final example of a professional copy is 1QS. This is a practically complete scroll of five sheets with eleven columns, two to three columns per sheet, and

---

160 4Q256 differs from both 4Q258 and 4Q260 in scroll height with ~12.5 cm; see Alexander and Vermes, DJD 26:41.

161 See also Tigchelaar, "'These Are the Names,'" 538–42.

162 Cross, "Palaeographic Dates of the Manuscripts," 57.

163 Alexander and Vermes, DJD 26:68–69.

164 Alexander and Vermes, DJD 26:66, 68, but cf. also Metso, *The Textual Development of the Community Rule*, 34 n. 50.

165 Cross, "Introduction," 4. See also, in general, Tov, *Scribal Practices and Approaches*, 84–90.

with an average height of ~24.1 cm and a scroll length of 1.86 m.[166] In addition, originally 1QSa was probably stitched to the end of 1QS, and 1QSb to 1QSa.[167]

The scribe of 1QS is often made out as a careless and less competent scribe with a relatively undisciplined calligraphy, but especially also because of the many errors and corrections, mainly in columns 7 and 8.[168] The scribe clearly knew how to execute the basic form of letters, but the impression of carelessness comes from the irregularity of individual letters. Many examples can be given, but compare, e.g., the *mem*s in column 3, the *ayin*s in column 5, or the *aleph*s in column 9 (although the aleph in איש in line 12 is beautiful, but, then again, this word and the final ואיש are horizontally irregularly arranged with the preceding part of line 12). There are clear irregularities in how the writing in different columns was executed. For example, columns 1–3 show irregular horizontal lines, whereas columns 4–6 show more regularity in this regard, yet still not completely straight horizontal lines. Columns 1–3 also show several instances of irregular inking. Columns 7–8 show great irregularity and many corrections.

If we compare 1QS with 1QIsa[a], which is thought to be earlier in date and also has a somewhat different writing style and slightly smaller average letter size, then the scribe of 1QS shows greater irregularity in his execution of the basic letter forms and also demonstrates greater inconsistency in his horizontal lining.

Is 1QS on the dividing line between professional and substandard, or is that too harsh a judgement of the writing quality and skills? We also have to take

---

166   Cross, "Introduction," 4.

167   On the evidence for stitching along the left side edge of the final sheet carrying 1QS 11, see Jokiranta, "Thinking About Ancient Manuscripts," 618; Michael Brooks Johnson, "One Work or Three? A Proposal for Reading 1QS-1QSa-1QSb as a Composite Work," *DSD* 25 (2018): 155 n. 51; Hempel, *The Community Rules from Qumran*, 17. Stitches on the left side of column 2 of 1QSa are clearly visible as is part of the next sheet and even the remains of some writing, parallel to lines 18–19 of 1QSa 2; see DJD 1: plate XXIV. For further discussion of the connection of 1QS with 1QSa and 1QSb, see, e.g., Hempel, *The Community Rules from Qumran*, 16–19; Nati, *Textual Criticism and the Ontology of Literature*, 46–47.

168   Cf., e.g., Ulrich, "4QSam[c]: A Fragmentary Manuscript," 1, 2; Tigchelaar, "In Search of the Scribe of 1QS," 450–52; Jokiranta, "Thinking About Ancient Manuscripts," 628; Hempel, *The Community Rules from Qumran*, 19. In terms of script style, Cross, "The Development of the Jewish Scripts," 158, 167 note 116 (1961), 22, 27 note 126 (2003), put 1QS as a Hasmonaean semiformal in the tradition of the Archaic semiformal, as exemplified by 4Q109 (4QQoh[a]) and 4Q504 (DibHam[a]), but also influenced at a number of points by the standard Hasmonaean style, by which he presumable meant the formal style. The problem is that Cross did not give much consideration to the Hasmonaean semiformal and no exemplars are given, except the two mentioned for Archaic/early Hasmonaean, 4Q109 and 4Q504; see also Tigchelaar, "Seventy Years of Palaeographic Dating," 267, 270.

BOOK PRODUCTION AND CIRCULATION IN ANCIENT JUDAEA 243

into account that the complete copy of 1QS has been preserved. If only remains of column 8 would have been preserved, then an assessment of it being a substandard copy would make sense. But other columns, e.g., column 4 or column 9, show better writing quality. Moreover, in terms of writing skills, there are worse examples of less competent writing skills than the scribe of 1QS, such as 4Q68 or 4Q56, though both of a different style and the latter also of later date (see section 3.1.1 and 3.1.2 above). 4Q56 would have been a sizeable bookroll containing the entire book of Isaiah and possibly with an average height of ~29 cm.[169]

This goes to show that entire works could be copied by unskilled scribes, and that on "a stately manuscript of thin, light brown leather with yellow tones" (4Q56) or on "fine white leather" (1QS).[170] With respect to the scribe of 1QS, it is difficult to decide whether he was an unskilled scribe, a moderately trained scribe, or a professional scribe that was for whatever reason careless in his writing. But it goes too far to regard 1QS as a whole as a substandard copy in terms of its writing quality. Rather, it seems to be somewhere in the lower spectrum of a professional copy.

4.2.2 Substandard Serekh Copies

Certainly, no extant Serekh manuscript would qualify as an elegant copy on the basis of its handwriting quality, but half of the copies are of substandard quality (and even over half of them if 4Q260 or 1QS were to be counted as such). This is relatively more than with the extant Isaiah copies, although no statistical conclusions of course can be drawn.

Despite the remains of two columns stitched together, too little writing is left of 5Q11 (5QS) to say much about it here,[171] except that it shows irregular handwriting (cf., e.g., *he*s and *tav*s) and that it probably was not a writing exercise if the evidence for text on two stitched together sheets would argue against that (cf. also 4Q68 in section 3.1.2 above). Although 5Q11 is written in relatively small letter size, it seems to be a substandard copy of an unskilled scribe.[172]

---

169   Ulrich, DJD 15:20.

170   Ulrich, DJD 15:19; Cross, "Introduction," 4.

171   Cf. also Jokiranta, "Thinking About Ancient Manuscripts," 620.

172   See also Milik DJD 3:180. As an aside, Józef T. Milik, "Milkî-ṣedeq et Milkî-reša' dans les anciens écrits juifs et chrétiens," *JJS* 23 (1972): 129, suggested that the scribe of 4Q280 ("rustic semiformal hand" from the first century BCE) also copied 5Q13 and perhaps 5Q11, among two more, but in DJD 3:181 Milik compared 5Q13, especially frg. 27, materially and palaeographically to 5Q11, dating 5Q13 to the first century CE.

The next substandard example in terms of letter size is 4Q263 (4QSⁱ), which consists now of two fragments, as recently one more fragment was identified.[173] The text that is preserved parallels that in 1QS 5:26–6:5 and in 4Q258 2:5–9, although 4Q263 seems to agree more with 4Q258 but for two cases where it sides with 1QS.[174] What remains of 4Q263 clearly represents far from regular handwriting,[175] shown by the variance in executing basic letter forms (especially the *lamed*s stand out, also in terms of their positioning vis-à-vis other letters such as in למלכאה, which is also a misspelling for למלאכה), the inconsistent spacing of letters within words, and the alternating thin strokes and thick strokes probably due to irregular inking.[176]

The editors characterized 4Q263 as a typical Herodian formal, but it is very different from other such Serekh copies such as 4Q256, 4Q258, or 4Q260 for that matter; look, e.g., at the *he*s in 4Q263. Tigchelaar observed that the script of 4Q263 is only formal in the sense that it is not cursive, and he also noted that the scribe alternated between formal and informal forms of the letters.[177] Yet, this very irregular and particular way of writing is not necessarily the work of an unskilled scribe. It is perhaps somewhat comparable to examples discussed earlier, such as 4Q62 (see section 3.1.2 above), though a bit more extreme in being careless. So, it may have been "a scribe who was not primarily concerned with the neat and correct appearance of their writing."[178] Only very little material is left, but perhaps the interlinear space of ~5 mm may be a further indication of 4Q263 being an excerpted copy of some sort.[179]

4Q259 (4QSᵉ) preserves material that correlates with text from 1QS 7:8 until 9:24 or 9:26, while somewhere in the middle of column 4 it continues, after the Statutes for the Maskil and instead of the final hymn, with calendrical material known as 4Q319 (4QOtot).[180] 4Q259/4Q319 demonstrates a distinct and irregular way of writing, also of mixed quality.[181] The scribe clearly knew the

---

173 Eibert Tigchelaar, "4Q263 (Sⁱ): Hand, Text, Another Fragment," *RevQ* 32 (2020): 267–71.

174 Tigchelaar, "4Q263 (Sⁱ)," 270; Hempel, *The Community Rules from Qumran*, 47.

175 Alexander and Vermes, DJD 26:197.

176 Tigchelaar, "4Q263 (Sⁱ)," 267–68, 269–70.

177 Tigchelaar, "4Q263 (Sⁱ)," 267, 269–70.

178 Tigchelaar, "4Q263 (Sⁱ)," 270.

179 Some of the possible Isaiah excerpts (see section 3.1.2 above) show wide interlinear space, such as 4Q62 (~4 mm), 4Q64 (varies, can be ~3 mm, can be ~5 mm), or 4Q66 (~5 mm), but not all of them do: 4Q67 varies from 2–3 mm and 4Q68 has ~2 mm.

180 Hempel, *The Community Rules from Qumran*, 29, 39–40, 266.

181 Cross, "Palaeographic Dates of the Manuscripts," 57, described 4Q259 as written in an unusual semicursive with mixed semicursive and semiformal script features, referring to semiformal and semicursive (looped) *tav* and dating it to the same time as 4Q398, 50–25 BCE. However, Józef T. Milik, *The Books of Enoch: Aramaic Fragments of Qumrân*

BOOK PRODUCTION AND CIRCULATION IN ANCIENT JUDAEA   245

basic forms of the letters, but there is much variance in the letter forms. There is irregularity in inking and letter size varies considerably. On some fragments, letter size can be as small as ~2 mm, e.g., *ayin* in 4Q259 2:12 (followed by a final *mem* of 4 mm height) to ~2.5–3 mm in that same column, while in other parts such as column 1 or column 3 the average letter height varies respectively between ~3.5–4.5 mm or between ~3.5–4 mm. Yet, sometimes the quality of writing looks maybe even nice, though still particular, such as intermittently in 4Q319 5. The spacing between letters within words varies from not awful to not excellent. All this gives a mixed impression of the scribe's writing skills, varying between substandard to skilled beyond basic training. There are two instances of Cryptic A script in 4Q259 3:3–4, possibly added by another scribe, although the reading of some letters is clearer than others.[182]

4Q259/4Q319 would have been a scroll of some significant size. The average scroll height has been estimated to be ~14.2 cm,[183] which would be slightly larger in height than 4Q256 (~12.5 cm) but not yet as large as 4Q257 (~20.1 cm) or 1QS (~24.1 cm). The copy 4Q259/4Q319 may have had at least nine columns and with an estimated column width of 13–15 cm,[184] the length of the scroll could have been at least between 1.17–1.35 m. The material reconstruction is difficult due to the many fragments that cannot be placed.[185]

This then is another example of a copy written by what seems an unskilled scribe, and it may be comparable to 4Q257 and 1QS, which were written by

---

Cave 4 (Oxford: Clarendon, 1976), 61 dated 4Q259 (there named 4QS^b and 4Q260; but see the explanation in DJD 26:21, 24) to the second half of the second century BCE. And Émile Puech, "L'alphabet cryptique A en 4QS^e (4Q259)," *RevQ* 18 (1998): 433–35, suggested to date 4Q259 in the first half of the first century BCE, preferably shortly after 100 BCE, contemporary to 1QS. Puech argued for this date on a combined basis of a palaeographic analysis of Cryptic A script, compared to 4Q298 and especially to 4Q249 and 4Q317, and on the basis of the C14 dating of 4Q317 (A. J. Timothy Jull, Douglas J. Donahue, Magen Broshi, and Emanuel Tov, "Radiocarbon Dating of Scrolls and Linen Fragments from the Judean Desert," *Radiocarbon* 37 [1995]: 11–19). Most scholars do not seem to decide on these suggested dates for 4Q259, but Hempel, *The Community Rules from Qumran*, 39, seemed to imply that she follows Milik and Puech, although it is not clear which date exactly, as Puech proposed a slightly later date than Milik and was in agreement with the date attributed to Cross by Milik that Puech notes (433 n. 14).

182 See, e.g., Metso, *The Textual Development of the Community Rule*, 53–54; Alexander and Vermes, DJD 26:145–46; Puech, "L'alphabet cryptique A"; Hempel, *The Community Rules from Qumran*, 39, 224–25.

183 Alexander and Vermes, DJD 26:130–31.

184 Alexander and Vermes, DJD 26:131.

185 Metso, *The Textual Development of the Community Rule*, 49–51; DJD 26:130–32; Shemaryahu Talmon, Jonathan Ben-Dov, and Uwe Glessmer, *Qumran Cave 4.XVI: Calendrical Texts*, DJD 21 (Oxford: Clarendon, 2001), 195–201.

moderately skilled but not highly professional scribes. However, the writing in 4Q259/4Q319 looks so much more particular and distinct than that in 4Q257 or 1QS that it does not seem apt to merely describe it as unskilled. One way to explain this unique or unusual handwriting is to suggest individual idiosyncrasy. Another possibility is to suggest a different geographical provenance of the scribe,[186] but apart from the style of the script that would not explain the other irregular and inconsistent features of the writing skills that are demonstrated by 4Q259/4Q319.

Hempel suggested that this manuscript may be what she calls an eclectic, avant-garde experiment by a scholar who inserted one of his calendric documents into a copy of the Serekh.[187] The analysis here further supports the understanding of 4Q259/4Q319 as the copy of a scholar-scribe. On the basis of the writing quality and skills, and in combination with the content matter of the text, especially its calendrical material, 4Q259/4Q319 may very well represent the personal bookroll of a learned individual.

From a material perspective, the size of 4Q259/4Q319 demonstrates that this was not some scrap material from someone practicing his writing skills. As distinct and particular though the handwriting may be, the better-looking parts of the mixed writing quality and skills can indicate that the scribe had attained at least a basic level of writing skills. Yet, as a bookroll copy the overall quality is substandard. This may indicate that this was not a copy produced for the broader circulation beyond that of the scribe. In terms of being a personal bookroll, 4Q259/4Q319 may have been something like a learned scribe's scribbled notes, adding calendrical considerations after the Statutes for the Maskil material from the Serekh.

From a content perspective, the calendrical concerns were quite complex, probably not the matter of elementary school training. While the structure of the Otot-text seems clear, there are basically two interpretations for the 294-year *otot* roster: the text provided either a mechanism to harmonize different sacred time-schemes, synchronizing the lunar and solar calendars within the *mishmarot* system of the 364-day calendar, counting the signs for doing so and integrating them in the jubilee system; or the *otot* roster was

---

186 Tigchelaar, "The Scribes of the Scrolls," 530.

187 Hempel, *The Qumran Rule Texts in Context*, 327. See also Charlotte Hempel, "A Tale of Two Scribes: Encounters with an Avant-Garde Manuscript of the Community Rules (4Q259)," in *Hokhmat Sopher: Mélanges offerts au Professeur Émile Puech en l'honneur de son quatre-vingtième anniversaire*, ed. Jean-Sébastien Rey and Martin Staszak, Études Bibliques 88 (Leuven: Peeters, 2021), 115–28.

BOOK PRODUCTION AND CIRCULATION IN ANCIENT JUDAEA   247

used for purposes of intercalation of the 364-day year with the tropical year of 365.25 days.[188]

Whatever the correct interpretation may be of the *otot* roster, the fact that this calendrical part was connected to Serekh material demonstrates this scribe's concern with certain learned information, and may also show a particular understanding of the connection between the Statutes for the Maskil and creation context and calendrical concerns as that relates to the opening rubric and first section of the final hymn in Serekh material.[189]

In this case, the substandard quality of handwriting indicates this not to have been a copy made on order by a professional scribe. If not for trade or for broader private circulation (see section 3.1.3 above for a broader sense of private), for whom then was this manuscript copied? It was copied for the scribe himself, although the possible insertion by another scribe in Cryptic A script in 4Q259 3:3–4 can indicate use by someone else but such a scenario does not have to conflict with the copy originally being meant for personal use. Therefore, the connection between this specific calendrical material and the Statutes for the Maskil may be the scribe's own doing. The content matter and the mixed quality of writing indicate this not to have been a learning exercise by a scribe in training but rather, I suggest, to have been the bookroll for the personal use of a learned individual, a scholar-scribe, who in his education had a basic scribal training.

The four extant fragments of 4Q255 (4QpapSª) represent a fascinating example of a reused manuscript, with two fragments preserving material from 1QS 1:1–5 and 3:7–12 while the other two cannot be exactly paralleled in 1QS. For the largest of these latter two fragments, fragment A, a connection with the Two Spirits Treatise has been suggested but recently Hempel suggested that there may also be a connection with the Statutes of the Maskil and the fragmentary introduction to the calendrical material in 4Q319 4.[190]

Like 4Q257, 4Q255 is on papyrus, but what makes it an exceptional Serekh copy is the fact that it is an opisthograph: 4Q255 was written on the back of another manuscript, 4Q433a (4QpapHodayot-like Text B).[191] Cross characterized the writing on 4Q255 as a crude, early cursive script and dated it to the

---

188 Mladen Popović, "Otot," in *The Eerdmans Dictionary of Early Judaism*, ed. John J. Collins and Daniel C. Harlow (Grand Rapids, MI: Eerdmans, 2010), 1013–1014.

189 Hempel, *The Community Rules from Qumran*, 33, 113, 266–268.

190 Alexander and Vermes, DJD 26:27–28; Hempel, *The Community Rules from Qumran*, 31–33.

191 4Q257 was perhaps also an opisthograph, but the traces of a few of words on the verso cannot be identified anymore.

second half of the second century BCE, preferably the late second century BCE,[192] but Ayhan Aksu recently suggested a slightly later date to the early first century BCE.[193] Scholars have debated which side was the recto and which side the verso and consequently which of the two texts was written before the other. Aksu, following Alexander and Vermes, made a strong case for 4Q255 having been written on the verso after 4Q433a had been written on the recto.[194]

With regard to the writing quality and skills evinced by 4Q255, the scribe was, first of all, very irregular in lining his writing horizontally and arranging his letters properly; some lines run even almost diagonal. His letters are written with great variance.[195] Interlinear space varies, from ~5 mm to often only ~3 mm interlinear space, which with an average letter size of 4.5–5 mm creates the impression of a very densely written surface. 4Q433a on the recto also shows some irregular lining but not like 4Q255 on the verso. The interlinear space can vary as well (~3–4 mm) and the average letter size of ~3.5–4 mm is slightly smaller than in 4Q255.[196] The writing quality looks better and 4Q433a gives the impression of having been written with more skill and attention.[197] While the writing style in 4Q433a can be characterized as semiformal, the script style in 4Q255 shows a mixture of cursive and semicursive.[198]

Both texts were written in different styles, presumably by different hands, and 4Q255 was written on the back (verso) of 4Q433a. This can be taken to

---

192   Cross, "Palaeographic Dates of the Manuscripts," 57; DJD 26:29–30; Metso, *The Community Rule*, 3; Hempel, *The Community Rules from Qumran*, 30; Nati, *Textual Criticism and the Ontology of Literature*, 48.

193   Ayhan Aksu, "A Palaeographic and Codicological (Re)assessment of the Opisthograph 4Q433a/4Q255," *DSD* 26 (2019): 1–19.

194   Aksu, "A Palaeographic and Codicological (Re)assessment." See also, e.g., Alexander and Vermes, DJD 26:28, 30; Tov, *Scribal Practices and Approaches*, 72; Hempel, *The Community Rules from Qumran*, 30; Nati, *Textual Criticism and the Ontology of Literature*, 48. George J. Brooke, "Choosing Between Papyrus and Skin: Cultural Complexity and Multiple Identities in the Qumran Library," in *Jewish Cultural Encounters in the Ancient Mediterranean and Near Eastern World*, ed. Mladen Popović, Myles Schoonover, and Marijn Vandenberghe, JSJSup 178 (Leiden: Brill, 2017), 126, also followed DJD 26:28, 30 regarding 4Q433a being on the recto and 4Q255 on the verso, yet, at 128, he also maintained the palaeographic dates given by the DJD editors so that 4Q255 has the earlier palaeographic date (125–100 BCE) and 4Q433a the later (75 BCE), which in this case is not possible if 4Q433a was to be written on the recto at an earlier date than 4Q255. For this confusion, see also Aksu, "A Palaeographic and Codicological (Re)assessment," 2.

195   Cf., e.g., *aleph, dalet, he, pe* in Aksu, "A Palaeographic and Codicological (Re)assessment," 15.

196   Eileen Schuller in Esther Chazon et al., *Qumran Cave 4.XX: Poetical and Liturgical Texts, Part 2*, DJD 29 (Oxford: Clarendon, 1999), 238, gives different measurements, especially for the interlinear space.

197   Cf. also Alexander, "Literacy among Jews in Second Temple Palestine," 17.

198   Cf. Aksu, "A Palaeographic and Codicological (Re)assessment."

BOOK PRODUCTION AND CIRCULATION IN ANCIENT JUDAEA 249

indicate that the scribe of 4Q255 reused the copy of 4Q433a in a different context, and that the original text, 4Q433a went defunct.[199]

For whom was 4Q255 copied? The fact that it was written in such poor manner on the back of another text suggested to scholars that it may have been an early draft or a personal, possibly scholarly copy of the Serekh.[200] A slightly different possibility is suggested by Hempel, who interpreted 4Q255 fragment A to contain material parallel to the hymnic material following the Statutes for the Maskil in 1QS and parallel to the calendrical introduction in 4Q319. She proposed to understand 4Q255 and 4Q433a together as part of a Community Rules manuscript with hymnic material following the statutes. This then could be evidence not so much of a draft or a personal copy, but of the efforts of scribes to collect and gather material at a time when the framework for the long text of the Serekh as most fully preserved in 1QS was still being drafted.[201] However, if 4Q255 was written on the verso later than, and perhaps also separately from, 4Q433a, then the material evidence does not support Hempel's interpretation because the statutes (4Q255) follow the hymnic material (4Q433a), and not the other way around. Moreover, the hymnic character of 4Q433a is doubtful. Eileen Schuller concluded that 4Q433a was more likely some type of extended sapiential-type reflection or instruction than a hymn.[202]

While the writing quality and skills evinced by the scribe in 4Q255 are substandard and 4Q433a makes a better impression in this regard, it would be difficult to qualify 4Q433a as a professional copy either because of the irregularity in interlinear spacing. The two interpretations for the character of this opisthograph by Alexander and Aksu on the one hand and Hempel on the other hand need not exclude each other. The writing quality and skills on both sides could be taken as evidence of works-in-progress by scholar-scribes. They knew how to write, the one better than the other, but they were not doing the copying work of a text available in some sort of edition, such as in the case of Isaiah, but rather the work of drafting or collecting and gathering various materials. Whether this happened separately or in tandem is difficult to determine, but can have consequences for how we think of a Serekh manuscript.

The final two examples of substandard quality Serekh copies are 4Q261 (4QS^g) and 4Q262 (4QS^h). The very little material that is left of 4Q261 can

---

199 Aksu, "A Palaeographic and Codicological (Re)assessment," 14.

200 Alexander and Vermes, DJD 26:30; Alexander, "Literacy among Jews in Second Temple Palestine," 17; Aksu, "A Palaeographic and Codicological (Re)assessment," 11–14.

201 Hempel, *The Community Rules from Qumran*, 33–34.

202 Schuller, DJD 29:239; eadem, "The Classification Hodayot and Hodayot-like (With Particular Attention to 4Q433, 4Q433A and 4Q440)," in *Sapiential, Liturgical and Poetical Texts from Qumran*, ed. Daniel K. Falk, Florentino García Martínez, and Eileen M. Schuller, STDJ 53 (Leiden: Brill, 2000), 182–93.

250 POPOVIĆ

sometimes be correlated with 1QS 5–7 with some shorter variants and possibly independent readings. With an interlinear space of ~4 mm little more than the average letter size (~4–4.5 mm), and sometimes even smaller, the writing makes a very dense impression, which is reinforced by the small spacing between words that is sometimes unclear. Fragment 3 shows evidence of ruling and the cursive/semicursive seems sometimes to have been written with some skill, although there is also a good deal of variance in the execution of the letter forms, especially in some of the smallest fragments preserved.

Regarding 4Q262, it is not clear whether the third fragment, fragment B, belongs together with the other two. It is very different in terms of proportion and arrangement of letters and lines. The material is difficult to connect with the Serekh except for fragment 1, which preserves material relating to 1QS 3:4–6. Whether this represents a Serekh copy, or some anthology or something else, depends also on the view one has, or the expectations one has, of what a Serekh copy was like.[203] In any case, 4Q262 shows irregularity in inking, variance in basic letter forms, and irregular execution of the letter strokes, indicating its substandard quality.

4.2.3 Implications of Writing Quality and Skills for the Question for Whom Serekh Manuscripts Were Copied

Based on the above, a preliminary consideration of the writing quality and skills in Serekh manuscripts makes it possible to differentiate between the evidence and to assess it in new ways, reinforcing also suggestions put forward by other scholars. Similar to the Isaiah manuscripts, here too the differentiation according to writing quality and skills demonstrates a diversity and pluriformity in the production of Serekh manuscripts.

An important difference is that, unlike for the Isaiah material, for the Serekh material we cannot reckon with a single edition to have been in circulation at the time. As James Nati succinctly observed,

> There is a clear tension that needs to be resolved in how we imagine a tradition such as the *Serekh*. It is, on the one hand, abundantly fluid, especially in comparison with other biblical books …. On the other hand, we have a collection of manuscripts, each of which constitutes a discrete physical object. At issue … is how to most productively hold these two facts in tandem.[204]

---

203   See, e.g., Jokiranta, "Thinking About Ancient Manuscripts," 620–21; Metso, *The Community Rule*, 5; Hempel, *The Community Rules from Qumran*, 46–47.

204   Nati, *Textual Criticism and the Ontology of Literature*, 237–38.

BOOK PRODUCTION AND CIRCULATION IN ANCIENT JUDAEA

Sarianna Metso and James Tucker argued that copies representing various stages of redaction were circulating simultaneously, without any particular copy representing the definitive one. Rather, the period of developing composition and the period of copying and creating textual variants were coterminous, while the fluidity of the material raises the question: what constitutes the Community Rule?[205] David Hamidović, who, like Metso and Tucker, also drew on Ulrich's concept of variant literary editions, tried to capture the textual fluidity not in terms of different versions but in terms of different editorial projects of the individual scribes that worked on a particular manuscript.[206] Nati took these considerations a step further by asking how scribes thought of their own task with respect to textual variation. He argued for 1QS and 4Q258 that, rather than being two manuscripts of a single work with textual variants, or even variant editions, they both claim for themselves two different essential qualities. These claims would have been part of the ways in which these texts were imagined in their context of production.[207]

It is difficult to approach how exactly the scribes behind what we categorize as Serekh manuscripts thought of their own task. Yet, through their handwriting, we come closer to certain aspects of the social context in which they were copying. By focusing on their writing quality and skills we can keep the two facts of textual fluidity and the manuscripts as discrete physical objects in tandem, and sharpen our understanding of what each piece of manuscript evidence may have represented for the one copying it as well as for those it was copied for.

For example, scholars have previously suggested that the smaller exemplars were portable and that the larger scrolls were used for study or reading in public.[208] 4Q258, 4Q260, and 4Q264 are then small and portable, but with an average height of ~4.4 cm 4Q264 stands apart from 4Q258 (~8.4 cm) and 4Q260 (~8.3 cm).

Moreover, 4Q264 is possibly not a bookroll copy at all but rather an excerpt copy of some sort from a professional scribe, perhaps a scribble for his own use. The fragment shows very small interlinear spacing, so that one may ask

---

205 Metso and Tucker, "The Changing Landscape of Editing Ancient Jewish Texts," 270–72. See also Jokiranta, "Thinking About Ancient Manuscripts." Hempel, *The Community Rules from Qumran*, 2, 34, suggested using the plural Community Rules manuscripts not only so as to challenge preconceived notions of what a Serekh manuscript should look like but also to indicate both the concurrent family resemblance and distinctiveness of the witnesses.

206 Hamidović, "Editing a Cluster of Texts," 198, 201–8; idem, "Living *Serakhim*," 69–84.

207 Nati, *Textual Criticism and the Ontology of Literature*, 165–214, 238–39.

208 Alexander and Vermes, DJD 26:5, 154, 201; Falk, "Material Aspects of Prayer Texts," 64; Hamidović, "Editing a Cluster of Texts," 201; Hempel, *The Community Rules from Qumran*, 44.

what kind of excerpt copy this may have been. Possibly there were excerpt copies for trade. But was 4Q264 a personal, individual one? Perhaps it is even possible to consider a scenario in which 4Q264 was a scrap paper that came from the bottom part of the sheet of another scroll and that was reused to put down, in quick and dense handwriting, this hymnic material from the Serekh.

Over against these smaller examples stand large examples such as 1QS (~24.1 cm) and 4Q257 (~20.1 cm). These can still be characterized as professional, albeit of a lower quality and skill level than other professional copies such as 4Q256 and 4Q258. Somewhat in between stands 4Q256 with an average height of ~12.5 cm. This illustrates the different formats used, over time, for Serekh copies of considerable length. But what to make of these different formats? 4Q256 could, conceivably, still count as a portable scroll but it is equally imaginable to have been used in a public setting for study or reading. Then again, portable does not stand over against public study or reading. These are different categories. If we take into account average letter size, then 1QS (3–3.5 mm) and 4Q257 (3.5–4 mm) might seem better equipped for public study or reading than 4Q256 (2–2.5 mm). I do not believe that the average letter size mattered in this case, and the better-quality writing of 4Q256 may have been a benefit in this regard. For that matter, the notions of "portability" and "public" with regard to the scrolls as material artefacts are in need of further reflection.

For the Serekh material there does not seem to be a correlation, in general, between the quality of writing and the length of the material being copied. In this regard, the Serekh material contrasts with the Isaiah copies, where manuscripts of everyday professional and elegant quality, in general, covered the whole book or the first or second half of the book and those lesser, substandard quality, generally, may have been excerpts or some even training exercises.

From the substandard copies, 4Q255 and 4Q259 stand out. Their writing quality and their content matter may indicate them to have been something like the result of works-in-progress by scholar-scribes, not copies of professional quality that would have been made on order for someone other than the scribes themselves. The analysis of the writing quality may support a scenario such as that suggested by Hempel, that 4Q259 (or a 4Q259-like *Vorlage*) was one of the sources used by the scribe of 1QS, and also her suggestion that 4Q255, together with 4Q257, represents a manuscript of the type used by the compiler(s) of 1QS when drawing up the framework of the long text of the Serekh.[209]

---

209   Hempel, *The Community Rules from Qumran*, 20, 21, 31–34, 36, 40–44, 62. Regarding 4Q259, see also Émile Puech, "Rémarques sur l'écriture de 1 QS VII–VIII," *RevQ* 10 (1979):

BOOK PRODUCTION AND CIRCULATION IN ANCIENT JUDAEA

The analysis of the writing quality and skills supports previous research that argued we should not treat all manuscript evidence as representing separate versions or editions of *the* Serekh. There were copies of considerable length in different formats that may have functioned in broader settings of studying or reading together, while others may have been personal copies by scholar-scribes, and then there were excerpts and possibly also training exercises.[210] Perhaps some copies exemplify not so much training in writing as learning by writing. Writing and copying helps memorization and learning,[211] and manuscripts could have been written as support of study and memorization.[212] This also means we need not assume that every manuscript that is now categorized as a Serekh manuscript served a different community, whether Essene, Yaḥad or otherwise; not every Serekh copy was a Serekh for a community somewhere.

5   Concluding Considerations

I claim no absolute judgements, distinctions, or categorizations on the basis of my palaeographic analysis regarding the writing style, quality, and skills of all Isaiah and Serekh manuscripts. But the approach has proven valuable from a heuristic perspective to get a better, differentiated understanding than before of the material evidence in terms of a manuscript's purpose or character and certain aspects of the social context of its copying.

---

43. When suggesting that 4Q259 was the source text used by the scribe(s) of 1QS Hempel, *The Community Rules from Qumran*, 40, suggests that textual variants can be attributed to the scribe of 1QS struggling with the idiosyncratic hand of 4Q259, but while his handwriting may be idiosyncratic it would not have been difficult to read. Instead of 4Q259, Alexander, "Literacy among Jews in Second Temple Palestine," 17–18 refers to 4Q255 as an example of a difficult to read exemplar, copying the text by eye, but while the mixture of cursive/semicursive may have made it perhaps somewhat of an effort for someone else to read I doubt it would have been very difficult.

210   Tigchelaar, "Elementary and Unskilled Hands," see at 31 minutes, observed that many Serekh manuscripts show elementary, unskilled handwriting and asked whether these are indicative for the Serekh as part of the curriculum of learning to write? However, I am not so sure that many can be seen as such; it seems clearer with a number of Isaiah manuscripts. 4Q262 was perhaps a training exercise? 4Q263 may have been an excerpted copy of some sort or perhaps a training exercise? These considerations are meant to stimulate further questioning into our criteria and assessment of writing quality and level.

211   Popović, "Reading, Writing, and Memorizing Together."

212   Tigchelaar, "Beautiful Bookhands and Careless Characters," see at 53 minutes. Hamidović, "Living *Serakhim*," 81, also invokes memorization, but in a different way, for a scenario in which after a group discussion scribes could record the changes by adding a new passage from memory.

My analysis and considerations are preliminary in so far as the twenty-two Isaiah copies and twelve Serekh copies are still a limited number of scrolls. These must be complemented by analyses of other batches of copies. Yet, the selection is useful to think about book production and circulation in a broader sense for ancient Judaea and in a specific sense for the people behind the scrolls from Qumran, as it contains complete bookroll copies (such as 1QIsa^a and 1QS), biblical and sectarian texts, and copies from various periods and from various Qumran caves and also from Murabba'at elsewhere in the Judaean Desert. It should be clear from the above that not all Isaiah manuscript evidence represents an edition of the biblical book, and that not all Serekh manuscript evidence represents a separate version or edition of *the* Serekh.

Here, I consider some of the general palaeographic conclusions regarding writing quality and skills, how these bear on the question for whom a manuscript was copied, and what that means for the social context of producing and circulating the Dead Sea Scrolls, also in relation to models of textual communities.

As a general, tentative conclusion I observe that what is striking when considering the writing style, quality, and skills in the Dead Sea Scrolls is, contrary to Johnson's assessment of the Oxyrhynchus papyri, not the overwhelming near uniformity and sheer dominance of professionalism. Rather, my analysis of the Isaiah and Serekh copies from the Judaean Desert demonstrates a diversity and pluriformity in their production and quality. Only the everyday professional may perhaps come nearest to representing somewhat of a homogenous grouping of copies, and this seems clearest for the formal Herodian-period script style. Often, whether for the formal hand or for what Cross has called the semiformal or the semicursive hand, the execution of these hands or styles, their quality, is not neat, especially, but not only, in copies from the Hasmonaean period.

Contrary to what Johnson has argued for the majority of very large scripts in the Oxyrhynchus papyri (see section 3.1 above), the scrolls do not show a very large script size to have been the norm for the highest quality professional or elegant copies. The Isaiah copies do not demonstrate such a correlation, while the Serekh copies with the smallest average letter size show, relatively, the best quality of handwriting, whereas those with a large letter size show the lowest quality of writing. Perhaps for the scrolls, smaller script size is to be associated with better quality copies, but this needs to be assessed in future research.

When it comes to Dead Sea Scrolls "deluxe" copies, this category will need to be considered anew in light of the analysis here. Thus far, scholars have mainly limited the focus on codicological dimensions when applying the deluxe category to copies, ignoring writing quality. Not only is this contrary to what has been observed for Greco-Roman writing culture, where the fine execution of the script was the distinguishing characteristic of a typical "deluxe" from an everyday production. But also, clearly badly written copies from Qumran cannot have been "deluxe" copies only on the basis of their codicological dimensions, though this is exactly what has been suggested, especially for specific copies of Isaiah but also for 1QS, as well as for copies of other texts. For example, both 4Q56 and 1QS have been assessed as possible deluxe copies, only on the basis of codicological dimensions. But the analysis of the quality of handwriting has shown it to be professional at best. Both of these manuscripts have been copied by unskilled or moderately skilled scribes, which disqualifies them to have been "deluxe."

Regarding scroll length, amount of text, and quality of handwriting, the Isaiah copies of everyday professional and elegant quality, in general, covered the whole book or the first or second half of the book and those of lesser, substandard quality, generally, may have been excerpts or some even training exercises, while such a correlation is not evident for the Serekh copies. However, copies like 4Q56 and 1QS show that entire works could be copied by unskilled or moderately skilled scribes. This evidence should caution against general inferences about a manuscript's purpose or character drawn from scroll length or amount of text only.

The palaeographic conclusions regarding the writing quality and skills bear on the question for whom a manuscript was copied, in a general sense of trade and private circumstances and in a specific sense of trained and untrained scribes, though these contexts often cannot be sharply separated.

In a specific sense, and following Johnson's distinction between book production and circulation, the Isaiah and Serekh copies present many examples of unskilled or untrained scribes producing lower quality copies, not all of which were actual bookrolls. Regarding Isaiah, we have reviewed a fair number of substandard copies that were probably not full editions but excerpts or even training exercises. These copies of unskilled scribes were most likely for the benefit of the scribe himself, whether for intellectual study of some sort (4Q62, 4Q65, 4Q66, 4Q67) or for writing training (4Q63). Regarding the Serekh copies, half of them are of substandard quality. These may have been personal copies by scholar-scribes (4Q255/4Q433a, 4Q259/4Q319), excerpts or possibly training exercises (4Q262, 4Q263). Yet, we should also allow for the possibility that excerpt collections of substandard quality could have been copied for others than the scribe, such as for private circulation (e.g., 4Q64 and 4Q68), or perhaps even for trade (4Q61), while in some cases it may not be possible to decide whether an excerpt copy was produced either for personal, private or even trade (4Q62a) or for personal or private (4Q264, if an excerpt). Circumstances may have changed also. So that what was originally, for example, a personal copy turned into a private, communal one. So, with Serekh copy 4Q259/4Q319 there is also the possibility that what was originally meant as a personal copy was further worked on by other scribes and may have circulated privately in a communal context.

In a general sense, the question is whether manuscripts were copied for a general market of book trade or for a private, communal context. I have argued for understanding "private," distinct from "individual" or "personal," in a broader sense to include a group of people (see section 3.1.3 above). A group or a social network, whether at one location or at various locations, provides a context in which manuscripts could conceivably have been produced by trained as well as untrained or unskilled scribes. I have discussed how the Great Isaiah Scroll was a communal, scholarly copy (see section 3.1.4 above). Whether that was intentional from the start or that is how it came to be used cannot be decided. But the continuous use of this manuscript as evidenced by the interventions of later scribes over possibly more than a century suggests that after its original production by two scribes it was read, used, and worked on in a private or communal setting, not in a market context. The idea that the scribe of 1QS intervened in the copy of 1QIsa[a] should be abandoned (see section 3.1.4.1 above). But the possible use of one of the readings in 1QIsa[a] in Pesher Habakkuk may be evidence to suggest that these two scrolls were used simultaneously for at least some period of time in the same social context of a private or communal setting.

As discussed above, there seems to be an assumption in the field that Qumran manuscripts were copied for the communal benefit of the community. But Wise suggested that the great majority of the scrolls constitute a cross-section of the book trade and Falk suggested a commercial market, also for sectarian rule texts (see section 1). Using Mur3 as an example, I argued that we have to reckon with different market circumstances and varying levels of quality in relation to supply and demand (see section 3.1.3). But such differentiation does not change that a careful consideration of the handwriting quality and skills shows that many of the Isaiah scrolls from the caves near Qumran are unlikely to have been produced for a general trade market. They were of too low quality for that. This does not only apply to substandard shorter copies or excerpts. A copy of a complete book could also be of questionable scribal quality. It is difficult to imagine how a copy such as 4Q56 could have been produced for a commercial market. So, contrary to Wise's suggestion, many of the scrolls from the caves near Qumran were not copied for the general book trade because they are of low writing quality and hardly market material; future research may further validate this.

The better-quality copies (elegant and professional) could conceivably have been produced for a general book trade. But often it is not possible to decide whether they were produced for a communal setting or for a commercial market context. How to decide whether professional copies of varying quality such as 1Q8, 4Q55, 4Q58, or an excerpt like 4Q61 were for a communal or a market context? Moreover, does it matter whether we are considering "biblical" or "sectarian" texts? It would seem that we would readily accept biblical copies to have been part of a book market and sectarian copies not so. Why? Is that because of the assumption that Qumran manuscripts were copied for the communal benefit of the community, and sectarian texts especially so? Is that because biblical texts would have been read by Jews more generally so that a book market is more feasible and sectarian texts were read only by Jews from a specific social network so that a book market would not have been feasible, for example, because of scale? Falk seems to have suggested a commercial market for sectarian rule texts but he gave no further explanation. Regarding the Serekh copies, half of them are of substandard quality and from those of professional quality only two, 4Q256 and 4Q258, seem to stand out for good but not deluxe writing quality, while 4Q264 is from a skilled scribe but possibly an excerpt of some sort. Were these kinds of Serekh copies, or the Isaiah copy 4Q57 with the divine name in palaeo-Hebrew characters, part of a commercial market of a specific social network? Here, our models of the textual communities determine how we envisage the social context of production and circulation.

When linking the site, the scrolls, and a group of people, palaeographic consideration of the writing quality and skills must be taken into account when looking at the scrolls as material evidence. Palaeography is a necessary method to study the scrolls as archaeological artefacts, and it should be part and parcel of any material philology approach. Thus, the diversity and pluriformity of the handwriting as discussed here can complement the much-studied textual pluriformity and fluidity to enhance our understanding of the literary and reading culture of ancient Judaea. As Tigchelaar reminded us, "The presence of scraps of writing exercises among the other scrolls of Qumran Cave 4 needs to be taken into account in any hypothesis about the collection in the caves."[213] Hempel discussed a number of texts from Cave 4 that appear less finessed and purposeful in their final shape to argue for their workaday quality.[214] White Crawford observed that the presence of notes and exercises in Cave 4 indicate the local nature of the collection as it is unlikely that such notes were transported to Qumran from elsewhere but must have been written at Qumran.[215] These hints of the real or "reality literature" can be reinforced by looking anew at the

---

213 Tigchelaar, "The Scribes of the Scrolls," 531.
214 Hempel, *The Qumran Rule Texts in Context*, 332–36; Hempel, *The Community Rules from Qumran*, 20.
215 White Crawford, *Scribes and Scrolls at Qumran*, 144.

written evidence through the lens of writing quality and skills. Any hypothesis that aims to explain the collections from Qumran must also take these aspects into account alongside other textual and archaeological approaches. Such an approach enables to differentiate not only between for whom a manuscript was likely copied but also where a manuscript was copied. Sometimes such an assessment entails a local explanation, but that does not mean of course that all written evidence was produced and circulated only locally.

If we ask for whom Serekh manuscripts were copied, the distinction between book production and book circulation may be different than for Isaiah manuscripts. With the Isaiah manuscripts it is clear that the extant copies certainly do not originate from the author, but how should we envisage that for the Serekh manuscripts? If we identify the Serekh manuscripts with the specific interests of a particular group or movement, then what does that mean for how we understand the production and circulation of such copies? If there was not a master copy or a single edition, what then was, in sociological terms, the source for circulation if not the author? On the basis of the above evidence and on the basis of a broader understanding of "private" as "communal," I suggest that a private, communal setting of a group or a social network provides a better context for understanding book production and circulation of such texts than does a trade or market context. There were Serekh copies of considerable length in different formats that may have functioned in broader settings of studying or reading together, next to scholars' personal copies, excerpts and training exercises. There was no publisher or other agent functioning as a gatekeeper. In sociological terms, the group acted as a gatekeeper for the production and circulation of texts. This gatekeeper function must have been the product of a complex social interaction, about which the extant sources from ancient Judaea do not tell us much. Fortunately, hints of this complex social interaction, hints of the real, can be glimpsed through the handwriting of the scribes of the Dead Sea Scrolls.

Bibliography

Aksu, Ayhan. "A Palaeographic and Codicological (Re)assessment of the Opisthograph 4Q433a/4Q255." *DSD* 26 (2019): 1–19.

Alexander, Philip S. "Literacy Among Jews in Second Temple Palestine: Reflections on the Evidence from Qumran." Pages 3–24 in *Hamlet on a Hill: Semitic and Greek Studies Presented to Professor T. Muraoka on the Occasion of his Sixty-Fifth Birthday*. Edited by Martin F. J. Baasten and Wido T. van Peursen. OLA 118. Leuven: Peeters, 2003.

Alexander, Philip S., and Géza Vermès, eds. *Qumran Cave 4.XIX: Serekh Ha-Yaḥad and Two Related Texts*. DJD 26. Oxford: Clarendon, 1998.

Baillet, Maurice, Józef T. Milik and Roland de Vaux, eds. *Les 'Petites Grottes'*. DJD 3. Oxford: Clarendon, 1962.

Baumgarten, Albert I. *The Flourishing of Jewish Sects in the Maccabean Era: An Interpretation.* JSJSup 55. Leiden: Brill, 1997.

Benoit, Pierre, Józef T. Milik, and Roland de Vaux, with contributions from Grace M. Crowfoot and Elizabeth Crowfoot, Adolf Grohmann, eds. *Les grottes de Murabba'ât.* DJD 2. Oxford: Clarendon, 1961.

Brooke, George J. "Choosing Between Papyrus and Skin: Cultural Complexity and Multiple Identities in the Qumran Library." Pages 119–35 in *Jewish Cultural Encounters in the Ancient Mediterranean and Near Eastern World.* Edited by Mladen Popović, Myles Schoonover, and Marijn Vandenberghe. JSJSup 178. Leiden: Brill, 2017.

Brooke, George J. "Isaiah in the Qumran Scrolls." Pages 429–50 in *The Oxford Handbook of Isaiah.* Edited by Lena-Sofia Tiemeyer. Oxford: Oxford University Press, 2021.

Burrows, Millar, John C. Trever, and William H. Brownlee, eds. *The Dead Sea Scrolls of St. Mark's Monastery, Volume 1: The Isaiah Manuscript and the Habakkuk Commentary.* New Haven, CT: American Schools of Oriental Research, 1950.

Cavallo, Guglielmo, and Herwig Maehler. *Hellenistic Bookhands.* Berlin: De Gruyter, 2008.

Chazon, Esther G. "Is *Divrei ha-me'orot* a Sectarian Prayer?" Pages 3–17 in *The Dead Sea Scrolls: Forty Years of Research.* Edited by Devorah Dimant and Uriel Rappaport. STDJ 10. Leiden: Brill, 1992.

Chazon, Esther, Torleif Elgvin, Esther Eshel, Daniel Falk, Bilhah Nitzan, Elisha Qimron, Eileen Schuller, David Seely, Eibert J. C. Tigchelaar, and Moshe Weinfeld, eds. *Qumran Cave 4.xx: Poetical and Liturgical Texts, Part 2.* DJD 29. Oxford: Clarendon, 1999.

Collins, John J. *Beyond the Qumran Community: The Sectarian Movement of the Dead Sea Scrolls.* Grand Rapids, MI: Eerdmans, 2010.

Cross, Frank Moore. "The Development of the Jewish Scripts." Pages 133–202 in *The Bible and the Ancient Near East: Essays in Honor of William Foxwell Albright.* Edited by G. Ernest Wright. Garden City, NY: Doubleday, 1961.

Cross, Frank Moore. "Introduction." Pages 1–5 in *Scrolls from Qumrân Cave 1: The Great Isaiah Scroll, the Order of the Community, the Pesher to Habakkuk.* Edited by Frank Moore Cross, David Noel Freedman, and James A. Sanders. Jerusalem: Albright Institute of Archaeological Research, 1972.

Cross, Frank Moore. "Palaeographic Dates of the Manuscripts." Page 57 in *The Dead Sea Scrolls: Hebrew, Aramaic, and Greek Texts with English Translations*, vol. 1: *Rule of the Community and Related Documents.* Edited by James H. Charlesworth. PTSDSSP 1. Tübingen and Louisville, KY: Mohr Siebeck and Westminster John Knox, 1994.

Cross, Frank Moore. *The Ancient Library of Qumran.* 3rd ed. Sheffield: Sheffield Academic Press, 1995.

Cross, Frank Moore. *Leaves from an Epigrapher's Notebook: Collected Papers in Hebrew and West Semitic Palaeography and Epigraphy.* HSS 51. Winona Lake, IN: Eisenbrauns, 2003.

Cross, Frank Moore, Donald W. Parry, Richard J. Saley, and Eugene Ulrich, eds. *Qumran Cave 4.XII: 1–2 Samuel*, DJD 17. Oxford: Clarendon, 2005.

Davies, Philip R. "The Judaism(s) of the Damascus Document." Pages 27–43 in *The Damascus Document: A Centennial of Discovery*. Edited by Joseph M. Baumgarten. STDJ 34. Leiden: Brill, 2000.

Davies, Philip R. "Sects from Texts: On the Problems of Doing a Sociology of the Qumran Literature." Pages 26–42 in *New Directions in Qumran Studies: Proceedings of the Bristol Colloquium on the Dead Sea Scrolls, 8–10 September 2003*. Edited by Jonathan G. Campbell, William J. Lyons, and Lloyd K. Pietersen. London: T&T Clark, 2005.

Falk, Daniel K. "Material Aspects of Prayer Manuscripts at Qumran." Pages 33–88 in *Literature or Liturgy? Early Christian Hymns and Prayers in their Literary and Liturgical Context in Antiquity*. Edited by Clemens Leonhard and Hermut Löhr. WUNT 2/363. Tübingen: Mohr Siebeck, 2014.

Flint, Peter W. "The Interpretation of Scriptural Isaiah in the Qumran Scrolls: Quotations, Citations, Allusions, and the Form of the Scriptural Source Text." Pages 1:389–406 in *A Teacher for All Generations: Essays in Honor of James C. VanderKam*. Edited by Eric F. Mason, Samuel I. Thomas, Alison Schofield, and Eugene Ulrich. JSJSup 153. 2 vols. Leiden: Brill, 2012.

García Martínez, Florentino, Eibert J. C. Tigchelaar, and Adam S. van der Woude, eds. *Qumran Cave 11.II: 11Q2–18, 11Q20–31*. DJD 23. Oxford: Clarendon, 1998.

Goldberg, Sander M. *Constructing Literature in the Roman Republic: Poetry and Its Reception*. Cambridge: Cambridge University Press, 2005.

Hamidović, David. "Living *Serakhim*: Process of Authority in the *Community Rule*." Pages 61–90 in *The Process of Authority: The Dynamics in Transmission and Reception of Canonical Texts*. Edited by Jan Dušek and Jan Roskovec. DCLS 27. Berlin: De Gruyter, 2016.

Hamidović, David. "Editing a Cluster of Texts: The Digital Solution." Pages 196–213 in *Ancient Worlds in Digital Culture*. Edited by Claire Clivaz, Paul Dilley, and David Hamidović. Digital Biblical Studies 1. Leiden: Brill, 2016.

Harding, Gerald Lankester. "Introductory: The Discovery, the Excavation, Minor Finds." Pages 3–7 in *Qumran Cave I*. DJD 1. Oxford: Clarendon, 1955.

Hartog, Pieter B. *Pesher and Hypomnema: A Comparison of Two Commentary Collections from the Hellenistic-Roman Period*. STDJ 121. Leiden: Brill, 2017.

Hempel, Charlotte. "Reflections on Literacy, Textuality, and Community in the Qumran Dead Sea Scrolls." Pages 69–82 in *Is There a Text in this Cave? Studies in the Textuality of the Dead Sea Scrolls in Honour of George J. Brooke*. Edited by Ariel Feldman, Maria Cioată, and Charlotte Hempel. STDJ 119. Leiden: Brill, 2017.

Hempel, Charlotte. "The Theatre of the Written Word: Reading the Community Rule with Steven Fraade." Pages 119–30 in *The Faces of Torah: Studies in the Texts and Contexts of Ancient Judaism in Honor of Steven Fraade*. Edited by Michal Bar-Asher Siegal, Tzvi Novick, and Christine Hayes. JAJSup 22. Göttingen: Vandenhoeck & Ruprecht, 2017.

Hempel, Charlotte. *The Community Rules from Qumran: A Commentary*. TSAJ 183. Tübingen: Mohr Siebeck, 2020.

Hempel, Charlotte. "A Tale of Two Scribes: Encounters with an Avant-Garde Manuscript of the Community Rules (4Q259)." Pages 115–28 in *Hokhmat Sopher: Mélanges offerts au Professeur Émile Puech en l'honneur de son quatre-vingtième anniversaire*. Edited by Jean-Sébastien Rey and Martin Staszak. Études Bibliques 88. Leuven: Peeters, 2021.

Iddeng, Jon W. "Publica aut peri! The Releasing and Distribution of Roman Books." *Symbloae Osloenses* 81 (2006): 58–84.

Johnson, Michael Brooks. "One Work or Three? A Proposal for Reading 1QS-1QSa-1QSb as a Composite Work." *DSD* 25 (2018): 141–77.

Johnson, William A. *Bookrolls and Scribes in Oxyrhynchus*. Studies in Book and Print Culture. Toronto: University of Toronto Press, 2004.

Johnson, William A. *Readers and Reading Culture in the High Roman Empire: A Study of Elite Communities*. Classical Culture and Society. Oxford: Oxford University Press, 2010.

Jokiranta, Jutta. "Thinking about Ancient Manuscripts as Information Processing." Pages 1:611–35 in *Sibyls, Scriptures, and Scrolls: John Collins at Seventy*. Edited by Joel Baden, Hindy Najman, and Eibert J. C. Tigchelaar. JSJSup 175. 2 vols. Leiden: Brill, 2017.

Jull, A. J. Timothy, Douglas J. Donahue, Magen Broshi, and Emanuel Tov. "Radiocarbon Dating of Scrolls and Linen Fragments from the Judean Desert." *Radiocarbon* 37 (1995): 11–19.

Justnes, Årstein. "The Hand of the Corrector in 1QIsaa XXXIII 7 (Isa 40,7–8). Some Observations." *Sem* 57 (2015): 205–10.

Keith, Chris. "Urbanization and Literate Status in Early Christian Rome: Hermas and Justin Martyr as Examples." Pages 187–204 in *The Urban World and the First Christians*. Edited by Steve Walton, Paul R. Trebilco, and David W. J. Gill. Grand Rapids, MI: Eerdmans, 2017.

Keith, Chris. *Gospel as Manuscript: An Early History of the Jesus Tradition as Material Artifact*. Oxford: Oxford University Press, 2020.

Kister, Menahem. "Wisdom Literature and Its Relation to Other Genres: From Ben Sira to Mysteries." Pages 13–47 in *Sapiential Perspectives: Wisdom Literature in Light of the Dead Sea Scrolls*. Edited by John J. Collins, Gregory E. Sterling, and Ruth A. Clements. STDJ 51. Leiden: Brill, 2004.

Lemaire, André. "Inscriptions du Khirbeh, des grottes et de ʿAïn Feshkha." Pages 341–88 in *Fouilles de Khirbet Qumrân et de Aïn Feshkha*. II, *Études d'anthropologie, de physique et de chimie*. Edited by Jean-Baptiste Humbert and Jan Gunneweg. NTOA.SA 3. Göttingen: Vandenhoeck & Ruprecht, 2003.

Lemaire, André. "Lire, écrire, étudier à Qoumrân et ailleurs." Pages 63–79 in *Qoumrân et la judaïsme du tournant de notre ère: Actes de la Table Ronde, Collège de France, 16 novembre 2004*. Edited by André Lemaire and Simon C. Mimouni. Collection de la Revue des études juives 40. Leuven: Peeters, 2006.

Longacre, Drew. "Disambiguating the Concept of Formality in Palaeographic Descriptions: Stylistic Classification and the Ancient Jewish Hebrew/Aramaic Scripts." *COMSt Bulletin* 5 (2019): 101–28.

Longacre, Drew. "Paleographic Style and the Forms and Functions of the Dead Sea Psalm Scrolls: A Hand Fitting for the Occasion?" *VT* 72 (2021): 67–92.

Longacre, Drew. "Comparative Hellenistic and Roman Manuscript Studies (CHRoMS): Scripts Interactions and Hebrew/Aramaic Writing Culture." *COMSt Bulletin* 7 (2021): 7–50.

Magness, Jodi. *The Archaeology of Qumran and the Dead Sea Scrolls*. Studies in the Dead Sea Scrolls and Related Literature. Grand Rapids, MI: Eerdmans, 2002.

Mandell, Alice. "When Form Is Function: A Reassessment of the *Marziḥu* Contract (*KTU* 3.9) as a Scribal Exercise." *Maarav* 23 (2019): 39–67.

Mason, Steve. "Of Audience and Meaning: Reading Josephus' *Bellum Judaicum* in the Context of a Flavian Audience." Pages 71–100 in *Josephus and Jewish History in Flavian Rome and Beyond*. Edited by Joseph Sievers and Gaia Lembi. Leiden: Brill, 2005.

Mason, Steve. "Josephus, Publication, and Audiences: A Response." *Zutot* 8 (2011): 81–94.

McDonnel, Myles. "Writing, Copying, and Autograph Manuscripts in Ancient Rome." *ClQ* 46 (1996): 469–91.

Metso, Sarianna. *The Textual Development of the Qumran Community Rule*. STDJ 21. Leiden: Brill, 1997.

Metso, Sarianna. *The Community Rule: A Critical Edition with Translation*. EJL 51. Atlanta, GA: SBL, 2019.

Metso, Sarianna, and James M. Tucker. "The Changing Landscape of Editing Ancient Jewish Texts." Pages 269–87 in *Reading the Bible in Ancient Traditions and Modern Editions: Studies in Memory of Peter W. Flint*. Edited by Andrew B. Perrin, Kyung S. Baek, and Daniel K. Falk. EJL 47. Atlanta, GA: SBL, 2017.

Milik, Józef T. *Ten Years of Discovery in the Wilderness of Judaea*. Translated by John Strugnell. London: SCM, 1959.

Milik, Józef T. "Milkî-ṣedeq et Milkî-rešaʿ dans les ancients écrits juifs et chrétiens." *JJS* 23 (1972): 95–144.

Milik, Józef T. *The Books of Enoch: Aramaic fragments of Qumrân Cave 4*. Oxford: Clarendon, 1976.

Milik, Józef T. "Numérotation des feuilles des rouleaux dans le scriptorium de Qumrân (Planches X et XI)." *Sem* 27 (1977): 75–81.

Mizzi, Dennis. "Archaeology of Qumran." Pages 17–36 in *T&T Companion to the Dead Sea Scrolls*. Edited by George J. Brooke and Charlotte Hempel, with the assistance of Michael DeVries and Drew Longacre. London: Bloomsbury, 2019.

Mizzi, Dennis, and Jodi Magness. "Was Qumran Abandoned at the End of the First Century BCE?" *JBL* 135 (2016): 301–20.

Mugridge, Alan. "Writing and Writers in Antiquity: Two 'Spectra' in Greek Handwriting." Pages 573–80 in *Proceedings of the 25th International Congress of Papyrology*. Edited by Traianos Gagos. Ann Arbor: Scholarly Publishing Office, The University of Michigan Library, 2010.

Mugridge, Alan. *Copying Early Christian Texts: A Study of Scribal Practice*. WUNT 362. Tübingen: Mohr Siebeck, 2016.

Nässelqvist, Dan. "Publication." Pages 319–20 in *The Dictionary of the Bible and Ancient Media*. Edited by Tom Thatcher, Chris Keith, Raymond F. Person, Jr., and Elsie R. Stern. London: Bloomsbury T&T Clark, 2017.

Nati, James. *Textual Criticism and the Ontology of Literature in Early Judaism: An Analysis of the* Serekh ha-Yaḥad. JSJSup 198. Leiden: Brill, 2022.

Pajunen, Mika S. "Reading Psalm and Prayer Manuscripts from Qumran." Pages 55–70 in *Material Aspects of Reading in Ancient and Medieval Cultures: Materiality, Presence and Performance*. Edited by Anna Krauß, Jonas Leipziger, and Friederike Schücking-Jungblut. Materiale Textkulturen 26. Berlin: De Gruyter, 2020.

Popović, Mladen. "Otot." Pages 1013–1014 in *The Eerdmans Dictionary of Early Judaism*. Edited by John J. Collins and Daniel C. Harlow. Grand Rapids, MI: Eerdmans, 2010.

Popović, Mladen. "Qumran as Scroll Storehouse in Times of Crisis? A Comparative Perspective on Judaean Desert Manuscript Collections." *JSJ* 43 (2012): 551–94.

Popović, Mladen. "The Ancient 'Library' of Qumran between Urban and Rural Culture." Pages 155–67 in *The Dead Sea Scrolls at Qumran and the Concept of a Library*. Edited by Sidnie White Crawford and Cecilia Wassén. STDJ 116. Leiden: Brill, 2016.

Popović, Mladen. "Reading, Writing, and Memorizing Together: Reading Culture in Ancient Judaism and the Dead Sea Scrolls in a Mediterranean Context." *DSD* 24 (2017): 447–70.

Popović, Mladen. "Multilingualism, Multiscripturalism, and Knowledge Transfer in the Dead Sea Scrolls and Graeco-Roman Judaea." Pages 46–71 in *Sharing and Hiding Religious Knowledge in Early Judaism, Christianity, and Islam*. Edited by Mladen Popović, Lautaro Roig Lanzillotta, and Clare Wilde. Judaism, Christianity, and Islam—Tension, Transmission, Transformation 10. Berlin: De Gruyter, 2018.

Popović, Mladen, Maruf A. Dhali, and Lambert Schomaker. "Artificial Intelligence Based Writer Identification Generates New Evidence for the Unknown Scribes of the Dead Sea Scrolls Exemplified by the Great Isaiah Scroll (1QIsaᵃ)." *PLoS ONE* 16/4 (2021): 1–28. doi.org/10.1371/journal.pone.0249769.

Puech, Émile. "Rémarques sur l'écriture de I QS VII–VIII." *RevQ* 10 (1979): 35–43.

Puech, Émile. "L'alphabet cryptique A en 4QSᵉ (4Q259)." *RevQ* 18 (1998): 429–35.

Puech, Émile. "Exercises de deux scribes à Khirbet Qumrân: KhQ 161 et KhQ 2207." *RevQ* 32 (2020): 43–56.

Quick, Laura. "Scribal Habits and Scholarly Texts: Codicology at Oxyrhynchus and Qumran." Pages 37–54 in *Material Aspects of Reading in Ancient and Medieval Cultures: Materiality, Presence and Performance*. Edited by Anna Krauß, Jonas Leipziger, Friederike Schücking-Jungblut. Materiale Textkulturen 26. Berlin: De Gruyter, 2020.

Regev, Eyal. *Sectarianism in Qumran: A Cross-Cultural Perspective*. Religion and Society 45. Berlin: De Gruyter, 2007.

Schofield, Alison. *From Qumran to the* Yaḥad: *A New Paradigm of Textual Development for The Community Rule*. STDJ 77. Leiden: Brill, 2009.

Schofield, Alison. "Forms of Community." Pages 533–46 in *T&T Companion to the Dead Sea Scrolls*. Edited by George J. Brooke and Charlotte Hempel, with the assistance of Michael DeVries and Drew Longacre. London: Bloomsbury, 2019.

Schuller, Eileen M. "The Classification Hodayot and Hodayot-like (With Particular Attention to 4Q433, 4Q433A and 4Q440)." Pages 182–93 in *Sapiential, Liturgical and Poetical Texts from Qumran*. Edited by Daniel K. Falk, Florentino García Martínez, and Eileen M. Schuller. STDJ 53. Leiden: Brill, 2000.

Starr, Raymond J. "The Circulation of Literary Texts in the Roman World." *ClQ* 37 (1987): 213–23.

Stegemann, Hartmut. *Die Essener, Qumran, Johannes der Täufer und Jesus: Ein Sachbuch*. Freiburg: Herder, 1993.

Talmon, Shemaryahu, Jonathan Ben-Dov, and Uwe Glessmer, eds. *Qumran Cave 4.XVI: Calendrical Texts*. DJD 21. Oxford: Clarendon, 2001.

Taylor, Joan E., Dennis Mizzi, and Marcello Fidanzio. "Revisiting Qumran Cave 1Q and Its Archaeological Assemblage." *PEQ* 149 (2017): 295–325.

Tigchelaar, Eibert J. C. "In Search of the Scribe of 1QS." Pages 439–52 in *Emanuel: Studies in Hebrew Bible, Septuagint, and Dead Sea Scrolls in Honor of Emanuel Tov*. Edited by Shalom M. Paul, Robert A. Kraft, Lawrence H. Schiffman, and Weston W. Fields. VTSup 94. Leiden: Brill, 2003.

Tigchelaar, Eibert J. C. "'These Are the Names of the Spirits of ...': A Preliminary Edition of *4QCatalogue of Spirits (4Q230)* and New Manuscript Evidence for the *Two Spirits Treatise (4Q257* and *1Q29a)*." *RevQ* 21 (2004): 529–47.

Tigchelaar, Eibert J. C. "Beautiful Bookhands and Careless Characters: An Alternative Approach to the Dead Sea Scrolls." Paper presented as the 8th Annual Rabbi Tann Memorial Lecture. University of Birmingham, 2018.

Tigchelaar, Eibert J. C. "The Scribes of the Scrolls." Pages 524–32 in *T&T Clark Companion to the Dead Sea Scrolls*. Edited by George J. Brooke and Charlotte Hempel, with the assistance of Michael DeVries and Drew Longacre. London: T&T Clark, 2019.

Tigchelaar, Eibert J. C. "Seventy Years of Palaeographic Dating of the Dead Sea Scrolls." Pages 258–78 in *Sacred Texts and Disparate Interpretations: Qumran Manuscripts Seventy Years Later: Proceedings of the International Conference Held at the John Paul II Catholic University of Lublin, 24–26 October 2017*. Edited by Henryk Drawnel. STDJ 133. Leiden: Brill, 2020.

Tigchelaar, Eibert J. C. "Elementary and Unskilled Hands." Paper presented at the Groningen conference on Digital Palaeography and Hebrew/Aramaic Scribal Culture. University of Groningen, 6–8 April 2021.

Tigchelaar, Eibert J. C. "The Scribes of the Dead Sea Scrolls: The Case of 4Q10." theo.kuleuven.be/apps/press/theologyresearchnews/2022/01/03/the-scribes-of-the-dead-sea-scrolls-the-case-of-4q10/.

Tov, Emanuel. *Scribal Practices and Approaches Reflected in the Texts Found in the Judean Desert.* STDJ 54. Leiden: Brill, 2004.

Trever, John C. "Preliminary Observations on the Jerusalem Scrolls." *BASOR* 111 (1948): 3–16.

Trever, John C. "A Paleographic Study of the Jerusalem Scrolls." *BASOR* 113 (1949): 6–23.

Ulrich, Eugene C. "4QSam^c: A Fragmentary Manuscript of 2 Samuel 14–15 from the Scribe of the Serek Hay-yaḥad (1QS)." *BASOR* 235 (1979): 1–25.

Ulrich, Eugene C. "Isaiah, Book of." Pages 1:384–88 in *Encyclopedia of the Dead Sea Scrolls.* Edited by Lawrence H. Schiffman and James C. VanderKam. 2 vols. Oxford: Oxford University Press, 2000.

Ulrich, Eugene C. "Identification of a Scribe Active at Qumran: 1QPs^b–4QIsa^c–11QM." Pages 201–10 in *Meghillot: Studies in the Dead Sea Scrolls V–VI. A Festschrift for Devorah Dimant.* Edited by Moshe Bar-Asher and Emanuel Tov. Jerusalem: Bialik Institute, 2007. (Hebrew)

Ulrich, Eugene C., and Peter W. Flint, with a contribution by Martin G. Abegg, Jr., eds. *Qumran Cave 1.II: The Isaiah Scrolls.* DJD 32. Oxford: Clarendon, 2010.

Ulrich, Eugene C., Frank Moore Cross, Russell E. Fuller, Judith E. Sanderson, Patrick W. Skehan, and Emanuel Tov, eds. *Qumran Cave 4.X: The Prophets.* DJD 15. Oxford: Clarendon, 1997.

Vaux, Roland de. *Archaeology and the Dead Sea Scrolls.* London: Oxford University Press, 1973.

White Crawford, Sidnie. *Scribes and Scrolls at Qumran.* Grand Rapids, MI: Eerdmans, 2019.

Wise, Michael O. "Accidents and Accidence: A Scribal View of Linguistic Dating of the Aramaic Scrolls from Qumran." Pages 103–51 in *Thunder in Gemini, and other Essays on the History, Language and Literature of Second Temple Palestine.* JSPSup 15. Sheffield: Sheffield Academic Press, 1994.

Wise, Michael O. *Language and Literacy in Roman Judaea: A Study of the Bar Kokhba Documents.* AYBRL. New Haven, CT: Yale University Press, 2015.

Yogev, Johnathan, and Shamir Yona. "A Trainee and a Skilled Ugaritic Scribe—KTU 1.12 and KTU 1.4." *ANES* 50 (2013): 237–42.

CHAPTER 7

4Q169 (Pesher Nahum) in Its Ancient Media Context

Pieter B. Hartog

1   Introduction

This article aims to situate 4Q169 (Pesher on Nahum) within its ancient media context. In the past decade, many studies on ancient media culture have seen the light, defining the topic increasingly as a central interest for those studying the ancient world. These studies address different themes, but all focus on forms and practices of communication.[1] Their governing principle is Marshall McLuhan's contention that "the medium is the message." As McLuhan explains:

> This is ... to say that the personal and social consequences of any medium—that is, of any extension of ourselves—result from the new scale that is introduced into our affairs by each extension of ourselves, or by any new technology.[2]

Following McLuhan's lead, media studies comprise the study of all phenomena and technologies that can be classified as means of communication. Studying a manuscript such as 4Q169 as an ancient medium, therefore, will amount to analysing what the manuscript aims to communicate and how it facilitates this communication of its contents.

The material features of ancient manuscripts offer clues to how they functioned as means of communication. It is no surprise, therefore, that the increasing attention to ancient media cultures intertwines with the rise of what some have called "new philology" or "material philology"—the study of pre-modern manuscripts as artefacts in their own rights rather than merely as carriers of

---

1   Cf. how Ray Person and Chris Keith describe ancient media studies not so much as a particular method, but rather as a general approach that studies "ancient communications culture." See Raymond F. Person, Jr. and Chris Keith, "Media Studies and Biblical Studies: An Introduction," in *The Dictionary of the Bible and Ancient Media*, ed. Tom Thatcher et al. (London: Bloomsbury, 2017), 1–15 (quote 1).

2   Marshall MacLuhan, *Understanding Media: The Extensions of Man*, introduction by Lewis H. Lapham (Cambridge, MA: The MIT Press, 1994), 7.

© PIETER B. HARTOG, 2023 | DOI:10.1163/9789004537804_008

texts. As Liv Lied has persuasively shown, both developments are indications of a broader move away from the study of origins to that of practices, which can be recognised in the humanities as a whole.[3] New Testament studies and Jewish Studies have tended to envision this move in slightly different ways. In studies on ancient Jewish literature, including the Dead Sea Scrolls, one will find references to new or material philology, but little engagement with media studies.[4] In New Testament studies, the situation is the reverse.[5] This presumably results from the different directions in which the fields have developed: much of Qumran scholarship has consisted of handling and editing the manuscripts as artefacts, whereas New Testament scholars have long had a particular interest in the oral traditions behind the New Testament writings. Given the overlaps between these perspectives, however, the aim of this volume to build bridges between the two disciplines and to develop a media approach towards the Dead Sea Scrolls is a welcome enterprise.

In what follows I will briefly survey some material characteristics of 4Q169. Subsequently I will argue that the contents of this manuscript constitute a written, narrativized representation of initially oral teachings and propose that 4Q169 served as an easy-to-carry copy, which served the dissemination of

---

3 Liv I. Lied, "Media Culture, New Philology, and the Pseudepigrapha: A Note on Method" (paper presented at the Annual Meeting of the SBL, Chicago, IL, 19 November 2012), 1–2.

4 E.g., Liv I. Lied, "*Nachleben* and Textual Identity: Variants and Variance in the Reception History of 2 Baruch," in *Fourth Ezra and Second Baruch: Reconstruction after the Fall*, ed. Matthias Henze and Gabriele Boccaccini, JSJSup 164 (Leiden: Brill, 2013), 403–28; Matthew P. Monger, "4Q216 and the State of Jubilees at Qumran," *RevQ* 26 (2014): 595–612; Liv I. Lied and Hugo Lundhaug, eds., *Snapshots of Evolving Traditions: Jewish and Christian Manuscript Culture, Textual Fluidity, and New Philology*, TUGAL 175 (Berlin: De Gruyter, 2017); Sarianna Metso and James M. Tucker, "The Changing Landscape of Editing Ancient Jewish Texts," in *Reading the Bible in Ancient Traditions and Modern Editions: Studies in Memory of Peter W. Flint*, ed. Andrew W. Perrin, Kyung S. Baek, and Daniel K. Falk, EJL 47 (Atlanta, GA: SBL, 2017), 269–87; Kipp Davis, "The Social Milieu of 4QJer[a] (4Q70) in a Second Temple Jewish Manuscript Culture: Fragments, Manuscripts, Variance, and Meaning," in *The Dead Sea Scrolls and the Study of the Humanities: Method, Theory, Meaning: Proceedings of the Eighth Meeting of the International Organization for Qumran Studies (Munich, 4–7 August, 2013)*, ed. Pieter B. Hartog, Samuel I. Thomas, and Alison Schofield, STDJ 125 (Leiden: Brill, 2018), 53–76. See also the programme for the 2014 conference on "Material Philology in the Dead Sea Scrolls": https://michaellanglois.org/medias/Material-Philology_DSS-Final-Program.pdf.

5 E.g., Holly E. Hearon and Philip Ruge-Jones, eds., *The Bible in Ancient and Modern Media: Story and Performance* (Eugene, OR: Cascade, 2009); Anthony Le Donne and Tom Thatcher, eds., *The Fourth Gospel in First-Century Media Culture*, LNTS 426 (London: T&T Clark, 2011); J. A. Loubser, *Oral and Manuscript Culture in the Bible: Studies on the Media Texture of the New Testament—Explorative Hermeneutics*, 2nd ed. (Eugene, OR: Cascade, 2013); Alan Kirk, *Q in Matthew: Ancient Media, Memory, and Early Scribal Transmission of the Jesus Traditions*, LNTS 564 (London: T&T Clark, 2016).

268   HARTOG

its contents across the various places in which members of the Qumran movement lived.

2 4Q169: Material Features

In this section I will discuss the material features of 4Q169 that I think shed light on the purpose and socio-historical background of this manuscript. I do not offer an exhaustive material treatment of 4Q169. I exclude, for instance, the remarkably wide intercolumn between 4Q169 3–4 iii–iv, which results from the practicalities of the production of this manuscript rather than from its intended purposes as a means of communication.[6]

2.1 *Handwriting*

The handwriting of most of the pesharim can be classified in general terms as trained, but not particularly well-executed.[7] John Strugnell has observed that many Pesher manuscripts are written in "mains hérodiennes semiformelles";[8] based on the similarities in handwriting Strugnell suggested that 4Q167 and 4Q168 were written by the same scribe.[9] More far-reaching is Ada Yardeni's suggestion that 4Q161, 4Q166, 4Q171, 4Q172, and perhaps 4Q167, can all be attributed to the same scribe.[10] Even if we do not accept Strugnell's and Yardeni's

---

6 The reason for this wide intercolumn is not entirely clear. It may be connected with the fact that column iii is the final column of a sheet and column iv the first of the next sheet, as suggested by George J. Brooke, "Aspects of the Physical and Scribal Features of some Cave 4 'Continuous' Pesharim," in *The Dead Sea Scrolls: Transmission of Traditions and Production of Texts*, ed. Sarianna Metso, Hindy Najman, and Eileen Schuller, STDJ 92 (Leiden: Brill, 2010), 135 n. 9. Shani Berrin (Tzoref), *The Pesher Nahum Scroll from Qumran: An Exegetical Study of 4Q169*, STDJ 53 (Leiden: Brill, 2004), 8, n. 23 suggests that the leather was brittle at this point, but this is difficult to check without examining the original manuscript (which I have not been able to do for this paper).

7 I would categorise the hands of 1QpHab, 4Q161, 4Q164, 4Q166, 4Q167, 4Q168, and 4Q171 in these terms. See Pieter B. Hartog, *Pesher and Hypomnema: A Comparison of Two Commentary Traditions from the Hellenistic-Roman World*, STDJ 121 (Leiden: Brill, 2017), 58–59. To this list I would now add 4Q170, on which Strugnell remarks: "L'écriture est de caractère « rustic semi-formal » mais distince de la main habituelle des *pešārîm*" ("Notes en marge du volume V des « Discoveries in the Judaean Desert of Jordan »," *RevQ* 7 [1970]: 210). The hands of 4Q162 and 4Q163 exhibit a rapid execution, whilst 4Q165 and 4Q169 are penned in neat, formal hands.

8 Strugnell, "Notes en marge," 186.

9 Strugnell, "Notes en marge," 204.

10 Ada Yardeni, "A Note on a Qumran Scribe," in *New Seals and Inscriptions: Hebrew, Idumean, and Cuneiform*, ed. Meir Lubetski, HBM 8 (Sheffield: Sheffield Phoenix, 2007), 287–98.

proposals, however,[11] their work shows that the similarities between the hands of the various Pesher manuscripts are substantial. These similarities may reflect the purposes and socio-historical background of these manuscripts.[12] If an analogy with teachers' and students' hands in Greek manuscripts, as outlined by Raffaella Cribiore, is allowed,[13] the type of handwriting one finds in the majority of Pesher manuscripts may support the scholarly-educational setting of these commentaries.

The handwriting of 4Q169, however, differs from that of most of the other pesharim in that it is a well-executed, formal hand. Strugnell speaks of a "main « formelle » de la fin de l'époque hasmonéenne, ou du commencement de l'hérodienne."[14] This formal handwriting may point to 4Q169 having fulfilled a less everyday purpose than most of the other Pesher manuscripts. Both Emanuel Tov, in his extensive study of scribal practices in the Dead Sea Scrolls, and scholars working on the Egyptian papyri associate formal hands—often in combination with other material features—with manuscripts that, as William Johnson has remarked, "not only contained high culture, but [were themselves] an expression of high culture."[15]

In this capacity, such manuscripts could fulfil different purposes. Johnson points to the display function of such manuscripts. Such display settings may not necessarily have involved reading: hardly literate owners of manuscripts may have put them on display as "as after-dinner entertainment,"[16] with the aesthetics of the manuscript—as a product of high culture—reflecting well on its owner. In other settings, formally written manuscripts may have been used for reading by a lector, presumably in a communal setting. The existence of reading communities in the ancient world did not necessarily imply widespread literacy, and many members of such reading communities would more

---

11   I tend to agree with scholars who assume that each Pesher manuscript was written by a different scribe. See, e.g., Emanuel Tov, *Scribal Practices and Approaches Reflected in the Texts Found in the Judean Desert*, STDJ 54 (Leiden: Brill, 2004), 258; Brooke, "Aspects," 141.

12   Cf. Hartog, *Pesher and Hypomnema*, 58–59.

13   Raffaella Cribiore points to parallels between the hands of teachers in model exercise and the hands of hypomnemata, writing that "[u]sually *hypomnemata* are written competently and quickly in neat hands that sometimes link some of the letters." See her *Writing, Teachers, and Students in Graeco-Roman Egypt*, ASP 36 (Atlanta, GA: Scholars Press, 1996), 100. With the exception of ligatures, which are rare in Pesher manuscripts, this characterisation of teachers' hands and the handwriting of commentaries also applies to the pesharim. Even so, some caution must of course be observed when applying characterisations of Greek writing—where the difference between formal and informal writing is usually clearer than it is in Hebrew writing—to manuscripts written in Hebrew.

14   Strugnell, "Notes en marge," 205.

15   William A. Johnson, "Toward a Sociology of Reading in Classical Antiquity," *AJP* 121 (2000): 612.

16   Johnson, "Sociology of Reading," 613.

often have heard texts being read to them rather than reading for themselves.[17] In other settings, formally written manuscripts possibly served as master copies for scribes copying their contents, or (as perhaps is the case with some of the so-called "deluxe scrolls" from Qumran) appropriated the idea of the master copy to present themselves as the most authoritative version of a textual tradition.

2.2 Intercolumns and Bottom Margins

Both in the Dead Sea Scrolls and in the Oxyrhynchus papyri collection, quickly written manuscripts tend to have narrower margins than those written in slower, more formal hands.[18] This tendency has been explained as reflecting the efficient use of material in manuscripts used for note taking or other everyday purposes: when taking notes, one would normally write more quickly and try to use as much of the writing material as possible.

Against this background, it seems unlikely that 4Q169 was used for note taking. With an average of 1.0–2.0 cm for top and 1.5–2.0 cm for bottom margins in the Qumran scrolls,[19] top margins in 4Q169 (measuring 1.5 cm or more) tend towards the larger side of Tov's scale, whereas bottom margins in this manuscript (measuring 2.8 cm or more[20]) are clearly large. Intercolumnar space in 4Q169 are likewise wide: they measure 1.5–2.4 cm, against an average of 1.0–1.5 cm in the Dead Sea Scrolls as a whole.[21] These measurements, alongside the small column height in 4Q169,[22] demonstrate that the scribe of 4Q169 did not intend to present as much information as he could in as little a space as

---

17 See Johnson, "Sociology of Reading"; idem, *Readers and Reading Culture in the High Roman Empire: A Study of Elite Communities* (New York, NY: Oxford University Press, 2010), esp. 17–31; Catherine Hezser, *Jewish Literacy in Roman Palestine*, TSAJ 81 (Tübingen: Mohr Siebeck, 2001), 451–73; Mladen Popović, "Reading, Writing, and Memorizing Together: Reading Culture in Ancient Judaism and the Dead Sea Scrolls in a Mediterranean Context," *DSD* 19 (2017): 446–69. Cf. also George J. Brooke's remark that "reading involved not just the repetition or rehearsal of the text, but some active participation in the realisation of the text, its oral performance" ("Reading, Searching and Blessing: A Functional Approach to Scriptural Interpretation in the יחד," in *The Temple in Text and Tradition: A Festschrift in Honour of Robert Hayward*, ed. R. Timothy McLay, LSTS 83 (London: T&T Clark, 2015), 146.

18 See William A. Johnson, *Bookrolls and Scribes in Oxyrhynchus* (Toronto: University of Toronto Press, 2004), 130–41 (esp. 135–36); Tov, *Scribal Practices*, 82–104, 125–30. As examples consider, e.g., 4Q165 (4QpIsaᵉ), which is written in a neat bookhand and has relatively large margins: its upper margins are average (0.9 cm), but its bottom margins are clearly large (2.5 cm). See Hartog, *Pesher and Hypomnema*, 83–84.

19 Tov, *Scribal Practices*, 99.

20 Tov, *Scribal Practices*, 100 gives a number of 2.3 cm or more.

21 Tov, *Scribal Practices*, 103.

22 See below.

possible. This is consistent with the handwriting of 4Q169, and confirms the idea that the manuscript served as a display copy of some sort.

2.3 Column Width and Height

Tov's study of the scribal features of the Dead Sea Scrolls implies (rather than states) averages of 11–13 cm for column width and 10–12.5 for column height.[23] What is more, Tov posits a correlation between column height and column width: the larger a column, the wider it tends to be.[24] Column dimensions in 4Q169 fall outside of Tov's average and contradict the correlation he found. Columns i and ii in this manuscript measure c. 16 cm and are clearly wide. Yet with an average height of 9.0–9.1 cm, columns in 4Q169 are also small. It has been suggested that this unusual distribution of the contents of the manuscript reflect an aesthetic ideal: if 4Q169 contained the entire book of Nahum and ratios between lemmata and interpretations remained constant throughout the roll, the manuscript would have contained 13 columns and thus resemble 1QpHab.[25] Apart from these two Pesher manuscripts, however, no other Qumran scroll seems to reflect this ideal, and the corresponding number of columns seems accidental.[26]

A more promising explanation for the small columns in 4Q169 comes from Józef Milik, who argued that the limited height of its columns defines 4Q169 as a pocket edition.[27] Such pocket editions are not uncommon in the scrolls: Milik gives some Aramaic examples as well as cases from "autres genres littéraires: commentaires, recueils de prières, règles."[28] Tov has pointed out that excerpted and abbreviated scriptural texts also occur in "scrolls of small dimensions."[29] The easy-to-carry format of these manuscripts would have facilitated their use

---

23   See Tov, *Scribal Practices*, 82–99. Tov's average column width is confirmed by Hartmut Stegemann, "Methods for the Reconstruction of Scrolls from Scattered Fragments," in *Archaeology and History in the Dead Sea Scrolls: The New York University Conference in Memory of Yigael Yadin*, ed. Lawrence H. Schiffman, JSPSup 8 (Sheffield: JSOT Press, 1990), 198, who writes that column widths in the Qumran scrolls "range from about 6 cm to about 20 cm."

24   Tov, *Scribal Practices*, 82.

25   Gregory L. Doudna, *4Q Pesher Nahum: A Critical Edition*, JSPSup 35, CIS 8 (Sheffield: Sheffield Academic Press, 2001), 37–38.

26   So also Brooke, "Aspects," 134–36.

27   It should not be ruled out that chance played a role as well. For instance, the size of the animal from whose skin this manuscript was produced would have affected the size of the manuscript.

28   Józef T. Milik, "Les modèles araméens du livre d'Esther dans la grotte 4 de Qumran," *RevQ* 15 (1992): 364.

29   Emanuel Tov, "Excerpted and Abbreviated Biblical Texts from Qumran," *RevQ* 16 (1995): 586.

in different locations,[30] e.g., "at the sick bed"[31] or during festivals.[32] In line with these suggestions it seems reasonable to assume that 4Q169 also travelled with its owner(s).

2.4 *Writing the Divine Name*

Hebrew manuscripts from the Hellenistic and Roman periods present the divine name either in square characters or in Paleo-Hebrew letters. The pesharim avoid the tetragrammaton in their interpretations—and sometimes also in their lemmata (4Q167). Previous scholarship has proposed several reasons for these different ways of handling the divine name. The most recent of these is George Brooke's suggestion that the differences reflect the different purposes of the manuscripts in which the divine name occurs:

> Perhaps manuscripts of pesharim with the divine name in square Hebrew were copies for expert use, such as being scribal base text exemplars or archive copies; those with the divine name in paleo-Hebrew might have been produced to be used by the less adroit, perhaps in public performance as the prophetic texts were studied afresh by novices and long-standing members in the community.[33]

Brooke's suggestion finds some support in 1QpHab—which appears to reflect the work of a teacher and a student and has the tetragrammaton in Paleo-Hebrew characters—as well as 4Q163, which presumably constituted a scholar's personal notes and presents the divine name in square letters.[34]

If Brooke's suggestion is endorsed, the presentation of the tetragrammaton in square characters in 4Q169 would imply that the manuscript was not meant

---

30   Cf. Philip S. Alexander, "Literacy among Jews in Second Temple Palestine: Reflections on the Evidence from Qumran," in *Hamlet on a Hill: Semitic and Greek Studies Presented to Professor T. Muraoka on the Occasion of his Sixty-Fifth Birthday*, ed. Martin F. J. Baasten and Wido Th. van Peursen, OLA 118 (Leuven: Peeters, 2003), 12, who argued that pocket editions of S were meant to be carried around by their owners. See also below on Alexander's suggestions.

31   As Florentino García Martínez, "Magic in the Dead Sea Scrolls," in *Qumranica minora II: Thematic Studies on the Dead Sea Scrolls*, ed. Eibert J. C. Tigchelaar, STDJ 64 (Leiden: Brill, 2007), 123 has suggested with regard to 11Q11.

32   As George J. Brooke, "Scripture and Scriptural Tradition in Transmission: Light from the Dead Sea Scrolls," in *The Scrolls and Biblical Traditions: Proceedings of the Seventh Meeting of the IOQS in Helsinki*, ed. George J. Brook et al., STDJ 103 (Leiden: Brill, 2012), 6 has argued for pocket editions of the *meghillot*.

33   Brooke, "Aspects," 149.

34   See more elaborately Hartog, *Pesher and Hypomnema*, 86–88.

to be read by everybody, but was intended to be used by experts who knew how to handle the divine name.

2.5 *Writing Material*

4Q169 is made of skin. This is not surprising in view of the Qumran collection as a whole: only 14% of the collection consists of papyri,[35] the rest of the scrolls—with the exception, of course, of the famous Copper Scroll[36]—are made of skin. Both this preference for skin and the predominantly literary character of the Qumran collection distinguish this scrolls collection from others in Hellenistic-Roman Palestine.[37] It appears that skin was the preferred material for writing literary works in Hellenistic-Roman Palestine. One reason for this was the availability of the material: the skins of sheep and goats were readily available for writing in Hellenistic and Roman Palestine, whereas papyrus had to be exported from Egypt.[38] Yet especially in the case of manuscripts meant to be in active use—such as subliterary manuscripts (to borrow a term from papyrology)[39] such as commentaries, paraphrases, or pocket editions like 4Q169—the durability of skin vis-à-vis papyrus may also have played a role. Although the Egyptian papyri show that subliterary works could be written on papyrus and that pocket editions on papyrus were a possibility, the durability of skin may have informed the preference for this material to write literary works in Hellenistic-Roman Palestine. If so, the fact that Pesher Nahum

---

35   Number taken from Tov, *Scribal Practices*, 45 (table 2).

36   On which see Joan Taylor's contribution to this volume.

37   Only Sdeir has yielded more leather than papyrus manuscripts (75 vs. 25%), but the sample there consists of only four manuscripts and should be approached with caution. In all other find sites, papyrus manuscripts constitute a clear majority ranging from 67% in Muraba'at to 100% in Jericho and several less significant localities. See the numbers in Tov, *Scribal Practices*, 45 (table 2).

38   On the Egyptian provenance of papyrus and its potential implications for the use of papyrus as a writing material in Hellenistic and Roman Palestine see Naphtali Lewis, *Papyrus in Classical Antiquity* (Oxford: Clarendon, 1974), 6–9; George J. Brooke, "Choosing between Papyrus and Skin: Cultural Complexity and Multiple Identities in the Qumran Library," in *Jewish Cultural Encounters in the Ancient Mediterranean and Near Eastern World*, ed. Mladen Popović, Myles Schoonover, and Marijn Vandenberghe, JSJSup 178 (Leiden: Brill, 2017), 119–35; Theo A.W. van der Louw and Pieter B. Hartog, "Physical and Economic Aspects of the Earliest Septuagint Papyri," *JJS* 72 (2021): 1–22.

39   The term "subliterary" is debated both for the qualitative assessment it may be taken to imply and for the strict distinction it seems to draw between subliterary and literary writing—a distinction which does not always work out in practice. Yet in the study of scholarly literature, or literature used in study contexts, the distinction may have some value, especially as a challenge to unreflective classifications of the Qumran scrolls collections as a "literary" collection.

274 HARTOG

is written on skin might correlate with the suggestion that 4Q169 served as a display copy for expert use.

2.6 *Interlinear Addition*[40]

A final physical feature of 4Q169 is the interlinear comment between 4Q169 1–2 3–5. This comment has often been taken as a scribal correction, most recently by Shani Tzoref, who has surmised that the comment was added "presumably to correct the omission of a citation and interpretation of the second half of Nah 1:4."[41] This view contradicts Tzoref's earlier reconstruction of these lines, which has a quotation of Nah 1:4aβ at the end of line 4 in the Pesher:

4 .... ולכלותם מעל פני [האדמה **וכול הנהרות החריב** פשרו על הכתיים

5a עם [מו[שליהם ...

5 אמלל ...

For reasons I elaborated elsewhere,[42] Tzoref's reconstruction of a *pēšer* formula after the lemma in line 4 is implausible. Instead, John Strugnell's reconstruction, which posits an interlinear addition between lines 3 and 4, is to be preferred:

4a פשרו על הכתיים]

4 ... ולכלותם מעל פני [הארץ .... וכל נהרות החריב]

5a עם [כל מו[שליהם אשר תתם ממשלתם]

5 אמלל וג״

If we follow Strugnell, this means that the entire interpretation dealing with Nah 1:4aβ is added between the lines in this column. As there is no reason why this interpretation should have been left out by accident, whereas there are abundant clues that 4Q169 and the other pesharim are no literary unities, it is plausible to assume that the interlinear comment in lines 4a and 5a constitutes an addition to an existing Pesher. This addition altered the literary structure of Pesher Nahum, since it isolated Nah 1:4aβ from its co-text and turned it into a lemma of its own, accompanying it with its own interpretation section.

---

40   Cf. my more elaborate treatment of this passage in "Interlinear Additions and Literary Development in 4Q163/*Pesher Isaiah C*, 4Q169/*Pesher Nahum*, and 4Q171/*Pesher Psalms A*," *RevQ* 28 (2016): 272–74.

41   Shani Tzoref, "Pesher Nahum," in *Outside the Bible: Ancient Jewish Writings Related to Scripture*, ed. Louis H. Feldman, James L. Kugel, and Lawrence H. Schiffman, 3 vols. (Philadelphia, PA: The Jewish Publication Society, 2012), 1:627.

42   Hartog, "Interlinear Additions," 272–73.

4Q169 (PESHER NAHUM) IN ITS ANCIENT MEDIA CONTEXT 275

This demonstrates that Pesher Nahum is a living text, subject to expansion and—perhaps—omission as it was transmitted.

3 From Oral Study to Written Text

The interlinear addition in 4Q169 1–2 3–5 demonstrates that Pesher Nahum has been subject to literary development. Some literary features of the Pesher offer clues to the same effect; Tzoref has argued, for instance, that 4Q169 3–4 i 6–8 are an addition to an earlier version of the Pesher.[43] This ongoing development of the Pesher raises the questions of how it came about and how it functioned within a variety of oral and written contexts.

The most likely *Sitz im Leben* for the oral traditions that were eventually incorporated into the pesharim is the study sessions of the Qumran movement. It is difficult to know for certain which forms these sessions took, but it is clear from the Qumran collection that the movement that collected these scrolls constituted, in Steven Fraade's words, a "studying community."[44] The studious character of the movement is evident, e.g., from the predominance of literary and subliterary manuscripts in the Qumran scrolls collection, as well as from the presence of manuscripts such as 1QpHab, which George Brooke has convincingly argued may be the work of a teacher and his student;[45] 4Q163, which probably contains the notes of one or more scholars;[46] and 4Q175, which contains homiletical or exegetical notes.

William Brownlee has suggested a two-stage development of the pesharim. The first stage consisted of oral teachings by the Teacher of Righteousness, whose "common method of teaching was that of the *pēšer*." These teachings would consist of scriptural quotations, followed by interpretations introduced "with some such expression as *pēšer had-dāvār ʾăšer*, or *pišrô ʿal*." At the second stage, "[t]hese oral interpretations were received and molded by the

---

43 Berrin (Tzoref), *Pesher Nahum Scroll*, 214.

44 Steven Fraade, "Interpretive Authority in the Studying Community at Qumran," in *Legal Fictions: Studies of Law and Narrative in the Discursive Worlds of Ancient Jewish Sectarians and Sages*, JSJSup 147 (Leiden: Brill, 2011), 37–67. On the study of Scripture at Qumran see also, e.g., Annette Steudel, "Die Rezeption authoritativer Texte in Qumran," in *Qumran und der biblische Kanon*, ed. Jörg Frey and Michael Becker, BTS 92 (Neukirchen-Vluyn: Neukirchener, 2009), 89–100; Brooke, "Reading, Searching and Blessing."

45 George J. Brooke, "Physicality, Paratextuality, and Pesher Habakkuk," in *On the Fringe of Commentary: Metatextuality in Ancient Near Eastern and Ancient Mediterranean Cultures*, ed. Sidney H. Aufrère, Philip S. Alexander, and Zlatko Pleše, OLA 232 (Leuven: Peeters, 2014), 180–81.

46 As I suggested in Hartog, *Pesher and Hypomnema*, 82–100 (esp. 100).

Essene Community" and "underwent reinterpretation within the study groups of Qumran, especially after the Teacher's death."[47] Note that Brownlee does not explicitly contrast an originally oral stage with a later written one. Rather, acknowledging that "[v]ariations in style, interpretation, and interest in the *pəšārîm* may reflect ... different generations of interpreters," Brownlee seems to allow for an ongoing oral (alongside a written) engagement with these commentaries. For Brownlee, the pesharim originated in oral study sessions of the Qumran movement, but continued to be further developed after having been written down.

Brownlee's model of the development of the pesharim is, in my viewpoint, essentially correct. I would however make two caveats. First, the study sessions from which the pesharim originated need not have yielded systematic expositions of the Hebrew Scriptures. In view of comparative evidence,[48] it seems likely that the pesharim go back to disparate interpretations which connected elements from the historical memories of those present in these study sessions with passages from the Scriptures. Only when written down did the pesharim come to assume a more systematic and narrative form. Second, the position of the Teacher of Righteousness within these study sessions is unclear. References to the Teacher in the Qumran scrolls are notoriously few, and most of them occur in late strata of the Qumran corpus, such as the latest parts of the D tradition or 1QpHab, one of the latest pesharim (at least in its current form).[49] This suggests that the persona of the Teacher was a latecomer at Qumran, which was developed to associate certain literary works or exegetical

---

47   All quotations are from William H. Brownlee, "The Background of Biblical Interpretation at Qumran," in *Qumrân: Sa piété, sa théologie et son milieu*, ed. Mathias Delcor, BETL 46 (Gembloux: Duculot, 1978), 188.

48   See below.

49   On the Teacher in the scrolls and as a persona to be remembered see Loren T. Stuckenbruck, "The Teacher of Righteousness Remembered: From Fragmentary Sources to Collective Memory in the Dead Sea Scrolls," in *Memory in the Bible and Antiquity: The Fifth Durham-Tübingen Research Symposium (Durham, September 2004)*, ed. Stephen C. Barton, Loren T. Stuckenbruck, and Benjamin G. Wold, WUNT 212 (Tübingen: Mohr, 2007), 75–94; idem, "The Legacy of the Teacher of Righteousness in the Dead Sea Scrolls," in *New Perspectives on Old Texts: Proceedings of the Tenth International Symposium of the Orion Center for the Study of the Dead Sea Scrolls and Associated Literature, 9–11 January, 2005*, ed. Esther G. Chazon, Betsy Halpern-Amaru, and Ruth A. Clements, STDJ 88 (Leiden: Brill, 2010), 23–49; George J. Brooke, "The 'Apocalyptic' Community, the Matrix of the Teacher and Rewriting Scripture," in *Authoritative Scriptures in Ancient Judaism*, ed. Mladen Popović, JSJSup 141 (Leiden: Brill, 2010), 37–53; Reinhard G. Kratz, "The Teacher of Righteousness and His Enemies," in *Is There a Text in This Cave? Studies in the Textuality of the Dead Sea Scrolls in Honour of George J. Brooke*, ed. Ariel Feldman, Maria Cioată, and Charlotte Hempel, STDJ 119 (Leiden: Brill, 2017), 515–32; Travis B. Williams, *History and Memory in*

practices with this mythical founding figure.[50] On this view the Teacher might belong at the end rather than the beginning of the development of the pesharim.

Comparative evidence supports the association of commentary writing—or more generally the production of subliterary writings—with study contexts. In contrast to most subliterary writings from the Qumran collection, Greek writings like paraphrases, commentaries, and word lists are attested in multiple versions. A comparison of these different versions shows that these subliterary writings tend to be particularly fluid and malleable.[51] This is due to their active use within study contexts: they transformed as they were read, studied, and interpreted. Manuscripts of literary works sometimes contain students' notes. At a later stage, such notes could be developed into full-blown commentaries.[52] Scholars, too, could take notes, and many subliterary papyri seem to contain notes scholars took for their scholarly work, but presumably also their teaching.[53] Commentaries in the papyri are thus closely affiliated with oral contexts of study and scholarship, and it is reasonable to assume a similar affiliation in the case of the pesharim.

At some point, however, the pesharim were written down. The fact that the Qumran commentaries as we now know them are carefully crafted writings,

---

the Dead Sea Scrolls: Remembering the Teacher of Righteousness (Cambridge: Cambridge University Press, 2019).

50 Cf. how Florentino García Martínez speaks of "the voice of the Teacher" (CD 20:28, 32 // 4Q267 3 7; 4Q270 2 i 2) as an authority-conferring strategy: "Beyond the Sectarian Divide: The 'Voice of the Teacher' as an Authority-Conferring Strategy in some Qumran Texts," in The Dead Sea Scrolls: Transmission of Traditions and Production of Texts, ed. Sarianna Metso, Hindy Najman, and Eileen M. Schuller, STDJ 92 (Leiden: Brill, 2010), 227–44. On the Teacher as a figure of authority and memory see also Angela Kim Harkins' work on the Teacher in the so-called Teacher Hymns; e.g., "Who is the Teacher of the Teacher Hymns? Re-Examining the Teacher Hymns Hypothesis Fifty Years Later," in A Teacher for All Generations: Essays in Honor of James C. VanderKam, ed. Eric F. Mason et al., JSJSup 153 (Leiden: Brill, 2012), 449–67.

51 Cf. how Ineke Sluiter contrasts "the stable written nature of the source-text" with "the improvised, oral aspects, and fluid nature, of the commentary" ("The Dialectics of Genre: Some Aspects of Secondary Literature and Genre in Antiquity," in Matrices of Genre: Authors, Canons, and Society, ed. Mary Depew and Dirk Obbink, CHSC 4 [Cambridge: Harvard University Press, 2000], 187).

52 Kathleen McNamee, Annotations in Greek and Latin Texts from Egypt, ASP 45 (Oakville, CT: American Society of Papyrologists, 2007), 49–62.

53 One important sign for such scholarly activity is the use of critical sigla. On these sigla see Kathleen McNamee, Sigla and Select Marginalia in Greek Literary Papyri, PB 26 (Brussels: Fondation Égyptologique Reine Élisabeth, 1992), Hartog, Pesher and Hypomnema, 71–77 (with references).

with their own plot and unity,[54] shows that the act of writing the pesharim down also involved a process of narrativization. On such processes Anthony Le Donne and Tom Thatcher write:

> One of the more significant cross-cultural strategies of redefinition involves narrativization, the process of organizing and structuring recollections in the form of stories with linear sequences. Beginnings, settings, climaxes and conclusions are (often subconsciously) imposed upon memories in order to arrange pertinent details.[55]

Only once written down do the pesharim turn into repositories of the historical memories—that is, history as remembered through and mediated by scriptural interpretation—of the Qumran movement. By imposing on the disparate memories developed in oral study sessions a narrative structure, a beginning, and—more important—a soon-to-come end, the pesharim come to present their readers with an overview of the history of the Qumran movement as remembered by that movement and understood in the light of their Scriptures. The pesharim as historical works—i.e., works that show an interest in presenting the past in a narrative fashion and by so doing aim to inform the present[56]—are, thus, scribal products whose efficacy depends on their writtenness.

These processes of writing and narrativization had two intimately related effects. To begin with, all narrativization, as Hayden White has shown, implies moralisation: as we imbue memories or disparate events with a plot, a beginning, and an ending, we make the story a carrier of particular moral convictions. In White's words:

> When it is a matter of recounting the concourse of real events, what other "ending" could a given sequence of such events have than a "moralizing" ending? What else could narrative closure consist of than the passage

---

54   On the narrative aspects of the pesharim see especially Bilhah Nitzan, *Pesher Habakkuk: A Scroll from the Wilderness of Judaea (1QpHab)* (Jerusalem: Bialik Institute, 1986) (Hebrew); Jutta Jokiranta, *Social Identity and Sectarianism in the Qumran Movement*, STDJ 105 (Leiden: Brill, 2013), 111–213.

55   Anthony Le Donne and Tom Thatcher, "Introducing Media Studies to Johannine Studies: Orality, Performance and Memory," in *The Fourth Gospel in First-Century Media Culture*, ed. Anthony Le Donne and Tom Thatcher, LNTS 426 (London: T&T Clark, 2011), 7.

56   Cf. the definition of George J. Brooke, "Types of Historiography in the Qumran Scrolls," in *Reading the Dead Sea Scrolls: Essays in Method*, EJL 39 (Atlanta, GA: SBL 2013), 183, which is endorsed by Shem Miller, "Traditional History and Cultural Memory in the Pesharim," *JSJ* 50 (2019): 352.

from one moral order to another? I confess that I cannot think of any other way of "concluding" an account of real events; for we cannot say, surely, that any sequence of real events actually comes to an end, that reality itself disappears, that events of the order of the real have ceased to happen. Such events could only have seemed to have ceased to happen when meaning is shifted, and shifted by narrative means, from one physical or social space to another .... Where, in any account of reality, narrativity is present, we can be sure that morality or a moralizing impulse is present too.[57]

White's comments are relevant if we seek to understand how the pesharim promote particular ingroup-outgroup distinctions on the basis of their historical memories.[58] Through their narrative depiction of history as remembered within the Qumran movement and their expectation that the final judgement is imminent, the pesharim bolster the identity of the group to which their authors belonged as being on the good side of history, whilst their enemies are portrayed as finding their end at the final judgement. The written representation of historical memory in the pesharim thus imparts on the readers of these commentaries the idea that they are part of a larger divine plan with history and will be vindicated in the end.

In addition to bolstering ingroup and outgroup identities, the writtenness of the pesharim bolsters the status of these commentaries as faithfully representing traditions from the early years of the Qumran movement. Consider in this context the connection between writing and transmission in, e.g., the book of Jubilees, a writing highly regarded by the movement in which the pesharim originated. Hindy Najman has shown that Jubilees exhibits a "fascination with writing."[59] This is evident, e.g., in Jubilees' repeated attribution of particular

---

57   Hayden White, "The Value of Narrativity in the Representation of Reality," *Critical Enquiry* 7 (1980): 26. See also idem, "The Narrativization of Real Events," *Critical Enquiry* 7 (1981): 793–98.

58   On ingroup-outgroup distinctions in the pesharim see Jokiranta, *Social Identity and Sectarianism*, 111–213; also Lloyd K. Pietersen, "'False Teaching, Lying Tongues and Deceitful Lips' (4Q169 frgs 3–4 2.8): The Pesharim and the Sociology of Deviance," in *New Directions in Qumran Studies: Proceedings of the Bristol Colloquium on the Dead Sea Scrolls, 8–10 September 2003*, ed. Jonathan G. Campbell, William J. Lyons, and Lloyd K. Pietersen, LSTS 52 (London: T&T Clark, 2005), 166–81.

59   Hindy Najman, "Interpretation as Primordial Writing: *Jubilees* and Its Authority Conferring Strategies," in *Past Renewals: Interpretative Authority, Renewed Revelation and the Quest for Perfection in Jewish Antiquity* (Leiden: Brill, 2010), 39–71 (esp. 41–49).

laws to the Heavenly Tablets on which they were written,[60] but also in its extensive description of Enoch as the first writer, who instigated a tradition of revealed knowledge, which was transmitted in writing from father to son until it reached Moses, the implied author of Jubilees.[61] Writing, on this view, symbolizes and safeguards the continuity of a tradition. At the same time, it allowed later tradents to write themselves into the tradition and present their own views and activities as being continuous with those of the first recipient of divine revelation. Thus Jubilees portrays Moses, its implied author, as continuing the tradition that Enoch started; the authors of Jubilees, in their turn, depict their own endeavours as Mosaic discourse.[62]

In like vein, the Pesher commentators, in 1QpHab 2:5–10, portray their own exegetical work as that of "the priest, in [whose heart] God has given [insig]ht to interpret all the words of his servants, the prophets" (1QpHab 2:8–9).[63] As Florentino García Martínez notes, the priest in this passage should not be equated with the Teacher; rather "[t]his Priest of the last days will ... have the same function the historical Teacher had, that is, to 'foretell the fulfilment of all the words of the Prophets'."[64] As I have argued elsewhere, the Priest in this passage is not just a person from the future: as the Pesher exegetes thought of themselves as living in the "latter days," the eschatological Priest, the successor of the now-deceased historical Teacher, had already manifested himself within the Qumran movement, namely, in the activities of those that heeded and transmitted the voice of the Teacher—i.e., the Pesher commentators.[65] Just as the authors of Jubilees write themselves into a Mosaic discourse, so the Pesher exegetes write themselves into the tradition that had allegedly begun with by the Teacher.

---

60   This attribution may not have originated with the author/compiler of Jubilees. Cf. Michael Segal's suggestion that Heavenly Tablets terminology in Jubilees is "an indication that the passages in which it is found belong to the redactional stratum; this terminology is a sign of the halakhic editor's contribution to this work" (*The Book of Jubilees: Rewritten Bible, Redaction, Ideology and Theology*, JSJSup 117 [Leiden: Brill, 2007], 31).

61   In addition to Najman, see Pieter B. Hartog, "Jubilees and Hellenistic Encyclopaedism," *JSJ* 50 (2019): 1–25 (13–16 on "Book Culture in Jubilees").

62   On Mosaic discourse see Hindy Najman, *Seconding Sinai: The Development of Mosaic Discourse in Second Temple Judaism*, JSJSup 77 (Leiden: Brill, 2003), esp. 41–69 on Jubilees and the Temple Scroll.

63   Reconstruction follows Elisha Qimron, *The Dead Sea Scrolls: The Hebrew Writings*, 3 vols. (Jerusalem: Yad Ben-Zvi, 2010–2014). Translations from the pesharim are my own.

64   García Martínez, "Beyond the Sectarian Divide," 241.

65   Pieter B. Hartog, "'The Final Priests of Jerusalem' and 'The Mouth of the Priest': Eschatological Development and Literary History in Pesher Habakkuk," *DSD* 24 (2017): 69–70.

This reference to Pesher Habakkuk, where the Teacher plays a prominent role, raises the issue of the absence of the Teacher from Pesher Nahum. As we have seen, the Teacher may belong to late strata in the Qumran literature, and his absence from Pesher Nahum might be related to the earlier date of this Pesher compared to, e.g., Pesher Habakkuk.[66] This argument is not without its problems, though: Pesher Habakkuk itself has undergone a literary development, and references to the Teacher appear to have been present already at earlier stages of this development than the one represented in the manuscript 1QpHab.[67] It seems worthwhile, therefore, to ponder other reasons for the absence of the Teacher from Pesher Nahum. Two such reasons may have been the interpretative possibilities offered by the base text or the historical memory/ies the exegete(s) responsible for this Pesher sought to communicate—or both. Compared to Habakkuk, with e.g. its neat רשע-צדיק distinction, Nahum appears to have offered its exegete fewer pegs to connect his base text with biographical memories regarding the Teacher. Moreover, Pesher Nahum appears to address a different period in the historical memory of its readers from the one treated in, e.g., Pesher Habakkuk or 4QPesher Psalms A: whereas the latter commentaries concentrate on the foundation of the movement, in which the Teacher is alleged to have played a major role, Pesher Nahum focuses on later confrontations between the movement and other Jewish and non-Jewish groups.[68] If not from the relatively early date of this Pesher, the absence of the Teacher from Pesher Nahum may therefore result from its contents. It need not imply that Pesher Nahum was not associated with the Teacher by its readers: perhaps the pesher genre itself, especially in its written, narrativized form, was connected to the persona of the Teacher from the outset.

Once written down, oral performances of the pesharim appear not to have ended, but rather to have continued alongside their written transmission. Signs for the written transmission of the pesharim are, e.g., the accidental repetition and subsequent deletion of the second ואשר in 4Q162 1:4; the omission and then addition of the second על in 1QpHab 7:1;[69] or the accidental omission

---

66   On the dating of the pesharim see Annette Steudel, "Dating Exegetical Texts from Qumran," in *The Dynamics of Language and Exegesis at Qumran*, ed. Devorah Dimant and Reinhard G. Kratz, FAT 2/35 (Tübingen: Mohr Siebeck, 2009), 39–53.

67   On the literary development of Pesher Habakkuk see Hartog, "'The Final Priests'," (with a discussion of previous proposals at 60–64).

68   Hartog, "Pesher as Commentary."

69   On this passage see Eibert J. C. Tigchelaar, "Dittography and Copying Lines in the Dead Sea Scrolls: Considering George Brooke's Proposal about 1QpHab 7:1–2," in *Is There a Text in This Cave? Studies in the Textuality of the Dead Sea Scrolls in Honour of George J. Brooke*, ed. Ariel Feldman, et al., STDJ 119 (Leiden: Brill, 2017), 293–307; Jutta Jokiranta, "Quoting, Writing, and Reading: Authority in *Pesher Habakkuk* from Qumran," in *Between Canonical*

of the ו- after פשר in 4Q169 3–4 iv 2. These scribal errors demonstrate that the copyists of these manuscripts copied their contents from written *Vorlagen*. At the same time, the pesharim were presumably performed orally. Ancient reading rarely implied silent reading, but often consisted of a lector or teacher reading out a text in front of an audience. It is difficult to reconstruct the exact settings in which such readings took place. I am not convinced that liturgical settings akin to the ones proposed by Gregory Snyder[70] are a better candidate than study sessions of the kind suggested by Brownlee,[71] although the two alternatives may not exclude each other. Yet regardless of how we envision these readings of the pesharim, many members of the Qumran movement familiar with the contents of these commentaries would have acquired their knowledge through hearing rather than (or, in addition to) reading.

The oral and written transmission of the pesharim intricately coincide in the additions to earlier pesharim which are found—either in the body of the manuscript or as interlinear annotations—in 1QpHab, 4Q163, 4Q169, and 4Q171. On the one hand, these additions probably reflect oral contexts in which the pesharim were read and, presumably, studied. These oral performances of the Qumran commentaries inspired new, disparate interpretations, which could be added at an appropriate point to the existing Pesher. On the other hand, these additions are at the same time already textualized, in that they take up language from other written versions of the pesharim. The addition in 4Q169 1–2 3–5, for instance, reads: ["Its interpretation concerns the Kittim] with [all] their [ru]lers, whose rule shall end." This reference to the rulers of the Kittim harks back to references to these rulers in the same column and elsewhere in 4Q169 (1–2 7; 3–4 i 3), and perhaps also to 4Q161 8–10 8.[72] The phrase "rule of the Kittim" finds a parallel in 1QM 1:6 (//4Q496 3 i 6), and both formulations occur in 1QpHab (2:13–14; 4:5, 10–12). The case of 1QpHab 2:5–10 is even clearer. This passage takes up language from other passages in the scrolls, most notably 4QpPs[a] and 1QpHab 6:12–7:18.[73] Even if originating from oral contexts, these additions occur in their manuscripts in narrativized form, taking up language from other, *written* pesharim.

---

    and Apocryphal Texts, ed. Jörg Frey et al., WUNT 419 (Tübingen: Mohr Siebeck, 2019), 185–212.

70   H. Gregory Snyder, "Naughts and Crosses: Pesher Manuscripts and Their Significance for Reading Practices at Qumran," *DSD* 7 (2000): 26–48.

71   On my problems with Snyder's proposals, see Hartog, *Pesher and Hypomnema*, 92–97.

72   These line numbers follow *DSSSE*.

73   Hartog, "'The Final Priests of Jerusalem,'" 68–70.

4   4Q169: A Travelling Manuscript

The pesharim originated from oral study sessions and were transmitted in combined oral and written contexts, most of them presumably also with a study purpose. In the case of 4Q169, its physical features suggest that the manuscript was read at different locations and constituted a travelling manuscript.

In his study of pocket editions among the Dead Sea Scrolls—including 4Q169—Milik argued that their main purpose was "la diffusion rapide et large des textes d'information, de propaganda, de consolation, de piété."[74] Such pocket editions need not all have served the same purpose. The neat handwriting and large margins of 4Q169 suggest that this manuscript was not just a personal copy of Pesher Nahum, but was intended for expert consultation. How should we envision the context in which such consultation took place?

It may be helpful to refer at this point to Alison Schofield's work on rule traditions within the Yaḥad. Rather than attributing these various rule traditions to diachronic development, Schofield proposed a "radial-dialogic model," in which these traditions originated in different localities that were each in dialogue with its centre, Qumran. As she writes:

> [S]tarting with the Teacher, eventually the *yaḥad*'s own center was formalized within a larger, coalescing movement. This new center then began codifying and transmitting its own traditions, which then were exchanged within the movement itself.[75]

Schofield was neither the first nor the last to propose that the home of the Yaḥad extended beyond Qumran; the idea that the movement whose texts were recovered from the Qumran caves lived in various places across Hellenistic-Roman Palestine is now widely accepted in Qumran scholarship.[76] The question remains whether Qumran should really be seen as the centre of the movement, and, if so, what kind of centre it constituted. Or perhaps the movement had multiple centres? In any event, it seems reasonable to assume that the Qumran movement was less centralised than had often been assumed, and

---

74   Milik, "Les modèles araméens," 364–65.

75   Alison Schofield, "Between Center and Periphery: The *Yaḥad* in Context," DSD 16 (2009): 341. See also eadem, *From Qumran to the Yaḥad: A New Paradigm of Textual Development for The Community Rule*, STDJ 77 (Leiden: Brill, 2009).

76   See, e.g., John J. Collins, *Beyond the Qumran Community: The Sectarian Movement of the Dead Sea Scrolls* (Grand Rapids, MI: Eerdmans, 2010); Charlotte Hempel, *The Qumran Rule Texts in Context: Collected Studies*, TSAJ 154 (Tübingen: Mohr Siebeck, 2013), 97–105.

that different traditions—or different forms of tradition—could be current simultaneously, in various localities inhabited by members of the movement.[77]

This model raises several intriguing questions. First, it may provide a new perspective on the emergence and development of similar, but not quite the same, traditions. In the case of the pesharim, for instance, one may wonder how the two pesharim on Hosea, the three pesharim on Psalms, or the five (or six, depending on how we classify 3Q4) pesharim on Isaiah may tie in with this model. Second, and more important for my purposes the model of a movement spread out across different localities in Hellenistic-Roman Palestine begs the question how exactly the dialogue—to use Schofield's term—between centre and periphery, or between different centres, crystallised.

In trying to answer this question, much must remain speculative. It seems not too far-fetched, however, to assume that one factor that facilitated this kind of dialogue was the travel of persons between the different places where members of the movement lived. Quite possibly we should think of the Qumran movement as a network, or a series of networks, through which knowledge was disseminated. What is more, the presence of pocket editions in the Qumran corpus shows that not only people, but also manuscripts, were on the move. Focusing on 4Q264—the smallest 4QS scroll in the Qumran corpus—Philip Alexander surmised that "at least some individuals possessed personal copies of some texts, since it is highly unlikely that miniature copies such as these would have been produced for general library use."[78] This comment may hold for other 4QS manuscripts, which can be classified as pocket editions as well (e.g., 4Q256, 4Q258, 4Q260, all included in Tov's list of "leather scrolls with a small writing block"[79]). The handwriting of these manuscripts may be informative of the persons who owned them: all 4QS manuscripts that may qualify

---

77 Schofield's theory has recently been criticised by Charlotte Hempel, who compares this radial-dialogic model with Cross's theory of "local texts" and emphasises the need to make sense of the occurrence of textual fluidity within one place: Qumran. Whilst Hempel is certainly correct in pointing out the risk of equating textual fluidity with geographical diversity, I would still say that the question how these two issues are related should be part of how we think of the Qumran movement as a network. Perhaps the focus should be on the question how textual fluidity functioned within a single, yet not wholly unified, movement. Geographical factors probably played a role, but, as Hempel stresses, should not too easily be taken as the main explanatory factor of what is doubtless a complex and multi-faceted issue. See Charlotte Hempel, "Reflections on Literacy, Textuality, and Community in the Qumran Dead Sea Scrolls," in *Is There a Text in This Cave? Studies in the Textuality of the Dead Sea Scrolls in Honour of George J. Brooke*, ed. Ariel Feldman et al., STDJ 119 (Leiden: Brill, 2017), 70–82 (esp. 70–73).

78 Alexander, "Literacy," 12.

79 Tov, *Scribal Practices*, 84–86. Tov includes 4Q264 as well.

as pocket editions exhibit trained hands; unless we assume that they were the work of professional scribes who barely had an inkling of what they were writing (which, of course, remains a possibility),[80] it seems safe to think of these manuscripts as personal copies belonging to experts within the movement who travelled from place to place, carrying their copy of the Serekh with them.[81]

4Q169 may fit this network context and belong to (a) travelling expert(s) within the Qumran movement. The manuscript does not seem to constitute a merely personal copy, however: its larger-than-usual margins and neat handwriting suggest that 4Q169 served as a master copy of some sort. The fact that, as far as we can tell, only one copy of Pesher Nahum existed at a time may support this view. Presumably, 4Q169 travelled around in the hands of (an) expert(s) within the Qumran movement and served as a vehicle to instil a set of historical memories on its members. In every location where the owner(s) of 4Q169 went, they would have presented the contents of the manuscript to those living in that place—most probably in oral fashion, though the possibility that 4Q169 served as a master copy for scribes producing their own copies of Pesher Nahum should not be discounted.[82] If study sessions took place in which 4Q169 was read and studied, these sessions would have aimed at unifying members of the Qumran movement living in various places around a shared set of experiences and memories.

If we compare 4Q169 with manuscripts of the other continuous pesharim, this scroll stands out as the most carefully produced Pesher. Even if no Pesher manuscript can be classified a truly deluxe copy,[83] 4Q169 does exhibit some tendencies in that direction. Might it be comparable to deluxe copies of other traditions, such as 1QS or 1QM? And if so, would it be too big a leap to think of these deluxe copies as reacting against the fluidity of earlier traditions, i.e., as attempts to create a stronger sense of overarching unity within the

---

80 Cf. Eibert Tigchelaar's comment that "[i]t is unknown to what extent there was a differentiation between those who composed or edited texts, and those who actually wrote them down and copied them" ("The Scribes of the Scrolls," in *T&T Clark Companion to the Dead Sea Scrolls*, ed. George J. Brooke and Charlotte Hempel, with the assistance of Michael DeVries and Drew Longacre [London: T&T Clark, 2019], 527).

81 But cf. Alexander's comments: "It is possible that the Qumran scribes did not distinguish all that consciously between formal and cursive styles. The formal style was the default. The cursive arose naturally out of it once the speed of the pen increased .... [I]t may be a mistake to suppose that [a scribe] is consciously choosing between two quite distinct styles, or in any way privileging one over the other" ("Literacy," 16).

82 I thank William Johnson for raising this possibility during the conference in London.

83 See Hartog, *Pesher and Hypomnema*, 84–85 (with discussion and references).

movement?[84] True, we have no indications that Pesher Nahum ever existed in various forms at the same time; and this may be why 4Q169 is not a truly deluxe production. But if we entertain the possibility that the different pesharim on Hosea, Isaiah, and Psalms did originate in various localities and are thus indicative of variety within the Qumran movement, is it possible that 4Q169 challenges this variety, offering a more unified approach towards the memory of the movement as an alternative? Such questions must for now remain open, but offer fruitful thought for future scholarship.

5 Conclusion

4Q169, containing a Pesher on Nahum, offers intriguing insights into ancient media culture. Like the other Qumran commentaries, this Pesher presumably originated from oral study sessions, which yielded disparate interpretations of passages from the Jewish Scriptures, reading them in light of the historical memories of the participants in these study sessions. When they were written down, the pesharim underwent a process of narrativization, which turned them into vehicles for the construction of a group identity and repositories of earlier knowledge, possibly even "the voice of the Teacher." These processes did not preclude the continued oral performance of the pesharim in reading sessions. In the case of 4Q169, these reading sessions appear to have taken place at different locations where members of the Qumran movement lived. The performance of this Pesher thus appears to have aimed to unite the members of this movement, who were spread out across Hellenistic-Roman Palestine, around a shared set of experiences and memories.

Acknowledgements

I thank Chris Keith, Travis Williams, and Loren Stuckenbruck for inviting me to their inspiring conference on "The Dead Sea Scrolls and Ancient Media

---

84 Such an assumption would be problematic on strictly palaeographical grounds; none of the large Cave 1 manuscripts seem to represent a late stage in the traditions to which they belong. At the same time, the long textual history of the S and M traditions, as well as the pesharim, should make us cautious to stake too much on palaeography. The continuing fluidity of the S and M traditions after the publication of 1QS and 1QM could indicate that these productions failed to fulfil the purposes intended for them. The same would be true for 4Q169, dated to 50–25 BCE (as per Webster, DJD 39:403). 1QpHab is a later Pesher manuscript (dated 1–50 CE; Webster, DJD 39:426) and reflects a fluid textual tradition.

Culture," and the other participants in that London conference for creating a lively forum for scholarly exchange. Earlier versions of this paper were presented at the Research Seminar of the Department of Theology and Religious Studies in Chester and the Amsterdam New Testament Seminar. I am grateful to the participants in both seminars for their feedback and suggestions.

Bibliography

Alexander, Philip. "Literacy among Jews in Second Temple Palestine: Reflections on the Evidence from Qumran." Pages 3–24 in *Hamlet on a Hill: Semitic and Greek Studies Presented to Professor T. Muraoka on the Occasion of his Sixty-Fifth Birthday*. Edited by Martin F.J. Baasten and Wido Th. van Peursen. OLA 118. Leuven: Peeters, 2003.

Berrin (Tzoref), Shani. *The Pesher Nahum Scroll from Qumran: An Exegetical Study of 4Q169*. STDJ 53. Leiden: Brill, 2004.

Brooke, George J. "The 'Apocalyptic' Community, the Matrix of the Teacher and Rewriting Scripture." Pages 37–53 in *Authoritative Scriptures in Ancient Judaism*. Edited by Mladen Popović. JSJSup 141. Leiden: Brill, 2010.

Brooke, George J. "Aspects of the Physical and Scribal Features of Some Cave 4 'Continuous' Pesharim." Pages 133–50 in *The Dead Sea Scrolls: Transmission of Traditions and Production of Texts*. Edited by Sarianna Metso, Hindy Najman, and Eileen Schuller. STDJ 92. Leiden: Brill, 2010.

Brooke, George J. "Scripture and Scriptural Tradition in Transmission: Light from the Dead Sea Scrolls." Pages 1–17 in *The Scrolls and Biblical Traditions: Proceedings of the Seventh Meeting of the IOQS in Helsinki*. Edited by George J. Brooke, Daniel K. Falk, Eibert J. C. Tigchelaar, and Molly M. Zahn. STDJ 103. Leiden: Brill, 2012.

Brooke, George J. "Types of Historiography in the Qumran Scrolls." Pages 175–92 in *Reading the Dead Sea Scrolls: Essays in Method*. EJL 39. Atlanta, GA: SBL, 2013.

Brooke, George J. "Physicality, Paratextuality and Pesher Habakkuk." Pages 175–93 in *On the Fringe of Commentary: Metatextuality in Ancient Near Eastern and Ancient Mediterranean Cultures*. Edited by Sidney H. Aufrère, Philip S. Alexander and Zlatko Pleše in association with C. J. Bouloux. OLA 232. Leuven: Peeters, 2014.

Brooke, George J. "Reading, Searching and Blessing: A Functional Approach to Scriptural Interpretation in the יחד." Pages 140–56 in *The Temple in Text and Tradition: A Festschrift in Honour of Robert Hayward*. Edited by R. Timothy McLay. LSTS 83. London: Bloomsbury, 2015.

Brooke, George J. "Choosing Between Papyrus and Skin: Cultural Complexity and Multiple Identities in the Qumran Library." Pages 119–35 in *Jewish Cultural Encounters in the Ancient Mediterranean and Near Eastern World*. Edited by Mladen Popović, Myles Schoonover, and Marijn Vandenberghe. JSJSup 178. Leiden: Brill, 2017.

Brownlee, William H. "The Background of Biblical Interpretation at Qumran." Pages 183–93 in *Qumrân: Sa piété, sa théologie et son milieu.* Edited by Mathias Delcor. BETL 46. Gembloux: Duculot, 1978.

Collins, John J. *Beyond the Qumran Community: The Sectarian Movement of the Dead Sea Scrolls.* Grand Rapids, MI: Eerdmans, 2010.

Cribiore, Raffaella. *Writing, Teachers, and Students in Graeco-Roman Egypt.* ASP 36. Atlanta, GA: Scholars Press, 1996.

Davis, Kipp. "The Social Milieu of 4QJer^a (4Q70) in a Second Temple Jewish Manuscript Culture: Fragments, Manuscripts, Variance, and Meaning." Pages 53–76 in *The Dead Sea Scrolls and the Study of the Humanities: Method, Theory, Meaning: Proceedings of the Eighth Meeting of the International Organization for Qumran Studies (Munich, 4–7 August, 2013).* Edited by Pieter B. Hartog, Samuel I. Thomas, and Alison Schofield. STDJ 125. Leiden: Brill, 2018.

Doudna, Gregory L. *4Q Pesher Nahum: A Critical Edition.* JSPSup 35. CIS 8. Sheffield: Sheffield Academic Press, 2001.

Fraade, Steven D. "Interpretive Authority in the Studying Community at Qumran." Pages 37–67 in *Legal Fictions: Studies of Law and Narrative in the Discursive Worlds of Ancient Jewish Sectarians and Sages.* JSJSup 147. Leiden: Brill, 2011.

García Martínez, Florentino. "Magic in the Dead Sea Scrolls." Pages 109–30 in *Qumranica minora II: Thematic Studies on the Dead Sea Scrolls.* Edited by Eibert J.C. Tigchelaar. STDJ 64. Leiden: Brill, 2007.

García Martínez, Florentino. "Beyond the Sectarian Divide: The 'Voice of the Teacher' as an Authority-Conferring Strategy in some Qumran Texts." Pages 227–44 in *The Dead Sea Scrolls: Transmission of Traditions and Production of Texts.* Edited by Sarianna Metso, Hindy Najman, and Eileen M. Schuller. STDJ 92. Leiden: Brill, 2010.

Harkins, Angela Kim. "Who is the Teacher of the Teacher Hymns? Re-Examining the Teacher Hymns Hypothesis Fifty Years Later." Pages 449–67 in *A Teacher for All Generations: Essays in Honor of James C. VanderKam.* Edited by Eric F. Mason, Samuel I. Thomas, Alison Schofield, and Eugene Ulrich. JSJSup 153. Leiden: Brill, 2012.

Hartog, Pieter B. "Interlinear Additions and Literary Development in 4Q163/*Pesher Isaiah C,* 4Q169/*Pesher Nahum,* and 4Q171/*Pesher Psalms A.*" *RevQ* 28/108 (2016): 267–77.

Hartog, Pieter B. "'The Final Priests of Jerusalem' and 'The Mouth of the Priest': Eschatology and Literary History in Pesher Habakkuk." *DSD* 24 (2017): 59–80.

Hartog, Pieter B. *Pesher and Hypomnema: A Comparison of Two Commentary Collections from the Hellenistic-Roman Period.* STDJ 121. Leiden: Brill, 2017.

Hartog, Pieter B. "Pesher as Commentary." Pages 92–116 in *The Dead Sea Scrolls and the Study of the Humanities: Method, Theory, Meaning: Proceedings of the Eighth Meeting of the International Organization for Qumran Studies (Munich, 4–7 August,*

2013). Edited by Pieter B. Hartog, Samuel I. Thomas, and Alison Schofield. STDJ 125. Leiden: Brill, 2018.

Hartog, Pieter B. "Jubilees and Hellenistic Encyclopaedism." *JSJ* 50 (2019): 1–25.

Hearon, Holly E., and Philip Ruge-Jones, eds. *The Bible in Ancient and Modern Media: Story and Performance*. Eugene, OR: Cascade, 2009.

Hempel, Charlotte. *The Qumran Rule Texts in Context: Collected Studies*. TSAJ 154. Tübingen: Mohr Siebeck, 2013.

Hempel, Charlotte. "Reflections on Literacy, Textuality, and Community in the Qumran Dead Sea Scrolls." Pages 70–82 in *Is There a Text in This Cave? Studies in the Textuality of the Dead Sea Scrolls in Honour of George J. Brooke*. Edited by Ariel Feldman, Maria Cioată, and Charlotte Hempel. STDJ 119. Leiden: Brill, 2017.

Hezser, Catherine. *Jewish Literacy in Roman Palestine*. TSAJ 81. Tübingen: Mohr Siebeck, 2001.

Johnson, William A. "Toward a Sociology of Reading in Classical Antiquity." *AJP* 121 (2000): 593–627.

Johnson, William A. *Bookrolls and Scribes in Oxyrhynchus*. Studies in Book and Print Culture. Toronto: University of Toronto Press, 2004.

Johnson, William A. *Readers and Reading Culture in the High Roman Empire: A Study of Elite Communities*. Classical Culture and Society. Oxford: Oxford University Press, 2010.

Jokiranta, Jutta. *Social Identity and Sectarianism in the Qumran Movement*. STDJ 105. Leiden: Brill, 2013.

Jokiranta, Jutta. "Quoting, Writing, and Reading: Authority in *Pesher Habakkuk* from Qumran." Pages 185–212 in *Between Canonical and Apocryphal Texts*. Edited by Jörg Frey, Claire Clivaz, Tobias Nicklas, and Jörg Röder. WUNT 419. Tübingen: Mohr Siebeck, 2019.

Kirk, Alan. *Q in Matthew: Ancient Media, Memory, and Early Scribal Transmission of the Jesus Traditions*. LNTS 564. London: T&T Clark, 2016.

Kratz, Reinhard G. "The Teacher of Righteousness and His Enemies." Pages 515–32 in *Is There a Text in This Cave? Studies in the Textuality of the Dead Sea Scrolls in Honour of George J. Brooke*. Edited by Ariel Feldman, Maria Cioată, and Charlotte Hempel. STDJ 119. Leiden: Brill, 2017.

Le Donne, Anthony, and Tom Thatcher, eds. *The Fourth Gospel in First-Century Media Culture*. LNTS 426. London: T&T Clark, 2011.

Le Donne, Anthony, and Tom Thatcher. "Introducing Media Studies to Johannine Studies: Orality, Performance and Memory." Pages 1–8 in *The Fourth Gospel in First-Century Media Culture*. Edited by Anthony Le Donne and Tom Thatcher. LNTS 426. London: T&T Clark, 2011.

Lewis, Naphtali. *Papyrus in Classical Antiquity*. Oxford: Clarendon, 1974.

Lied, Liv I. "Media Culture, New Philology, and the Pseudepigrapha: A Note on Method." Paper presented at the Annual Meeting of the SBL. Chicago, IL, 19 November 2012.

Lied, Liv I. "*Nachleben* and Textual Identity: Variants and Variance in the Reception History of 2 Baruch." Pages 403–28 in *Fourth Ezra and Second Baruch: Reconstruction after the Fall*. Edited by Matthias Henze and Gabriele Boccaccini. JSJSup 164. Leiden: Brill, 2013.

Lied, Liv I., and Hugo Lundhaug, eds. *Snapshots of Evolving Traditions: Jewish and Christian Manuscript Culture, Textual Fluidity, and New Philology*. TUGAL 175. Berlin: De Gruyter, 2017.

Loubser, J. A. *Oral and Manuscript Culture in the Bible: Studies on the Media Texture of the New Testament—Explorative Hermeneutics*. 2nd ed. Eugene, OR: Cascade, 2013.

Louw, Theo A.W. van der, and Pieter B. Hartog. "Physical and Economic Aspects of the Earliest Septuagint Papyri." *JJS* 72 (2021): 1–22.

MacLuhan, Marshall. *Understanding Media: The Extensions of Man*. Introduction by Lewis H. Lapham. Cambridge, MA: The MIT Press, 1994.

McNamee, Kathleen. *Sigla and Select Marginalia in Greek Literary Papyri*. PB 26. Brussels: Fondation Égyptologique Reine Élisabeth, 1992.

McNamee, Kathleen. *Annotations in Greek and Latin Texts from Egypt*. ASP 45. Oakville, CT: American Society of Papyrologists, 2007.

Metso, Sarianna, and James M. Tucker. "The Changing Landscape of Editing Ancient Jewish Texts." Pages 269–87 in *Reading the Bible in Ancient Traditions and Modern Editions: Studies in Memory of Peter W. Flint*. Edited by Andrew W. Perrin, Kyung S. Baek, and Daniel K. Falk. EJL 47. Atlanta, GA: SBL, 2017.

Milik, Józef T. "Les modèles araméens du livre d'Esther dans la grotte 4 de Qumran." *RevQ* 15/59 (1992): 321–99.

Miller, Shem. "Traditional History and Cultural Memory in the Pesharim." *JSJ* 50 (2019): 348–70.

Monger, Matthew P. "4Q216 and the State of Jubilees at Qumran." *RevQ* 26/104 (2014): 595–612.

Najman, Hindy. *Seconding Sinai: The Development of Mosaic Discourse in Second Temple Judaism*. JSJSup 77. Leiden: Brill 2003.

Najman, Hindy. "Interpretation as Primordial Writing: Jubilees and Its Authority Conferring Strategies." Pages 39–71 in *Past Renewals: Interpretative Authority, Renewed Revelation and the Quest for Perfection in Jewish Antiquity*. Leiden: Brill, 2010.

Nitzan, Bilhah. *Pesher Habakkuk: A Scroll from the Wilderness of Judaea (1QpHab)*. Jerusalem: Bialik Institute, 1986. (Hebrew).

Person, Jr., Raymond F., and Chris Keith. "Media Studies and Biblical Studies: An Introduction." Pages 1–15 in *The Dictionary of the Bible and Ancient Media*. Edited by Tom Thatcher, Chris Keith, Raymond F. Person, and Elsie R. Stern. London: Bloomsbury, 2017.

Pietersen, Lloyd K. "'False Teaching, Lying Tongues and Deceitful Lips' (4Q169 frgs 3–4 2.8): The Pesharim and the Sociology of Deviance." Pages 166–81 in *New Directions in Qumran Studies: Proceedings of the Bristol Colloquium on the Dead Sea Scrolls, 8–10 September 2003*. Edited by Jonathan G. Campbell, William J. Lyons, and Lloyd K. Pietersen. LSTS 52. London: T&T Clark, 2005.

Popović, Mladen. "Reading, Writing, and Memorizing Together: Reading Culture in Ancient Judaism and the Dead Sea Scrolls in a Mediterranean Context." *DSD* 19 (2017): 446–69.

Qimron, Elisha. *The Dead Sea Scrolls: The Hebrew Writings*. 3 vols. Jerusalem: Yad Ben-Zvi, 2010–2014.

Schofield, Alison. *From Qumran to the* Yaḥad: *A New Paradigm of Textual Development for The Community Rule*. STDJ 77. Leiden: Brill, 2009.

Schofield, Alison. "Between Center and Periphery: The *Yaḥad* in Context." *DSD* 16 (2009): 330–50.

Segal, Michael. *The Book of Jubilees: Rewritten Bible, Redaction, Ideology and Theology*. Leiden: Brill, 2007.

Sluiter, Ineke. "The Dialectics of Genre: Some Aspects of Secondary Literature and Genre in Antiquity." Pages 183–203 in *Matrices of Genre: Authors, Canons, and Society*. Edited by Mary Depew and Dirk Obbink. CHSC 4. Cambridge: Harvard University Press, 2000.

Snyder, H. Gregory. "Naughts and Crosses: Pesher Manuscripts and Their Significance for Reading Practices at Qumran." *DSD* 7 (2000): 26–48.

Stegemann, Hartmut. "Methods for the Reconstruction of Scrolls from Scattered Fragments." Pages 189–220 in *Archaeology and History in the Dead Sea Scrolls: The New York University Conference in Memory of Yigael Yadin*. Edited by Lawrence H. Schiffman. JSPSup 8. Sheffield: JSOT Press, 1990.

Steudel, Annette. "Die Rezeption autoritativer Texte in Qumran." Pages 89–100 in *Qumran und der biblische Kanon*. Edited by Jörg Frey and Michael Becker. BTS 92. Neukirchen-Vluyn: Neukirchener, 2009.

Steudel, Annette. "Dating Exegetical Texts from Qumran." Pages 39–53 in *The Dynamics of Language and Exegesis at Qumran*. Edited by Devorah Dimant and Reinhard G. Kratz. FAT 2/35. Tübingen: Mohr Siebeck, 2009.

Strugnell, John. "Notes en marge du volume V des « Discoveries in the Judaean Desert of Jordan »." *RevQ* 7/26 (1970): 163–276.

Stuckenbruck, Loren T. "The Teacher of Righteousness Remembered: From Fragmentary Sources to Collective Memory in the Dead Sea Scrolls." Pages 75–94 in *Memory in the Bible and Antiquity: The Fifth Durham-Tübingen Research Symposium (Durham, September 2004)*. Edited by Stephen Barton, Loren T. Stuckenbruck and Benjamin G. Wold. WUNT 212. Tübingen: Mohr Siebeck, 2007.

Stuckenbruck, Loren T. "The Legacy of the Teacher of Righteousness in the Dead Sea Scrolls." Pages 23–49 in *New Perspectives on Old Texts: Proceedings of the Tenth International Symposium of the Orion Center for the Study of the Dead Sea Scrolls and Associated Literature, 9–11 January, 2005.* Edited by Esther G. Chazon, Betsy Halpern-Amaru, and Ruth A. Clements. STDJ 88. Leiden: Brill, 2010.

Tigchelaar, Eibert J. C. "Dittography and Copying Lines in the Dead Sea Scrolls: Considering George Brooke's Proposal about 1QpHab 7:1–2." Pages 293–307 in *Is There a Text in This Cave? Studies in the Textuality of the Dead Sea Scrolls in Honour of George J. Brooke.* Edited by Ariel Feldman, Maria Cioată, and Charlotte Hempel. STDJ 119. Leiden: Brill, 2017.

Tigchelaar, Eibert J. C. "The Scribes of the Scrolls." Pages 524–32 in *T&T Clark Companion to the Dead Sea Scrolls.* Edited by George J. Brooke and Charlotte Hempel, with the assistance of Michael DeVries and Drew Longacre. London: T&T Clark, 2019.

Tov, Emanuel. "Excerpted and Abbreviated Biblical Texts from Qumran." *RevQ* 16 (1995): 581–600.

Tov, Emanuel. *Scribal Practices and Approaches Reflected in the Texts Found in the Judean Desert.* STDJ 54. Leiden: Brill, 2004.

Tzoref, Shani. "Pesher Nahum." Pages 1:623–35 in *Outside the Bible: Ancient Jewish Writings Related to Scripture.* Edited by Louis H. Feldman, James L. Kugel, and Lawrence H. Schiffman. 3 vols. Philadelphia, PA: The Jewish Publication Society, 2012.

White, Hayden. "The Value of Narrativity in the Representation of Reality." *Critical Enquiry* 7 (1980): 5–27.

White, Hayden. "The Narrativization of Real Events." *Critical Enquiry* 7 (1981): 793–98.

Yardeni, Ada. "A Note on a Qumran Scribe." Pages 287–98 in *New Seals and Inscriptions: Hebrew, Idumean, and Cuneiform.* Edited by Meir Lubetski. HBM 8. Sheffield: Sheffield Phoenix, 2007.

CHAPTER 8

The Copper Scroll: The Medium, the Context and the Archaeology

Joan E. Taylor

1 Introduction

As a communication, there is no more mystifying an example than the Copper Scroll (3Q15). Among the Dead Sea Scrolls, it appears anomalous. Among examples of communications in the ancient world, it is unique. It looks like a list of places where treasure may be found, but some have considered this more fantasy than reality. However, if we consider it initially in terms of its materiality, context and archaeology, the likelihood of it being a listing of real treasure is strong. The materiality of the Copper Scroll indicates that it was composed by people with access to considerable wealth, but that it was inscribed and hidden in a hurry. The Mishnaic Hebrew language has long suggested a second-century dating, yet scholars often resist this, and rely on diverse arguments to insist it should be counted as first-century. In this discussion, the focus will be on the Copper Scroll as a form of communication, with its materiality and archaeological context foregrounded. We shall see that the second-century language of the communication can be seen to cohere with a second-century scenario that would explain its hiding, inside a cave full of jars.

2 Finding and Opening

The Copper Scroll (3Q15) was discovered in the survey explorations done jointly by the American Schools of Oriental Research, the Palestine Archaeological Museum and the École Biblique et Archéologique Français (EBAF) on March 20, 1952. It was found in a cave labelled GQ8 (Grotte de Qumran 8) by "Team G", a party made up of local Bedouin workers and headed by Henri de Contenson.[1] Located some 800 m from Cave 1Q, it is about 2 km from Kh. Qumran (see

---

1 Originally it was labelled G8: Team G, Cave 8.

© JOAN E. TAYLOR, 2023 | DOI:10.1163/9789004537804_009

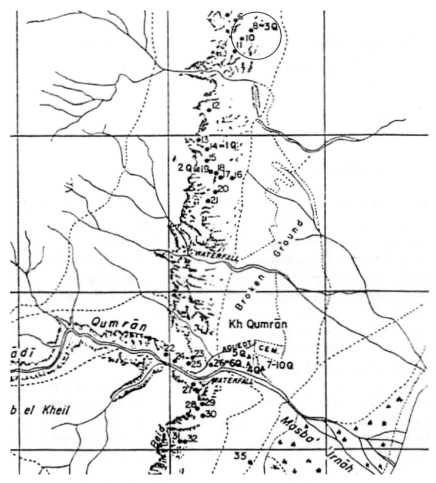

FIGURE 8.1 Jack Ziegler's plan of the Qumran caves area. Detail with marking
COURTESY OF THE EBAF

Figure 8.1). A photograph shows the excavation of the cave in progress with de Contenson and the Bedouin workers outside it (Figure 8.2).[2] Since this cave also contained fragments of parchment and papyrus manuscripts it was

---

2 Note that the cave is to the left of the figures in the photograph in Figure 8.2. It has been a common error to consider the cave to be the one behind the figures, for example in the photographs available for reproduction at Zev Radovan's website, www.bibleandpictures.com; thus Google searches present this cave (erroneously). Radovan has explained to me in an email of 28/3/19 that this was identified for him by Hanan Eshel, but, if so, this was one of Eshel's rare mistakes.

THE COPPER SCROLL 295

FIGURE 8.2 Henry de Contenson (top image, left) with three Bedouin workers outside Cave 3Q. Note the position of Cave 3Q is to the left, to the east. In the foreground, to the south, excavation equipment is located, not behind the figures. A large pile of excavated soil and debris lies on the steep slope at the front of the picture, along with boulders. It appears that the original front and south side of the cave collapsed sometime in the past. Black and white photograph
COURTESY OF AMERICAN SCHOOLS OF ORIENTAL RESEARCH

then re-designated as Cave 3Q.[3] The manuscripts include small fragments of Psalms, Ezekiel, Lamentations, Jubilees, and some unidentified works, pieces left over after the scrolls themselves were removed or perished. However, it is the Copper Scroll that is the most extraordinary find.

As we see from the photograph taken at the time of its discovery (Figure 8.3), this was not actually one intact scroll, but rather it was separated into two rolls. The larger of the two rolls was positioned on a kind of small rocky protrusion at the bottom of the cave wall, with the smaller one tucked in underneath. It is a frequent mistake of publication to show the rolls in an incorrect position, but the clue is in the measuring stick found in one of the images, which needs to be horizontal, not vertical.

ASOR's William Reed and others originally assumed that the rolls were made of bronze, but they were confirmed as oxidised copper upon analysis by experts at the British Museum and Johns Hopkins University.[4] The rolls were then treated with a cellulose varnish to preserve them from deterioration. For some time they remained unopened, lying on white cloth in the Palestine Archaeological Museum, Jerusalem (Figure 8.4),[5] while much debate ensued about how the rolls could possibly be read. Scholars tried to work out the letters on the basis of the impressions on the exterior sides.[6] After some protracted negotiations, the first (smaller) roll was delivered to the Manchester Institute of Science and Technology and opened by Henry Wright Baker, through the agency of John Allegro, in October 1955. As John Allegro described it, "A steel rod was run through the centre of the roll and then lowered into a cradle running on rails directly beneath a small (1 ¾″) circular saw".[7] Given the success of the operation, the larger roll was opened early in the following year.

John Allegro has provided an excellent photographic record of the Copper Scroll's original state before and after opening. Allegro also shot valuable movie footage of the cutting open of the rolls, which is available online as a result of the work of the Leverhulme-funded Dispersed Qumran Cave Artefacts and Archival Sources (DQCAAS) project,[8] a collaboration between myself, Marcello

---

3   Roland de Vaux, "Exploration de la Région de Qumran," *RB* 60 (1953): 540–61; Maurice Baillet, Józef T. Milik and Roland de Vaux, ed., *Les 'Petites Grottes'*, DJD 3 (Oxford: Clarendon, 1962), 7–8, 201.
4   William L. Reed, "The Qumran Caves Expedition of March, 1952," *BASOR* 135 (Oct., 1954): 12.
5   John Allegro, "The Copper Scroll from Qumran," *Restaurator* 1 (1969): 13–19.
6   Karl G. Kuhn, "Les Rouleaux de Cuivre de Qumran," *RB* 61 (1954): 193–205.
7   Allegro, "Copper Scroll," 14.
8   Allegro's photographs and slides have also been digitised and are available online at the website https://dqcaas.com.

FIGURE 8.3 The Copper Scroll at the time of its discovery in March, 1952. Note that there is a small rocky protrusion above the lower scroll, and the upper larger scroll sits unevenly on top of this. Black and white photograph
COURTESY OF AMERICAN SCHOOLS OF ORIENTAL RESEARCH

FIGURE 8.4 Unopened rolls of the Copper Scroll on display in the Palestine Archaeological Museum. Note green (oxidised) coloration of the rolls, the damage to the outside edge of the larger scroll (lost top sections of columns III–VIII) and the line of small rivet holes at the bottom inside edge of the smaller scroll (ahead of column IX). Photo: John Allegro. Colour slide held by Manchester Museum: John Allegro
COURTESY OF THE ALLEGRO ESTATE

Fidanzio and Dennis Mizzi.[9] In these early photographs taken of the rolls, we can see that the oxidisation has led to a green dusting over the outer surface of the rolls, and also observe the depth of the letters, visible on the front and back of the thin sheets of metal (Figure 8.5).

The cutting through of the rolls in October 1955 and January 1956 resulted in 23 sections, which were carefully photographed by John Allegro and transcribed by projecting the photographs and tracing the images (at approximately 2.5 times their size), and a full set of these transcriptions exists in the John Rylands library (Hebrew MS 56) and in the Allegro image collection of Manchester University Museum. The rolls were then sent back to the Jordan

[9] See https://dqcaas.com/2016/11/24/1953-film-of-cutting-open-of-the-copper-scroll/. The Leverhulme-funded project has sought to document archival and artefactual material from the Qumran caves now found in different collections, private and public, worldwide. The digitisation of the film footage was done by Flying Pig studios and the work of scanning the slides was done by Sandra Jacobs with permission from Judy Brown, John Allegro's daughter, and Manchester Museum.

FIGURE 8.5 Detail of letters pressed into the copper scroll (second roll). Sections 16 to 18 = columns 9–10. Photo: John Allegro. Black and white print and negative held by Manchester Museum
COURTESY OF THE ALLEGRO ESTATE

Archaeological Museum in Amman, where they remained on display until 2004. In the 1990s, after significant deterioration, they were sent for conservation to the Laboratoire EDF-Valectra in Paris, supported by the Institut Français d'Archéologie du Proche Orient and EBAF. The EDF team undertook metallurgical studies, chemical analysis, X-ray imagery and produced high quality digital positive and X-ray images that have been made available in a magnificent two-volume scientific work. They also produced a set of twenty exact replicas of the Scroll, in collaboration with Facsimile Editions of London,[10] with the combined industry enabling epigrapher Émile Puech to propose new

---

10 See https://facsimile-editions.com/cs/.

readings.[11] The restored Copper Scroll is now on display in the new Jordan Museum in Amman. However, by far the best record of the original condition of the Copper Scroll may be seen in the photographs taken by John Allegro shortly after it was opened.[12]

3 The Copper Scroll as Communication

The Copper Scroll is by genre a list, very similar to a treasury list, as Michael Wise and David Wilmot have identified.[13] Set out in twelve columns, unlike a normal treasury list for silver, gold and precious items deposited in a temple in certain locations, this list indicates hiding places in a landscape. The treasure is vast, far beyond what we could imagine would be the property of an individual or even a group, unless they are the rulers of a nation or the treasure is from a large public institution. This treasure seems to come from a Temple, treasure which was secreted away in 64 (or perhaps 61) locations, and Karl Kuhn argued already in 1956 that it must relate to the Jerusalem Temple.[14] The enormous size of the treasure indicates this, as well as the fact that there is cultic terminology (e.g. references to tithe vessels, priestly vestments, incense). John Allegro followed suit, and invested much effort trying to understand the precise locations of this treasure, even searching for it.[15] Others have followed in his footsteps, on the ground, often with elaborate theories about where the treasure could be located and what kind of treasure it is.[16] But some scholars have doubted that this could possibly be the Jerusalem Temple treasure,

---

11 Daniel Brizemeure, Noël Lacoudre and Émile Puech, *Le Rouleau de cuivre de la grotte 3 de Qumrân (3Q15): expertise, restauration, epigraphie*, STDJ 55/1–2, 2 vols. (Leiden: Brill/ École Biblique et Archéologique Française de Jérusalem/EDF Foundation, 2006).

12 See https://dqcaas.com/allegro-manchester-copper-scroll/. Note that small pieces that fell off the scroll were lost even at the time of its first publication by Józef Milik, "Le rouleau de cuivre provenant de la grotte 3Q (3Q15)," in *Les 'Petites Grottes'*, ed. Maurice Baillet, Józef T. Milik, and Roland de Vaux, DJD 3 (Oxford: Clarendon, 1962), 212.

13 See Michael O. Wise, "David J. Wilmot and the Copper Scroll," in *Copper Scroll Studies*, ed. George J. Brooke and Philip J. Davies (London: T&T Clark International, 2002), 291–309. Wise and Wilmot point to very similar treasury lists in marble inscriptions from the Temple of Apollo on Delos. See also Jesper Høgenhaven, *The Cave 3 Copper Scroll: A Symbolic Journey*, STDJ 132 (Leiden: Brill, 2020), 167–72.

14 Karl G. Kuhn, "Der gegenwärtige Stand der Erforschung der in Palästina neu gefundenen hebräischen Handschriften 33. Bericht über neue Qumranfunde und über die Öffnung der Kupferrollen." *TLZ* 81 (1956): 541–46.

15 John Allegro, *The Treasure of the Copper Scroll* (Garden City, NY: Doubleday, 1960).

16 See for these the op-ed by Robert Cargill, "On the Insignificance and Abuse of the Copper Scroll," July 2009, at https://www.bibleinterp.com/opeds/copper.html.

THE COPPER SCROLL

301

arguing instead that it relates to a sectarian or Essene community who lived at Qumran.[17] Émile Puech has suggested that the Copper Scroll could not have been deposited after 68 CE, when the Romans captured the site.[18] He has suggested that after disaffected Essene priests left Jerusalem with the Teacher of Righteousness in 152 BCE, they amassed Temple tithes they refused to send to the Temple, burying all these ahead of 68 CE.[19]

But, in the opinion of the initial editor of the *editio princeps*, Józef Milik, the entire treasure was a complete fantasy.[20] There was no actual activity of secreting anything. Milik looked to supposed parallels, for example the *Treatise of the Vessels (Massekhet Kelim)*.[21] However, in genre the *Treatise of the Vessels*, a midrash of late antiquity, is not identical at all.[22] It is written in past tense and describes a story of the hiding of treasure of the First Temple ahead of the Babylonian destruction. This treasure is based on biblical artefacts recorded in Exodus, Kings and Chronicles, and the developed story brings in a number of biblical figures, for example Jeremiah, Zechariah, Baruch, Ezra.[23] The narrative of the treasure's hiding is the focus, and the story includes help from angelic

---

17   So initially Kuhn, "Les rouleaux de cuivre," 204–205; Andre Dupont-Sommer, *The Essene Writings from Qumran* (Oxford: Basil Blackwell, 1961), 379–93, Stephen Goranson, "Sectarianism, Geography and the Copper Scroll," *JJS* 43 (1992): 282–87.

18   Émile Puech, "Some Results of the Restoration of the Copper Scroll by EDF Mecenat," in *The Dead Sea Scrolls Fifty Years after their Discovery 1947–1997: Proceedings of the Jerusalem Congress, July 20–25, 1997*, ed. Lawrence H. Schiffman, Emanuel Tov, James C. VanderKam and Galen Marquis (Jerusalem: Israel Exploration Society, 2000), 893.

19   Émile Puech, *The Copper Scroll Revisited*, STDJ 112, trans. David E. Orton (Leiden: Brill, 2015), 18–22 and see also Émile Puech, Noël Lacoudre, in collaboration with Farah Mébarki, "The Mysteries of the 'Copper Scroll,' Qumran and the Dead Sea Scrolls: Discoveries, Debates, the Scrolls and the Bible," *NEA* 63/3 (2000): 152–53.

20   E.g. "the bronze catalogue describes purely imaginary treasures belonging to Jewish folklore of the Roman period": Józef T. Milik, "The Copper Document from Cave III of Qumran: Translation and Commentary," *ADAJ* 4–5 (1960): 137; idem, "Le rouleau de cuivre de Qumran (3Q 15)," *RB* 66 (1959): 322; idem, "Le rouleau de cuivre," DJD III, 278–81. Others who suggest the treasure is legendary include: L. H. Silberman, "A Note on the Copper Scrolls," *VT* 10 (1960): 77–79, and Sigmund Mowinckel, "The Copper Scroll—An Apocryphon?" *JBL* 76 (1957): 261–65.

21   See James R. Davila, "Treatise of the Vessels (*Massekhet Kelim*)," in *Old Testament Pseudepigrapha: More Noncanonical Scriptures*, ed. Richard Bauckham, James Davila, Alex Panayotov (Grand Rapids, MI: Eerdmans, 2013), 1:393–409. The Hebrew text is found in Adolph Jellinek, *Beth ha-Midrasch: Sammlung kleiner Midraschim und Vermischter Abhandlungen aus der ältern jüdischen Literatur* (Leipzig: F. Nies, 1876), 2:xxvi–xxvii, 88–91 (no. XIII),

22   See Wise, "David Wilmot," 293–96.

23   See James R. Davila, "Scriptural Exegesis in the *Treatise of the Vessels*, a Legendary Account of the Hiding of the Temple Treasures," in *With Letters of Light: Studies in the Dead Sea Scrolls, Early Jewish Apocalypticism, Magic and Mysticism in Honor of Rachel Elior*, ed.

beings, with the treasure destined to be revealed when the Messiah comes at the Eschaton. In contrast, the Copper Scroll inventory is extremely bald: it is a list of findspots, with nothing about the circumstances of hiding, and nothing suggests a grand revelation. There are no eschatological indications.

Doubts about the scroll as indicating the hiding places of real treasure continue, and both Steve Weitzmann and Jesper Høgenhaven can niftily argue that the treasure is both real and imagined.[24] They have both suggested that the so-called Lindian Chronicle, a record on a marble stele in Rhodes, dated 99 BCE, is a parallel that illustrates such a mix. It has some similarity of structure and composition, and presents a full list of votive gifts belonging to the temple of Athena Lindia, with careful citations of evidence, even though it also notes that only a few of these treasures currently survived. Since many of these gifts are associated with legendary figures, it is assumed they are largely imaginary.[25] However, beyond this being a list of treasures, one may question it as a comparable communication. While this listing was designed ultimately to promote the status of the sacred site, the priestly authors claimed these votive gifts existed and were carefully verifying the memories of these: it is not so much a mix of real and imagined, but of locatable and lost. Many Medieval Christian relics were associated with biblical and legendary origins, but the actual objects were real. Moreover, unlike the Lindian Chronicle, the Copper Scroll cites no proof for anything and the sacred site from which they came is only barely implied; items are simply to be found in various locations. If anything, the proof is in the finding: dig at a certain number of cubits and there the treasure will be. The Copper Scroll is thus a list of instructions to enable findings.

4 Medium

I would like here to look not so much at the contents of the scroll, or turn over the difficulties of its reading and interpretation, but rather think about the artefact itself as a vehicle of communication. This approach aligns with what William Johnson has done in looking at the "Pragmatics of Reading" at the outset in his study of readers and reading culture in the high Roman Empire,

---

Daphne V. Arbel and Andrei A. Orlov, Ekstasis: Religious Experience from Antiquity to the Middle Ages 2 (Berlin: De Gruyter, 2011), 45–61.

24 Steven Weitzman, "Absent but Accounted for: A New Approach to the Copper Scroll," *HTR* 108 (2015): 423–47, and see Høgenhaven, *Cave 3 Copper Scroll*, passim.

25 See the discussion in Høgenhaven, *Cave 3 Copper Scroll*, 201–207, supporting Weitzman.

THE COPPER SCROLL   303

when he begins in examining the bookroll itself—the scroll and the writing on it—as an artefact.[26]

Put plainly, we need to consider the physical medium for the communication.[27] Today we think of "content" on a certain "platform". In the ancient world, where literacy was minimal, "content" was of course largely spoken, communicated orally and remembered and retold. When written down, it could be contained on different platforms: e.g. on stone, wood, pottery, papyrus, wax tablets, plaster, papyrus and parchment, but the bookroll was the prime choice for libraries in elite circles. In encountering artefacts with written content, we know intuitively that content chiselled on marble or made out of black tesserae in a mosaic is likely to be different from something written in ink on an ostracon. We often "get" the differences the moment we see an object, understanding immediately that we are reading a tomb epitaph, for example, or a writing exercise, by an object's appearance and its materiality, even before we even begin to think of genre, or read a single letter. When the content alone is reproduced in a book, however, as a collection of written words printed on a page, formatted consistently, we lose the information the medium of the communication itself provides: a message that we often pick up unwittingly. The intuitive understanding needs to be something we bring to our conscious awareness: the substance of the platform in which the content is found should give us clues about the nature of the content.

In this case, the content is communicated by writing on a metal surface. The quality copper (99% copper, 1% tin), rather than the usual fine leather (a type of parchment), of most of the scrolls, needs to be noticed. When Wright Baker wrote a report about his opening of the rolls, he noted that the substance was "presumably a naturally impure copper",[28] that is it was not artificially mixed with tin to create the tin content but raw copper which contained tin. Likely extracted nearby at the copper mines of the Wadi Faynan, as well as further south at Timna, this substance of raw copper was well beyond the means of most people.[29]

---

26   William A. Johnson, *Readers and Reading Culture in the High Roman Empire: A Study of Elite Communities* (Oxford: Oxford University Press, 2010), 17–31.

27   See Høgenhaven, *Cave 3 Copper Scroll*, 141–44, 158–60.

28   Henry Wright Baker, "Notes on the Opening of the 'Bronze' Scrolls from Qumran," *BJRL* 39 (1956): 46; idem, "Notes on the Opening of the Copper Scrolls from Qumran," in *Les 'Petites Grottes'*, ed. Maurice Baillet, Józef T. Milik and Roland de Vaux, DJD 3 (Oxford: Clarendon, 1962), 204.

29   See Andreas Hauptman, *The Archaeometallurgy of Copper: Evidence from Faynan, Jordan* (New York, NY: Springer, 2007), 154–56; G. W. Barker, et al., "The Wadi Faynan Project, Southern Jordan: A Preliminary Report on Geomorphology and Landscape Archaeology," *Levant* 29 (1997): 19–25; Zeidan A. Kafafi, "New Insights on the Copper Mines of Wadi

In regard to the writing, it was done by pressing into the copper a metal point, shaped like a very fine slotted screwdriver point (see Figure 8.5). The scribe[30] had three instruments that could achieve the effect: one straight and two curved. Each letter's form was pressed into the copper, and because of the instruments the letters were quite large, up to 1 cm high. It would have taken much longer to press these letters than to scrawl with stylus and ink, and the scribe may not have been expert. There are mistakes and corrections, and uneven spacing, which may indicate haste.[31] One may wonder here whether the tools used for the creation of the letters were made for purpose, or employed secondarily when they were otherwise intended for other crafts, perhaps leatherworking.

One should remember that the letters could not be formed without annealing the copper first, in order to make it soft. To anneal it, the copper would have been heated, by fire, and then plunged into cold water, which renders it pliable for a time. However, hammering or bending causes it to harden. The execution of the writing would presumably have required the expertise of a metal-worker while the letters were pressed by a scribe. One can only imagine the peculiar conditions of the execution.

The letters as created are often unclear, making reading difficult. There are not many precise names of locations in the Copper Scroll, and some disappear when the Hebrew text is read differently. For example, in the letters of the scroll, it is nearly impossible in most cases to distinguish between tau, he and ḥet, or daleth and resh, bet and kaph, or yod and waw, and other letters are also difficult to determine. Place names might be read, but some may also be descriptions. For example, at the very beginning of the Scroll (1:1–2), Milik determined a place name and thus read: "In Khorebbeh,".[32] Likewise, Lefkovits has a place name: "In Haruvah (or: in the ruin)", reading a waw in the first word rather than a yod.[33] Puech reads a yod, as Allegro, and translates, "In 'the Ruin'"[34]

Faynan/Jordan," *PEQ* 146 (2014): 263–80; Beno Rothenberg, *Timna: Valley of the Biblical Copper Mines* (London: Thames and Hudson, 1972); idem, "The Arabah in Roman and Byzantine Times in the Light of New Research," in *Roman Frontier Studies 1967: Proceedings of the Seventh International Congress*, ed. Shimon Applebaum (Tel Aviv: Tel Aviv University, 1971), 211–33.

30 Following Puech's identification of only one scribe, see *Copper Scroll Revisited*, 3, n. 11.

31 Bargil Pixner, "Unravelling the *Copper Scroll* Case: A Study on the Topography of 3Q15," *RevQ* 11 (1983): 326–27.

32 Milik, "The Copper Document," 139; idem, "Rouleau de cuivre de Qumran," 323; idem, "Rouleau de cuivre," 285.

33 Judah Lefkovits, *The Copper Scroll (3Q15): A Reevaluation, A New Reading, Translation, and Commentary*, STDJ 25 (Leiden: Brill, 1999), 94.

34 Puech, *Copper Scroll Revisited*, 121.

THE COPPER SCROLL   305

though he identifies that "the Ruin" is actually a place-name—Horebbeh.[35] But Martínez reads the same words simply as: "In the ruin".[36] Høgenhaven adds some descriptive detail to the term: "In the small ruin".[37] From word to word as one goes through the text there are many alternative readings, indicated in different transcriptions and translations.

Since expert readers of Hebrew puzzle over basic letter recognition, there is a mismatch between a highly expensive and unusual writing surface and the technical quality of what is written on it, One might expect a high-quality substance to contain a high-quality script, and perfectly clarity. We associate beautiful marble with beautiful chiseled letters.[38] However, the lines are uneven, the edges of the twelve columns are rough, and the letters are badly done, especially towards the end when the scribe squashes in as many letters as possible, as if assuming there is little room on the sheet, only to find there is space spare at the finish.[39] Again, one imagines the peculiar circumstances of the execution of the writing on this particular surface.

Why write on copper at all? If we look to comparative examples of writing inscribed directly on fine copper (or other fine metals) in antiquity, we only have tiny pieces, largely in the form of amulets called *lamellae*, on which there was writing punched or inscribed on thin metal sheets that were then rolled up, placed in containers and worn around the neck.[40] A good example of such

---

35 Puech, *Copper Scroll Revisited*, 26. He notes that this was still known in the Byzantine period as Chorembe, located in the Wadi Nuweimeh, north-east of Jericho, which is the Valley of Achor in Byzantine texts.

36 Florentino García Martínez, *The Dead Sea Scrolls Translated: The Qumran Texts in English*, 2nd ed. (Leiden: Brill, 1996), 461, modified in Florentino García Martínez and Eibert J. C. Tigchelaar, *The Dead Sea Scrolls Study Edition* (Leiden: Brill, 1997), 233: "the ruin which is in the valley of Acor, under the steps."

37 Høgenhaven, *Cave 3 Copper Scroll*, 239.

38 Poor quality lettering on valuable surfaces may be found if the letters are extremely small, like on gemstones.

39 Høgenhaven (*Cave 3 Copper Scroll*, 146) suggests the scribe may have decided to leave the space blank for aesthetic reasons. It is hard to accept this, since corresponding unclear and squashed letters do not really provide aesthetic satisfaction.

40 Such *lamellae* are widely known from the Mediterranean world, see Roy D. Kotansky, *Greek Magical Amulets: The Inscribed Gold, Silver, Copper and Bronze Lamellae*, Part 1: *Published Texts of Known Provenance*, Papyrologica Coloniensia 22/1 (Opladen: Westdeutscher Verlag, 1994). A number of these have been found in the region of Israel-Palestine and are of Jewish provenance. See Joseph Naveh and Saul Shaked, *Magic Spells and Formulae: Aramaic Incantations of Late Antiquity* (Jerusalem: Magnes, 1993); idem, *Amulets and Magic Bowls: Aramaic Incantations of Late Antiquity*, 3rd ed. (Jerusalem: Magnes, 1998); Rivka Elitzur-Leiman, "A Copper Amulet," in *Khirbet Wadi Ḥammam: A Roman-Period Village and Synagogue in the Lower Galilee*, ed. Uzi Leibner, Qedem Report 13 (Jerusalem: Hebrew University of Jerusalem, 2018), 616–19; Hanan Eshel and Rivka Leiman, "Jewish Amulets Written on Metal Scrolls," *Journal of Ancient Judaism* 1 (2010): 189–99; Moïse

an amulet, now in the Palestine Exploration Fund, was found in a Roman tomb in Samaria in the 1930s.[41] The amulet was comprised by two rolls of silver that had been housed in a slim copper case, 31.2 mm and 10 mm high respectively (Figure 8.6). The silver amulets found in Ketef Hinnom were similarly small.[42] By contrast, the Copper Scroll is huge. It was originally not two rolls but one entity measuring 2.46 m by 28 cm (= ca. 8 feet long and 0.9 foot wide), though only 0.76 to 1 mm (= 0.03 to 0.04 inches) in thickness, made up of three pieces (ca. 81 cm long) rivetted together. Wright Baker defined the thickness as "three or four times that of a post card".[43] Its thickness is significant because for a plaque that was intended to be seen one would expect it to be thicker. Indeed, Wright Baker noted—against the assumption of de Vaux—that it would have been impossible to consider this as anything suitable for hanging up, and there are no hanging holes.[44] The one hole near the edge of the first section indicating it was fixed at some point can be understood as a peg hole "used to hold the metal onto the scribe's table."[45]

It was in two rolls because one of these had broken off at the time it was rolled, but clearly the intention was that it should have been a single entity, and Wright Baker identified that this indicates haste. The varying thickness of the material would at any rate have made it difficult to roll it evenly at speed. There was no effort to reattach the broken piece. In addition, the copper itself would not have easily allowed re-rolling and there is no evidence such re-rolling took place.[46] There is even the thumb marks of the principal roller on the innermost sheet. As John Allegro writes, "The rolling of the document had apparently been done in a hurry. This was shown not only by the broken line

---

Schwab, "Une amulette judéo-araméenne," *JA* 7 (1906): 1–15; Louis-Hugues Vincent, "Amulette judeo-arameenne," *RB* 5 (1908): 382–94; James A. Montgomery, "Some Early Amulets from Palestine," *JAOS* 31 (1911): 272–81; Andre Dupont-Sommer, "Deux lamelles d'argent à inscription hébréo-araméenne trouvées à Ağabeyli (Turquie)," *Jahrbuch für Kleinasiatische Forschung* 1 (1950–51): 201–17; Emmanuele Testa, *L'huile de la foi: L'onction des malades sur une lamelle du 1er siècle*, Publications du Studium Biblicum Franciscanum: Collectio minor 3 (Jerusalem: Magnes, 1967); Felix Klein-Franke, "Eine aramäische Tabella devotionis (T.Colon. inv. nr. 6)," *ZPE* 7 (1971): 47–52; Jeremy D. Smoak, "Words Unseen: The Power of Hidden Writing," *BAR* 44.1 (2018): 52–59, 70.

41   PEF 2049. See Christa Müller-Kessler, T. Crichton Mitchell and Marilyn I. Hockey, "An Inscribed Silver Amulet from Samaria," *PEQ* 139 (2007): 5–19.

42   Gabriel Barkay, "The Priestly Benediction on Silver Plaques from Ketef Hinnom Jerusalem," *Tel Aviv* 19 (1992): 139–192.

43   Wright Baker, "Notes 'Bronze'," 45; idem, "Notes Copper," 203.

44   *Contra* de Vaux, "Exploration," 557–58, who thought it would have been on display in the community buildings before it was placed in the cave.

45   Wright Baker, "Notes 'Bronze'," 54; idem, "Notes Copper," 209.

46   Wright Baker, "Notes 'Bronze'," 45; idem, "Notes Copper," 203.

FIGURE 8.6 Silver scroll amulet (PEF AO2049) found in Samaria, two rolls 31.2 mm and 10 mm high
COURTESY OF THE PALESTINE EXPLORATION FUND, LONDON

of rivets that had split the document into two parts, but by the way the end of the scroll had been forcibly bent round to make the first turn, the indentations of the person's thumbs being clearly visible where he had creased the soft metal."[47] They should have carefully reheated the scroll. Copper conducts heat easily and quickly and heating could have facilitated the rolling, but instead they bent it around and broke off a piece, and left it as is.

Once rolled, then, that was it, unlike a parchment or papyrus scroll that could be rolled and unrolled multiple times. It would have hardened. There would have been an expectation of reheating by people of the future who

---

47   Allegro, "The Copper Scroll from Qumran," 15.

would unroll it, but it could not simply be opened up and read *in situ*, unlike a parchment or papyrus scroll. We think again of the *lamellae*, which were rolled up and then placed in containers to be worn, rather than frequently read. The inscriptions on *lamellae* are designed to protect the wearer, and could contain both prophylactic messages or curses, but they are not public. The Copper Scroll contents are prescriptive: this is a list of places, with no apparent prophylactic value, but the information is likewise secret, in that a list of hiding places of treasure should not be available for everyone to find. The Copper Scroll content was then—as with a *lamella*—intended to be hidden, like the treasure itself.

There has been nothing exactly like this ever found. Nevertheless, further afield, there is another copper scroll of larger size than the *lamellae* that is now in the Schøyen Collection, Norway. Measuring 58 × 26 cm, it was a foundation deed at the consecration of a Buddhist stupa in the fifth century, from the region of Talaqan in northern Afghanistan, and this was also written on fine copper, intended to be rolled up, to be put inside the stupa itself.[48] While it is nowhere near as long as the Copper Scroll from Cave 3Q, its width is comparable and, like the Copper Scroll from Qumran, a key feature is its intended secrecy.

Given that the material of the scroll should be a major consideration in its interpretation, one needs to ask why copper was preferable to parchment or papyrus. The most obvious answer is that writing on copper was intended to last, as with the Talaqan example. It could not be damaged by water and its high melting point (1083 Celsius, or 1981 Fahrenheit) means it could also survive fires. So here the substance of the writing material coheres with the contents of the work, in that it is an expensive treasure in itself, containing evidence of hiding places of treasure, and it is to be secret and built to last. This implies that whatever historical crisis caused the hiding of the treasure, those who hid it had a fairly dismal view of their own survival. It is like a time capsule, made for the future.

In the *Treatise of the Vessels* there is mention that a list of treasure was written on לוח נחושת (2.11.J), "a tablet/board of copper/bronze,"[49] which may bring

---

48 Jens Braarvig and Fredrik Liland, eds, *Traces of Gandhāran Buddhism: An Exhibition of Ancient Buddhist Manuscripts in the Schøyen Collection* (Oslo: Hermes Publishing, in collaboration with Amarin Printing and Publishing Public Co. Ltd: Bangkok, 2010), 91–101; Gudrun Melzer, with Lore Sander. "A Copper Scroll Inscription from the Time of Alchon Huns," in *Buddhist Manuscripts III*, ed. Jens Braarvig and Mark Allon, Manuscripts in the Schøyen Collection 7 (Oslo: Hermes, 2006), 251–78.

49 Jellinek, *Beth ha-Midrasch*, 88.

THE COPPER SCROLL

to mind the Copper Scroll.[50] We may justifiably ask where such a notion comes from and what it means.

Interestingly Steven Weitzmann has pointed out a parallel for this kind of object in the writings of Pausanias.[51] In Book 4 (26.8), of his *Description of Greece* (ca. 150 CE), Pausanias tells the story of the Messenians who had long ago preserved the mysteries of the Great Goddesses on thin metal, rolled up into a scroll that was discovered after many generations hidden away in a bronze urn buried between two trees on a mountainside. While Weitzmann uses this as an example of how the Copper Scroll and its treasure could "fall somewhere between reality and myth",[52] what is interesting here to me is the mentality that associates writing on thin metal and its long survival over time. As Pausanias tells the story, the recovery of this metal scroll leads to the refoundation or renaissance of the Messenians and re-establishment of their temples 287 years after they were vanquished by the Spartans.

Wise (Wilmot) and Weitzmann, and also Høgenhaven,[53] use comparanda of bronze plaques,[54] but the material of the Copper Scroll is not bronze, and so comparison with bronze plaques does not really help us. References to these plaques have sometimes loosely indicated that the objects in question are made of copper, when this is not so. For example, Wise and Wilmot pointed to "use of copper" for a Demotic text from Medinet Habu, Luxor, now in Cairo's Egyptian Museum (CG 30691), which has inscribed letters in a two-column list, front and back; but it is a bronze tablet not a copper sheet.[55]

Bronze has a much higher tin content, about 12%, and includes zinc and other metals. It has a lower melting point (950 degrees Celsius or 1742 degrees Fahrenheit). It does not have the malleability of annealed copper, so one cannot press script right on to it, but rather it was and is used for inscriptions done by bronze casting. Hot metal is poured into a mould which has the inscription written in mirror image, and then the bronze hardens and the mould is

---

50 Davila, "Treatise of the Vessels," 400, n. 20. Józef T. Milik translates this as "bronze plaque" (see "Notes d'epigraphie et de topographie palestiniennes," *RB* 66 [1959]: 572). One may incidentally note that this is understood to be a separate list of items to the Treatise of Vessels itself, which itself was not inscribed on anything.

51 Steven Weitzman, "Myth, History and Mystery in the Copper Scroll," in *The Idea of Biblical Interpretation: Essays in Honor of James L. Kugel*, ed. Hindy Najman and Judith H. Newman (Leiden: Brill, 2003), 239–55.

52 Weitzmann, "Absent," 428.

53 Høgenhaven, *Cave 3 Copper Scroll*, 159–60.

54 Wise, "David Wilmot," 303–304; Weitzmann, "Absent," 433, 435.

55 Wise, "David Wilmot," 304; Sven P. Vleeming, *Some Coins of Artaxerxes and Other Short Texts in the Demotic Script Found on Various Objects Gathered from Many Publications*, Studia Demotica 5 (Leuven: Peeters, 2001), 38.

removed. It is hard and resilient, ideal for use in a public place. In short, comparisons between different media need to be quite precise.

5   Writing

In terms of the content of the scroll, it is written in Hebrew. The orthography is distinctive and the language is generally identified as an early form of Mishnaic Hebrew with a number of Greek loanwords, and even mysterious Greek letter sequences. The Mishnaic style is quite different from any other text from the Dead Sea Scrolls corpus, and includes use of the ending ין‎- instead of ים‎- for the masculine plural, and use of של‎, "of", with about 50 words consistent with Mishnaic Hebrew usage.[56] As Jesper Høgenhaven concludes: "The language of the Copper Scroll is closer to M[ishnaic] H[ebrew] than to any other known type of Hebrew. In particular, the vocabulary of 3Q15 is strikingly similar."[57]

Despite the Mishnaic style, most scholars follow the palaeography of Frank Moore Cross, who identified the script as peculiar but still coming from the mid-first century, though this was not entirely accepted.[58] Many have suggested the Copper Scroll comes from just before the Second Temple was destroyed in 70 CE, matching it with the dating of Qumran Period II. However, Milik decided differently: "As to the date of the document, further study of the complex and disparate data, discussed in detail in DJD III, makes us now lean towards the period between the two Jewish wars against the Romans, giving the year 100 as a round number."[59]

The inclusion and influence of Greek is distinctive in relation to other Dead Sea Scrolls.[60] Of 930 texts at Qumran only 27 are in Greek, with all but one

---

56   Al Wolters, "The Copper Scroll," in *The Dead Sea Scrolls after Fifty Years: A Comprehensive Assessment*, ed. Peter W. Flint and James C. Vanderkam (Leiden: Brill, 1998–99), 1:304.

57   Høgenhaven, *Cave 3 Copper Scroll*, 25, and see his discussion 154–56.

58   See Al Wolters, "Literary Analysis and the *Copper Scroll*," in *Intertestamental Essays in Honour of Józef Tadeusz Milik*, ed. Zdzisław Jan Kapera, Qumranica Mogilanensia 6 (Kraków: Enigma Press, 1992), 239–52.

59   Milik, "Copper Document," 137; idem, "Rouleau de Cuivre," 322. For detailed an analysis of the text and its relationship with Mishnaic Hebrew, see Al Wolters, "The Copper Scroll and the Vocabulary of Mishnaic Hebrew," *RevQ* 14 (1989–90): 483–95; idem, "Literary Analysis," 239–52; cf. also Frank Moore Cross, "Excursus on the Palaeographical Dating of the Copper Document," in *Les 'Petites Grottes'*, ed. Maurice Baillet, Józef T. Milik, and Roland de Vaux, DJD 3 (Oxford: Clarendon, 1962), 217–21.

60   See Matthew Richey, "The Use of Greek at Qumran: Manuscript and Epigraphic Evidence for a Marginalised Language," *DSD* 19 (2012): 177–97. A small amount of Greek is indicated in ostraca, inscriptions and a stamp from Qumran, showing its use for economic

THE COPPER SCROLL   311

being scriptural or liturgical, not original compositions. The documentary text 4Q350, a cereal list written on the back of a scrap of an older para-biblical Hebrew manuscript including the tetragrammaton (4Q460), likely is the work of someone in the Roman garrison at Qumran post 68 CE.[61] Also, among Qumran texts, only in the Copper Scroll do we find Greek loanwords.[62]

Greek loanwords can be identified early on in the Aramaic of the Book of Daniel (second century BCE) in defining certain types of musical instruments,[63] which presumably would relate to specific objects involved in Greek-style music, thus testifying to cultural influence, but loanwords for other vocabulary are another matter. Such general loanwords are, outside the Copper Scroll, first attested in documents from the Bar Kokhba period. Letters from Bar Kokhba himself (P.Yadin 54 and 57) include Greek loanwords: כאספליה from ἐν ἀσφαλεία, and אובלסה from ὄχλος.[64] The reason that so many Greek loanwords appear in such texts, and broadly in Mishnaic Hebrew, is usually explained by the fact that from sometime in the second century Greek superseded Aramaic (and Hebrew) as the main language of Palestine.[65]

In the Copper Scroll the Greek loan words are related to both architecture and objects. This suggests that the author(s) of the Copper Scroll existed in a linguistic environment in which Greek terminology was employed for such things.

As Bargil Pixner argued, the mysterious Greek letter sequences most likely refer to people with Greek names responsible for burying certain caches.

---

transactions see Richey, "Greek", 187–89; David Hamidović, "Do Qumran Inscriptions Show Hellenization of Qumran Residents?" in *Names in a Multi-Lingual, Multi-Cultural, and Multi-Ethnic Contact: Proceedings of the 23rd International Congress of Onomastic Sciences, August 17–22, 2008, York University, Toronto, Canada*, ed. Wolfgang Ahrens et al. (Toronto: York University, 2009), 465–72. However, the question is how all well these can be definitively assigned to the period before the garrison took over the site in 68 CE.

61   Hannah Cotton and Erik Larson, "4Q460/4Q350 and Tampering with Qumran Texts in Antiquity," in *Emanuel: Studies in Hebrew Bible, Septuagint, and Dead Sea Scrolls in Honor of Emanuel Tov*, ed. Shalom M. Paul et al., VTSup 94 (Leiden: Brill, 2003), 113–25.

62   Jan Joosten, "Hebrew, Aramaic and Greek in the Qumran Scrolls," in *The Oxford Handbook of the Dead Sea Scrolls*, ed. Timothy H. Lim and John J. Collins (Oxford: Oxford University Press, 2010), 355, and see Florentino García Martínez, "Greek Loanwords in the Copper Scroll," in *Jerusalem, Alexandria, Rome: Studies in Ancient Cultural Interaction in Honour of A. Hilhorst*, ed. Florentino García Martínez and Gerard P. Luttikhuizen, JSJSup 82 (Leiden: Brill, 2003), 119–45.

63   In Dan. 3:5, 7, 10 and 15. García Martínez, "Greek Loanwords," 147; Pierre Grelot, "L'orchestre de Daniel III, 5,7,10,15," *VT* 29 (1979): 23–38.

64   Scott D. Charlesworth, "Recognizing Greek Literacy in Early Roman Documents from the Judaean Desert," *BASP* 51 (2014): 188.

65   Daniel Sperber, *Greek in Talmudic Palestine* (Ramat-Gan: Bar Ilan University Press, 2012).

He read ΚΕΝ ΧΑΓ ΗΝ ΘΕ ΔΙ ΤΡ ΣΚ respectively as names found in Josephus: Κενεδαιος, Χαγειρας, Ηνναφην, Θεβουτις, Διοφαντος, Τρυφον, Σκοπας,[66] though one could cast the net wider. But this only begs the question: why *Greek* names?[67]

Scholars have long debated the extent of Greek spoken in the context of the nascent church in Judaea.[68] Certainly the language was present, especially in the Greek cities of the Decapolis and the coast. Nevertheless, for Jews it was secondary to Aramaic and Hebrew, with the latter still likely dominant in Jerusalem.[69] This is the key issue here. Despite what may have been true for Galilean marketplaces, Josephus explicitly states that his Greek learning—probably gained in his long period in Rome (*Ag. Ap* 1.1)—was extremely unusual for elite scholarly priests like him in Jerusalem; rather, his contemporaries overtly scorned anyone gaining accomplishment, judging it "common" (*Ant.* 20.262–264).[70] Preservation of the national tongue is linked with a desire to maintain national and religious identity over against various linguistic, cultural and religious threats.[71] Therefore, in the period prior to 70 CE, it would be difficult to argue that the Jerusalem scholarly elite was bathed in Greek influence, despite the existence of Greek as a language spoken and written in economic transactions and by Diaspora visitors (as the Diaspora-focused Theodotion inscription, ossuaries, ostraca and tomb inscriptions indicate). Greek language was present, but not sufficiently to impact on Aramaic or Hebrew as written down at this time by the scholarly elite. For example, a letter like 4QMMT does not contain a single Greek loan-word. Instead, Qumran Hebrew outside the Copper Scroll has numerous *Aramaic* loanwords,[72] but not Greek. Within other Hebrew texts from the Qumran caves, Greek lettering is only found in

---

66   Pixner, "Unravelling," 335.

67   As asked and explored with different possible answers by Richey, "Greek," 194–95.

68   See Jan N. Sevenster, *Do You Know Greek? How Much Greek Could the First Jewish Christians Have Known?* NovTSup 19 (Leiden: Brill, 1968).

69   Chaim Rabin, "The Historical Background of Qumran Hebrew," *ScrHier* 4 (1958): 144–61, and see idem, "Hebrew and Aramaic in the First Century," in *The Jewish People in the First Century*, ed. Shmuel Safrai and Menahem Stern (Philadephia: Fortress, 1976), 1007–39.

70   It is a common misconception that Hebrew was not a spoken language in first century Jerusalem, but this has repeatedly been shown to be erroneous: Moses H. Segal, "Mishnaic Hebrew and its Relation to Biblical Hebrew and to Aramaic," *JQR* 20 (1908): 647–737; William Chomsky, "What was the Jewish Vernacular during the Second Commonwealth?" *JQR* 42 (1951): 193–212; Joshua Grintz, "Hebrew as the Spoken and Written Language in the Last Days of the Second Temple Period," *JBL* 79 (1960): 32–47.

71   Seth Schwartz, "Language, Power and Identity," *Past and Present* 148 (1995): 21–31.

72   Joosten, "Hebrew, Aramaic and Greek," 358. For the scholarly debate, see Høgenhaven, *Cave 3 Copper Scroll*, 22–25.

THE COPPER SCROLL   313

the cryptic alphabet of 4Q186.[73] 4Q464:8 refers to the "holy tongue", that will
be restored in the Eschaton, when the people become again "pure of speech"
(line 9). This is linked with the Testament of Judah (25.1–3) where likewise the
one people of the Lord will speak one language, and in Jubilees 12.25–7 Hebrew
is the "language of the creation".[74] Why then insert Greek into this language?

One may then justifiably ask whether the Copper Scroll might belong to
the period through to early second century, as countenanced by both Albright
and Milik. This has long been mooted. Ernest-Marie Laperrousaz,[75] followed
by Ben-Zion Luria[76] and Manfred Lehmann,[77] have argued that the Copper
Scroll is a second-century artefact. They have suggested that it must relate
either to treasures connected to cultic activity in the Bar Kokhba period
(Laperrousaz), or to a third temple that existed at this time (Luria), or perhaps the treasure comprised the temple tithes and taxes collected between
the years 70 and 135 CE, probably in the first century (Lehmann). Lehmann
in particular noted the technical terms in כלי דמע, "vessels of heave-offering"
(1:9–10, III:2–3; XI:4, 10, 14; XII:6–7, cf. t. Maʿaś. Š. 5.1); *lagin* (לגין; 1:9) is from
Greek *lagunos* (λάγυνος), a type of vessel referred to in the Mishnah for stor-
ing heave-offerings (m. Ter. 9.5). The "second tithe" in Deut 14:22–26 had to be
eaten in Jerusalem, but without a Temple it had to be redeemed for money or
left unredeemed (m. Maʿaś. Š. 5.7). Likewise, with the accumulation of money
or precious metals designed to be consecrated to the Sanctuary, a baraitha preserved in the Babylonian Talmud (b. ʿAbod. Zar. 13a; b. Bek. 53a; b. Yoma 66a;
b. Šeqal. 22a) states that these "should be taken to the Dead Sea", a body of water
that would corrode the images.[78] Thus Lehmann, for such reasons, associated
the accumulation of these things with a point after the Temple was actually
destroyed.

---

73   Høgenhaven, *Cave 3 Copper Scroll*, 153.
74   Michael Stone and Esther Eshel, "The Holy Language at the End of Days in Light of a
      Qumran Fragment," *Tarbiz* 62 (1993–94): 169–77 (Hebrew); Steven Weitzman, "Why Did
      the Qumran Community Write in Hebrew?" *JAOS* 119 (1999): 35–45.
75   Ernest-Marie Laperrousaz, "Remarques sur l'origine des rouleaux de cuivre decouverts
      dans la grotte 3 de Qumran," *RHR* 159 (1961): 157–72; idem, "La grotte 3 de Qoumran et le
      « Rouleau de Cuivre »," in *Qoumrân et les Manuscrits de la mer Morte. Un cinquantenaire*,
      ed. Ernest-Marie Laperrousaz (Paris: Éditions du Cerf, 1997), 207–13.
76   Ben-Zion Luria, *The Copper Scroll from the Desert of Judah* (Jerusalem: Kiryath Sepher,
      1963) (Hebrew).
77   Manfred R. Lehmann, "Identification of the *Copper Scroll* Based on Its Technical Terms,"
      RevQ 5 (1964): 97–105; idem, "Where the Temple Tax Was Buried: The Key to Understanding
      the Copper Scroll," *BAR* 19 (Nov./Dec. 1993): 38–42.
78   Lehman, "Identification."

It is these latter suggestions about the Copper Scroll that are most intriguing to me, since the placement of the scroll in a time-frame that stretches through to the second century would make better sense of the language itself, as written, and give us further insight into the purpose of the communication. The question though is how late after the destruction of the Temple this hiding of tithes, taxes and other items could have taken place. Might this burying take us all the way through to the time of Bar Kokhba?

6   Bar Kokhba

Bar Kokhba—rightly Shimon Bar-Kosiba[79]—is himself a mystery. While it is clear that he led a Judaean revolt against the Romans ca. 132–135 CE, when his rebellion was quashed with enormous force, little is known about him from texts. For this revolt, we have no Josephus, and therefore little evidence to form a historical narrative. It seems unrest was sparked by an announcement by the Roman Emperor Hadrian:[80] Dio Cassius (*Roman History* 69.12–14) states that when Hadrian visited Judaea *en route* from Egypt to Syria (ca. 129–130 CE), he ordered that a new temple to Jupiter Capitolinus should be constructed on the Temple Mount and that Jerusalem should be rebuilt as a Roman colony, Aelia Capitolina ("The City of the Capitoline Gods"). The resulting Judaean revolt was widespread, and the results were catastrophic. Dio Cassius records that the Romans sent their best generals and massive numbers of troops, and soon 50 of the secret outposts of the rebels[81] were destroyed, 985 towns and villages were razed, 580,000 Judean fighting men were killed in battle and countless numbers of people died from starvation, disease and the burning of the towns and villages: "So, almost all of Judaea was turned into a wilderness".[82]

Given the insufficiencies of extant texts informing us of events, archaeological evidence has provided vital clues that enable us to understand the Revolt more holistically. Clearly, like the scholarly elite in Jerusalem at the time of

---

79   See Hanan Eshel, "The Bar Kochba Revolt, 132–135 CE," in *The Cambridge History of Judaism*, vol. 4: *The Late Roman-Rabbinic Period*, ed. Steven T. Katz (Cambridge: Cambridge University Press, 2006), 105–27.

80   See Dio Cassius, *Roman History* 69.12.1; cf. Eusebius, *Hist. eccl.* 4.6.1, 3; Barn. 16.4.

81   Many of these have been found; see Amos Kloner and Boaz Zissu, "Hiding Complexes in Judaea: An Archaeological and Geographical Update on the Area of the Bar Kochba Revolt," in *The Bar Kokhba Revolt Reconsidered: New Perspectives on the Second Jewish Revolt against Rome*, ed. Peter Schäfer, TSAK 100 (Tübingen: Mohr Siebeck, 2003), 181–82. We now know of over 125 subterranean hiding settlement-complexes in the Shephalah, Hebron mountains and Bethel region.

82   *Roman History* 69.14.2.

THE COPPER SCROLL   315

Josephus, this administration also favored Hebrew and wrote legends on their coins in paleo-Hebrew script. In P.Yadin 52, the author Soumaios apologises that he wrote in Greek because of an inability to write in Hebrew, but clearly expected a reader to understand,[83] which is consistent with a scenario in which the Greek language had gained ground.

In the Bar Kokhba silver coinage we see the façade of the Temple sanctuary.[84] From coins, we also learn that a Temple administration existed under a high priest named Eleazar.[85] Functions of the priesthood seem to have continued into this time.[86] This is not to say that Bar Kokhba ever rebuilt the Jerusalem Temple as such. As Lehmann has noted, it is not necessary to have a Temple building in Jerusalem for there to be Temple treasure, because some form of cult could continue without a building. Lehmann has argued that this treasure may never have been in Jerusalem, but rather stored up in various safe localities over some time. I have previously noted how Josephus describes everything to do with the Temple cult and Jewish law as still functioning through to the 90s of the first century, even though the Temple was destroyed.[87] Josephus, while always referring in the past tense to the Temple as a building, refers to the continuation of sacrifices in the present (e.g., *Ag. Ap.* 2.193–8). We should not be surprised by this: if your synagogue or church is destroyed, it does not mean you give up on worship and religious practice. After all, the conceptual template of the Temple in Exodus was a moveable tent of meeting in the desert: Judaean cultic practice was not tied to having a built structure in Jerusalem.

What we know about the Copper Scroll would cohere well then with what we know of the period after 70 CE through to the Bar Kokhba revolt, when cultic operations of some kinds continued with the hope of rebuilding the Jerusalem Temple. Tithes and taxes were "redeemed," that is, converted into money and precious metal. The evidence suggests that there was an ongoing cult and the hope of a rebuilt structure for it, and so we may quite appropriately imagine a scenario in which the High Priest and chief priests sought finally to hide what they could of what was in reality the state treasury as much as

---

83   As Catherine Hezser points out: *Jewish Literacy in Roman Palestine*, TSAJ 81 (Tübingen: Mohr Siebeck, 2001), 279.

84   See Leo Mildenberg, *The Coinage of the Bar Kokhba War*, ed. Patricia Erhart Mottahedeh, Typos: Monographien zur antiken Numismatik 6 (Aarau: Sauerländer, 1984).

85   See Emil Schürer, *The History of the Jewish People in the Age of Jesus Christ*, ed. Geza Vermes, Fergus Millar and Matthew Black (Edinburgh: T&T Clark, 1973), 1:544.

86   Philip Alexander, "What Happened to the Jewish Priesthood after 70?" in *A Wandering Galilean: Essays in Honour of Sean Freyne*, ed. Zuleika Rodgers, with Margaret Daly-Denton and Anne Fitzpatrick-McKinley, JSJSup 132 (Leiden: Brill, 2009), 29–30.

87   Joan E. Taylor, "Parting in Palestine," in *Partings: How Judaism and Christianity Became Two*, ed. Hershel Shanks (Washington, DC: Biblical Archaeology Society, 2013), 87–104.

Judean cultic funds, assuming rightly that the most horrendous circumstances would prevail.

Historically, there have always been problems in ascribing the Copper Scroll to the time of the First Revolt and the functioning Jerusalem Temple.[88] It is hard to imagine how the ancient Jewish legal school of the Essenes—as envisaged—could have played a part in hiding it. Allegro had to suggest that Qumran was briefly overtaken by the same revolutionary factions that held Jerusalem from 66 CE to make a case.[89]

Even with this switch, it is hard to imagine a scenario in which a scroll listing buried Jerusalem Temple treasure was taken to a Qumran cave in order to hide it, sometime before the Romans came and laid siege to Jerusalem. In 68 CE Qumran itself was burnt and occupied by the Romans, as they secured the region of Jericho through to En Gedi. The historian Josephus describes the arrival of Vespasian's army in Jericho and the northern Dead Sea (*War* 4.443–50), and the site of Qumran was clearly damaged at this point, as verified by evidence of Roman arrowheads and burning; the site was then occupied by a Roman garrison through to *c*.113 CE (Qumran Period III).[90] Thus the scroll would have been carefully hidden away right in the path of an invading army *before* 68. We would also have to imagine a situation in which people in league with the revolutionaries in Jerusalem journeyed a long way in order to then hide the scroll, without anyone knowing or noting that a large amount of cultic treasure was mysteriously missing. As for why the Scroll was not retrieved after the First Revolt, there seems to be an assumption that all Essenes were utterly annihilated when their site at Qumran was destroyed, which is at variance, again, with Josephus. His testimony in *Ant.* 18.18–22 indicates Pharisees, Sadducees and Essenes were still the principal legal schools in Judaea the 90s; Judaea remained a functioning province.[91]

---

88   So Dupont-Sommer, "Les rouleaux de cuivre," 28–29.

89   Allegro, *Treasure*, 124–25.

90   I have previously suggested that most of the extant scrolls comprise the remainder of a large cache buried in the caves around Qumran over a long period of time before 68 CE, and these were placed there by Essenes who lived at Qumran, reflecting their very high esteem for "ancient writings" (*War* 2.136, cf. *War* 2.159; *Ant.* 13.311). See Joan E. Taylor, 'Buried Manuscripts and Empty Tombs: The *Genizah* Hypothesis Reconsidered,' in *'Go Out and Study the Land' (Judges 18:2): Archaeological, Historical and Textual Studies in Honor of Hanan Eshel*, ed. Aren M. Maeir, Jodi Magness, and Lawrence Schiffman, JSJSup 148 (Leiden: Brill, 2011), 269–316, and with revisions in eadem, *The Essenes, the Scrolls and the Dead Sea* (Oxford: Oxford University Press, 2012), 282–95.

91   For the survival of the legal schools through to the Bar Kokhba Revolt see Taylor, *Essenes, Scrolls*, 167–72.

Moreover, Josephus indicates that the Temple treasure stayed in Jerusalem. The priests delivered this to Titus in 70 CE, when the Romans took the city (*War* 6.390–91). The Romans carried off and exhibited in an extravagant public procession what they understood to be the Temple treasure found in Jerusalem (*War* 6.282; 7.148), some of this being displayed until today on the Arch of Titus in Rome.[92] That wealthy people of Jerusalem could not get their goods out of the city is indicated by what Josephus states in *War* 7.114–15: after the war the Roman soldiers and Jewish captives managed to dig up gold, silver and precious furniture which the desperate owners had buried underground *in the city*. And the treasure seized by the Romans from the Temple was so vast it furnished the Temple of Peace in Rome, and continued to be known about (and transferred around) for centuries to come.[93] The whole point of Josephus' account is that no Temple treasure was secreted away anywhere; it was all, very sadly, lost to the Romans.

As an alternative theory, Puech's idea that the treasure was accumulated by Essene priests alienated from the Temple, who stored massive amounts of tithes and other items separately over many years, relies on a fundamental assertion of the Essenes' total separation from the Jerusalem Temple, but this is simply not what is stated by Josephus. As far as the Scrolls are concerned, attitudes to the issues concerning the Temple administration and purity are complex, and Hanne von Weissenberg has helpfully noted that "the group responsible for the authoring of 4QMMT, even though criticizing the current practices at the Jerusalem Temple, still considered it to be the only legitimate cultic place".[94] The theory relies on an outdated notion of a small, sectarian Qumran community that had nothing to do with Jerusalem and the Temple.

As for the extraordinary idea that any priests collected up and withheld tithes, artefacts and funds destined otherwise for the Temple, this does not square with the fact that Josephus and Philo both esteem the much-respected Essenes very highly and would hardly do so of a Temple-rejecting and tithe-hoarding marginal splinter group. The Essene prophet Menahem is apparently in the Temple when he predicts that Herod will be king (*Ant.* 15.368–71).[95]

---

92   For a critique of the "Jerusalem Temple treasure" hypothesis, see Goranson, "Sectarianism," 285.

93   See Sean Kingsley, *God's Gold: A Quest for the Lost Temple Treasures of Jerusalem* (London: John Murray, 2006); Joan E. Taylor, "The Nea Church: Were the Temple Treasures Hidden Here?" *BAR* 34/1 (2008): 50–59, 82.

94   Hanne M. von Weissenberg, "The *Centrality* of the *Temple* in 4QMMT," in *The Dead Sea Scrolls: Texts and Context*, ed. Charlotte Hempel, STDJ 90 (Leiden: Brill, 2010), 298.

95   For further discussion see Taylor, *Essenes, Scrolls and the Dead Sea*, 97–99.

7   The Archaeological Context of Cave 3Q

At this point, we need to turn back to the artefact itself. We have already concluded that the scroll was written and rolled up in haste and placed in a cave soon after its completion. What can we learn further about it if we examine the archaeological context in which it was found?

As noted above, Cave 3Q was excavated in March 1952, by a team headed by Henri de Contenson, and was turned over quite thoroughly. What was left as a large opening was actually a cut into the original cave, because the front part had collapsed in antiquity (see below). It was excavated again in 1986, by a team led by Joseph Patrich.[96]

William Reed stated in his report on the discovery of the Copper Scroll rolls that "[t]he date of the pottery with which they were associated, and the similarity of several small pieces of inscribed parchment in Cave 3Q to the Dead Sea Scrolls make it certain that the rolls were placed on the floor of the cave prior to 70 AD"[97] However, in terms of this evidence, in fact not all items in the cave were catalogued. Those that were are listed as being: 5 jars, one of which had the letter *teth* written twice; 21 lids; 2 jugs; and a lamp. De Vaux also noted there were uncatalogued fragments of around 30 cylindrical jars, and fragments of at least 5 lids,[98] which—assuming cylindrical jars usually contained scrolls—indicates that the original number of manuscripts placed in this cave would have been considerable. The "inscribed parchment" that survived have been identified as parts of Ezekiel (3Q1), Psalms (3Q2), Lamentations (3Q3), a pesher on Isaiah (3Q4), Jubilees (3Q5), an unidentified hymn (3Q6), probably the Testament of Judah (3Q7), and some unidentified texts (3Q14).

However, the dating of the pottery in Qumran caves is actually very difficult because many of the forms of the mid-first century continued on into the second century, and the typology of Qumran cylindrical jars has never been linked definitively to chronological parameters. The one indicative (or diagnostic) item of pottery is the lamp, and it is now missing from the Qumran stores. Fortunately, it was drawn and published in DJD III, where it was identified originally as a "Herodian" type lamp correlating with Qumran Period II

---

96   Joseph Patrich, "Khirbet Qumran in Light of New Archaeological Explorations in the Qumran Caves," in *Methods of Investigation of the Dead Sea Scrolls and the Khirbet Qumran Site: Present Realities and Future Prospects*. ed. Michael O. Wise, Norman Golb, John J. Collins, and Dennis G. Pardee, Annals of the New York Academy of Sciences 722 (New York, NY: New York Academy of Sciences, 1994), 77.

97   Reed, "Qumran Caves Expedition," 10.

98   De Vaux, *"Petites Grottes,"* 7–8, 201.

THE COPPER SCROLL   319

(ca. 4 CE through to 68 CE).[99] Since the 1950s and 1960s, the chronological parameters of lamps overall have been refined. Jolanta Młynarczyk has published a new analysis and drawing in her study on Qumran lamps, and she dates this lamp differently than de Vaux.[100] From her study it is clear that this type of lamp itself indeed is a "Herodian" (knife-pared or spatulate) lamp, but the type (036.2) made and used from the first century CE (or very late first century BCE) through to the middle of the second century CE.[101] Thus, taken on its own, the vitally important lamp suggests a use of the cave anywhere between these parameters.

Normally one would consider an object in the light of the assemblage in which it is found in the same stratum, unless there are intrusive artefacts and/or stratigraphical disturbances. However, sequences of deposits in caves are often difficult to understand, because caves do not usually have much of a stratigraphy. In terms of sequences, earthquake falls can provide some perspectives. Without rockfall, and especially if the cave entrance is sealed for a time, objects deposited 100 years apart can easily lie on the same level.

So what do we know about the morphology of the cave? From the original descriptions[102] and Patrich's re-excavation and important plan, on which Figure 8.7 is based, it is apparent that Cave 3Q was originally part of a larger cave (10 m wide), but the front had collapsed, leaving only a smaller cavity.[103] When the explorers of 1952 found Cave 3Q, the way into the cave was sealed shut with fallen rocks, but potsherds intermixed with these gave a clue to the

---

99 Baillet, Milik and de Vaux, "*Petites Grottes*," Fig. 5:6, Pl. VII.

100 It was not included in the original study of Qumran lamps made by Jolanta Młynarczyk, "Terracotta Oil Lamps from Qumran," *RB* 120 (2013): 99–133, but was included in her subsequent study, "Terracotta Oil Lamps (Roland de Vaux's Excavation of the Caves)," in *The Caves of Qumran: Proceedings of the International Conference, Lugano 2014*, ed. Marcello Fidanzio, STDJ 118 (Leiden: Brill, 2016), 115, and see Fig. 7.6, p. 120. She states in terms of the analysis: "GQ 8–12 (Qumran Type 036.2, see Figure 7.6). Nozzle with a part of wall and lamp top; traces of burning at wick hole. Extant L.4.9, extant W. 4.6; W. nozzle 2.9. Fabric: gritty but dense, dark reddish brown with partial dark grey core and many minute white grits; surface: beige to light grey (interpreted as couverte blanche by Baillet, Milik and de Vaux), rather smooth" (115). She labels the cave GQ 8–12, in line with the original caves expedition numeration. Since some readers may not know that GQ 8 is indeed Cave 3Q they may not understand the significance of her discussion.

101 Młynarczyk, "Terracotta Oil Lamps," 108–12; idem, "Caves," 113.

102 For useful summaries of reports of the discoveries in Cave 3Q and Contenson's own views, see Laperrousaz, "La grotte 3 de Qoumran," 207–13.

103 De Vaux, "*Petites Grottes*," 7, states that this is 3 × 2 m. wide but this is all that survives of a larger collapsed cave, apparently stretching to the south, where the workmen are digging in Fig. 8.2.

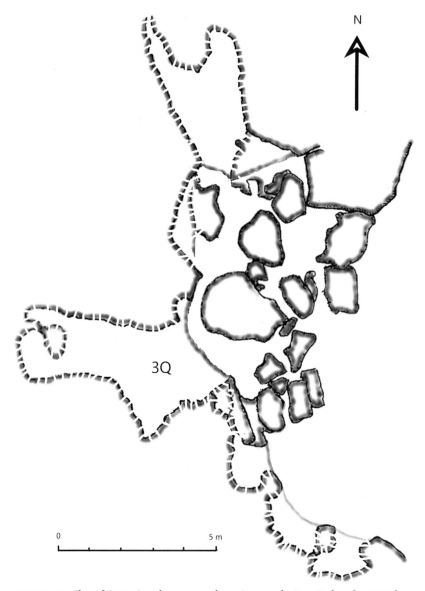

FIGURE 8.7 Plan of Cave 3Q and its surroundings. Drawing by Joan Taylor after Patrich, "Khirbet Qumran," Figure 2, 77

archaeological team that they should break through this stone collapse.[104] The initial team found sherds *under* the outer fallen rocks, from pottery that would

---

104 See Roland de Vaux, *Archaeology and the Dead Sea Scrolls* (London: Oxford University Press, 1973), 95: "Its mouth had been blocked and the Bedouin did not know of its existence"; cf. idem, "Exploration," 555.

THE COPPER SCROLL   321

originally have been well within the cave. The original entrance had collapsed away. The excavation team cleared away collapse blocking the cave with picks, as can been seen in the ASOR photograph taken at the time (Figure 8.2).[105] From the photograph it is clear that the cave lay west of large fallen boulders. There is excavated soil thrown eastwards, lying under where the men are standing behind a large boulder, and also excavation utensils in front of a boulder, with another area of excavated soil. Contenson seems to be leaning with his right arm on an obscured boulder. This means they excavated westwards from the boulders into the subterranean area they understood to be Cave 3Q.

Inside the cave there was a quantity of broken jars and lids mixed with debris. At the back of this area there were layers of fallen shingle in which there were fragments of textiles, blackened leather, and the manuscript fragments, with just a few sherds. While Reed stated that the rolls were on the floor of the cave,[106] elsewhere, the two rolls are described as being on a "ledge" or "niche" in the northern part of the cave. The two rolls of the Copper Scroll were found lying, one of top of the other against the wall of the cave, behind a large boulder, near the corner to the main chamber.[107] The rolls were also set apart, away from the broken jars and lids. But the boulders, as can be seen from Figure 8.2a, lay outside the subterranean cavity, not inside.

Pixner, who clarified matters with Contenson for his article, wrote that it was *after* the deposit of the Copper Scroll and the jars in the cave that "[a] huge part of the ceiling caved in right in front of it, hiding the C[opper] S[croll] in a sort of niche and barring all access to it."[108] So the cave collapse at the front of the cave was a cave collapse in front of the Copper Scroll.

Reed suggested that the cave itself was "apparently closed by a severe earthquake shortly after the rolls were placed in it".[109] However, while the collapse of the front part of the cave is certain, there was a question about whether the boulder collapse was "shortly after" the deposit of either the manuscripts or the Copper Scroll. Clearly, at some point the cave ceiling collapse smashed surrounding jars, with the sherds and their contents buried in 30–40 cm of

---

105   See Jean-Baptiste Humbert, "Cacher et se cacher à Qumrân: grottes et refuges. morphologie, fonctions, anthropologie," in *The Caves of Qumran: Proceedings of the International Conference, Lugano 2014*, ed. Marcello Fidanzio, STDJ 118 (Leiden: Brill, 2016), 44–45, Figs 2.9A and 2.9B.

106   Reed, "Qumran Caves Expedition," 12.

107   See de Vaux, "*Petites Grottes*," 201. Noting the enormous stone that was assumed to have fallen *after* the deposit of the rolls, de Vaux writes, "un énorme bloc est tombé du plafond très peu en avant des rouleaux et c'est une chance qu'ils aient été préserves."

108   Pixner, "Unravelling," 327.

109   Reed, "Qumran Caves Expedition," 12.

debris.[110] The Copper Scroll is itself testimony to a major event of post-deposit collapse because stone dust was pushed deep inside the interstices of the rolls, as Wright Baker observed:[111]

> The extremely fine compacted powder of stone-dust which completely filled the interstices of the scroll could usually, when accessible, be removed by brushing, but in some places, apparently in the presence of moisture, had formed an intensely hard stony layer which instantly blunted a steel tool and could only be removed by grinding or by prising the separate grains apart. In some places this matter formed a rough layer intensely bonded to the body material of the scrolls and sometimes locked areas of contact; at others it had the appearance of loosely attached stone droplets, or of a stalactitic incrustation covering thick layers of the green matter.

However, it is not clear when the collapse happened that propelled so many particles inside the scroll. At some point the collapse of the front part of the cave destroyed the original entrance, to the east, but rendered it accessible for some time to rats and other animals: rats nests found in the western passage testified to their healthy appetite for ancient manuscripts.[112] These manuscripts were available to the rats for consumption, and therefore their activity took place after the jars were smashed and the manuscripts within them were exposed and vulnerable.[113] Contenson noted that other animals used the cave, because there was a smelly layer to dig through:

> Le sol était constitué sur une trentaine de centimètres d'une poussière malodorante qui révélait la fréquentation de la grotte par les chauves-souris, les hyènes et les damans.
>
> C'est à l'emplacement des nids de ces derniers, sympathiques rongeurs dont la chair rappelle celle du lapin de garenne, que l'on retrouvait les

---

110 De Vaux, "*Petites Grottes*," 7–8.

111 Wright Baker, "Notes 'Bronze'," 48; idem, "Notes Copper," 205.

112 De Vaux, "Exploration," 555, 557; idem, "*Petites Grottes*," 8; Pixner, "Unravelling," 327–28.

113 For the archaeological evidence for the burial of manuscripts wrapped in linen being placed inside the cylindrical jars in different Qumran caves, see discussion in Taylor, *Essenes, Scrolls and Dead Sea*, 282–95, though my initial acceptance that linen was impregnated with bitumen to seal the jars was unwarranted. The jars were more likely sealed with clay jar stoppers.

THE COPPER SCROLL 323

morceaux de tissus, de cuir noirci et quelques petits fragments de parchemin inscrit.[114]

This clearly also indicates that the animals were feeding very well on something in the cave: the many manuscripts.

However, when in 1986 the team headed by Joseph Patrich re-excavated Cave 3Q,[115] it was noted that an ancient very much larger cave had suffered partial collapse long ago. This ancient cave had two arms, one to the west and one to the north, with a central area where the boulders now lay (presently outside) (see Figure 8.7). Patrich's team broke boulders to check if any sherds were located under these and found nothing but sherds from the Chalcolithic era.[116] This confirms it was only the western 'arm' and its environs that was the Roman-era Cave 3Q as defined by the initial excavation team in 1952. There is nevertheless a question about how far to the east the cave of the Roman era stretched. If we do not know this, we cannot say whether the Copper Scroll was near the front of the cave, or some way in.

Earthquakes can open and close entrances to caves over the centuries many times, and in this earthquake zone we cannot really know how many times the entrance could have been blocked up—by humans or earthquakes—and opened again, or how many times jars were smashed by rockfall. A cave closed in antiquity can be open now, and vice versa. We cannot know the processes of the collapse of the front part of the cave. If manuscripts (in the jars, with lids) were placed in 3Q before 68 CE, and the cave was sealed shut by people, we could well imagine a scenario in which the cave was subject to an earthquake that opened it, only to have another earthquake collapse the opening, and a further earthquake collapse more of the cave inside, and so on.[117]

Archaeological remains in this region testify to the fact that in ca. 135 CE Bar Kokhba refugees were looking for caves here: as mentioned above, we know

---

114 Henri de Contenson, "La découverte et la fouille de la grotte au « Rouleau de Cuivre »," in *Qoumrân et les Manuscrits de la mer Morte. Un cinquantenaire*, ed. Ernest-Marie Laperrousaz (Paris: Éditions du Cerf, 1997), 205.

115 Patrich, "Khirbet Qumran," 77.

116 Patrich states: "During periods Ib and II at Qumran the shape of this cave was very much like that at the start of our excavation. It was a quite open recess, exposed to daylight, not a deep and dark cave suitable for hiding precious writings" ("Khirbet Qumran," 77). This does not at all cohere with what the first excavators reported, that the cave was entirely blocked up by rockfall. Patrich seems to be describing the state of the cave in the Chalcolithic period, not the Roman.

117 Pixner suggests that there was no way of getting to the niche in which the Copper Scroll was found with the ceiling collapse of the main chamber, but, as noted, this ceiling collapse happened after the Copper Scroll was deposited.

of many other caves in the immediate vicinity where Bar Kokhba refugees hid from the Romans; they even encamped at Qumran.[118] It is possible that a cave previously sealed was open, on account of an earthquake. There was a strong earthquake recorded as happening ca. 113–115 CE, which would be after (we may presume) the jars with manuscripts were placed in the cave, and this earthquake probably caused severe damage and rifts in the Qumran settlement itself, finishing off any chance of settlement (Period III) at the site.[119] Strangely, an early newspaper report states that the Copper Scroll was found with Bar Kokhba coins,[120] but these were never mentioned again. The type of lamp could give us a clue not to the time of the deposit of the jars, but of the Copper Scroll.

There is one body of archaeological evidence from Cave 3Q that might have held the clue to more refined dating: the organic remains. These included fragments of leather and textiles, all of which could be radiocarbon dated. However, most of the textiles discovered by Contenson had gone missing at the time of the Qumran textile study undertaken by Mireille Bélis.[121] She noted one bag of uncleaned linen with some wood. No textiles were found in the excavation done by Patrich, and, in terms of the current IAA holdings, they have no organic remains from Cave 3Q.[122]

In short, the archaeological context of Cave 3Q indicates that the Copper Scroll was deposited in a cave either at the same time as or after many cylindrical jars containing manuscripts were deposited, and at some point(s) later the eastern ceiling and entrance of this Roman-era cave collapsed. The material artefact, the language and the archaeology suggest it could well have been deposited after 68 CE.

Oddly, Jesper Høgenhaven notes that de Vaux observed that the cylindrical jars must have touched the low ceiling of this cave, and thus "[t]his description

---

118   Joan E. Taylor, "The Qumran Caves in their Regional Context: A Chronological Review with a Focus on Bar Kokhba Assemblages," in *The Caves of Qumran: Proceedings of the International Conference, Lugano 2014*, ed. Marcello Fidanzio, STDJ 118 (Leiden: Brill, 2016), 7–33.

119   Taylor, *Essenes, Scrolls and Dead Sea*, 265.

120   Report in the *New York Times*, Tuesday, April 1st, 1952, less than 2 weeks after the discovery. This article was based on the report by the Religious News Service from Jerusalem, March 31, 1952 and appeared on p. 13, col. 6, see Lefkovits, *Copper Scroll*, 2. However, de Vaux later indicated that no coins were found in any of the caves, "Exploration," 553.

121   Mireille Bélis, "Les Textiles," in *Khirbet Qumran and 'Aïn Feshkha II: Études d'anthropologie, de physique et de chimie*, ed. Jean-Baptiste Humbert and Jan Gunneweg, NTOA, Series archaeologica 3 (Gottingen: Vandenhoeck & Ruprecht; Fribourg: Editions universitaires, 2003), 253.

122   Orit Shamir, Curator of IAA Organic Materials Unit, email of 29/4/19.

THE COPPER SCROLL   325

makes the assumption of a second deposit in the very same cave extremely difficult."[123] This implies that the people who record 64 caches of treasure buried in numerous locations (a procedure that would have required exceptional labor) were absolutely deterred by having to crawl into the depths of a dark cave full of jars in order to bury the crucial item that revealed the whereabouts of the hiding places. Surely, such a cave would have seemed an ideal location to hide it.

In fact, even with an assumption that the boulders fell after the deposit of the rolls, de Vaux himself thought that the rolls could possibly be a later deposit, and adopted an agnostic position in print.[124] He wrote: "Ces indices archéologiques ne suffisent pas à prouver que les rouleaux ont été déposés après la poterie et les autres textes mais ils ne s'opposent pas à une telle conclusion." Milik more firmly thought they were a later deposit.[125] Indeed, Contenson, excavator of the cave, responding to the queries of Laperoussaz, by directly affirming the rolls could well belong to the time of the Second Revolt.

> Pour ce qui est de la grotte 3Q, je reconnais que ses [de Vaux's] descriptions manquent de précision. Je suis tout à fait convaincu par l'opinion du P. de Vaux que les rouleaux de cuivre ont pu être déposés plus tard que les manuscrits, ainsi que par les arguments de Milik et les tiens pour une date liée à la Seconde Révolte Juive.[126]

8   Readers

The final point to consider here in terms of the communication of the scroll is the intended readers. We have seen that the medium for the content was likely chosen for its longevity at a time that there was a threat to the survival of not only the treasure but also the nation. The writing, rolling of the scroll and hiding away were all done quickly.

The communication was thus preserved, but for whom? Given that the medium was intended to preserve content for some point in the future, in this case the audience is imagined. We can assume a character for them by implied

---

123   Høgenhaven, *Cave 3 Copper Scroll*, 145, noting de Vaux, "Exploration," 555.
124   De Vaux, "*Petites Grottes*," 201.
125   Milik, "Rouleau de cuivre," 277.
126   Laperrousaz, "La grotte 3 de Qoumran," 210, quoting personal correspondence with Contenson.

indicators within the content. We will here consider briefly what is implied in order to define better the rationale for the communication.

In the first place, there is the matter of the Scroll's hiddenness, and not for a prophylactic reason. It is hidden to be found at some point and read. It is assumed that the future readers can read the language and the script in which it is written. In the second century, in Judaea, there is a question about the extent of real literacy, with Catherine Hezser arguing for little literacy, and Michael Wise arguing for somewhat more, on the basis of material from the Bar Kokhba period.[127] While Aramaic was the main spoken language of Galilee and wider Syria, with Nabataean on the east of the Dead Sea and Greek spoken in numerous Hellenistic cities, here we have a Mishnaic Hebrew text, which assumes that the readers understood a language that was largely the preserve of Judaeans.[128]

The future readers are also assumed to be Judaean, and quite local, in that they are expected to know locations without any explanation. The communication begins without introduction and with a simple indication of buried treasure, if we read the beginning as: "In the ruin which is in the Valley of Achor, under the steps leading eastward ..." (I:1–2). The readers apparently are meant to know where the Valley of Achor is, and that there is a ruin in it. There are numerous places identified that imply an expectation of naming continuity. For example, early on there is a place named Kohlit or Kahelet (I:9).[129] The entire document finishes with mention of another copy of the document buried in a place north of Kahelet (XII:10); it is therefore clear through the internal logic of the text that Kahelet is a central locus for the burial of the treasure. But this location is not a famous place known in our literature from the Roman period, or from biblical literature, and yet it is assumed the reader knows where it is. One would need to have lived in Judaea, or inherit information about Judaea, to know this.

The author may have hoped that the names of places would be remembered for a long time, and that the places themselves would remain relatively unchanged, but clearly there is a sense that the readers are expected to be able to navigate the geography, the water systems and structures, as if these would endure and be recognizable. The readers are not then imagined as outsiders.

---

127   Hezser, *Jewish Literacy*; Michael O. Wise, *Language and Literacy in Roman Judaea: A Study of the Bar Kokhba Documents*, AYBRL (New Haven, CT: Yale University Press, 2015). For variant types of literacy, see Chris Keith, *Jesus' Literacy: Scribal Culture and the Teacher from Galilee*, LNTS 413 (London: Bloomsbury T&T Clark, 2011), 71–123.

128   See the survey of current thinking on spoken language in Wise, *Language and Literacy*, 11–13.

129   Lefkovits, *Copper Scroll*, 185.

THE COPPER SCROLL 327

They are locals who read Hebrew, and know this environment, even if they are the generations of the future. They are fellow Jews, who will use this treasure again, as restorers, who will know what to do with the treasure. They know the artefacts, they understand the significance of the quantities of things, and yet they are not aware of the hiding places until they read the content of the Scroll, as if oral continuity might not be reliable or sufficient. It is assumed that they will be able to unroll the Scroll (annealing it anew) and read it, without the help of a cutting blade. They are thus a kind of dream group of the future, a source of hope for final victory despite imminent annihilation. Such annihilation is implied, or else there is no reason for the treasure to be hidden. The Copper Scroll was written to be hidden, then, but also the content was preserved with an expectation that it would be retrieved, read, and acted upon.

9   Conclusion

In this paper we have re-visited the Copper Scroll as a type of communication by considering initially the medium in which the content is found. The material of copper is particularly fine, and probably employed for its longevity. This implies that those responsible for the content were an elite group who could afford copper, and who could write and read Hebrew. They sought to send a message to a future group in circumstances that were particularly threatening. The style of language and script employed would match with what we know of Hebrew in the second or later centuries, and therefore in this study the historical circumstances of the Bar Kokhba revolt in 132–135 CE were explored and evidence was found to indicate that a Temple cult was maintained at this time. Thus, the scroll would fit a scenario in which priestly circles sought to preserve the cult treasure and artefacts from an advancing Roman army at a time Judaeans were suffering a horrific genocide. The "success" of the Roman program of annihilation was absolute. Unlike the circumstances after 70 CE, now there was no one to retrieve this document.

We considered the archaeology of Cave 3Q, and noted that the original entrance on the eastern side of the cave collapsed close to where the rolls were placed, but we do not know how far in they were located in the Roman-era cave, because the original entrance is gone. They were clearly not positioned right at the back (in the west), or in among the jars. Nothing precludes us from suggesting that the Copper Scroll was left as a deposit in the second century, very carefully hidden and left there for future readers. These readers, implied in the content, are imagined as local and elite, knowledgeable about locations and able to read Hebrew, and assumed as having aspirations to restore the cult once the treasure is retrieved. The Copper Scroll is ultimately, in this case, a testimony of hope.

Bibliography

Alexander, Philip S. "What Happened to the Jewish Priesthood after 70?" Pages 3–34 in *A Wandering Galilean: Essays in Honour of Sean Freyne*. Edited by Zuleika Rodgers, with Margaret Daly-Denton and Anne Fitzpatrick-McKinley. JSJSup 132. Leiden: Brill, 2009.

Allegro, John M. *The Treasure of the Copper Scroll*. Garden City, NY: Doubleday, 1960.

Allegro, John M. "The Copper Scroll from Qumran." *Restaurator* 1 (1969): 13–19.

Baillet, Maurice, Józef T. Milik and Roland de Vaux, eds. *Les 'Petites Grottes'*. DJD 3. Oxford: Clarendon, 1962.

Baker, Henry Wright. "Notes on the Opening of the 'Bronze' Scrolls from Qumran." *BJRL* 39 (1956): 45–56.

Baker, Henry Wright. "Notes on the Opening of the Copper Scrolls from Qumran." Pages 203–10 in *Les 'Petites Grottes'*. Edited by Maurice Baillet, Józef T. Milik and Roland de Vaux. DJD 3. Oxford: Clarendon, 1962.

Barkay, Gabriel. "The Priestly Benediction on Silver Plaques from Ketef Hinnom Jerusalem." *Tel Aviv* 19 (1992): 139–92.

Barker, G. W., O. H. Creighton, D. D. Gilbertson, C. O. Hunt, D. J. Mattingly, S. J. McLaren, D. C. Thomas, and G. C. Morgan. "The Wadi Faynan Project, Southern Jordan: A Preliminary Report on Geomorphology and Landscape Archaeology." *Levant* 29 (1997): 19–40.

Bélis, Mireille. "Les Textiles." Pages 206–76 in *Khirbet Qumran and 'Aïn Feshkha* II: *Études d'anthropologie, de physique et de chimie*. Edited by Jean-Baptiste Humbert and Jan Gunneweg. NTOA, Series archaeologica 3. Gottingen: Vandenhoeck & Ruprecht; Fribourg: Editions universitaires, 2003.

Braarvig, Jens, and Fredrik Liland, eds. *Traces of Gandhāran Buddhism: An Exhibition of Ancient Buddhist Manuscripts in the Schøyen Collection*. Oslo: Hermes Publishing, in collaboration with Amarin Printing and Publishing Public Co. Ltd: Bangkok, 2010.

Brizemeure, Daniel, Noël Lacoudre, and Émile Puech. *Le Rouleau de cuivre de la grotte 3 de Qumrân (3Q15): expertise, restauration, epigraphie*. 2 vols. STDJ 55/1–2. Leiden: Brill/École Biblique et Archéologique Française de Jérusalem/EDF Foundation, 2006.

Cargill, Robert. "On the Insignificance and Abuse of the Copper Scroll," July 2009, at https://www.bibleinterp.com/opeds/copper.html.

Charlesworth, Scott D. "Recognizing Greek Literacy in Early Roman Documents from the Judaean Desert." *BASP* 51 (2014): 161–89.

Chomsky, William. "What was the Jewish Vernacular during the Second Commonwealth?" *JQR* 42 (1951): 193–212.

Contenson, Henri de. "La découverte et la fouille de la grotte au « Rouleau de Cuivre »." Pages 205–206 in *Qoumrân et les Manuscrits de la mer Morte. Un cinquantenaire.* Edited by Ernest-Marie Laperrousaz. Paris: Éditions du Cerf, 1997.

Cotton, Hannah, and Erik Larson. "4Q460/4Q350 and Tampering with Qumran Texts in Antiquity." Pages 113–25 in *Emanuel: Studies in Hebrew Bible, Septuagint, and Dead Sea Scrolls in Honor of Emanuel Tov.* Edited by Shalom M. Paul, Robert A. Kraft, Lawrence H. Schiffman, and Weston W. Fields. VTSup 94. Leiden: Brill, 2003.

Cross, Frank Moore. "Excursus on the Palaeographical Dating of the Copper Document." Pages 217–221 in *Les 'Petites Grottes'.* Edited by Maurice Baillet, Józef T. Milik, and Roland de Vaux. DJD 3. Oxford: Clarendon, 1962.

Davila, James R. "Scriptural Exegesis in the *Treatise of the Vessels*, a Legendary Account of the Hiding of the Temple Treasures." Pages 45–61 in *With Letters of Light: Studies in the Dead Sea Scrolls, Early Jewish Apocalypticism, Magic and Mysticism in Honor of Rachel Elior. Edited by* Daphne V. Arbel and Andrei A. Orlov. Ekstasis: Religious Experience from Antiquity to the Middle Ages 2. Berlin: De Gruyter, 2011.

Davila, James R. "Treatise of the Vessels (*Massekhet Kelim*)." Pages 1:393–409 in *Old Testament Pseudepigrapha: More Noncanonical Scriptures.* Edited by Richard J. Bauckham, James R. Davila, Alex Panayotov. Grand Rapids, MI: Eerdmans, 2013.

Dupont-Sommer, Andre. "Deux lamelles d'argent à inscription hébréo-araméenne trouvées à Ağabeyli (Turquie)." *Jahrbuch für Kleinasiatische Forschung* 1 (1950–51): 201–17.

Dupont-Sommer, Andre. *The Essene Writings from Qumran.* Oxford: Basil Blackwell, 1961.

Elitzur-Leiman, Rivka. "A Copper Amulet." Pages 616–19 in Uzi Leibner (ed.), *Khirbet Wadi Ḥammam: A Roman-Period Village and Synagogue in the Lower Galilee.* Edited by Uzi Leibner. Qedem Report 13. Jerusalem: Hebrew University of Jerusalem, 2018.

Eshel, Hanan. "The Bar Kochba Revolt, 132–135 CE." Pages 105–27 in *The Cambridge History of Judaism*, vol. 4: *The Late Roman-Rabbinic Period.* Edited by Steven T. Katz. Cambridge: Cambridge University Press, 2006.

Eshel, Hanan, and Rivka Leiman. "Jewish Amulets Written on Metal Scrolls." *Journal of Ancient Judaism* 1 (2010): 189–99.

García Martínez, Florentino. *The Dead Sea Scrolls Translated: The Qumran Texts in English.* 2nd ed. Leiden: Brill, 1996.

García Martínez, Florentino. "Greek Loanwords in the Copper Scroll." Pages 119–45 in *Jerusalem, Alexandria, Rome: Studies in Ancient Cultural Interaction in Honour of A. Hilhorst.* Edited by Florentino García Martínez and Gerard P. Luttikhuizen. JSJSup 82. Leiden: Brill, 2003.

García Martínez, Florentino, and Eibert J. C. Tigchelaar. *The Dead Sea Scrolls Study Edition.* 2 vols. Leiden: Brill, 1997.

Goranson, Stephen. "Sectarianism, Geography and the Copper Scroll." *JJS* 43 (1992): 282–87.

Grelot, Pierre. "L'orchestre de Daniel III, 5,7,10,15." *VT* 29 (1979): 23–38.

Grintz, Joshua. "Hebrew as the Spoken and Written Language in the Last Days of the Second Temple Period." *JBL* 79 (1960): 32–47.

Hamidović, David. "Do Qumran Inscriptions Show Hellenization of Qumran Residents?" Pages 465–72 in *Names in a Multi-Lingual, Multi-Cultural, and Multi-Ethnic Contact: Proceedings of the 23rd International Congress of Onomastic Sciences, August 17–22, 2008, York University, Toronto, Canada.* Edited by Wolfgang Ahrens, André Lapierre, Grant Smith, María Figueredo, and Sheila Embleton. Toronto: York University, 2009.

Hauptman, Andreas. *The Archaeometallurgy of Copper: Evidence from Faynan, Jordan.* New York, NY: Springer, 2007.

Hezser, Catherine. *Jewish Literacy in Roman Palestine.* TSAJ 81. Tübingen: Mohr Siebeck, 2001.

Høgenhaven, Jesper. *The Cave 3 Copper Scroll: A Symbolic Journey.* STDJ 132. Leiden: Brill, 2020.

Humbert, Jean-Baptiste. "Cacher et se cacher à Qumrân: grottes et refuges. morphologie, fonctions, anthropologie." Pages 34–63 in *The Caves of Qumran: Proceedings of the International Conference, Lugano 2014.* Edited by Marcello Fidanzio. STDJ 118. Leiden: Brill, 2016.

Jellinek, Adolph. *Beth ha-Midrasch: Sammlung kleiner Midraschim und Vermischter Abhandlungen aus der ältern jüdischen Literatur.* Leipzig: F. Nies, 1876.

Johnson, William A. *Readers and Reading Culture in the High Roman Empire: A Study of Elite Communities.* Classical Culture and Society. Oxford: Oxford University Press, 2010.

Joosten, Jan. "Hebrew, Aramaic and Greek in the Qumran Scrolls." Pages 351–74 in *The Oxford Handbook of the Dead Sea Scrolls.* Edited by Timothy H. Lim and John J. Collins. Oxford: Oxford University Press, 2010.

Kafafi, Zeidan A. "New Insights on the Copper Mines of Wadi Faynan/Jordan." *PEQ* 146 (2014): 263–80.

Keith, Chris. *Jesus' Literacy: Scribal Culture and the Teacher from Galilee.* LNTS 413. London: Bloomsbury, 2011.

Kingsley, Sean. *God's Gold: A Quest for the Lost Temple Treasures of Jerusalem.* London: John Murray, 2006.

Klein-Franke, Felix. "Eine aramäische Tabella devotionis (T.Colon. inv. nr. 6)." *ZPE* 7 (1971): 47–52.

Kloner, Amos, and Boaz Zissu. "Hiding Complexes in Judaea: An Archaeological and Geographical Update on the Area of the Bar Kochba Revolt." Pages 181–216 in *The Bar Kokhba Revolt Reconsidered: New Perspectives on the Second Jewish Revolt against Rome*. Edited by Peter Schäfer. TSAK 100. Tübingen: Mohr Siebeck, 2003.

Kotansky, Roy D. *Greek Magical Amulets: The Inscribed Gold, Silver, Copper and Bronze Lamellae*, Part 1: *Published Texts of Known Provenance*. Papyrologica Coloniensia 22/1. Opladen: Westdeutscher Verlag, 1994.

Kuhn, Karl G. "Les Rouleaux de Cuivre de Qumran." *RB* 61 (1954): 193–205.

Kuhn, Karl G. "Der gegenwärtige Stand der Erforschung der in Palästina neu gefundenen hebräischen Handschriften 33. Bericht über neue Qumranfunde und über die Öffnung der Kupferrollen." *TLZ* 81 (1956): 541–46.

Laperrousaz, Ernest-Marie. "Remarques sur l'origine des rouleaux de cuivre decouverts dans la grotte 3 de Qumran." *Revue de l'histoire des religions* 159 (1961): 157–72.

Laperrousaz, Ernest-Marie. "La grotte 3 de Qoumran et le « Rouleau de Cuivre »." Pages 207–13 in *Qoumrân et les Manuscrits de la mer Morte. Un cinquantenaire*. Edited by Ernest-Marie Laperrousaz. Paris: Éditions du Cerf, 1997.

Lefkovits, Judah. *The Copper Scroll (3Q15): A Reevaluation, A New Reading, Translation, and Commentary*. STDJ 25. Leiden: Brill, 1999.

Lehmann, Manfred R. "Identification of the *Copper Scroll* Based on Its Technical Terms." *RevQ* 5 (1964): 97–105.

Lehmann, Manfred R. "Where the Temple Tax Was Buried: The Key to Understanding the Copper Scroll." *BAR* 19 (Nov./Dec. 1993): 38–42.

Luria, Ben-Zion. *The Copper Scroll from the Desert of Judah*. Jerusalem: Kiryath Sepher, 1963. (Hebrew).

Melzer, Gudrun, with Lore Sander. "A Copper Scroll Inscription from the Time of Alchon Huns." Pages 251–78 in *Buddhist Manuscripts III*. Edited by Jens Braarvig and Mark Allon. Manuscripts in the Schøyen Collection 7. Oslo: Hermes, 2006.

Mildenberg, Leo. *The Coinage of the Bar Kokhba War*. Edited by Patricia Erhart Mottahedeh. Typos: Monographien zur antiken Numismatik 6. Aarau: Sauerländer, 1984.

Milik, Józef T. "Le rouleau de cuivre de Qumran (3Q 15)." *RB* 66 (1959): 321–57.

Milik, Józef T. "The Copper Document from Cave III of Qumran: Translation and Commentary." *Annual of the Department of Antiquities of Jordan* 4–5 (1960): 137–55.

Milik, Józef T. "Le rouleau de cuivre provenant de la grotte 3Q (3Q15)." Pages 201–99 in *Les 'Petites Grottes'*. Edited by Maurice Baillet, Józef T. Milik, and Roland de Vaux. DJD III. Oxford: Clarendon, 1962.

Młynarczyk, Jolanta. "Terracotta Oil Lamps from Qumran." *RB* 120 (2013): 99–133.

Młynarczyk, Jolanta. "Terracotta Oil Lamps (Roland de Vaux's Excavation of the Caves)." Pages 109–22 in *The Caves of Qumran: Proceedings of the International Conference, Lugano 2014*. Edited by Marcello Fidanzio. STDJ 118. Leiden: Brill, 2016.

Montgomery, James A. "Some Early Amulets from Palestine." *JAOS* 31 (1911): 272–81.

Mowinckel, Sigmund. "The Copper Scroll—An Apocryphon?" *JBL* 76 (1957): 261–65.

Müller-Kessler, Christa, T. Crichton Mitchell, and Marilyn I. Hockey. "An Inscribed Silver Amulet from Samaria." *PEQ* 139 (2007): 5–19.

Naveh, Joseph, and Saul Shaked. *Magic Spells and Formulae: Aramaic Incantations of Late Antiquity.* Jerusalem: Magnes, 1993.

Naveh, Joseph, and Saul Shaked. *Amulets and Magic Bowls: Aramaic Incantations of Late Antiquity.* 3rd ed. Jerusalem: Magnes, 1998.

Patrich, Joseph. "Khirbet Qumran in Light of New Archaeological Explorations in the Qumran Caves." Pages 73–95 in *Methods of Investigation of the Dead Sea Scrolls and the Khirbet Qumran Site: Present Realities and Future Prospects.* Edited by Michael O. Wise, Norman Golb, John J. Collins, and Dennis G. Pardee. Annals of the New York Academy of Sciences 722. New York, NY: New York Academy of Sciences, 1994.

Pixner, Bargil. "Unravelling the *Copper Scroll* Case: A Study on the Topography of 3Q15." *RevQ* 11 (1983): 323–66.

Puech, Émile. "Some Results of the Restoration of the Copper Scroll by *EDF Mecenat.*" Pages 889–94 in *The Dead Sea Scrolls Fifty Years after their Discovery 1947–1997: Proceedings of the Jerusalem Congress, July 20–25, 1997.* Edited by Lawrence H. Schiffman, Emanuel Tov, James C. VanderKam and G. Marquis. Jerusalem: Israel Exploration Society, 2000.

Puech, Émile. *The Copper Scroll Revisited.* STDJ 112. Translated by David E. Orton. Leiden: Brill, 2015.

Puech, Émile, Noël Lacoudre, in collaboration with Farah Mébarki. "The Mysteries of the 'Copper Scroll,' Qumran and the Dead Sea Scrolls: Discoveries, Debates, the Scrolls and the Bible." *NEA* 63/3 (2000): 152–53.

Rabin, Chaim. "The Historical Background of Qumran Hebrew." *ScrHier* 4 (1958): 144–61.

Rabin, Chaim. "Hebrew and Aramaic in the First Century." Pages 1007–39 in *The Jewish People in the First Century.* Edited by Shmuel Safrai and Menahem Stern. Philadelphia: Fortress, 1976.

Reed, William L. "The Qumran Caves Expedition of March, 1952." *BASOR* 135 (Oct., 1954): 8–13.

Richey, Matthew. "The Use of Greek at Qumran: Manuscript and Epigraphic Evidence for a Marginalised Language." *DSD* 19 (2012): 177–97.

Rothenberg, Beno. "The Arabah in Roman and Byzantine Times in the Light of New Research." Pages 211–33 in *Roman Frontier Studies 1967: Proceedings of the Seventh International Congress.* Edited by Shimon Applebaum. Tel Aviv: Tel Aviv University, 1971.

Rothenberg, Beno. *Timna: Valley of the Biblical Copper Mines.* London: Thames and Hudson, 1972.

Schürer, Emil. *The History of the Jewish People in the Age of Jesus Christ*. Revised ed. Edited by Géza Vermes, Fergus Millar, and Matthew Black. Edinburgh: T&T Clark, 1973–1987.

Schwab, Moïse. "Une amulette judéo-araméenne." *JA* 7 (1906): 1–15.

Schwartz, Seth. "Language, Power and Identity in Ancient Palestine." *Past and Present* 148 (1995): 3–47.

Segal, Moses H. "Mishnaic Hebrew and its Relation to Biblical Hebrew and to Aramaic." *JQR* 20 (1908): 647–737.

Sevenster, Jan N. *Do You Know Greek? How Much Greek Could* the *First Jewish Christians Have Known?* NovTSup 19. Leiden: Brill, 1968.

Silberman, L. H. "A Note on the Copper Scrolls." *VT* 10 (1960): 77–79.

Smoak, Jeremy D. "Words Unseen: The Power of Hidden Writing." *BAR* 44.1 (2018): 52–59, 70.

Sperber, Daniel. *Greek in Talmudic Palestine*. Ramat-Gan: Bar Ilan University Press, 2012.

Stone, Michael, and Esther Eshel. "The Holy Language at the End of Days in Light of a Qumran Fragment." *Tarbiz* 62 (1993–94): 169–77. (Hebrew).

Taylor, Joan E. "The Nea Church: Were the Temple Treasures Hidden Here?" *BAR* 34/1 (2008): 50–59, 82.

Taylor, Joan E. "Buried Manuscripts and Empty Tombs: The Qumran Genizah Theory Revisited." Pages 269–315 in *'Go Out and Study the Land' (Judges 18:2): Archaeological, Historical and Textual Studies in Honor of Hanan Eshel*. Edited by Aren M. Maeir, Jodi Magness, and Lawrence Schiffman. JSJSup 148. Leiden: Brill, 2011.

Taylor, Joan E. *The Essenes, the Scrolls, and the Dead Sea*. Oxford: Oxford University Press, 2012.

Taylor, Joan E. "Parting in Palestine." Pages 87–104 in *Partings: How Judaism and Christianity Became Two*. Edited by Hershel Shanks. Washington, DC: Biblical Archaeology Society, 2013.

Taylor, Joan E. "The Qumran Caves in their Regional Context: A Chronological Review with a Focus on Bar Kokhba Assemblages." Pages 7–33 *The Caves of Qumran: Proceedings of the International Conference, Lugano 2014*. Edited by Marcello Fidanzio. STDJ 118. Leiden: Brill, 2016.

Testa, Emmanuele. *L'huile de la foi: L'onction des malades sur une lamelle du 1er siècle*. Publications du Studium Biblicum Franciscanum: Collectio minor 3. Jerusalem: Magnes, 1967.

Vaux, Roland de. "Exploration de la Région de Qumran." *RB* 60 (1953): 540–61.

Vaux, Roland de. *Archaeology and the Dead Sea Scrolls*. London: Oxford University Press, 1973.

Vincent, Louis-Hugues. "Amulette judeo-arameenne." *RB* 5 (1908): 382–94.

Vleeming, Sven P. *Some Coins of Artaxerxes and Other Short Texts in the Demotic Script Found on Various Objects Gathered from Many Publications*. Studia Demotica 5. Leuven: Peeters, 2001.

Weissenberg, Hanne M. von. "The Centrality of the Temple in 4QMMT." Pages 293–305 in *The Dead Sea Scrolls: Texts and Context*. Edited by Charlotte Hempel. STDJ 90. Leiden: Brill, 2010.

Weitzman, Steven. "Why Did the Qumran Community Write in Hebrew?" *JAOS* 119 (1999): 35–45.

Weitzman, Steven. "Myth, History and Mystery in the Copper Scroll." Pages 239–55 in *The Idea of Biblical Interpretation: Essays in Honor of James L. Kugel*. Edited by Hindy Najman and Judith H. Newman. Leiden: Brill, 2003.

Weitzman, Steven. "Absent but Accounted for: A New Approach to the Copper Scroll." *HTR* 108 (2015): 423–47.

Wise, Michael O. "David J. Wilmot and the Copper Scroll." Pages 291–309 in *Copper Scroll Studies*. Edited by George J. Brooke and Philip R. Davies. London: T&T Clark International, 2002.

Wise, Michael O. *Language and Literacy in Roman Judaea: A Study of the Bar Kokhba Documents*. AYBRL. New Haven, CT: Yale University Press, 2015.

Wolters, Al. "The Copper Scroll and the Vocabulary of Mishnaic Hebrew." *RevQ* 14 (1989–90): 483–95.

Wolters, Al. "Literary Analysis and the *Copper Scroll*," Pages 239–52 in *Intertestamental Essays in Honour of Józef Tadeusz Milik*. Edited by Zdzisław Jan Kapera. Qumranica Mogilanensia 6. Kraków: Enigma Press, 1992.

Wolters, Al. "The Copper Scroll." Pages 1:302–24 in *The Dead Sea Scrolls after Fifty Years: A Comprehensive Assessment*. Edited by Peter W. Flint and James C. Vanderkam. 2 vols. Leiden: Brill, 1998–1999.

CHAPTER 9

Curated Communities: Refracted Realities at Qumran and on Social Media

Charlotte Hempel

This study explores the intriguing interface of the presentation of the collective community in the Dead Sea Scrolls and the question of how and whether this can be related to the real-life experiences of a particular movement.[1] I will draw on recent research on the question of the self-presentation, audiences and interaction in social media. I chose this lens since the issue of how reality is represented and refracted in online interactions has been problematized and illuminated vociferously by social scientists and others working on representations of the self in online environments.

1   Reality and Textuality in the Dead Sea Scrolls

The scrolls found in the eleven Scroll Caves at and near Khirbet Qumran have always seemed to take both scholars and the wider public into another age. In a visceral manner we imagined ourselves able to enter the world of an ancient Jewish community by exploring the site and the caves as well as the breathtaking materiality of scrolls and fragments that are over two thousand years old. The emotional response of several scholars who touched the material early on is palpable and even infectious. For Eleazar Sukenik, Professor of Archaeology at the Hebrew University of Jerusalem, to travel across a city divided into military zones in times of war to lay eyes on some of the most ancient Hebrew and Aramaic texts ever seen was clearly an emotionally intense encounter that still touches us today as we read and reflect on the account. Sukenik's son Yigael Yadin published his father's recollections of being presented with

---

1   I am grateful to the organizers and participants at the stimulating conference at St Mary's University Twickenham that gave rise to this volume. I would also like to thank Dr Karen Patel and Dr Craig Hamilton, both alumni of Birmingham City University, for opening windows into the world of media studies, the members of the Sheffield Institute for Interdisciplinary Biblical Studies (SIIBS) at the University of Sheffield as well my colleagues and students at the University of Birmingham for opportunities to discuss earlier versions of the argument presented here.

© CHARLOTTE HEMPEL, 2023 | DOI:10.1163/9789004537804_010

recently discovered scrolls for examination in the house of an antiquities dealer in Bethlehem on the same day as the United Nations voted on the Partition of Palestine and the end of the British Mandate (29 November 1947). Sukenik wrote,

> My hands shook as I started to unwrap one of them. I read a few sentences. It was written in beautiful Biblical Hebrew. The language was like that of the Psalms, but the text was unknown to me. I looked and looked, and I suddenly had the feeling that I was privileged by destiny to gaze upon a Hebrew Scroll which had not been read for more than two thousand years. [...] But the identity of the text still eluded me. I looked up the Apocryphal books in my library to see if I could find parallels, but there were none. *Here, then, were original texts.*[2]

One gets the impression that whereas we have been reading and studying witnesses to the biblical and early Jewish past, in the case of the Dead Sea Scrolls we are face to face with it. The discovery of the oldest manuscripts of the Hebrew Bible bestowed a sense of reality on the antiquity of the Bible.[3] Comparable palpable points of contact between the Scrolls and the New Testament as well as legal debates attested in rabbinic sources compiled centuries later confirmed the sense of verisimilitude of those religious texts and their scholarly evaluation. We note an infusion of energy infecting scholars and their publics[4] to whom the notion of having a kind of corroboration for the antiquity of normative Christian and Jewish sources was appealing.

Similarly, scholars trained in historical critical terms discovered the questions that comprised their training—in areas such as source and redaction

---

2   Yigael Yadin, *The Message of the Scrolls*, Christian Origins Library (New York, NY: Crossroad, 1992), 23–24 (emphasis added).

3   For recent research that challenges provenance narratives of archaeological discoveries see Mark Goodacre, "How Reliable is the Story of the Nag Hammadi Discovery?" *JSNT* 35 (2013): 303–22; Rebecca J. W. Jefferson, "Deconstructing 'the Cairo Genizah:' A Fresh Look at Genizah Manuscript Discoveries in Cairo before 1897," *JQR* 108 (2018): 422–48; Årstein Justness, "Fake Fragments, Flexible Provenances: Eight Aramaic 'Dead Sea Scrolls' from the 21st Century," in *Vision, Narrative, and Wisdom in the Aramaic Texts from Qumran*, ed. Mette Bundvad and Kasper Siegismund, STDJ 131 (Leiden: Brill, 2020), 242–71, and Brent Nongbri, "Finding Early Christian Books at Nag Hammadi and Beyond," *Bulletin for the Study of Religion* 45 (2016): 11–19.

4   See danah m. boyd, "Taken Out of Context: American Teen Sociality in Networked Publics," (PhD diss., University of California, Berkeley, 2008).

criticism,[5] *Fortschreibung*,[6] the formation of the Bible[7] and the canon,[8] pseudepigraphy and rewriting[9] as well as scribal practices[10]—on occasion illustrated in the Scrolls as if in a textbook from two thousand years ago. A

---

5 See, e.g., John Barton, "Source Criticism," *ABD* 6:162–65; Barton, "Redaction Criticism," *ABD* 5:644–47 and Charlotte Hempel, "Sources and Redaction in the Dead Sea Scrolls: The Growth of Ancient Texts," in *Rediscovering the Dead Sea Scrolls: An Assessment of Old and New Approaches and Methods*, ed. Maxine L. Grossman (Grand Rapids, MI: Eerdmans, 2010), 162–81; Reinhard G. Kratz, "Biblical Scholarship and Qumran Studies," in *T&T Clark Companion to the Dead Sea Scrolls*, ed. George J. Brooke and Charlotte Hempel, with the assistance of Michael DeVries and Drew Longacre (London: Bloomsbury, 2019), 204–15, and Reinhard Müller and Juha Pakkala, eds., *Insights into Editing in the Hebrew Bible and the Ancient Near East: What Does Documented Evidence Tell us about the Transmission of Authoritative Texts* (Leuven: Peeters, 2017).

6 Reinhard G. Kratz, *Historical and Biblical Israel: The History, Tradition, and Archives of the History of Israel and Judah* (Oxford: Oxford University Press, 2015), 75–92.

7 See Eugene C. Ulrich, "The Bible in the Making: The Scriptures Found at Qumran," in *The Bible at Qumran: Text, Shape, and Interpretation*, ed. Peter W. Flint, Studies in the Dead Sea Scrolls and Related Literature (Grand Rapids, MI: Eerdmans, 2001), 51–66; idem, *The Dead Sea Scrolls and the Developmental Composition of the Bible* (Leiden: Brill, 2015); James C. VanderKam, *The Dead Sea Scrolls and the Bible* (Grand Rapids, MI: Eerdmans, 2012). See also David Carr, *The Formation of the Hebrew Bible: A New Reconstruction* (Oxford: Oxford University Press, 2011); Charlotte Hempel, *Qumran Rule Texts in Context: Collected Studies*, TSAJ 154 (Tübingen: Mohr Siebeck, 2013), 229–99; Karel van der Toorn, *Scribal Culture and the Making of the Hebrew Bible* (Cambridge, MA: Harvard University Press, 2007) and Sidnie White Crawford, *Scribes and Scrolls at Qumran* (Grand Rapids, MI: Eerdmans, 2019), 217–22.

8 See Hindy Najman, "The Vitality of Scripture Within and Beyond the 'Canon,'" *JSJ* 43 (2012): 497–518; Timothy H. Lim, *The Formation of the Jewish Canon* (New Haven, CT: Yale University Press, 2013); James C. VanderKam, "Questions of Canon Viewed Through the Dead Sea Scrolls," in *The Canon Debate*, ed. Lee M. McDonald and James A. Sanders (Peabody, MA: Hendrickson, 2002), 91–109, and Eva Mroczek, "The Hegemony of the Biblical in the Study of Second Temple Literature," *JAJ* 6 (2015): 1–35.

9 Hindy Najman, *Seconding Sinai: The Development of Mosaic Discourse in Second Temple Judaism*, JSJSup 77 (Leiden: Brill 2003); Eva Mroczek, *The Literary Imagination in Jewish Antiquity* (New York, NY: Oxford University Press, 2016); Molly M. Zahn, "Parabiblical Literature/Rewritten Scripture," in *T&T Clark Companion to the Dead Sea Scrolls*, ed. George J. Brooke and Charlotte Hempel, with the assistance of Michael DeVries and Drew Longacre (London: Bloomsbury, 2019), 378–85, and most recently Molly M. Zahn, *Genres of Rewriting in Second Temple Judaism: Scribal Composition and Transmission* (Cambridge: Cambridge University Press, 2020).

10 Cf. Malachi Martin, *The Scribal Character of the Dead Sea Scrolls*, 2 vols (Louvain: Publications Universitaires, 1958); Emanuel Tov, *Scribal Practices and Approaches Reflected in Texts Found in the Judean Desert*, STDJ 54 (Leiden: Brill, 2004), and Eibert J. C. Tigchelaar, "The Scribes of the Scrolls," in *T&T Clark Companion to the Dead Sea Scrolls*, ed. George J. Brooke and Charlotte Hempel, with the assistance of Michael DeVries and Drew Longacre (London: Bloomsbury, 2019), 524–32.

striking example was a seminal article by Jerome Murphy-O'Connor whose conclusion that the first four columns of the Community Rule were added after the bulk of the remaining seven columns of 1QS—arrived at solely on the basis of a single manuscript—was dramatically confirmed by the publication of an ancient manuscript of the Rule (4Q258 [4QS^d]) that started with the equivalent of 1QS column 5.[11] And this is not even to speak of the exuberance of riches the Dead Sea Scrolls have brought to the fields of Textual Criticism,[12] including Septuagint and Samaritan Studies. Just as the Dead Sea Scrolls injected a huge dose of trust in the antiquity of biblical manuscripts that have a good semblance to what would become the scriptures of Judaism and Christianity, they also affirmed the credibility of the Septuagint and the Samaritan Pentateuch. Thus, the Scrolls revealed Hebrew manuscripts that confirm the antiquity and importance of ancient Greek translations of the Hebrew Bible[13] as well as manuscripts used by the Samaritan scribes from a time before the latter community had parted company with the Jews of Palestine.[14]

Another area where the Scrolls appeared to confirm ancient accounts concerns the classical sources on the Essenes. With the prolific first century Jewish

---

11   See Jerome Murphy-O'Connor, "La genèse littéraire de la Règle de la Communauté," *RB* 76 (1969): 533–37 and the refinements offered by Jean Pouilly, *La Règle de la Communauté de Qumrân: Son évolution littéraire*, CahRB 17 (Paris: Gabalda, 1976). On the evidence of the Cave 4 manuscripts see Philip S. Alexander and Geza Vermes, *Qumran Cave 4.XIX: Serekh Ha-Yaḥad and Two Related Texts*, DJD 26 (Oxford: Clarendon, 1998); Sarianna Metso, *The Textual Development of the Qumran Community Rule*, STDJ 21 (Leiden: Brill, 1997); idem, *The Serekh Texts*, CQS 9/LSTS 62 (London: T&T Clark, 2007); Charlotte Hempel, *The Community Rules from Qumran: A Commentary* (Tübingen: Mohr Siebeck, 2020); idem, *Qumran Rule Texts in Context*, 109–19 and Alison Schofield, *From Qumran to the Yaḥad: A New Paradigm of Textual Development for the Community Rule*, STDJ 77 (Leiden: Brill, 2009).

12   See George J. Brooke, "The Qumran Scrolls and the Demise of the Distinction Between Higher and Lower Criticism," in *New Directions in Qumran Studies*, ed. Jonathan G. Campbell, William J. Lyons, and Lloyd K. Pietersen, LSTS 52 (London: T&T Clark, 2005), 26–42; Armin Lange, "7.2.1 Ancient Manuscript Evidence," in *Textual History of the Bible*, General Editor Armin Lange. Consulted online on 19 April 2020 http://dx.doi.org/.ezproxyd.bham.ac.uk/10.1163/2452-4107_thb_COM_0007020100; Emanuel Tov, *Textual Criticism of the Hebrew Bible*, 3rd ed. (Minneapolis, MN: Fortress, 2012).

13   Cf. Timothy Michael Law, *When God Spoke Greek: The Septuagint and the Making of the Christian Bible* (Oxford: Oxford University Press, 2013); Ulrich, *Developmental Composition of the Bible*, 229–49; Emanuel Tov, *The Greek and Hebrew Bible: Collected Essays on the Septuagint*, VTSup 72 (Leiden: Brill, 1999).

14   See Robert T. Anderson and Terry Giles, *The Samaritan Pentateuch: An Introduction to Its Origin, History, and Significance for Biblical Studies*, RBS 72 (Atlanta, GA: SBL, 2012); Gary Knoppers, *Jews and Samaritans: The Origin and History of their Early Relations* (Oxford: Oxford University Press, 2019), and Ulrich, *Developmental Composition of the Bible*, 215–27.

historian Josephus, for example, we score double points—so to speak—since Josephus is often taken to tally with the Scrolls while the Scrolls are implicitly seen to confirm the reliability of Josephus. In both cases the picture painted of the Essenes and the people behind the Scrolls exudes a virtuous quality. While the relationship of both bodies is indeed worthy of scrutiny, both literatures have rightly been read with more nuance in recent years. Scholars like Steve Mason, for instance, have highlighted the circularity of the arguments put forward as well as the complexity of each body of literature. It is crucial to avoid reading one body of evidence in light of the other before closely analysing each in their own right. As Mason has convincingly shown, both Philo and Josephus outline a portrayal of the Essenes that closely mirrors more widespread notions of ideals of virtue associated with exceptional groups in antiquity, including also Spartans.[15]

Among the sectarian texts from Qumran the Community Rule has long been a special case. While this text is often read as what I have called "reality literature,"[16] such an approach was challenged by the publication of ten at times radically different manuscripts of this text from Cave 4. In order to accommodate the new evidence, a number of scholars have sought to reconcile the ancient manuscripts of the Community Rule from Qumran with a variety of lived realities. Thus, Sarianna Metso has argued that the Community Rule manuscripts constitute written records of once oral deliberation.[17] However, given deliberations, such as exchanging counsel, are portrayed as an ongoing part of communal life in the Community Rule[18] it is difficult to see how literary production could keep pace with events. In a later publication Metso develops her position with more nuance and proposes that what we may call the minutes of oral decisions were used in an educational context.[19] Alison Schofield and John Collins propose a correspondence between communal life and different manuscripts of the Community Rule in a range of geographically

---

15   See Steve Mason, "Essenes," in *The Encyclopedia of Ancient History*, ed. Roger S. Bagnall et al. (London: Blackwell, 2013), 2501–2503; idem, "Essenes and Lurking Spartans in Josephus' *Judean War*: From Story to History," in *Making History: Josephus and Historical Method*, ed. Zuleika Rogers (Leiden: Brill, 2007), 219–61 and Joan E. Taylor, *The Essenes, the Scrolls and the Dead Sea* (Oxford: Oxford University Press, 2012).

16   Hempel, *Qumran Rule Texts in Context*, 8.

17   Sarianna Metso, "In Search of the *Sitz im Leben* of the *Community Rule*," in *The Provo International Conference on the Dead Sea Scrolls: Technological Innovations, New Texts, and Reformulated Issues*, ed. Donald W. Parry and Eugene Ulrich, STDJ 30 (Leiden: Brill, 1999), 306–15.

18   See especially 1QS 6–7.

19   Sarianna Metso, "Methodological Problems in Reconstructing History from Rule Texts Found at Qumran," *DSD* 11 (2004): 315–35, 333.

spread out communities by suggesting various Rules were each applied in a series of settlements and subsequently brought to Khirbet Qumran in a crisis situation.[20]

My own approach has been to challenge prominent readings of the material as reality literature captured by a candid camera fed by the efforts of our ancient scribes.[21] However, I nevertheless perceive a degree of verisimilitude with lives on the ground behind some of the material. It is this sense that the Dead Sea Scrolls, including the Rule texts,[22] are both sophisticated literary creations on a par with the emerging Bible but also appear to reflect a constructed reality that led me to explore the similarly complex presentation of the self on social media.

Beyond the Rule texts recent research on 4QMMT has challenged initial assessments of the composition as a stash of six (draft) letters by the Teacher of Righteousness to his nemesis the Wicked Priest.[23] Moreover, in an excellent early monograph on the Qumran Hymn Scroll—the manuscript Sukenik wrote about in his journal entry quoted above—Svend Holm-Nielsen rightly emphasized that this composition resembles the work of the poets behind the biblical Psalms rather than reflecting intimate outpourings of individuals including the Teacher of Righteousness.[24] In fact, in the extract cited above Sukenik already referred to the resemblance between the Hodayot and the Psalms.[25] More recently Angela Harkins critiqued prevalent readings of the

---

20 Schofield, *From Qumran to the* Yaḥad and John J. Collins, *Beyond the Qumran Community: The Sectarian Movement of the Dead Sea Scrolls* (Grand Rapids, MI: Eerdmans, 2010).

21 See Charlotte Hempel, "Self-Fashioning in the Dead Sea Scrolls: Thickening the Description of What Rule Texts Do," in *Social History of the Jews within the Ancient World*, ed. Jonathan Ben-Dov and Michal Bar-Asher Siegal, TSAJ (Tübingen: Mohr Siebeck, 2021), 49–66) and Hempel, *Qumran Rule Texts in Context*, 1–21.

22 For details on representative texts that belong to this category—especially, though not exclusively, the Community Rule, the Damascus Document, the Rule of the Congregation and 4QMiscellaneous Rules—see Hempel, *Rule Texts in Context*, 1 and idem, "Rules," in *T&T Clark Companion to the Dead Sea Scrolls*, George J. Brooke and Charlotte Hempel, with the assistance of Michael DeVries and Drew Longacre (London: Bloomsbury, 2019), 405–12.

23 For analysis of the so-called halakhic letter 4QMMT see Maxine Grossman, "Reading *4QMMT*: Genre and History," *RevQ* 20 (2001): 3–22; Steven D. Fraade, "To Whom It May Concern: 4QMMT and Its Addressee(s)," *RevQ* 19 (2000): 507–26. See also, most recently, the comprehensive discussion of 4QMMT including a new edition in Reinhard G. Kratz, ed., *Interpreting and Living God's Law at Qumran: Miqsat Ma'aśe ha-Torah, Some of the Works of the Torah (4QMMT)*, Sapere 37 (Tübingen: Mohr Siebeck, 2020) and Charlotte Hempel, "The Dead Sea Scrolls: Challenging the Particularist Paradigm," in *Torah, Temple, Land: Constructions of Judaism in Antiquity*, ed. Bernd Schröter, TSAJ 184 (Tübingen: Mohr Siebeck, forthcoming).

24 Svend Holm-Nielsen, *Hodayot: Psalms from Qumran* (Aarhus: Universitetsforlaget, 1960).

25 Yadin, *Message of the Scrolls*, 23.

CURATED COMMUNITIES

so-called Teacher Hymns as expressions of the anxieties and inner life of the Teacher of Righteousness.[26]

Finally, several scholars have offered critical discussions on how we approach history in the Dead Sea Scrolls and other early Jewish literature. Here Philip Davies was, as so often, an intellectual trail blazer with his 1987 collection *Behind the Essenes*.[27] I would like to share a typically eloquent example of Davies' approach,

> We cannot expect [...] objectively to restore the historical integrity of texts which once spoke to citizens of our world in another time [...] But we can intellectually construe a history which offers a critically plausible account of the texts as relics of the past. [...] its idiom is that of possibility and probability, its instincts sometimes empathy and imagination ...[28]

Maxine Grossman's seminal monograph *Reading for History in the Damascus Document: A Methodological Study* credits the influence of Davies and advocates a New Historiography approach to the Damascus Document and acknowledges that

> our historical approach to the Dead Sea Scrolls needs to move away from a view of the Scrolls only as "historical evidence" and toward a recognition that they are, themselves, literary texts presenting ideological constructions of history and not simple statements of fact.[29]

---

26 Angela K. Harkins, "Who is the Teacher of the Teacher Hymns? Re-Examining the Teacher Hymns Hypothesis Fifty Years Later," in *A Teacher for All Generations: Essays in Honor of James C. VanderKam*, ed. Eric Mason et al., JSJSup 153 (Leiden: Brill, 2012), 449–67; idem, *Reading with an "I" to the Heavens: Looking at the Qumran Hodayot through the Lens of Visionary Traditions*, Ekstasis 3 (Berlin: De Gruyter, 2012); see also Carol Newsom, *The Self as Symbolic Space: Constructing Identity and Community at Qumran*, STDJ 52 (Leiden: Brill, 2004), 287–351.

27 Philip R. Davies, *Behind the Essenes: History and Ideology in the Dead Sea Scrolls*, BJS 94 (Atlanta, GA: Scholars Press, 1987). See also more recently idem, "Historiography," in *T&T Clark Companion to the Dead Sea Scrolls*, ed. George J. Brooke and Charlotte Hempel, with the assistance of Michael DeVries and Drew Longacre (London: Bloomsbury, 2019), 228–36. See also Hayim Lapin, "Dead Sea Scrolls and the Historiography of Ancient Judaism," in *Rediscovering the Dead Sea Scrolls: An Assessment of Old and New Approaches and Methods*, ed. Maxine L. Grossman (Grand Rapids, MI: Eerdmans, 2010), 108–27.

28 Davies, *Behind the Essenes*, 10.

29 Maxine L. Grossman, *Reading for History in the Damascus Document: A Methodological Study*, STDJ 45 (Leiden: Brill, 2002), x.

Moreover, Steven Fraade has problematized the relationship of the imagined and the real in ancient legal literature in the provocatively titled volume *Legal Fictions: Studies of Law and Narrative in the Discursive Worlds of Ancient Jewish Sectarians and Sages*. He introduces his approach as follows,

> the following studies repeatedly emphasize the complex ways in which both Qumran and early rabbinic textual practices provide not only important representations of their respective historical worlds and world views, but ongoing constructions of their places in the sacred history of Israel, whether real or imagined or imagined as real ...[30]

Having reviewed a spectrum of scholarly assessments of our ability to access historical and social realities reflected in the Dead Sea Scrolls and ancient Jewish legal literature I will now turn to some reflections on the customary distinction between documentary and literary texts that is particularly prominent in discussions of texts that have emerged from archaeological contexts.[31]

2 Documentary and Literary Texts

Scholars like Averil Cameron, Judith Lieu and others have rightly stressed the extent to which texts serve to create rather than reflect reality.[32] While observations of the scarcity of documentary texts among the finds from Qumran have become a common place,[33] literary texts from Qumran are commonly read as documentary literature, almost as if they have come down to us via a blog or vlog from the Judean Desert. Apart from producing naïve readings, such an approach overlooks the shared literary conventions that characterize

---

30 Steven D. Fraade, *Legal Fictions: Studies of Law and Narrative in the Discursive Worlds of Ancient Jewish Sectarians and Sages*, JSJS 147 (Leiden: Brill, 2011), 14–15.

31 See, e.g., James G. Keegan, "The History of the Discipline," in *The Oxford Handbook of Papyrology*, ed. Roger S. Bagnall (Oxford: Oxford University Press, 2009), 59–78.

32 See Averil Cameron, *Christianity and the Rhetoric of Empire: The Development of Christian Discourse* (Berkeley, CA: University of California Press, 1991), 21 and Judith M. Lieu, *Christian Identity in the Jewish and Graeco-Roman World* (Oxford: Oxford University Press, 2004), 27–62.

33 See Mladen Popović, "The Manuscript Collection: An Overview," in *T&T Clark Companion to the Dead Sea Scrolls*, ed. George J. Brooke and Charlotte Hempel, with the assistance of Michael DeVries and Drew Longacre (London: Bloomsbury, 2019), 37–50; Ian Werrett, "Is Qumran a Library?" in *The Dead Sea Scrolls at Qumran and the Concept of a Library*, ed. Sidnie White Crawford and Cecilia Wassén, STDJ 116 (Leiden: Brill, 2016), 78–105 and White Crawford, *Scribes*, 257–60.

CURATED COMMUNITIES 343

these narratives as much as they do texts that would become the Hebrew Bible, the Gospels, or the Mishnah. If educated ancient Jews were driven by ideology in portraying "the imagined as real"—as Steven Fraade calls it[34]—then the folks behind the Scrolls were part of the same intellectual and cultural milieu. This is not to say that there is nothing real to be recovered from reading the Scrolls, but simply to remind ourselves that the sorts of literary and rhetorical strategies we see driving the agenda in other ancient Jewish literature are almost certainly also drivers in the Scrolls.

Entries in the Oxford English Dictionary on Documentary and Literary include two semantic strands that are of particular relevance for our enquiry:

1. The adjective "literary" and the noun "literature" convey a sense of the elevated quality or merit of a work. Importantly the terminology is described as encompassing both fiction and non-fiction. The adjective is first attested in Francis Bacon, *The Advancement of Learning* Ch. IV (1605) where he bemoans the lack of a literary history as still "wanting" and advocates "The design of this work should be, to relate from the earliest accounts of time, what particular kinds of learning [101] and arts flourished, in what ages, and what parts of the world" and is to include "the most famous sects and controversies of learned men." It would appear Bacon may well have incorporated the Dead Sea Scrolls in such a work had they been available.[35]

2. The entry for "documentary" notes under (4) a meaning in the realm of the "Factual, realistic; applied esp. to a film or literary work." This semantic range almost collapses the distinction between literary and documentary by allowing for a documentary literary work.[36]

As far as the Dead Sea Scrolls are concerned, Emanuel Tov employs a distinction between documentary and non-documentary.[37] In his Introduction on the sources for his project he notes,

> The analysis pertains to all the texts from the Judean Desert, non-documentary (literary) as well as documentary, with special emphasis on literary texts.[38]

---

34 Fraade, *Legal Fictions*, 15.

35 See "Literary, adj. and n.," OED Online. March 2020. Oxford University Press. https://www.oed.com/view/Entry/109067?redirectedFrom=literary (accessed May 16, 2020).

36 "Documentary, adj. and n.," OED Online. March 2020. Oxford University Press. https://www.oed.com/view/Entry/56332?redirectedFrom=documentary (accessed May 16, 2020).

37 Tov, *Scribal Practices*.

38 Tov, *Scribal Practices*, 3.

Jürgen Zangenberg's essay on "Archaeology, Papyri and Inscriptions," in the *Eerdmans Dictionary of Early Judaism* begins with an opening sentence that distinguishes between "literary texts" and "material culture," the latter being the focus of his attention.[39] Zangenberg goes on to include the archaeological remains from Qumran which are characterised by their "religious character" in a section on "Textual Discoveries from Palestine."[40] We note a very interesting profile in the use of the terms "texts" and "documents" in Zangenberg's piece which shows a preference to refer to documents when it comes to the finds from sites elsewhere in the Judean desert such as Wadi Muraba'at and Naḥal Ḥever which revealed a large number of legal documents and letters. The Qumran material is almost exclusively referred to as comprising texts, manuscripts, or books. There are two exceptions, however. The obvious exception is a reference to a small number of documentary texts from Qumran.[41] A more subtle exception occurs in Zangenberg's description of the material we are concerned with presently, which is referred to in the following terms,

> Slightly more than a third of the corpus, around 250 manuscripts, are recognized by most scholars as *documents* that reflect the ideology and practices of a particular sect ....[42]

Finally, Eibert Tigchelaar's excellent overview over the Dead Sea Scrolls in the same volume emphasizes the significance of the finds as "the largest collection of Jewish religious texts from the Second Temple period."[43] Tigchelaar allots a special place to the Rule texts, which "give an unprecedented insight into aspects of the formation, organization, practices and beliefs of early Jewish groups or movements ..."[44]

In sum, my sense is that texts like the Community Rule—while presented as part of the literary and religious material from Qumran—are often singled out for their verisimilitude with the presumed practices of a movement. Such a reading might invite a new category of what I would call "docu-literature," "docu-lit" for short. Before moving to recent research on self-presentation on

---

39 Jürgen Zangenberg, "Archaeology, Papyri and Inscriptions," in *Eerdmans Dictionary of Early Judaism*, ed. John J. Collins and Dan Harlow (Grand Rapids, MI: Eerdmans, 2010), especially 201 and 226–27.

40 Zangenberg, "Archaeology, Papyri and Inscriptions," 226–31.

41 Zangenberg, "Archaeology, Papyri and Inscriptions," 227.

42 Zangenberg, "Archaeology, Papyri and Inscriptions," 226 (emphasis added).

43 Eibert J. C. Tigchelaar, "The Dead Sea Scrolls," in *Eerdmans Dictionary of Early Judaism*, ed. John J. Collins and Dan Harlow (Grand Rapids, MI: Eerdmans, 2010), 163.

44 Tigchelaar, "The Dead Sea Scrolls," 178.

CURATED COMMUNITIES

social media it will be helpful to turn to the work of the sociologist Erving Goffman on the presentation of the self in every-day life.

3 Erving Goffman's Dramaturgical Reading of Everyday Life

Goffman was a vastly influential American Canadian sociologist whose book *The Presentation of Self in Every Day Life* first appeared in 1956 and is exerting significant influence on current scholarly analyses of Social Media Networks.[45] According to Goffman, all of us engage in "socialized" performances in our daily lives.[46] Our performances are witnessed by a variety of audiences whose presence has an effect on the performance. Goffman further adopted the concept of "behaviour settings" from Roger Barker's 1968 work *Ecological Psychology* that stresses norms and conventions which apply to particular settings.[47] Finally, Goffman distinguishes between two regions in everyday behavior. He identifies "the front region" and "the back region" which can be likened to the stage and backstage area of a theatre.[48] Goffman suggests that "impression management" is associated with the stage whereas a more chaotic space is found "backstage."[49] In private homes, for example, the reception rooms would be the stage whereas adult bedrooms and private bathrooms represent the back region where performances might be contradicted.

Several of Goffman's insights permit a more nuanced reading of the Dead Sea Scrolls. Thus, the idea of an aspect of "backstage" activity can include performances that fail to acknowledge unpleasant or unremarkable tasks that make the performance possible.[50] As far as the Dead Sea Scrolls are concerned we may ask what happens if we go below stairs *Downton Abbey* style. Neither the ancient texts nor modern scholars have directed our attention to those who took care of tedious and menial jobs that inevitably made the life of literary production, devotion, prayer, and fellowship possible. While I did not set out to uncover the equivalent of "below stairs" at Qumran, I stumbled across it as I was puzzling about a particular group of texts. In an article entitled "Who is Making Dinner at Qumran?" I stressed that what is often translated as the pure meals and pure drink of the community does not, in fact, speak

---

45　Erving Goffman, *The Presentation of Self in Everyday Life* (London: Penguin, 1990).

46　Goffman, *Presentation of Self*, 44.

47　Roger Barker, *Ecological Psychology: Concepts and Methods for Studying the Environment of Human Behavior* (Stanford, CA: Stanford University Press, 1968).

48　Goffman, *Presentation of Self*, 109–40.

49　Goffman, *Presentation of Self*, 202–30.

50　Goffman, *Presentation of Self*, 53.

of *eating* and *drinking* but rather of *touching* the purity and the pure liquid of the community.[51] I then put this important detail into conversation with references to harvesting foods that are susceptible to impurity by *touch*. This close reading of the texts suggests the admissions process described in the Community Rule would allow new members to get to work by supporting the harvest, preparing, and serving food before partaking themselves. Such a reading of the texts presupposes a more broadly skilled workforce and would sit well with the analysis of the site proposed by the archaeologist Dennis Mizzi who identifies Qumran as associated with a sectarian community with dedicated resources to agro-industrial efforts, especially the date industry.[52]

A small number of texts reveal potential glimpses of the literary "green room" or back region such as The Overseer's Record of Rebukes (4Q477). Such a record may also have played a role in the literary performance intended to shame those named in it, either for the purpose of oral proclamation or signaled by the powerful impact of the inscription of one's name in such an unfavorable context.[53]

On the level of scribal culture we are dealing with a shared setting of behavior in ancient literary production, such as the manufacture of a *de luxe* manuscript containing communal rules, the production and use of which can be understood as a kind of performance. The notion of *de luxe* scrolls was developed by Emanuel Tov with particular reference to torah scrolls.[54] Inscribing a large scale scroll like 1QS with descriptions of the organization associated with the movement that settled for a time at Qumran can only be an endeavor conceived by an elite with the necessary economic and intellectual capital at their disposal.[55] Moreover, a close reading of the organizational material makes it clear that authority is assigned to community leaders who operate almost

---

51   See Charlotte Hempel, "Who is Making Dinner at Qumran?" *JTS* 63 (2012): 49–65.

52   Cf. Dennis Mizzi, "Archaeology of Qumran," in *T&T Companion to the Dead Sea Scrolls*, ed. George J. Brooke and Charlotte Hempel (London: Bloomsbury, 2019), 31 where he draws attention to the discovery of quantities of dates and date pits, date honey in jars as well as an ostracon that refers to the owner of a palm grove.

53   See also Mary Beard, "Writing and Religion: Ancient Literacy and the Function of the Written Word in Roman Religion," in *Literacy in the Roman World*, ed. Mary Beard et al. (Ann Arbor, MI: Journal of Roman Archaeology, 1991), 35–58.

54   Emanuel Tov, *Textual Criticism of the Hebrew Bible, Qumran, Septuagint: Collected Essays*, VTSup 167 (Leiden: Brill, 2015), 3:160–161.

55   See further Charlotte Hempel, "Bildung und Wissenswirtschaft im Judentum zur Zeit des Zweiten Tempels," in *Was ist Bildung in der Vormoderne?*, ed. Peter Gemeinhardt, Studies in Education and Religion in Ancient and Pre-Modern History in the Mediterranean and Its Environs 4 (Tübingen: Mohr Siebeck, 2020), 229–44.

exclusively through the spoken word.[56] Literary performance, as represented also by the production of Community Rule manuscripts, constitutes a form of Goffmanian "impression management" targeted at multiple audiences. One audience were those associated with the textual community associated with the Scrolls.[57] On the basis of the analysis of medievalist Brian Stock, such a textual community can include members not able to access texts unaided.[58] Drawing on Stock's insights, I have argued elsewhere that the movement associated with Dead Sea Scrolls drew on the unacknowledged contributions and labor of members that lacked the literary skills of the educated scribal constituency that we have customarily imagined as settling at Qumran in the first century BCE.[59] Quite a different audience are those engaged in the literary production of ancient texts including the Dead Sea Scrolls found at Qumran, who were themselves performing an act of impression management by signaling the prestige of their role in creating compositions that are both literarily and materially "up there" with manuscripts of the emerging Bible.[60] Even *if* the producers of some of the material discovered at and near Qumran had withdrawn

---

56   An exception occurs in 1QS 9:9–10 and 4Q258 7:9. Whilst we have a reference there to "the first rules" (משפטים) to guide the judgment of members until the arrival of the eschatological prophet and the two messiahs, this statement comes at the back of an admonition not to deviate from the council of the law (מכול עצת התורת) which presupposes the authority of the spoken word. In addition, the material also attests a close relationship to CD 20:31, see further Philip R. Davies, *Sects and Scrolls: Essays on Qumran and Related Topics*, SFSHJ 134 (Atlanta, GA: Scholars Press, 1996), 141 and Hempel, *Qumran Rule Texts in Context*, 123–36.

57   Brian Stock, *The Implications of Literacy: Written Language and Models of Interpretation in the Eleventh and Twelfth Centuries* (Princeton, NJ: Princeton University Press, 1983), 522. See also Mladen Popović, "Qumran as Scroll Storehouse in Times of Crisis? A Comparative Perspective on Judaean Desert Manuscript Collections," *JSJ* 43 (2012): 551–94 and idem, "The Ancient 'Library' of Qumran between Urban and Rural Culture," in *Qumran and the Concept of a Library*, ed. Sidnie White Crawford and Cecilia Wassén, STDJ 116 (Leiden: Brill, 2016), 155–67.

58   On the issue of the dating of the communal occupation of the site see See Jodi Magness, *The Archaeology of Qumran and the Dead Sea Scrolls* (Grand Rapids, MI: Eerdmans, 2002), 47–72; Dennis Mizzi, "Qumran Period I Reconsidered: An Evaluation of Several Competing Theories," *DSD* 22 (2015): 1–42 and idem, "Archaeology of Qumran," 21–24.

59   See Charlotte Hempel, "Reflections on Literacy, Textuality, and Community in the Qumran Dead Sea Scrolls," in *Is There a Text in this Cave? Studies in the Textuality of the Dead Sea Scrolls in Honour of George J. Brooke*, ed. Ariel Feldman, Maria Cioată and Charlotte Hempel, STDJ 119 (Leiden: Brill, 2017), 69–82.

60   Thus, William Johnson has comprehensively demonstrated how ancient manuscripts shed light on "socio-cultural models of behaviour," see William A. Johnson, *Readers and Reading Culture in the High Roman Empire: A Study of Elite Communities* (New York, NY: Oxford University Press, 2010), 188.

from a larger collective of literarily minded Jews, these literary creatives were nevertheless socialized in the cultural value system of elevated literary circles.

Building on Goffman's approach, Bernie Hogan, a sociologist based at the Oxford Internet Institute in the UK, stresses the prominence of what he calls social media "exhibitions" which reflect the hand of a "virtual curator" playing a significant role.[61] Hogan suggests, "In an era of social media, [...] data traces do not merely document our passage in life's play but mediate our parts" and emphasizes the "ephemeral" quality of a performance over against the much more carefully constructed role of a recorded performance that can be engaged with in various contexts. As conceived by Hogan, curators filter and order the items to be put on display in a social media context as much as in a museum. Related to the idea of moving beyond the ephemeral is the work of the Africanist and cultural anthropologist Karin Barber on the anthropology of texts. After noting the *reflexive* nature of texts which are committed to writing "to attract attention and outlast the moment," Barber argues, "Textual traditions can be seen as a community's ethnography of itself."[62]

Hogan's notion of a curated and mediated identity offers a helpful lens for our conceptualization of the complex relationship of text to reality in the Qumran Rule texts in particular. What emerges from such a perspective is a curated community that displays a semblance to social phenomena in the real world but not a precise representation of them. In 2009 the Fashion and Style section of *The New York Times* published a piece by Alex Williams on the verb "curate." Williams cites a pertinent comment from Tina Brown, founding editor of online news and opinion outlet *The Daily Beast*: "The Daily Beast doesn't aggregate. It sifts and sorts, and curates. We're as much about what's not there as what is."[63] I contend something similar takes place in ancient texts also.

4   A Stake in the Ancient Jewish Literary Landscape

As far as the Rule texts are concerned it is indeed likely that these texts reflect several real movements.[64] However, the portrayals of the movements that

---

61   Bernie Hogan, "The Presentation of Self in the Age of Social Media: Distinguishing Performances and Exhibitions Online," *Bulletin of Science, Technology and Society* 30 (2010): 377–86.

62   Karin Barber, *The Anthropology of Texts, Persons and Publics* (Cambridge: Cambridge University Press, 2007), 4.

63   See Alex Williams, "On the Tip of Creative Tongues" *The New York Times*, Section ST, page 1, 2 October 2009.

64   On the differences between the accounts of the camp movement in the Damascus Document and what is described in the Community Rule see Hempel, *Qumran Rules Texts*

CURATED COMMUNITIES

emerge are carefully curated by scribes whose aim it was to create a particular perception of the movements. Moreover, there was no need to produce highly labor- and cost intensive scrolls of the Rule texts for the movements to go about their business. The textualization is to a large extent driven by a desire to claim a share in the ancient Jewish literary landscape. Moreover, those who shaped the literary presentation of the communities were not only drawing on an actual community but also intended to influence actual communities.[65] Thus, I have argued elsewhere that what I have called the Long Text of the Community Rule with its Covenant Ceremony and the Teaching on the Two Spirits appears to frame the communal regulations in 1QS 5–7 with introductory columns intended to counteract a lack of commitment on the part of community members.[66]

As Chris Keith and Raymond Person put it, ancient Jewish literary production constituted "specialized trade skills."[67] They go on to observe,

> The biblical world—at least, the world of the late Second Temple period—attributed high social value to the sacred and legal written texts that the large majority of people could not read.[68]

We need to recognize that considerable social and cultural value is attached also to the non-biblical material attested in the Dead Sea Scrolls.[69] danah boyd, a specialist on technology and social media, has couched the findings of her Berkeley dissertation on teenage online identities in terms of "writing identity into being online."[70] Her insights translate to the present enquiry as writing identity into being "on-scroll."

---

 in Context, 1–150 as well as Alison Schofield, "Forms of Community," in *T&T Companion to the Dead Sea Scrolls*, ed. George J. Brooke and Charlotte Hempel (London: Bloomsbury, 2019), 533–46 and further literature cited there.

65 See also Johnson, *Readers and Reading Culture*, 13, 41 and 65.

66 Charlotte Hempel, "The Long Text of the *Serekh* as Crisis Literature," *RevQ* 27 (2015): 3–24. See further Newsom, *Self as Symbolic Space*, 91–190 and already Murphy-O'Connor, "La genèse littéraire," 528–49.

67 Raymond P. Person, Jr. and Chris Keith, "Media Studies and Biblical Studies: An Introduction," in *The Dictionary of the Bible and Ancient Media*, ed. Tom Thatcher et al. (London: Bloomsbury T&T Clark, 2017), 4.

68 Person and Keith, "Media Studies and Biblical Studies," 4.

69 Cf. Johnson's pertinent observation that "each *literary program* seems to map onto the social ambitions and cultural traditions of the time," *Reading and Reading Culture*, 15–16.

70 boyd, "American Teen Sociality in Networked Publics," 119–69.

5 Conclusion

Our investigation of the interface of reality and textuality has uncovered a complex and symbiotic web of cross-fertilization. A strong case can be made in favor of acknowledging the complexity of the interface of life and text also in the Qumran sectarian texts. It is standard practice in scholarship on the Hebrew Bible and, indeed, the New Testament, to operate with a great deal of caution when mining the sources for the historical Jesus, Isaiah or Hezekiah. Moreover, the vogue for taking complex compositions such as the Community Rule as reflecting one community at one time has outlived its usefulness.[71] We are more likely to get a glimpse of some kind of social reality in the smaller building blocks that were eventually incorporated into complex literary artefacts. An excellent example is the account of the social support network for the most vulnerable where a "tax system" of two days' wages per month is outlined in the Damascus Document (CD 14:12–17 and 4QDᵃ [4Q266] 10 i 5–10). Particularly striking is the combination of terms employed to refer to the community. In addition to more familiar language such as "the many" (הרבים) and "camps" (מחנות) we also come across the distinctive language of "the association" (החבר) in the statement,

> *all* the work of the association (עבודת החבר) and *no* [*house of the association shall be cut off from*] *their* [*hand*].[72]
>
> CD 14:16–17; reconstructed with aid of 4Q266 [Dᵃ] 10 i 9–10 in *italics*

The term "association" (חבר) which occurs twice in this brief context suggests that some of this material was amalgamated into the camp movement framework that predominates in the Damascus Document.[73] While we cannot be sure that what we learn here reflects social realities, the passage warrants close attention since it breaks up a dominant frame of reference. Both the terminology and the substance of advocating a collective economic enterprise

---

71 See also Metso, "Methodological Problems," 322.

72 4Q266 10 i 9 begins this statement with "and for all" (ולכול), see Joseph M. Baumgarten, *Qumran Cave 4.XIII: The Damascus Document (4Q266–4Q273)*, DJD 18 (Oxford: Clarendon, 1996), 72–74; Charlotte Hempel, *The Damascus Texts*, CQS 1 (Sheffield: Sheffield Academic Press, 2000), esp. 40–41 and idem, *The Laws of the Damascus Document: Sources, Tradition and Redaction*, STDJ 29 (Leiden: Brill, 1998), 131–40.

73 Further, Hempel, *Damascus Texts*.

resemble later rabbinic accounts on the *ḥaburah* which also include רבים (*rabbim*) terminology.[74]

Beyond portraying potential glimpses of social reality, the act of committing such texts to writing conveys status to the anonymous scribes, the manuscripts and the communities they reflect. These inscribed communities only partially resemble life on the ground. The best way to conceive of the final product is of a blended textuality that draws on social realities which are skillfully curated in texts that also stake a claim in the thriving literary landscape of ancient Judaism. The scribes responsible for the high-quality manuscripts we are dealing with were metaphorically shouting: "Look at us and our community. We belong here among others who claim texts can maintain and repair the relationship of the Jewish people to God."

Bibliography

Alexander, Philip S., and Geza Vermes. *Qumran Cave 4.XIX: Serekh Ha-Yaḥad and Two Related Texts*. DJD 26. Oxford: Clarendon, 1998.

Anderson, Robert T., and Terry Giles. *The Samaritan Pentateuch: An Introduction to Its Origin, History, and Significance for Biblical Studies*. RBS 72. Atlanta, GA: SBL, 2012.

Barber, Karin. *The Anthropology of Texts, Persons and Publics*. Cambridge: Cambridge University Press, 2007.

Barker, Roger. *Ecological Psychology: Concepts and Methods for Studying the Environment of Human Behavior*. Stanford, CA: Stanford University Press, 1968.

Barton, John. "Source Criticism." Pages 162–65 in *The Anchor Bible Dictionary: Volume 6: Si–Z*. Edited by David Noel Freedman. New York, NY: Doubleday, 1992.

Barton, John. "Redaction Criticism." Pages 644–47 in *The Anchor Bible Dictionary: Volume 5: O–Sh*. Edited by David Noel Freedman. New York, NY: Doubleday, 1992.

Baumgarten, Joseph M., ed. *Qumran Cave 4.XIII: The Damascus Document (4Q266–4Q273)*. DJD 18. Oxford: Clarendon, 1996.

Beard, Mary. "Writing and Religion: Ancient Literacy and the Function of the Written Word in Roman Religion." Pages 35–58 in *Literacy in the Roman World*. Edited by Mary Beard, et al. Ann Arbor, MI: Journal of Roman Archaeology, 1991.

---

74   See Saul Lieberman, "The Discipline of the So-Called Dead Sea Manual of Discipline," *JBL* 71 (1952): 199–206 and, more recently, Fraade, *Legal Fictions*, 125–143 as well as Lawrence H. Schiffman, *Reclaiming the Dead Sea Scrolls: The History of Judaism, the Background to Christianity, the Lost Library of Qumran* (Philadelphia, PA: Jewish Publication Society, 1994), 104–105 and Hempel, *Community Rules from Qumran*, 171–216.

boyd, danah m. "Taken Out of Context: American Teen Sociality in Networked Publics." PhD diss. University of California, Berkeley, 2008.

Brooke, George J. "The Qumran Scrolls and the Demise of the Distinction Between Higher and Lower Criticism." Pages 26–42 in *New Directions in Qumran Studies*. Edited by Jonathan G. Campbell, William J. Lyons, and Lloyd K. Pietersen. LSTS 52. London: T&T Clark, 2005.

Cameron, Averil. *Christianity and the Rhetoric of Empire: The Development of Christian Discourse*. Berkeley, CA: University of California Press, 1991.

Carr, David M. *The Formation of the Hebrew Bible: A New Reconstruction*. Oxford: Oxford University Press, 2011.

Collins, John J. *Beyond the Qumran Community: The Sectarian Movement of the Dead Sea Scrolls*. Grand Rapids, MI: Eerdmans, 2010.

Davies, Philip R. *Behind the Essenes: History and Ideology in the Dead Sea Scrolls*. BJS 94. Atlanta, GA: Scholars Press, 1987.

Davies, Philip R. *Sects and Scrolls: Essays on Qumran and Related Topics*. SFSHJ 134. Atlanta, GA: Scholars Press, 1996.

Davies, Philip R. "Historiography." Pages 228–36 in *T&T Clark Companion to the Dead Sea Scrolls*. Edited by George J. Brooke and Charlotte Hempel, with the assistance of Michael DeVries and Drew Longacre. London: Bloomsbury, 2019.

Fraade, Steven D. "To Whom It May Concern: 4QMMT and Its Addressee(s)." *RevQ* 19 (2000): 507–26.

Fraade, Steven D. *Legal Fictions: Studies of Law and Narrative in the Discursive Worlds of Ancient Jewish Sectarians and Sages*. JSJS 147. Leiden: Brill, 2011.

Goffman, Erving. *The Presentation of Self in Everyday Life*. London: Penguin, 1990.

Goodacre, Mark. "How Reliable is the Story of the Nag Hammadi Discovery?" *JSNT* 35 (2013): 303–22.

Grossman, Maxine L. "Reading *4QMMT*: Genre and History." *RevQ* 20 (2001): 3–22.

Grossman, Maxine L. *Reading for History in the Damascus Document: A Methodological Study*. STDJ 45. Leiden: Brill, 2002.

Harkins, Angela K. "Who is the Teacher of the Teacher Hymns? Re-Examining the Teacher Hymns Hypothesis Fifty Years Later." Pages 449–67 in *A Teacher for All Generations: Essays in Honor of James C. VanderKam*. Edited by Eric Mason, Samuel I. Thomas, Alison Schofield, and Eugene Ulrich. JSJSup 153. Leiden: Brill, 2012.

Harkins, Angela K. *Reading with an "I" to the Heavens: Looking at the Qumran Hodayot through the Lens of Visionary Traditions*. Ekstasis 3. Berlin: De Gruyter, 2012.

Hempel, Charlotte. *The Laws of the Damascus Document: Sources, Tradition and Redaction*. STDJ 29. Leiden: Brill, 1998.

Hempel, Charlotte. *The Damascus Texts*. CQS 1. Sheffield: Sheffield Academic Press, 2000.

Hempel, Charlotte. "Sources and Redaction in the Dead Sea Scrolls: The Growth of Ancient Texts." Pages 162–81 in *Rediscovering the Dead Sea Scrolls: An Assessment of Old and New Approaches and Methods*. Edited by Maxine L. Grossman. Grand Rapids, MI: Eerdmans, 2010.

Hempel, Charlotte. "Who is Making Dinner at Qumran?" *JTS* 63 (2012): 49–65.

Hempel, Charlotte. *Qumran Rule Texts in Context: Collected Studies*. TSAJ 154. Tübingen: Mohr Siebeck, 2013.

Hempel, Charlotte. "The Long Text of the *Serekh* as Crisis Literature." *RevQ* 27 (2015): 3–24.

Hempel, Charlotte. "Reflections on Literacy, Textuality, and Community in the Qumran Dead Sea Scrolls." Pages 69–82 in *Is There a Text in this Cave? Studies in the Textuality of the Dead Sea Scrolls in Honour of George J. Brooke*. Edited by Ariel Feldman, Maria Cioată, and Charlotte Hempel. STDJ 119. Leiden: Brill, 2017.

Hempel, Charlotte. "Rules." Pages 405–12 in *T&T Clark Companion to the Dead Sea Scrolls*. George J. Brooke and Charlotte Hempel, with the assistance of Michael DeVries and Drew Longacre. London: Bloomsbury, 2019.

Hempel, Charlotte. "Bildung und Wissenswirtschaft im Judentum zur Zeit des Zweiten Tempels." Pages 229–44 in *Was ist Bildung in der Vormoderne*? Edited by Peter Gemeinhardt. Studies in Education and Religion in Ancient and Pre-Modern History in the Mediterranean and Its Environs 4. Tübingen: Mohr Siebeck, 2020.

Hempel, Charlotte. *The Community Rules from Qumran: A Commentary*. TSAJ 183. Tübingen: Mohr Siebeck, 2020.

Hempel, Charlotte. "The Dead Sea Scrolls: Challenging the Particularist Paradigm." Forthcoming in *Torah, Temple, Land: Ancient Judaism(s) in Context*. Edited by Bernd Schröter. TSAJ. Tübingen: Mohr Siebeck.

Hempel, Charlotte. "Self-Fashioning in the Dead Sea Scrolls: Thickening the Description of What Rule Texts Do." Forthcoming in *Social History of the Jews within the Ancient World*. Edited by Jonathan Ben-Dov and Michal Bar-Asher Siegal. TSAJ. Tübingen: Mohr Siebeck.

Hogan, Bernie. "The Presentation of Self in the Age of Social Media: Distinguishing Performances and Exhibitions Online." *Bulletin of Science, Technology and Society* 30 (2010): 377–86.

Holm-Nielsen, Svend. *Hodayot: Psalms from Qumran*. Aarhus: Universitetsforlaget, 1960.

Jefferson, Rebecca J. W. "Deconstructing 'the Cairo Genizah:' A Fresh Look at Genizah Manuscript Discoveries in Cairo before 1897." *JQR* 108 (2018): 422–48.

Johnson, William A. *Readers and Reading Culture in the High Roman Empire: A Study of Elite Communities*. Classical Culture and Society. Oxford: Oxford University Press, 2010.

Justnes, Årstein. "Fake Fragments, Flexible Provenances: Eight Aramaic 'Dead Sea Scrolls' from the 21st Century." Pages 242–71 in *Vision, Narrative, and Wisdom in the Aramaic Texts from Qumran*. Edited by Mette Bundvad and Kasper Siegismund. STDJ 131. Leiden: Brill, 2020.

Keegan, James G. "The History of the Discipline." Pages 59–78 in *The Oxford Handbook of Papyrology*. Edited by Roger S. Bagnall. Oxford: Oxford University Press, 2009.

Knoppers, Gary. *Jews and Samaritans: The Origin and History of their Early Relations*. Oxford: Oxford University Press, 2019.

Kratz, Reinhard G. *Historical and Biblical Israel: The History, Tradition, and Archives of the History of Israel and Judah*. Oxford: Oxford University Press, 2015.

Kratz, Reinhard G. "Biblical Scholarship and Qumran Studies." Pages 204–15 in *T&T Clark Companion to the Dead Sea Scrolls*. Edited by George J. Brooke and Charlotte Hempel, with the assistance of Michael DeVries and Drew Longacre. London: Bloomsbury, 2019.

Kratz, Reinhard G., ed. *Qumran 4QMMT: Some Precepts of the Law*. Sapere. Tübingen: Mohr Siebeck, 2020.

Lange, Armin. "7.2.1 Ancient Manuscript Evidence." in *Textual History of the Bible*, General Editor Armin Lange. Consulted online on 19 April 2020 http://dx.doi.org /.ezproxyd.bham.ac.uk/10.1163/2452-4107_thb_COM_0007020100.

Lapin, Hayim. "Dead Sea Scrolls and the Historiography of Ancient Judaism." Pages 108–27 in *Rediscovering the Dead Sea Scrolls: An Assessment of Old and New Approaches and Methods*. Edited by Maxine L. Grossman. Grand Rapids, MI: Eerdmans, 2010.

Law, Timothy Michael. *When God Spoke Greek: The Septuagint and the Making of the Christian Bible*. Oxford: Oxford University Press, 2013.

Lieberman, Saul. "The Discipline of the So-Called Dead Sea Manual of Discipline." *JBL* 71 (1952): 199–206.

Lieu, Judith M. *Christian Identity in the Jewish and Graeco-Roman World*. Oxford: Oxford University Press, 2004.

Lim, Timothy H. *The Formation of the Jewish Canon*. New Haven, CT: Yale University Press, 2013.

Magness, Jodi. *The Archaeology of Qumran and the Dead Sea Scrolls*. Studies in the Dead Sea Scrolls and Related Literature. Grand Rapids, MI: Eerdmans, 2002.

Martin, Malachi. *The Scribal Character of the Dead Sea Scrolls*. Bibliothèque du Muséon 44–45. Louvain: Publications universitaires, 1958.

Mason, Steve. "Essenes and Lurking Spartans in Josephus' *Judean War*: From Story to History." Pages 219–61 in *Making History: Josephus and Historical Method*. Edited by Zuleika Rogers. Leiden: Brill, 2007.

Mason, Steve. "Essenes." Pages 2501–2503 in *The Encyclopedia of Ancient History*. Edited by Roger S. Bagnall, Kai Brodersen, Craige B. Champion, Andrew Erskine, and Sabine R. Huebner. London: Blackwell, 2013.

Metso, Sarianna. *The Textual Development of the Qumran Community Rule*. STDJ 21. Leiden: Brill, 1997.

Metso, Sarianna. "In Search of the *Sitz im Leben* of the *Community Rule*." Pages 86–93 in *The Provo International Conference on the Dead Sea Scrolls: Technological Innovations, New Texts, and Reformulated Issues*. Edited by Donald W. Parry and Eugene Ulrich. STDJ 30. Leiden: Brill, 1998.

Metso, Sarianna. "Methodological Problems in Reconstructing History from Rule Texts Found at Qumran." *DSD* 11 (2004): 315–35.

Metso, Sarianna. *The Serekh Texts*. LSTS 62. London: T&T Clark, 2007.

Mizzi, Dennis. "Qumran Period I Reconsidered: An Evaluation of Several Competing Theories." *DSD* 22 (2015): 1–42.

Mizzi, Dennis. "Archaeology of Qumran." Pages 17–36 in *T&T Companion to the Dead Sea Scrolls*. Edited by George J. Brooke and Charlotte Hempel, with the assistance of Michael DeVries and Drew Longacre. London: Bloomsbury, 2019.

Mroczek, Eva. "The Hegemony of the Biblical in the Study of Second Temple Literature." *JAJ* 6 (2015): 1–35.

Mroczek, Eva. *The Literary Imagination in Jewish Antiquity*. Oxford: Oxford University Press, 2016.

Müller, Reinhard, and Juha Pakkala. eds. *Insights into Editing in the Hebrew Bible and the Ancient Near East: What Does Documented Evidence Tell us about the Transmission of Authoritative Texts*. Leuven: Peeters, 2017.

Murphy-O'Connor, Jerome. "La genèse littéraire de la Règle de la Communauté." *RB* 76 (1969): 528–49.

Najman, Hindy. *Seconding Sinai: The Development of Mosaic Discourse in Second Temple Judaism*. JSJSup 77. Leiden: Brill 2003.

Najman, Hindy. "Interpretation as Primordial Writing: Jubilees and Its Authority Conferring Strategies." Pages 39–71 in *Past Renewals: Interpretative Authority, Renewed Revelation and the Quest for Perfection in Jewish Antiquity*. Leiden: Brill, 2010.

Najman, Hindy. "The Vitality of Scripture Within and Beyond the 'Canon'." *JSJ* 43 (2012): 497–518.

Newsom, Carol A. *The Self as Symbolic Space: Constructing Identity and Community at Qumran*. STDJ 52. Leiden: Brill, 2004.

Nongbri, Brent. "Finding Early Christian Books at Nag Hammadi and Beyond." *Bulletin for the Study of Religion* 45 (2016): 11–19.

Person, Jr., Raymond F., and Chris Keith. "Media Studies and Biblical Studies: An Introduction." Pages 1–15 in *The Dictionary of the Bible and Ancient Media*. Edited by Tom Thatcher, Chris Keith, Raymond F. Person, Jr., and Elsie R. Stern. London: Bloomsbury, 2017.

Popović, Mladen. "Qumran as Scroll Storehouse in Times of Crisis? A Comparative Perspective on Judaean Desert Manuscript Collections." *JSJ* 43 (2012): 551–94.

Popović, Mladen. "The Ancient 'Library' of Qumran between Urban and Rural Culture." Pages 155–67 in *The Dead Sea Scrolls at Qumran and the Concept of a Library*. Edited by Sidnie White Crawford and Cecilia Wassén. STDJ 116. Leiden: Brill, 2016.

Popović, Mladen. "The Manuscript Collection: An Overview." Pages 37–50 in *T&T Clark Companion to the Dead Sea Scrolls*. Edited by George J. Brooke and Charlotte Hempel, with the assistance of Michael DeVries and Drew Longacre. London: Bloomsbury, 2019.

Pouilly, Jean. *La Règle de la Communauté de Qumrân: Son évolution littéraire*. CahRB 17. Paris: Gabalda, 1976.

Schiffman, Lawrence H. *Reclaiming the Dead Sea Scrolls: The History of Judaism, the Background to Christianity, the Lost Library of Qumran*. Philadelphia, PA: Jewish Publication Society, 1994.

Schofield, Alison. *From Qumran to the* Yaḥad: *A New Paradigm of Textual Development for The Community Rule*. STDJ 77. Leiden: Brill, 2009.

Schofield, Alison. "Forms of Community." Pages 533–46 in *T&T Companion to the Dead Sea Scrolls*. Edited by George J. Brooke and Charlotte Hempel, with the assistance of Michael DeVries and Drew Longacre. London: Bloomsbury, 2019.

Stock, Brian. *The Implications of Literacy: Written Language and Models of Interpretation in the Eleventh and Twelfth Centuries*. Princeton, NJ: Princeton University Press, 1983.

Taylor, Joan E. *The Essenes, the Scrolls, and the Dead Sea*. Oxford: Oxford University Press, 2012.

Tigchelaar, Eibert J. C. "The Dead Sea Scrolls." Pages 163–80 in *Eerdmans Dictionary of Early Judaism*. Edited by John J. Collins and Dan Harlow. Grand Rapids, MI: Eerdmans, 2010.

Tigchelaar, Eibert J. C. "The Scribes of the Scrolls." Pages 524–32 in *T&T Clark Companion to the Dead Sea Scrolls*. Edited by George J. Brooke and Charlotte Hempel, with the assistance of Michael DeVries and Drew Longacre. London: T&T Clark, 2019.

Toorn, Karel van der. *Scribal Culture and the Making of the Hebrew Bible*. Cambridge, MA: Harvard University Press, 2009.

Tov, Emanuel. *The Greek and Hebrew Bible: Collected Essays on the Septuagint*. VTSup 72. Leiden: Brill, 1999.

Tov, Emanuel. *Scribal Practices and Approaches Reflected in the Texts Found in the Judean Desert*. STDJ 54. Leiden: Brill, 2004.

Tov, Emanuel. *Textual Criticism of the Hebrew Bible*. 3rd ed. Minneapolis, MN: Fortress, 2012.

Tov, Emanuel. *Textual Criticism of the Hebrew Bible, Qumran, Septuagint: Collected Essays*. VTSup 167. Leiden: Brill, 2015.

Ulrich, Eugene C. "The Bible in the Making: The Scriptures Found at Qumran." Pages 51–66 in *The Bible at Qumran: Text, Shape, and Interpretation*. Edited by Peter

W. Flint. Studies in the Dead Sea Scrolls and Related Literature. Grand Rapids, MI: Eerdmans, 2001.

Ulrich, Eugene C. *The Dead Sea Scrolls and the Developmental Composition of the Bible*. Leiden: Brill, 2015.

VanderKam, James C. "Questions of Canon Viewed Through the Dead Sea Scrolls." Pages 91–109 in *The Canon Debate*. Edited by Lee M. McDonald and James A. Sanders. Peabody, MA: Hendrickson, 2002.

VanderKam, James C. *The Dead Sea Scrolls and the Bible*. Grand Rapids, MI: Eerdmans, 2012.

Werrett, Ian. "Is Qumran a Library?" Pages 78–105 in *The Dead Sea Scrolls at Qumran and the Concept of a Library*. Edited by Sidnie White Crawford and Cecilia Wassén. STDJ 116. Leiden: Brill, 2016.

White Crawford, Sidnie. *Scribes and Scrolls at Qumran*. Grand Rapids, MI: Eerdmans, 2019.

Williams, Alex. "On the Tip of Creative Tongues." *The New York Times*, Section ST, page 1, 2 October 2009.

Yadin, Yigael. *The Message of the Scrolls*. Christian Origins Library. New York, NY: Crossroad, 1992.

Zahn, Molly M. "Parabiblical Literature/Rewritten Scripture." Pages 378–85 in *T&T Clark Companion to the Dead Sea Scrolls*. Edited by George J. Brooke and Charlotte Hempel, with the assistance of Michael DeVries and Drew Longacre. London: Bloomsbury, 2019.

Zahn, Molly M. *Genres of Rewriting in Second Temple Judaism: Scribal Composition and Transmission*. Cambridge: Cambridge University Press, 2020.

Zangenberg, Jürgen. "Archaeology, Papyri and Inscriptions." Pages 201–35 in *Eerdmans Dictionary of Early Judaism*. Edited by John J. Collins and Dan Harlow. Grand Rapids, MI: Eerdmans, 2010.

CHAPTER 10

Orality and Written-ness in the Dead Sea Scrolls: Where Have We Got to and Where Are We Going?

George J. Brooke

1 Introduction

What motivates this paper? In 2017 I was honoured to receive a very handsome collection of essays for a 65th birthday present. The book was on the theme of textuality, broadly conceived. The discovery and publication of multiple versions of several compositions found in the caves at and near Qumran has raised acutely the issue for the student of Judaism as to what might constitute a text. The Festschrift prepared for me was entitled *Is There a Text in This Cave?*[1] The play on the title of the famous book by Stanley Fish was deliberate.[2] However, as the subtitle of his work discloses, Fish had been concerned primarily with how multiple readers of any single text create multiple texts through their reading strategies, their interpretative lenses, and so on, so that any single text becomes manifold through its readers. The issues facing those engaging with the Dead Sea Scrolls concern not just readers but also those involved in the production and transmission of texts in antiquity. The challenge of the variegated evidence of textual vitality[3] from the Qumran caves requires something more than the well-developed approaches of historical criticism whose tenets overwhelmingly explain variety through the identification of multiple sources, the discernment of multi-layered editing processes and the assumption of the scribal corruption of texts.[4] My motivation is thus to engage with

---

1 Ariel Feldman, Maria Cioată, and Charlotte Hempel, eds., *Is There a Text in This Cave? Studies in the Textuality of the Dead Sea Scrolls in Honour of George J. Brooke*, STDJ 119 (Leiden: Brill, 2017).

2 Stanley E. Fish, *Is There a Text in This Class?: The Authority of Interpretive Communities* (Cambridge, MA: Harvard University Press, 1980).

3 I borrow the language of vitality from Hindy Najman, "The Vitality of Scripture Within and Beyond the 'Canon'," *JSJ* 43 (2012): 497–518; Najman uses the term to express how authoritative texts have a vital significance in several ways, not least in generating further textual production.

4 A helpful collection of essays indicating worthwhile directions of travel is Raymond F. Person Jr. and Robert Rezetko, eds., *Empirical Models Challenging Biblical Criticism*, AIL 25 (Atlanta, GA: SBL, 2016).

© GEORGE J. BROOKE, 2023 | DOI:10.1163/9789004537804_011

the manuscript media to move towards a more satisfactory set of descriptions and explanations of the multiform data.

My own assumption is that the manuscript media from the Qumran caves and the other material evidence is part of a complex cultural context in which traits from both east and west were mixed together in ways which we do not yet fully appreciate.[5] In addition while much has been achieved in appreciating all this material by those of the first and second generations, mostly biblical scholars of one sort or another, it has long been time to involve the scholarly insights of other disciplines and to transform the endeavour into a multi-disciplinary enterprise, as some have indeed attempted for some specific matters with particular reference to the social sciences.[6] The 2017 article on the Scrolls by Bennie Reynolds in the generally highly informative *Dictionary of the Bible and Ancient Media* is largely a descriptive summary of the Scrolls themselves and barely addresses the issues at stake for the Scrolls as media.[7] I offer this study as a somewhat programmatic contribution that attempts to set out a set of issues and problems that seem to me to be facing students of the Dead Sea Scrolls in relation to orality and written-ness; the distinction of those two facets in terms of textual formation, transmission and performance is done primarily for heuristic purposes—part of what is needed is attention to what Shem Miller has offered for the Scrolls, namely some understanding of oral-written texts.[8]

---

5   From this perspective in relation to orality and literacy it is important for scholars of Second Temple period Jewish texts to consider the way that the study of classical texts has been in the vanguard. For the post Parry-Lord generation, for the study of primary oral tradition, see, e.g., Geoffrey S. Kirk, *Homer and the Oral Tradition* (Cambridge: Cambridge University Press, 1976); Rosalind Thomas, *Oral Tradition and Written Record in Classical Athens*, Cambridge Studies in Oral and Literate Culture (Cambridge: Cambridge University Press, 1989). For residual orality, which is perhaps more important for consideration of the Dead Sea Scrolls, see, e.g., the insightful studies in the series Orality and Literacy in the Ancient World (Leiden: Brill).

6   See, e.g., Eyal Regev's sociological analysis of introvertionist sectarian communities: Eyal Regev, *Sectarianism in Qumran: A Cross-Cultural Perspective*, Religion and Society 45 (Berlin: De Gruyter, 2007); or the use of social psychology by Jutta Jokiranta, "Black Sheep, Outsiders, and the Qumran Movement: Social-Psychological Perspectives on Norm—Deviant Behaviour," in *Social Memory and Social Identity in the Study of Early Judaism and Early Christianity*, ed. Samuel Byrskog, Raimo Hakola and Jutta Jokiranta, NTOA/SUNT 116 (Göttingen: Vandenhoeck & Ruprecht, 2016), 151–73.

7   Bennie H. Reynolds, III, "Dead Sea Scrolls and Other Judean Desert Texts," in *The Dictionary of the Bible and Ancient Media*, ed. Tom Thatcher et al. (London: T&T Clark, 2017), 74–80.

8   Shem Miller, "The Oral-Written Textuality of Stichographic Poetry in the Dead Sea Scrolls," *DSD* 22 (2015): 162–88; idem, "'Sectual' Performance in Rule Texts," *DSD* 25 (2018): 17–18; see further idem, *Dead Sea Media: Orality, Textuality, and Memory in the Scrolls from the Judean*

2   The Problem of Written-ness

A first point is almost too basic to mention. The discovery of skin, papyrus and copper scrolls from the late Second Temple period, together with some inscribed potsherds, encouraged scholars to focus almost exclusively on what was written. What was written, written-ness and writing have become the principal subjects of study. Priority has been given to the written evidence and several other aspects of the texts have been overlooked. Amongst those overlooked aspects are the nature of the scrolls as archaeological artefacts in need of a finds context, the character of the scrolls in terms of their material culture, shape, size and presentation, and the need to consider in detail how the material remains challenge some of the basic tenets of historical criticism. It seems that many scholars when they use the Dead Sea Scrolls in their work begin with an available edition of the texts in printed or electronic form and not with images of the fragmentary remains, even though for the most part those are now readily available on the Leon Levy website (deadseascrolls.org.il). The tide is turning and there are many instances of scholarly contributions where the material evidence is presented and problematized, but there is still room for more nuanced handling of the primary evidence, engaging with it not just as written text.

In fact, this is not a new phenomenon. A concern with being written has been noticed by scholars in the texts themselves, namely their own attention to what is written. In other words, some of the compositions show a self-awareness about matters of media. For example, in relation to the citation of authoritative sources, things are recognised as "written in the book of Isaiah the prophet" (4Q174 1–2 i 15), or engraved, for example, "in the heavenly tablets."[9] Such explicit attention to written-ness might reflect an implicit anxiety about the relative statuses of what is spoken and what is written or a concern to make explicit a shift in authority structures in some circles, a shift from the oral to the written, a shift which was to become ever more significant in the period after the destruction of the Temple in 70 CE when text and customary practice demoted temple and land as the key markers of Jewish identity.

Desert, STDJ 129 (Leiden: Brill, 2019), esp. 116–87, Chapter 3 on "Oral-Written Textuality" and Chapter 4 on "Oral-Written Register."

9   See, e.g., James C. VanderKam, "The Putative Author of the Book of Jubilees," *JSS* 26 (1981): 209–17; repr. in idem, *From Revelation to Canon: Studies in the Hebrew Bible and Second Temple Judaism*, JSPSup 62 (Leiden: Brill, 2000), 439–47 on Jubilees; Hindy Najman, "The Symbolic Significance of Writing in Ancient Judaism," in *The Idea of Biblical Interpretation: Essays in Honor of James L. Kugel*, ed. Hindy Najman and Judith H. Newman, JSJSup 83 (Leiden: Brill, 2004), 139–73.

The attention to the written artefact has had a knock-on effect in relation to the scholarly understanding of some of the manuscripts themselves. I have in mind the discussion of re*written* Bible, which has then been applied to various compositions amongst the Dead Sea Scrolls corpus as if the process of production and transmission was exclusively or almost exclusively about writing and re-writing. But what if priority was given to speech and oral performance in relation to such works; then there is a different feel, a different set of possibilities. Perhaps the discussion should rather be of re-spoken Torah, or re-oralised Torah; it is then possible to re-imagine the processes of production and transmission of the text in ways that give greater place to contexts in which teaching and instruction and their oral character have a leading role. I like to think that I played a small part in signalling this quite a while ago when in discussions about how 4Q365 and its associated manuscripts might be named; rather than the use of the label "rewritten," I suggested the use of the designation "reworked": Reworked Pentateuch was indeed the designation adopted.[10] "Reworked" how? Orally or in writing, or both as oral-written? And, then, there is of course the basic question: are not all texts "reworkings"?

3   The Problem of Orality

Several issues can be mentioned in relation to orality itself. The first matter concerns what seems to be a dearth of studies that have sought to place the Scrolls in relation to orality, particularly as that has played a significant role in discussions of the last thirty years or more about how the scriptures of the Hebrew Bible came to be the way they are, especially through various contexts in the Second Temple period. This might simply be the corollary of my opening point, that the very nature of the manuscripts as written material has inhibited scholars. In fact, on the Orion Center Bibliography, there is only one article from the over 23,000 items listed from the last twenty-five years or so that uses the term in its title;[11] a search will give you items concerning m*orality*, immo*rality*, temp*orality*, even corp*orality*, but not orality plain and simple! There

---

10   The opportunity for such a contribution occurred while I was a research fellow at the Annenberg Institute, Philadelphia, in 1992, where Emanuel Tov and Sidnie White Crawford were working on the principal edition of 4Q365 and related compositions and were seeking advice on suitable designations.

11   The important study by Jason Silverman, "The Media of Influence: Orality, Literacy, and Cultural Interaction," in *Persepolis and Jerusalem: Iranian Influence on the Apocalyptic Hermeneutic*, ed. Jason M. Silverman, LHBOTS 558 (London: T&T Clark, 2012), 175–205.

are a few more items that use the word oral, but without the contributions of Shem Miller even they are few and far between.

A second more general observation in relation to orality concerns the scholarly debates in related fields that might restrict treatment of the Dead Sea Scrolls themselves. Three traditional approaches can be mentioned. To begin with there is the long-standing and somewhat problematic view that orality belongs to social settings that are exemplary of "primitive" groups. Then, secondly, partly as a development of such ideas, orality is linked principally or exclusively to the pre-written stages of text composition. Here the influence of New Testament scholars can be discerned. I suspect that a lack of manuscript evidence has encouraged many New Testament scholars to be concerned for longer with questions of orality, since almost certainly they have nothing written from the first century in any case. New Testament scholars have indeed moved forwards,[12] so that orality is seen as significant in more ways than merely in the formation of texts. For example, some prominence has been given to memory studies,[13] a method also applied by some to the Scrolls.[14] And lastly, thirdly, there are the parameters of discussion associated with the persistent but regularly refined notions of oral and written Torah;[15] to what

---

12   See, e.g., the stimulating set of essays in Tom Thatcher, ed., *Jesus, the Voice, and the Text: Beyond the Oral and the Written Gospel* (Waco, TX: Baylor University Press, 2008).

13   See, e.g., Anthony Le Donne, *The Historiographical Jesus: Memory, Typology, and the Son of David* (Waco, TX: Baylor University Press, 2009); Robert K. McIver, *Memory, Jesus, and the Synoptic Gospels*, RBS 59 (Atlanta, GA: SBL, 2011); Chris Keith, "Social Memory Theory and Gospels Research: The First Decade," *Early Christianity* 6 (2015): 354–76 (Part One), 517–42 (Part Two). Although Le Donne's study is based on his Durham PhD thesis, it is interesting to note that memory studies are significantly absent from a slightly earlier Durham product, James D. G. Dunn, *Jesus Remembered*, Christianity in the Making 1 (Grand Rapids, MI: Eerdmans, 2003); on pp. 197–98 Dunn discusses memorization only in describing the contribution of Birger Gerhardsson.

14   See, e.g., Loren T. Stuckenbruck, "The Teacher of Righteousness Remembered: From Fragmentary Sources to Collective Memory in the Dead Sea Scrolls," in *Memory in the Bible and Antiquity: The Fifth Durham-Tübingen Research Symposium (Durham, September 2004)*, ed. Stephen Barton, Loren T. Stuckenbruck and Benjamin G. Wold, WUNT 212 (Tübingen: Mohr Siebeck, 2007), 75–94; George J. Brooke, "Memory, Cultural Memory and Rewriting Scripture," in *Rewritten Bible after Fifty Years: Texts, Terms, or Techniques? A Last Dialogue with Geza Vermes*, ed. József Zsellengér, JSJSup 166 (Leiden: Brill, 2014), 119–36; idem, "Praying History in the Dead Sea Scrolls: Memory, Identity, Fulfilment," in *Function of Psalms and Prayers in the Late Second Temple Period*, ed. Mika Pajunen and Jeremy Penner, BZAW 486 (Berlin: De Gruyter, 2017), 305–19; Travis B. Williams, *History and Memory in the Dead Sea Scrolls: Remembering the Teacher of Righteousness* (Cambridge: Cambridge University Press, 2019).

15   See, e.g., Martin Jaffee, *Torah in the Mouth: Writing and Oral Tradition in Palestinian Judaism 200 BCE–400 CE* (New York, NY: Oxford University Press, 2001).

extent such paradigms are relevant to the study of the evidence in the period when certain texts were moving from authority to canon, but were not yet fixed, is a matter for discussion.[16]

In my opinion none of those three approaches is adequate to the task of engaging with the role of orality in relation to the understanding of the textuality of the Dead Sea Scrolls. There needs to be a place for the spoken and the read word, as those who pay attention to oral literature strongly indicate, with the read word belonging technically to the area of residual orality. This is most obvious when trying to understand the role of key terms such as *'āmar* or *qārā'*. For the latter, for instance, its use in 1QS 6:7–8 ("And the Many shall be on watch together for a third of each night of the year in order to read [*qr'*] the book, explain the regulation, and bless together") does not necessarily mean that a manuscript was held in the hand of the reader and presented in a monochrome voice; rather reading was much more likely to have been the performance and re-presentation of the text, voiced with emphasis and cadence, and probably glossed. It is such reading processes, each understood in some kind of context, that might begin to explain some of the multiple variants, both major and minor, in the so-called biblical Scrolls found in the caves.

4 The Challenges of the Intellectual Traditions of Orality Studies

Orality Studies can be characterised briefly as having three phases, and those three phases have created a set of opportunities and accompanying problems for the appreciation of ancient texts.

The first phase for students of Biblical Studies belongs most clearly with the insights and focus of scholars such as Hermann Gunkel (1862–1932) whose approach to the development of some biblical texts, built in some measure on nineteenth-century views about the recoverability of the *ipsissima verba* of the prophets, was a willingness to engage with contemporary insights that were emerging from the study of longstanding traditions of story-telling, both as those were observed in various European contexts, but perhaps more significantly in non-European non-written societies. So, on the one hand, there were

---

16 Those and other methodological issues are set out by Shemaryahu Talmon, "Oral Tradition and Written Transmission, or the 'Heard' and the 'Seen' Word in Judaism of the Second Temple Period," in *Jesus and the Oral Gospel Tradition*, ed. Henry Wansbrough, JSNTSup 64 (Sheffield: Sheffield Academic Press, 1991), 121–58, repr. in idem, *Text and Canon of the Hebrew Bible: Collected Studies* (Winona Lake, IN: Eisenbrauns, 2010), 85–124. Talmon is right to point out the inadequacies of Werner Kelber's dismissal of Qumran evidence and to construct an argument for its relevance.

the collectors and re-presenters of all kinds of myths and fairy stories, from the brothers Grimm through George Macdonald (1824–1905) and Andrew Lang (1844–1912), so that one of the finest scholars of the Jewish and Christian so-called apocryphal texts, Montague Rhodes James (1862–1936), was also a highly regarded teller of mystery tales and ghost stories. Moses Gaster (1856–1939) represents such intellectual activity for Eastern Europe. And, on the other hand, the explorers, missionary workers, and students of nascent social and cultural anthropology were providing information and creating patterns of understanding that prioritised oral tradition, especially story-telling. All this created what we might call the problem of the "primitive," namely that pre-literate societies could be characterised as oral, and by overly simplistic transference, the pre-written stages of a literary composition were most likely also oral. Worth holding onto might be the notion of the priority of orality, but its workings need full integration within the complex processes of the formation and transmission of "oral-written" texts within a carefully described set of cultural parameters.

In a second phase, which is not uncommonly referred to as the Parry—Lord period, the descriptive and analytical concerns of scholars were refined.[17] As such it was more often noticed that orality was not just primitive or the key to understanding the pre-written form of texts, but a major part in understanding their transmission. Nevertheless, the key issue that emerged might be characterised as the problem of the universal, a problem that has been both influential and generally helpful in the formulation of theoretical approaches based in the social sciences, but which is also now recognized as insufficiently nuanced in accounting for the culturally local and specific.[18] In addition, insufficient attention seems to have been paid by scholars interested in using the insights of these scholars to the way in which texts are defined as such. No performance of a "text" is ever the same as another; "texts" are narrative frames rather than items memorized verbatim. Worth holding onto in relation to the Scrolls is the way in which texts are both stable and unstable at the same time.[19]

---

17   See, e.g., Milman Parry, *The Making of Homeric Verse: The Collected Papers of Milman Parry*, ed. Adam Parry (Oxford: Clarendon Press, 1971); Albert Lord, *The Singer of Tales*, Harvard Studies in Comparative Literature 24 (Cambridge, MA: Harvard University Press, 1960).

18   The problem of the universal in this regard is clearly visible in the system of classifying folktales constructed by Antti Aarne, *The Types of the Folktale: A Classification and Bibliography*, trans. and ed. Stith Thompson (Helsinki: Suomalainen Tiedeaketemia, 1928).

19   From the field of textual criticism in English Literature, the remarks of Peter Shillingsburg on textual variation are pertinent: see Peter Shillingsburg, *Textuality and Knowledge: Essays* (University Park, PA: University of Pennsylvania Press, 2017), Chapters 4 ("Some Functions of Textual Criticism," 48–63), 5 ("Responsibility for Textual Changes in Long-Distance

More recently still, in a third phase, of which current scholars are the immediate heirs and participants, orality has been engaged with in finer detail as part of particular sub-disciplines, such as memory studies,[20] dialectology, socio-linguistics, communication and media studies, and the neurosciences. For the neurosciences, I have been intrigued by what is now known about various types of eye movement and how the brain, culturally informed, even moulded, processes what is seen. There are four types of movement: saccades, smooth pursuit movements, vergence movements, and vestibulo-ocular movements. Each kind of eye movement has a different function. In reading it is saccades (French for "jerk") that are at play: "they are rapid, ballistic movements of the eyes that abruptly change the point of fixation and they can range in amplitude from the small movements made while reading, for example, to the much larger movements made while gazing around a room. Saccades can be elicited voluntarily, but occur reflexively whenever the eyes are open."[21] In the reading or dictation of a written text, residual orality, how much of oral performance is interfered with by rapid eye movement? For cases of homoioarchton or homoioteleuton might intentional eye movement enable deliberate omission in some instances, whereas at other times the reflex activity could cause an accidental omission? Here, faced with the ongoing and in many respects increasing fragmentation of knowledge, it is difficult to determine an overall picture of how orality should be understood and located in the scheme of things. Nevertheless, worth holding onto for the study of the Scrolls are the variegated ways that orality is both individually and socially embodied.

5   The Ongoing Search for the Archetype and the Marginalization of Orality and Textual Fluidity

Beyond the theoretical opportunities and problems associated with orality studies, there are problems associated with how written texts have been understood, not least in the study of the Hebrew Bible/Old Testament. Some of those approaches and their problems are still around, not least because of the Dead Sea Scrolls. I will give a little focus to what is at stake by considering briefly and perhaps in a slightly distorted fashion some of the concerns of the

---

Revisions," 64–82), 8 ("How Literary Works Exist," 115–33), and 9 ("Convenient Scholarly Editions," 134–44).

20   For the study of particular variants see, e.g., William A. Tooman, "Authenticating Oral and Memory Variants in Ancient Hebrew Literature," *JSS* 64 (2019): 91–114.

21   Dale Purves et al., *Neuroscience*, 5th ed. (Sunderland, MA: Sinauer Associates, 2001), 223–50.

Hebrew Bible: A Critical Edition. That project has as its goal the production of a written text of each book of the Hebrew Bible which will purport to be the earliest from of the written text attainable through the application of standard norms of textual criticism. Why is this relevant? It is relevant in a context like that of this set of conference proceedings because such editorial aspirations have been stimulated in large measure because of the finds coming from the Judean wilderness.

One of the key issues in that editorial project concerns how the evidence of the Dead Sea Scrolls is treated. Of course, the Scrolls can be used in varieties of ways, but in this instance, they are not treated as objects in their own right but as the means to an end quite apart from them. And the application of the norms of classical textual criticism results in the understanding of variants chiefly as indications of error, together with an attitude to text that gives priority to views about the transmission of texts from one written form to another, so that the role of orality in both the formation and transmission of texts is minimized or sidestepped altogether.

Here is one small example. The possibility that the so-called biblical Scrolls would facilitate the search for textual archetypes was anticipated in those editions of Dead Sea Scroll manuscripts that came out of Harvard in the 1980s and 1990s; under the aegis of Frank Moore Cross, Harvard had become a bastion for rigorous text criticism of a sophisticated but traditional sort. In the principal edition of 4QGen[g] there is a variant in the text of Gen 1:5 which is described as follows by James Davila its editor:

> יומם T[ONJF(P)] Syr] יום MT, SP, LXX, OL, V. The reading in 4QGen[g] etc. seems to be a systematic alteration of original יום in Gen 1:1–2:4a wherever the word is used in an abstract sense (1:5, 14, 16, 18). Of these only the present passage is preserved in 4QGen[g], but T[ONJF(P)] Syr have the Aramaic equivalent of יומם for each dialect in each case. When the reference is to a specific day the word corresponding to יום is always used (1:5, 8, 13, 19, 23, 31, 2:2, 3; none of these references is preserved after 1:13 in 4QGen[g]). It is possible that the alteration arose from a dittography of mem in an early MS or one written in Palaeo-Hebrew script. In either case there would have been no distinction between medial and final mem. Once the error was present it could easily have spread to other passages where it seemed appropriate.[22]

---

22   James Davila, "7. 4QGenesis[g]," in *Genesis to Numbers*, DJD XII (Oxford: Clarendon Press, 1994), 59.

That interpretation of the variant describes scribal activity that is understood as probably having been based on an error. The reading is evidently secondary, but Davila has concluded that it is the result of dittography.

In his theoretical underpinning of *The Hebrew Bible: A Critical Edition*, Ronald Hendel writes as follows:

> The secondary reading יומם is a LBH usage, meaning not "by day" (as it does in CBH) but "daytime." The LBH meaning derives from Aramaic יממא (Joosten 2008: 95–97). This revision disambiguates the meaning of יום ("day"), which can mean a (whole) day or daytime (as in English and other languages). "Daytime" clarifies the obvious contextual sense of יום[1] in 1:5, whereas יום[2] means "(whole) day." The Targums and Peshitta have the same reading in vv. 14, 16, and 18, suggesting a Hebrew parent text with יומם in these verses also (4QGen[g] lacks these portions).[23]

There is a significant shift here away from the explanation of a variant as a scribal error towards seeing it as a secondary interpretative reading of a problematic text. Nevertheless, the aim overall is not to enjoy the vitality of the variant but to use it to assist in the determination of the earliest reconstructable form of written archetype for the book of Genesis. The place of orality in any process of textual transmission is ignored.

There is an intriguing corollary to the way in which the biblical Scrolls have been turned by some towards the construction of written archetypes. That corollary emerges neatly from consideration of Susan Niditch's wise insights of long ago, namely that attention to the formation of texts in such ways also gives priority to the written over the oral in terms of sources. She has written:

> Turning our ancestors into ourselves, we call the Israelites 'people of the book' and reinforce this proverbial image of a community well versed in the skills of literacy with scholarly treatments of the last century that seek to explain the genesis of the Hebrew Bible and to explore the relationships between the literature and actual Israelites. For example, behind the documentary hypothesis associated with Julius Wellhausen but still influential today is the assumption that written layers or sources—the earliest dating back to the Davidic monarchy of the tenth century BCE—underlie large portions of scripture.
>
> These written sources, it is suggested, were woven together and edited in a cumulative process of writing. Other more recent studies emphasize

---

23 Ronald Hendel, *Steps to a New Edition of the Hebrew Bible* (Atlanta, GA: SBL, 2017), 36.

'intertextuality' in the Bible, one writer's quotation of another's written, fixed text. Other scholars regard large portions of scripture as the product of modern-style literati or of ancient historiographers, all of whom rely upon the resources or reflect the values of an essentially literate culture.

Neglected in all these approaches is the importance of the oral world for understanding the Bible's written words.[24]

Niditch's words speak for themselves, but for me it is interesting to note her attention, by way of example, to how source criticism of the Old Testament has undermined the role of orality. I think that it is no accident that scholars such as Ronald Hendel, deeply immersed in a highly refined text-critical project of a traditional sort, are also those who are proponents of the so-called neo-documentary hypothesis.

What might be proposed as an antidote to this ongoing tendency towards the marginalization of orality in some quarters? It is especially worth holding on to the idea that at least in some cultural contexts, even after writing has taken place, the oral form of a text retains its authority as determinative of the next written instantiation of the text. In the rest of this paper I will suggest some steps for how the balance between the oral and the written can be reworked for the better appreciation of the evidence of the Dead Sea Scrolls and I will raise some questions that might be taken into account as the Scrolls are used to provide evidence of a particular oral-written culture.

6 Searching for Evidence of Orality in the Dead Sea Scrolls

There are three matters of scribal practice that provide evidence for orality in the transmission of texts. These are matters of residual orality, as technically defined.[25] These matters have been commented upon generally by Martin Jaffee in his 2001 monograph where he characterizes Second Temple Judaism as a scribal phenomenon in which orality belonged in some limited measure to the production of texts and their subsequent performance, a practice that resulted in multiple versions of authoritative traditions in particular.[26]

First, orality is discernible in scribal copying practice. The first location of evidence for orality has long been noted and this concerns those variants from

---

24 Susan Niditch, *Oral World and Written Word* (Louisville, KY: Westminster John Knox, 1996), 1.

25 By McLuhan and others, see Silverman, "The Media of Influence," 101.

26 Jaffee, *Torah in the Mouth*, 26–27.

some previously known compositions that can best be understood as involving a process of dictation or of visual error, deliberate or unintentional. In all of this it is important to recall that the Hebrew and Aramaic texts are written without vocalisation, though there are various additional vowel-letters in differing orthographies. Thus, a scribe might be visually copying from an exemplar and misread or misremember that exemplar as he rehearses the text into written form in its new copy. Or, as the recipient of the exemplar through dictation he might misconstrue what he was hearing, perhaps because of homophony or because he expected to hear something else. Those are cases of the classic oral/aural transmission changes. Most substantially recently, Raymond Person has indicated how some of the variants in 1QIsa[a] are best explained by the "oral mindset" of the scribes that produced the text.[27]

But the representation of a tradition in multiple ways, multiformity, is evidence of the need for the text critic to take account of the way scribes might be deemed to be oral performers of the tradition.[28] At one level this is evident in the multiple text types that exist in the pre-canonical era. For Person such multiformity indicates that

> the ancient Israelite scribes were performers of their traditions in ways analogous to oral bards .... Each manuscript represents the broader tradition as an imperfect instantiation of the broader tradition that existed, on the one hand, in the interplay of coexisting parallel written texts, none of which alone can possibly represent the fullness of the tradition, and, on the other hand, in the mental text in the collective memory of the people.[29]

---

27   Raymond Person, "The Ancient Israelite Scribe as Performer," *JBL* 117 (1998): 601–9; idem, *The Deuteronomistic History and the Book of Chronicles: Scribal Works in an Oral World*, AIL 6 (Leiden: Brill, 2010). Person's work is used favourably by David M. Carr, "Orality, Textuality, *and* Memory: The State of Biblical Studies," in *Contextualizing Israel's Sacred Writings: Ancient Literacy, Orality, and Literary Production*, ed. Brian B. Schmidt, AIL 22 (Atlanta, GA: SBL, 2015), 163.

28   As has been argued in relation to Anglo-Saxon poetry by A. Nicholas Doane, "The Ethnography of Scribal Writing and Anglo-Saxon Poetry: Scribe as Performer," *Oral Tradition* 9 (1994): 429–39; Doane is cited approvingly by Susan Niditch, *Oral World and Written Word*, 75.

29   Raymond Person, "Text Criticism as a Lens for Understanding the Transmission of Ancient Texts in Their Oral Environments," in *Contextualizing Israel's Sacred Writings: Ancient Literacy, Orality, and Literary Production*, ed. Brian B. Schmidt, AIL 22 (Atlanta, GA: SBL, 2015), 197.

Person uses the so-called Reworked Pentateuch manuscripts as primary evidence for his approach. Those manuscripts have recently come to be recognized as Torah or Pentateuch, but their variations indicate the need for multiple forms of the same tradition to be accounted for in some manner. The role of orality in such accounts has yet to be adequately determined and described.

Second, orality is discernible in paratextual indicators. Most manuscripts display evidence that might be interpreted as indicating a role for oral performance. Here it is probably important to distinguish between oral performance through memory and that through reading. The Dead Sea Scrolls provide some evidence for what we can most readily recognize as reading performance. The most obvious features are various paragraphing techniques that nearly all manuscripts display. Those indicate how compositions are broken into units that are manageable for various reading purposes, perhaps particularly liturgical reading.[30]

Sometimes marginal marks in a manuscript highlight material that might require special attention in reading or indicate something about the earlier history of the composition in which an oral stage has probably played a part. There are a set of saltire crosses in the margins of Pesher Habakkuk, but one of them has a slightly different appearance and seems to be more akin to a Hebrew ʾalef. It occurs at a point at which the commentary on part of Habakkuk has been extended, as internal textual evidence seems to confirm. Was that supplementation the result solely of an editorial writing process by a scribe working at his desk or was it the result of someone hearing a more elaborate discussion, perhaps even participating in it orally, and then making real the fruits of that discussion the next time the Pesher is copied out, perhaps after an earlier copy of the composition has received a marginal gloss?[31]

In addition, there has been a very long-standing discussion of the use of paleo-Hebrew for the divine name in some manuscripts, both what might be deemed scriptural and others that were probably not.[32] Was the change of font,

---

30   On sense units in the Scrolls see Emanuel Tov, *Scribal Practices and Approaches Reflected in the Texts Found in the Judean Desert*, STDJ 54 (Leiden: Brill, 2004), 131–66.

31   See George J. Brooke, "Physicality, Paratextuality and Pesher Habakkuk," in *On the Fringe of Commentary: Metatextuality in Ancient Near Eastern and Ancient Mediterranean Cultures*, ed. Sidney H. Aufrère, Philip S. Alexander and Zlatko Pleše in association with C. J. Bouloux, OLA 232 (Leuven: Peeters, 2014), 175–93. For how someone *hearing* Pesher Habakkuk might construe its authority see Jutta Jokiranta, "Quoting, Writing, and Reading: Authority in Pesher Habakkuk from Qumran," in *Between Canonical and Apocryphal Texts: Processes of Reception, Rewriting and Interpretation in Early Judaism and Early Christianity*, ed. Jörg Frey, Claire Clivaz and Tobias Nicklas, WUNT 419 (Tübingen: Mohr Siebeck, 2019), 185–211.

32   See Tov, *Scribal Practices and Approaches*, 238–46.

ORALITY AND WRITTEN-NESS IN THE DEAD SEA SCROLLS 371

the use of such letters in some manuscripts by some scribes a straightforward act of respect for the *nomina sacra* or was it that in combination with a desire to allow for readers to anticipate the divine name and pronounce an alternative euphemism?

Third, orality can be discerned in compositions that refer to community activities.[33] Evidence of orality is found in several instances in the Scrolls where community activities are described and some kind of oral performance seems likely. Such contexts for orality will be discussed further below, but here it is worth drawing attention to the emic description of what takes place in the community every night: "And the Congregation shall watch in community for a third of every night of the year, to read the Book and to study the Law and to bless together" (1QS 6:6–8).[34] Elsewhere I have proposed that the three activities referred to here may be much richer than might be supposed.[35] Shem Miller has largely endorsed my views in a recent study.[36] Reading the Book might well involve an active oral participation in the text as received so that there is oral rephrasing of the text in its representation.[37] The example cited earlier in this paper of the addition of a single *mem* in Gen 1:5 in 4QGen^g, is to my mind an exegetical plus perhaps produced through oral glossing. My own view is that many of the so-called re-writings in the scriptural compositions as now found in the Qumran caves are in fact based upon re-readings, that is, in part at least, they are oral in nature. Something similar might be said about the variations in Synoptic Gospel materials.

Then there is what Vermes and others call "study" (*drš*), which one imagines is an oral activity like the two other matters, reading and blessing. As such it is important to ask how such oral searching of what has been read might be pursued. I am inclined to think that it was a mixture of recalling the authoritative interpretations of earlier members of the congregation, perhaps even of the

---

33 As is pointed out by Shem Miller, "'Sectual' Performance in Rule Texts," 18–37.

34 Trans. Geza Vermes, *The Complete Dead Sea Scrolls in English* (London: Penguin Books, 2004), 105.

35 George J. Brooke, "Reading, Searching and Blessing: A Functional Approach to Scriptural Interpretation in the דרש," in *The Temple in Text and Tradition: A Festschrift in Honour of Robert Hayward*, ed. R. Timothy McLay, LSTS 83 (London: Bloomsbury T&T Clark, 2015), 140–56.

36 Miller, "'Sectual' Performance in Rule Texts," 22–26; idem, *Dead Sea Media*, 48–53. See also his further discussion of this passage in this collection of essays.

37 This is to provide a brief description of the reading community implied by the text; cf. the demarcation and description of some exemplary communities in classical antiquity by William A. Johnson, *Readers and Reading Culture in the High Roman Empire: A Study of Elite Communities*, Classical Culture and Society (New York, NY: Oxford University Press, 2010).

Teacher of Righteousness himself, together with the offering of fresh insights which then needed oral scrutiny by fellow-seekers. Paul Mandel has argued strongly that it is principally a matter of oral instruction in the law.[38]

And as for blessing, on the basis of the blessings that survive amongst the compositions on the manuscripts from the Qumran caves a considerable number are variations on or adaptations of the Aaronic benediction from Numbers 6.[39] Although there might be some communal prayers of blessing, perhaps learnt by heart and recited together from memory, one can readily imagine that rather than giving a fixed or set blessing, the president of the session might offer an oral improvisation on a known blessing formula to create a specific benediction for the moment. In fact, it is likely that blessings and other formulae, such as the apotropaic poems of 11Q11, need to be considered as performative speech acts of some kind, bringing into actuality what they state when pronounced.[40]

7 Education and Literacy

The study of educational practices in the movement attested in the Scrolls from the caves at and near Qumran is in its infancy.[41] The clearest statement concerning the education of a sectarian is to be found in the so-called Rule of the Congregation (1QSa). The composition shares several features with the Damascus Document and may well reflect life in part of the sectarian movement before the occupation of Qumran by some small section of it.

1QSa describes two kinds of education. The first concerns the edification of all the members of the congregation, perhaps especially those who are

---

38   Paul D. Mandel, *The Origins of* Midrash: *From Teaching to Text*, JSJSup 180 (Leiden: Brill, 2017), chapter 3.

39   See Bilhah Nitzan, *Qumran Prayer and Religious Poetry*, STDJ 12 (Leiden: Brill, 1994), 145–71.

40   See the discussion stimulated by John L. Austin, *How to Do Things with Words: the William James Lectures delivered at Harvard University in 1955*, ed. James O. Urmson (Oxford: Clarendon Press, 1962); and John R. Searle, *Speech Acts: An Essay in the Philosophy of Language* (Cambridge: Cambridge University Press, 1969).

41   I tried to describe some of what is currently known in George J. Brooke, "Some Aspects of Education in the Sectarian Scrolls from Qumran," in *Jewish Education from Antiquity to the Middle Ages: Studies in Honour of Philip S. Alexander*, ed. George J. Brooke and Renate Smithuis, AJEC 100 (Leiden: Brill, 2017), 11–42. See also the essays in "Part 1: Pedagogy in Second Temple Judaism: From *Musar* to Paideia" in Karina Martin Hogan, Matthew Goff, and Emma Wasserman, eds., *Pedagogy in Ancient Judaism and Early Christianity*, EJL 41 (Atlanta, GA: SBL, 2017). See also the contribution by Travis B. Williams to this volume.

joining: "When they come, they shall summon them all, the little children and the women also, and they shall read (*qr'*) into their ears all the precepts of the Covenant and shall expound (*hbyn*) to them all their statutes that they may no longer stray in their errors." This education involves reading and teaching, with teaching likely to include oral instruction in received authoritative interpretations of the statutes. The second kind of education concerns what happens to each young male member of the movement: "From his youth they shall instruct (*lmd*) him in the Book of Meditation and shall teach (*śkl*) him, according to his age, the precepts (*hwq*) of the Covenant. He shall be educated in their statutes for ten years ..." Here the curriculum seems to extend beyond the Torah, though there has been much discussion of what the precise referent of *seper Hagi/u* might be, and the reference to "their statutes" implies that any text of scriptural authority was also to be associated with its interpretation that had in some way itself become statutory and authoritative within the community. What was given priority in this ten-year process? Oral competence and reading skill or writing or a mixture of both? Many descriptions of education in antiquity highlight the view exemplified by Socrates: "He would be a very simple person, and quite a stranger to the oracle of Thamus [king of Egypt] or Ammon, who should leave in writing or receive in writing any art under the idea that the written word would be intelligible or certain; or who deemed that writing was at all better than knowledge and recollection of the same matters" (Plato, *Phaedrus*).[42] That view gives priority to the spoken word over the written text and was echoed by many others, such as Alcidamas writing against the Sophists.[43] But was orality the educational priority for the movement part of which took up residence at Qumran as André Lemaire has suggested?[44]

What were the relative merits of memorisation and oral skills, including reading, on the one hand and writing on the other? Literacy defines those skills that are linked to reading and writing, and so there is some overlap in the categories.[45] But it is not clear that all members of the movement associated with the Qumran site were taught to write. Some certainly were, since writing

---

42 Cited by Thomas Römer and Philip R. Davies, "Introduction," in *Writing the Bible: Scribes, Scribalism and Script*, ed. Thomas Römer and Philip R. Davies, Bible World (Durham: Acumen, 2013), 1.

43 See Mark Joyal, Iain McDougall, and John C. Yardley, *Greek and Roman Education* (London: Routledge, 2009), 94–95.

44 André Lemaire, "Lire, écrire, étudier à Qoumrân et ailleurs," in *Qoumrân et le judaïsme du tournant de notre ère: actes de la Table ronde, Collège de France, 16 novembre 2004*, ed. André Lemaire and Simon C. Mimouni, Collection de la RÉJ 40 (Leuven: Peeters, 2006), 63–79.

45 Silverman, "The Media of Influence," 100.

exercises of various kinds survive. And some of those who were scribes in the community had enhanced specialist skills, either in the writing of specialist fonts beyond those of Aramaic script (paleo-Hebrew and Cryptic scripts), or in the writing of tefillin through micrography, or in the presentation of specialist texts such as apotropaic amulets. While writing might be a common skill, with some scribes having specialist expertise, reading and oral performance seems to have been a sectarian requirement, at least for all men.

8 The Contexts for Oral (and Oral-Written) Literature

In this section, encouraged by Miller's helpful studies,[46] I simply wish to articulate a few of those settings for speech which "have an ambition beyond ordinary conversation."[47] These are the initial contexts in which a composition would be published or re-published; these settings are the basis for a textual community of some sort.[48] In addition, Shemaryahu Talmon has commented as follows: "In the milieu which engulfed all streams of Judaism at the turn of the era, a text was by definition an aural text, a *spoken* piece of writing, a performed story. The words of the message must be actually heard, so that there will be an intake by which the receptor is bound. It follows that in reference to the behaviour of sacred traditions, the real opposition was not *oral versus written*, but rather *voiced* versus *silent*. 'Orality' and 'textuality' were both deemed handmaidens of 'aurality'."[49]

A first context for the use of texts orally has already been indicated in what has been said about education in which it seems that both the Torah and other received traditions, not necessarily written ones, were expounded in the light of authoritative interpretations.

A second context for the discussion of texts would be council meetings. The Rule texts describe meetings of either part or the whole of the (male) community in a particular place. At such meetings some individual cases were considered, not least those that seemed to require discipline. I agree to some extent with Talmon that MMT is indicative of a composition based upon halakhic reasoning mostly concerning purity issues. However, whereas he considers its

---

46 Miller, "'Sectual' Performance in Rule Texts," 18–37; Miller has described performance of oral-written texts in local chapter meetings, nightly study sessions, general membership meetings, the covenant renewal ceremony, admission procedures, and at the meeting of Israel in the last days. See also idem, *Dead Sea Media*, 45–62.

47 Kristen H. Lindbeck, "Review: Martin Jaffee," in *JAAR* 71 (2003): 698.

48 See the contribution by Mladen Popović to this volume.

49 Talmon, *Text and Canon of the Hebrew Bible: Collected Studies*, 115.

origin to be in writing, perhaps deriving from a pinax, with a single author, I am more inclined to see it as a summary of views based on collective opinion orally derived, with each "concerning" representing the introduction of a conciliar decision on a particular topic; it reads like a set of minutes compiled in the form of an epistle. The multiple copies of the text suggest that the composition was subsequently used in public settings in the community, perhaps educational ones.[50]

Then, thirdly, there are study sessions of reading, searching and blessing, all three activities being oral and the last two probably involving the use of memorised texts as well as improvisation of some kind.[51] Alongside the instruction in the law might also be placed the searching of the prophets, as attested in the pesharim.[52]

And fourthly, there are cultic practices. Nowhere is it made precisely explicit what happened in regular prayer or worship services, either as individual or as communal activities.[53] Nevertheless, texts such as the description of the annual covenant ceremony in the Cave 1 version of the Rule of the Community or the instructions to the priests in the War Rule, strongly indicate something of how various rituals should proceed.[54] There was a place for both the spoken and the written word in such rites; and, in addition, it is important that some consideration should be given to the roles of rhythm, sonority and music in assisting in verbalisation.[55] Indeed Talmon has drawn attention to the inauguration ritual to which a new entrant to the yaḥad is subjected: "When he

---

50   As is also suggested by Marvin Miller, *Performances of Ancient Jewish Letters: From Elephantine to MMT*, JAJSup 20 (Göttingen: Vandenhoeck & Ruprecht, 2015), 258–63.

51   Elsewhere in this volume Cecilia Wassén wonders whether such study sessions might be best contextualized in a meal setting.

52   See the contribution by Bärry Hartog to this volume.

53   See, e.g., Shem Miller, "The Role of Performance and the Performance of Role: Cultural Memory in the Hodayot," *JBL* 137 (2018): 359–82; see also the contribution by Jutta Jokiranta to this volume of essays.

54   In my mind as I write this paragraph I have the stimulating essay by Jay Fisher, "Spoken Prayers and Written Instructions in the Central Italian Cultural Koinē and Beyond," in *Between Orality and Literacy: Communication and Adaptation in Antiquity*, ed. Ruth Scodel, Mnemosyne Sup 367, Orality and Literacy in the Ancient World 10 (Leiden: Brill, 2014), 197–217.

55   For the classical texts see, e.g., Mark W. Edwards, *Sound, Sense, and Rhythm: Listening to Greek and Latin Poetry*, Martin Classical Lectures 1998 (Princeton, NJ: Princeton University Press, 2002). Amongst the Scrolls the War Rule refers to several different types of musical instrument, as does the Psalm at the end of 1QS. On the significance of music in oral culture, see the comments on the Kalapalo community by Robert N. Bellah, *Religion in Human Evolution: From the Paleolithic to the Axial Age* (Cambridge, MA: Belknap Press, 2011), 138–42.

hears the curses of this [the *Yaḥad*] covenant ... which are audibly proclaimed in this ceremony, he will take upon himself all injunctions announced" (1QS 2:12–14).[56] The large number of written liturgical texts, not least the extra Psalm compositions that have come to light in the compositions found in the caves, indicates the importance of the written word. "These songs," Talmon states, "were not exclusively preserved as oral tradition, viz., as oral Torah, but rather were handed down in writing and became part of the Yaḥad's written Torah."[57]

9   Do the Written Scrolls Indicate Individualisation?

One of Walter Ong's suggestions was that a social or cultural context in which there was increasing presentation of text in written form could be characterized as one in which the place and the role of the individual became possible.[58] He was not suggesting naively that oral cultures are social and written ones individualistic, but that there might be a tendency in social structures and norms predominantly in one direction as any group moved from a predominantly oral culture which required social interaction towards one in which writing was increasingly privileged. There seems to be some justification in his approach in the way smart phones are changing discourse patterns throughout the world and causing the strong individuation of communication which can also have wide social implications.

Two comments are worthwhile. First, there is the moral self. Carol Newsom, in particular, has recently begun to disclose how the individual moral self was articulated in Second Temple Judaism, especially the Dead Sea Scrolls.[59] She has found some plausible and significant parallels with moves in the wider Hellenistic world. Intriguingly much of her insight is based on her thorough studies of various liturgical texts. And that takes one immediately to the second matter, namely individual prayer. The existence of several tefillin in various caves is a strong indicator that textuality could be appropriated by the individual through his regular embodied prayer practice. The texts in the tefillin case were not designed to be read; the micrography inhibited that. The texts symbolise the role, place, and power of the individual.

---

56   Talmon, *Text and Canon of the Hebrew Bible: Collected Studies*, 122–23.

57   Talmon, *Text and Canon of the Hebrew Bible: Collected Studies*, 110.

58   Walter J. Ong, *Orality and Literacy: The Technologizing of the Word*, 2nd ed. (London: Routledge, 2002), 77–114.

59   Carol A. Newsom, *The Spirit within Me: Self and Agency in Ancient Israel and Second Temple Judaism*, AYBRL (New Haven, CT: Yale University Press, 2021).

ORALITY AND WRITTEN-NESS IN THE DEAD SEA SCROLLS 377

Second, any sense of a move towards individualisation requires some consideration also of the politics of orality and written-ness. In her contribution to a volume of essays on the *Politics of Orality* Margalit Finkelberg has argued that Plato's *Phaedrus* is not so much about the relative merits of the oral and the written as it is concerned with Plato's concern to exercise control over higher knowledge. She has suggested that Plato saw writing as the realm of mass culture, making texts and the ideas they contain available to all, though without the skills that enable the text to be interrogated. What was more important to him was his downgrading of writing because he wished to retain control.[60]

Whatever might be the case with the most appropriate understanding of the text of the Phaedrus, the question arises concerning the various politics of the spoken and written words. In what ways are the collecting of written Scrolls in various caves acts of control? What are the politics of libraries in the ancient world? Are manuscripts in fact the democratization of text? As Finkelberg's reading of Plato implies, did the elites of the movement part of which ended up at Qumran give priority to the spoken word, to the rhetoric of scriptural interpretation or to the written word, received inspiration? Or was there a fine balance of the revealed and the hidden that is only revealed to the insider, the *niglaot* and the *nistarot*, of prophecy and pesher? And what of all the variety in the manuscripts for any one composition in the light of the politics of orality and written-ness?

10   What Contribution Might Performance Criticism Make?

In New Testament Studies some considerable room has been given to the possible advantages of including the perspectives of performance criticism in the better understanding of the transmission of texts. Such promotion of a particular approach has not been without its critics.[61] Little has yet been done with the Scrolls through the explicit application of performance criticism,[62] though there is increasing interest in the place of liturgical practice and ritual performance within the life of the sect and its constituent parts, and

---

60   Margalit Finkelberg, "Elitist Orality and the Triviality of Writing," in *Politics of Orality*, ed. Craig Cooper, Mnemosyne Supplement 280, Orality and Literacy in Ancient Greece 6 (Leiden: Brill, 2007), 293–305.

61   See, e.g., Larry W. Hurtado, "Oral Fixation and New Testament Studies? 'Orality', 'Performance' and Reading Texts in Early Christianity," *NTS* 60 (2014): 321–40.

62   An exception is the study mentioned above more than once by Miller, "'Sectual' Performance in Rule Texts," 18–37.

inasmuch as those matters might reflect on Jewish cultic and spiritual practice more broadly.

In his 1991 essay on "Oral Tradition and Written Transmission" Talmon implied much about the necessary performance of texts without setting his comments within the framework of any performance theory as such. He gave pride of place to the three exhortations preserved in the Damascus Document each of which begins with the formula *w'th šm'w* (CD 1:1; 2:2, 14), "and now listen," followed by a string of exhortations. He remarks, perhaps with a little too much romantic historical imagination: "If these speeches can indeed be ascribed to the Teacher, we may confidently assume that they were submitted to writing almost simultaneously with their oral delivery, or after a minimal lapse of time .... It seems that in the transfer of the Teacher's message from one medium to the other, the one-time oral tradition became written transmission without undergoing any spectacular changes. Nothing gives reason for presuming that a dramatic hermeneutic shift occurred when his spoken words became written text. It would seem, quite to the contrary, that the written version retained the original wording, as much as the cadences of oral delivery, and the typical structure of a speech or an oration."[63]

In his consideration of the use of letters in Judaism of the Second Temple period through the lens of performance criticism, Marvin Miller has reconsidered MMT in terms of how orality would play a role in its composition in various stages and in its presentation to its recipient. In addition, its subsequent use within the community seems to indicate its use for didactic or reference purposes in settings where its contents would have been voiced.[64] There is likely much more to be said under this category, not least as the letter format seems to imply a journey of some kind as if the text was especially suitable for making a journey.[65]

11 Are Orality and Writing Gendered?

This question has been provoked by Joanna Dewey's study *Women on the Way*,[66] which gives a prominent place to Christian women's story-telling in the late first century CE. I am not sure how to answer the question in relation to

---

63 Talmon, *Text and Canon of the Hebrew Bible: Collected Studies*, 124.

64 Miller, *Performances of Ancient Jewish Letters*, 247–66.

65 See the comments by Bärry Hartog in this volume on the possibility of considering 4Q169 as a travelling manuscript.

66 Joanna Dewey, "Women on the Way: A Reconstruction of Late First-Century Women's Story-Telling," in *The Bible in Ancient and Modern Media: Story and Performance*, ed. Holly

the Scrolls without falling into various stereotypical essentialist traps and false-hoods, such as that women gossip and men control. Nevertheless, it is worth asking whether the Dead Sea Scrolls might offer something on camp fires and story-telling. Whether or not story-telling is a particularly female activity, it is noticeable that the narratives amongst the Dead Sea Scrolls seem to belong to the pre-sectarian period. Most well-known are the Genesis Apocryphon and the Book of Tobit, both of which were Aramaic compositions, though the Scrolls also indicate that Tobit was translated into Hebrew and copied several times. Perhaps the movement that was responsible for variously putting the Scrolls in the Caves was not a group that created its own stories.

Though the classical treatments of Homer imagine a masculine represen-tation of his poetry, the activities of pre-sectarian, perhaps predominantly Aramaic-speaking, female sympathisers of the Essenes or of early Christian women could have been the primary vehicles for the oral transmission of cer-tain traditions.[67]

12   Conclusion

In sum, the plethora of written evidence in the 900 or more manuscripts from the caves at and near Qumran should not lead the modern reader to suppose that that movement prioritised writing in all things. There is plenty of evidence of orality, not least residual orality, alongside the possibility that written-ness encouraged the democratisation of the text, just as the *miqdash 'adam* (4Q174), the human sanctuary, democratised the temple and its priesthood. Through fresh reconsiderations of the oral and the written in creative juxtaposition and interaction with one another, the vitality of texts in the Qumran corpus can be repositioned as indicative of kinds of textuality that challenge certain inherited scholarly paradigms. Consideration of the Scrolls as media allows for the scholarly combination of thinking about material culture together with thoughts on the nature of textuality, both of which could help answer the question: Is there a text in this cave?

E. Hearon and Philip Ruge-Jones, Biblical Performance Criticism 1 (Eugene, OR: Cascade Books, 2009), 36–48.

67   Note the role of women in educating Tobit (Tob 1:8) and in the nurture of Timothy (Acts 16:1; 2 Tim 1:5).

Bibliography

Aarne, Antti. *The Types of the Folktale: A Classification and Bibliography*. Translated and edited by Stith Thompson. Helsinki: Suomalainen Tiedeaketemia, 1928.

Austin, John L. *How to Do Things with Words: the William James Lectures delivered at Harvard University in 1955*. Edited by James O. Urmson. Oxford: Clarendon Press, 1962.

Bellah, Robert N. *Religion in Human Evolution: From the Paleolithic to the Axial Age*. Cambridge, MA: Belknap Press, 2011.

Brooke, George J. "Memory, Cultural Memory and Rewriting Scripture." Pages 119–36 in *Rewritten Bible after Fifty Years: Texts, Terms, or Techniques? A Last Dialogue with Geza Vermes*. Edited by József Zsellengér. JSJSup 166. Leiden: Brill, 2014.

Brooke, George J. "Physicality, Paratextuality and Pesher Habakkuk." Pages 175–93 in *On the Fringe of Commentary: Metatextuality in Ancient Near Eastern and Ancient Mediterranean Cultures*. Edited by Sidney H. Aufrère, Philip S. Alexander and Zlatko Pleše in association with C.J. Bouloux. OLA 232. Leuven: Peeters, 2014.

Brooke, George J. "Reading, Searching and Blessing: A Functional Approach to Scriptural Interpretation in the יחד." Pages 140–56 in *The Temple in Text and Tradition: A Festschrift in Honour of Robert Hayward*. Edited by R. Timothy McLay. LSTS 83. London: Bloomsbury T&T Clark, 2015.

Brooke, George J. "Praying History in the Dead Sea Scrolls: Memory, Identity, Fulfilment." Pages 305–19 in *Function of Psalms and Prayers in the Late Second Temple Period*. Edited by Mika Pajunen and Jeremy Penner. BZAW 486. Berlin: De Gruyter, 2017.

Brooke, George J. "Some Aspects of Education in the Sectarian Scrolls from Qumran." Pages 11–42 in *Jewish Education from Antiquity to the Middle Ages: Studies in Honour of Philip S. Alexander*. Edited by George J. Brooke and Renate Smithuis. AJEC 100. Leiden: Brill, 2017.

Carr, David. "Orality, Textuality, *and* Memory: The State of Biblical Studies." Pages 161–74 in *Contextualizing Israel's Sacred Writings: Ancient Literacy, Orality, and Literary Production*. Edited by Brian B. Schmidt. AIL 22. Atlanta, GA: SBL, 2015.

Davila, James. "7. 4QGenesis^g." Pages 57–60 in *Genesis to Numbers*. Edited by Eugene C. Ulrich and Frank Moore Cross. DJD 12. Oxford: Clarendon Press, 1994.

Dewey, Joanna. "Women on the Way: A Reconstruction of Late First-Century Women's Story-Telling." Pages 36–48 in *The Bible in Ancient and Modern Media: Story and Performance*. Edited by Holly E. Hearon and Philip Ruge-Jones. Eugene, OR: Cascade Books, 2009.

Doane, A. Nicholas. "The Ethnography of Scribal Writing and Anglo-Saxon Poetry: Scribe as Performer." *Oral Tradition* 9 (1994): 429–39.

Dunn, James D. G. *Jesus Remembered*. Christianity in the Making 1. Grand Rapids, MI: Eerdmans, 2003.

Edwards, Mark W. *Sound, Sense, and Rhythm: Listening to Greek and Latin Poetry.* Martin Classical Lectures 1998. Princeton, NJ: Princeton University Press, 2002.

Feldman, Ariel, Maria Cioată, and Charlotte Hempel, eds. *Is There a Text in This Cave? Studies in the Textuality of the Dead Sea Scrolls in Honour of George J. Brooke.* STDJ 119. Leiden: Brill, 2017.

Finkelberg, Margalit. "Elitist Orality and the Triviality of Writing." Pages 293–305 in *Politics of Orality.* Edited by Craig Cooper. Mnemosyne Supplement 280, Orality and Literacy in Ancient Greece 6. Leiden: Brill, 2007.

Fish, Stanley E. *Is There a Text in This Class?: The Authority of Interpretive Communities.* Cambridge, MA: Harvard University Press, 1980.

Fisher, Jay. "Spoken Prayers and Written Instructions in the Central Italian Cultural Koinē and Beyond." Pages 197–217 in *Between Orality and Literacy: Communication and Adaptation in Antiquity.* Edited by Ruth Scodel. Mnemosyne Sup 367, Orality and Literacy in the Ancient World 10. Leiden: Brill, 2014.

Hendel, Ronald. *Steps to a New Edition of the Hebrew Bible.* Atlanta, GA: SBL, 2017.

Hogan, Karina Martin, Matthew Goff, and Emma Wasserman, eds. *Pedagogy in Ancient Judaism and Early Christianity.* EJL 41. Atlanta, GA: SBL, 2017.

Hurtado, Larry W. "Oral Fixation and New Testament Studies? 'Orality', 'Performance' and Reading Texts in Early Christianity." *NTS* 60 (2014): 321–40.

Jaffee, Martin. *Torah in the Mouth: Writing and Oral Tradition in Palestinian Judaism 200 BCE–400 CE.* New York, NY: Oxford University Press, 2001.

Johnson, William A. *Readers and Reading Culture in the High Roman Empire: A Study of Elite Communities.* Classical Culture and Society. New York, NY: Oxford University Press, 2010.

Jokiranta, Jutta. "Black Sheep, Outsiders, and the Qumran Movement: Social-Psychological Perspectives on Norm–Deviant Behaviour." Pages 151–73 in *Social Memory and Social Identity in the Study of Early Judaism and Early Christianity.* Edited by Samuel Byrskog, Raimo Hakola, and Jutta Jokiranta. NTOA/SUNT 116. Göttingen: Vandenhoeck & Ruprecht, 2016.

Jokiranta, Jutta. "Quoting, Writing, and Reading: Authority in Pesher Habakkuk from Qumran." Pages 185–211 in *Between Canonical and Apocryphal Texts: Processes of Reception, Rewriting and Interpretation in Early Judaism and Early Christianity.* Edited by Jörg Frey, Claire Clivaz, and Tobias Nicklas. WUNT 419. Tübingen: Mohr Siebeck, 2019.

Joyal, Mark, Iain McDougall, and John C. Yardley. *Greek and Roman Education.* London: Routledge, 2009.

Keith, Chris. "Social Memory Theory and Gospels Research: The First Decade." *Early Christianity* 6 (2015): 354–76 (Part One), 517–42 (Part Two).

Kirk, Geoffrey S. *Homer and the Oral Tradition.* Cambridge: Cambridge University Press, 1976.

Le Donne, Anthony. *The Historiographical Jesus: Memory, Typology, and the Son of David*. Waco, TX: Baylor University Press, 2009.

Lemaire, André. "Lire, écrire, étudier à Qoumrân et ailleurs." Pages 63–79 in *Qoumrân et le judaïsme du tournant de notre ère: actes de la Table ronde, Collège de France, 16 novembre 2004*. Edited by André Lemaire and Simon C. Mimouni. Collection de la RÉJ 40. Leuven: Peeters, 2006.

Lindbeck, Kristen H. "Review: Martin Jaffee, *Torah in the Mouth: Writing and Oral Tradition in Palestinian Judaism 200 BCE–400 CE* (New York, NY: Oxford University Press, 2001)." *JAAR* 71 (2003): 698–701.

Lord, Albert. *The Singer of Tales*. Harvard Studies in Comparative Literature 24. Cambridge, MA: Harvard University Press, 1960.

Mandel, Paul D. *The Origins of* Midrash: *From Teaching to Text*. JSJSup 180. Leiden: Brill, 2017.

McIver, Robert K. *Memory, Jesus, and the Synoptic Gospels*. RBS 59. Atlanta, GA: SBL, 2011.

Miller, Marvin Lloyd. *Performances of Ancient Jewish Letters: From Elephantine to MMT*. JAJSup 20. Göttingen: Vandenhoeck & Ruprecht, 2015.

Miller, Shem. "The Oral-Written Textuality of Stichographic Poetry in the Dead Sea Scrolls." *DSD* 22 (2015): 162–88.

Miller, Shem. "The Role of Performance and the Performance of Role: Cultural Memory in the Hodayot." *JBL* 137 (2018): 359–382.

Miller, Shem. "'Sectual' Performance in Rule Texts." *DSD* 25 (2018): 15–38.

Miller, Shem. *Dead Sea Media: Orality, Textuality, and Memory in the Scrolls from the Judean Desert*. STDJ 129. Leiden: Brill, 2019.

Najman, Hindy. "The Symbolic Significance of Writing in Ancient Judaism." Pages 139–73 in *The Idea of Biblical Interpretation: Essays in Honor of James L. Kugel*. Edited by Hindy Najman and Judith H. Newman. JSJSup 83. Leiden: Brill, 2004.

Najman, Hindy. "The Vitality of Scripture Within and Beyond the 'Canon'." *JSJ* 43 (2012): 497–518.

Newsom, Carol A. *The Spirit within Me: Self and Agency in Ancient Israel and Second Temple Judaism*. AYBRL. New Haven, CT: Yale University Press, 2021.

Niditch, Susan. *Oral World and Written Word*. Louisville, KY: Westminster John Knox, 1996.

Nitzan, Bilhah. *Qumran Prayer and Religious Poetry*. STDJ 12. Leiden: Brill, 1994.

Ong, Walter J. *Orality and Literacy: The Technologizing of the World*. 2nd ed. London: Routledge, 2002.

Parry, Milman. *The Making of Homeric Verse: The Collected Papers of Milman Parry*. Edited by Adam Parry. Oxford: Clarendon Press, 1971.

Person, Jr., Raymond. "The Ancient Israelite Scribe as Performer." *JBL* 117 (1998): 601–609.

Person, Jr., Raymond. *The Deuteronomistic History and the Book of Chronicles: Scribal Works in an Oral World.* AIL 6. Leiden: Brill, 2010.

Person, Jr., Raymond. "Text Criticism as a Lens for Understanding the Transmission of Ancient Texts in Their Oral Environments." Pages 197–216 in *Contextualizing Israel's Sacred Writings: Ancient Literacy, Orality, and Literary Production.* Edited by Brian B. Schmidt. AIL 22. Atlanta, GA: SBL, 2015.

Person, Raymond F. Jr., and Robert Rezetko, ed. *Empirical Models Challenging Biblical Criticism.* Ancient Israel and Its Literature 25. Atlanta, GA: SBL, 2016.

Purves, Dale, George J. Augustine, David Fitzpatrick, William C. Hall, Anthony-Samuel LaMantia, Richard D. Mooney, Michael L. Platt, and Leonard E. White. *Neuroscience.* 5th ed. Sunderland, MA: Sinauer Associates, 2001.

Regev, Eyal. *Sectarianism in Qumran: A Cross-Cultural Perspective.* Religion and Society 45. Berlin: De Gruyter, 2007.

Reynolds III, Bennie H. "Dead Sea Scrolls and Other Judean Desert Texts." Pages 74–80 in *The Dictionary of the Bible and Ancient Media.* Edited by Tom Thatcher, Chris Keith, Raymond F. Person, Jr., and Elsie R. Stern. London: Bloomsbury, 2017.

Römer, Thomas, and Philip R. Davies. "Introduction." Pages 1–9 in *Writing the Bible: Scribes, Scribalism and Script.* Edited by Thomas Römer and Philip R. Davies. Bible World. Durham: Acumen, 2013.

Searle, John R. *Speech Acts: An Essay in the Philosophy of Language.* Cambridge: Cambridge University Press, 1969.

Shillingsburg, Peter. *Textuality and Knowledge: Essays.* University Park, PA: University of Pennsylvania Press, 2017.

Silverman, Jason. "The Media of Influence: Orality, Literacy, and Cultural Interaction." Pages 175–205 in *Persepolis and Jerusalem: Iranian Influence on the Apocalyptic Hermeneutic.* Edited by Jason M. Silverman. LHBOTS 558. London: T&T Clark, 2012.

Stuckenbruck, Loren T. "The Teacher of Righteousness Remembered: From Fragmentary Sources to Collective Memory in the Dead Sea Scrolls." Pages 75–94 in *Memory in the Bible and Antiquity: The Fifth Durham-Tübingen Research Symposium (Durham, September 2004).* Edited by Stephen Barton, Loren T. Stuckenbruck and Benjamin G. Wold. WUNT 212. Tübingen: Mohr Siebeck, 2007.

Talmon, Shemaryahu. "Oral Tradition and Written Transmission, or the 'Heard' and the 'Seen' Word in Judaism of the Second Temple Period." Pages 121–58 in *Jesus and the Oral Gospel Tradition.* Edited by Henry Wansbrough. JSNTSup 64. Sheffield: Sheffield Academic Press, 1991. Reprinted as pages 85–124 in Shemaryahu Talmon, *Text and Canon of the Hebrew Bible: Collected Studies.* Winona Lake, IN: Eisenbrauns, 2010.

Thatcher, Tom, ed. *Jesus, the Voice, and the Text: Beyond the Oral and the Written Gospel.* Waco, TX: Baylor University Press, 2008.

Thomas, Rosalind. *Oral Tradition and Written Record in Classical Athens.* Cambridge Studies in Oral and Literate Culture. Cambridge: Cambridge University Press, 1989.

Tooman, William A. "Authenticating Oral and Memory Variants in Ancient Hebrew Literature." *JSS* 64 (2019): 91–114.

Tov, Emanuel. *Scribal Practices and Approaches Reflected in the Texts Found in the Judean Desert*. STDJ 54. Leiden: Brill, 2004.

VanderKam, James C. "The Putative Author of the Book of Jubilees." *JSS* 26 (1981): 209–17. Reprinted as pages 439–47 in James C. VanderKam, *From Revelation to Canon: Studies in the Hebrew Bible and Second Temple Judaism*. JSPSup 62. Leiden: Brill, 2000.

Vermès, Géza. *The Complete Dead Sea Scrolls in English*. Revised edition. London: Penguin, 2004.

Williams, Travis B. *History and Memory in the Dead Sea Scrolls: Remembering the Teacher of Righteousness*. Cambridge: Cambridge University Press, 2019.

CHAPTER 11

Rituals as Media: Shared, Embodied, and Extended Knowledge Mediation in Rituals

Jutta Jokiranta

1 Introduction

According to the famous slogan "the medium is the message," coined by Marshall McLuhan, the message cannot be understood separately from the medium that delivers it, and the medium itself has consequences that are not obvious in the contents of the message.[1] From this perspective, *rituals* call for special treatment. If media are understood as forms of communication to store and deliver information, rituals can be explored as important media that are often found at the crossroads of oral and written practices and include learned embodied practices.[2] This is a comparative enterprise to see what is special about this medium and to explore how the medium (and its technology), not just the information, has an effect—often slowly, implicitly, and structurally—on societal practices, norms, and values, and what the unintended consequences of the medium might be.

The history of rituals is as long as the history of humankind, and thus this technology of communication is quite old. Yet among media studies, rituals have had a mixed position: they are central to the ways in which commemorative

---

1 Marshall McLuhan, *Understanding Media: The Extensions of Man* (New York, NY: McGraw-Hill, 1964). Following in the footsteps of McLuhan, it is important to look beyond the obvious, into the non-obvious effects that the new forms of media enable, encourage, or accelerate. "This is merely to say that the personal and social consequences of any medium—that is, of any extension of ourselves—result from the new scale that is introduced into our affairs by each extension of ourselves, or by any new technology" (7).

2 Günther Thomas, "Communication," in *Theorizing Rituals: Issues, Topics, Approaches, Concepts*, ed. Jens Kreinath, Jan Snoek, and Michael Stausberg (Leiden: Brill, 2008), 321–43, outlines five ways in which rituals and communication can be viewed together, mainly from an analytical perspective: (1) rituals contain verbal communication, (2) rituals are communication via symbols, (3) rituals have hidden grammars that communicate structural categories, (4) rituals are action without meaning, and (5) any communication system can have ritual aspects in it. He then proceeds to seek a sixth, multidimensional approach. I will touch upon at least 1–4 of these links, but will organize my analysis differently, from the perspective of cognition.

© JUTTA JOKIRANTA, 2023 | DOI:10.1163/9789004537804_012

practices transmit and construct collective memory and rehearse the master narratives of a community, but often they are not addressed as a medium in their own right.[3]

Recently, ritual studies have been revived, but with some new questions. In today's secular societies, scholars ask: Why do rituals persist?[4] Why do people engage in obscure activities where the cause-and-consequence patterns repel normal logic and continue to invest time and resources in them? What good are rituals? Behind the attempt to explain ritual behavior in the modern world is a more profound attempt to identify the role of religion in human evolution. Rituals are one example of coordinated action that supposedly played a role in the selective advantages of human ancestors and enabled the formation of groups larger than immediate kin and the emergence of more complex cognitive abilities that require nurture to develop.[5]

Another central focus arises from theories that aim to overcome the dominant body-mind dualism. The human mind is not a disembodied thing—although it is very natural to think so. We tend to assume that we can perceive, reason, and imagine without our bodies, but this is merely an illusion. All human conceptual thinking is deeply embedded in our being corporeal organisms and in interaction with our environment. Starting from the fact that we discover ourselves through movement, there is no human self without relations to other humans, and all propositional thinking ("higher" operations) is grounded in structures and dimensions of the body ("lower" operations).[6]

---

3 Especially the work of Maurice Halbwachs and Jan Assmann on collective memory and cultural memory have touched upon rituals from this perspective; see, e.g., Tom Thatcher, Chris Keith, Raymond F. Person, Jr., and Elise R. Stern, eds., *The Dictionary of the Bible and Ancient Media* (London: Bloomsbury T&T Clark, 2017), 60, 70.

4 E.g., Robert N. McCauley, *Why Religion Is Natural and Science Is Not* (Oxford: Oxford University Press, 2011).

5 E.g., Ara Norenzayan, *Big Gods: How Religion Transformed Cooperation and Conflict* (Princeton, NJ: Princeton University Press, 2013). This is not to take a stance in the debate over whether religion had an adaptionist function in human evolution or whether it is a by-product of other evolutionary traits. For a critique of the fact that evolutionary questions are often by-passed, see Radek Kundt, "Making Evolutionary Science of Religion an Integral Part of Cognitive Science of Religion," in *Evolution, Cognition, and the History of Religion: A New Synthesis. Festschrift in Honour of Armin W. Geertz*, ed. Anders Klostergaard Petersen, Ingvild Sælid Gilhus, Luther H. Martin, Jeppe Sinding Jensen, and Jesper Sørensen (Leiden: Brill, 2019), 141–58. Note that cooperation is not a purely positive phenomenon; theorists recognize its destructive potential (as in warfare) or negative side (exclusion of outsiders), too.

6 Mark Johnson, *The Meaning of the Body: Aesthetics of Human Understanding* (Chicago: The University of Chicago Press, 2007). Our bodies are designed to hide their functions so that when we see, we are not aware of our seeing but only of the target of the seeing, whereas when we experience, we do not feel the operations of the organs but only the resulting

Ritual actions are no different from ordinary actions in that they employ the human body as the instrument; yet, they do have some special features that make them especially interesting from the point of view of human cognition and communication.

Here, media studies have long understood that humans are more than their individual bodies and brains. Media are extensions of the human, but so too is the human a product of technology. In the field of the cognitive science of religion, such investigation could be phrased in terms of bio-cultural evolution: how human capacities direct and modify forms of culture and how cultures in turn shape human cognition and practices.[7] Technology is not an independent vehicle, but rather something that enables humans to shape themselves. Human agency is relational and embedded in its environment.

In this essay, I will seek ways in which approaching rituals as media might offer a framework for study rather than attempt an overall analysis of relevant (Qumran) texts. When *texts* are addressed, our immediate concern is restricted to how we can study rituals as (historical) practices. We risk studying merely their narrow literary representations or the scrolls as a medium of thin ritual description. Surely, much of ritual praxis remains unknown to us and is unmediated via textual means. Even if we were certain that the words in the scrolls were exactly the ones recited in rituals, ritual experiences include so much more context-dependent and bodily information that the remaining reconstruction would be very shallow. On the other hand, ritual theorists have long noted that even the anthropological and ethnographic observation of rituals does not provide direct access into the practices; anthropological work is in some respects analogous to the interpretation of texts.[8] The medium, whether the ritual practice as practice (including engagement with texts or not) or the text itself, in any case, is not reflecting the "real" world so much as it *is* the real world where information about social relations, the cosmos, and God are established and transmitted.[9]

---

feeling. Thus, we have an illusion of an independent mind sensing and having ideas *of* the body but not *through* the body.

7   See Armin Geertz, "Brain, Body and Culture: A Biocultural Theory of Religion," MTSR 22 (2010): 304–21. Cognition is not approached as distinct operations of the brain; it is extended, embedded, enactive, and embodied—thus, human culture could be seen as extensive extended cognition.

8   See Catherine Bell, *Ritual: Perspectives and Dimensions* (Oxford: Oxford University Press, 1997), 67.

9   See Richard Cavell, *Remediating McLuhan* (Amsterdam: Amsterdam University Press, 2016), 21.

2 What (Obvious) Information Is Mediated in Rituals?

Rituals are of many types and so is the information mediated through them. To start with, I will roughly divide the types of information mediated through rituals into four categories: factual, normative, meta-, and motivational information. The next section will focus on ritual as multimedia events (both verbal and nonverbal) and the ways in which this information is delivered.

Factual information is basic information about *who* and *what*. In life-cycle rituals, for example, it has to do with who is born, transformed, or has died. Judean purity practices deliver information on childbirths, cures from diseases, male and female sexual conditions, and deaths. Different vows and promises deliver information about human needs and wishes—and they tell us who is sick and in need of help. Factual information includes basic facts about time, such as when the Sabbath begins and when the annual festivals take place. It may also include secondary information, such as how good the harvest was during a seasonal festival.

Factual information could be delivered via other media, simply by mouth-to-mouth communication or via verbal announcements. Rituals do more and are meant to do more. They are organized to deliver *normative information*: norms, values, and beliefs. These include all kinds of communication about God, human beings, and the cosmos. Thus, sacrificial practices transmit, at least in some views, knowledge about the desired order of things in the created cosmos;[10] purity practices signal the boundaries of sacred space and time; festival traditions transmit memories of Israel's history and God's acts for his people; the Sabbath observance transmits, for example, belief in the proper cyclic order of the cosmos: God rested, so humans should rest and let others rest. Transmitted knowledge is always contextual, and no single theory on the meaning of a ritual practice can be presented. This normative and mythic aspect of rituals often points towards the *symbolic* meanings *behind* ritual actions, and it causes participants and observers to seek out the underlying meanings of each action, actor, or object.[11] Often ritual experts are harnessed to give the correct interpretations.

Meta-information is information that may not be explicit or primary in the ritual itself but is derived at a meta level. Meta-information includes knowledge about the statuses, hierarchies, and relations between people: for example,

---

10   Jonathan Klawans, *Purity, Sacrifice, and the Temple: Symbolism and Supersessionism in the Study of Ancient Judaism* (Oxford: Oxford University Press, 2005).

11   See Bell, *Ritual*, 33–46, for a structuralist attempt to find the hidden grammar behind the obvious social systems.

RITUALS AS MEDIA   389

who is the religious expert from whom to seek help, what counts as work (Sabbath), when is a wife's fertile period of the month (ritual purity), or who is a trustworthy member of the community? Significant meta-information for a community is communicated via this last type of *identity* information: who belongs—who is an insider and who is an outsider—and who participates in the rituals and who does not: who is a pious, healthy, or wealthy member of the community.[12] In the words of George Brooke, "liturgy defines in a particular way and with particular words the community that prays and praises."[13] Ritual participation controls change and the accepted identity expression; it contributes directly to information about selfhood. As such, rituals impose and enforce *social order* by negotiating and legitimizing social distinctions.[14]

Yet a further aspect of rituals has to do with the urge and compulsory feeling of an individual to engage in ritualized activities. Efficacious rituals are meant to accomplish and change something, not just to deliver symbolic messages. I call this *motivational information*: why does the ritual matter, what does it do, and why is it dangerous to overlook it? Supernatural agents have a role in many rituals; rituals are not just a human endeavor. Ritual theories also suggest that if only the symbolic, the meaning side mattered in rituals, participants would become tired. Rituals need the efficacy side, the notion that something really changes, to motivate participation. Rituals do not convey a message, but rather they are the language itself through which things are done.[15] This motivational information may precede the practice itself: one's own emotions or urges communicate to oneself the need to engage in action and the possibility of the ritual to respond to those emotions.

The Qumran movement not only maintained and modified existing ritual practices but developed its own ritual practices. It had *more* or *other information* to mediate than what could be delivered through existing practices. Ritual practices were needed to mediate identities, and not only at the factual and normative level but also at the meta- and motivational levels, providing an

---

12   Roy A. Rappaport, *Ritual and Religion in the Making of Humanity* (Cambridge: Cambridge University Press, 1999), speaks of the self-referential, indexical messages (as opposed to canonical messages) that ritual behavior sends.

13   George J. Brooke, "Aspects of the Theological Significance of Prayer and Worship in the Qumran Scrolls," in *Prayer and Poetry in the Dead Sea Scrolls and Related Literature*, ed. Jeremy Penner, Ken M. Penner, and Cecilia Wassén, STDJ 98 (Leiden: Brill, 2012), 39.

14   See Bell, *Ritual*, 23–29, for a functionalist attempt to reveal the social function of rituals.

15   E.g., Robert N. McCauley and E. Thomas Lawson, *Bringing Ritual to Mind: Psychological Foundations of Cultural Forms* (Cambridge: Cambridge University Press, 2002); Harvey Whitehouse, *Modes of Religiosity: A Cognitive Theory of Religious Transmission* (Walnut Creek, CA: AltaMira Press, 2004).

understanding of one's role in relation to that of the elite knowing ones. How do the rituals transmit this knowledge? What are the mechanisms?

3 How Is Information Mediated in Rituals?

Rituals are a special kind of activity that can be distinguished from the mundane by their repetition, their frequency, and also their goal demotion:[16] they achieve something by a logic that is not obvious to an outside observer. Rituals are not only organized to mediate some explicit teachings or traditions (symbolic information),[17] they also convey information that is needed for the coordination of collective action, identity formation, bodily experience, motivation and emotions, even wellbeing. Recently, Risto Uro has discussed rituals and religious knowledge from three cognitive perspectives in the study of Early Christianity.[18] I base my discussion below on his outline to explore three ways in which rituals mediate information and are in turn mediated by it:
- rituals mediate shared (common) knowledge
- rituals mediate (grounded) embodied and memorable knowledge
- extended (embedded, situated) knowledge mediates rituals

3.1 Rituals Mediate Shared Knowledge

First, (collective) rituals generate common (shared) knowledge. According to Michael Chwe, "public ceremonies are powerful not simply because they transmit meaning from a central source to each audience member but because they let audience members know what other members know."[19] This common knowledge makes it possible for people to coordinate action, as they trust that the others know the same things and they want to participate only if the others also participate.

---

16   Rappaport, *Ritual and Religion in the Making of Humanity.*

17   In their role of mediating symbolic information and abstract ideas, rituals can be compared to other means of learning existing knowledge, such as education. If the purpose is to transmit information about Israel's history, one can study a scroll or hear it read and explained. Deep learning comes through hearing something dozens of times and by doing it oneself. Institutionalized education naturally employs many similar techniques as collective rituals. Yet, this aspect covers only part of what rituals do.

18   Risto Uro, *Ritual and Christian Beginnings: A Socio-Cognitive Analysis* (Oxford: Oxford University Press, 2016), 154–77. For studying early Christian baptism, Uro outlines three cognitive approaches to ritual knowledge as "rituals generate embodied knowledge;" "rituals generate common (shared) knowledge;" "rituals accommodate extended knowledge."

19   Michael Suk-Young Chwe, *Rational Ritual: Culture, Coordination and Common Knowledge* (Princeton, NJ: Princeton University Press, 2003), abstract.

One obvious Qumran case for a novel collective ritual where such shared information is created was the annual covenant renewal, in which members were also ranked:

> They shall do as follows annually, all the days of Belial's dominion: the priests shall pass in review first, ranked according to their spiritual excellence, one after another. Then the Levites shall follow, and third all the people by rank, one after another, in their thousands and hundreds and fifties and tens. Thus shall each Israelite know his proper standing in the *Yahad* of God, an eternal society. None shall be demoted from his appointed place, none promoted beyond his foreordained rank. (1QS 2:19–23)[20]

Knowing who was part of the covenant was important knowledge for people who normally—probably—lived spread out across the land. It was necessary to know what rank one had, to know who the novices were, and to know that everyone else knew so that the members could continue to strive for perfection in their everyday life. This has at least three aspects to it. First, had one relied only on small-group gatherings and a few superiors who could supervise the members' conduct, it would have been easier to defect and leave the group—even such an expression of disapproval would then be known only to a small circle of people. When a member knew that their position was annually being evaluated, their behavior was a larger issue: it mattered to the whole covenant.

Secondly, one knew whom to trust and whom to follow; those below you in the hierarchy were not the ones likely to help you proceed and improve your position. Thirdly, one knew that others knew: if your position was low, you would need to prove yourself to convince others that you deserve more; if your position was high, you would need to convince others that you deserved such a position. If you received an invitation to the covenant ceremony without knowing who else was going, would you go? Each person's motivation to participate increases the more they know that the others are participating. Just knowing the message (e.g., that God has formed a new/renewed covenant to

---

20   Unless otherwise noted, the translations of the scrolls follow Emanuel Tov, ed., *The Dead Sea Scrolls Electronic Library: Texts and Images*. Partially based on *The Dead Sea Scrolls Reader*, edited by Donald W. Parry and Emanuel Tov, morphological analysis by Martin Abegg, Jr., produced by Noel B. Reynolds, associate producer Kristian Heal (Leiden: Brill, 2006).

which one can join) is not enough; some messages need the metaknowledge of others knowing what you know.[21]

Human groups also have other problems to solve that extend beyond the coordination problem (should I participate—are others participating?). One is the "free-rider" problem: why should I invest in this group if I could get the benefits in any case? Rituals may increase the level of trust and cooperation among those who signal their commitment through "costly signals," and thus make these groups more sustainable. By participating in time-consuming and arduous, stressful, or concretely costly rituals, members may tell others that they are committed, trustworthy members.[22]

We must remember, however, that the text for the covenant renewal as it is represented in the Community Rule Scroll 1QS does not mediate the ritual to us nor to its users: some words and structure of actions are given, but not others. Is this intentional? The confession of sins is rather pronounced in 1QS since such collective confession is found quoted only here and in the Damascus Document (CD 20:28–30) and is not a typical discourse found in the rules elsewhere. It thus has a specific place within the covenant entry, since those who *know to confess* are those who receive the blessing. Prior to this, the priests are said to rehearse God's great deeds and the Levites are said to pronounce Israel's wicked deeds, but these words are not given. One can easily imagine a traditional view of history provided here: both salvation history and a history of breaking the covenant. This particular scribal representation left room for creative oral uses of history by not fixing it in traditional terms. Perhaps space was opened for a retelling of the cosmic history, as presented in columns 1QS 3–4, in the form of the discourse on two spirits.

Nevertheless, we should not overestimate the information that was shared among the covenanters. Each Serekh ha-Yahad (S) manuscript presents a certain type of "user platform."[23] Here, 1QS is an anomaly with its long discourse on the two spirits and information about a divine plan and determination.[24] Some information in the discourse—that God has not only set two opposing

---

21   Chwe, *Rational Ritual*, 8–12.

22   Joseph A. Bulbulia and Richard Sosis, "Signalling Theory and the Evolution of Religious Cooperation," *Religion* 41 (2011): 363–88; see also Richard Sosis, "Do Religions Promote Cooperation? Testing Signaling Theories of Religion," in *The Cognitive Science of Religion: A Methodological Introduction to Key Empirical Studies*, ed. D. Jason Slone and William W. McCorkle Jr. (London: Bloomsbury, 2019), 155–62, and the literature therein.

23   Jutta Jokiranta, "What is 'Serekh ha-Yahad (S)'? Thinking About Ancient Manuscripts as Information Processing," in *Sibyls, Scriptures, and Scrolls: John Collins at Seventy*, ed. Joel Baden, Hindy Najman, and Eibert Tigchelaar, JSJS 175 (Leiden: Brill, 2016), 1:611–35.

24   Charlotte Hempel, "The Long Text of the Serekh as Crisis Literature," *RevQ* 27 (2015): 3–24.

powers to have dominion over the world, but has also determined the spirits of truth and injustice by which *each individual* walks (1QS 3:17–18; 4:23c–26)—is rare and may *not* have been common knowledge in the movement.[25] Consider this information:

> According to the inheritance of a person in truth he acts with righteousness and thus detests injustice and according to his allocation in the lot of injustice he acts wickedly because of it and thus loathes truth. For God has put them in place in equal measure until the agreed end and the renewal. And He knows the actions of their deeds for all periods of [eterni]ty and He has given them as an inheritance to the children of humanity so that they may know good [and evil and He deter]mines the fate for all the living according to the spirit of each person [] visitation. (1QS 4:24–26)[26]

Imagine that this piece of information was e-mailed to the covenant members using the "bcc" (blind carbon copy) function of email: you would now know this information but you would not know who else knew.[27] How would you react? The fellows whom you thought were on your side might actually turn out to be working on the side of evil. But they might not know that you were aware of this possibility, and you might not want to raise this accusation against them. Cooperation and trust would be severely risked. On the other hand, if this information was shared, for example in the covenant ritual, then everyone would know that others knew that you might be compromised in your spirit—and thus the motivation to participate and be among the ones who *know* to confess their sins and supervise their behavior would increase.[28]

---

25   For a suggestion of textual development within the discourse, see Meike Christian, "The Literary Development of the 'Treatise of the Two Spirits' as Dependent on Instruction and the Hodayot," in *Law, Literature, and Society in Legal Texts from Qumran: Papers from the Ninth Meeting of the International Organization for Qumran Studies, Leuven 2016*, ed. Jutta Jokiranta and Molly M. Zahn, STDJ 128 (Leiden: Brill, 2019), 153–84.

26   Translation by Charlotte Hempel, *The Community Rules from Qumran: A Commentary*, TSAJ 183 (Tübingen: Mohr Siebeck, 2020). I thank Prof. Hempel for sharing the work with me prior to publication.

27   See Chwe, *Rational Ritual*, 14.

28   Peter Porzig, "The Place of the 'Treatise of the Two Spirits' (1QS 3:13–4:26) within the Literary Development of the Community Rule," in *Law, Literature, and Society in Legal Texts from Qumran*, 127–52, makes the connection between the idea of "being a sinner and righteous at the same time" in the Discourse of the Two Spirits and the final hymn in 1QS 10–11.

No-one can be sure that all knowledge in a public ritual becomes shared knowledge, but rituals have tools to facilitate that this is so. Rituals often use formalized language and thus already limit the choice of words and expressions.[29] In the covenant renewal, the formality of the confession, blessings and curses, and the "amen" responses ensure that they remain "pure" in their genre, no-one freely adds other elements, and thus, there are restrictions on the flexibility of the information. Ritual does not require faith, merely participation.

Repetition marks things as common knowledge. According to Michael Chwe, "in terms of common knowledge generation, when a person hears something repeated, not only does she get the message, she knows it is repeated and hence knows that it is more likely that others have heard it."[30] For example, in another section of 1QS, in the midst of rules and strict hierarchies according to which one needs to submit to superiors, the repetition of the term מתנדבים, "those who volunteer" (six times in 1QS 5:1–22), underlines the fact that one has freely joined the movement and one knows others know this, even though one's reality may be full of commitments and restrictions emanating from above.

Furthermore, the movement did not rely on annual meetings only, but also on repetitive, frequent, small-group meetings. Not only prayer, but education and the study of texts became ritualized.[31] The mention of collective assemblies in 1QS 6:2–3, "they shall eat, pray and deliberate communally," could be understood as a completely oral activity. Later in the same passage (1QS 6:6–8), we hear about the continuous study of the *torah* in every group of ten, as well as the nightly reading of the "document" (ספר) by the *rabbim*.[32] As suggested by Charlotte Hempel, praying and the nightly reading can be associated with apotropaic practices to safeguard members from demonic threats during the nighttime or time of testing.[33] However, these sentences are one of a few indications of how frequently the members met ("day and night," "for the first of every night of the year"), and it is doubtful whether we can take them at face value and believe that all people could afford to make such a daily investment.[34]

---

29 Thomas, "Communication," 332–35.

30 Chwe, *Rational Ritual*, 4, also 27–30.

31 On the kind of experience that would most likely be aroused by the reading, see Angela Kim Harkins, "The Emotional Re-Experiencing of the Hortatory Narratives Found in the Admonition of the Damascus Document," *DSD* 22 (2015): 285–307.

32 For the three activities, see George J. Brooke, "Reading, Searching and Blessing: A Functional Approach to Scriptural Interpretation in the יחד," in *The Temple in Text and Tradition: A Festschrift in Honour of Robert Hayward*, ed. R. Timothy McLay, LSTS 83 (London: Bloomsbury, 2015), 143 n. 10.

33 Hempel, *Community Rules*, 176–78.

34 See Hempel, *Community Rules*, and idem, *The Qumran Rule Texts in Context: Collected Studies* (Tübingen: Mohr Siebeck, 2013), 79–105, for a discussion on how various types of

In any case, the work of William Johnson is relevant: "When one asks why literature is so important within these communities, the answer in part must be circular: these communities construct themselves as exclusive domains on the basis of their knowledge of, and facility with, literary texts."[35] If we envision that all ten persons or else one person at a time are *able to study the torah* (1QS 6:6–7), this would then set them apart from the illiterate majority and be a huge achievement.[36] Thus, the passage tells us a lot about the ideal construction of the reading and studying of the text: it is continuous (cf. Josh 1:8; Deut 6:6–9), systematic, and structured; it takes place collectively and engages all present; it occupies a great deal of time. Furthermore, this community could afford it and they had the necessary skills and resources for it. They were both open and concealed about their knowledge: it was shared among the participants but concealed from others.[37]

Michael Chwe also explains how coordination becomes an issue in collective action, such as rebelling against the regime. If you believe others will submit to the leading authority, you are more likely to do the same, but if you believe most others will rebel, you are more likely to join in the rebellion.[38] This is an interesting aspect if we think of the Qumran movement as a subversive movement to the Hasmonean regime that, while it did not openly revolt, created a network to offer alternative ways to promote one's position, an alternative system of education, and a quasi-military structure.[39] A sufficient

---

gatherings are put together in this material. Note also that 1QS 6:6–7a is not preserved in any of the Cave 4 S manuscripts.

35   William A. Johnson, *Readers and Reading Culture in the High Roman Empire: A Study of Elite Communities*, Classical Culture and Society (Oxford: Oxford University Press, 2010), 203. See also Mladen Popović, "Reading, Writing, and Memorizing Together: Reading Culture in Ancient Judaism and the Dead Sea Scrolls in a Mediterranean Context," *DSD* 24 (2017): 447–70.

36   Not everyone was literate in such a community; see Hempel, *Community Rules*, 13. Compare Roman reading practises by William A. Johnson, "Constructing Elite Reading Communities in the High Empire," in *Ancient Literacies: The Culture of Reading in Greece and Rome*, ed. Holt N. Parker and William A. Johnson (Oxford: Oxford University Press, 2009), 320–30.

37   For more on such a "knowledge economy," see Charlotte Hempel, "Bildung und Wissenswirtschaft im Judentum zur Zeit des Zweiten Tempels," in *Was ist Bildung in der Vormoderne?* ed. Peter Gemeinhardt, Studies in Education and Religion in Ancient and Pre-Modern History in the Mediterranean and Its Environs 4 (Tübingen: Mohr Siebeck, 2020), 229–44.

38   Chwe, *Rational Ritual*, 11, 19–25.

39   See Jutta Jokiranta, "Competitors to Middle Maccabees: Evidence from the Dead Sea Scrolls," in *The Middle Maccabees: Archaeology, History, and the Rise of the Hasmonean Kingdom*, ed. Andrea M. Berlin and Paul J. Kosmin, Archaeology and Biblical Studies Series (Atlanta, GA: SBL, 2021), 363–78.

number of people needed to have shared knowledge (know that others were going to participate) in order to create and maintain a sustainable network. Chwe also explains how, by establishing their own weights, measures, and calendar, the French revolution solved the other coordination problem, that of getting people to signal shared knowledge about the new government:

> A person might not know the extent to which other people support a new regime but would know that others consented at least to using its new weights and measures ... Changing weights, measures, and the calendar is particularly effective not simply because they change the way that a given individual thinks about the revolution or the physical world, but because they change how individuals interact with each other; they change what an individual knows about other individuals.[40]

The calendar example brings forward a tempting idea regarding the role of the 364-day calendar in the Qumran movement. Could the calendar or some other institution or legal innovation have been a way of enhancing shared knowledge in the case of the Qumran movement? Creating a new symbol for the new association is not enough; the symbol must enjoy sufficient agreement and become common knowledge. However, we must not draw hasty conclusions, as we do not know which halakhic practices were strictly unique to the Qumran movement, and the calendar most probably was not an innovation made by the movement.[41] The possibility that some purity or Sabbath practices, for example, may have functioned as such signals could be further explored. Sabbath rules are a unique form of ritual practice since they *ban* activities rather than command them. Such rules have a strong potential to convey identity information: the more the people follow specific rules (of what is prohibited) and allow for less individual choice, the more those people come to be associated with a certain circle or movement of people. What one does *not* do can be more of a powerful message than what one does, since adding ritual actions is often easier than taking them away. However, in order to be an effective means to mark coordinated action and draw group boundaries, the banned activities must somehow *play a symbolic role and be significant and*

---

40 Chwe, *Rational Ritual*, 27. Furthermore, the role of strong and weak links is related to the spread of information. Strong-link networks are ones where everyone knows each other and tend to be friends; there, knowledge is likely to become shared. Weak-link networks include a person's friends' friends, who tend not to be the person's friends; weak links may be more effective at spreading information to a larger group of people, Chwe, *Rational Ritual*, 6, 61–66. See further below.

41 E.g., Vered Noam, "Stringency in Qumran: A Reassessment," *JSJ* 40 (2009): 342–55.

observable in the socio-cultural environment. Thus, things related to the starting time of the Sabbath, maximum distances of movement, a ban on work done in public (e.g., business, court, agriculture), and proper clothing would work as publicly observable actions, whereas restrictions in cooking, baby-sitting, and carrying things within the household would not (see CD 10–11).[42]

Furthermore, whereas weak ties (contacts with acquaintances, friends' friends) are important for spreading new information across distinct networks, they are not always sufficient for adopting new, risky, costly, or controversial information. Such information or practices may require further reinforcement—by having close friends or a great number of people adopt the information, or by being acquainted with the new information through several channels.[43] The secrecy and exclusive gatherings may have decelerated the outsiders' (or other inside-groups') knowledge of the Qumran movement's beliefs and practices; yet the members' everyday practices had the potential to spread to new clusters of people if the "bridge" was wide enough (e.g., several people around you started to exhibit a certain behavior).

3.2   *Rituals Mediate Embodied Knowledge*

Following recent work that abolishes mind-body and inner-outer dualisms, we may say that *any* cognition is embodied cognition. We do not have inner mental states that represent the outer world to us, but rather our bodies engage in organism-environment coordination in ways that allow us to function purposefully in changing (physical, social, and cultural) environments. Cognition and meaning-making require brains, bodies, and interaction with the environment.[44] The sensorimotor system that allows interaction with the environment is multimodal: the input from one sensory area (such as *seeing* an object) often activates other areas too (such as the potentiality to *grasp* things that are seen, their tactile features), and one piece of modal information is continuously being connected with others in the brain.[45] Further, neural patterns may be similar in the actual event and in the later recollection or representation

---

42   See Lutz Doering, *Schabbat: Sabbathalacha und -praxis im antiken Judentum und Urchristentum*, TSAJ 78 (Tübingen: Mohr Siebeck, 1999).

43   Damon Centola and Michael Macy, "Complex Contagions and the Weakness of Long Ties," *American Journal of Sociology* 113 (2007): 702–34. Simple contagion takes place when one contact is enough to cause the new party to adopt the piece of information or practice, and complex contagion takes place when the new party requires several contacts or several exposures to the same information before adopting it.

44   Johnson, *The Meaning of the Body*, esp. 113–34.

45   Johnson, *The Meaning of the Body*, 160–62, notes that understanding is a form of simulation.

of the event. According to the theory of grounded cognition, "the brain areas that represent an entity or event in actual experience also represent it conceptually in its absence."[46] When a person is exposed to food cues, for example, the same brain networks are activated as when consuming food.

What significance does this have for understanding rituals? Rituals are just one environment and setting, but they engage bodies and senses in a governed manner, and understanding cognition as embodied helps us to understand various aspects of rituals as media.

First, while the previous section was about shared knowledge between people, another important aspect of ritualized actions is that they convey information *to the body itself*. Especially in a state of anxiety when people face uncontrollable or unnamable threats, they may resort to repetitive, rigid, seemingly meaningless actions to gain a sense of control over the situation.[47] To take an example from ethnographic research that has sought to investigate this mechanism: Richard Sosis interviewed the residents of a Northern Israelite village during the Second Intifada and found that women who reported intensive recitation of psalms showed lower levels of anxiety and were more likely to continue with their normal lives than women who did not recite psalms.[48] In a stressful setting where things are unpredictable, a sense of doing something is better than doing nothing. Moreover, doing something repetitiously is better than doing something once or randomly.

Turning to evidence from the Qumran movement, we may ask: Was there a heightened sense of threat? If so, could the many psalm texts or exorcist texts or other ritual activities be used to relieve it? To answer the first question, this naturally varied from individual to individual. Most people experience some occasions of uncontrollable threat during their lifetime (illness or the threat

---

46   Jing Chen, Esther K. Papies, and Lawrence W. Barsalou. "A Core Eating Network and Its Modulations Underlie Diverse Eating Phenomena," *Brain and Cognition* 110 (2016): 24. See also Lawrence W. Barsalou, "Grounded Cognition," *Annual Review of Psychology* 59.1 (2008): 617–45.

47   Pascal Boyer and Pierre Liénard, "Why Ritualized Behavior? Precaution Systems and Action Parsing in Developmental, Pathological and Cultural Rituals," *Behavioral and Brain Sciences* 29 (2006): 595–613, explain the psychological mechanism involved in this behavior, which is related to the mechanism in OCD (obsessive compulsory disorder), but which also occurs in childhood and life crises. See also Martin Lang, Jan Krátký, John Shaver, Danijela Jerotijević, and Dimitry Xygalatas, "Is Ritual Behavior a Response to Anxiety?" in *The Cognitive Science of Religion: A Methodological Introduction to Key Empirical Studies*, ed. D. Jason Slone and William W. McCorkle Jr. (London: Bloomsbury, 2019), 181–91.

48   See Richard Sosis, "Can Rituals Reduce Stress during War? The Magic of Psalms," in *The Cognitive Science of Religion: A Methodological Introduction to Key Empirical Studies*, ed. D. Jason Slone and William W. McCorkle Jr. (London: Bloomsbury, 2019), 193–202. Sosis concentrated on women, since Jewish males normally participate in many ritual activities.

RITUALS AS MEDIA

of violence); there was much unrest during the time of the Qumran movement's existence. But the heightened sense of threat was also created within the movement via its ideology regarding the periodization of time: they were witnessing the time of Belial, a time of testing (e.g., 1QS 1:17–18; 3:12–4:26). Fear is a powerful tool and can be used to motivate people to modify their behavior in a certain way. The direction they took may indeed have involved prayers and psalms but also the ritualized study of texts and careful observance of purity, as discussed above. Songs of the Sabbath Sacrifice (4Q400–407) are often referred to as good candidates for transcendental experience, but their repetitive, formulaic language (esp. songs 6–8) may also be considered suitable for meditative recitation to relieve stress.[49] I have elsewhere looked at the Qumran Berakhot (4Q286) from a similar perspective: detailed lists are optimal for occupying one's attention.[50] Several texts in the Qumran corpus are meant to ward off evil (e.g., 11QApocryphal Psalms [11Q11], Songs of the Sage [4Q510–511]).[51] But in theory, any psalms deemed protective could have been used for similar purposes, and also in private. Moreover, texts in the *tefillin* and the praxis of *wearing texts*, including the divine name, in material form had a significant role in this respect.[52] One may also wonder if the detailed halakhic study, the results of which are seen in numerous scrolls from Qumran, could address a similar need to focus attention on doing.

---

49 The difficulty is that we do not know if they were recited all year round or only for the first quarter of the year. For more on mysticism, see Annette Evans, "Songs of the Sabbath Sacrifice, Song Thirteen: Ambiguity, Mysticism, and Cognitive Neuroscience," *JSem* 28 (2019): 1–17.

50 Jutta Jokiranta, "Ritualization and Power of Listing in 4QBerakhot[a] (4Q286)," in *Is There a Text in this Cave?: Studies in the Textuality of the Dead Sea Scrolls in Honour of George J. Brooke*, ed. Ariel Feldman, Maria Cioată and Charlotte Hempel, STDJ 119 (Leiden: Brill, 2017), 438–58.

51 See, e.g., Esther Eshel, "Apotropaic Prayers in the Second Temple Period," in *Liturgical Perspectives: Prayer and Poetry in the Light of the Dead Sea Scrolls: Proceedings of the Fifth International Symposium of the Orion Center for the Study of the Dead Sea Scrolls and Associated Literature, 19–23 January 2000*, ed. Esther G. Chazon, STDJ 48 (Leiden: Brill, 2003), 69–88; Mika S. Pajunen, "How to Expel a Demon: Form- and Tradition-Critical Assessment of the Ritual of Exorcism in 11Qapocryphal Psalms," in *Crossing Imaginary Boundaries: The Dead Sea Scrolls in the Context of Second Temple Judaism*, ed. Mika S. Pajunen and Hanna Tervanotko, Publications of the Finnish Exegetical Society 108 (Helsinki: Finnish Exegetical Society, 2015), 128–61.

52 Yehudah Cohn, *Tangled Up in Text: Tefillin and the Ancient World*, BJS 351 (Providence, RI: Brown Judaic Studies, 2008), argues that the practice was an innovation during the Second Temple period, inspired by magical amulets of the Greeks and associated with the length of days in the land (Deut 11:21). For more Qumran evidence, see Yonatan Adler, "The Distribution of Tefillin Finds among the Judean Desert Caves," in *The Caves of Qumran: Proceedings of the International Conference, Lugano 2014*, ed. Marcello Fidanzio, STDJ 118 (Leiden: Brill, 2016), 161–73.

Secondly, whereas in ritualized recitation it may not matter if one understands the words of the psalms or not, in other respects rituals may seek to engage the imagination and capture tangible experiences. Again, we are restricted to the textual evidence, but one thing to note is just how common concrete images are in texts that probably were used in ritual settings. Examples are numerous. Consider this brief example from the Songs of the Sage (4Q510–511), which are praises to God in order to gain protection from evil spirits (4Q510 1 4–8):

> [Sing for joy, O righteous ones,] *vacat?* for the God of Wonder.
> The psalms of his glory are for the upright.
> [And   let] all those who are blameless exalt Him! *vacat*
> With the lyre of salvation they [shall ope]n their mouths for God's compassion.
> They shall seek His manna.
> > 4Q511 10 7–9

The context in which these songs were used had primed the hearers to be aware of (unseen) dangers and threats; the preceding text paints the picture of the "present dominion of wickedness" (4Q511 10 3). The quoted text exhorts the righteous to join in the praises (which ward off evil), and thus "seek His manna." This raises the question: Which is more important for the understanding of this phrase, to connect manna to the miraculous food provided during the desert wondering of the Israelites (Exodus 16), or to understand that manna is some sort of (positively valued) eatable substance? The manna is primed here by the preceding phrase: "They shall open their mouths for God's compassion." In seeking to understand the text, I claim that the primary level comes from being able to intuitively connect manna to food cues that activate one's neural networks with respect to food and eating. The secondary levels of understanding come via activating memories and knowledge of wilderness traditions—these are the intertextual links we as scholars are so keen on identifying. In doing so, we may miss how the texts work at a primary, bodily level and how they might work for hearers and participants without the same cultural knowledge. All vocabulary connected to the senses influence the experience, accessibility, and attractiveness of the ritual. The more such elements are present, the easier it is for the participant to use basic mundane knowledge to process and anticipate the information.[53]

---

53   Lawrence W. Barsalou, Aron K. Barbey, W. Kyle Simmons, and Ava Santos, "Embodiment in Religious Knowledge," *Journal of Cognition & Culture* 5 (2005): 44, speak about three

Thirdly, we may note the significance of these concrete images and of bodily engagement regardless of whether you participate in the ritual yourself, observe it, or only encounter it in textual form (listening or reading). Let us turn back to the covenant ritual of 1QS, where the priests, the Levites, and the people were said to pass (יעבורו) to the covenant in three turns (Priests, Levites, people), as quoted above (1QS 2:19–23). We have no way of knowing if this sort of action took place annually or how it took place, but if it did, it most probably was a distressing situation for all the groups: the ceremonial procession not only demonstrated the group to which one belonged, but also one's rank within the group. The verb עבר may be understood metaphorically as describing the resulting order of "passing," evidenced, for example, in a written register, but it may also just as easily point to a concrete movement of people (also activating the memory of Israel crossing the river Jordan), since the text otherwise indicates ceremonial features (such as collective, liturgical words and responses). The solemn setting would likely have caused people to attach special meaning to this movement of bodies: one's cosmic status depends on one's concrete place among other bodies of people. There is also evidence that mere observing may cause similar heart-rate synchrony with those participating in an anxiety-arousing event.[54] But even just the act of *hearing* this text annually, without the actual movement or ceremony, could activate the sensorimotor systems connected to movement, to imagination of the procession of multiple groups, and to the shift from one place to another. Drawing people into the idea of movement and passing across a border had consequences for how the abstract idea of covenant was perceived and understood: when one simulated her/his own position among the ranked, the covenant became yet more concrete and compelling.

Furthermore, bodily states influence cognition and information processing, and ritual experiences may vary accordingly. In a hungry state, people simulate the taste and reward value of foods more than when they are not hungry.[55] In empirical tests, bodily states may be induced by, for example, activating certain stereotypes and then investigating how they influence behavior. When in

---

encoding factors: the subject-performed task (SPT) benefit, the location benefit, and the concreteness benefit.

54   Dimitris Xygalatas, *The Burning Saints: Cognition and Culture in the Fire-Walking Rituals of the Anastenaria* (Bristol: Equinox, 2012), 182–83, studied the fire-walking ritual in Northern Greek villages, and he measured a similar heart rate among those performing the fire walking and the local spectators who were merely sitting and watching the performance. However, the synchrony did not extend to non-local spectators, who did not share the contextual knowledge and expectations as the local residents.

55   Chen et al., "A Core Eating Network," 24. People are also more likely to simulate the taste and reward of tasty, unhealthy foods than of less flavorful healthy foods.

one experiment subjects were primed with the "elderly" concept, they walked more slowly to the elevator.[56] Judith Newman has suggested that the language of prostration in the hymns contributes to the humble making of the wisdom teacher: moving your body or simulating movement contributes to the affective responses in the body.[57]

Fourthly, the fact that conceptual thinking is deeply embedded in bodily postures, conditions, and experiences with the concrete world is also strongly suggested by *conceptual metaphor theory*. Metaphors are embodied in us, and metaphoric thinking is our way of making sense of the world. As George Lakoff and Mark Johnson have shown, humans understand abstract things in terms of concrete things, and there is evidence that the processing of abstract ideas involves the corresponding sensorimotor structures.[58] These structures include image schemas having to do with orientation, amount, or position, for example (such as VERTICALITY, SCALARITY, CONTAINER schemas: UP IS GOOD, MORE IS GOOD, INSIDE-OUTSIDE). Conceptual metaphors make use of bodily experiences (e.g., UNDERSTANDING IS *SEEING*), and these (unconscious) patterns lie behind various linguistic expressions ("I *see* what you mean"). A growing number of studies have analyzed metaphors in biblical materials from this perspective. Let us go back to our first example from the Songs of the Sage:

---

56 E.g., Barsalou et al., "Embodiment in Religious Knowledge." However, Doyen et al., "Behavioral Priming: It's All in the Mind, but Whose Mind?" PLoS ONE 7(1) (2012): e29081, famously addressed problems in priming studies as they were not able to replicate the earlier test.

57 Judith H. Newman, "Embodied Techniques: The Communal Formation of the Maskil's Self," *DSD* 22 (2015): 249–66. Most of the ways in which such rituals encoded information in bodily movements and postures have been lost to us. One ritual that almost certainly engaged the body was ritual purification. Washing the impurity away by water and immersing the whole body may have felt as concrete as washing away dirt and sweat, although, according to some archaeological assessments, this experience may have not been refreshing, but rather have involved stagnant water in a dark place; see Rick Bonnie, "Bath/Mikveh," in *Brill Encyclopedia of Early Christianity Online*, ed. David G. Hunter, Paul J. J. van Geest, Bert Jan Lietaert Peerbolte (Leiden: Brill, 2019).

58 George Lakoff and Mark Johnson, *Metaphors We Live By* (Chicago: University of Chicago Press, 2003); Zoltán Kövecses and Réka Benczes. *Metaphor: A Practical Introduction*, 2nd ed. (Oxford: Oxford University Press, 2010); Johnson, *The Meaning of the Body*, 165–206.

RITUALS AS MEDIA   403

[רננו צדיקים] *vac?* באלוהי פלא

[Sing for joy, O righteous ones,]
vacat? for the God of Wonder.

ולישרים תהלי כ[בודו]

The psalms of [his glory] are for the upright.

[ ] י[רוממוהו כול תמימי דרך *vac*

[And let] all those who are blameless exalt Him! *vacat*

בכנור יש[ועות יפת]חו פֿת לרחמי אל

With the lyre of sal[vation they shall ope]n their mouths for God's compassion.

ידרושו למנו *vacat*

They shall seek His manna. *vacat*

4Q511 10 7–9

The short section includes many types of metaphors. It uses the orientation metaphor RIGHT/STRAIGHT IS GOOD in the expression ישרים, "the upright (people),"[59] and the orientation metaphor UP IS GOOD in the exhortation ירוממוהו, "let [them] exalt him" (from the root רום, "be high").[60] The expression תמימי דרך, "the blameless of the way," is a common expression in the scrolls, and it employs the conceptual metaphor LIFE IS A WAY. The expression כנור ישועות, "the lyre of victories," makes use of the fact that lyres are played in victory celebrations and connected to joy (e.g., Neh 12:27; 1 Chr 15:16, 28); yet, here the ישועות does not refer so much to victories but to salvation from danger and help in need: the players of the lyre are not (only) opening their mouths for song and praise but, like helpless babies or chicks, they open their mouth for nourishment, God's compassion (cf. Ps 81:10; 147:9; Isa 10:14). Thus, one understands the sentence from various integrated perspectives (e.g., PRAISING IS BEING NOURISHED) and concrete movements (mouths are opened both for eating and for speaking/singing/playing).

Another example of a text that could have been used in a ritual setting shows the saturation of conceptual metaphors behind the many linguistic expressions. The hymn in the Hodayot (1QH[a]) 10 describes the troubles of the singer:

> I thank you, O Lord, that you have placed my soul in the bundle of the living and that you have protected me from all the snares of the pit; f[o]r ruthless people have sought my life when I hold fast to your covenant.

---

59   This may also be a more complex blend of, for example, the orientation metaphor and the conceptual metaphor PEOPLE ARE PATHS (cf. ישרי דרך in 1QH[a] 10:12, and 1QS 4:2, where paths, not people, are the object of making straight).

60   The processing of such orientation information may also affect bodily movements and postures: for example, with things that are normally up, one's eyes, face, and hand often also move upwards; see Barsalou et al., "Embodiment in Religious Knowledge," 27.

They are a council of deception and a congregation of Belial. They do not know that my station comes from you and that by your kindness you save my life, for from you come my steps.

And because of you they have threatened my life, so that you may be glorified in the judgment of the wicked and manifest your strength through me before mortal beings, for by your kindness do I stand.

And I myself said, "Warriors have encamped against me; they have surrounded (me) with all their weapons of war. Arrows for which there is no cure destroy, and the blade of the spear is like fire that devours trees. Like the roar of mighty waters is the tumult of their shout, a cloudburst and tempest to destroy a multitude. When their waves mount up, deception and vanity burst forth toward the constellations."

But as for me, even when my heart melted like water, my soul held fast to your covenant. And as for them, the net they spread against me seized their feet, and the snares they hid for my life, they themselves fell into them. But my feet stand upon level ground. Far away from their assembly I will bless your name.[61]

> 1QHᵃ 10:22–32

In this passage, the scribe makes use of hunting imagery, war imagery, and water metaphors. It is difficult to tell which aspects of the hymn should *not* be taken figuratively, as describing concrete events rather than experiences or feelings. But the opportunity to take them figuratively is readily apparent and makes the hymn appealing to many situations. When one is safe, one is "in the bundle (צרור) of the living" (SECURITY IS CLOSED BUNDLE/PURSE; CONTAINER SCHEME). When one feels threatened, one encounters "snares" (DANGER IS HUNTER'S TRAP). When one feels God's help, one's "steps" are with God (LIFE IS WALKING/JOURNEY). When one has opponents, they "camp" and surround their enemy (CONFLICT IS SIEGE). Many such metaphors may have become conventional, but they nevertheless contribute to the lived experience in hearing such a hymn. If a prayer or hymn had very few such concrete cues as to where to focus one's attention, it became more laborious to learn and transmit. Our example also reveals how abstract ideas—for example, human agency and the dilemmas humans face—are conceptualized in metaphoric terms: "But as for me, even when my heart melted like water, my soul held fast to your covenant."

---

61 Translation by Eileen M. Schuller and Carol A. Newsom, *The Hodayot (Thanksgiving Psalms): A Study Edition of 1QHᵃ* (Atlanta, GA: SBL, 2012), 33–35.

RITUALS AS MEDIA   405

Such cues in the text may also create experiences that are often called altered states of consciousness. We all know from experience that when we "dwell" on something that takes our full attention, we suddenly discover how time has passed without us noticing it, or we "come back down to earth," feeling that we had been elsewhere for a while, with our mind having wandered off before returning to the present moment. The final question is whether embodied language and the engagement of the body in rituals may also make for more memorable experiences. An early idea in the cognitive science of religion was that minimally counterintuitive concepts are better recalled.[62] That is, those concepts and ideas that violate ontological categories—such as walking trees or talking tables—are memorable because they catch our attention, but at the same time are not too difficult to understand.[63] However, not all tests support this idea, and it has also been suggested that the role of different cultural expectations is an important variable.[64] Rituals often contain actions that also violate everyday (cultural, learned) expectations: for example, after the confession of sins, one might expect a petition for forgiveness, yet in the covenant ceremony of 1QS this is lacking.[65] Likewise, emotional arousal does not automatically increase the accuracy of recollection; rather, emotions increase one's trust in the memories.[66]

3.3 Rituals Rely on Extended Knowledge, and Extended Knowledge Mediates Ritual Practice

Humans do not carry all information in their bodies, but also make use of interactions with their environment and material objects, such as written texts,

---

62   Pascal Boyer and Charles Ramble, "Cognitive Templates for Religious Concepts: Cross-Cultural Evidence for Recall of Counter-Intuitive Representations," *Cognitive Science* 25 (2001): 535–64.

63   Catchy novel concepts spread easily, but for example the use of the division into sons of "light and darkness" seems to have spread more efficiently among modern scrolls scholars than the producers of the scrolls themselves—if judged by the occurrences, which are fairly few in the scrolls.

64   Michaela Porubanova, "Is Memory Crucial for Transmission of Religious Ideas?" in *The Cognitive Science of Religion*, 93–100.

65   Daniel K. Falk, "Petition and Ideology in the Dead Sea Scrolls," in *Prayer and Poetry in the Dead Sea Scrolls and Related Literature*, ed. Jeremy Penner, Ken M. Penner, and Cecilia Wassén, STDJ 98 (Leiden: Brill, 2012), 136.

66   E. A. Phelps, "Emotion's Impact on Memory," in *Memory and Law*, ed. L. Nadel and W. P. Sinnott-Armstrong (Oxford: Oxford University Press, 2013), 7–28. Early theorists in the cognitive science of religion also identified two basic ways in which religious (oral) traditions may seek to ensure the transmission of complex ideas: by frequent repetition and by high emotional arousal; see Whitehouse, *Modes of Religiosity*; McCauley and Lawson, *Bringing Ritual to Mind*.

symbols, and architecture, and that environment affects their cognition (just think of the modern discussion on how mobile technology affects our ability to concentrate).[67] The first implication of this extended knowledge with respect to rituals is obvious: written texts can contain more words than one individual can recite by heart, and such texts serve as a counter-force to the speed of change that takes place through transmission. For a literate and well-trained person, it may require less effort to start reading than reciting from memory, although in reading Hebrew or Aramaic, which requires fluency in the language, oral experiences may still have played a major role. Scholars have noted how the scrolls and codices differed from each other and changed practices, but less research has been done on how scrolls of different size or quality may have affected the user's cognition and ability to process information.[68]

But the second implication is no less important: it is the role of material elements to trigger emotions and memories and attract attention. Tefillin were referred to above as amulet-like objects used for protection, and from the Judaean identity perspective, it may have been significant that they were *inscribed* objects, so as to distinguish them from other amulets.[69] Another prime example are the stepped pools and stone vessels that spread during the Hasmonean and Herodian time: the material forms, perhaps emulating other existing material culture (cf. Greek baths and Idumean hip-baths; stone vessels resembled metal objects rather than pottery), visually and spatially signaled the importance of purity.[70] Without such structures, purification was harder to witness—anyone could wash and launder their clothes in any place with water—but the stepped pools added a space to visit, making the practice comparable to sacrifices that had to be brought to the Temple. If the pools were in individual houses, the changes may have been visible only within the household. (Were the pools shared by male and female, master and slave, what about host and guest?). If the pools were located in connection with gathering

---

67   Lambros Malafouris, "The Brain-Artefact Interface (BAI): A Challenge for Archaeology and Cultural Neuroscience," *Social Cognitive and Affective Neuroscience* 5 (2010): 264–73; John A. Teske, "From Embodied to Extended Cognition," *Zygon* 48 (2013): 759–87; Richard Menary, ed., *The Extended Mind* (Cambridge, MA: MIT Press, 2010).

68   However, see contributions mentioned in Williams, "Textuality and the Dead Sea Scrolls"; Johnson, *Readers and Reading Culture*; Eva Mroczek, *The Literary Imagination in Jewish Antiquity* (Oxford: Oxford University Press, 2016); Eva Mroczek, "Early Jewish Literature," in *Dictionary of the Bible and Ancient Media*, 101–109.

69   Cohn, *Tangled Up in Text*, 87–92.

70   Stuart S. Miller, *At the Intersection of Texts and Material Finds: Stepped Pools, Stone Vessels, and Ritual Purity Among the Jews of Roman Galilee*, JSJSup 16 (Göttingen: Vandenhoeck & Ruprecht, 2015); Yonatan Adler, "The Hellenistic Origins of Jewish Ritual Immersion," *JJS* 69 (2018): 1–21; Rick Bonnie, *Being Jewish in Galilee, 100–200 CE: An Archaeological Study* (Turnhout: Brepols Publishers, 2019).

places, agricultural estates, tombs, and the Temple, then they could have served as public reminders for people of the threats involved in impurity (and sin). Thus, they could become identity markers—even though this was not their intended purpose.

Some texts testify to prayer practices in connection with purification (4Q414). Purification performed with recited words feels intuitively more effective than mere immersion without any adjacent communication, similar to how blessing feels more effective with bodily gestures (like hands spread above a person) than without them.[71] Again, correct purification according to the rules is the desired message, but the manner of purification and its semi-public nature (in stepped pools, by immersion) may invite other ritualized activities (prayer), and the nature of the message changes with the medium.[72] Prayers in general structured sacred time for the members of the Qumran movement.[73] They could also implement a Temple service outside the Temple, using the language of worship and thus verbalizing the Temple and reactivating experiences from the Temple.[74] Rituals re-create mini-worlds and virtual realities.

4 Conclusions

In conclusion, rituals are effective mediators of many types of knowledge. Collective rituals create the *shared knowledge* needed to coordinate action, to make sure everyone receive that knowledge (e.g., by repetition). They facilitate

---

71   Paul Rozin and Carol Nemeroff, "The Laws of Sympathetic Magic: A Psychological Analysis of Similarity and Contagion," in *Cultural Psychology: Essays on Comparative Human Development*, ed. James W. Stigler, Richard A. Shweder and Gilbert Herdt (Cambridge: Cambridge University Press, 1990), 205–32, mention the laying on of hands as example of positive contagion.

72   Ari Mermelstein, "Emotional Regimes, Ritual Practice, and the Shaping of Sectarian Identity: The Experience of Ablutions in the Dead Sea Scrolls," *BibInt* 24 (2016): 492–513, discusses how the sectarian purification practice mediates foundational beliefs about the movement, especially the nothingness, of human beings, the gift of divine election, and the boundary between insiders and outsiders. Purification denotes the redemption that will be realized fully in the future.

73   See Daniel K. Falk, *Daily, Sabbath, and Festival Prayers in the Dead Sea Scrolls*, STDJ 27 (Leiden: Brill, 1998); Jeremy Penner, *Patterns of Daily Prayer in Second Temple Period Judaism*, STDJ 104 (Leiden: Brill, 2012); idem, "Mapping Fixed Prayers from the Dead Sea Scrolls onto Second Temple Period Judaism," *DSD* 21 (2014): 39–63; Jeremy Penner, Ken M. Penner, and Cecilia Wassén, eds., *Prayer and Poetry in the Dead Sea Scrolls and Related Literature*, STDJ 98 (Leiden: Brill, 2012).

74   For more on the construction of an experience of progression throughout the liturgical cycle, see Daniel K. Falk, "Liturgical Progression and the Experience of Transformation in Prayers from Qumran," *DSD* 22 (2015): 267–84.

cooperation and trust by enabling participants to signal their commitment. Rituals mediate *embodied knowledge* because they arouse emotions and enhance self-relatedness, employ mechanisms that reduce anxiety, encode information in the body, engage imagination, and reveal the conceptual metaphors that ground human thinking. Rituals rely on *extended knowledge*—by rehearsing and visualizing master narratives, structured in time, data that is transmitted over generations in textual form becomes collective memory and the basis for communal identity. Knowledge situated in material objects and the environment, such as in stepped pools or tefillin, carry and modify ritual practice via their form and "user-interface": stepped pools invite comprehensive immersion instead of a mere pouring of water and create a more visible, (semi-)public, structured practice, and tefillin mark the bodies that belong to the land and live on in it.

I have touched upon a few possible ways in which the rich evidence in the scrolls might be further investigated. Ritual is old technology, but it can be endlessly varied according to new contexts and situations. The human body is its instrument, especially the social human body, which learns from others and derives its motivation from others. My emphasis was on rituals as types of media, not on their success or failure as means of communication. The information was divided into factual, normative, meta-, and motivational information. In the end, we may come back to the question of how the medium is the message: What (unexpected) consequences can rituals have for a knowledge economy? What might be the consequences that occur because of new technology or the various forms that the technology takes?

I discussed the way in which the material presence of stepped pools changed the nature and role of purification. It has also been suggested that when the purity rules were being systematized and more detailed information transmitted about purification,[75] female purification practices became equal to those of male participants, and gender difference was diminished (though Leviticus 15 did not perceive females as active agents in purification, only as passive transmitters of impurity). Males became equally vulnerable since their purity demanded self-control. Such consequences were not the aim of scribal practices and elaborations on the purity rules, but they could influence the way in which gender was perceived in the movement.[76]

---

75   E.g., Ian C. Werrett, *Ritual Purity and the Dead Sea Scrolls*, STDJ 72 (Leiden: Brill, 2007). See also important suggestions on the legal attitudes of scribes who created halakhot by Jonathan Vroom, *The Authority of Law in the Hebrew Bible and Early Judaism: Tracing the Origins of Legal Obligation from Ezra to Qumran*, JSJSup 187 (Leiden: Brill, 2018).

76   Jessica M. Keady, *Vulnerability and Valour: A Gendered Analysis of Everyday Life in the Dead Sea Scrolls Communities*, LSTS 91 (London: Bloomsbury, 2017).

The obvious message of collective rituals is to make a group of strangers come to see themselves as one body. But bringing people together in a specific manner can also have undesired consequences. An undesired outcome of such a ritual would be dropping out from participation; envy or anger; challenging of authority. The covenant renewal, in light of 1QS, was about entering into the covenant and hearing its blessings and curses (see Deuteronomy 27–30), but when the blessings and curses were detached from the individual's moral behavior and attached to determined divine lots, as in 1QS, the unintended consequence was the problem of sinful acts of the righteous. This called for the development and articulation of inner anthropology, as we saw in 1QS 4. Another unintended consequence was that the ritual activities (sacrifice and purification) of those outside the covenant had to be deemed ineffective (1QS 3:1–12). This demanded condemning one's neighbors, maintaining even stronger boundaries with earlier ingroup members than with outgroup members, and drawing attention to maintaining boundaries rather than achieving the mission—a mission impossible in the end.

Bibliography

Adler, Yonatan. "The Distribution of Tefillin Finds among the Judean Desert Caves." Pages 161–73 in *The Caves of Qumran: Proceedings of the International Conference, Lugano 2014.* Edited by Marcello Fidanzio. STDJ 118. Leiden: Brill, 2016.

Adler, Yonatan. "The Hellenistic Origins of Jewish Ritual Immersion." *JJS* 69 (2018): 1–21.

Barsalou, Lawrence W., Aron K. Barbey, W. Kyle Simmons, and Ava Santos. "Embodiment in Religious Knowledge." *Journal of Cognition & Culture* 5 (2005): 14–57.

Barsalou, Lawrence W. "Grounded Cognition." *Annual Review of Psychology* 59.1 (2008): 617–45.

Bell, Catherine. *Ritual: Perspectives and Dimensions.* Oxford: Oxford University Press, 1997.

Bonnie, Rick. *Brill Encyclopedia of Early Christianity Online.* Edited by David G. Hunter, Paul J. J. van Geest, and Bert Jan Lietaert Peerbolte. Leiden: Brill, 2019.

Bonnie, Rick. *Being Jewish in Galilee, 100–200 CE: An Archaeological Study.* Turnhout: Brepols Publishers, 2019.

Boyer, Pascal, and Pierre Liénard. "Why Ritualized Behavior? Precaution Systems and Action Parsing in Development, Pathological and Cultural Rituals." *Behavioral and Brain Sciences* 29 (2006): 595–613.

Boyer, Pascal, and Charles Ramble. "Cognitive Templates for Religious Concepts: Cross-Cultural Evidence for Recall of Counter-Intuitive Representations." *Cognitive Science* 25 (2001): 535–64.

Brooke, George J. "Aspects of the Theological Significance of Prayer and Worship in the Qumran Scrolls." Pages 36–54 in *Prayer and Poetry in the Dead Sea Scrolls and Related Literature.* Edited by Jeremy Penner, Ken M. Penner, and Cecilia Wassén. STDJ 98. Leiden: Brill, 2012.

Brooke, George J. "Reading, Searching and Blessing: A Functional Approach to Scriptural Interpretation in the יחד." Pages 140–56 in *The Temple in Text and Tradition: A Festschrift in Honour of Robert Hayward.* Edited by R. Timothy McLay. LSTS 83. London: Bloomsbury, 2015.

Bulbulia, Joseph A., and Richard Sosis. "Signalling Theory and the Evolution of Religious Cooperation." *Religion* 41 (2011): 363–88.

Cavell, Richard. *Remediating McLuhan.* Amsterdam: Amsterdam University Press, 2016.

Centola, Damon, and Michael Macy. "Complex Contagions and the Weakness of Long Ties." *American Journal of Sociology* 113.3 (2007): 702–34.

Chen, Jing, Esther K. Papies, and Lawrence W. Barsalou. "A Core Eating Network and Its Modulations Underlie Diverse Eating Phenomena." *Brain and Cognition* 110 (2016): 20–42.

Christian, Meike. "The Literary Development of the 'Treatise of the Two Spirits' as Dependent on Instruction and the Hodayot." Pages 153–84 in *Law, Literature, and Society in Legal Texts from Qumran: Papers from the Ninth Meeting of the International Organization for Qumran Studies, Leuven 2016.* Edited by Jutta Jokiranta and Molly M. Zahn. STDJ 128. Leiden: Brill, 2019.

Chwe, Michael Suk-Young. *Rational Ritual: Culture, Coordination and Common Knowledge.* Princeton, NJ: Princeton University Press, 2003.

Cohn, Yehudah. *Tangled Up in Text: Tefillin and the Ancient World.* Providence, RI: Brown Judaic Studies, 2008.

Doering, Lutz. *Schabbat: Sabbathalacha und -praxis im antiken Judentum und Urchristentum.* TSAJ 78. Tübingen: Mohr Siebeck, 1999.

Doyen, Stéphane, Olivier Klein, Cora-Lise Pichon, Axel Cleeremans, and Jan Lauwereyns. "Behavioral Priming: It's All in the Mind, but Whose Mind?" *PLoS ONE* 7(1) (2012): e29081.

Eshel, Esther. "Apotropaic Prayers in the Second Temple Period." Pages 69–88 in *Liturgical Perspectives: Prayer and Poetry in the Light of the Dead Sea Scrolls: Proceedings of the Fifth International Symposium of the Orion Center for the Study of the Dead Sea Scrolls and Associated Literature, 19–23 January 2000.* Edited by Esther G. Chazon. STDJ 48. Leiden: Brill, 2003.

Evans, Annette. "Songs of the Sabbath Sacrifice, Song Thirteen: Ambiguity, Mysticism, and Cognitive Neuroscience." *Journal for Semitics* 28.1 (2019): 1–17.

Falk, Daniel K. *Daily, Sabbath, and Festival Prayers in the Dead Sea Scrolls.* STDJ 27. Leiden: Brill, 1998.

Falk, Daniel K. "Petition and Ideology in the Dead Sea Scrolls." Pages 135–59 in *Prayer and Poetry in the Dead Sea Scrolls and Related Literature*. Edited by Jeremy Penner, Ken M. Penner, and Cecilia Wassén. STDJ 98. Leiden: Brill, 2012.

Falk, Daniel K. "Liturgical Progression and the Experience of Transformation in Prayers from Qumran." *DSD* 22 (2015): 267–84.

Geertz, Armin. "Brain, Body and Culture: A Biocultural Theory of Religion." *Method and Theory in the Study of Religion* 22 (2010): 304–21.

Harkins, Angela Kim. "The Emotional Re-Experiencing of the Hortatory Narratives Found in the Admonition of the Damascus Document." *DSD* 22 (2015): 285–307.

Hempel, Charlotte. *The Qumran Rule Texts in Context: Collected Studies*. Tübingen: Mohr Siebeck, 2013.

Hempel, Charlotte. "The Long Text of the Serekh as Crisis Literature." *RevQ* 27 (2015): 3–24.

Hempel, Charlotte. "Bildung und Wissenswirtschaft im Judentum zur Zeit des Zweiten Tempels." Pages 229–44 in *Was ist Bildung in der Vormoderne?* Edited by Peter Gemeinhardt. Tübingen: Mohr Siebeck, 2019.

Hempel, Charlotte. *The Community Rules from Qumran: A Commentary*. TSAJ 183. Tübingen: Mohr Siebeck, 2020.

Johnson, Mark. *The Meaning of the Body: Aesthetics of Human Understanding*. Chicago, IL: The University of Chicago Press, 2007.

Johnson, William A. *Readers and Reading Culture in the High Roman Empire: A Study of Elite Communities*. Classical Culture and Society. Oxford: Oxford University Press, 2010.

Jokiranta, Jutta. "What is '*Serekh ha-Yahad* (S)'? Thinking About Ancient Manuscripts as Information Processing." Pages 611–35 in *Sibyls, Scriptures, and Scrolls: John Collins at Seventy*. Joel S. Baden, Hindy Najman, and Eibert J. C. Tigchelaar. JSJSup 175. Leiden: Brill, 2016.

Jokiranta, Jutta. "Ritualization and Power of Listing in 4QBerakhot[a] (4Q286)." Pages 438–58 in *Is There a Text in this Cave? Studies in the Textuality of the Dead Sea Scrolls in Honour of George J. Brooke*. Edited by Ariel Feldman, Maria Cioată and Charlotte Hempel. STDJ 119. Leiden: Brill, 2017.

Jokiranta, Jutta. "Competitors to Middle Maccabees: Evidence from the Dead Sea Scrolls." Forthcoming in *The Middle Maccabees: From the Death of Judas through the Reign of John Hyrcanus (ca. 160–104 BCE): New Archaeological and Historical Perspectives*. Edited by Andrea M. Berlin and Paul J. Kosmin. Archaeology and Biblical Studies Series. Atlanta, GA: SBL.

Keady, Jessica M. *Vulnerability and Valour: A Gendered Analysis of Everyday Life in the Dead Sea Scrolls Communities*. LSTS 91. London: Bloomsbury, 2017.

Klawans, Jonathan. *Purity, Sacrifice, and the Temple: Symbolism and Supersessionism in the Study of Ancient Judaism*. Oxford: Oxford University Press, 2005.

Kundt, Radek. "Making Evolutionary Science of Religion an Integral Part of Cognitive Science of Religion." Pages 141–58 in *Evolution, Cognition, and the History of Religion: A New Synthesis. Festschrift in Honour of Armin W. Geertz*. Edited by Anders Klostergaard Petersen, Ingvild Sælid Gilhus, Luther H. Martin, Jeppe Sinding Jensen, and Jesper Sørensen. Leiden: Brill, 2019.

Kövecses, Zoltán, and Réka Benczes. *Metaphor: A Practical Introduction*. 2nd ed. Oxford: Oxford University Press, 2010.

Lakoff, George, and Mark Johnson. *Metaphors We Live By*. Chicago, IL: University of Chicago Press, 2003.

Lang, Martin, Jan Krátký, John Shaver, Danijela Jerotijević, and Dimitry Xygalatas. "Is Ritual Behavior a Response to Anxiety?" Pages 181–91 in *The Cognitive Science of Religion: A Methodological Introduction to Key Empirical Studies*. Edited by D. Jason Slone and William W. McCorkle Jr. London: Bloomsbury, 2019.

Malafouris, Lambros. "The Brain-Artefact Interface (BAI): A Challenge for Archaeology and Cultural Neuroscience." *Social Cognitive and Affective Neuroscience* 5.2–3 (2010): 264–73.

McCauley, Robert N. *Why Religion Is Natural and Science Is Not*. Oxford: Oxford University Press, 2011.

McCauley, Robert N., and E. Thomas Lawson. *Bringing Ritual to Mind: Psychological Foundations of Cultural Forms*. Cambridge: Cambridge University Press, 2002.

McLuhan, Marshall. *Understanding Media: The Extensions of Man*. New York, NY: McGraw-Hill, 1964.

Menary, Richard., ed. *The Extended Mind*. Cambridge, MA: MIT Press, 2010.

Mermelstein, Ari. "Emotional Regimes, Ritual Practice, and the Shaping of Sectarian Identity: The Experience of Ablutions in the Dead Sea Scrolls." *BibInt* 24 (2016): 492–513.

Miller, Stuart S. *At the Intersection of Texts and Material Finds: Stepped Pools, Stone Vessels, and Ritual Purity Among the Jews of Roman Galilee*. Göttingen: Vandenhoeck & Ruprecht, 2015.

Mroczek, Eva. *The Literary Imagination in Jewish Antiquity*. New York, NY: Oxford University Press, 2016.

Mroczek, Eva. "Early Jewish Literature." Pages 101–9 in *The Dictionary of the Bible and Ancient Media*. Edited by Tom Thatcher, Chris Keith, Raymond F. Person, Jr., and Elise R. Stern. London: Bloomsbury T&T Clark, 2017.

Newman, Judith H. "Embodied Techniques: The Communal Formation of the Maskil's Self." *DSD* 22 (2015): 249–66.

Noam, Vered. "Stringency in Qumran: A Reassessment." *JSJ* 40 (2009): 342–55.

Norenzayan, Ara. *Big Gods: How Religion Transformed Cooperation and Conflict*. Princeton, NJ: Princeton University Press, 2013.

Pajunen, Mika. "How to Expel a Demon: Form- and Tradition-Critical Assessment of the Ritual of Exorcism in 11Qapocryphal Psalms." Pages 128–61 in *Crossing Imaginary Boundaries: The Dead Sea Scrolls in the Context of Second Temple Judaism*. Edited by Mika Pajunen and Hanna Tervanotko. Publications of the Finnish Exegetical Society 108. Helsinki: Finnish Exegetical Society, 2015.

Parker, Holt N., and William A. Johnson. *Ancient Literacies: The Culture of Reading in Greece and Rome*. Oxford: Oxford University Press, 2009.

Penner, Jeremy. *Patterns of Daily Prayer in Second Temple Period Judaism*. STDJ 104. Leiden: Brill, 2012.

Penner, Jeremy. "Mapping Fixed Prayers from the Dead Sea Scrolls onto Second Temple Period Judaism." *DSD* 21 (2014): 39–63.

Penner, Jeremy, Ken M. Penner, and Cecilia Wassén, eds. *Prayer and Poetry in the Dead Sea Scrolls and Related Literature*. STDJ 98. Leiden: Brill, 2012.

Phelps, E. A. "Emotion's Impact on Memory." Pages 7–28 in *Memory and Law*. Edited by L. Nadel and W. P. Sinnott-Armstrong. Oxford: Oxford University Press, 2013.

Popović, Mladen. "Reading, Writing, and Memorizing Together: Reading Culture in Ancient Judaism and the Dead Sea Scrolls in a Mediterranean Context." *DSD* 24 (2017): 447–70.

Porubanova, Michaela. "Is Memory Crucial for Transmission of Religious Ideas?" Pages 93–100 in *The Cognitive Science of Religion: A Methodological Introduction to Key Empirical Studies*. Edited by D. Jason Slone and William W. McCorkle Jr. London: Bloomsbury, 2019.

Porzig, Peter. "The Place of the 'Treatise of the Two Spirits' (1QS 3:13–4:26) within the Literary Development of the Community Rule." Pages 127–52 in *Law, Literature, and Society in Legal Texts from Qumran: Papers from the Ninth Meeting of the International Organization for Qumran Studies, Leuven 2016*. Edited by Jutta Jokiranta and Molly M. Zahn. STDJ 128. Leiden: Brill, 2019.

Rappaport, Roy A. *Ritual and Religion in the Making of Humanity*. Cambridge: Cambridge University Press, 1999.

Rozin, Paul, and Carol Nemeroff. "The Laws of Sympathetic Magic: A Psychological Analysis of Similarity and Contagion." Pages 205–32 in *Cultural Psychology: Essays on Comparative Human Development*. Edited by James W. Stigler, Richard A. Shweder, and Gilbert Herdt. Cambridge: Cambridge University Press, 1990.

Schuller, Eileen M., and Carol A. Newsom. *The Hodayot (Thanksgiving Psalms): A Study Edition of 1QHª*. Atlanta, GA: SBL, 2012.

Sosis, Richard. "Can Rituals Reduce Stress during War? The Magic of Psalms." Pages 193–202 in *The Cognitive Science of Religion: A Methodological Introduction to Key Empirical Studies*. Edited by D. Jason Slone and William W. McCorkle Jr. London: Bloomsbury, 2019.

Sosis, Richard. "Do Religions Promote Cooperation? Testing Signaling Theories of Religion." Pages 155–62 in *The Cognitive Science of Religion: A Methodological Introduction to Key Empirical Studies*. Edited by D. Jason Slone and William W. McCorkle, Jr. London: Bloomsbury, 2019.

Teske, John A. "From Embodied to Extended Cognition." *Zygon* 48.3 (2013): 759–87.

Thatcher, Tom, Chris Keith, Raymond F. Person, Jr., and Elise R. Stern, eds. *The Dictionary of the Bible and Ancient Media*. London: Bloomsbury T&T Clark, 2017.

Thomas, Günther. "Communication." Pages 321–43 in *Theorizing Rituals: Issues, Topics, Approaches, Concepts*. Edited by Jens Kreinath, Jan Snoek, and Michael Stausberg. Leiden: Brill, 2008.

Tov, Emanuel E., ed. *The Dead Sea Scrolls Electronic Library: Texts and Images*. Partially based on *The Dead Sea Scrolls Reader*. Edited by Donald W. Parry and Emanuel Tov. Morphological analysis by Martin Abegg, Jr. Produced by Noel B. Reynolds. Associate producer Kristian Heal. Leiden: Brill, 2006.

Uro, Risto. *Ritual and Christian Beginnings: A Socio-Cognitive Analysis*. Oxford: Oxford University Press, 2016.

Vroom, Jonathan. *The Authority of Law in the Hebrew Bible and Early Judaism: Tracing the Origins of Legal Obligation from Ezra to Qumran*. JSJSup 187. Leiden: Brill, 2018.

Werrett, Ian C. *Ritual Purity and the Dead Sea Scrolls*. STDJ 72. Leiden: Brill, 2007.

Whitehouse, Harvey. *Modes of Religiosity: A Cognitive Theory of Religious Transmission*. Walnut Creek, CA: AltaMira Press, 2004.

Xygalatas, Dimitris. *The Burning Saints: Cognition and Culture in the Fire-Walking Rituals of the Anastenaria*. Bristol: Equinox, 2012.

CHAPTER 12

Rations, Refreshments, Reading, and Revelation: The Multifunction of the Common Meal in the Qumran Movement

Cecilia Wassén

1 Introduction

The members of the Qumran movement came together regularly for social activities. The lines in 1QS 6:2–3 describe the key parts of these gatherings, "They shall eat together (יחד), together they shall bless, and together they shall take counsel."[1] According to this sentence the members got together particularly for communal meals. Moreover, the meal is a common topic in sectarian literature, found in texts such as the Community Rule (1QS), the Damascus Document (CD, D), the Rule of the Congregation (1QSa), Tohorot A (4Q274), Ordinances^c (4Q514), and Miscellaneous Rules (4Q265). These texts include various regulations concerning meals, which include seating order, procedures, leaders, purity, and penalties. Taken together these documents point to the prominence of the communal meal within the movement. Hence, it is likely that, like other associations in the Greco-Roman world, the meal was the central social event for the members, as Matthias Klinghardt has argued. Still few scholars have recognized that the common meal was the main occasion for the gatherings. In this study, I will demonstrate the centrality of the common meal in the movement and analyze the structure of the meal and its components. I will address the questions: What did the members of the Qumran movement do at their common meal apart from eating, and why did the meal require ritual purity of the participants? A comparison between meal practices of the Qumran sectarians and other Greco-Roman associations in light of the common banquet traditions may provide some insight into these questions. I will not engage with the question of whether the sectarians performed their own sacrifices at Khirbet Qumran as Jodi Magness and Jean Baptiste

---

1 Matthias Klinghardt, *Gemeinschaftsmahl und Mahlgemeinschaft: Soziologie und Liturgie früh-christlicher Mahlfeiern*, Texte und Arbeiten zum neutestamentlichen Zeitalter 13 (Tübingen: Francke, 1996).

© CECILIA WASSÉN, 2023 | DOI:10.1163/9789004537804_013

Humbert argue.[2] Although I will briefly comment on the seating arrangements at Qumran, my focus will be on the role of the common meal among the great majority of members who lived at different places around the land.

2   The Character of the Qumran Movement

In order to discuss the gatherings, I need to clarify my understanding of the social context of the sectarian regulations. I concur with those scholars who have criticized the traditional understanding of the Qumran movement as consisting of two distinct branches based on marital status, represented by the Community Rule (1QS) on the one hand, and the Damascus Document (D), on the other. Scholars such as John Collins, Alison Schofield, and Jutta Jokiranta reconstruct the movement as more complex and less structured than the early paradigm.[3] One reason is the overlapping organizational terminology in various sectarian rules, which points to interchanges of various kinds between different groups in the movement.[4] So Schofield, for example, highlights the great variety in the use of the terms *yaḥad* and *edah* in the scrolls, which point to a more varied communal organization than a mere twofold division of the sect. The simple fact that the rules 4Q265 and 1QSa, in which marriage is taken for granted, share terminology with both S and D gives reason to pause.

---

2   Jodi Magness, "Were Sacrifices Offered at Qumran? The Animal Bone Deposits Reconsidered," *JAJ* 7 (2016): 5–34; Jean-Baptiste Humbert, "L'espace sacré à Qumrân: propositions pour l'archéologie," *RB* 101 (1994): 161–214.

3   Alison Schofield, *From Qumran to the Yaḥad: A New Paradigm of Textual Development for The Community Rule*, STDJ 77 (Leiden: Brill, 2009); John J. Collins, *Beyond the Qumran Community: The Sectarian Movement of the Dead Sea Scrolls* (Grand Rapids, MI: Eerdmans, 2010); Jutta Jokiranta, "Black Sheep, Outsiders, and the Qumran Movement: Social-Psychological Perspectives on Norm-Deviant Behaviour," in *Social Memory and Social Identity in the Study of Early Judaism and Early Christianity*, ed. Samuel Byrskog, Raimo Hakola, and Jutta Jokiranta, NTOA/SUNT 116 (Göttingen: Vandenhoeck & Ruprecht, 2016), 151–73.

4   Sarianna Metso highlights that there are several other documents, apart from the well-known rules, that also reflect communal organizations: 4Q477 (Rebukes) 4Q275 (Communal Ceremony), 4Q279 (Four Lots), and 5Q13 (Rule). She describes 4Q477 like 4Q265 as a kind of hybrid with features particular for both S and D. In particular, 4Q265 mentions women and children and also includes the term *yaḥad*. She argues that scholars should also take these small manuscripts into consideration when reconstructing the movement since their fragmentary nature is no reason for dismissing them. When we bring these small manuscripts into the discussion the picture gets quite complex. See Sarianna Metso, "Problems in Reconstructing the Organizational Chart of the Essenes," *DSD* 16 (2009): 388–415, especially 395–97.

RATIONS, REFRESHMENTS, READING, AND REVELATION   417

This new perspective also calls into question the close link between the Community Rule and Qumran, which has previously been taken for granted. Importantly, John Collins points out that 1QS also assumes multiple habitations of the members. He highlights 1QS 6:1–4:[5]

> In this way they shall behave in all their places of residence (בכול מגוריהם). Whenever one fellow meets another, the junior shall obey the senior in work and in money. They shall eat together (יחד), together they shall bless and together they shall take counsel. In every place where there are ten men of the council of the community (היחד), there should not be missing among them a priest.[6] (1QS 6:1–4)

Thereby, according to Collins, rather than referring to an elite, single group the term *yahad* is an umbrella term for several communities.[7] He writes, "S clearly provides for several small communities, with a quorum of ten, and cannot be

---

5 Some scholars prefer to consider these lines an interpolation, e.g., Metso and Charlotte Hempel, but fragments of the text appear also in 4QS^d, which according to Metso is older than 1QS. See John J. Collins, "The Yaḥad and 'the Qumran Community,'" in *Biblical Traditions in Transmission: Essays in Honour of Michael A. Knibb*, ed. Charlotte Hempel and Judith M. Lieu, JSJSup 111 (Leiden: Brill, 2006), 87–88. See also Sarianna Metso, "Whom Does the Term Yaḥad Identify?" in *Defining Identities: We, You, and the Other in the Dead Sea Scrolls: Proceedings of the Fifth Meeting of the IOQS in Groningen*, ed. Florentino García Martínez and Mladen Popović, STDJ 70 (Leiden: Brill, 2008), 68–71. Her main argument is that the segment displays distinct features compared to the rest of the organizational rules in 1QS 5–7. According to Metso: "An argument can be made that the passage may have originated in a different setting, described that which happened somewhere else than in the community behind the Serek, and then may have been secondarily borrowed and inserted into the Serek" (68). Nevertheless, in light of Jokiranta's review of the manuscripts, the texts related to S were not stable (Jutta Jokiranta, "What Is 'Serekh Ha-Yahad [S]'? Thinking About Ancient Manuscripts as Information Processing," in *Sibyls, Scriptures, and Scrolls: John Collins at Seventy*, ed. Joel S. Baden, Hindy Najman, and Eibert J. C. Tigchelaar, JSJSup 175.1 [Leiden: Brill, 2017], 611–35). Hence, even if this passage were inserted (into which text?) later than other parts it is difficult to evaluate what this would mean. The passage 1QS 6:1–8 was obviously meaningful to the scribe/s putting this together. Metso argues that the passage refers to travelling fellows in spite of the expression מגורים from גור "to dwell" (75). Charlotte Hempel, on her part, detects three layers within the segment 1QS 6:1–8 which in turn reflect a development in the organization; see Charlotte Hempel, "Emerging Communal Life and Ideology in the S Tradition," in *Defining Identities: We, You, and the Other in the Dead Sea Scrolls: Proceedings of the Fifth Meeting of the IOQS in Groningen*, ed. Florentino García Martínez and Mladen Popović, STDJ 70 (Leiden: Brill, 2008), 44–49. This line of reasoning gets highly speculative.
6 Trans. Collins, *Beyond*, 66.
7 Collins, *Beyond*, 10.

regarded as the rule for a single community at Qumran."[8] Furthermore, about Khirbet Qumran, he states:

> At most, Qumran was one settlement of the Yahad. It was never the Yahad in its entirety .... The Yahad, and still more the new covenant of the Damascus Rule, was not an isolated monastic community, as has sometimes been imagined, it was part of the religious association spread widely throughout the land.[9]

This line of reconstruction is convincing, based on the arguments stated above. This leads to the question as to the function and status of the community at Qumran. What was Qumran, then, if not the main center of the sect and the site of its leaders? Sidnie White Crawford suggests that Qumran was the central library and a scribal center of the Essenes.[10] In her analysis of the whole library at Qumran she highlights the diverse character and scribal features. For our purpose, it is important that she agrees with the assessment by Collins and Schofield that the library contained minor collections from various Judean Essene communities. She notes, "This collecting activity from around Judea would account for the large size of the collection in the number of scribal hands found in it, as well as the fact that certain key sectarian and affiliated texts are preserved in multiple copies."[11] White Crawford still finds it plausible that the scribes at Qumran lived according to the Community Rule because it fits the best: "If a particular rule was being followed in the Qumran settlement,

---

8   Collins, *Beyond*, 5. In contrast, Russell C. D. Arnold, *Social Role of Liturgy in the Religion of the Qumran Community*, STDJ 60 (Leiden: Brill, 2005), 87, argues that whereas the section pertains to the community at Qumran, it was designed to ensure that meetings at other places resembled that of meals at Qumran.

9   Collins, *Beyond*, 208. In comparison, Eyal Regev argues that both S and D reflect small social organizations of local communities. Yet he states concerning these two branches, "from a strictly sociological perspective they were two independent sects, affiliated with the same religious movement" (Eyal Regev, "Between Two Sects: Differentiating the Yaḥad and the Damascus Covenant," in *Dead Sea Scrolls: Texts and Context*, Charlotte Hempel, STDJ 90 [Leiden: Brill, 2010], 436). He writes, "I do not list marriage and family life as a difference between the two groups since I believe that the Yahad were not celibates" (436 n.19). At the same time, he criticizes Wassén and Jokiranta for downplaying the differences between D and S regarding family life, wealth, ownership of slaves, and the Temple (439 n.26). See Cecilia Wassén and Jutta Jokiranta, "Groups in Tension: Sectarianism in the Damascus Document and the Community Rule," in *Sectarianism in Early Judaism: Sociological Advances*, Bibleworld (London: Equinox Pub, 2007), 205–45.

10   Sidnie White Crawford, *Scribes and Scrolls at Qumran* (Grand Rapids, MI: Eerdmans, 2019), 317–18.

11   White Crawford, *Scribes*, 411.

RATIONS, REFRESHMENTS, READING, AND REVELATION 419

that rule would most likely have been some form of S."[12] In contrast, I would argue that is not possible to say anything about which rule or combination of rules were normative at Qumran. We only have a general sense.

Rather than associating the Qumran movement primarily with the scribal center at Qumran, then, we should imagine the members living in various places in the country as reflected in both D and S. My view is that the movement was made up of a mix of members, some married and some not, who lived all over the country. One manifestation of different types of membership was in the varying levels of economic commitment of the members to the sect. In this regard D, with the requirement of contributing two days salary a month (CD 14:12–13), diverges conspicuously from the stipulated merging of property in 1QS (1QS 6:22). Yet, members still retained some control over their property according to 1QS 7:6–8, since they are assumed to be able to refund any common property they have wasted. Families would more naturally fall under the stipulations from D, that is, to contribute two days salary a month, while single men more easily could have handed over their property to the movement when joining. At the same time, young men who grew up in sectarian families may have chosen to remain celibate while continuing to live at home, i.e., in a family household. Widows or widowers may have opened up their homes for unmarried members and so on. With a movement spread all over the country, there are numerous possibilities for all kinds of different living arrangements. Some initiates may have lived together whereas others got together less frequently. When and why did these members meet? The many regulations in sectarian texts pertaining to communal meals suggest that members got together in particular for meals, similar to other voluntary associations in the Greco-Roman world, which I will turn to next.

3   The Qumran Movement and Other Voluntary Associations

There is no doubt that the organization of the Qumran movement formed a distinct association within Jewish society, with its own rules for entry, expulsion, and membership. Like other associations in the Greco-Roman world, it filled a social space in between the civic society and the household. John Kloppenborg explains:

> Between poles of the family and the polis there existed a large number of more or less permanent private associations, guilds, or clubs, organized

---

12   White Crawford, *Scribes*, 276.

around an extended family, the cult of a deity or hero, an ethnic group in diaspora, a neighborhood, or a common trade or profession. Most of these associations had cultic aspects and most served broadly social goals.[13]

The question is whether the Qumran movement can be compared to non-Jewish associations in function and character, or whether it should be considered a group isolated from any influence from the larger world in this respect. Since the ground breaking work by Hans Bardtke[14] in the 1960s many scholars, such as Sandra Walker-Ramisch,[15] Moshe Weinfeld,[16] Matthias Klinghardt,[17] and Yonder Gillihan[18] have highlighted similar characteristics of the Qumran movement compared to that of Greco-Roman associations, including voluntary membership, hierarchy, officials, regulations, initiation, decision making, common meals, duties, and penalties.[19] Notably, the term *yaḥad* (יחד), "community," is the Hebrew equivalent of the Greek *koinon* (κοινόν or κοινωνία), a regular term for association.[20] Despite the common starting point, the conclusions by these scholars differ. Benedikt Eckhardt puts it succinctly:

> The definition of the groups behind the Dead Sea Scrolls as associations can be used either to "normalize" their relations with mainstream society in light of Greek parallels, or to emphasize a categorical difference between them and the Greek associations.[21]

---

13   John S. Kloppenborg and Richard S. Ascough, eds., *Greco-Roman Associations: Texts, Translations, and Commentary II: Attica, Central Greece, Macedonia, Thrace*, BZNW 181 (Berlin: De Gruyter, 2011), 1.

14   Hans Bardtke, "Die Rechtstellung der Qumran Gemeinde," *TLZ* 86 (1961): 93–104.

15   Sandra Walker-Ramisch, "Graeco-Roman Voluntary Associations and the Damascus Document: A Sociological Analysis," in *Voluntary Associations in the Graeco-Roman World*, ed. John S. Kloppenborg and Brian Wilson (London: Routledge, 1996), 128–45.

16   Moshe Weinfeld, *The Organizational Pattern and the Penal Code of the Qumran Sect: A Comparison with Guilds and Religious Associations of the Hellenistic-Roman Period*, NTOA 2 (Göttingen: Vandenhoeck & Ruprecht, 1986).

17   Matthias Klinghardt, *Gemeinschaftsmahl und Mahlgemeinschaft*.

18   Yonder Moynihan Gillihan, *Civic Ideology, Organization, and Law in the Rule Scrolls: A Comparative Study of the Covenanters' Sect and Contemporary Voluntary Associations in Political Context*, STDJ 97 (Leiden: Brill, 2012).

19   Gillihan, *Civic Ideology, Organization, and Law in the Rule Scrolls*, 22.

20   Bruno W. Dombrowski, "היחד in 1QS and Τὸ Κοινόν: An Instance of Early Greek and Jewish Synthesis," *HTR* 59 (1966): 293–307.

21   Benedikt Eckhardt, "Temple Ideology and Hellenistic Private Associations," *DSD* 24 (2017): 411.

While listing many parallels to non-Jewish associations, Weinfeld still argues that the Qumran movement was a very different group. Similarly, Walker-Ramisch compares the organization behind D with Roman collegia and highlights various differences, including the geographic spread of the D group, the exclusive nature of the congregation, and its negative attitude towards the general society.[22] Furthermore, Eckhardt notes that the common affiliation with a sanctuary in the classical Hellenistic associations is lacking in the case of the Qumran movement, given the unique position of the Jerusalem temple in Jewish society.[23] By comparison, he argues other associations could build their own sanctuaries.[24] At the same time, he makes the important observation that the Qumran movement shared religion as its focal point with these various associations. The most thorough study so far is that by Gillihan who demonstrates the analogies between the Covenanters (as he prefers to call the members) and Greco-Roman associations, on the one hand, and philosophical schools, on the other. According to him, the parallels are striking and the Covenanters should be considered a type of association. In his view, the critical attitude towards society does not disqualify the Covenanters from being considered an association; instead, he points to other groups that similarly rejected the legitimacy of the state and "developed alternative civic ideology," like Paul's *ekklesiai* and some philosophical schools.[25] He explains, "Alternative civic ideology enables members of associations to imagine themselves as citizens of a superior commonwealth."[26]

Why do we find these similarities? Previous studies, such as Weinfeld's, discussed the influence of Greco-Roman associations in a general sense. Gillihan, for his part, is skeptical to any direct influence by other associations, and instead proposes that the Covenanters, just like other associations, developed an internal organization patterned on institutions of the civic society of the

---

22 Walker-Ramisch, "Graeco-Roman," 130. See the critique of her analysis by Gillihan, *Civic Ideology*, 50–53. He notes that "members of philosophical schools occasionally came into conflict with state authorities for their criticism of the status quo, as happened with some Stoics under Nero and Vespasian" (51).

23 Eckhardt, "Temple Ideology."

24 "Building a new temple community was presented by Hellenistic associations as an expansion of the religious field constituted by civic sanctuaries and festivals. It was the logical way for a private association to gain acceptance" (Benedikt Eckhardt, "The Yahad in the Context of Hellenistic Group Formation," in *T&T Clark Companion to the Dead Sea Scrolls*, ed. George J. Brooke and Charlotte Hempel, with the assistance of Michael DeVries and Drew Longacre [London: T&T Clark, 2019], 92).

25 Gillihan, *Civic Ideology*, 79. For a critique of this approach, see Eckhardt, "Temple Ideology," 411.

26 Gillihan, *Civic Ideology*, 73.

cities and the state.[27] Hence, their ideology developed in interaction with state ideology, but at the same time, for the Covenanters the Torah was the source of inspiration and legitimization:

> The Covenanters' civic ideology presented a response to and critique of the Hasmonean state. Their organization and regulation show extensive familiarity with Judean offices, laws, and the temple cult. Nevertheless, ... the Covenanters crafted their society by drawing not only upon actual organization and laws of Judea, but also upon other sources, most importantly the Torah.[28]

In my view, Gillihan demonstrates that the Qumran movement displays considerable similarities with other associations and he makes a plausible case for some of the reasons for these analogies. Nevertheless, in contrast to Gillihan, I assume that there was direct influence, in particular given the similarities in terminology between Greco-Roman associations (*koinon, thiasos, synagoge, synodos, or collegium*) and Jewish ones (*synagoge, synodos* among other labels).[29] Indeed, many scholars argue quite convincingly that synagogues made up a Jewish type of association, both in the diaspora and in the land.[30] Furthermore, we should take into account that "there was significant diversity"

---

27 Gillihan, *Civic Ideology*, 66. He alleges that most scholars "attempt to explain all organizational features on the basis of 'influence,' if engagement with Hellenistic-Roman culture is admitted, or 'exegesis' if it is denied." Gillihan explains: "Whether state-affiliated associations are formed by private or state initiative, their organization and ideology inevitably will be affected by their affiliation with state institutions and will reflect the rationally constructed social patterns of the institutions with which they are affiliated" (71).

28 Gillihan, *Civic Ideology*, 74.

29 Philip A. Harland, *Dynamics of Identity in the World of the Early Christians: Associations, Judeans, and Cultural Minorities* (New York, NY: Continuum, 2009), 36–46. *Ekklesia* ("assembly"), although not widely used among associations, was also used for synagogues; see Ralph Korner, "Ekklēsia as a Jewish Synagogue Term: Some Implications for Paul's Socio-Religious Location," *Journal of the Jesus Movement in its Jewish Setting* 2 (2015): 53–78.

30 Matthias Klinghardt, "The Manual of Discipline in the Light of Statutes of Hellenistic Associations," in *Methods of Investigation of the Dead Sea Scrolls and the Khirbet Qumran Site: Present Realities and Future Prospects*, ed. Michael Owen Wise, John J. Collins, and Dennis G. Pardee, Annals of the New York Academy of Sciences 722 (New York, NY: New York Academy of Sciences, 1994), 258–63. Harland, *Dynamics of Identity*; Richard S. Ascough, "Paul, Synagogues, and Associations: Reframing the Question of Models for Pauline Christ Groups," *Journal of the Jesus Movement in its Jewish Setting* 2 (2015): 51: "We must drop the dichotomous either/or categorization and re-frame the discussion around the comparative exploration of similarities and differences across all types of Greco-Roman associations, including synagogues and Christ groups, in order to move forward in our understanding of the complex interactions reflected in all of our texts, sacred

among Greco-Roman associations and it is therefore a mistake to compare the Qumran movement to the Greco-Roman groups as if they made up a homogeneous phenomenon.[31] Different types of societies served a variety of functions. Similarly, Jewish associations, or synagogues, made up different types of institutions, to which I will return below. According to Philip Harland, Greco-Roman associations attracted members from different kinds of social networks, including a shared ethnic identity or geographic origin; occupation; neighborhood; links to the sanctuary of a particular deity (or deities); or an extended household. Hence, like other immigrant groups Judeans in the Diaspora formed associations based on ethnic origins.[32] Similarly, Richard Ascough asserts, "we should see synagogues as a different manifestation of 'association,' bearing both similarities to and differences from other manifestations of associations."[33]

For understanding the nature of the assemblies (synagogues) in the land of Israel, it is important to distinguish between two different types of synagogues, namely the public municipal synagogue and the association synagogue, as Anders Runesson argues. Public synagogues had a wide function as locations for town or city administration, law courts, storage for legal archives, as well as for reading and teaching the Torah publicly on the Sabbaths.[34] Given that people in antiquity did not distinguish between secular and religious spheres, as many tend to do today, both liturgical and religious activities took place alongside civic tasks at public synagogues. In contrast to the municipal synagogue, which was open to everyone, the association synagogues were for members only and had their own rules for membership and meetings just like Graco-Roman associations.[35] Thus, according to Runesson, the assemblies within the Qumran movement represented association synagogues, along the

---

or otherwise." See also Anders Runesson, *Origins of the Synagogue: A Socio-Historical Study*, CBNT 37 (Stockholm: Almquest & Wiksell, 2001).

31   On the diversity of Greco-Roman associations, see Philip A. Harland, ed., *Greco-Roman Associations: Texts, Translations, and Commentary*, vol. 2: *North Coast of the Black Sea, Asia Minor*, BZNW 204 (Berlin: De Gruyter, 2014), 2.

32   See Philip A. Harland, *Associations, Synagogues and Congregations: Claiming a Place in Ancient Mediterranean Society* (Minneapolis, MN: Fortress, 2013), 1, 30.

33   Ascough, "Paul," 39.

34   Anders Runesson, "The Historical Jesus, the Gospels, and First-Century Jewish Society: The Importance of the Synagogue for Understanding the New Testament," in *A City Set on a Hill: Essays in Honor of James F. Strange*, ed. Daniel A. Warner and Donald D. Binder (Mountain Home, AR: BorderStone Press, 2014), 269. He notes, "What makes the situation in Galilee and Judea unique within this larger context is the coterminous existence of the public synagogues, i.e., the town and city assemblies, and the association synagogues" (270).

35   Runesson, "Historical," 272.

line of those of the Pharisees and the "synagogue of the Freedmen" described in Acts 6:9. Whereas Jewish synagogues in the diaspora were usually open forms of institutions, the secluded association of the Therapeutai was an exception. Nevertheless, both types of institutions had a focus on reading and interpretation of Scripture. Runesson also highlights the similarity between association synagogues in Palestine and the Diaspora synagogues in having communal meals, which is also true for Graco-Roman associations in general.[36] We may conclude that reading and interpreting Scripture as well as commensality made up important activities among the assemblies (or the synagogues) in general, and, as we will see, also of the Qumran movement. Indeed, as I argue they may have taken place at the same occasion.

4 The Meals of the Greco-Roman Associations

As mentioned, many associations were linked to a particular deity and a sanctuary.[37] Since the worship involved ritual sacrifices, the god's part, often consisting of thighbones and tails, was normally burnt on the altar. Then members shared the remains of the victims after the priests had received their due.[38] The ritual of sacrifice was enveloped within two communal acts, a procession and a meal, which also meant that sharing the meal was an integral part of the sacrifice.[39] In other words, a cultic meal was the central activity of many associations. Harland emphasizes the importance of common meals: "Offerings of sacrificial victims, other foods, and libations with accompanying banquets were the touchstone of corporate piety in the Greco-Roman world and we can assume that they were a regular part of the lives of most associations."[40] While noting the anachronism in using terms like "religious," Harland emphasizes that the religious purpose of the associations extended to their common meals. According to him, scholars often fail to recognize that the meal after a sacrifice was a religious activity and not simply a festive banquet.

---

36   Runesson, "Historical," 273.

37   Kloppenborg states: "It is a good working hypothesis that most of these clubs met for the purpose of sociability, usually connected with some cultic activity" (Kloppenborg and Ascough, *Greco-Roman Associations*, 5).

38   Gunnel Ekroth, "A Room of One's Own? Exploring the Temenos Concept as Divine Property," in *Stuff of the Gods: The Material Aspects of Religion in Ancient Greece*, ed. J. Wallensten, M. Haysom, and M. Mili, forthcoming.

39   Jørgen Podemann Sørensen, "The Sacrificial Logic of Cultic Meals in Antiquity," *Early Christianity* 7 (2016): 447–67. He notes, "Greek sacrifice typically begins and ends with expressions of communality and civilization: A procession and a meal" (457).

40   Harland, *Associations, Synagogues and Congregations*, 57.

Instead, Harland points to inscriptions and reliefs featuring banquet scenes that emphasize the honoring of the gods or a specific deity.[41] He explains,

> Cultic life in antiquity had to do with appropriately honoring gods and goddesses through rituals of various kinds, especially sacrificial offerings, in ways that ensured the safety and protection of human groups and their members. Moreover, the forms which such honors could take do not necessarily coincide with modern or western preconceptions of what being "religious" means.[42]

Dining facilities are found in many large sanctuaries, but the ensuing meals could be taken elsewhere as well.[43] Paul, for example, is familiar with the custom of dining in the *temenos*, which also apparently some Christ-believers in Corinth would do: "For if others see you, who possess knowledge, eating in the temple of an idol, might they not, since their conscience is weak, be encouraged to the point of eating food sacrificed to idols?" (1 Cor 8:10). Some clubs had their own facilities that typically would include a sanctuary and a banquet hall, which confirms the importance of sacrifices and the ensuing meals.[44] Hal Taussig—an expert on ancient meals—notes, "The cultural emergence of

---

41   Harland, *Associations, Synagogues and Congregations*, 45. Cf. Charles H. Cosgrove, "Banquet Ceremonies Involving Wine in the Greco-Roman World and Early Christianity," *CBQ* 79 (2017): 308.

42   Harland, *Associations, Synagogues and Congregations*, 50.

43   Ekroth explains: "Although dining facilities are found in many sanctuaries, dining inside the *temenos* was not always a given fact. The size of *temene* vary greatly and in some cases there seems only to have been room for the god and his or her property and needs, with little space for the human worshippers. In some sanctuaries, such as Brauron, the structures for dining dominate" ("A Room of One's Own,").

44   Harland, *Associations, Synagogues and Congregations*, 53–56. Some buildings, probably of less wealthy associations, lacked these facilities; see Richard S. Ascough, "Social and Political Characteristics of Greco-Roman Association Meals," in *Meals in the Early Christian World: Social Formation, Experimentation, and Conflict at the Table*, ed. Dennis E. Smith and Hal Taussig (New York, NY: Palgrave Macmillan, 2012), 59–72. Ascough describes the Pergamon banquet hall of the Dionysiac *Bukoloi* ("cowherds"), from the second to fourth century CE (AGRW B6) with *triclinia* that could accommodate about 70 diners (63); a building of a wealthy association of carpenters (*fabri tignuari*) from the second to fourth century CE in Ostia contains four dining rooms that could accommodate "up to a dozen diners, indicating that 40 to 50 participants were expected on a regular basis" (64). And he notes, "At the same time, there is no standard architectural form to which association buildings conform, and thus the identification of buildings as belonging to an association must be based on inscriptions or on contents" (63). The close ties to sanctuaries are evident in many inscriptions, although details are missing. Kloppenborg states, "Sacrifices, temples, priesthoods, and officers are mentioned frequently, but very little data exists, for example, as to the precise procedures for the selection of officers, or

the associations in the Hellenistic era cannot be separated from the Hellenistic meal. The association's main activity was the meal together. The meal constituted a major component of the social bonding for the association."[45]

Given the importance of common meals within associations, it is somewhat surprising that few scholars studying the Dead Sea Scrolls have made the connection between the common meals within the Qumran movement and those in the Greco-Roman associations.[46] Gillihan explains the significance of the shared meals:

> Communal meals, συσσιτία, were part of public and private life in the *poleis* throughout the Mediterranean world. Most occurrences of the term in the literature refer to the habit of citizens or officials dining together, but the practice was also one of the most common features of private voluntary associations: rules for communal meals appear in the statutes of numerous associations.[47]

Still, pointing to the uncertain historical background concerning the meetings of the Many in the Rule texts, he does not speculate much about the function or character of the common meals of the Covenanters.[48]

---

how access to temples was negotiated, or details about the sacrificial rites" (Kloppenborg and Ascough, *Greco-Roman Associations*, 4.

45   Hal Taussig, *In the Beginning Was the Meal: Social Experimentation and Early Christian Identity* (Minneapolis, MN: Fortress, 2009), 34.

46   Scholars who focus on ancient meals, however, compare the Qumran material with sources on associations; see e.g., Esther Kobel, *Dining with John: Communal Meals and Identity Formation in the Fourth Gospel and Its Historical and Cultural Context*, BIS 109 (Leiden: Brill, 2011), 111–71; Dennis E. Smith, *From Symposium to Eucharist: The Banquet in the Early Christian World* (Minneapolis, MN: Fortress, 2003), 152–59. Cf. also Hugo Antonissen, "The Banquet Culture on New Jerusalem, An Aramaic Text from Qumran," in *Vision, Narrative, and Wisdom in the Aramaic Texts from Qumran: Essays from the Copenhagen Symposium, 14–15 August, 2017*, ed. Mette Bundvad and Kasper Siegismund, STDJ 131 (Leiden: Brill, 2019), 52–77.

47   Gillihan, *Civic Ideology*, 22.

48   "Exactly how commensality, blessing, and deliberation went together we do not know. Some claim that the Yaḥad's meals were eaten as 'sacral affairs,' like the consumption of offerings in the temple. But nothing in the rules for meals suggests that they had cultic purpose. We do not know if assemblies of the Many followed, preceded, or included communal meals" (Gillihan, *Civic Ideology*, 341).

5   The Connection between the Admission and Meals in the Qumran Movement

When and why did these members meet? The many regulations in sectarian texts pertaining to communal meals suggest that members assembled together in particular for meals, similar to other voluntary associations in the Greco-Roman world.[49] Often, the regulations for meals and meetings of various kinds overlap and are hard to distinguish from each other. The most likely reason for this is that these gatherings usually took place after one another as part of the same occasion. Initiates would likely get together at the Sabbath and festivals when, in addition to taking part in religious celebrations and liturgies, they would share meals. Nevertheless, those members who lived together would of course eat together on a regular basis. Thereby, there was a distinction between formal meals, when at least ten members shared a meal (1QSa 2:22; 1QS 6:3–4), and other, everyday meals. The level of formality would also depend on whether the meal took place during the Sabbath or other holiday, or on a regular day of the week.

New members were examined before being accepted as members of the Qumran association, a process that took a year for outsiders, according to the Damascus Document (CD 15:5–16:5/ 4Q266 8 i; xiii 11–13). In contrast, the Community Rule and Miscellaneous Rules (4Q265)[50] give evidence of a highly structured system whereby the novice passed through two stages of acceptance, which is reminiscent of Josephus' description. According to 1QS 6:13–23, an initiate who successfully passed the examinations could touch "the purity of the many" הטהרת הרבים after a year, while he is allowed to touch "the drink of the many" המשקה הרבים only after a second year. The term הטהרה "the purity" appears in different contexts and clearly refers to more items than food.[51] Although food is not mentioned in the regulations for the admission

---

49   I will not go into the texts that provide purity regulations in connection to meals, i.e., primarily Tohorot A (4Q274) and Ordinances^c (4Q514), since the main topic in this study is not purity. I have analyzed these texts in detail previously; see e.g., Cecilia Wassén, "The (Im)Purity Levels of Communal Meals within the Qumran Movement," *Journal of Ancient Judaism* 7 (2016): 102–22.

50   The brief fragmentary instruction concerning admission procedure in 4Q265 4 ii 1–9 appears similar to 1QS 6:13–23, concerning a two year process. The title of the leader in 4Q265 4 ii 6, המבקר על היחד, is reminiscent of המבקר אשר לרבים "the Overseer for the Many" in CD 15 and המבקר על הרבים in 1QS 6:12.

51   Friedrich Avemarie argues that the term *hatohorah* primarily refers to "pure food for the full members of the community" but also more broadly includes the quality 'purity' of vessels, clothing and even persons. See Friedrich Avemarie, "'Tohorat Ha-Rabbim' and 'Mashqeh Ha-Rabbim': Jacob Licht Reconsidered," in *Legal Texts and Legal Issues: Proceedings of the Second Meeting of the International Organization for Qumran Studies,*

process, it is commonly assumed that "the purity of the many" pertains to food in particular, since it is juxtaposed with drink or liquid, which is evident in the common translation of the phrase הטהרת הרבים as "pure food."[52]

> When he approaches the council of the community he must not touch the purity of the many הטהרת הרבים, until he has been examined concerning his spirit and his work until one full year is completed, nor shall he have any share in the property of the many ... He must not touch the drink of the many המשקה הרבים until he has completed a second year among the men of the community.[53] (1QS 6:16–21)

Nevertheless, there are different views as to what the terms specifically involve and how they relate to communal meals. These prescriptions must be understood in light of penalties of exclusion from הטהרה "the purity," or טהרת הרבים, "the purity of the many," in cases of transgressions in S (1QS 6:24–7:25), D (CD 14:20–22; 4Q266 10 i 14–ii 15), and 4Q265 (4Q265 4 i 2–ii 2).[54] These penalties are combined with food rations: in 4Q265 the food is reduced by a half (4Q265 4 i 8), while in 1QS it is reduced by a quarter (1QS 6:25). Although the precise punishment behind the term נענש (be punished) is not evident in the fragmentary texts of D (e.g., 4Q266 10 ii 1), we may assume a similar meaning.

Several scholars argue for a wide connotation of the references to pure food and pure drink and point to the heightened susceptibility of liquid to transmit impurity in order to explain the difference between the two stages.[55] Charlotte Hempel goes into much detail in her reconstruction of the regulations, arguing that novices were not trusted to handle food items or liquid: "The regulations

---

    Cambridge 1995, Published in Honour of Joseph M. Baumgarten, ed. Moshe Bernstein, Florentino García Martínez, and John Kampen, STDJ 23 (Leiden: Brill, 1997), 215–29. Similarly, Geza Vermes explains that the terms "purity" and "purities" designate "ritually pure food ... as well as the vessels and utensils on which it is contained or cooked ... also garments" (*The Complete Dead Sea Scrolls in English* [London: Allen Lane, 1997], 33).

52   The translation by Elisha Qimron reads "the pure-food" in *The Dead Sea Scrolls: Hebrew, Aramaic, and Greek Texts with English Translations*, vol. 1: *Rule of the Community and Related Documents*, ed. James H. Charlesworth (Tübingen/Louisville, KY: Mohr Siebeck/ Westminster John Knox Press, 1994), 29.

53   The translation of this and other passages of 1QS are based on Charlesworth, *The Dead Sea Scrolls*, vol. 1, unless stated otherwise.

54   The term "the purity" is reconstructed in 4Q265 and D.

55   For example, Yair Furstenberg states, "During the two-year process, the candidate proceeds between three levels of purity: at first, he is impure and prohibited to touch the sect's pure food; during the second year he is allowed to touch only dry foodstuff, and only at the end of the process he is considered pure also with respect to liquids" ("Initiation and the Ritual Purification from Sin: Between Qumran and the Apostolic Tradition," *DSD* 23 [2016]: 381).

RATIONS, REFRESHMENTS, READING, AND REVELATION 429

for admission lays down the restrictions on touching pure food and utensils and pure liquids (including the juices of ripe fruit) anywhere in the process of food consumption and preparation, serving, and only ultimately consumption."[56] Hanna Harrington similarly assumes that "the purity" applies to all communal food and all food items: "Ordinary food was eaten in a state of purity, that is, communal food, the *tohorah*, was harvested, stored and eaten in a state of purity; all members had to bathe before eating it (1QS 5:13; cf. *War* 2.129)."[57] This scenario assumes a similar setting as Khirbet Qumran where members lived and worked together, which is not necessarily the implied setting of S. In any case, although the term "the purity" carries a wider connotation than food, the main practical application of the admission regulations would be in relation to communal pure meals. Josephus also links the admission of members to participation at common meals.[58] In other words, full membership meant taking part of the communal meals (*War* 2.138–139), which is quite similar to the Community Rule. Only after three years was a successful adherent able to join the diners at the common meal:

> For after this exhibition of endurance, his character is tested for two years more, and only then, if found worthy, is he enrolled in the society. But, before he might touch the common food πρὶν δὲ τῆς κοινῆς ἅψασθαι τροφῆς, he is made to swear tremendous oaths. (*War* 2.139)[59]

At the same time, the gradual access to pure food and pure drink raises other questions. It is hard to envision how a novice would be allowed to participate at a meal but not receive anything to drink. Russell Arnold points out the inherent problem from the point of view of the full members:

> In this scenario, we are faced with a situation in which mid-level initiates were granted access to the common meal, but were restricted from partaking of anything to drink. Even if they were seated, according to rank,

---

56 Charlotte Hempel, "Who Is Making Dinner at Qumran?" *JTS* 63 (2012): 62.

57 Hannah Harrington, *The Purity Texts*, CQS 5 (New York, NY: T&T Clark, 2004), 23.

58 Scholars differ widely on the relationship between the Qumran movement and the Essenes. I side with those scholars who assume that the Essenes represent the continuation of the Qumran movement. We should remember that Josephus and Philo are writing their accounts almost two centuries after the rules of S and D were composed and from an outsider's perspective. We should be as critical of the description of the Essenes in the classical sources as we are with other ancient historiographical works. For an initiated evaluation of the sources, see Collins, *Beyond*, 122–65.

59 Josephus, *The Jewish War, Books 1–2*, trans. H. St. J. Thackeray, LCL 203 (Cambridge, MA: Harvard University Press, 1927). Similarly, he explains that uninitiated persons were not allowed to enter the refectory (2.129).

at the far end of the room, would not their very presence still have put the members at risk of impurity because liquids were present?[60]

There are different suggestions for solutions to the problem.[61] An intriguing suggestion is offered by Klinghardt, who claims that the "drink of the many" המשקה הרבים refers to the symposium, the drinking party that comprised the second part of the meal in a traditional banquet.[62] This is in line with his argument that 1QS 6:2–3 ("together they shall eat, together they shall bless, together they shall take counsel") refers to the activities of the ordinary gatherings, that is the meals, and not three separate gatherings, parallel to other Greco-Roman associations (see below).[63] The rules about readmission after a serious transgression in 1QS 7:19–20 demonstrate that the expression "drink of the many" relates to meals and not liquids in general:

> If he returns he shall be punished (for) two years: in the first (year) he must not touch the pure food of the many and in the second he must not touch the pure drink of the many, and he shall sit behind all the men of the community.[64]

Accordingly, during his second year—not touching the pure drink but being able to partake of the meal—he shall sit behind the others, presumably at the meal (when eating). At these meals where members sat according to rank (cf. 1QS 6:4, 8–11 and 1QSa 2:17–22), to sit behind the others indicates a non-ranking. Hence, when he is finally admitted, he will be ranked ("be listed in his place") and he will be asked concerning judgment (7:21). In light of Klinghardt's reconstruction we may understand that these parts are related; once an adherent is

---

60   Arnold, *Social Role of Liturgy*, 91.
61   Arnold argues for a broad connotation of both "the purity of the many" and "the drink of the many," suggesting that exclusion from each one imply exclusion from the communal meals. Hence, only full members would have allowed access to communal meals (*Social Role of Liturgy*, 90–92). Often, however, scholars do not see any practical problems in the regulations but simply rephrase the passage, e.g., Harrington, *Purity*, 24, states, "Candidates for membership in the community were put on probation and examined for a whole year before they were allowed to eat the communal food; at least two years of probation was were necessary in order to drink communal liquids." Cf. Per Bilde, "The Common Meal in the Qumran-Essene Communities," in *Meals in a Social Context: Aspects of the Communal Meal in the Hellenistic and Roman World*, ed. Hanne Sigismund Nielsen and Inge Nielsen, Aarhus Studies in Mediterranean Antiquity (Aarhus: Aarhus University Press, 1998), 52–53.
62   Klinghardt, *Gemeinschaftsmahl*, 244–49.
63   Klinghardt, "The Manual of Discipline," 261.
64   Based on the translation in Charlesworth, *The Dead Sea Scrolls*, vol. 1.

RATIONS, REFRESHMENTS, READING, AND REVELATION   431

readmitted he is allowed to give his judgment, presumably at the symposium part of the meal, when counselling took place (1QS 6:4, 9–13):

> When he has completed two years, the many shall be asked concerning his affairs. If they allow him to draw near he shall be enlisted in this place, and afterwards he may be asked concerning judgment. (1QS 7:20–21)

In my view, "the purity of the many" or "the purity" refers to special communal meals eaten in full purity. This is in contrast to regular communal meals when full purity was not required, as is evident in Tohorot A (4Q274) and 4QOrdinances[c] (4Q514). These texts give prescriptions concerning meals for mildly impure people, the ones in the process of purifying.[65] In other words, we should distinguish between special formal meals and regular meals eaten by members when full purity was not necessary. The mistake that scholars often make is mixing the categories of regular meals and special, pure meals. It is not clear how often members assembled together for common meals. The instructions in 1QS 6 imply that they got together every day, which may have been the case for those members who lived together, who could also study the Torah every night. But, the frequency by which members had common meals would certainly vary according to living arrangements. The instruction in 1QSa 2:22 regarding meals for the members "when as many as ten men meet together" also indicate that this was not always the case. Finally, it is noteworthy that the entry regulations concern participation at meals. If the members primarily met in connection to communal meals, then the entry rules simply spell out what membership in this association meant in concrete terms, that is, participation at meals.

6   The Character of the Meals and Meetings in the Qumran Association

Already in 1996 Klinghardt argued that the common meals in the Qumran movement was the main occasion for their meetings.[66] He makes a strong case for the interpretation that 1QS 6:2–3 relates to different elements of a meal rather than to three different communal activities as suggested by Lawrence Schiffman among others.[67] Hence, the instructions for assemblies entail three parts according to lines 2–3: "together they shall eat, together they shall bless,

---

65   Wassén, "(Im)Purity."
66   Klinghardt, *Gemeinschaftsmahl.*
67   Lawrence H. Schiffman, "Communal Meals at Qumran," *RevQ* 10 (1979): 50.

together they shall take counsel." Klinghardt compares this to the common meals of the Greco-Roman associations. The standard model for Greek banquets always included three parts: a communal meal (*deipnon*), a ceremonial libation followed by various religious ceremonies, and the *symposium*, a drinking party.[68] The libation divided the two parts of the meal and was always dedicated to a god or gods. Thus the libation in a sense expressed dedication of the whole meal to a particular god.[69] Although there were some variations in the customs of banquets around the turn of the Era,[70] Dennis Smith, whose research focuses on ancient meals, explains that the pattern remained remarkably consistent. Thus, regardless of the occasion, there was a common banquet tradition.[71] The Greek banquet traditions had spread around the Mediterranean and Jews also shared these meal customs.[72] Nevertheless, like other Jewish associations, the Qumran sect replaced the libation with prayers (cf. m. Ber. 6.1).[73] It should be noted that the libation was not the only religious expression during the meal but there would be other rituals of admiration such as songs to express gratitude to the gods.[74] We may compare this to the Jewish customs in general in antiquity of singing particular hymns and saying traditional blessings at meals. In the Qumran texts, saying the blessings makes up a central part of the meal with the priest leading the ceremony, which I will turn to next.

---

68   Klinghardt, "Manual of Discipline," 261–62. His reasoning is supported by e.g., Metso, "Whom Does the Term Yaḥad Identify?," 73; John J. Collins, "Forms of Community in the Dead Sea Scrolls," in *Emanuel: Studies in Hebrew Bible, Septuagint, and Dead Sea Scrolls in Honor of Emanuel Tov*, ed. Shalom M. Paul et al., VTSup 94 (Leiden: Brill, 2003), 103; Arnold, *Social Role of Liturgy*, 87.

69   Taussig, *In the Beginning*, 32.

70   Cosgrove, "Banquet."

71   Smith, *From Symposium*, 2, states, "The meals at which they gathered also tended to follow the same basic form, customs, and rules regardless of the group, occasion, or setting. They followed the form of the banquet, the traditional evening meal, which had become the pattern for all formalized meals in the Mediterranean world in this period. In this sense, the banquet can be called a social institution in the Greco-Roman world."

72   Smith, *From Symposium*, 133–72. He concludes: "Jewish meals of the Second Temple period are seen to be embedded in the Greco-Roman banquet tradition in form, ideology, and literary descriptions. Though there were some distinctive aspects to Jewish meal traditions, these are best interpreted as subdivisions of the general banquet tradition and often can be seen as variations of common aspects of that tradition" (172).

73   Dennis E. Smith, "Meals," in *The Eerdmans Dictionary of Early Judaism*, ed. John J. Collins and Daniel C. Harlow (Grand Rapids, MI: Eerdmans, 2010), 924–26; Susan Marks, "In the Place of Libation: Birkat Hamazon Navigates New Ground," in *Meals in Early Judaism: Social Formation at the Table*, ed. Susan Marks and Hal Taussig (New York, NY: Palgrave Macmillan, 2014), 71–97.

74   Taussig, *In the Beginning*, 32.

RATIONS, REFRESHMENTS, READING, AND REVELATION 433

Two rule texts provide explicit prescriptions concerning the order for common meals, 1QS 6:2–5 and 1QSa 2:17–22. The latter concerns a meal, often called a "messianic meal" because it is presided over by the priest and the messiah. Although 1QSa explicitly provides regulations for the end time (1QSa 1:1), including the presence of the messiah at the meal, the rules still likely applied to the present-time community who saw itself as living in the end of time. The two sets of regulations share several features: the prominence of the priest, the blessings over the food and wine, and the hierarchical seating order. The regulations for meals in 1QSa 2:17–22 and 1QS 6 both highlight the importance of the blessings. 1QSa 2:17–22 reads:

> [When] they gather [at the] communal [tab]le, [having set out food and w]ine so the communal table is set (18) [for eating] and [the] wine (poured) for drinking, none [may re]ach for the first portion (19) of the food or [the wine] before the Priest. For [he] shall [bl]ess the first portion of the food (20) and the wine, [reac]hing for the food first. Afterw[ard] the Messiah of Israel [shall re]ach (21) for the food. [Finally,] ea[ch] member of the whole congregation of the Yahad [shall give a bl]essing, [in descending order of] rank. This procedure shall govern (22) every me[al], provided at least ten me[n are ga]thered together[75]

We may compare the instructions with those in 1QS 6:2b–8:

> (2b) Together they shall eat, (3) together they shall bless, together they shall take counsel. And in every place where there are ten men (belonging to) the Council of the Community, there must not be lacking among them a man (who is) (4) a priest. And each member shall sit according to his rank before him, and in thus they shall be asked for the council concerning every matter. When the table has been prepared for eating, or the new wine (5) for drinking, the priest shall be the first to stretch out his hand, in order to bless the first (produce of) the food לחם (6) and the new wine. And in the place in which the ten assemble there should not be missing a man to interpret the law day and night, (7) always, one relieving another. The Many shall spend the third of every night of the year

---

75   Translation based on Michael Wise, Martin Abegg Jr., and Edward Cook, *The Dead Sea Scrolls: A New Translation* (New York: HarperSanFrancisco, 1996). Although לחם is usually translated "bread," it refers to the food on the table. In addition, the wine תירוש is often translated "new wine," but it can also simply mean "wine" (the same term is used in 1QS 6:4).

together, reading from the book, interpreting the regulations, (8) and saying blessings together.[76]

I take all of these regulations as pertaining to different parts of the meal. Hence, "the third of every night" refers to the dinner that took place in the evening, or after sunset at the beginning of the night. In line with the common banquet pattern, then, the meal proper of the sectarians was followed by prayers and, likely at times, more elaborate ceremonies, and subsequently by meetings of various kinds, such as deliberations, or "counselling" (1QS 6:3), and studying Scripture (more on that below).[77] At the same time, and in contrast to the common banquets, the meal according to 1QS and 1QSa was also preceded by blessings.[78] The activities at the communal meeting would correspond to the symposium, which traditionally consisted of drinking diluted wine, discussions (a popular topic by Greek and Roman authors), and different forms of entertainment, typically music by a flute girl and sometimes party games.[79] It is revealing that the instructions concerning studying of the law follow the prescriptions for the meal. Referring to 1QS 6:6–8, Smith notes that studying the Torah in group ("together") can be compared to the philosophical symposium tradition whereby the entertainment consisted of learned discussions.[80] In other words, the community meal consisted of two parts, the meal proper and the ensuing symposium. At the same time, there does not seem to be a strict division between eating and drinking, since the blessings over food and wine were pronounced at the same time. Thereby, they seem to have been drinking some wine already at the first part of the meal, which was also possible at meals in the Greco-Roman tradition; the key distinction for the Qumran communities is between eating (dining with or without some drinking) and the ensuing symposium (drink and entertainment, which took the form of learned discussion).

The subsequent regulations found in 1QS 6:8–13 concern the session of the Many, which pertains to an assembly larger than ten (1QS 6:3–7). They prescribe the proper conduct for conversations, including seating order, taking turns according to rank, not interrupting one another, and the responsibilities of the host, in this case the examiner. These regulations are consistent with

---

76   Translation based on Collins, *Beyond*, 66.

77   Pointing to the prescriptions for the meal in 1QSa 2:10–22, Eileen Schuller suggests that the extensive blessings in 1QSb for the instructor to bless the community members, the priests, and the Messiah may have taken place at communal meals (Eileen M. Schuller, *The Dead Sea Scrolls: What Have We Learnt?* [Louisville, KY: WJK, 2006], 58).

78   Gillihan, *Civic*, 343, calls this a "major problem." I do not agree.

79   Smith, *From Symposium*, 27–38, 47–65.

80   Smith, *From Symposium*, 154.

RATIONS, REFRESHMENTS, READING, AND REVELATION   435

Greek symposium etiquette. Accordingly, these regulations likely pertain to the symposium part of the communal meal.

> This is the rule for the session of the many: each (member) in his order. The priests shall sit first, the elders second, and the rest of all the people shall sit each (member) in his order. And thus they shall be asked concerning judgment, concerning any counsel, and anything which is for the many, each man presenting his knowledge to the council of the community. No man may speak during the speech of his fellow before his brother has finished speaking. He may not also speak before one whose registered rank is before him. The man who is asked may speak only in his turn. At a session of the many no man may say anything which is not according to the interest of the many. (1QS 6:8–11)

We find similar prescriptions for an association of Zeus Hypsistos from Philadelphia in Egypt that dates from mid-first century BCE:

> Further everyone must obey the leader and his assistant in matters concerning the association (*koinon*) and they shall be present for all occasions that have been prescribed for them, at meetings (*synlogous*), gatherings (*synagōga*), and outings (*apodēmia*). It is not lawful for anyone of them … to establish factions, or to depart from the brotherhood (*phatra*) of the leader to join another brotherhood, or for men to argue about one another's genealogies at the banquet (*symposion*) or to abuse one another verbally at the banquet, or to chatter or to indict or accuse another, or to resign for the course of the year, or to be absent from the banquet[81]

The list of penalties in the Qumran texts suggests that the members did not always observe the proper etiquette according to the regulations.

We may get further hints about what happened at the symposium from descriptions of the Therapeutai and the Essenes. Both Philo and Josephus highlight the common meal of the Essenes (Philo, *Hypoth.* 11.5; *Prob.* 85–86). Philo emphasizes their unity at the meals, explaining that they were "living together in societies, forming comradeships and having common meals" οἰκοῦσι δ'ἐν ταυτῷ κατὰ θιάσους, ἑταιρίας καὶ συσσίτια πεποιημένοι. According to Josephus the Essenes shared a meal twice a day, with prior purifications and changing of clothes. He states: "They approach the dining room as if it were some [kind of] sanctuary τέμενος" (*War* 2.129). Josephus' description has

---

81 Richard S. Ascough, Philip A. Harland, and John S. Kloppenborg, *Associations in the Greco-Roman World: A Sourcebook* (Waco, TX: Baylor University Press, 2012), 177.

been influential in interpreting the common meal as a sacred meal and as an everyday event. It is interesting that he highlights the leading role of the priest in saying the prayers and that they speak in turn, without interrupting each other, which is reminiscent of the regulations in the rule texts from Qumran. Josephus does not explain what the Essenes were discussing during meals, but if we were to guess we might suggest reading and interpreting Scripture reminiscent of Philo's description of the Therapeutai.

Of course the drinking party could be rowdy business in some groups. Some of the penalties listed in the rules for the associations indicate that much as we saw above. This is also something that Paul complains about when writing to the Corinthians concerning their common meals: "When you come together, it is not really to eat the Lord's supper. For when the time comes to eat, each of you goes ahead with your own supper, and one goes hungry and another becomes drunk" (1 Cor 11:20–21). We should note, however, that the wine was diluted, only the libation consisted of undiluted wine. The common proportions were five parts water and two parts wine or three parts water and one of wine.[82] It was also common for ancient authors to complain about the symposic behaviour of others while asserting the pious character of their own or their favoured ones. Philo uses this literary convention when he contrasts the sober symposium of the Therapeutai with those of other more luxurious ones with which he is familiar in contemporary literature and in society in general (*Contempl.* 40–63).[83] The account of these lavish banquets appear quite exaggerated.[84]

> I wish also to speak of their common assemblages and the cheerfulness of their convivial meals as contrasted with those of other people. Some people when they have filled themselves with strong drink behave as though they had drunk not wine but some witch's potion charged with frenzy and madness and anything more fatal that can be imagined to overthrow their reason. (Philo, *Contempl.* 40).[85]

---

82   Smith, *From Symposium*, 32.

83   Jonathan Brumberg-Kraus, "Contrasting Banquets: A Literary Commonplace in *Philo's On the Contemplative Life* and Other Greek and Roman Symposia," in *Meals in Early Judaism: Social Formation at the Table*, ed. Susan Marks and Hal Taussig (New York, NY: Palgrave Macmillan, 2014), 163–74. He highlights passages such as the one by Athanaeus: "But in the symposium of Epicurus there is an assemblage of flatterers praising one another, while the symposium of Plato is full of men who turn their noses up in jeers at one another; for I pass over in silence what is said about Alcibiades. In Homer, on the other hand, only sober symposia are organized" (Athenaeus, *Deipn.* 182a); quotation on 163.

84   See Brumberg-Kraus, "Contrasting Banquets," 165.

85   All translations of Philo are from *Philo, Volume 9*, trans. F. H. Colson, LCL 363 (Cambridge, MA: Harvard University Press, 1954).

RATIONS, REFRESHMENTS, READING, AND REVELATION 437

In Philo's description of the special banquets of the Therapeutai every seventh week, this meal was unique in its simplicity, consisting of water instead of wine, no meat, and only bread with some seasoning. The women and men reclined on opposite sides. In contrast to other examples of literary symposia there are no dialogues among participants at the banquets, instead one speaker expounded Scripture while the others were quiet.

> But when the guests have laid themselves down arranged in rows, as I have described, and the attendants have taken their stand with everything in order ready for their ministry, the President of the company, when a general silence is established—here it may be asked when is there no silence—well at this point there is silence even more than before so that no one ventures to make a sound or breathe with more force than usual—amid this silence, I say, he discusses some question arising in the Holy Scriptures or solves one that has been propounded by someone else (*Contempl.* 75)

> When then the President thinks he has discoursed enough and both sides feel sure that they have attained their object, the speaker in the effectiveness with which his discourse has carried out his aims, the audience in the substance of what they have heard a universal applause arises showing a general pleasure in the prospect of what is still to follow. (*Contempl.* 79)

After the exposition, the President initiates the singing of hymns after which the meal is served. After the banquet the men and women continue singing hymns into the night. The austerity and the silence appears exaggerated and even utopian. Jonathan Brumberg-Kraus argues that Philo rejects the symposium literary tradition made up of dialogues, discussions, and conflicts in order to keep any disagreement out of the meal. Instead for Philo the general agreements and unity of the participants captures his "utopian idealization of the Therapeutae community."[86] It is apparent from Philo's description of Essene synagogues that his ideal of learning and acquiring wisdom is through one wise person instructing others while the group remains silent.[87] For our purpose, it is important to note that exposition of Scripture was an integral

---

86 Brumberg-Kraus, "Contrasting Banquets," 170.
87 "For that day has been set apart to be kept holy and on it they abstain from all other work and proceed to sacred spots which they call synagogues. There, arranged in rows according to their ages, the younger below the elder, they sit decorously as befits the occasion with attentive ears. Then one takes the books and reads aloud and another of especial proficiency comes forward and expounds what is not understood" (Philo, *Prob.* 81–82).

part of the banquet, although it took place prior to, rather than subsequent to, the actual meal.

In the case of the meals within the Qumran community, the interpretation of Scripture likewise appears to be a communal activity, although the priests may have had a leading role, as 1QS 6:7–8 reads: "The Many shall spend the third of every night of the year together reading from the book, interpreting the regulations, and saying blessings together." The reading and interpreting of the book were done together. Mladen Popović compares the reading practices of the community of the Dead Sea Scrolls with the reading culture in general in the Mediterranean in antiquity which considered reading as a social activity.[88] Likewise, he points to Philo's account of synagogue practices among the Essenes that consists of reading and interpretation of Scripture ("Then one takes the books and reads aloud and another of especial proficiency comes forward and expounds what is not understood"; *Prob.* 82). This is similar to the description in the Theodotus inscription from Jerusalem that explains that the synagogue was built for reading the law and for instruction of the commandments. These examples show that reading and interpreting texts took place in deeply social contexts.[89]

But the communal aspect is particularly emphasized in 1QS, which describes reading and studying text as a social event that the members do "together" יחד (1QS 6:6–8).[90] As Popović explains, although not everyone was literate, in the sense of being able to read and write, they could still take part in interpretive discussions of a text. And, since the reading was a communal event, it was important that the reading was done aloud by someone proficient. Popović notes that the regulation prohibiting priests who cannot pronounce the words properly from reading the Torah aloud demonstrates the importance that the reader had the right pronunciation (4Q266 5 ii). Popović quite appropriately calls the Qumran community a "textual community," explaining that "the textual community is a social entity where the texts—materially and content wise—take centre stage."[91]

Although the Qumran movement, as I have emphasized, was spread around the country, it is relevant to consider the dining facilities at Khirbet Qumran. Roland de Vaux identified locus 77 (L77), the largest hall measuring 22 × 4.5 meters with plastered walls and floor, as the dining hall. The discovery of

---

88 Mladen Popović, "Reading, Writing, and Memorizing Together: Reading Culture in Ancient Judaism and the Dead Sea Scrolls in a Mediterranean Context," *DSD* 24 (2017): 447–70.

89 Popović, "Reading," 453–56.

90 Popović, "Reading," 451–52.

91 Popović, "Reading," 452.

RATIONS, REFRESHMENTS, READING, AND REVELATION 439

ca. 1000 dishes in the adjacent room (L86) indicated that the big hall was used as the refectory.[92] Nevertheless, Dennis Mizzi has identified a smaller room, L4, which de Vaux described as an assembly room, as the actual dining room of the community. A unique feature is the low benches, about 40 cm deep and 10 to 20 cm high, running alongside the walls. Mizzi argues that these benches were used as support for wooden benches for sitting, not reclining.[93] He points to similar structures at dining halls in antiquity such as dining rooms at the sanctuary of Demeter in Corinth and in a private home in Dura Europos. He also provides several strong arguments for L4 as the main dining hall, including the close proximity to the kitchen and the discovery of a large number of vessels used for dining and cooking.[94] The size of the room provides a more intimate setting than that of L77 and it would be an ideal setting for meals where all participants would be able to partake in discussions and listening to each other. In comparison, L77 may bring up associations of a school cafeteria which is about "eating" rather than "dining," as Susan Marks remarks.[95] Indeed, Mizzi highlights the multi-function possibility of the assembly room:

L4 could have been used for meetings, prayer, study, reading, and dining. Indeed, some of these activities were intricately intertwined in the ancient world. For example, several classical and Jewish sources demonstrate that eating, drinking, and learned conversation (in lieu of music and entertainment) were two sides of the same coin.[96]

The studying of texts would likely be a proper activity at the communal meals at the symposium part, together with prayers and blessings as 1QS 6:7–8 suggests.

---

92 Roland de Vaux, *Archaeology and the Dead Sea Scrolls* (Oxford: Oxford University Press, 1973), 10–11, 32; cf. Jodi Magness, *The Archaeology of Qumran and the Dead Sea Scrolls*, Studies in the Dead Sea Scrolls and Related Literature (Grand Rapids, MI: Eerdmans, 2002), 53.

93 Accordingly, the plastered platform protected the wooden benches from moisture when the floor was washed, Dennis Mizzi, "From the Judaean Desert to the Great Sea: Qumran in a Mediterranean Context," *DSD* 24 (2017): 401–2; cf. de Vaux, *Archaeology*, 10–11, 32; Magness, *Archaeology*, 51.

94 Based on information from Jean-Baptiste Humbert, Mizzi explains, "Around one hundred pottery vessels were discovered in L4", consisting of "jars, plates, bowls, goblets, cooking pots, kraters, flasks, jugs, and juglets" ("From the Judaean," 402). He identifies the plastered "basin" as a brazier, used to keep the food warm (403).

95 Susan Marks, "Reconsidering Reclining at Qumran," *Journal of Ancient Judaism* 7 (2016): 87–88.

96 Mizzi, "From the Judaean," 405.

A possible scenario would be that one person read a text from the Scriptures, which was discussed within the group under the guidance of a priest.

7 Interpretation as Revelation

We know from the communal rules that the reading and interpretation of authoritative texts was an exclusive activity for members only and was also considered a revelatory experience. This aspect explains in part why certain meals ("the purity") required full purity of the participants. Whereas scholars usually explain the strict purity regulations in connection to meals by pointing to the obvious risk of transmission of impurity between members through food and drinks, there may be additional reasons when we consider the activities during the symposium and the interpreting of Scripture. Alex Jassen demonstrates how reading and interpreting Scripture among the sectarians in a sense continued the prophetic tradition and can best be described as inspired exegesis. He argues that the members viewed their halakhah, their interpretation of the law, as part of a progressive revelation of the law.[97] This understanding of exegesis is clearly stated in the famous passage from 1QS 8:14–16 concerning the true meaning of Isaiah 40:3:

> They shall separate themselves from the session of the men of deceit in order to depart into the wilderness to prepare there the Way of the Lord; as it is written: "In the wilderness prepare the way of the Lord, make level in the desert a highway for our God" (Isaiah 40:3). This (alludes to) the study of the Torah which he commanded through Moses to do, according to everything which has been revealed (from) time to time, and according to that which the prophets have revealed by his Holy Spirit.

Thus Moses, as well as the ancient prophets, are seen as the recipients of divine revelation and the sectarians as their heirs.[98] Evidently, this does not only apply to halakhah but also interpretation of the texts in the form of pesharim and more.[99] It is noteworthy for our purpose that the continuation of the discourse turns immediately to touching the purity/ pure food (1QS 8:17–19).

---

97   Alex P. Jassen, *Mediating the Divine: Prophecy and Revelation in the Dead Sea Scrolls and Second Temple Judaism*, STDJ 68 (Leiden: Brill, 2007), 332.

98   Jassen, *Mediating*, 334–35.

99   Jassen, *Mediating*, 343–62.

> No man belonging to the Covenant of the Yahad who flagrantly deviates from any commandment is to touch the pure food belonging to the holy men. Further, he is not to participate in any of their deliberations until all his works have been cleansed from evil, so that he is again able to walk blamelessly. They shall admit him into deliberations by the decision of the general membership.

In my view, the association between studying (1QS 8:14–16) and touching the purity (1QS 8:17–19) came very naturally since many of these interpretive activities took place at special pure meals.[100] Jassen points out that the Holy Spirit is often the agent that transmits divine knowledge to the humans, which is apparent in the Hodayot. For example, 1QHᵃ 6:23–24 reads:

> And as for me, I know from the understanding that comes from you that through your goodwill toward a p[er]son you mul[tiply his portion] in your holy spirit. Thus you draw him closer to your understanding.[101]

The hymnist is also convinced that God has given him "the spirit of knowledge" (1QHᵃ 4:36). The same assertion is made in 1QHᵃ 5:35–36: "And I, your servant, know by means of the spirit that you have placed in me". In a similar vein, in 1QS it is through the Holy Spirit that God will purify the world so that the righteous "may have insight into the knowledge of the most high and the wisdom of the sons of heaven בני שמים וחכמת עליון בדעת" (1QS 4:22). The most structured forms of interpretation are found in the pesharim; they provide a deeper understanding of Scripture. The interpretations are typically introduced by the phrase, פשרו "its interpretation" or הדבר פשר "the interpretation of the passage," but the authors rarely dwell on the means of their interpretation. It is evident, however, that the interpretation is considered divinely inspired and is understood to be a continuation of the prophetic tradition.[102] Thus, the Teacher of Righteousness speaks the words "from the mouth of God" (1QpHab 2:2–3; cf. 2:7–10; 7:1–5). It is likely, as James Charlesworth claims, that the spirit was assumed to be active also in this case.[103]

---

100   Wassén, "(Im)Purity."

101   All citations of 1QHᵃ are taken from Eileen M. Schuller and Carol A. Newsom, *The Hodayot (Thanksgiving Psalms): A Study Edition of 1QHᵃ* (Atlanta, GA: SBL, 2012), 22–23. Cf. 1QHᵃ 13:11, 28.

102   Timothy H. Lim, *Pesharim*, CQS 3 (London: Sheffield Academic Press, 2002), 76–77.

103   James H. Charlesworth, "Revelation and Perspicacity in Qumran Hermeneutics?" in *The Dead Sea Scrolls and Contemporary Culture: Proceedings of the International Conference*

In addition to the Holy Spirit, we should not forget the angels as transmitters of divine knowledge, as in 1QS 4:22 (above). This is consistent with their traditional role as God's messengers. For example, they appear as heavenly guides in stories of ascent into heavens, such as in 1 Enoch 1–36; they are interpreters of dreams or visions as in Daniel 7; and sometimes they simply show up in dreams and visions to deliver a message, as occurs frequently at the beginning of Luke's Gospel (e.g., Luke 1:26–38). The Sabbath Songs emphasize the superior knowledge of the angels who frequently are called wise. Indeed, according to Carol Newsom, knowledge is the most prominent quality attributed to angels in the Sabbath Songs.[104] There are also references to the teaching of angels, for example, "from their mouths (come) teachings concerning all matters of holiness" (4Q400 1 i 17).[105] According to the War Scroll, the sharing of knowledge with the angels belongs to the eschaton (1QM 17:8). Nonetheless, a hymn that appears unrelated to the theme of war (1QM 10:8b–16) juxtaposes the insights that come from seeing and listening to the angels with learning the statutes (from Torah), thereby giving the impression that the knowledge concerns present reality (from the point of the author):

> Who is like Your people Israel, whom You have chosen for Yourself from all
> the peoples of the lands; the people of the saints of the covenant, learned
>   in the
> statutes, enlightened in understan[ding] those who hear the glorious
>   voice and
> see the holy angels, whose ears are open; hearing deep things. (1QM
>   10:8b–11)

Similarly, the hymnist of 1QH[a], who labels himself as a "spirit" claims to have communion with the angels who in this context are called "spirits of

---

Held at the Israel Museum, Jerusalem (July 6–8, 2008), ed. Adolfo D. Roitman, Lawrence H. Schiffman, and Shani Tzoref, STDJ 93 (Leiden: Brill, 2011), 161–62.

104 Carol A. Newsom, *Songs of the Sabbath Sacrifice: A Critical Edition*, HSS 27 (Atlanta, GA: Scholars, 1985), 30. See e.g., 4Q400 1 17; 2 1; 2 3; 2 7; 4Q403 1 14; 1 24; also the following: "in the chiefs of praise-offering are tongues of knowledge" (4Q405 23 ii 12) and "they declare His regal Majesty according to their knowledge" (4Q400 2 3).

105 For a survey of the various roles of angels in early Jewish documents, see Cecilia Wassén, "Angels and Humans: Boundaries and Synergies," in *Celebrating the Dead Sea Scrolls: A Canadian Collection*, ed. Jean Duhaime, Peter Flint and Kyung Baek, EJL 30 (Atlanta, GA: SBL, 2011), 523–39; cf. Cecilia Wassén, "Good and Bad Angels in the Construction of Identity in the Qumran Movement," in *Gottesdienst und Engel im antiken Judentum und fruhen Christentum*, ed. Jörg Frey and Michael Jost, WUNT 2/446 (Tübingen: Mohr Siebeck, 2017), 71–97.

RATIONS, REFRESHMENTS, READING, AND REVELATION   443

knowledge" (1QH[a] 11:22–24).[106] These passages express a fundamental belief that the members have a close relationship with the angels, even to the point where they belong in the community of divine beings. In this context we may recall the prohibition in D and 1QSa for impure people, as well as persons with blemishes or physical handicaps, to take part in certain meetings because of the presence of the holy angels. So, 1QSa 2:2–9 reads:

> And anyone who is afflicted in his flesh or the hands, lame or blind or deaf or dumb, or if he stricken with a blemish in his flesh visible to the eyes; or a (tottering) old man who cannot maintain himself within the congregation; these may not enter to stand firm within the congregation of men of the name, for holy angels are in the council.[107]

These restrictions concern meetings of different kinds: "And when there will be a convocation of the entire assembly for judgment or for the council of the community, or for a convocation of war, they shall sanctify them(selves) for three days, so that everyone who comes shall be pre[pared for the coun]cil" (1QSa 1:25–26). At these occasions the members had to be fully pure by starting their purification three days in advance.[108] The passage is followed by the regulations for "the feast for the council of the community" (1QSa 2:17–22 cited earlier) when the Messiah and the priest shall lead the congregation in their communal meal, with blessings over the wine and bread. These regulations also apply to every meal when as many as ten men meet together, as the section ends (1QSa 2:22). These two segments concerning the exclusion of blemished members and the feast of the council of the community belong together, since the same terms are used for the events, namely עצת היחד. It is not farfetched to relate the purity restrictions at these special meals with the belief

---

106 "And a perverted spirit you have purified from great sin that it might take its place with the host of the holy ones and enter into community with the congregation of the children of heaven. And you cast for a person an eternal lot with the spirits of knowledge רוחות דעת, that he might praise your name in the common rejoicing and recount your wonderful acts before all your works" (1QH[a] 11:22–23).

107 Similarly, 4Q266 8 i 6b–9 (par. CD 15:15–17; 4Q270 6 ii 8–9) excludes the physically handicapped and blemished people from participating at meetings, also with reference to the presence of angels (cf. 1QM 7:3–6). For the theme of communion with angels in the Dead Sea Scrolls, see Björn Frennesson, "In a Common Rejoicing": Liturgical Communion with Angels in Qumran, Studia Semitica Upsaliensia 14 (Uppsala: Acta Universitatis Upsaliensis, 1999).

108 Sanctification in this context refers to purification patterned on the commandments at Mount Sinai before the theophany in Exodus (19:10–11) when Israelites abstained from sexual relations and washed their clothes, preparing for "the third day."

in the presence of angels, which gave the meals an aura of sacredness. With no sinful transgressors or ritually impure initiates present, the symposia provided the ideal environment for interpreting Scripture with the guidance of spiritual beings.

8 Conclusion and Summary

The sectarian rules demonstrate that the common meal in the Qumran movement was of central importance. Membership meant gaining access to the communal meals, which provided, as I argue, the basic setting for most of the communal activities. In short, membership in the association was manifested at the table. The communal meal when ten or more were assembled together was formally structured with hierarchical seating and a strict order of speech, and it took place under the guidance of a priest. At the same time, there is a distinction between ordinary, everyday meals that some of the sectarians may have frequently eaten together, and the special meals, "the pure meal," that was more of a formal event, which included at least ten members and had a sacred ambiance. The latter has been the focus of this study. In agreement with Klinghardt and other scholars who focus on ancient meals, I maintain that the formal sectarian common meals consisted of two main parts, a dining part and a symposium. This is consistent with a general banquet tradition of the Greco-Roman world that entailed certain shared social norms and customs.

Acceptance into the society was a two-step process whereby novices could attend the dining part at first, and only as full members take part of the second part, the symposium. Stringent regulations restricted attendance to the symposium and only full members who also were ritually pure were allowed access, which gave the event an exclusive character. In light of the practices in other Greco-Roman associations, the joint meal most likely provided a common setting for multiple activities. 1QS 6:7–8 may well describe the ordinary activities that took place at the later part of the meal, namely "reading from the book, interpreting the regulations, and saying blessings together." If so, in addition to eating, the members of the Qumran movement engaged in various activities, including prayers, blessings, deliberations of various kinds, as well as reading and interpreting Scripture at their meals. These were communal activities. I proposed that the demand for ritual purity at these meals was only partly due to the risk of transmitting impurity at such occasions. Another important reason was the sacred character of the exegesis, which was conceived as a revelatory enterprise. In the presence of the divine, in the form of angels and the Holy Spirit who inspired the sectarians in their readings, full ritual purity was essential. Hence, within the Qumran movement, transmission of knowledge and the development of new insights and interpretation of Scripture often took place in the context of the communal meal, particularly where ten or more were gathered in compliance with the regulations.

Acknowledgments

I would like to thank Chris Keith and Travis Williams for inviting me to a highly stimulating conference on ancient media culture and the Scrolls at St Mary's University in Twickenham and for taking such a good care of the participants during the stay.

Bibliography

Antonissen, Hugo. "The Banquet Culture on New Jerusalem, An Aramaic Text from Qumran." Pages 52–77 in *Vision, Narrative, and Wisdom in the Aramaic Texts from Qumran: Essays from the Copenhagen Symposium, 14–15 August, 2017*. Edited by Mette Bundvad and Kasper Siegismund. STDJ 131. Leiden: Brill, 2019.

Arnold, Russell C. D. *Social Role of Liturgy in the Religion of the Qumran Community*. STDJ 60. Leiden: Brill, 2005.

Ascough, Richard S. "Social and Political Characteristics of Greco-Roman Association Meals." Pages 59–72 in *Meals in the Early Christian World: Social Formation, Experimentation, and Conflict at the Table*. Edited by Dennis E. Smith and Hal Taussig. New York, NY: Palgrave Macmillan, 2012.

Ascough, Richard S. "Paul, Synagogues, and Associations: Reframing the Question of Models for Pauline Christ Groups." *JJMJS* 2 (2015): 27–52.

Ascough, Richard S., Philip A. Harland, and John S. Kloppenborg, eds. *Associations in the Greco-Roman World: A Sourcebook*. Waco, TX: Baylor University Press, 2012.

Avemarie, Friedrich. "'Tohorat Ha-Rabbim' and 'Mashqeh Ha-Rabbim': Jacob Licht Reconsidered." Pages 215–29 in *Legal Texts and Legal Issues: Proceedings of the Second Meeting of the International Organization for Qumran Studies, Cambridge 1995, Published in Honour of Joseph M. Baumgarten*. Edited by Moshe Berstein, Florentino García Martínez, and John Kampen. STDJ 23. Leiden: Brill, 1997.

Bardtke, Hans. "Die Rechtstellung der Qumran Gemeinde." *TLZ* 86 (1961): 93–104.

Bilde, Per. "The Common Meal in the Qumran-Essene Communities." Pages 145–66 in *Meals in a Social Context: Aspects of the Communal Meal in the Hellenistic and*

Roman World. Edited by Hanne Sigismund Nielsen and Inge Nielsen. Aarhus Studies in Mediterranean Antiquity 1. Aarhus: Aarhus University Press, 1998.

Brumberg-Kraus, Jonathan. "Contrasting Banquets: A Literary Commonplace in Philo's *On the Contemplative Life* and Other Greek and Roman Symposia." Pages 163–74 in *Meals in Early Judaism: Social Formation at the Table*. Edited by Susan Marks and Hal Taussig. New York, NY: Palgrave Macmillan, 2014.

Charlesworth, James H. ed. *The Dead Sea Scrolls: Hebrew, Aramaic, and Greek Texts with English Translations*, vol. 1: *Rule of the Community and Related Documents*. PTSDSSP. Tübingen: Mohr Siebeck; Louisville, KY: Westminster John Knox Press, 1994.

Charlesworth, James H. "Revelation and Perspicacity in Qumran Hermeneutics?" Pages 161–80 in *The Dead Sea Scrolls and Contemporary Culture: Proceedings of the International Conference Held at the Israel Museum, Jerusalem (July 6–8, 2008)*. Edited by Adolfo D. Roitman, Lawrence H. Schiffman, and Shani Tzoref. STDJ 93. Leiden: Brill, 2011.

Collins, John J. "Forms of Community in the Dead Sea Scrolls." Pages 97–111 in *Emanuel: Studies in Hebrew Bible, Septuagint, and Dead Sea Scrolls in Honor of Emanuel Tov*. Edited by Shalom M. Paul Robert A. Kraft, Lawrence H. Schiffman, and Weston W. Fields. VTSup 94. Leiden: Brill, 2003.

Collins, John J. "The Yaḥad and 'the Qumran Community.'" Pages 81–96 in *Biblical Traditions in Transmission: Essays in Honour of Michael A. Knibb*. Edited by Charlotte Hempel and Judith Lieu. JSJSup 111. Leiden: Brill, 2006.

Collins, John J. *Beyond the Qumran Community: The Sectarian Movement of the Dead Sea Scrolls*. Grand Rapids, MI: Eerdmans, 2010.

Cosgrove, Charles H. "Banquet Ceremonies Involving Wine in the Greco-Roman World and Early Christianity." *CBQ* 79 (2017): 299–316.

Dombrowski, Bruno. "היחד in 1QS and Τὸ Κοινόν: An Instance of Early Greek and Jewish Synthesis." *HTR* 59 (1966): 293–307.

Eckhardt, Benedikt. "Temple Ideology and Hellenistic Private Associations." *DSD* 24 (2017): 407–23.

Eckhardt, Benedikt. "The Yahad in the Context of Hellenistic Group Formation." Pages 86–96 in *T&T Clark Companion to the Dead Sea Scrolls*. Edited by George J. Brooke and Charlotte Hempel, with the assistance of Michael DeVries and Drew Longacre. London: T&T Clark, 2019.

Ekroth, Gunnel. "A Room of One's Own? Exploring the Temenos Concept as Divine Property." *Stuff of the Gods: The Material Aspects of Religion in Ancient Greece*. Edited by J. Wallensten, M. Haysom, and M. Mili, forthcoming.

Frennesson, Björn. *"In a Common Rejoicing": Liturgical Communion with Angels in Qumran*. Studia Semitica Upsaliensia 14. Uppsala: Acta Universitatis Upsaliensis, 1999.

Furstenberg, Yair. "Initiation and the Ritual Purification from Sin: Between Qumran and the Apostolic Tradition." *DSD* 23 (2016): 365–94.

Gillihan, Yonder Moynihan. *Civic Ideology, Organization, and Law in the Rule Scrolls: A Comparative Study of the Covenanters' Sect and Contemporary Voluntary Associations in Political Context.* STDJ 97. Leiden: Brill, 2012.

Harland, Philip A. *Associations, Synagogues and Congregations: Claiming a Place in Ancient Mediterranean Society.* Minneapolis, MN: Fortress, 2003.

Harland, Philip A. *Dynamics of Identity in the World of the Early Christians: Associations, Judeans, and Cultural Minorities.* New York, NY: Continuum, 2009.

Harland, Philip A., ed. *Greco-Roman Associations: Texts, Translations, and Commentary*, II: *North Coast of the Black Sea, Asia Minor.* BZNW 204. Berlin: De Gruyter, 2014.

Harrington, Hannah. *The Purity Texts.* CQS 5. New York, NY: T&T Clark, 2004.

Hempel, Charlotte. "Emerging Communal Life and Ideology in the S Tradition." Pages 43–61 in *Defining Identities: We, You, and the Other in the Dead Sea Scrolls: Proceedings of the Fifth Meeting of the IOQS in Groningen.* Edited by Florentino García Martínez and Mladen Popović. STDJ 70. Leiden: Brill, 2008.

Hempel, Charlotte. "Who Is Making Dinner at Qumran?" *JTS* 63 (2012): 49–65.

Humbert, Jean-Baptiste. "L'espace sacré à Qumrân: propositions pour l'archéologie." *RB* 101 (1994): 161–214.

Jassen, Alex P. *Mediating the Divine: Prophecy and Revelation in the Dead Sea Scrolls and Second Temple Judaism.* STDJ 68. Leiden: Brill, 2007.

Jokiranta, Jutta. "What is '*Serekh ha-Yahad* (S)'? Thinking About Ancient Manuscripts as Information Processing." Pages 611–35 in *Sibyls, Scriptures, and Scrolls: John Collins at Seventy.* Joel S. Baden, Hindy Najman, and Eibert J. C. Tigchelaar. JSJSup 175. Leiden: Brill, 2016.

Jokiranta, Jutta. "Black Sheep, Outsiders, and the Qumran Movement: Social-Psychological Perspectives on Norm–Deviant Behaviour." Pages 151–73 in *Social Memory and Social Identity in the Study of Early Judaism and Early Christianity.* Edited by Samuel Byrskog, Raimo Hakola and Jutta Jokiranta. NTOA/SUNT 116. Göttingen: Vandenhoeck & Ruprecht, 2016.

Josephus. *The Jewish War, Books 1–2.* Translated by H. St. J. Thackeray. LCL 203. Cambridge, MA: Harvard University Press, 1927.

Klinghardt, Matthias. "The Manual of Discipline in the Light of Statutes of Hellenistic Associations." Pages 251–67 in *Methods of Investigation of the Dead Sea Scrolls and the Khirbet Qumran Site: Present Realities and Future Prospects.* Edited by Michael O. Wise, Norman Golb, John J. Collins, and Dennis G. Pardee. Annals of the New York Academy of Sciences 722. New York, NY: New York Academy of Sciences, 1994.

Klinghardt, Matthias. *Gemeinschaftsmahl Und Mahlgemeinschaft: Soziologie Und Liturgie Frühchristlicher Mahlfeiern.* TANZ 13. Tübingen: Francke, 1996.

Kloppenborg, John S., and Richard S. Ascough, eds. *Greco-Roman Associations: Texts, Translations, and Commentary* II: *Attica, Central Greece, Macedonia, Thrace*. BZNW 181. Berlin: De Gruyter, 2011.

Kobel, Esther. *Dining with John: Communal Meals and Identity Formation in the Fourth Gospel and Its Historical and Cultural Context*. BIS 109. Leiden: Brill, 2011.

Korner, Ralph. "Ekklēsia as a Jewish Synagogue Term: Some Implications for Paul's Socio-Religious Location." *Journal of the Jesus Movement in its Jewish Setting* 2 (2015): 53–78.

Lim, Timothy H. *Pesharim*. CQS 3. London: Sheffield Academic Press, 2002.

Magness, Jodi. *The Archaeology of Qumran and the Dead Sea Scrolls*. Studies in the Dead Sea Scrolls and Related Literature. Grand Rapids, MI: Eerdmans, 2002.

Magness, Jodi. "Were Sacrifices Offered at Qumran? The Animal Bone Deposits Reconsidered." *JAJ* 7 (2016): 5–34.

Marks, Susan. "In the Place of Libation: Birkat Hamazon Navigates New Ground." Pages 71–97 in *Meals in Early Judaism: Social Formation at the Table*. Edited by Susan Marks and Hal Taussig. New York, NY: Palgrave Macmillan, 2014.

Marks, Susan. "Reconsidering Reclining at Qumran." *JAJ* 7 (2016): 86–101.

Metso, Sarianna. "Whom Does the Term Yaḥad Identify?" Pages 63–84 in *Defining Identities: We, You, and the Other in the Dead Sea Scrolls: Proceedings of the Fifth Meeting of the IOQS in Groningen*. Edited by Florentino García Martínez and Mladen Popović. STDJ 70. Leiden: Brill, 2008.

Metso, Sarianna. "Problems in Reconstructing the Organizational Chart of the Essenes." *DSD* 16 (2009): 388–415.

Mizzi, Dennis. "From the Judaean Desert to the Great Sea: Qumran in a Mediterranean Context." *DSD* 24 (2017): 378–406.

Newsom, Carol A. *Songs of the Sabbath Sacrifice: A Critical Edition*. HSS 27. Atlanta, GA: Scholars, 1985.

Philo. *Philo, Volume 9*. Translated by F. H. Colson. LCL 363. Cambridge, MA: Harvard University Press, 1954.

Podemann Sørensen, Jørgen. "The Sacrificial Logic of Cultic Meals in Antiquity." *Early Christianity* 7 (2016): 447–67.

Popović, Mladen. "Reading, Writing, and Memorizing Together: Reading Culture in Ancient Judaism and the Dead Sea Scrolls in a Mediterranean Context." *DSD* 24 (2017): 447–70.

Regev, Eyal. "Between Two Sects: Differentiating the Yaḥad and the Damascus Covenant." Pages 431–49 in *Dead Sea Scrolls: Texts and Context*. Edited by Charlotte Hempel. STDJ 90. Leiden: Brill, 2010.

Runesson, Anders. *Origins of the Synagogue: A Socio-Historical Study*. CBNT 37. Stockholm: Almquest & Wiksell, 2001.

Runesson, Anders. "The Historical Jesus, the Gospels, and First-Century Jewish Society: The Importance of the Synagogue for Understanding the New Testament."

Pages 265–97 in *A City Set on a Hill: Essays in Honor of James F. Strange*. Mountain Home, AR: BorderStone Press, 2014.

Schiffman, Lawrence H. "Communal Meals at Qumran." *RevQ* 10 (1979): 45–56.

Schofield, Alison. *From Qumran to the* Yaḥad*: A New Paradigm of Textual Development for The Community Rule*. STDJ 77. Leiden: Brill, 2009.

Schuller, Eileen M. *The Dead Sea Scrolls: What Have We Learnt?* Louisville, KY: Westminster John Knox Press, 2006.

Schuller, Eileen M., and Carol A. Newsom. *The Hodayot (Thanksgiving Psalms): A Study Edition of 1QHa*. Atlanta, GA: SBL, 2012.

Smith, Dennis E. *From Symposium to Eucharist: The Banquet in the Early Christian World*. Minneapolis, MN: Fortress, 2003.

Smith, Dennis E. "Meals," Pages 924–26 in *The Eerdmans Dictionary of Early Judaism*. Edited by John J. Collins and Daniel C. Harlow. Grand Rapids, MI: Eerdmans, 2010.

Taussig, Hal. *In the Beginning Was the Meal: Social Experimentation and Early Christian Identity*. Minneapolis, MN: Fortress, 2009.

Vaux, Roland de. *Archaeology and the Dead Sea Scrolls*. London: Oxford University Press, 1973.

Vermès, Géza. *The Complete Dead Sea Scrolls in English*. London: Allen Lane, 1997.

Walker-Ramisch, Sandra. "Graeco-Roman Voluntary Associations and the Damascus Document: A Sociological Analysis." Pages 128–45 in *Voluntary Associations in the Graeco-Roman World*. Edited by John S. Kloppenborg and Brian Wilson. London: Routledge, 1996.

Wassén, Cecilia, and Jutta Jokiranta. "Groups in Tension: Sectarianism in the Damascus Document and the Community Rule." Pages 205–45 in *Sectarianism in Early Judaism: Sociological Advances*. Edited by David J. Chalcraft. London: Equinox, 2007.

Wassén, Cecilia. "Angels and Humans: Boundaries and Synergies." Pages 523–39 in *Celebrating the Dead Sea Scrolls: A Canadian Collection*. Edited by Jean Duhaime, Peter Flint, and Kyung Baek. EJL 30. Atlanta, GA: SBL, 2011.

Wassén, Cecilia. "The (Im)purity Levels of Communal Meals within the Qumran Movement." *JAJ* 7 (2016): 102–22.

Wassén, Cecilia. "Good and Bad Angels in the Construction of Identity in the Qumran Movement." Pages 71–97 in *Gottesdienst und Engel im Antiken Judentum und Fruhen Christentum*. Edited by Jörg Frey and Michael Jost. WUNT 2/446. Tübingen: Mohr Siebeck, 2017.

Weinfeld, Moshe. *The Organizational Pattern and the Penal Code of the Qumran Sect: A Comparison with Guilds and Religious Associations of the Hellenistic-Roman Period*. NTOA 2. Göttingen: Vandenhoeck & Ruprecht, 1986.

White Crawford, Sidnie. *Scribes and Scrolls at Qumran*. Grand Rapids, MI: Eerdmans, 2019.

PART 3

Future Perspectives on the Dead Sea Scrolls and Ancient Media

∵

CHAPTER 13

Mediated Textuality: Ambient Orality and the Dead Sea Scrolls

Maxine L. Grossman

Media:

1. the main *means of mass communication* (broadcasting, publishing, and the internet) regarded collectively. "their demands were publicized by the media"
2. plural form of medium.

Medium:

1. an agency or *means of doing something.* "using the latest technology as a medium for job creation"
2. a means by which something is *communicated or expressed.* "here the Welsh language is the medium of instruction"
3. *the intervening substance* through which impressions are conveyed to the senses or a force acts on objects at a distance. "radio communication needs no physical medium between the two stations"[1]

1 Introduction

In his introduction to ancient media culture, Travis B. Williams observes that media studies "focuses on the ways that various forms of communication impact culture."[2] This impact includes but is not limited to "manuscript production, education, oral tradition, ritualization, [and] memory."[3] The interplay of orality and writtenness—in modes of preservation, communication, and cultural formation—takes a central role in this process, as do such important factors as the materiality of the means of communication and its context in a larger social setting.

---

1 Google definition search, March 18, 2022; on the social context for this resource, see Oxford Languages, https://languages.oup.com/google-dictionary-en/ (italics mine).

2 Williams, "Studies in Ancient Media Culture," 10. I am grateful to Travis Williams and Chris Keith for inviting me to join this project at a relatively late stage and for their patience and generosity throughout the process.

3 Williams, "Studies in Ancient Media Culture," 10.

© MAXINE L. GROSSMAN, 2023 | DOI:10.1163/9789004537804_014

In reading the thought-provoking essays in this volume, I was struck by the multivalent conceptions of "media" available to us. Our scholarly analysis benefits from recent work in the field of mass communication, even as such engagement highlights the very different dynamics of textual production associated with scribal practice and the scrolls movement. Further attention to factors like education, the scribes who copied the scrolls, and the dynamic of curation lends important insight to our understanding of textual production and transmission.

As with "media," awareness of the "medium" of communication is similarly provocative. Engagement with textual and oral tradition in ancient Judaism and biblical studies often focuses more on *what* is communicated—the wording and meaning of texts and their theological implications—than it does on *how* it is communicated. A media studies approach, as the articles in this volume illustrate, allows for attention to other important aspects of the communication process. A medium can also be "an agency or means of doing something" or "the intervening substance" through which it is done, which shifts our focus from the *process* of communication ("media") and the *materiality* of that communication (as material "medium") to the social and cultural *contexts* in which communication can be, if you will, *mediated*.

Attention to the cultural spaces associated with the scrolls allows us to engage with media studies in ways that are generative for our understandings of textuality and orality as multilayered and relational. To the extent that these cultural settings provide a context for experience of texts, there is something valuable in thinking about the "intervening substance" in which they take place. What ideas were "in the air" for participants in the scrolls movement, and how did that *ambient* experience of orality and textuality contribute to their understanding of the meanings of their textual and oral traditions? Without falling too far into speculation, can we understand such a cultural space as an element in the larger process, as well?

George Brooke, in his powerful contribution to this volume, begins his discussion with reference to Stanley Fish and audience-oriented criticism. Fish, in turn, reminds us of the centrality of the reader and, by extrapolation, the reciter and the listener, in assigning meaning to texts in any form. While the editors of Brooke's recent Festschrift asked the question, "Is there a Text in this Cave?" Fish would ask something just slightly different. Without an audience, Fish observes, "the meaning" of a text is at best nascent.[4] This in turn suggests

---

4 Ariel Feldman, Maria Cioată, and Charlotte Hempel, eds., *Is there a Text in this Cave? Studies in the Textuality of the Dead Sea Scrolls in Honour of George J. Brooke*, STDJ 119 (Leiden: Brill, 2017).

MEDIATED TEXTUALITY 455

that there is indeed no text *in the cave*; the text exists only when it makes its way to "the class" (where Fish considers it), or—better, for the sources addressed in this volume—to the community, the congregation, or the Covenant group.

In responding to the essays in this volume, I will focus on several important topics. The first of these is the dynamic tension between orality and writtenness, not only in material form but also, or even especially, in light of ideological framings of their respective value. Attention to ambient orality will provide an opportunity to engage with treatments of ritual and ritual performance in these essays, and it will also serve as a pivot point toward a discussion of materiality. Consideration of the materiality of media, with attention to ritual objects, scribal practice, and the curation of the scrolls, will in turn provide grounding for some concluding thoughts on mediated textuality and ambient orality in the Dead Sea Scrolls.

2 Orality and Writtenness in Performance, Tradition, and Everyday Life

In this volume, the concept of orality is wide-ranging, referring to "the various ways that individuals and groups communicate through oral media, including any means of support that makes such communication possible."[5] This statement reflects a long history of scholarship beyond the first generations of work on orality and writtenness, which viewed the two as successive stages of cultural development marked by a Great Divide: "when literacy finally developed within a society, this media shift marked a significant cultural revolution."[6] An important contribution of the articles in this volume is their engagement with the *intersecting* dynamics of literacy and orality, as they manifest and shape communication in the scrolls movement.

Attention to intersections of oral and literate composition runs through the articles in this volume. Pieter Hartog identifies the pesher texts in particular as a product of "oral study sessions, which yielded disparate interpretations of passages from the Jewish Scriptures, reading them in light of the historical memories of the participants in these study sessions .... These processes did not preclude the continued oral performance of the pesharim in reading sessions."[7] Shem Miller shares this perception of the dynamic development of certain kinds of texts through a combination of oral and written stages,

---

5   Williams, "Studies in Ancient Media Culture," 10–11.
6   Williams, "Studies in Ancient Media Culture," 23.
7   Hartog, "4Q169 (Pesher Nahum)," 286.

noting Sarianna Metso's treatment of the Community Rule and her observation that it "was not to serve as a lawbook, but rather as a record of judicial decisions and *an accurate report of oral traditions*."[8] George Brooke takes a similar approach to the rule texts and MMT, which "reads like a set of minutes compiled in the form of an epistle."[9] Miller's engagement with this dynamic process rewards quoting at length:

> On the one hand, the Dead Sea Scrolls were not texts frozen in written media; rather, they were dynamic discourses that represented spoken words (speech) heard in shifting contexts of oral performance (reading). For the Jews who used them, they functioned as reference points for study, reading, and memorization. Moreover, as oral mediums, they stored the oral interpretive traditions and oral traditional texts of the communities associated with the Scrolls. On the other hand, both the social context of the Scrolls and the descriptions of oral performance in the Scrolls demand an influential place for orality in our reconstructions of daily life.[10]

From this rich passage, I would highlight three observations in particular, related to the dynamics of oral performance, the multivalent significance of "oral tradition," and orality as an element of daily life.

2.1 *Performance*

Several of our authors address the concept of performance and the impact of performance theory on an understanding of orality in an ancient Jewish setting. Brooke remarks on the vibrant quality that would have accompanied oral performances, which would include "re-presentation of the text, voiced with emphasis and cadence, and probably glossed,"[11] further noting that the capacity for such reading performance would have been expected of members of the sectarian movement.[12] Miller and Charlotte Hempel emphasize the contextualized setting of such practices, in which the audience plays an equally important role: "Oral performance may be defined as the reading, recitation,

---

8   Sarianna Metso, "In Search of the *Sitz im Leben* of the *Community Rule*," in *The Provo International Conference on the Dead Sea Scrolls: Technological Innovations, New Texts, and Reformulated Issues*, ed. Donald W. Parry and Eugene Ulrich, STDJ 30 (Leiden: Brill, 1998), 86–93, cited in Shem Miller, "Is there a Spoken Voice," 149 (original italics).

9   Brooke, "Orality and Written-ness," 375.

10   Miller, "Is there a Spoken Voice," 151.

11   Brooke, "Orality and Written-ness," 363.

12   Brooke, "Orality and Written-ness," 368–72.

MEDIATED TEXTUALITY   457

or enactment of a text *before an audience*,"[13] Miller notes. Hempel further emphasizes that performances "are witnessed by a variety of audiences whose presence has an effect on the performance."[14] Pesher, again, is the quintessential example, which—like rabbinic midrash—reflects both an action and the composition that results from it. Hartog thus comments that, "oral performances of the Qumran commentaries inspired new, disparate interpretations, which could be added at an appropriate point to the existing Pesher."[15]

These insights on performance are important, and I would argue that we can push them even further by emphasizing their intersection. If Brooke is right, then sectarian performers must be thought of as *both* "author" and "audience" of a set of readings, which would take place within a social collective that they comprised but also experienced contextually. To put it another way, individual performance would always be experienced within a collective dynamic that reflected on and reinforced the sense of self of individual sectarians, while asserting, undergirding, and potentially reshaping the values of the group as a whole. Carol Newsom's influence is obvious here,[16] but I would add two other thinkers to the mix: Fish, once more, and Judith Butler.

An emphasis on Fish is necessary to really push the idea of audience *as* author, without losing sight of the nuances of such a relational dynamic. Metso (quoted in Miller) and Hartog are particularly attentive to this creative process, which has, if I may be forgiven, an important *always already* quality about it. Pesher, as a process, sets this scene nicely. It begins with a scriptural lemma, one that has authoritative priority if not canonically-fixed content, but it is experienced orally and collectively through the process Brooke describes: recitation in a collective setting. Interpretive—and potentially *authoritative* interpretive—performance ensues, resulting in a new understanding of the original text, and in the creation of a new oral textual standard to then be understood again. This hermeneutical cycle has a variety of implications, in that it creates new textual meaning as well as new texts, which contributing to the authority of its performers as textual interpreters but also, reciprocally, audience-participants as well. Fish would push this still further by noting that audience interpretations are constrained by collective norms but that differences of understanding ("what is a text?") are not only possible but entirely to be expected within a collective. The seeds of dispute are intrinsic to the process,

---

13   Miller, "Is there a Spoken Voice," 137.
14   Hempel, "Curated Communities," 345.
15   Hartog, "4Q169 (Pesher Nahum)," 282.
16   Carol Newsom, *The Self as Symbolic Space: Constructing Identity and Community at Qumran*, STDJ 52 (Leiden: Brill, 2004).

since interpreters as performers may be inspired to different understandings of texts while sharing claims to the authoritative origins of their views. The audience—in hearing, internalizing, processing, and echoing—may validate the lector's presentation of the text, but they may also reflect back on it and carry it forward in new and contradictory ways.

This engagement with the performative underscores the dynamics of a process and reframes texts (scriptural, interpretive, legal) as elements of the process itself. The result is reminiscent (to me, at least) of another approach to the performative, that of Judith Butler. Her approach is committed to a recognition of performance not in a single moment or a particular dramatic setting but as a constituting experience. Particular identity qualities serve not merely to describe a phenomenon; rather, they constitute and reinforce that phenomenon in always-ongoing ways. Shamelessly stealing from her treatment of gender, I would similarly like to insist that:

> In this sense, [sectarian identity] is not a noun, but neither is it a set of free-floating attributes, for we have seen that the substantive effect of [sectarianism] is performatively produced and compelled by the regulatory practices of [sectarian] coherence .... [Sectarian identity] proves to be performative—that is, constituting the identity it is purported to be.[17]

Orality and writtenness remain relevant in this context, but as aspects of a larger social formation and in the context of a larger authoritative tradition from which they draw and to which they contribute. Performance, similarly, expands the bounds of individual behaviors and becomes instead the constitutive elements for both individual identity and large-scale social practice.

2.2 Oral Tradition

Like performativity, the concept of oral tradition is layered. Miller again provides a starting point in his definition of "tradition" as "a multivalent body of established thought, meaning, or interpretation." Oral tradition manifests when "this tradition is composed, performed, or received orally (in part or in whole)."[18] Tradition binds a group together in light of a perceived shared history; as such, it is "designed to be stored and transmitted."[19]

---

17 Judith Butler, *Gender Trouble: Feminism and the Subversion of Identity* (New York, NY: Routledge, 1990), 24–25.
18 Miller, "Is there a Spoken Voice," 140–141.
19 Miller, "Is there a Spoken Voice," 141.

But tradition in this sense is not a neutral repository. In writing or "speaking" themselves back into their inherited traditions, ancient Jewish interpreters expressed strong views about the authority of those traditions and the proper contexts for their transmission. Thus, for example, Hartog observes that, "just as the authors of Jubilees write themselves into a Mosaic discourse, so the Pesher exegetes write themselves into the tradition that had allegedly begun with the Teacher."[20] Writing itself, in contrast with orality, "symbolises and safeguards the continuity of a tradition,"[21] at least in the context of the scrolls movement.

Precisely the opposite valuation is articulated in early rabbinic literature, which views a particular oral transmission of Torah as the one to be valued and privileged.[22] This privileging of orality should not be read in general terms. While the classical rabbis did debate the general value of "the oral" and "the written" conceptually, recognizing the presence of the sacred in material form (e.g., scriptural texts that "render the hands unclean"),[23] the orality of rabbinic tradition in fact refers to a *specific* transmission from Sinai, an Oral Torah that passed through a single line of tradents and supported a particular set of authoritative claims.[24] The scrolls movement, too, had an oral tradition, but it was not this Oral Torah. As Miller observes, "the gap between Sinai and the sect was not bridged by a chain of authoritative oral tradition but rather by progressive revelation of law to members and leaders of the sectarian communities associated with the scrolls."[25]

Ancient Jewish orality, these articles suggest, needs to be understood in light of some very particular contexts. Transmission of tradition also requires and in fact contributes to its adaptation. Appeals to authority negotiate the oral/textual divide. And "orality" itself can refer to a specific rabbinic claim, and not only to a contextualizing frame of reference. A shift of focus to orality in

---

20   Hartog, "4Q169 (Pesher Nahum)," 280.

21   Hartog, "4Q169 (Pesher Nahum)," 280.

22   See Brooke, "Orality and Written-ness," 358–84; Martin S. Jaffee, *Torah in the Mouth: Writing and Oral Tradition in Palestinian Judaism, 200 BCE–400 CE* (New York, NY: Oxford University Press, 2001).

23   See the discussion in Jodi Magness, "Scrolls and Hand Impurity," in *The Dead Sea Scrolls: Texts and Context*, ed. Charlotte Hempel, STDJ 90 (Leiden: Brill, 2010), 89–97.

24   Pirkei Avot 1.1–18 traces the lineage of the Oral Torah from Sinai to Rabban Shimon ben Gamliel, beginning with the assertion that "Moses received the Torah at Sinai and transmitted it to Joshua, Joshua to the elders, and the elders to the prophets, and the prophets to the Men of the Great Assembly" (Avot 1.1). See Amram Tropper, *Wisdom, Politics, and Historiography: Tractate Avot in the Context of the Graeco-Roman Near East* (New York, NY: Oxford University Press, 2004).

25   Miller, "Is there a Spoken Voice," 147.

the context of daily life in the scrolls movement can help to clarify the situation further.

2.3   *Daily Life*

Alongside engagement with literary and oral tradition and alongside the performative engagement with texts, I found myself searching these articles for attention to everyday lived experience and what I might classify as the *ambient orality* of life in the scrolls movement. How did scripture manifest in spoken word? How did individual and collective identity formation happen in the spaces outside of worship or study: in the menial work of lower-status group members (per Hempel),[26] in meals both formal and ordinary (per Cecilia Wassén), and in contexts where "foolish words" might have significant and potentially lasting implications for a member's place in the collective?[27] Ambient orality—the words and concepts that were "in the air" among members of the movement—is conceptually closer to a discussion of religious experience or cognition than it is to the oral/written binary of textuality, but it remains an important point of consideration as we explore these concepts in particular social frames.

A word of caution is in order, as both Williams and Wassén demonstrate in their contributions. Past treatments of the scrolls have attempted to connect individual documents to specific communities, or to read the entire collection of the scrolls as a unitary library for a single community, as Williams has observed.[28] Wassén argues for another approach, one that views the scrolls as evidence for a movement, not a single group, and for habitation in related, networked small groups.[29] She further observes that participation in the scrolls movement would "fill a social space in between the civic society and the household."[30] Such a space would necessarily be diverse and potentially wide-ranging in its social scale. For members of the movement living in a neighborhood or community of scrolls sectarians, their experience of the movement might indeed resemble—or replace—that of the household. Group members living in a more diverse setting, among outsiders in a large city, or simply at a

---

26   Hempel, "Curated Communities," 345–48.

27   1QS 7:9: "whoever utters foolish words aloud [is punished for] three months."

28   Williams, "Textuality and the Dead Sea Scrolls," 90–97.

29   Wassén, "Rations, Refreshments," 415–49. On this approach to the scrolls movement, see esp. Alison Schofield, *From Qumran to the Yahad: A New Paradigm of Textual Development for the Community Rule*, STDJ 77 (Leiden: Brill, 2009), and John J. Collins, *Beyond the Qumran Community: The Sectarian Movement of the Dead Sea Scrolls* (Grand Rapids, MI: Eerdmans, 2010).

30   Wassén, "Rations, Refreshments," 419.

MEDIATED TEXTUALITY

remove from their compatriots, might view their special identity as precisely the thing that causes them to stand out as distinct. From this perspective, daily life experiences for participants in the scrolls movement might have included a push-pull of sameness and difference that would be shaped and supported by their everyday choices around speech and referentiality.

A last caveat on lived experience for participants in the scrolls movement concerns the concepts associated with literacy and orality. My own sense is that we need to be careful with the concept of literacy, and even more so with the idea of illiteracy, since these would be highly contextualized and would operate, especially in lived experience, in highly contextualized ways. Williams notes a spectrum of skills from "signature literacy" to "semi-literate" and fully-literate capacities, and he remarks as well on individual capacities for varied literacy in multiple languages.[31] Such ranges of literacy should also be understood in terms of contextualized cultural competence. In particular social settings, within and outside movement boundaries, specialized terminology and even language of usage might vary widely. As one can attest after attempting to buy a pound of grapes at a metric-based market, contextualized competence rapidly distinguishes outsiders and insiders from one another.

Negotiating the complexities of literate and non-literate participation in a common movement also requires deep reconsideration of the social roles associated with textuality and orality. To this end, an important through-line in this volume is the work of Brian Stock, whose understanding of *textual communities* precisely attends to the oral/literate dynamics that structure religious movements whose participants vary in their experience of authoritative textual tradition. Stock's approach is relevant for scrolls scholarship, not only because it recognizes that participants in a movement will vary in their access to traditional texts, but also because it recognizes the power dynamics implicit in that differential. Hempel draws upon Stock in her important reminder about the internal diversity of the scrolls movement, which might be identifiable for its "educated scribal constituency," but which would have included unacknowledged participants of lower status, as well.[32] Other authors in the volume (DeVries and Jokiranta, Miller, Popović) engage with Stock's treatment of textual communities, as well, and I think a renewed attention to his work will be valuable for our understanding of textual authority in the social context of the scrolls movement.[33]

---

31   Williams, "Studies in Ancient Media Culture," 12–14.

32   Hempel, "Curated Communities," 347.

33   Engagement with Stock is explicit in Miller, "Is there a Spoken Voice," 139–41; and DeVries and Jokiranta, "Ritual Studies and the Scrolls," 168. Popović, "Book Production," 199–265,

2.4   Ritual, Ritualization, and Ambient Ritual Action

Several of the contributions to this volume engage with ritual theory and the place of ritual in a media-studies approach to the scrolls. Both the comprehensive presentation of ritual theory by Michael DeVries and Jutta Jokiranta and the fascinating engagement with ritual *as* media by Jokiranta alone point toward important possibilities for thinking about ritual in light of orality, literacy, and lived experience.

Rituals themselves may be small or large, formal or informal, but a culture of ritual is one that incorporates not only examples of specific bounded practice (ritual as "an action whose performance is attributed special significance in accordance with existing cultural guidelines")[34] but also an extension beyond them to the ritualization of more ordinary behavior and ultimately to a general atmosphere in which the language and cultural formations of ritual find their way into everyday lived experience. Anyone who has lived in a house where a pre-teen is preparing for a bar or bat mitzvah is familiar with the fact that ritual content easily escapes ritual bounds. Having heard (or sung) the opening lines of the Torah service in the shower, we recognize that words have sound, meaning, and an emotional feel that extends beyond the constraints of particular religious moments. Nor is this a uniquely Jewish value, as the similarly ambient sounds of Christian hymn-singing demonstrate. A favorite young-adult novel from the mid-20th century makes casual reference to such ambient orality: "[Mother] went downstairs singing *Onward, Christian Soldiers*, which she always sang when she felt she needed courage,"[35] and later, "It was not until she reached the foot of the stairs that she realized she was humming *Come Thou Fount of Every Blessing*, just as she had heard her mother hum it."[36]

Study of the scrolls reveals quantities of liturgies, prayers, and hymns in standalone textual settings, as well as copious and virtuoso engagements with scripture in rule texts and pesharim.[37] Perhaps these might allow us, with caution, to imagine the language—sung or spoken—that could have permeated

---

does not reference Stock directly, but see Popović, "Reading, Writing, and Memorizing Together: Reading Culture in Ancient Judaism and the Dead Sea Scrolls in a Mediterranean Context," *DSD* 24 (2017): 447–70, esp. 450, for insights on Stock's work that highlight its relevance for future scrolls scholarship.

34   Williams, "Studies in Ancient Media Culture," 38.

35   Elisabeth Ogilvie, *Blueberry Summer* (New York, NY: Scholastic Book Services, 1956), 13.

36   Ogilvie, *Blueberry Summer*, 70–71.

37   For an unpacking of one example of such virtuosity, see Maxine L. Grossman, "Cultivating Identity: Textual Virtuosity and 'Insider' Status," in *Defining Identities: We, You, and the Other in the Dead Sea Scrolls*, ed. Florentino García Martínez and Mladen Popović, STDJ 70 (Leiden: Brill, 2008), 1–11.

the lived experience of the members of the scrolls movement. This is something of an ironic claim: an argument from silence about the role of sound in the everyday life of a scrolls sectarian. But DeVries and Jokiranta engage with several authors who explore these possibilities. First, in response to Robert Kugler's treatment of ritual theory and the scrolls, they highlight his argument that "rituals were so pervasive within community life that every facet of experience was imbued with a religious quality."[38] In a second engagement, here of Russell Arnold's treatment of ritual, they note his position that "extensive liturgical tradition at Qumran fulfills a social function, the formation of a community in which all aspects of communal life were directed toward maintaining perfect holiness in obedience to God's commands and the coming day of restoration."[39]

Jokiranta carries the discussion forward still further in her single-authored chapter on ritual as media. "Rituals are just one environment and setting, but they engage bodies and senses in a governed manner, and understanding cognition as embodied helps us to understand various aspects of rituals as media," Jokiranta remarks.[40] She notes in addition that rituals "are often found at the crossroads of oral and written practices and include learned embodied practices"[41] and that rituals provide factual information but also speak to normative, meta- and motivational content. All of these observations are relevant for contextualizing ritual in lived social experience. Against an earlier strand in ritual theory, Jokiranta rightly argues that "rituals do not convey a message, but rather they are the language through which things are done." And the "things" that are done are culturally formative: asserting collective norms and values, arguing for particular reality claims, and, for our scrolls practitioners, claiming space within and in response to the larger ritual world of ancient Judeans.

Wassén adds another layer to this discussion of ritual, introducing meals as an aspect of the movement's ritual experience. She cites Hal Taussig on the idea that for ancient associations, "the meal constituted a major component of the social bonding for the association."[42] She views meals as a part of the regular

---

38 DeVries and Jokiranta, "Ritual Studies and the Scrolls," 168, engaging with Robert A. Kugler, "Making All Experience Religious: The Hegemony of Ritual at Qumran," *JSJ* 33 (2002): 131–52.

39 DeVries and Jokiranta, "Ritual Studies and the Scrolls," 169, engaging with Russell C. D. Arnold, *The Social Role of Liturgy in the Religion of the Qumran Community*, STDJ 60 (Leiden: Brill, 2006).

40 Jokiranta, "Rituals as Media," 398.

41 Jokiranta, "Rituals as Media," 385.

42 Wassén, "Rations, Refreshments," 426, quoting Hal Taussig, *In the Beginning Was the Meal: Social Experimentation and Early Christian Identity* (Minneapolis, MN: Fortress Press, 2009), 34.

gatherings of the movement, including those that took place on Sabbaths and festivals, where religious celebrations and liturgies would also be part of the experience;[43] she also distinguishes between meals eaten in purity and ordinary meals.[44] Meals are not only a ritual but a medium of communication.

Attention to ritual as media carries us quickly to the material context of experience. Thus, Jokiranta observes, "Humans do not carry all information in their bodies, but also make use of interactions with their environment and material objects, such as written texts, symbols, and architecture, and that environment affects their cognition."[45] Pivoting to a discussion of materiality and the material will allow us to return to questions of performativity and ambient orality while understanding textual evidence at its most specific and grounded.

2.5 *Materiality and the Material*

Jokiranta's treatment of shared and embodied knowledge in the context of ritual recognizes the potency of material objects and embodiment in a spatial context. Recent scrolls scholarship has most extensively engaged with "material textuality" by focusing on manuscripts, their para- or meta-textual elements, and the scribal practices associated with them. To this discussion, the present volume contributes other examples of the material in a scrolls context. Alongside manuscripts and evidence for scribal practice, consideration of the examples provided by tefillin, group meals, and dynamics of curation, taken together, push us to think more deeply about textuality and orality as lived experience, in a material realm.

2.6 *Scribal Practice*

The materiality of manuscripts and the dynamics of scribal practice have been the topic of serious attention by scrolls scholars for at least the last two decades.[46] Several of the essays in this volume bring a media studies approach to that conversation in ways that highlight relational dynamics of texts, social contexts, scribes, and audiences. Joan Taylor, for example, in her exploration of the Copper Scroll, explores its materiality as an important nexus of meaning, "the artefact itself as a vehicle of communication."[47] With deft consideration of the tensions at work here, Taylor reminds us of the many strange

---

43 Wassén, "Rations, Refreshments," 426–31.
44 Wassén, "Rations, Refreshments," 426–31.
45 Jokiranta, "Rituals as Media," 405–406.
46 The history of this field of study is particularly marked by the publication of scroll's editor Emanuel Tov's rich volume, *Scribal Practices and Approaches Reflected in the Texts Found in the Judean Desert*, STDJ 54 (Leiden: Brill, 2004).
47 Taylor, "The Copper Scroll," 302.

aspects of this "document": inscribed on expensive material but in a hand that appears awkward at best;[48] hidden, but for the purpose of being found; and featuring wording that would make transparent sense only to people who are already familiar with what it means to convey.[49] The Copper Scroll has never quite made sense to me, and it still doesn't, quite, but Taylor's engagement with the implications of its materiality as an "insider" text clarifies the picture considerably.

As a general rule, the scribal hands that are discussed in this volume tend not to reflect particularly "professional," let alone "elegant" standards, especially when considered in light of standards of book production and circulation in the Roman empire more generally.[50] Thus, Mladen Popović observes, "a careful consideration of the handwriting quality and skills in relation to the character of the copies may show that many of the scrolls from the caves near Qumran were not for the general trade market."[51] Pieter Hartog draws a similar conclusion with regard to the scribal hands of the pesher texts, which he considers "trained, but not particularly well-executed."[52]

In some ways, such a finding confirms what we might already claim to know: that scribes associated with the Qumran scrolls were less likely to be paid professionals and more likely to be copying manuscripts for use within the movement. But other implications also follow, including Popović's provocative suggestion that manuscript writing itself might have had communal value as a practice, allowing for "not so much training in writing as learning by writing." This observation with regard to scribal practice and identity formation is interesting in itself, but it also has striking implications for our understanding of the history of the texts, since "we need not assume that every manuscript that is now categorized as a Serekh manuscript served a different community, whether Essene, Yaḥad or otherwise; not every Serekh copy was a Serekh for a community elsewhere."[53]

2.7   *Communication through Curation*

Attention to curation is another interesting contribution of this volume. Charlotte Hempel compares the scrolls authors to participants in social media, noting that they create "a curated community which displays a semblance to social phenomena in the real world but not a precise representation of them … the portrayals of the movements that emerge are carefully curated by scribes

48   Taylor, "The Copper Scroll," 303–305.
49   Taylor, "The Copper Scroll," 303–305.
50   Popović, "Book Production," 199–265.
51   Popović, "Book Production," 256.
52   Hartog, "4Q169 (Pesher Nahum)," 268.
53   Popović, "Book Production," 253.

whose aim it was to create a particular perception of the movements."[54] I would argue that material curation of some scrolls texts has also been an important aspect of our understanding of the scrolls. The well-preserved manuscript remains from Cave 1 argue this point in their own way and demonstrate its potential for success: the classic Essene Hypothesis is as much a product of precisely which texts were gathered together and so carefully preserved in linens, jars, and a single cave as it is a product of academic interpretation of text and artifact. The choice to carefully preserve a different cluster of scrolls (imagine, by way of example, the discovery of a single cave containing carefully preserved copies of MMT, the Damascus Document, and the Temple Scroll) might have led to an equally authoritative modern narrative around a very different picture of ancient Jewish sectarianism. This is a point worth remembering.

Curation as authority formation may also be present in the *deluxe* manuscripts from Qumran. Hartog notes that such manuscripts may have been created by scribes who "appropriated the idea of the master copy to present themselves as the most authoritative version of a textual tradition."[55] Deluxe copies of sectarian texts (1QS, 1QM, and here, 4Q169) might also be "reacting against the fluidity of earlier traditions, i.e., as attempts to create a stronger sense of overarching unity within the movement."[56] Hempel adds the element of performance to this discussion, noting that the use of high quality materials and careful writing styles in such deluxe manuscripts creates an opportunity for scribes to "argue" materially for the value of their content and the credit that should be given to their scribal tradition.[57]

2.8 *Words as Worn*

Tefillin provide an interesting point of conclusion for this exploration of materiality, texts, and ritual in light of lived experience. Tefillin as material objects touch almost every point of our discussion. They manifest the authority of scripture in written form, while obscuring that textual content by presenting it in the tiniest of scribal writing.[58] Later rabbinic disputes would center on the precise content of the passages contained within tefillin, but such scribal orthopraxy is not yet evident in the examples from among the scrolls, which vary in content and composition.[59] We lack evidence for precisely when and how tefillin were worn (during prayer? more generally? as a means of focusing

---

54 Hempel, "Curated Communities," 348–49.

55 Hartog, "4Q169 (Pesher Nahum)," 270.

56 Hartog, "4Q169 (Pesher Nahum)," 285–86.

57 Hempel, "Curated Communities," 348–49.

58 Brooke, "Orality and Written-ness," 376.

59 Martin G. Abegg, Jr., "The Linguistic Analysis of the Dead Sea Scrolls: More Than (Initially) Meets the Eye," in *Rediscovering the Dead Sea Scrolls: An Assessment of Old and New*

MEDIATED TEXTUALITY

on the divine, or for apotropaic reasons?), but we know from ancient sources that they might serve to communicate spiritual intentionality or might be perceived to communicate hypocrisy instead.[60]

Wearing words—like hearing or reciting them, like reading them on a page—has a ritual quality to it, but would that ritual quality be foregrounded in the mind of a member of the scrolls movement, or would it be yet another example—like eating meals, like reading scripture—of ordinary, if perhaps "para-ritual" (ritualized), daily practice, what one "simply does" as a member of the movement? Further, would a group member's tefillin stand out from those of other Judeans, enhancing a sense of separateness in their specificity, or would they serve to mark a point of commonality more generally between them?

Jokiranta deals with this complex phenomenon thoughtfully. "Knowledge situated in material objects and the environment, such as in stepped pools or tefillin, carry and modify ritual practice via their form and 'user-interface,'" she remarks. "Ritual is old technology, but it can be endlessly varied according to new contexts and situations. The human body is its instrument, especially the social human body, which learns from others and derives its motivation from others."[61]

Such motivation can manifest in ways that are surprising, even for participants in the ritual itself. Raphael Magarik, writing on Twitter, reflects a present-day example of that tension in this way: "Had my 20-year-old, bar mitzvah tefillin checked: totally invalid, even to my untrained eye. Feeling unexpectedly gutted, as if I'd been betrayed by an old friend."[62]

3 Ambient Orality and Mediated Textuality: Some Concluding Thoughts

The gap between the manuscript evidence available to us today and the actual experiences of people and their texts in antiquity is one that we should probably approach with caution. Precisely in their representational capacity, as

---

Approaches and Methods, ed. Maxine L. Grossman (Grand Rapids, MI: Eerdmans, 2010), 48–68.

60   Matt 23:5: "[The Pharisees] do all their deeds to be seen by others; for they make their phylacteries broad and their fringes long."

61   Jokiranta, "Rituals as Media," 408.

62   Raphael Magarik (@RaffiMagarik), 5:32 PM Feb 15, 2022·Twitter for iPhone, https://twitter .com/RaffiMagarik/status/1493714839545552897. Accessed Feb. 16. 2022.

Charlotte Hempel shows, many of the scrolls are not so much a record of unmediated historical information as an example of "reality literature," the product of "sophisticated literary creations ... [that] appear to reflect a constructed reality."[63] Textual verisimilitude is a problem, I would argue, in light of Steven Fraade's lovely observation (quoted by Hempel) that such texts "provide not only important representations of their respective historical worlds and world views, but ongoing constructions of their places in the sacred history of Israel, whether real or imagined or imagined as real."[64]

In some ways, all of our studies of the past begin with things that we "imagine as real," but media studies provides some truly helpful resources for lending strength and nuance to the claims we make. Most striking to me, from the articles in this volume, is our profound responsibility to understand orality and literacy as *mutually comprising forces* in a *dynamic*—truly dynamic—process of *contextualized* textual production. Texts do have authors (at least some of the time) and manuscripts do have scribes, but experiences of textuality in first century Jewish culture were heard and spoken as much as read and written. As Miller affirms, quoting Shemaryahu Talmon's view of first century Jewish culture, "a text was by definition an aural text, a spoken writing, a performed story."[65] For Miller, and I would argue for us as well, the question then becomes: "*how* do we hear this voice today?"[66]

Media studies is not alone in attempting to listen to the past in this way. Since the landmark publication of Carol Newsom's *The Self as Symbolic Space* in 2004, scrolls scholars have sought to hear the voice of the scrolls movement by means of attention to the social and sociological,[67] the experiential,[68]

---

63   Hempel, "Curated Communities," 340.

64   Steven D. Fraade, *Legal Fictions: Studies of Law and Narrative in the Discursive Worlds of Ancient Jewish Sectarians and Sages.* JSJS 147 (Leiden: Brill, 2011), 14–15; quoted in Hempel, "Curated Communities," 342.

65   Shemaryahu Talmon, "Oral Tradition and Written Transmission, or the Heard and the Seen Word in Judaism of the Second Temple Period," in *Jesus and the Oral Gospel Tradition*, ed. Henry Wansbrough, JSNTSup 64 (Sheffield: Sheffield Academic, 1991), 121–58, esp. 150, cited in Miller, "Is there a Spoken Voice," 135.

66   Miller, "Is there a Spoken Voice," 135 (italics original).

67   For example, David Chalcraft, ed., *Sectarianism in Early Judaism: Sociological Advances* (London: Equinox, 2007); Eyal Regev, *Sectarianism in Qumran: A Cross-Cultural Perspective* (Berlin: De Gruyter, 2007); Jutta Jokiranta, *Social Identity and Sectarianism in the Qumran Movement*, STDJ 105 (Leiden: Brill, 2013).

68   This subfield has been shaped by two edited volumes: Frances Flannery, Colleen Shantz, and Rodney A. Werline, eds., *Experientia, Volume 1: Inquiry into Religious Experience in Early Judaism and Christianity*, SBL Symposium Series 40 (Atlanta, GA: SBL, 2008) and Colleen Shantz and Rodney A. Werline, eds., *Experientia, Volume 2: Linking Text and Experience*, EJL 35 (Atlanta, GA: SBL, 2012). In the latter volume, two articles focus specifically on religious experience and the scrolls: Carol A. Newsom, "Religious Experience

MEDIATED TEXTUALITY

the emotional,[69] and the cognitive.[70] My own treatment in this response essay works at the intersection of several of these approaches but focuses on consideration of possible *social contexts* for the *lived experience* of scrolls movements participants, and the *ambient orality* they might have experienced in those contexts. The question I would ask is not only what did the sectarians *say*, but what did they *hear*, in their own daily lives, and in their moments of self-reflection and their experiences of self-formation?

In presenting the idea of ritual as a form of media, Jokiranta makes the observation that "transmitted knowledge is always contextual."[71] Media studies demonstrates for us some of the multiple contexts through which knowledge might be transmitted, both within the evidence for the scrolls movement and in our present-day rendering of its voice. Media-focused approaches, in combination with attention to the cognitive, the emotional, and especially the material, open the door to more complicated questions about the lived experiences of our ancient Jewish sectarians.

In asking not only what was written in ancient tefillin but perhaps also how their wearers felt about them; in pursuing not only the scriptural referentiality of the Thanksgiving Hymns, but also what it might have felt like to sing them as a means of gathering one's strength and or being reminded of one's place among the holy, this combination of approaches pushes us to think about the ancient scrolls movement in its larger Jewish, religious, experiential contexts. In their communication of sacred and social claims, but also in the tools they used and the contexts through which they worked, the authors, scribes, and auditors of the Dead Sea Scrolls found agency, expressed themselves, and conveyed impressions through an intervening social reality. Media studies is a valuable resource for exploring precisely *how* they did those things, and

---

in the Dead Sea Scrolls: Two Case Studies, 205–22 and Angela Kim Harkins, "Religious Experience through the Lens of Critical Spatiality: A Look at Embodiment Language in Prayers and Hymns," 223–42.

69 Ari Mermelstein and Angela Kim Harkins have been especially influential in the study of emotion and the scrolls, through a variety of articles and book publications. See, e.g., Mermelstein, *Power and Emotion in Ancient Judaism: Community and Identity in Formation* (Cambridge: Cambridge University Press, 2021); Harkins, *Reading with an "I" to the Heavens: Looking at the Qumran Hodayot through the Lens of Visionary Traditions* (Berlin: De Gruyter, 2012) is grounded in the study of religious experience but also engages with emotion and cognition.

70 The field of cognitive studies in religion is among the most recent to reach the study of the scrolls. See, e.g., Petri Luomanen, Ilkka Pyysiäinen, and Risto Uro, eds., *Explaining Christian Origins and Early Judaism: Contributions from Cognitive and Social Science*, BibInt 89 (Leiden: Brill, 2008), esp. Jutta Jokiranta, "Social Identity in the Qumran Movement: The Case of the Penal Code," 277–98.

71 Jokiranta, "Rituals as Media," 388.

Bibliography

Abegg, Martin G., Jr. "The Linguistic Analysis of the Dead Sea Scrolls: More Than (Initially) Meets the Eye." Pages 48–68 in *Rediscovering the Dead Sea Scrolls: An Assessment of Old and New Approaches and Methods*. Edited by Maxine L. Grossman. Grand Rapids, MI: Eerdmans, 2010.

Arnold, Russell C. D. *The Social Role of Liturgy in the Religion of the Qumran Community*. STDJ 60. Leiden: Brill, 2006.

Butler, Judith. *Gender Trouble: Feminism and the Subversion of Identity*. New York, NY: Routledge, 1990.

Chalcraft, David, ed. *Sectarianism in Early Judaism: Sociological Advances*. London: Equinox, 2007.

Collins, John J. *Beyond the Qumran Community: The Sectarian Movement of the Dead Sea Scrolls*. Grand Rapids, MI: Eerdmans, 2010.

Feldman, Ariel, Maria Cioată, and Charlotte Hempel, eds. *Is there a Text in this Cave? Studies in the Textuality of the Dead Sea Scrolls in Honour of George J. Brooke*. STDJ 119. Leiden: Brill, 2017.

Flannery, Frances, Colleen Shantz, and Rodney A. Werline, eds. *Experientia, Volume 1: Inquiry into Religious Experience in Early Judaism and Christianity*. SBLSymS 40. Atlanta, GA: SBL, 2008.

Fraade, Steven D. *Legal Fictions: Studies of Law and Narrative in the Discursive Worlds of Ancient Jewish Sectarians and Sages*. JSJS 147. Leiden: Brill, 2011.

Grossman, Maxine L. "Cultivating Identity: Textual Virtuosity and 'Insider' Status." Pages 1–11 in *Defining Identities: We, You, and the Other in the Dead Sea Scrolls*. Edited by in Florentino García Martínez and Mladen Popović. STDJ 70. Leiden: Brill, 2008.

Harkins, Angela K. *Reading with an "I" to the Heavens: Looking at the Qumran Hodayot through the Lens of Visionary Traditions*. Ekstasis 3. Berlin: De Gruyter, 2012.

Harkins, Angela K. "Religious Experience through the Lens of Critical Spatiality: A Look at Embodiment Language in Prayers and Hymns." Pages 223–42 in *Experientia, Volume 2: Linking Text and Experience*. Edited by Colleen Shantz and Rodney A. Werline. EJL 35. Atlanta, GA: SBL, 2012.

Jaffee, Martin S. *Torah in the Mouth: Writing and Oral Tradition in Palestinian Judaism, 200 BCE–400 CE*. New York, NY: Oxford University Press, 2001.

Jokiranta, Jutta. "Social Identity in the Qumran Movement: The Case of the Penal Code." Pages 277–98 in *Explaining Christian Origins and Early Judaism: Contributions from Cognitive and Social Sciences*. Edited by Petri Luomanen, Ilkka Pyysiäinen, and Risto Uro. BibInt 89. Leiden: Brill, 2007.

Jokiranta, Jutta. *Social Identity and Sectarianism in the Qumran Movement*. STDJ 105. Leiden: Brill, 2013.

Kugler, Robert A. "Making All Experience Religious: The Hegemony of Ritual at Qumran." *JSJ* 33 (2002): 131–52.

Luomanen, Petri, Ilkka Pyysiäinen, and Risto Uro, eds. *Explaining Christian Origins and Early Judaism Contributions from Cognitive and Social Science*. BIS 89. Leiden: Brill, 2008.

Magness, Jodi. "Scrolls and Hand Impurity." Pages 89–97 in *The Dead Sea Scrolls: Texts and Context*. Edited by Charlotte Hempel. STDJ 90. Leiden: Brill, 2010.

Mermelstein, Ari. *Power and Emotion in Ancient Judaism: Community and Identity in Formation*. Cambridge: Cambridge University Press, 2021.

Metso, Sarianna. "In Search of the *Sitz im Leben* of the *Community Rule*." Pages 86–93 in *The Provo International Conference on the Dead Sea Scrolls: Technological Innovations, New Texts, and Reformulated Issues*. Edited by Donald W. Parry and Eugene Ulrich. STDJ 30. Leiden: Brill, 1998.

Newsom, Carol A. *The Self as Symbolic Space: Constructing Identity and Community at Qumran*. STDJ 52. Leiden: Brill, 2004.

Newsom, Carol A. "Religious Experience in the Dead Sea Scrolls: Two Case Studies." Pages 205–22 in *Experientia, Volume 2: Linking Text and Experience*. Edited by Colleen Shantz and Rodney A. Werline. EJL 35. Atlanta, GA: SBL, 2012.

Ogilvie, Elisabeth. *Blueberry Summer*. New York, NY: Scholastic Book Services, 1956.

Popović, Mladen. "Reading, Writing, and Memorizing Together: Reading Culture in Ancient Judaism and the Dead Sea Scrolls in a Mediterranean Context." *DSD* 24 (2017): 447–70.

Regev, Eyal. *Sectarianism in Qumran: A Cross-Cultural Perspective*. Religion and Society 45. Berlin: De Gruyter, 2007.

Schofield, Alison. *From Qumran to the* Yahad*: A New Paradigm of Textual Development for the Community Rule*. STDJ 77. Leiden: Brill, 2009.

Shantz, Colleen, and Rodney A. Werline, ed. *Experientia, Volume 2: Linking Text and Experience*. EJL 35. Atlanta, GA: SBL, 2012.

Talmon, Shemaryahu. "Oral Tradition and Written Transmission, or the Heard and the Seen Word in Judaism of the Second Temple Period." Pages 121–58 in *Jesus and the Oral Gospel Tradition*. Edited by Henry Wansbrough. JSNTSup 64. Sheffield: Sheffield Academic, 1991.

Taussig, Hal. *In the Beginning Was the Meal: Social Experimentation and Early Christian Identity*. Minneapolis, MN: Fortress, 2009.

Tov, Emanuel. *Scribal Practices and Approaches Reflected in the Texts Found in the Judean Desert*. STDJ 54. Leiden: Brill, 2004.

Tropper, Amram. *Wisdom, Politics, and Historiography: Tractate Avot in the Context of the Graeco-Roman Near East*. New York, NY: Oxford University Press, 2004.

CHAPTER 14

The Dead Sea Scrolls: A View from New Testament Studies

Chris Keith

When Tom Thatcher, Raymond Person, Jr., Elsie Stern, and I were editing the *Dictionary of the Bible and Ancient Media* (T&T Clark, 2017), we were, from the beginning of the project through to its publication and period of review, intensely aware that we were only scratching the surface of the significance of media studies for the respective fields of Hebrew Bible and ancient Judaism, Second Temple Judaism, New Testament and early Christianity, and rabbinic Judaism.[1] Before *DBAM* was published, we were already assembling a list of further entries that we might add to a second edition if we ever had the opportunity.[2] In addition to other factors, our cognizance of opportunities missed was due to the fact that the *status quaestionis* seemed to be unfolding in front of us, outpacing our attempts to corral it. Every month a new article, monograph, or collection of essays appeared on orality, textuality, literacy, illiteracy, memory, book culture, scribal culture, performance, or some other aspect of ancient Jewish and Christian media cultures. The prodigious output of scholarship was actively carving out a sizable interdisciplinary subdiscipline with the cultures of the ancient Mediterranean at its center.[3] Eventually we had to draw a line and go to press just for the sake of the publication of the volume.

Since that time, the growth of this discussion has continued unabated. The goal of the 2019 conference at the Centre for the Social-Scientific Study of the Bible (later named Centre for the Study of Judaism and Christianity in Antiquity) was to capture some of this research as it directly relates to the Qumran community and Dead Sea Scrolls. As the Centre's director at the time and one of the organizers of that conference, it is my pleasure to respond to

---

1   Tom Thatcher et al., eds., *The Dictionary of the Bible and Ancient Media* (London: Bloomsbury T&T Clark, 2017).

2   In their overview of ritual studies in this volume, DeVries and Jokiranta, "Ritual Studies," 164, are kind enough to contribute to the effort by rightly noting our omission of "ritual."

3   The vitality of this discussion is also partly responsible for my and William A. Johnson's creation of a new monograph series at Oxford University Press, the Cultures of Reading in the Ancient Mediterranean monograph series.

© CHRIS KEITH, 2023 | DOI:10.1163/9789004537804_015

THE DEAD SEA SCROLLS: A VIEW FROM NEW TESTAMENT STUDIES   473

the proceedings of the conference from the external perspective of someone whose research focuses on the New Testament and early Christianity.

1   Brief Overview of Media Criticism in New Testament Studies

To the extent that ancient media studies has played a role in the long history of New Testament scholarship, it has thus far done so predominantly in the form of reflection on the oral transmission of tradition. Scholars in various subdisciplines have observed the impact of orality and aurality in some form or another for well over a century, though these media states have typically played only supporting roles in the discussion. For example, New Testament textual critics—historically as manuscript-oriented of a subdiscipline as there is—have always acknowledged the role of errors of speaking and hearing in the production of some variants. A popular textbook notes the common confusion of sounds resulting in, for example, ἔχωμεν and ἔχομεν at Rom 5:1 or νῖκος and νεῖκος at 1 Cor 15:54.[4] Even more complex scenarios also exist, such as the occurrence of καυχήσωμαι (P[46] ℵ A B), καυθήσομαι (C D F G L), and καυθήσωμαι (K Ψ) in the manuscript tradition at 1 Cor 13:3. In positing such so-called "errors arising from faulty hearing"[5] during dictation or perhaps from a copyist reading aloud to himself as he copies, New Testament textual critics have included a role for the effects of orality in their scholarly edifice. This point needs to be stated clearly in light of the present trend of (rightly) emphasizing the thorough interaction of orality and textuality in essentially all transmission contexts in antiquity, which often takes as its starting point the so-called and now discredited "Great Divide"[6] between orality and textual-ity assumed by previous generations: although New Testament textual critics sometimes used "oral tradition" as a last-effort explanation[7] when possible written sources of readings were exhausted and infrequently reflected on it in a sustained manner, there *was* nevertheless awareness that orality and aurality impacted the transmission of early Christian tradition.

---

4   Bruce M. Metzger and Bart D. Ehrman, *The Text of the New Testament: Its Transmission, Corruption, and Restoration*, 4th ed. (New York, NY: Oxford University Press, 2005), 254–57.
5   Metzger and Ehrman, *Text*, 254.
6   Rafael Rodríguez, "Great Divide," *DBAM*, 163–64.
7   They were not alone. In roughly the same generation, P. Gardner-Smith, *Saint John and the Synoptic Gospels* (Cambridge: Cambridge University Press, 1938), throughout appealed to oral tradition without any sustained discussion of its characteristics, and mainly to keep his theory of Johannine independence in tact in the face of evidence to the contrary.

474   KEITH

Similarly, historical Jesus research has always had to contend with the so-called *agrapha*, the "unwritten" traditions about Jesus.[8] These traditions eventually were written down, but the assumption has frequently been that they circulated orally, perhaps even as some of the "many others things" that Jesus did according to John 21:25, until someone eventually recorded them in manuscripts[9] or the writings of an early church father.

Even the very earliest theories about the writing of the Gospels included a role for oral transmission. According to Eusebius's fourth-century citation of Clement of Alexandria (late second/early third century CE), Mark composed his Gospel because "the hearers" (τῶν ἀκροατῶν) of Peter's "unwritten teaching" (τῇ ἀγράφῳ διδασκαλίᾳ) in Rome were not satisfied and desired "written notes (διὰ γραφῆς ὑπόμνημα) of the teaching passed down to them."[10] Thus, in one form or another, orality and its effects have been factored into thinking about the origins of Jesus traditions from early on and in a number of discourses.

It is nevertheless also the case that orality and oral tradition did not take center stage until much later. The spotlight came, arguably, with the advent of form criticism and its antecedents, initially with Hermann Gunkel and the *religionsgeschictliche Schule* and then prominently with Martin Dibelius and Rudolf Bultmann.[11] That statement is arguable (among other reasons) because one

---

8   For overviews, see Otfried Hofius, "Außerkanonische Herrenworte," in *Antike christliche Apokryphen in deutscher Übersetzung*, eds. Christoph Markschies and Jens Schröter, 2 vols. (Tübingen: Mohr Siebeck, 2012), 1:184–89; Chris Keith, "Introduction: Jesus Outside and Inside the New Testament," in *Jesus among Friends and Enemies*, ed. Chris Keith and Larry W. Hurtado (Grand Rapids, MI: Baker Academic, 2011), 3–5; Christoph Markschies, "Außerkanonische Jesusüberlieferung," in *Antike*, 1:181–3; William D. Stroker, *Extracanonical Sayings of Jesus*, RBS 18 (Atlanta, GA: Scholars, 1989); Robert E. Van Voorst, *Jesus Outside the New Testament: An Introduction to the Ancient Evidence* (Grand Rapids, MI: Eerdmans, 2000), 179–85.

9   Some examples are prominent and well-known, such as the *pericope adulterae*, which occurs in many manuscripts at John 7:53–8:11 and elsewhere (see now Jennifer Knust and Tommy Wasserman, *To Cast the First Stone: The Transmission of a Gospel Story* [Princeton, NJ: Princeton University Press, 2019]). Others are less well-known. For example, after Matt 20:28, only Codex Bezae (D) and Codex Beratinus (Φ) have the following *agraphon*: "But seek to increase from that which is small, and to become less from that which is greater."

10   Eusebius, *Hist. eccl.* 2.15.1 (my translation). For a proposal for viewing the Gospels as ὑπομνήματα, see Matthew D. C. Larsen, *Gospels before the Book* (New York, NY: Oxford University Press, 2018), though I have argued that this proposal works better for some aspects of Gospel production in the early centuries than others in Chris Keith, *The Gospel as Manuscript: An Early History of the Jesus Tradition as Material Artifact* (New York, NY: Oxford University Press, 2020), 49–64.

11   See the undervalued study of Sang-Il Lee, *Jesus and Gospel Traditions in Bilingual Context: A Study in the Interdirectionality of Language*, BZNW 186 (Berlin: De Gruyter 2012), 1–73, but especially 2–16.

could easily question whether oral tradition, in reality, took a center-stage role. With the benefit of hindsight, these scholars' attention to the dynamics of oral tradition were embryonic, but here at least we see New Testament scholars ascribing a prominent role to it. For form critics, oral tradition was crucial because it was tantamount to the preliterary stage of transmission. Similar to Clement of Alexandria, they envisioned a tidy and unidirectional oral-to-written transmission history for the Jesus tradition. And under such a scheme, "orality" became the prized means of getting "behind" the written text and thus to an earlier stage of the community's history. Directly related to this point, for the form critics, oral tradition was less significant for any distinct media characteristics than for its usefulness in serving as the (false) division between the early, illiterate Palestinian Christianity and later, comparably more literate (though not yet fully literary) Hellenistic Christianity that produced the Gospels.[12] Oral tradition and its effects largely remained undertheorized but were nevertheless conceptually and heuristically important to form criticism.

Then came Werner Kelber. The current status of the study of orality and, to some extent, textuality, in New Testament studies is a direct result of Kelber. In his 1983 *The Oral and the Written Gospel*, Kelber gave oral tradition the theoretical attention it deserved. He enlisted, among others, the Parry-Lord school, Ruth Finnegan, Eric Havelock, and Jack Goody, and thereby brought the study of oral tradition in New Testament studies into direct interdisciplinary conversation with the relevant advances in the Humanities.[13] The book even included a Foreword from Walter J. Ong and its later republication in 1997 was in a monograph series edited by John Miles Foley. Kelber's explicit purpose was to address form criticism's failure to engage these interdisciplinary developments. His primary argument was that the transition from oral Jesus tradition to written Jesus tradition was neither logical nor inevitable, as the form critics had assumed, but cataclysmic because it forever froze the previously vibrant, living Jesus tradition into the stillness of textual death.[14] For Kelber, there

---

12   Martin Dibelius, *From Tradition to Gospel*, trans. Bertram Lee Woolf, SL 124 (New York, NY: Charles Scribner's Sons, 1934), 5, 9, 39, 234; Rudolf Bultmann, *The History of the Synoptic Tradition*, trans. John Marsh (Peabody: Hendrickson, 1963), 3, 5, and cf., e.g., his proposal for the development of the I-sayings in the respective communities on p. 163. For further discussion, see Chris Keith, *Jesus' Literacy: Scribal Culture and the Teacher from Galilee*, LHJS 8/LNTS 413 (London: T&T Clark, 2011), 32–34.

13   Werner H. Kelber, *The Oral and the Written Gospel: The Hermeneutics of Speaking and Writing in the Synoptic Tradition, Mark, Paul, and Q* (Philadelphia, PA: Fortress, 1983).

14   See especially Kelber, *Oral*, 44–139. Kelber was not the only one criticizing the form critics' tradition model. Birger Gerhardsson, *Memory and Manuscript: Oral Tradition and Written Transmission in Rabbinic Judaism and Early Christianity* with *Tradition and Transmission in Early Christianity*, Biblical Resource Series (Grand Rapids, MI: Eerdmans, 1998), originally published in 1961, similarly had as its main target form criticism's undertheorized

were important tradition-critical, socio-historical, historiographical, and even Christological and theological ramifications of this media transition.

In the roughly forty years since the publication of *The Oral and the Written Gospel*, scholars have affirmed robustly Kelber's assertion that orality was a major factor in the transmission of the Jesus tradition while disagreeing with exactly why it was a major factor, and further what impacts it had. Notably, among the critics of the early Kelber is the later Kelber, who has increasingly come to recognize that the written medium exhibited many of the characteristics of living, sprawling, culturally embedded and ever-adapting tradition that he earlier associated almost strictly with oral tradition.[15]

The post-Kelber discussion has witnessed at least four major developments, the first three of which one can trace, to one extent or another, directly to Kelber's work and responses to it, especially among scholars active in the Bible in Ancient and Modern Media SBL unit.[16] The first development within the post-Kelber discussion is the emergence of performance criticism in Biblical Studies, whose first generation of practitioners were Kelber devotees such as David Rhoads, Richard Horsley, Whitney Shiner, and Joanna Dewey.[17]

The second development of the post-Kelber discussion in New Testament studies, and one that has sometimes proceeded as a reaction to perceived excesses of the first,[18] is a greater inclusion of textuality as an intertwined,

---

notion of oral tradition. Kelber's initial response to Gerhardsson was both appreciative and critical (*Oral*, 8–13) and unfortunately repeated inaccurate portrayals of Gerhardsson by Morton Smith and Jacob Neusner, for which Neusner subsequently apologized in his Foreword to the 1998 edition of Gerhardsson's *Memory and Manuscript* (xxv–xlvi). Kelber later wrote a fuller treatment of Gerhardsson's work in Werner H. Kelber, "The Work of Birger Gerhardsson in Perspective," in *Jesus in Memory: Traditions in Oral and Scribal Perspectives*, eds. Werner H. Kelber and Samuel Byrskog (Waco, TX: Baylor University Press, 2009), 173–206. Similarly, E. P. Sanders, *The Tendencies of the Synoptic Tradition*, SNTSMS 9 (Cambridge: Cambridge University Press, 1969), was a critical response to form criticism's tradition model.

15 See especially Werner H. Kelber, "Orality and Biblical Scholarship: Seven Case Studies," in his *Imprints, Voiceprints, and Footprints of Memory: Collected Essays of Werner H. Kelber*, RBS 74 (Atlanta, GA: SBL, 2013), 297–331, and "The History of the Closure of Biblical Texts," in *Imprints*, 413–40. Influential on Kelber in this regard, among other studies, was David C. Parker, *The Living Text of the Gospels* (Cambridge: Cambridge University Press, 1997).

16 Thomas E. Boomershine, "Bible in Ancient and Modern Media Research Unit (Society of Biblical Literature)," in *DBAM*, 36–40. See also the helpful survey in Holly E. Hearon, "The Implications of Orality for Studies of the Biblical Text," in *Performing the Gospel: Orality, Memory, and Mark*, eds. Richard A. Horsley, Jonathan A. Draper, and John Miles Foley (Minneapolis, MN: Fortress, 2006), 3–20.

17 David Rhoads, "Performance Criticism (Biblical)," in *DBAM*, 281–89.

18 Cf. Larry W. Hurtado, "Oral Fixation and New Testament Studies? 'Orality', 'Performance' and Reading Texts in Early Christianity," *NTS* 60 (2014): 321–40; Dan Nässelqvist, *Public*

THE DEAD SEA SCROLLS: A VIEW FROM NEW TESTAMENT STUDIES 477

interpenetrating, ever-present factor in the oral media environment of Second Temple Judaism and the early Jesus movement. Scholars now recognize that there was never a purely oral Jesus movement nor a purely textual one. Completely illiterate followers of Jesus came in contact with writing on contracts, coinage, and signage; and it was normal for specially-educated artisan scribes capable of compositional literacy or even calligraphy to read aloud to themselves and others, re-oralizing the writing before them. Thus, illiterates interacted with written tradition and literates interacted with oral tradition because both forms of media—as well as other forms such as ritual, visual, and monumental—were common features even in a culture where literacy was relatively low.[19] Scholars have therefore refined their approaches to account, for example, for the *interaction* of orality and textuality or, more practically, the places of books and written tradition *within* largely oral environments. Examples of greater nuance are Elder's forwarding of a "mixed-media approach"[20] and Rodríguez's helpful suggestion that scholars think of orality as a *characteristic* of the culture of Jesus and his earliest followers rather than as an *ontic reality* with traceable boundaries concerning what it is and is not.[21]

The third post-Kelber development has been the emergence of memory approaches. The flow of applications of one of several memory theories to New Testament studies has origins in several tributaries,[22] but at least one tributary has been scholars who saw in social memory theory a tradition model that included and expanded upon what they had been trying to model with cultural-anthropological studies of orality. Kelber himself was an early influence in this regard[23] and the first full application of social memory theory to New Testament studies in English—Kirk and Thatcher's 2005 *Semeia*—was a product of the Mapping Memory Consultation, which formed out of and

---

    Reading in Early Christianity: Lectors, Manuscripts, and Sound in the Oral Delivery of John 1–4, NovTSup 163 (Leiden: Brill, 163), esp. 2–16.

19   On kinds and levels of literate status, see further Keith, *Jesus' Literacy*, 71–123.

20   Nicholas A. Elder, *The Media Matrix of Early Jewish and Christian Narrative*, LNTS 612 (London: T&T Clark, 2019).

21   Rafael Rodríguez, *Oral Tradition and the New Testament: A Guide for the Perplexed* (London: T&T Clark, 2014).

22   Chris Keith, "Social Memory Theory and Gospels Research: The First Decade (Part One)," *Early Christianity* 6.3 (2015): 354–76; "Social Memory Theory and Gospels Research: The First Decade (Part Two)," *Early Christianity* 6.4 (2015): 517–42.

23   Inter alia, Werner H. Kelber, "Language, Memory, and Sense Perception in the Religious and Technological Culture of Antiquity and the Middle Ages," in *Imprints*, 103–32; "Memory's Desire or the Ordeal of Remembering: Judaism and Christianity," in *Imprints*, 187–215.

eventually was absorbed back into the Bible in Ancient and Modern Media SBL unit.[24] At least in English-speaking New Testament scholarship, scholars who were already paying attention to oral tradition were the first who started paying attention to memory in a sustained manner.[25]

The fourth relevant post-Kelber development has been the integration of the study of manuscripts and material culture into media studies. Although this development is arguably a variant of the second development noted above—the full integration of textuality and orality in the scholarly apparatus—the impetus for this fourth development came more strongly from New Testament textual critics and scholars of book culture. In a 2013 essay on "The Social History of Early Christian Scribes," Haines-Eitzen refers to this development as "the material turn" in "the study of early Christianity" and describes it as "a renewed interest in the physical features of our earliest Christian scribes and readers, about Christian ideologies of text and their interpretation, and how books intersected with religious identity."[26] Resembling and, to a great degree, running parallel to, the application of the so-called "new philology" in Biblical Studies, this specific trend in studies of early Christianity tends also to stem from scholars who were applying William A. Johnson's sociology of ancient reading cultures to the Jesus movement.[27]

The post-Kelber state of media studies among scholars of the New Testament and early Christianity has therefore witnessed a heightened attention to the complexity of the ancient media environment, the social settings in which

---

24   Alan Kirk and Tom Thatcher, eds., *Memory, Tradition, and Text: Uses of the Past in Early Christianity*, SemSt 52 (Atlanta, GA: SBL, 2005). The application of cultural memory theory to the New Testament was well underway in Germany by this time in the 1990s scholarship of Cilliers Breytenbach and Jens Schröter (Keith, "Social Memory Theory and Gospels Research [Part One]," 355–6).

25   This point seems true also for James D. G. Dunn, whose massive *Jesus Remembered*, Christianity in the Making 1 (Grand Rapids, MI: Eerdmans, 2003), foregrounds memory in the title but, as many reviewers have noted, analyzes the Jesus tradition on the basis of orality studies rather than memory studies. See further James D. G. Dunn, *The Oral Gospel Tradition* (Grand Rapids, MI: Eerdmans, 2013).

26   Kim Haines-Eitzen, "The Social History of Early Christian Scribes," in *The Text of the New Testament in Contemporary Research: Essays on the Status Quaestionis*, eds. Bart D. Ehrman and Michael W. Holmes, 2nd ed., NTTSD 42 (Leiden: Brill, 2013), 486.

27   Haines-Eitzen, "Social," 479, cites Johnson on the first page of her essay alongside others. For others, see those listed in Keith, *Gospel*, 18 n. 1. Cf., however, Christoph Markschies, "What Ancient Christian Manuscripts Reveal about Reading (and About Non-Reading)," in *Material Aspects of Reading in Ancient and Medieval Cultures: Materiality, Presence and Performance*, ed. Anna Krauß, Jonas Leipziger and Friederike Schücking-Jungblut, Materiale Textkulturen 26 (Berlin: De Gruyter, 2020), 197–215, who takes a similar approach with no mention of Johnson's work.

THE DEAD SEA SCROLLS: A VIEW FROM NEW TESTAMENT STUDIES

tradition was actualized, and the place of material culture within those various actualizations.

2 Engaging the Scrolls

Although one could write the history of media criticism in New Testament studies from a variety of other perspectives and include other aspects, such as literacy studies or cultural anthropology, these four developments—performance criticism, textuality, memory, and materiality—are notable because they appear prominently in the essays in this volume on the Dead Sea Scrolls.

The masterful overviews of orality and textuality in Scrolls scholarship by Miller, Williams, and Brooke, as well as the Introduction by Williams strongly attest the growing trend of positing a full integration of oral tradition and written tradition, and rightly so. Each understands orality as something that must be conceptualized in tandem with manuscripts and vice versa. Miller correctly refers to the *yaḥad* as "an oral-textual community." He positions this claim as an instance of Scrolls scholarship catching up to theories already prevalent in Hebrew Bible and New Testament scholarship, but one could equally shift the viewpoint to say that Scrolls scholarship has given us further, and concrete, illustrations of Second Temple transmission practices that augment prior theorizations.

An interesting irony involving 1QS 6, which features throughout the essays in this volume, illustrates the complexity of the discussion concerning how scholars envision the interaction or orality and textuality. Miller cites the description of the community's activities in 1QS 5 and 6, including the public reading of the law in the latter, in order to demonstrate the prominent, even authoritative, role of oral performance and discussion in the community. Miller is concerned to demonstrate that dismissals of oral authority are inappropriate. I have otherwise appealed to 1QS 6 in order to argue that purely oral conceptions of what is portrayed as happening particularly at 1QS 6:7 with the phrase לקרוא בספר, and even more specifically the interpretations of this phrase as recitation *sans* manuscript by Jaffee and Horsley, underappreciate the fact that "reading" at Qumran, whatever else it might entail, involved manuscripts.[28] (That is not to say that "recitation" is never a possible meaning

---

28   Keith, *Gospel*, 167. See Martin S. Jaffee, *Torah in the Mouth: Writing and Oral Tradition in Palestinian Judaism, 200 BCE–400 CE* (New York, NY: Oxford University Press, 2001). Horsley advances this understanding in multiple publications; as an example, see Richard

for קרא,[29] only that it is not here.) Miller wishes to retain the oral dynamics of what is portrayed in this text in the face of those who wish to emphasize writtenness to the exclusion of orality; I wish to emphasize the textual and material dynamics of what is portrayed in this text in the face of those who wish to emphasize orality to the exclusion of writtenness. As far as I can tell, we are both correct. Brooke had earlier wisely held these dynamics in appropriate tension: "Reading seems to be more than recitation from text or memory; it seems to involve comprehension and even some kind of active engagement with the text as it was performed."[30] My point presently in drawing attention to these different, though complementary, perspectives is simply to reiterate that scholars are increasingly recognizing the thoroughly intertwined nature of orality and textuality in the media environments of Qumran and the rest of antiquity.

In addition to Miller's and Brooke's essays, Hartog's study of 4Q169 raises the possibility of the performative reading of manuscripts. He posits that this manuscript could have emerged from oral study sessions and been the possession of a traveling pedagogue. Hartog's careful study answers for me a question that Brooke's overview implicitly raises. Brooke presents where the discussion has been, where it is, and where it will go, but I wonder also about how exactly we measure progress. To state the matter another way, we have become exceedingly accomplished at demonstrating that the media cultures of antiquity were more complex than our scholarly forebears acknowledged, but less accomplished at explaining how this demonstration offers us greater clarity in concrete ways on particular instantiations of tradition. I cite an example from my world of New Testament studies. Previous media critics of the Gospel of Mark have sought to demonstrate its prior existence as oral tradition by identifying supposedly residual oral psychodynamics within its narrative. Rodríguez has detailed Joanna Dewey's prior treatment of *inclusio* in Mark's Gospel in this regard, and has drawn attention to the inevitable result of attempting to identify something as a *particularly* oral characteristic on the basis of its occurrence in an unquestionably *written* source: "The very fact that these written features work perfectly well in oral narratives as well as in written narratives

---

S. Horsley, *Scribes, Visionaries, and the Politics of Second Temple Judaism* (Louisville, KY: Westminster John Knox, 2007).

29 Rebecca Sharbach Wollenberg, "The Dangers of Reading as We Know It: Sight Reading as a Source of Heresy in Early Rabbinic Traditions," *JAAR* 85 (2019): 709–45.

30 George Brooke, "Reading, Searching and Blessing: A Functional Approach to Scriptural Interpretation in the יחד," in *The Temple in Text and Tradition: A Festschrift in Honour of Robert Hayward*, ed. R. Timothy McLay, LSTS 82 (London: Bloomsbury T&T Clark, 2015), 29.

THE DEAD SEA SCROLLS: A VIEW FROM NEW TESTAMENT STUDIES   481

reveals the absurdity of calling them *oral* features in any restrictive sense. The features themselves are neither necessarily oral nor necessarily written. They are features of both oral and written narratives."[31]

Acknowledgement of complexity is admittedly a form of clarity and progress. It nevertheless remains the case that successfully arguing that "orality" and "textuality" should be conceptualized as, for example, a spectrum of overlapping and interpenetrating characteristics rather than neatly juxtaposed things-in-themselves, is different than showing where on that theoretical spectrum a particular performance, text, proclamation, etc., dwells, *and furthermore how we even know that and what significance it has*. The task before us now is to figure out how to move beyond the discussion stalling out at descriptions of complexity before we resort to finding the most scholarly ways possible to say "It could be either" in response to questions about particular traditions. I get the impression sometimes that we—and I certainly indict myself here—know that we are asking the wrong questions but continue to do so because we do not yet know which other ones to ask.

Much work in this vein undoubtedly remains, but Hartog has provided a case study for at least one way that progress can be profitably made. He incorporates the latest advances in media criticism with detailed attention to manuscript features, situating his study as a contribution to the "new philology." Most important, Hartog deploys concrete information on 4Q169 as a material artifact, such as its column measurements, margin size, handwriting characteristics, or treatment of the divine name, within a plausible scenario with exactly the right amount of historical imagination. He imaginatively reconstructs the reading culture(s) around 4Q169 in light of its material characteristics.

Similarly mining manuscripts' material features for information, Popović's essay interrogates the Isaiah and Serekh scrolls for what they can tell us about the users of the tradition, and more specifically the likely person or persons for whom the specific manuscripts were copied. Popović's research will be immensely useful for future scrolls scholars if for no other reason than its provision of an inaugural, and comprehensive, handwriting analysis of these two groups of manuscripts. Popović has previously led the field in applying William Johnson's work to the manuscripts of Qumran, and here he continues by employing the three categories of handwriting analysis that Johnson developed for Oxyrhynchus manuscripts—deluxe, everyday professional, and substandard. He concludes that many of these manuscripts were likely made for the personal usage of the scribes who copied them. Beyond this contribution, however, Popović also argues in an excursus, and on the basis of handwriting

---

31   Rodríguez, *Oral*, 63–64.

analysis, against the theory that the scribe of 1QS was responsible for insertions in 1QIsaᵃ.

Stepping back from the arguments of Hartog and Popović, as well as Taylor (see immediately below), I am struck at how this new work at the intersection of media studies and manuscript studies reveals the degree to which the field has left behind one of the more significant developments in the humanities over the past fifty years, namely poststructuralism's "death of the author" movement. Without overstating the evidence and while also holding in tension the variety of historical scenarios that are possible, these scholars replace agnosticism about authorial circumstances with scholarly trained historical imagination, boldly and convincingly showing that we can know quite a bit about the authors, or at least copyists, of these manuscripts based on the material artifacts they left behind. May their tribe increase.

Another example of exacting attention to detail combined with historical imagination leading to a plausible historical reconstruction is Taylor's impressive essay on 3Q15, the so-called Copper Scroll. Similar to Hartog's discussion of 4Q169, Taylor dwells at length on the material characteristics of 3Q15, to the extent that this essay would function well as an assigned introduction to this artifact. Taylor shows that, although metal scrolls are not entirely unheard of in antiquity, 3Q15 is unquestionably a rare and curious artifact in Palestinian Judaism. Taylor observes how the writing surface and act of rolling it indicates that it was perhaps not meant to be read, or at least not by many—"once rolled," she says, "that was it".[32] A heating process was required to unroll the scroll, so if there was an imagined audience, it was severely restricted to some kind of blacksmith-scribe artisans capable of accomplishing such a task. Her conception of the audience thus stems directly from her assessment of the realia, and in this way we once again witness the material characteristics enabling imaginative reconstructions of possible reading communities. Taylor also engages the evidence concerning the physical environs of cave 3 and its archaeological stages, carefully proposing a scenario in which 3Q15 was deposited later into cave 3Q, after 68 CE and after which the ceiling collapsed. The result is an enriching essay that takes the reader into the chronological, geographical, and archaeological surroundings of this distinct piece of written material.

With the essays by DeVries and Jokiranta, Jokiranta, and Wassén, the concept of a "reading community" gains specificity in ways similar to, yet also beyond, what Johnson does in his studies on the elite Roman readers of the high empire. These essays, the first of which introduces ritual theory(ies) and their application thus far in Scrolls scholarship, the second of which addresses

---

32 Taylor, "The Copper Scrolls," 307.

the ritual mediation of transmission in Qumran, and the third of which addresses meal contexts as points of transmission, indicate to me, one of the most promising lines of future research in Jewish and Christian book cultures of antiquity. Although one could cite many contributions from these essays, two in particular stand above the others as prospects for even further research. The first, which is demonstrated by DeVries and Jokiranta's introductory essay, is how ritual functions as a language in and of itself. Similar to its verbal counterpart, ritual language has a grammar all its own and carries tradition of its own. The second, strongly related contribution, stems from this observation, and concerns the fact that ritual is *embodied* language. Jokiranta emphasizes this point, but equally Wassén's essay, which demonstrates how commensality was a central context for tradition transmission in the *yaḥad*, during which social order, etc., was manifested, forces us to acknowledge the imagined role of human actors in these rituals. Their observations once more underscore the important role of scholarly trained historical imagination as we confront the limits of what we can know, but also have an awareness of unknown matters.

Finally, I address Hempel's important essay on the curation of ancient and modern communities, which has some overlaps with recent discussion of "memory" in historical Jesus studies.[33] Hempel's discussion is strongly reminiscent of the impact of media studies on historical Jesus research. Indeed, to my knowledge the most substantial discussion of the concept of "refraction" of the past, to which her subtitle alludes, is Anthony Le Donne's seminal contribution to the memory discussion in *The Historiographical Jesus*.[34] Furthermore, I have used the phrase "the new historiography" to describe a recent shift in Gospels studies,[35] just as Hempel uses the phrase here to describe Maxine Grossman's approach to the Damascus Document.[36] These similarities of jargon are not deliberate replications, but neither are they unrelated; I think they can be understood as attempts in two different, though related, subdisciplines in Jewish and Mediterranean studies to describe a cresting wave of change in how scholars understand the past and how we study it. In both domains, there has been an increasing loss of confidence in scholarly abilities to delineate neatly between "myth" and "history."

---

33   For an earlier, thorough, engagement of memory studies in Scrolls scholarship, see Travis B. Williams, *History and Memory in the Dead Sea Scrolls: Remembering the Teacher of Righteousness* (Cambridge: Cambridge University Press, 2019).

34   Anthony Le Donne, *The Historiographical Jesus: Memory, Typology, and the Son of David* (Waco, TX: Baylor University Press, 2009), 13–14, 50–59.

35   Keith, "Social Memory Theory and Gospels Research: The First Decade (Part Two)," 527–9.

36   Hempel, "Curated Communities," 341. See Maxine L. Grossman, *Reading for History in the Damascus Document: A Methodological Study*, STDJ 45 (Leiden: Brill, 2002).

There is little in Hempel's careful essay with which I could disagree or improve. Her approach to curation is distinct and a welcomed nuance. Drawing on Erving Goffman's work and its applications in current studies of social media, Hempel reminds us that even "reality" is a curated reality. We already have an implicit understanding of these dynamics in contemporary life. Few of us, for example, need to be told that "reality" television is not "reality" but a carefully crafted version of it that may or may not have any resemblance to what we accept as reality. And while many scholars in the fields of Second Temple Judaism and Early Christianity readily acknowledge that our ancient texts do not easily yield the "reality" of the ancient actors portrayed in them, Hempel reminds us further of *the degree to which that fact is true*. Commendably, however, Hempel does not swing the pendulum and declare that such a state of affairs renders historical enquiry impossible. Rather, she notes that the ancient curation was happening at the moment of textual inception, as ancient scribes were already busy making a bid for their texts within the "ancient Jewish literary landscape." To merge her insights with similar recent insights in historical Jesus research, we could perhaps observe that historical enquiry must start with this fundamental insight into the hermeneutical nature of historiographical activity and assessment of that activity, though it need not cease there. Or, in the helpful words of Ruben Zimmermann, "Es gibt keine Historie jenseits des Textes. Aber es gibt Historie durch den Text und als Text."[37] Hempel reminds us similarly that all texts are curated texts.

3 Conclusion

I have learned immensely from these essays. In my capacity as an interested observer from a related, nevertheless external, field of study, I have focused here upon points of confluence and promise. One thing that these contributions, and the conference that preceded them, has confirmed is that we editors of *DBAM* were right in feeling that our work at the time was offering only a glimpse of the blossoming discourse on ancient media culture as it relates to the fields of Biblical Studies.

---

37   Ruben Zimmermann, "Geschichtstheorien und Neues Testament: Gedächtnis, Diskurs, Kultur und Narration in der historiographischen Diskussion," *Early Christianity* 2 (2011): 440.

Bibliography

Boomershine, Thomas E. "Bible in Ancient and Modern Media Research Unit (Society of Biblical Literature)." Pages 36–40 in *The Dictionary of the Bible and Ancient Media*. Edited by Tom Thatcher, Chris Keith, Raymond F. Person, Jr., and Elsie R. Stern. London: Bloomsbury, 2017.

Brooke, George J. "Reading, Searching and Blessing: A Functional Approach to Scriptural Interpretation in the יחד." Pages 140–56 in *The Temple in Text and Tradition: A Festschrift in Honour of Robert Hayward*. Edited by R. Timothy McLay. LSTS 83. London: Bloomsbury, 2015.

Bultmann, Rudolf. *The History of the Synoptic Tradition*. Translated by John Marsh. Peabody: Hendrickson, 1963.

Dibelius, Martin. *From Tradition to Gospel*. Translated by Bertram Lee Woolf. SL 124. New York, NY: Charles Scribner's Sons, 1934.

Dunn, James D. G. *Jesus Remembered*. Christianity in the Making 1. Grand Rapids, MI: Eerdmans, 2003.

Dunn, James D. G. *The Oral Gospel Tradition*. Grand Rapids, MI: Eerdmans, 2013.

Elder, Nicholas A. *The Media Matrix of Early Jewish and Christian Narrative*. LNTS 612. London: T&T Clark, 2019.

Gardner-Smith, P. *Saint John and the Synoptic Gospels*. Cambridge: Cambridge University Press, 1938.

Gerhardsson, Birger. *Memory and Manuscript: Oral Tradition and Written Transmission in Rabbinic Judaism and Early Christianity*. Translated by Eric J. Sharpe. ASNU 22. Lund: C. W. K. Gleerup, 1961.

Grossman, Maxine L. *Reading for History in the Damascus Document: A Methodological Study*. STDJ 45. Leiden: Brill, 2002.

Haines-Eitzen, Kim. "The Social History of Early Christian Scribes." Pages 479–95 in *The Text of the New Testament in Contemporary Research: Essays on the Status Quaestionis*. Edited by Bart D. Ehrman and Michael W. Holmes. 2nd ed. NTTSD 42. Leiden: Brill, 2013.

Hearon, Holly E. "The Implications of Orality for Studies of the Biblical Text." Pages 3–20 in *Performing the Gospel: Orality, Memory, and Mark*. Edited by Richard A. Horsley, Jonathan A. Draper, and John Miles Foley. Minneapolis, MN: Fortress, 2006.

Hofius, Otfried. "Außerkanonische Herrenworte." Pages 184–89 in *Antike christliche Apokryphen in deutscher Übersetzung*. Band 1: *Evangelien und Verwandtes*. Edited by Christoph Markschies and Jens Schröter. Tübingen: Mohr Siebeck, 2012.

Horsley, Richard A. *Scribes, Visionaries, and the Politics of Second Temple Judaism*. Louisville, KY: Westminster John Knox, 2007.

Hurtado, Larry W. "Oral Fixation and New Testament Studies? 'Orality', 'Performance' and Reading Texts in Early Christianity." NTS 60 (2014): 321–40.

Jaffee, Martin S. *Torah in the Mouth: Writing and Oral Tradition in Palestinian Judaism, 200 BCE–400 CE*. Oxford: Oxford University Press, 2001.

Keith, Chris. "Introduction: Jesus Outside and Inside the New Testament." Pages 3–5 in *Jesus among Friends and Enemies*. Edited by Chris Keith and Larry W. Hurtado. Grand Rapids, MI: Baker Academic, 2011.

Keith, Chris. *Jesus' Literacy: Scribal Culture and the Teacher from Galilee*. LNTS 413. London: Bloomsbury, 2011.

Keith, Chris. "Social Memory Theory and Gospels Research: The First Decade." *Early Christianity* 6 (2015): 354–76 (Part One), 517–42 (Part Two).

Keith, Chris. *Gospel as Manuscript: An Early History of the Jesus Tradition as Material Artifact*. New York, NY: Oxford University Press, 2020.

Kelber, Werner H. *The Oral and the Written Gospel: The Hermeneutics of Speaking and Writing in the Synoptic Tradition, Mark, Paul, and Q*. Philadelphia, PA: Fortress, 1983.

Kelber, Werner H. "The Work of Birger Gerhardsson in Perspective." Pages 173–206 in *Jesus in Memory: Traditions in Oral and Scribal Perspectives*. Edited by Werner H. Kelber and Samuel Byrskog. Waco, TX: Baylor University Press, 2009.

Kelber, Werner H. *Imprints, Voiceprints, and Footprints of Memory: Collected Essays of Werner H. Kelber*. RBS 74. Atlanta, GA: SBL, 2013.

Kelber, Werner H. "Language, Memory, and Sense Perception in the Religious and Technological Culture of Antiquity and the Middle Ages." Pages 103–32 in idem, *Imprints, Voiceprints, and Footprints of Memory: Collected Essays of Werner H. Kelber*. RBS 74. Atlanta, GA: SBL, 2013.

Kelber, Werner H. "Memory's Desire or the Ordeal of Remembering: Judaism and Christianity." Pages 187–215 in idem, *Imprints, Voiceprints, and Footprints of Memory: Collected Essays of Werner H. Kelber*. RBS 74. Atlanta, GA: SBL, 2013.

Kelber, Werner H. "Orality and Biblical Scholarship: Seven Case Studies." Pages 297–331 in idem, *Imprints, Voiceprints, and Footprints of Memory: Collected Essays of Werner H. Kelber*. RBS 74. Atlanta, GA: SBL, 2013.

Kelber, Werner H. "The History of the Closure of Biblical Texts." Pages 413–40 in idem, *Imprints, Voiceprints, and Footprints of Memory: Collected Essays of Werner H. Kelber*. RBS 74. Atlanta, GA: SBL, 2013.

Kirk, Alan, and Tom Thatcher, eds. *Memory, Tradition, and Text: Uses of the Past in Early Christianity*. SemeiaSt 52. Atlanta, GA: SBL, 2005.

Knust, Jennifer, and Tommy Wasserman. *To Cast the First Stone: The Transmission of a Gospel Story*. Princeton, NJ: Princeton University Press, 2019.

Larsen, Matthew D. C. *Gospels before the Book*. New York, NY: Oxford University Press, 2018.

Le Donne, Anthony. *The Historiographical Jesus: Memory, Typology, and the Son of David*. Waco, TX: Baylor University Press, 2009.

Lee, Sang-Il. *Jesus and Gospel Traditions in Bilingual Context: A Study in the Interdirectionality of Language.* BZNW 186. Berlin: De Gruyter, 2012.

Markschies, Christoph. "Außerkanonische Jesusüberlieferung." Pages 181–83 in *Antike christliche Apokryphen in deutscher Übersetzung.* Band 1: *Evangelien und Verwandtes.* Edited by Christoph Markschies and Jens Schröter. Tübingen: Mohr Siebeck, 2012.

Markschies, Christoph. "What Ancient Christian Manuscripts Reveal About Reading (and About Non-Reading)." Pages 197–216 in *Material Aspects of Reading in Ancient and Medieval Cultures: Materiality, Presence and Performance.* Edited by Anna Krauß, Jonas Leipziger and Friederike Schücking-Jungblut. Materiale Textkulturen 26. Berlin: De Gruyter, 2020.

Metzger, Bruce M., and Bart D. Ehrman. *The Text of the New Testament: Its Transmission, Corruption, and Restoration.* 4th ed. New York, NY: Oxford University Press, 2005.

Nässelqvist, Dan. *Public Reading in Early Christianity: Lectors, Manuscripts, and Sound in the Oral Delivery of John 1–4.* NovTSup 163. Leiden: Brill, 2016.

Parker, David C. *The Living Text of the Gospels.* Cambridge: Cambridge University Press, 1997.

Rhoads, David. "Performance Criticism (Biblical)." Pages 281–89 in *The Dictionary of the Bible and Ancient Media.* Edited by Tom Thatcher, Chris Keith, Raymond F. Person, Jr., and Elsie R. Stern. London: Bloomsbury, 2017.

Rodríguez, Rafael. *Oral Tradition and the New Testament: A Guide for the Perplexed.* London: Bloomsbury, 2014.

Rodríguez, Rafael. "Great Divide." Pages 163–64 in *The Dictionary of the Bible and Ancient Media.* Edited by Tom Thatcher, Chris Keith, Raymond F. Person, Jr., and Elsie R. Stern. London: Bloomsbury, 2017.

Sanders, E. P. *The Tendencies of the Synoptic Tradition.* SNTSMS 9. Cambridge: Cambridge University Press, 1969.

Stroker, William D. *Extracanonical Sayings of Jesus.* RBS 18. Atlanta, GA: Scholars, 1989.

Thatcher, Tom, Chris Keith, Raymond F. Person, Jr., and Elise R. Stern, eds. *The Dictionary of the Bible and Ancient Media.* London: Bloomsbury T&T Clark, 2017.

Voorst, Robert E. van. *Jesus Outside the New Testament: An Introduction to the Ancient Evidence.* Grand Rapids, MI: Eerdmans, 2000.

Williams, Travis B. *History and Memory in the Dead Sea Scrolls: Remembering the Teacher of Righteousness.* Cambridge: Cambridge University Press, 2019.

Wollenberg, Rebecca Sharbach. "The Dangers of Reading as We Know It: Sight Reading as a Source of Heresy in Early Rabbinic Traditions." *JAAR* 85 (2019): 709–45.

Zimmermann, Reuben. "Geschichtstheorien und Neues Testament: Gedächtnis, Diskurs, Kultur und Narration in der historiographischen Diskussion." *Early Christianity* 2 (2011): 417–44.

CHAPTER 15

The Dead Sea Scrolls: A Classicist's View

William A. Johnson

1 The Reading Community

1.1 *Tribal Exoticism*

Book 5 of Pliny the Elder's *Natural History* contains a description of the geography and tribes of north Africa, moving from the northeast coast of Africa (present-day Morocco) to Egypt and then to the eastern Mediterranean, taking in the Roman province of Syria Palestina along the way. In his three geographical books (Books 4–6) Pliny only rarely adds to his account of the landscape and towns anything beyond the names of peoples (the *gens*, or "tribe," as we will translate), and, when he does, his focus is on exotic people in remote areas. In Book 5 at Chapter 45 he summarizes the Ethiopic tribes who live far off in the desert: the Atlas tribe who do not use names and curse the rising and setting of the sun; the Cave-Dwellers, a tribe that eats only snakes and speaks by making squeaking sounds; another tribe that does not practice marriage but shares women promiscuously; one where the people go naked and do not engage in battle; finally and most remotely, a tribe without heads, with mouths and eyes attached to their chests, and another with feet like leather thongs whose nature is to crawl rather than to walk.[1] These details at Chapter 45 constitute Pliny's lone excursus on remote peoples in the 151 chapters of Book 5—aside from his spectacular account of the Essenes at chapter 73.

Despite its familiarity, it is worthwhile to pause for a moment not only to consider the context but also to review both the details and rhetoric that Pliny deploys.[2] We hear there of the tribe of the Essenes—"marvelous beyond all the tribes of the earth!" Pliny says—who renounce all sexual desire and have

---

1 These rare tribal accounts vary in the type and degree of exoticism: in Book 6, for example, in his account of the tribes around and above Scythia, Pliny omits most of the exotic details reported about these peoples in Herodotus. His motivation then is not simply the presentation of exoticism.

2 For a detailed analysis of the passage from Pliny see also Joan E. Taylor, *The Essenes, the Scrolls, and the Dead Sea* (Oxford: Oxford University Press, 2012), 131–40, who however focuses on how Pliny's depiction creates an "exaggerated caricature, with only some very superficial correlations with Josephus and Philo" (133), that is, she examines Pliny more for reliability as a source in comparison with other sources than on his own terms.

© WILLIAM A. JOHNSON, 2023 | DOI:10.1163/9789004537804_016

THE DEAD SEA SCROLLS: A CLASSICIST'S VIEW 489

among them only men, no women, have no money, and have "palm trees as their (sole) companions." Yet, Pliny tells us, the tribe is able to maintain steady numbers by a constant influx of refugees "weary of life and the vicissitudes of fortune" who come to the Essenes' remote location and adopt their ways. Thus, through a thousand ages—"incredible as it is to say!" (*incredibile dictu!*)—a tribe into which no one is born lives on forever, as other men's fatigue with life provides the fertility necessary to maintain continuity (*gens aeterna est in qua nemo nascitur, tam fecunda illis aliorum vitae paenitentia est*). Pliny places that remote location roughly near the west coast of the Dead Sea above the fortress of Masada and the *wadi* of Engada (Ein Gedi), that is, at the northwestern edge. This, of course, is the basis for the identification of Qumran with the Essene community.

Also well-known is the long and more sympathetic account of the Essenes in Josephus (*War* 2.120–161, cf. *Ant.* 18.11, 18–22), whose account supports the idea of a closed-off, ascetic, and celibate Jewish community who share property in common. In Josephus, however, the Essenes are not refugees who have removed themselves to the desert but are communities settled "in large numbers in every town" and who maintain their numbers by initiating new members—proselytizing, that is—and bringing up the orphaned children of others, training all to the strict, reverent ways that characterize this community. Their strict piety and purity and communal living is also emphasized by Philo (*Prob.* 75–88, cf. *Hypoth.* 11), which seems to have been one of the sources for Josephus.[3]

As historians, we are trained to regard elements of these accounts with appropriate caution, whether we focus on the "thousand ages" mentioned by Pliny, or on Josephus's report that "most" Essenes live to be close to one hundred years old (*War* 2.151) or that they boast fortune-tellers who "seldom if ever err" in their predictions (159). But we also use these reports, almost the only information we have, to frame the ways that we think, to connect the dots and to try to construct history. That quite natural impulse has led more than a generation of scholars to attach the Dead Sea Scrolls, be it loosely or tightly, to the "Qumran community" and/or to an Essene or Essene-like sect. The Pliny passage is used as the link that ties together the archaeological site with the Essenes; from Josephus the studiousness of the community is pointed

---

3 Philo, however, has the Essenes residing in villages only, avoiding the cities. For a magisterial review of the current state of the question for the "Essene Hypothesis," see Jonathan Klawans, "The Essene Hypothesis: Insights from Religion 101," *DSD* 23 (2016): 51–78. For detailed analysis of the reports in Philo and Josephus, see Chapters 2 and 3 in Taylor, *The Essenes, the Scrolls.* Taylor also argues (in Chapter 6) that a report in Synesius of a remark in Dio Chrysostom is an additional, independent source for the link between Essenes and the Dead Sea.

to, though more often the focus is on the special reverence for Moses (145) or the "books of the sect" (142) or the "holy books" (159)[4] than on the medicinal and magical books that Josephus particularly highlights (136).[5]

It is not my purpose, nor do I have the requisite expertise, to comment on the advantages and disadvantages, solutions and problems, afforded by the various forms of the Essene narrative. But that it *is* a narrative, a framing construct, is important, since the way things are framed has so large an impact on the way the dots are connected and the history that is written. This is obvious, but I start exactly here in order to highlight an aspect of that narrative that is not often enough remarked. From the point of view of a Greek, or a Roman, the behaviors described are very strange. That a group of men would declare celibacy, renounce women, seclude themselves—whether off in the desert or not—and live a strict regimen according to an elaborate set of seemingly arbitrary rules is almost entirely without analogue in Greco-Roman society.[6] The voice of Pliny in the passage cited is one describing a hard-to-believe marvel: people who are fantastically weird.[7] This is not a neutral report. Modern buy-in to the Essene narrative, which seems still quietly to lurk beneath more cautious phrases like the "Qumran movement," runs then in three directions. (1) It creates a frame that delimits the ways that the data are analyzed. One wonders how differently these manuscripts might be viewed if the Pliny passage did not exist, and it is provocative to reflect upon the assumptions made by scholars of Asia as they speculate about the mysterious Cave Library among the Mogao caves complex in Dunhuang, China, a site with intriguing parallels.[8] But there is also another direction. (2) The Essene narrative also

---

4   "Books of the sect" comes up in a general description of the group; "holy books," however, is not a general remark, but occurs in the context of the members who claim the ability to tell the future.

5   "They display an extraordinary interest in the writings of the ancients, singling out in particular those which make for the welfare of soul and body; with the help of these, and with a view to the treatment of diseases, they make investigations into medicinal roots and the properties of stones [i.e. amulets]."

6   As often noted, extreme Pythagoreans form something of an analogue, though it is weak. Another exceptionally weird group are the priests of Cybele, who self-castrate and thereby maintain celibacy. But in general the Essenes as presented in Pliny (or Philo/Josephus) exhibit behaviors that will have seemed very exotic to a Roman or Greek.

7   The same word is chosen by Taylor, *The Essenes, the Scrolls*, 136; she with justice cites the habit of collecting marvels in antiquity (*mirabilia* literature: 133–34), and declares the Pliny account a "paradox" (133: rightly) and a "parody" (139: misleadingly, in my view).

8   The objects in the sealed cave, mostly scrolls, are said to number close to 50,000; and described as five cubic meters of materials. Speculation on the nature of the collection and the reason for the sealing of the cave range widely, and are all problematic because of the variety to the contents. Three prominent possibilities are: (1) a monastic library (+ certain

suggests some respects in which sociocultural comparisons from elsewhere in antiquity may be at best approximate, or even misleading, since the sect involved is so very eccentric from a broader Mediterranean perspective. And, finally: (3) It prioritizes "the" social group behind the texts, rather than looking at the texts as communications over time that urge varying, particular ways to construct society.[9]

1.2   *Reading Culture*

I have read with interest and pleasure Mladen Popović's extensive engagement with ways that my work on reading cultures in the Roman high empire might be suggestive for understanding the "textual community" that constitutes the "people behind the scrolls" (the first phrase being from Brian Stock and the second his own).[10] Nonetheless, it will be useful to suggest ways by which we can perhaps extend or refine his remarks further. Much of what he culls from my *Readers and Reading Culture* volume is taken from the chapter on Aulus Gellius, which describes a reading community that is focused on a certain type of high literary elitism. As I put it:

> Gellius ... craft[s] his own set of reader expectations, which focus relent-lessly on intellectual endeavor as it plays out in two arenas: in the learned discussion surrounding the *magistri* [that is, the leaders of the learned group], and in private study and writing subsequent and preliminary to learned discussion .... The *magistri* are in practice commentators—on matters literary, linguistic, rhetorical, philosophical, ethical. They are also,

---

administrative records?) hidden away at a time of invasion and crisis; (2) a depository for battered texts whose method of disposal was limited by the fact of their "sacred" character (like a *genizah*!); (3) offerings made by pilgrims and other travelers to a revered monk, placed in a cave that was closed when it filled up. For an overview of these and other hypotheses, see Yoshirō Imaeda, "The Provenance and Character of the Dunhuang Documents," *Memoirs of the Toyo Bunko* 66 (2008): 81–102.

9   In general, see my *Readers and Reading Culture in the High Empire* (Oxford: Oxford University Press, 2010) for this constructivist view, esp. 200–206. Charlotte Hempel argues along similar lines in her contribution to this volume ("Curated Communities," 342), setting herself in alignment with those who "have rightly stressed the extent to which texts serve to create rather than reflect reality."

10   Mladen Popović, "Reading, Writing, and Memorizing Together: Reading Culture in Ancient Judaism and the Dead Sea Scrolls in a Mediterranean Context," *DSD* 24 (2017): 447–70; cf. also his contribution in this volume (Popović, "Book Production," 199–265). The main point of reference for Popović is my *Readers and Reading Culture*. The phrase "textual community" originates with Brian Stock, *The Implications of Literacy: Written Language and Models of Interpretation in the 11th and 12th Centuries* (Princeton, NJ: Princeton University Press, 1983).

and even especially, commentators on the other commentators on these matters. To be learned is not simply to know one's Vergil, but to know that for a given line in [Vergil's] *Georgics* (2.247), most write *amaro* at the end, but Hyginus in his *Commentaries* cites an ancient manuscript in which *amaror* is written; and one should also know what (e.g.) Favorinus says about whether Hyginus is right .... [A]s presented in Gellius, the elite fascination and entertainment is not so much in, say, the writing of poetry or oratory, nor even in its reading; but rather in knowing the literature, and indeed the commentators on the literature, so as to be able to comment learnedly upon the literature and its commentators.[11]

This then is a natural point of focus for Popović, who in his writings repeatedly characterizes "the movement behind the Dead Sea Scrolls" as "consisting of Jewish intellectuals or scholars who were deeply engaged with their ancestral traditions, and with a high level of sophistication."[12] The elements he brings out from my *Readers and Reading Culture* thus naturally center around "scholarly readers" like those depicted in Gellius, who often work together in groups, with one reading aloud and others interrupting, asking questions, commenting, asking the reader to repeat the text; who sometimes form groups to work over texts while excerpting and performing other written exercises; who in the contexts of a new work being read compete to memorize snatches or even entire passages; who demand a lector who can read aloud so as to bring the meaning out from a text written in *scriptio continua*, that is without spaces—in analogue, as Popović puts it, to the "non-vocalized Hebrew and Aramaic scrolls" that are characteristic of the Dead Sea texts.[13]

1.3 *Mastery of Language; Access and Control*

While reading how my own work might dovetail with suggestions for the socio-cultural context of the Dead Sea texts I find at least as interesting the elements Popović has chosen not to include. Some seem suggestive. Within the Gellius materials are two areas that may be productive in trying to conjure "the people behind the scrolls." The first is the mastery of language motif. Much of what Gellius and his associates do revolves around philological disputes: what a given archaic word or phrase means, whether a given archaic word or expression is appropriate in contemporary elite compositions, whether a given word

---

11   Johnson, *Readers and Reading Culture*, 108–109.

12   Popović, "Reading, Writing, and Memorizing Together," 449, a common stance among Dead Sea Scrolls scholars.

13   Popović, "Reading, Writing, and Memorizing Together," 459.

THE DEAD SEA SCROLLS: A CLASSICIST'S VIEW 493

occurs in this or that "approved" ancient author (think how well you have to know your texts to be able to cite on the fly an occurrence of a rare word, or to state accurately that it does *not* occur in, say, Plato and Demosthenes!). My analysis in *Readers and Reading Culture* focused on the mastery of language motif as a core feature of a particular elite in-group in second-century Rome. Displaying and improving this mastery of language is what they got together to do; it was hard, very hard, to gain the necessary habits of mind and knowledge-set, taking years and years of intense study; their particular style of language mastery put them in direct competition with other text-oriented in-groups, such as contemporary poets or lovers of poetry, for example, over whom they declared superiority as the ones who were the tastemakers, who because of their deep learning best decided which archaic texts were a meaningful and appropriate subject of study, which contemporary or near-contemporary commentators were worth knowing and citing, which of the new poets were worth paying attention to. Gellius was part of a strange archaizing movement that privileged selected secular texts from the Latin and Greek yesteryear and new compositions full of archaic words and expressions, and thus the parallel is not exact. But surely one possible context for an assembly of texts like the Dead Sea Scrolls might be as a consequence of the formation of an in-group of self-identified "scholars" whose reason to get together would be to study, absorb, memorize, and debate among themselves selected ancient, inscrutable, linguistically difficult texts they held as "sacred"; to train themselves to certain habits of reading, absorbing, memorizing, commenting, and writing; and along the way to train others.[14] Because the group is profoundly eccentric from the broad Mediterranean point of view, this happens not (as in Gellius) for advantage within the society at-large, whether social or monetary or otherwise, but for status and influence within a self-secluded, non-elite community of common-property religious ascetics.

The problem with this sort of argument is that it is deeply embedded within the Essene narrative. The line of argument works only if the Dead Sea Scrolls were in fact brought together and studied and if the Qumran caves are not,

---

14   On mastery of *sacred* language as a social identifier and hierarchical marker, see Steve Delamarter, "Sociological Models for Understanding the Scribal Practices in the Biblical Dead Sea Scrolls," in *Rediscovering the Dead Sea Scrolls: An Assessment of Old and New Approaches and Methods*, ed. Maxine L. Grossman (Grand Rapids, MI: Eerdmans, 2010), 192: "[The] unique function of language in religious communities creates a fabulously efficient sociological mechanism that separates outsiders from 'normal insiders' (the ordinary members of the community) and 'deep insiders' (priests and other such persons) …. There is a clear correlation between mastery of the sacred language of a community and influence in the community."

for example, a sacred-text burial site.[15] The same limitation is true for another elemental feature of the ideal reading community depicted in Gellius and not taken up by Popović: the access and control of texts motif. In Gellius, this plays out in particular ways. First, the learned in Gellius's ideal community not only know many, many obscure works, but also know where to find them—the only known copy will be found in the library of Rome's Temple of Peace, for example, or in the library of a particular, named elite individual. The situation in Gellius, as it happens, connects to a broad set of Greco-Roman habits as regards book access and knowledge for ambitious intellectuals in this period. The availability of a wide range of books depended not so much on a book trade in our sense, but on the book collections of individuals, the formation of circles of similarly minded "friends" around those individuals, the network of *literati* who know where to go to find what, and the presence of trained copyists for hire or, in the circles of the wealthy, for loan. In the Roman world of the late republic and early empire we hear of the library of Lucullus, the "richest man" of his era (Diodorus Siculus 4.21.4), a library which specialized in works of Greek philosophy, and which is depicted as a magnet for powerful intellectual elites, including Cicero and Cato; we know of the library discovered at Herculaneum, which was a specialist collection of Epicurean texts, kept in a magnificent villa by the sea for appropriate insiders to visit and study; we know from Suetonius that the wealthy satirist Persius owned a library of seven hundred volumes of the Stoic Chrysippus that he left to the influential intellectual and teacher Cornutus. We also hear incidentally of large general collections accumulated by particularly wealthy and powerful men with deep intellectual interests: Cicero's fabulously rich and well-connected friend Atticus; the consular Herodes Atticus, a friend of the emperor Hadrian, who donated the theater of his name that we still admire on Athens' acropolis;[16] Marcus Aurelius's teacher Fronto. From many indications, we best understand the Greco-Roman custom of dedicating a newly composed work to someone as a move to get one's own work within the exclusionary zone that is the book collection of an

---

15   Joan Taylor has recently revived the *genizah* hypothesis (see *The Essenes, the Scrolls*); for summaries of archaeological evidence that seem to counter it, see Devorah Dimant, *History, Ideology and Bible Interpretation in the Dead Sea Scrolls*, FAT 90 (Tübingen: Mohr Siebeck, 2014), 233–35, and Mladen Popović, "Qumran as Scroll Storehouse in Times of Crisis? A Comparative Perspective on Judaean Desert Manuscript Collections," *JSJ* 43 (2012): 583–85.

16   Herodes inherited the library of Favorinus, to which he will have added significantly, one assumes. All the examples in this paragraph are treated in my chapter on Roman libraries, "Libraries and Reading Culture in the High Empire," in *Ancient Libraries*, ed. Jason König, Katerina Oikonomopoulou, Greg Woolf (Cambridge: Cambridge University Press, 2013), 347–63.

influential and wealthy man. The sociological aspect of such book collections is, then, particularly suggestive. As I wrote in an article offering an account of the sociology of Roman libraries, "*Sociologically*, a central use of a library in the Greco-Roman context is to focus the circle of readers, and also of writers, more particularly around the *vir magnus*, the Great Man, much as the physical space of the Great Man's villa does .... Moreover, by virtue of the selective nature of the collections, libraries are an important component in determining what forms the subject of *studia* ['what to study']—important, that is, in the negotiation of which texts are considered to have enduring value."[17]

The parallels are, again, inexact, but it is not hard to reimagine the Teacher of Righteousness and other leaders as the builders of a specialist collection of particular interest to a religious insider group; the construction of a sense of exclusive access to rare materials whose study then becomes a central activity for at least some members of the group; the sharing of resources, including existing books as well as the common-property leather, ink, and pens to make more; and the training of in-house copyists to create both books to retain and books to share with allied communities. All of these are, after all, features essentially analogous to the libraries of Roman elite and the circles that made use of them. Again, however, the analogy depends on the fragile assumption of the centrality of a group like the Essenes.[18]

1.4   *Writing and the Circulation of Texts*

I now turn to a different aspect of Greco-Roman reading communities that does not require an Essene-like group to constitute a suggestive parallel. Among those obscure works mentioned in Gellius, whose location is known only by the in-group, are autographs that are explicitly not "published" but circulated in very limited form among friends or, if a teacher, among pupils.[19] Of such texts, Gellius makes remarks such as, "[the commentaries of Publius Nigidius Figulus are written] more as an aid to his own memory than for the instruction of readers" (*Attic Nights* 17.7.5).[20] As it happens, we know quite a lot about this particular type of exclusionary in-group behavior through its visibility in the writings of Galen, arguably the greatest and certainly the most

---

17   Johnson, "Libraries and Reading Culture," 361.

18   On the sociological power of *sharing* as it relates to books and lectors see Johnson, "Libraries and Reading Culture," 359–61. The question of whether the scrolls represent a "library" or in some other way a collection of texts is much debated: see Williams ("Textuality and the Dead Sea Scrolls," 90–97) for discussion with extensive bibliography.

19   For discussion of how ancient notions of publication and circulation intersect with the texts from Qumran, see Popović ("Book Production," 199–265).

20   Johnson, *Readers and Reading Culture*, 131–32.

prolific medical writer of his era (the second century CE). Galen with typical self-preening wrote a work, *On My Own Books*, which catalogues and describes the circumstances of creation for many of his 350 works, and along the way provides us with a lot of fascinating detail about book production and circulation. Galen presents himself, plausibly, as the center of an intellectual coterie made up of "friends and companions" interested in medicine and philosophy. He, then, is the master and the others his followers. These followers are not strictly pupils, since there is no fee involved for this wealthy man. Moreover, his followers include not only doctors-in-training, but experienced medical men from around the Mediterranean, as well as the intellectually curious from among the most influential thinkers and politically powerful men in Rome.[21] These then were the "friends and companions" who attended his lectures and exhibitions, and with whom he interacted over the texts of Hippocrates and Aristotle and others.

Now the writings of Galen that mimic those oral behaviors—writings of a discursive lecture or interactive commentary on ancient texts—have an interesting pattern of creation.[22] Galen, for instance, complains that many of his works circulate under the names of others, explaining "that they were given without inscription [of the author's name] to friends or pupils, having been written with no thought for publication, but simply at the request of those individuals, who had desired a written record of lectures they had attended. When in the course of time some of these individuals died, their successors … began to pass the writings off as their own" (*On My Own Books*, 10). That theme, of writing a book on demand for a friend, recurs again and again. Galen tells us that the long list of his works marked as "for Beginners" were "dictated to young men at the beginning of their studies or in some cases presented to friends at their request" (11–12). With some exaggeration, Galen elsewhere states, "I have not written a single book [of the commentary type] except by request of one or another of my friends or companions, particularly when they are setting out on a long journey and think that it would be helpful to have a reminder/commentary (*hypomnema*) on the things I've said and demonstrated" (*Commentary on Hippocrates, Epidemics III* 17A.576K). Galen often emphasizes that such commentaries were only to be shared with those already initiated into his (or similar) teachings. Over and over again, Galen insists that his writings be reserved for those who have worked hard to master the ancients, commanding his readers, for example, not to proceed further in

---

21   A paradigmatic example is the consular Flavius Boethus (see Johnson, *Readers and Reading Culture*, 78–80).

22   Johnson, *Readers and Reading Culture*, 85–91.

reading his treatise until they have gained a thorough knowledge of this or that specific Hippocratic text.[23] Illustrative is the interesting proviso that Galen attaches to a commentary on Aristotle's *Categories*, also written at a friend's request: "[I gave it to him] with the firm instruction that he should only show it to students who had already read the *Categories* with a teacher, or at least made a start with other commentaries" (42–43). Galen also repeatedly makes clear that these individualized commentaries "written for friends" were provided as unique copies. In Galen's world, then, it was normal to hand over a physical bookroll to one or more "friends" which could act as a substitute for the continued teaching of Galen himself, as intellectual benefit and guidance for the friends and others—including others remote in time—wanting to enter these exclusive Galenic circles. In Greco-Roman contexts such practices seem particularly characteristic of intellectuals interested in medicine, philosophy, and philology,[24] where commentary on an ancient text, both oral and written, was a common activity. The practice of using writings to substitute for a distant teacher has a long history: one thinks equally of the Seventh Letter of Plato and of the letter-treatises of Augustine of Hippo, for example. Again, and finally, it is not hard to see possible analogues here for how the commentaries known as the *Pesharim* might have come about, and the exclusive circles to whom such commentaries were probably aimed.

2   The Scribes behind the Scrolls

Locating the writers behind the scrolls is at least as perplexing as situating the readers and their possible communities. Worth emphasizing, once again, is the degree to which the framing narrative for those people we imagine as the writers—the "scribes"—informs a productive path towards understanding. Here there is wide divergence among Dead Sea Scrolls scholars, with imaginings that roam from "professional" scribes to authoritative priestly author-scribes to a highly literate community making personal copies.[25] Behind

---

23   Popović points to a similar mindset for Philo's ideal reader in *On the Special Laws*, 4.160–67 ("Reading, Writing, and Memorizing Together," 464–66).

24   On the commonalities see especially Kendra Eshelman, *The Social World of Intellectuals in the Roman Empire: Sophists, Philosophers, and Christians; Greek Culture in the Roman Empire* (Cambridge: Cambridge University Press, 2012).

25   For a good overview with bibliography, see Eibert J. C. Tigchelaar, "The Scribes of the Scrolls," in *T&T Clark Companion to the Dead Sea Scrolls*, ed. George J. Brooke and Charlotte Hempel, with the assistance of Michael DeVries and Drew Longacre (London: T&T Clark, 2019), 524–32.

these imaginings are, again, assumed sociocultural contexts, and as a starting point it may help to be more specific about what a "scribe" meant in adjacent Mediterranean scribal cultures.

2.1 Scribes in the Greco-Roman World

In his magisterial essay on the copyists who produced the hundreds of surviving literary and paraliterary texts[26] in Greco-Roman Oxyrhynchus, Peter Parsons wisely remarks,

> [T]he very word 'scribe' can mislead. It suggests a professional member of a sacred calling: such as the Egyptian scribe, proudly depicted in sculpture, transmitting texts and informing administration under the eye of Thoth himself; or the monastic scribe, with his special place in a religious institution, governed by firm rules .... By contrast, the book-transcriber of Roman Egypt has a low profile: anonymous, uncommemorated in art, featureless except in the rare aside to the reader.[27]

Under Hellenized Rome, a "scribe" (Greek *grammateus*, Latin *scriba*) in the first instance denoted an official who was concerned with the writing of things, like the processing of contracts and petitions, and the keeping of records. This official typically worked for an association (such as the "scribe of the guards") or in a governmental bureau (such as the "scribe of the polity"). The liturgical system allowed competent writers to be drafted, as it were, from the elite educated class in order fulfill important writing tasks.[28] Such officials, even when elite, need not be the ones doing the writing: as the much-cited case of the "village scribe" (*komogrammateus*) Petaus has taught us, the "scribe" need not himself be literate.[29] Those looking at cross-comparative evidence from Greece and Rome need forewarning that there is a regrettable slippage in how

---

26   "Paraliterary" is the term currently favored among papyrologists for texts that are not documentary but not fully literary, such as commentaries, lists, hypotheses, mythographic writings, etc.

27   Peter Parsons, "Copyists of Oxyrhynchus," in *Oxyrhynchus: A City and its Texts*, ed. Alan K. Bowman et al. (London: Egypt Exploration Society, 2007), 262–70.

28   For this sort of liturgical encumbrance, see Rodney Ast, "Writing and the City in Later Roman Egypt: Towards a Social History of the Ancient 'Scribe'," CHS *Research Bulletin* 4/1 (2015) [URL http://nrs.harvard.edu/urn-3:hlnc.essay:AstR.Writing_in_the _City_in_Later_Roman_Egypt.2016], who focuses on the late antique period but gives a summary overview, with references, for the earlier period.

29   P.Petaus 2: see H. C. Youtie, "Pétaus, fils de Pétaus, ou le scribe qui ne savait pas écrire," *Chronique d'Égypte* 41 (1966): 127–43.

THE DEAD SEA SCROLLS: A CLASSICIST'S VIEW   499

scholars of Greece and Rome speak about ancient scribes. Papyrologist Rodney
Ast has recently and rightly complained:

> [T]he title "scribe," which properly denotes a professional copyist or
> clerk, is used very freely in disciplines such as papyrology and paleog-
> raphy to describe nearly every kind of writer, from the tax collector who
> authored a receipt, to the concerned father who wrote a letter to his son.
> In such contexts, it ignores the identity of the agent responsible for a
> piece of writing, meaning little more than "hand." Such indiscriminate
> use of the term reflects complacency on our part and an unwillingness to
> look beyond the text at the individual responsible for creating it. So the
> problem is part social as well, or a failure on our part to address social
> forces behind the production of texts of any given type.[30]

We might, then, best use the phrase "trained copyist" (Greek (*biblio*)*graphos*,
Latin *librarius*) for those who went through the rigorous practice necessary
to produce the literary and paraliterary texts that survive in the papyrological
record. As Parsons makes clear, this functional person is low status enough to
leave a light imprint.[31] Hardly any are known by name. We know from literary
sources that they could be in-house slaves or freedmen trained to the task for
the use of elite and their associates; public-facing "booksellers" (*librarii*) were
often also the copyists, since a basic bookseller function was to make books
to order.[32] We know from the Price Edict of Diocletian that Greek and Roman
copyists were paid by the line, and that the lines were charged at different rates
depending on how slowly and carefully the writing was done. We know from
close study of surviving bookrolls[33] that this was a highly trained profession
with many details of manufacture that distinguish its products. Such bookrolls
were written in columns with a particular look and set of stylistic markers,
such as the distinctive lean to the columns of writing that papyrologists call
"Maas' Law." Script styles fall within traditional types and, whether calligraphic
or more plain, individual letters in literary bookrolls were distinct and highly

---

30   Ast, "Writing and the City," §1.1.

31   Parsons's essay ("Copyists of Oxyrhynchus") works through in some detail the many questions we have yet to answer about Greco-Roman copyists.

32   Latin *librarius* thus refers to (1) trained copyist and (2) bookseller, since the bookseller
was often both, or had in-house copyists to serve the function.

33   Bookroll (or "book roll") is the technical term used by Classicists to denote a papyrus roll
(scroll) containing an unexcerpted literary text. For a close study of the formal features
that characterized bookrolls, including those cited here, see my *Bookrolls and Scribes in
Oxyrhynchus* (Toronto: Toronto University Press, 2004).

legible; and the column layout was exacting, such that the measurement from column to column typically varies no more than ±1.5 mm—the width of a pen's nib! Though apprentice contracts of any type are rare among Greco-Egyptian documents, we can infer that such copyists, like other artisans, were trained from a young age to perform this exacting task.[34] What is distinctive here for our purposes is the severe disconnect between book production and authorship or readership. As I have repeatedly emphasized in my own work, there is no technological impediment for a literate individual from picking up a pen and copying out a text onto a roll, and amateurs certainly did sometimes write out a literary (and more commonly a paraliterary) text for their own purposes, or as a gesture towards an honored friend. But the bookroll in Greco-Roman antiquity typically had a highly distinctive look, a look determined by culture and executed by people trained to the task. Such bookrolls were not the products of the leisured elite who were the authors and readers of the literary texts. The Greco-Roman world would deem exotic, then, the idea of a scribal community of private intellectuals making their own copies, as is often surmised for the Qumran scrolls.

2.2   *Scribes in Mesopotamia*

Meanwhile, to the east in Mesopotamia, a strong contrast to Greco-Roman habits of producing literary and paraliterary texts can be found in first millennium BCE cuneiform culture, which continued well past the conquest by Alexander. As Eleanor Robson puts it:

> Gradually the emphasis shifted ... from the transmission of [literary works] through memory and recitation (with concomitant textual flexibility) towards an increasing dependence on copying out manuscripts (and careful recording of sources) in the first millennium BC. A parallel tradition of editorial work, commentary-writing and recording the oral traditions around texts also developed at the same time. So far as we know, all of those engaged in such literary and scholarly activities made their livelihoods from this knowledge, whether through royal patronage, priestly employment, or solicitation of private clients for performance of ritual. As far as we can tell, there was no wealthy, leisured class for whom intellectual activities were optional, if challenging, pastimes.[35]

---

34   The few existing contracts seem to be for occupations that might involve talent as well as practice, such as flute-playing or weaving. We do have two examples of apprentice contracts for shorthand writers: P.Oxy. IV.724 and XLI.2988.

35   Eleanor Robson, "Reading the Libraries of Assyria and Babylonia," in *Ancient Libraries*, ed. Jason König, Katerina Oikonomopoulou, Greg Woolf (Cambridge: Cambridge University Press, 2013), 40, a consensus view. The footnote to her paragraph reads, "This aspect

THE DEAD SEA SCROLLS: A CLASSICIST'S VIEW   501

To be sure, the difficulty of mastering the complexities of cuneiform script
and the ancient languages the script represented pushed naturally towards a
more closed-off and distinct scribal profile. But behind this depiction are also
critical differences, by contrast with the Greco-Roman writer, in the kinds of
literary and paraliterary texts in view and in the socioeconomic pressures that
drive the activity of writing, as well as in readership and use. In her study of
three substantial tablet collections of nondocumentary texts beyond that of
the palace at Nineveh, Robson discovers that one, based on direct royal patronage, centered around "omens, incantations and ritual to provide divinely
authorised guidance to the crown"; another, the remains of a scribal school run
by a priestly family in the hinterland, emphasized "incantations, (non-royal)
ritual, medicine and literature"; and the last, a collection of records but also
scholarly writings of a few priestly families employed at a city temple, had "a
tight focus on astronomy, lamentations and ritual ... closely aligned to [their]
professional interests" as "lamentation priests and astronomers of the god
Anu."[36] These priestly "families" are not necessarily hereditary, but the product of a tight apprenticeship system.[37] By the first millenium, there developed
two levels for the scribal apprentice. The first was more basic in its aims but
still required a considerable knowledge-set; the second, more advanced, training had three specialist branches, in divination, exorcism, and lamentation,
that had their own curricula and practices, including substantial interpretative
and performance elements.[38] Within the context of the palace at Nineveh, the
"vast copying operation" that led to the royal library could be surprisingly inat-
tentive to exact copying of texts and more attentive to practice: "It is remarkable that the scribes to whom Ashurbanipal entrusted the constitution of his
library were not content to recopy the originals exactly as they were when

---

     of ancient Mesopotamian society, so striking to Classicists, goes largely unremarked in
     Assyriological circles." A detailed and accessible recent account of Mesopotamian reading
     culture can be found in Dominique Charpin, *Reading and Writing in Babylon* (Cambridge:
     Harvard University Press, 2010); and, with more focus on education, David M. Carr, *Writ-
     ing on the Tablet of the Heart: Origins of Scripture and Literature* (Oxford: Oxford Univer-
     sity Press, 2005), 17–46. See also Popović, "Reading, Writing, and Memorizing Together,"
     who at 453 quotes Charpin (p. 67), "In Mesopotamia, there was no 'free' reading: no one is
     ever depicted reading for pleasure."

36   Robson, "Reading the Libraries of Assyria and Babylonia," 55. The first collection is that
     Kalbu Ezida, from the eighth and seventh centuries BCE; the second is that at Hurizina,
     active *c.*718–610; the last is the tablet room in the Reš temple in Uruk, *c.*220–170 BCE.

37   See Charpin, *Reading and Writing in Babylon*, 17–53 (on scribal families: 50–51) and Carr,
     Writing on the Tablet of the Heart, 20–23. Calling the master scribe "father" and the pupil
     "son," just as in ancient acting and musical performance groups, need not imply a biologi-
     cal relationship.

38   Charpin, *Reading and Writing in Babylon*, 48–49, with bibliography.

the scribes received them. Their work as *editors* is particularly evident in the omen texts."[39]

Here, then, the copying of traditional texts, the composing of commentaries on or editorial adjustments to those texts, and the priestly action or consultation depending on those texts, are tightly bound. Divination and ritual are core, with only occasional and incidental ramifications into the "literary": works like myths and epics that we think of as literary entertainment are unusual and found in the context of prayer and ritual.[40] Tradent, copyist, interpreter, and often also the user (i.e., the performer) are one and the same. The Mesopotamian "scribe," in short, is much like a member of a priestly caste who relies for income on private or royal patronage, offerings from worshippers, or the training of others.[41] The figure is of a priest-scribe but of a particular sort; in any case both teasingly similar to and materially different from the author-scribes or "scribal community" sometimes imagined for the scrolls.[42]

2.3 Scribes in Judaea

How much did either the Greco-Roman or Mesopotamian scribal profile map onto those who wrote or copied the Dead Sea Scrolls? In his discussion of the ancient Jewish scribes, Emmanuel Tov offers this depiction, relying (as he makes clear) on Rabbinic sources:

> The term *soferim* involves the combined activities of the copying of text, especially of Scripture and other sacred documents, and an intimate knowledge of the documents, and it is often difficult to decide which nuance of the term is intended .... [M]ost *soferim* were skilled in both aspects of the profession.[43]

---

39 Charpin, *Reading and Writing in Babylon*, 197–98. Emphasis original. Similarly, Carr, *Writing on the Tablet of the Heart*, 34: "We see literary creativity at every stage of Mesopotamian history. The question, however, is how this creativity is expressed. In the earliest stages [chronologically], scribes tended to adapt and create traditions freely, while in the later stages scribes tended to recombine and translate older traditions, sometimes creating new material but retrojecting it backward."

40 Charpin, *Reading and Writing in Babylon*, 196.

41 Egyptian temple scribes functioned not unlike this depiction, but other Egyptian scribes worked more along the line of the *grammateus* figure in Greco-Roman Egypt already described. For a comprehensive and recent overview, see Jennifer Cromwell and Eitan Grossman, eds., *Scribal Repertoires in Egypt from the New Kingdom to the Early Islamic Period* (Oxford: Oxford University Press, 2017).

42 Carr, *Writing on the Tablet of the Heart*, 47–61, discusses reasons to suppose direct Mesopotamian influence on education in ancient Israel.

43 Emanuel Tov, *Scribal Practices and Approaches Reflected in the Texts Found in the Judean Desert*, STDJ 54 (Leiden: Brill, 2004), 12.

THE DEAD SEA SCROLLS: A CLASSICIST'S VIEW   503

This proto-Rabbinic model is appealingly similar to the Mesopotamian model, but is it right?[44] The luxury rolls found beside personal documents in the Judaean desert refuge caves seem rather to be the products of skilled copyists in service to wealthy families than priest-scribes.[45] If we agree with Michael Wise when he writes about the way that "Hebrew literacy ... served to fashion and sustain elites, as literacy did elsewhere in the Greco-Roman world,"[46] what elite do we have in mind? Is it an elite like that of the Greeks who in an act of group enculturation used their leisure to immerse themselves in texts produced by low-status trained copyists? Or is the context comparable to that of Mesopotamia, in which the elite are not only the patrons but also the "scribes," who claim and perform *mastery* of the texts? In short, the degree to which the "scribe" runs with or against the grain of the idea of "scholar" or "elite" depends largely on the baggage we bring to those terms, which is a matter of complex cultural assumptions rather than of tidy definition.

3   Conclusion

I end with a caveat. My many years of work on Greco-Roman bookrolls and ancient reading cultures has focused upon trying to tease apart the differences, subtle and not, among a variety of sociocultural groups, even while also recognizing some commonalities. While I hope that some of these comparisons to Greco-Roman reading and writing practices prove provocative, we must be careful not to fall into the trap of thinking, "this is how ancient readers or writers went about it," as if ancient readers and writers all worked alike. And in the case of the Dead Sea Scrolls, we must be particularly cautious when using such parallels to think with: as Pliny reminds us, from the Greco-Roman perspective, the habits of such a people were "marvelous beyond all the tribes of the earth."

---

44   For a sharp rebuke of the tendency to let later Rabbinic materials influence views on the society behind the Dead Sea Scrolls, see Delamarter, "Sociological Models for Understanding Scribal Practices," 183–85.

45   See Kipp Davis, "Paleographical and Physical Features of the Dead Sea Scrolls in the Museum of the Bible Collection: A Synopsis," in *Dead Sea Scrolls Fragments in the Museum Collection*, ed. Emanuel Tov, Kipp Davis, and Robert Duke, Publications of Museum of the Bible 1 (Leiden: Brill, 2016), 19–35 and Popović, "Qumran as Scroll Storehouse," 554, 573–88. Further references and discussion will be found in Williams, "Textuality and the Dead Sea Scrolls," 71–134.

46   Michael O. Wise, *Language & Literacy in Roman Judaea: A Study of the Bar Kokhba Documents*, AYBRL (New Haven, CT: Yale University Press, 2015), 303.

Acknowledgments

I offer here an essay by way of provocation rather than a rounded scholarly view. I appreciate deeply the chance to meet and interact with the tight group of distinguished DSS scholars at what proved an unusually stimulating conference; and I give my thanks to the organizers for their kind invitation.

Bibliography

Ast, Rodney. "Writing and the City in Later Roman Egypt: Towards a Social History of the Ancient 'Scribe'." *CHS Research Bulletin* 4/1 (2015). 6 sections. Persistent URL: http://nrs.harvard.edu/urn-3:hlnc.essay:AstR.Writing_in_the_City_in_Later_Roman_Egypt .2016.

Carr, David M. *Writing on Tablets of the Heart: Origins of Scripture and Literature.* Oxford: Oxford University Press, 2005.

Charpin, Dominique. *Reading and Writing in Babylon.* Cambridge: Harvard University Press, 2010.

Cromwell, Jennifer, and Eitan Grossman, eds. *Scribal Repertoires in Egypt from the New Kingdom to the Early Islamic Period.* Oxford: Oxford University Press, 2017.

Davis, Kipp. "Paleographical and Physical Features of the Dead Sea Scrolls in the Museum of the Bible Collection: A Synopsis." Pages 19–35 in *Dead Sea Scrolls Fragments in the Museum Collection.* Edited by Emanuel Tov, Kipp Davis, and Robert Duke. Publications of Museum of the Bible 1. Leiden: Brill, 2016.

Delamarter, Steve. "Sociological Models for Understanding the Scribal Practices in the Biblical Dead Sea Scrolls." Pages 182–97 in *Rediscovering the Dead Sea Scrolls: An Assessment of Old and New Approaches and Methods.* Edited by Maxine L. Grossman. Grand Rapids, MI: Eerdmans, 2010.

Dimant, Devorah. *History, Ideology and Bible Interpretation in the Dead Sea Scrolls.* FAT 90. Tübingen: Mohr Siebeck, 2014.

Eshelman, Kendra. *The Social World of Intellectuals in the Roman Empire: Sophists, Philosophers, and Christians; Greek Culture in the Roman Empire.* Cambridge: Cambridge University Press, 2012.

Imaeda, Yoshirō. "The Provenance and Character of the Dunhuang Documents." *Memoirs of the Toyo Bunko* 66 (2008): 81–102.

Johnson, William A. "Toward a Sociology of Reading in Classical Antiquity." *AJP* 121 (2000): 593–627.

Johnson, William A. *Bookrolls and Scribes in Oxyrhynchus.* Studies in Book and Print Culture. Toronto: University of Toronto Press, 2004.

Johnson, William A. "Constructing Elite Reading Communities in the High Empire." Pages 320–30 in *Ancient Literacies: The Culture of Reading in Greece and Rome*. Edited by William A. Johnson and Holt N. Parker. Oxford: Oxford University Press, 2009.

Johnson, William A. *Readers and Reading Culture in the High Roman Empire: A Study of Elite Communities*. Classical Culture and Society. Oxford: Oxford University Press, 2010.

Johnson, William A. "Libraries and Reading Culture in the High Empire." Pages 347–63 in *Ancient Libraries*. Edited by Jason König, Katerina Oikonomopoulou, and Greg Woolf. Cambridge: Cambridge University Press, 2013.

Klawans, Jonathan. "The Essene Hypothesis: Insights from Religion 101." *DSD* 23 (2016): 51–78.

Parsons, Peter. "Copyists of Oxyrhynchus." Pages 262–70 in *Oxyrhynchus: A City and its Texts*. Edited by Alan K. Bowman, R. A. Coles, Nikolaos Gonis, Dirk Obbink, and Peter Parsons. London: Egypt Exploration Society, 2007.

Popović, Mladen. "Qumran as Scroll Storehouse in Times of Crisis? A Comparative Perspective on Judaean Desert Manuscript Collections." *JSJ* 43 (2012): 551–94.

Popović, Mladen. "Reading, Writing, and Memorizing Together: Reading Culture in Ancient Judaism and the Dead Sea Scrolls in a Mediterranean Context." *DSD* 24 (2017): 447–70.

Robson, Eleanor. "Reading the Libraries of Assyria and Babylonia." Pages 38–56 in *Ancient Libraries*. Edited by Jason König, Katerina Oikonomopoulou, and Greg Woolf. Cambridge: Cambridge University Press, 2013.

Stock, Brian. *The Implications of Literacy: Written Language and Models of Interpretation in the Eleventh and Twelfth Centuries*. Princeton, NJ: Princeton University Press, 1983.

Taylor, Joan E. *The Essenes, the Scrolls, and the Dead Sea*. Oxford: Oxford University Press, 2012.

Tigchelaar, Eibert J. C. "The Scribes of the Scrolls." Pages 524–32 in *T&T Clark Companion to the Dead Sea Scrolls*. Edited by George J. Brooke and Charlotte Hempel, with the assistance of Michael DeVries and Drew Longacre. London: T&T Clark, 2019.

Tov, Emanuel. *Scribal Practices and Approaches Reflected in the Texts Found in the Judean Desert*. STDJ 54. Leiden: Brill, 2004.

Wise, Michael O. *Language and Literacy in Roman Judaea: A Study of the Bar Kokhba Documents*. AYBRL. New Haven, CT: Yale University Press, 2015.

Youtie, H. C. "Pétaus, fils de Pétaus, ou le scribe qui ne savait pas écrire." *Chronique d'Égypte* 41 (1966): 127–43.

Index of Modern Authors

Aarne, Antti   364n18
Abegg, Martin G.   86n64, 87n70, 202n8, 391n20, 466n59
Achtemeier, Paul J.   28n66
Adams, Samuel L.   113, 114n176
Adcock, James Seth   170n57
Adler, Yonatan   170n59, 185n123, 185n124, 399n52, 406n70
Adriaens, Annemie   73n9, 74n10, 75n13
Agha, Asif   136n5
Aguila, Mario I.   167n47
Ahrens, Wolfgang   311n60
Aitken, James K.   77n25
Aksu, Ayhan   248–249, 248n193, 248n194, 248n195, 248n198, 249n199, 249n200
Alexander, Philip S.   78n29, 82n47, 84n58, 100, 100n116, 103, 104n132, 105n137, 107n149, 111, 111n166, 111n167, 112n170, 113n172, 113n173, 175n82, 178n96, 207n30, 215n75, 221n100, 237n148, 237n149, 238n150, 239–240, 239n151, 239n154, 240n155, 240n157, 240n158, 240n159, 241n160, 241n163, 241n164, 244n175, 245n182, 245n183, 245n184, 247n190, 248, 248n194, 248n197, 249, 249n200, 251n208, 253n209, 272n30, 275n45, 284, 284n78, 285n81, 315n86, 338n11, 370n31
Allegro, John   107, 107n148, 296–300, 296n5, 296n7, 300n15, 304, 306, 307n47, 316n89
Allen, Garrick V.   21n42, 22n45, 22n46, 92n89
Allon, Mark   308n48
Ames, Frank R.   42n117
Amoresano, Angela   74n12
Anderson, Francis I.   87n66
Anderson, Jeff S.   174, 174n79, 174n80
Anderson, Robert T.   338n14
Andrews, Edward D.   16n27
Andrist, Patrick   21n42, 21n43
Antes, Peter   159n20
Applebaum, Shimon   304n29
Arbel, Daphne V.   302n23
Arnold, Russell C. D.   167n47, 169, 169n54, 169n55, 169n56, 171–172, 171n67, 175, 175n83, 178n99, 418n8, 429, 430n60, 430n61, 432n68, 463, 463n39

Ascough, Richard S.   420n13, 422n30, 423, 423n33, 424n37, 425n44, 435n81
Askin, Lindsey A.   1n2, 92n89
Assman, Aleida   141n31
Assmann, Jan   36, 36n97, 37, 141n31, 386n3
Ast, Rodney   498n28, 499, 499n30
Aufrère, Sidney H.   275n45, 370n31
Augustine, George J.   365n21
Aune, David E.   13n13
Austin, John L.   159n18, 173n73, 372n40
Avemarie, Friedrich   427n51

Baasten, Martin F. J.   78n29, 216n75, 272n30
Babcock, Bryan C.   39n102
Bacon, Francis   343
Baden, Joel S.   100n119, 114n176, 147n61, 176n86, 202n9, 392n23, 417n5
Baek, Kyung S.   98n113, 99n114, 169n56, 202n9, 267n4, 442n105
Bagnall, Roger S.   73n5, 339n15, 342n31
Bailey, Kenneth E.   26n59
Baillet, Maurice   219n92, 296n3, 300n12, 303n28, 310n59, 319n99
Baker, David W.   15n21
Balentine, Samuel E.   38n101, 40n110, 167n45, 167n47
Balla, Marta   73n9
Balogh, József   28n64
Banton, Michael   39n105
Bar-Asher Siegal, Michal   206n30, 340n21
Bar-Asher, Moshe   87n69, 88n71
Barber, Karin   348, 348n62
Barbey, Aron K.   400n53, 402n56, 403n60
Bardtke, Hans   420, 420n14
Bar-Gal, Gila Kahila   75n13
Bar-Ilan, Meier   15n22, 15n23, 76n16, 111n165
Barkay, Gabriel   306n42
Barker, G. W.   303n29
Barker, Roger   345, 345n47
Barsalou, Lawrence W.   398n46, 400n53, 401n55, 402n56, 403n60
Barstad, Hans M.   37n98
Barthélemy, Dominique   73n6
Barton, John   337n5
Barton, Stephen C.   35n90, 276n49, 362n14
Batsch, Christophe   180n105

INDEX OF MODERN AUTHORS

Bauckham, Richard J.   32n80, 301n21
Bauman, Richard   136n5
Baumgarten, Albert I.   91n83, 112n168, 217n83
Baumgarten, Joseph M.   146n58, 204n21, 350n72
Beard, Mary   346n53
Becker, Michael   275n44
Bélis, Mireille   324, 324n121
Bell, Catherine   3, 38n100, 41n114, 156n2, 157, 157n3, 157n7, 158n9, 159n20, 161, 161n25, 161n26, 161n27, 162, 162n28, 162n29, 166n43, 167, 167n46, 168, 168n48, 168n49, 168n52, 169–173, 172n69, 173n73, 177, 177n92, 177n93, 181, 387n8, 388n11, 389n14
Bellah, Robert N.   375n55
Benczes, Réka   402n58
Ben-Dov, Jonathan   185n122, 245n185, 340n21
Benoit, Pierre   227n115
Ben Zvi, Ehud   25n55, 34, 34n87, 35n88
Bergen, Wesley J.   40n109
Berlin, Andrea M.   395n39
Bernstein, Moshe   428n51
Berti, Monica   93n93
Bibb, Bryan D.   167n45
Bienkowski, Piotr   108n153
Bij de Vaate, Alice   105n139, 105n140
Bilde, Per   430n61
Binder, Donald D.   423n34
Bíró, Tamas   45n131
Birolo, Leila   74n12
Black, Matthew   315n85
Blenkinsopp, Joseph   37n98
Bloch, Maurice   173n73
Boccaccini, Gabriele   91n85, 92n86, 102n126, 103n127, 112n169, 267n4
Bockmuehl, Markus N. A.   35n90, 100n116
Boda, Mark J.   167n45, 167n47
Bohak, Gideon   175n82
Bonaduce, Ilaria   74n12
Bond, Andrew D.   74n12
Bonnie, Rick   402n57, 406n70
Boomershine, Thomas E.   476n16
Botha, Pieter J. J.   15n23, 16n24, 27n60, 28n66, 29n70
Bouloux, C. J.   370n31
Bourdieu, Pierre   163, 164n37, 172n70, 173, 175
Bowen Savant, Sarah   72n3
Bowman, Alan K.   498n27

Boyd, Danah M.   336n4, 349, 349n70
Boyd, Gregory A.   16n28
Boyer, Pascal   45, 45n129, 162, 162n31, 176n88, 398n47, 405n62
Braarvig, Jens   308n48
Brady, Miryam T.   182n113
Brady, Monica   182n112, 183n115
Brettler, Marc   37n98
Brizemeure, Daniel   300n11
Brooke, George J.   5, 76n18, 77n25, 78, 78n27, 78n28, 79n32, 79n36, 80n36, 81n43, 89n79, 97n107, 104, 104n133, 108, 108n153, 108n154, 111n168, 115n180, 135, 139, 139n17, 168n48, 175n82, 178n96, 179n100, 182n112, 184n118, 199n1, 201n8, 203n10, 205n21, 219n93, 226n113, 233n131, 234n133, 248n194, 268n6, 269n11, 270n17, 271n26, 272, 272n32, 272n33, 273n38, 275, 275n44, 275n45, 276n49, 278n56, 285n80, 300n13, 337n5, 337n9, 337n10, 346n52, 349n64, 362n14, 370n31, 371n35, 372n41, 389, 389n13, 394n32, 421n24, 454, 456–457, 456n9, 456n11, 456n12, 459n22, 466n58, 479–480, 480n30, 497n25
Broshi, Magen   73n7, 75n13, 89n77, 245n181, 338n12, 340n22, 341n27, 342n33
Brownlee, William H.   230n122, 275–276, 276n47, 282
Brumberg-Kraus, Jonathan   436n83, 436n84, 437, 437n86
Bulbulia, Joseph A.   163n34, 392n22
Bull, Christian H.   45n131
Bülow-Jacobsen, Adam   73n5
Bultmann, Rudolf   26, 474, 475n12
Bundvad, Mette   336n3
Burnyeat, M. F.   30n73
Burrows, Millar   230n122
Butler, Judith   457–458, 458n17
Butticaz, Simon   35n90
Buzi, Paolo   22n45
Byrskog, Samuel   32n80, 359n6, 416n3, 476n14

Callaway, Phillip R.   109n157
Cameron, Averil   342, 342n32
Campbell, Jonathan G.   87n66, 205n21, 279n58, 338n12
Cansdale, Lena   94n96

INDEX OF MODERN AUTHORS

Capua, Francesco di   28*n*64
Caquot, André   104*n*136, 106*n*146
Cargill, Robert   300*n*16
Carlson, Stephen C.   20*n*39
Carr, David M.   14*n*19, 25*n*56, 137, 137*n*9, 337*n*7, 369*n*27, 501*n*35, 501*n*37, 502*n*39, 502*n*42
Carrez, Maurice   106*n*145
Cavallo, Guglielmo   217*n*83, 217*n*86
Cavell, Richard   387*n*9
Centola, Damon   397*n*43
Cerquiglini, Bernard   20*n*40
Chalcraft, David   468*n*67
Champion, Craige B.   339*n*15
Chancey, Mark A.   110*n*163
Charlesworth, James H.   82*n*47, 102*n*124, 107*n*148, 238*n*150, 428*n*52, 428*n*53, 430*n*64, 433*n*75, 441, 441*n*103
Charlesworth, Scott D.   14*n*17, 311*n*64
Charpin, Dominique   501*n*35, 501*n*37, 501*n*38, 502*n*39, 502*n*40
Chartier, Roger   97*n*108
Chazon, Esther G.   87*n*67, 102*n*125, 143*n*44, 170*n*61, 182*n*113, 206*n*27, 248*n*196, 276*n*49, 399*n*51
Chen, Jing   398*n*46, 401*n*55
Chomsky, William   312*n*70
Christian, Meike   393*n*25
Christie, Peter   12*n*8
Chwe, Michael Suk-Young   175, 175*n*84, 390, 390*n*19, 392*n*21, 393*n*27, 394–396, 394*n*30, 395*n*38, 396*n*40
Cioată, Maria   84*n*57, 109*n*155, 135*n*1, 138*n*13, 176*n*89, 215*n*72, 276*n*49, 281*n*69, 284*n*77, 347*n*59, 358*n*1, 399*n*50, 454*n*4
Clark Wire, Antoinette   29*n*70
Clark, W. P.   30*n*73
Claußen, Carsten   95*n*99, 95*n*100
Cleeremans, Axel   402*n*56
Clements, Ruth A.   87*n*69, 102*n*125, 143*n*44, 182*n*113, 233*n*130, 276*n*49
Clivaz, Claire   72*n*3, 90*n*80, 202*n*9, 282*n*69, 370*n*31
Cohen, Shaye J. D.   12*n*9
Cohn, Yehudah B.   185*n*123, 399*n*52, 406*n*69
Coles, R. A.   498*n*27
Collins, John J.   86*n*64, 89*n*76, 91*n*85, 92*n*86, 93*n*91, 111*n*166, 142, 142*n*34, 142*n*35, 142*n*38, 167*n*47, 172, 172*n*68, 172*n*69, 172*n*70, 172*n*71, 180*n*105, 205*n*21, 206–207, 206*n*28, 208, 208*n*35, 233*n*130, 247*n*188, 283*n*76, 311*n*62, 318*n*96, 339, 340*n*20, 344*n*39, 344*n*43, 416–418, 416*n*3, 417*n*5, 417*n*6, 417*n*7, 418*n*8, 418*n*9, 422*n*30, 429*n*58, 432*n*68, 432*n*73, 434*n*76, 460*n*29
Colombini, Maria Perla   74*n*12
Contenson, Henri de   293–295, 318, 321–322, 323*n*114, 324–325
Coogan, Jeremiah   22*n*46
Coogan, Michael D.   15*n*21, 105*n*138
Cook, Johann   86*n*65
Cooper, Craig   377*n*60
Coote, Robert B.   24*n*53, 145*n*53
Cosgrove, Charles H.   425*n*41, 432*n*70
Cotte, Marine   73*n*9
Cottle, Simon   165*n*42, 165*n*42
Cotton, Hannah M.   110*n*161, 311*n*61
Couldry, Nick   165*n*43
Craffert, Pieter F.   16*n*24
Crawford, Matthew R.   22*n*46
Creighton, O. H.   303*n*29
Crenshaw, James L.   11*n*5
Cribiore, Raffaella   12*n*11, 14*n*16, 269, 269*n*13
Cromwell, Jennifer   502*n*41
Crook, Zeba A.   33*n*82
Cross, Frank Moore   81*n*41, 88*n*73, 203*n*11, 203*n*14, 207*n*30, 215, 215*n*73, 218*n*91, 220*n*97, 230*n*123, 231, 231*n*127, 234, 234*n*133, 238*n*150, 241*n*162, 241*n*165, 242*n*60, 242*n*168, 243*n*170, 244*n*181, 248*n*192, 254, 284*n*77, 310, 310*n*59, 366
Crowfoot, Elizabeth   227*n*115
Crowfoot, Grace M.   227*n*115
Cui, Xi   166*n*44
Czachesz, István   32*n*79, 45, 45*n*131, 46*n*131, 171*n*66

Dahmen, Ulrich   87*n*69
Daise, Michael   170, 170*n*61, 170*n*62
Daly-Denton, Margaret   315*n*86
Damasio, Antonio   176, 176*n*87
Daunton-Fear, Andrew   107*n*148
Davies, Graham   11*n*7
Davies, Philip R.   37*n*98, 89*n*75, 89*n*78, 204*n*21, 300*n*13, 341, 341*n*27, 341*n*28, 347*n*57, 373*n*42

Davila, James R. 92*n*86, 167*n*47, 183*n*117, 301*n*21, 301*n*23, 309*n*50, 366–367, 366*n*22

Davis, Kipp 82*n*46, 98*n*113, 113*n*173, 169*n*56, 267*n*4, 503*n*45

Day, John 11*n*7

Day, Juliette 40*n*110, 43*n*120, 43*n*123, 44*n*124, 46*n*131, 167*n*45

Delamarter, Steve 89*n*78, 493*n*14, 503*n*44

Delcor, Mathias 106*n*146, 276*n*47

Dell, Katharine J. 77*n*25

DeMaris, Richard E. 40*n*110, 43*n*120, 43*n*123, 44*n*124, 46*n*131, 46*n*134, 167*n*45

De Marsico, Maria 90*n*80

Demsky, Aaron 15*n*21

Depew, Mary 277*n*51

De Troyer, Kristin 142*n*37, 170*n*57

DeVries, Michael 3, 76*n*18, 81*n*43, 89*n*79, 168*n*48, 175*n*82, 178*n*96, 179*n*100, 182*n*112, 184*n*118, 199*n*1, 203*n*10, 205*n*21, 285*n*80, 337*n*5, 337*n*9, 337*n*10, 340*n*22, 341*n*27, 342*n*33, 421*n*24, 461, 461*n*33, 462–463, 463*n*38, 463*n*39, 472*n*2, 482–483

Dewey, Joanna 24*n*51, 27*n*60, 27*n*63, 29*n*70, 378, 378*n*66, 476, 480

Dhali, Maruf 90*n*80, 230, 230*n*124, 234*n*134

Dibelius, Martin 26, 474, 475*n*12

Diehl, Judy 43*n*122

Dik, Joris 73*n*9, 74*n*10, 75*n*13

Dilley, Paul 202*n*9

Dimant Devorah 87*n*67, 89*n*77, 99*n*115, 100*n*116, 206*n*27, 281*n*66, 494*n*15

Diringer, David 73*n*4

Długosz, Dariusz 93*n*91

Doane, A. Nicholas 369*n*28

Doering, Lutz 185*n*122, 397*n*42

Dombrowski, Bruno W. 420*n*20

Donahue, Douglas J. 245*n*181

Doré, Joseph 106*n*145

Doudna, Greg 74*n*12, 94*n*96, 271*n*25

Douglas, Mary 158*n*8

Doyen, Stéphane 402*n*56

Draper, Jonathan A. 26*n*57, 26*n*59, 476*n*16

Drawnel, Henryk 72*n*2, 215*n*74

Driscoll, Matthew James 71*n*1

Duhaime, Jean 442*n*105

Duke, Robert 113*n*173, 503*n*45

Dunn, James D. G. 26*n*59, 362*n*13, 478*n*25

Dunne, John Anthony 92*n*89

Dupont-Sommer, Andre 301*n*17, 306*n*40, 316*n*88

Duranti, Alessandro 136*n*5

Durkheim, Émile 157, 157*n*5, 158

Dušek, Jan 202*n*9

Eberhart, Christian A. 40*n*110, 170*n*59

Eckhardt, Benedikt 179*n*102, 420–421, 420*n*21, 421*n*23, 421*n*24, 421*n*25

Eddy, Paul Rhodes 16*n*28

Edelman, Diana V. 34*n*87, 38*n*88, 37*n*98

Edwards, Mark 375*n*55

Edwards, Morgan J. 44*n*125

Ehlich, Konrad 141*n*31

Ehrman, Bart D. 20*n*38, 473*n*4, 473*n*5, 478*n*26

Ekroth, Gunnel 424*n*38, 425*n*43

Elder, Nicholas A. 10*n*3, 477*n*20

Elgvin, Torleif 82, 82*n*46, 82*n*48, 91*n*85

Elitzur-Leiman, Rivka 305*n*40

Ellman, Barat 37*n*98

Embleton, Sheila 311*n*60

Emerton, J. A. 11*n*5

Epp, Eldon J. 17*n*30, 20*n*38

Erhart Mottahedeh, Patricia 315*n*84

Erskine, Andrew 339*n*15

Eshel, Esther 15*n*21, 105*n*137, 182*n*112, 182*n*113, 183*n*115, 313*n*74, 399*n*51

Eshel, Hanan 305*n*40, 314*n*79

Eshelman, Kendra 497*n*24

Esler, Philip F. 35*n*90, 45*n*131

Evans, Annette 399*n*49

Evans, Craig A. 13*n*13, 16*n*26, 17*n*29, 31*n*77, 85*n*61

Evans, Paul S. 25*n*56

Eve, Eric 24*n*52

Faigenbaum-Golovin, Shira 14*n*20

Falk, Daniel K. 75*n*14, 76*n*15, 77*n*24, 79*n*32, 81*n*43, 95*n*100, 99*n*114, 167*n*45, 167*n*47, 168*n*48, 169*n*56, 173–174, 173*n*76, 174*n*77, 180*n*105, 180*n*106, 181, 181*n*109, 181*n*110, 181*n*111, 202*n*9, 208–209, 209*n*42, 214*n*70, 216, 216*n*77, 216*n*78, 228, 240*n*155, 240*n*159, 249*n*202, 251*n*208, 256–257, 267*n*4, 272*n*32, 405*n*65, 407*n*73, 407*n*74

Fassberg, Steven E. 87*n*69

INDEX OF MODERN AUTHORS

Feder, Yitzhaq   39n102

Feldman, Ariel   84n57, 109n155, 135n1, 138n13, 176n89, 182n113, 215n72, 276n49, 281n69, 284n77, 347n59, 358n1, 399n50, 454n4

Feldman, Louis H.   274n41

Ferguson, Everett   16n26, 17n30

Fewster, Gregory P.   98n112

Fidanzio, Marcello   106n144, 185n123, 233n132, 298, 319n100, 321n105, 324n118, 399n52

Fields, Weston W.   88n72, 208n36, 311n61, 432n68

Fiensy, David A.   106n143

Figueredo, María   311n60

Finkelberg, Margalit   377, 377n60

Finkelstein, Israel   14n20

Finnegan, Ruth   24n51, 135, 136n3, 475

Fish, Stanley   358, 358n2, 454–455, 457

Fishbane, Simcha   15n23, 111n165

Fisher, Jay   375n54

Fitzmyer, Joseph A.   81n41

Fitzpatrick, David   365n21

Fitzpatrick-McKinley, Anne   315n86

Flannery, Frances   468n68

Flint, Peter W.   76n16, 81n41, 85n61, 87n70, 98n113, 169n56, 202n8, 219n92, 220n96, 230n123, 230n125, 231, 231n128, 233n131, 234n133, 236n143, 310n56, 337n7, 442n105

Floyd, Michael H.   25n55

Focken, Friedrich-Emanuel   112n170

Foley, John Miles   23n49, 24n53, 26n57, 27, 27n62, 141, 141n26, 141n27, 141n29, 142, 142n36, 143n41, 475, 476n16

Forbes, A. Dean   87n66

Foster, Paul   16n28, 33n82

Foucault, Michel   162

Fraade, Steven D.   13n15, 102n125, 103n130, 112n168, 145, 145n52, 145n53, 275, 275n44, 340n23, 342–343, 342n30, 343n34, 351n74, 468, 468n64

Freedman, David Noel   87n66, 88n73, 230n123

Frennesson, Björn   443n107

Frey, Jörg   87n67, 95n99, 95n100, 275n44, 282n69, 370n31, 442n105

Freyne, Sean   115n180

Fuller, Russell E.   220n97

Fuller, Steve W.   157n4

Furstenberg, Yair   428n55

Gagos, Traianos   218n89

Galano, Eugenio   74n12

Gamble, Harry Y.   13n13, 28n66

Gammie, John G.   140n23

Gane, Roy E.   40n110, 45n128

García Martínez, Florentino   95n100, 236n147, 249n202, 272n31, 277n50, 280, 280n64, 305, 305n36, 311n62, 311n63, 417n5, 428n51, 462n37

Gardner-Smith, P.   473n7

Gathercole, Simon   22n45

Gault, Brian P.   83, 83n53, 83n54

Gavrilov, A. K.   30n73

Geertz, Armin W.   159n20, 387n7

Geertz, Clifford   39, 39n105, 158, 158n13, 173n73

Geest, Paul J. J. van   402n57

Gemeinhardt, Peter   346n55, 395n37

Genette, Gérard   21, 21n41

Gennep, Arnold van   41n114

Gerber, Yana   14n20

Gerhardsson, Birger   26n57, 475n14

Geyer-Fouché, Ananda   86n64

Gilbert, Maurice   11n4

Gilbertson, D. D.   303n29

Gilders, William K.   40n109, 41n112, 176n90

Giles, Terry   338n14

Gilhus, Ingvild Saelid   386n5

Gill, David W. J.   228n118

Gilliard, Frank D.   30n73

Gillihan, Yonder Moynihan   420–422, 420n18, 420n19, 421n22, 421n25, 421n26, 422n27, 422n28, 426, 426n47, 426n48, 434n78

Gleaves, G. Scott   13n14

Glessmer, Uwe   245n185

Goff, Matthew J.   102n126, 103, 103n131, 106, 106n142, 109n156, 372n40

Goffman, Erving   345, 345n45, 345n46, 345n48, 345n49, 345n50, 484

Golb, Norman   89n76, 93n91, 94n96, 318n96

Goldberg, Sander M.   210n48

Goldschlaeger, A.   15n23

Gonis, Nikolaos   498n27

Goodacre, Mark   336n3
Goodblatt, David M.   75n13
Goody, Jack   23n50, 475
Goranson, Stephen   113n174, 301n17, 317n92
Gordon, Robert P.   11n7
Gorman Jr., Frank H.   38n101, 166n45
Grabbe, Lester L.   180n105
Greenberg, Moshe   136, 136n6
Greenblatt, Charles   75n13
Greenspahn, Frederick E.   41n112
Greenstein, Edward L.   136, 137n7
Gregory, Andrew   72n3, 90n80
Grelot, Pierre   106n145, 311n63
Grimes, Ronald L.   38n100, 156n1, 156n2,
   159n20, 161n25, 162, 162n30, 163, 163n35,
   164, 164n38, 164n39, 164n40, 166n43,
   167, 167n46
Grintz, Joshua   312n70
Grohmann, Adolf   227n115
Grossman, Eitan   502n41
Grossman, Maxine L.   5, 6, 86n64, 89n78,
   101n120, 175n84, 337n5, 340n23, 341,
   341n27, 341n29, 462n37, 467n59, 483,
   483n36, 493n14
Gruenwald, Ithamar   38n101, 166n45
Gunkel, Hermann   22, 363, 474
Gunneweg, Jan   73n9, 74n10, 74n12, 75n13,
   105n137, 205n22, 324n121
Gurry, Peter J.   20n39

Hachlili, Rachel   105n137
Hadas-Lebel, Mireille   104n136
Hahn, Oliver   74n10, 74n11, 75n13
Haigh, Rebekah   181n108
Haines-Eitzen, Kim   12n12, 478, 478n26,
   478n27
Hakola, Raimo   359n6, 416n3
Halbwachs, Maurice   33, 34, 34n86, 386n3
Hall, William C.   365n21
Halliday, M. A. K.   136n5
Halpern-Amaru, Baruch   143n44
Halpern-Amaru, Betsy   102n125, 170n61,
   276n49
Hamidović, David   72n3, 90n80, 202n9, 251,
   251n206, 251n208, 253n212, 311n60
Haran, Menahem   11n5
Harding, Gerald Lankester   233n132
Hardmeier, Christof   141n31

Harkins, Angela Kim   173, 173n74, 173n75,
   277n50, 340, 341n26, 394n31, 469n68,
   469n69
Harland, Philip A.   422n29, 422n30, 423–
   425, 423n31, 423n32, 424n40, 425n41,
   425n42, 425n44, 435n81
Harlow, Daniel C.   247n188, 344n39, 344n43,
   432n73
Harrington, Hannah K.   169n57, 170n59,
   184n118, 429, 429n57, 430n61
Harris, William V.   16n25, 17n29, 111n165, 137,
   137n11
Harrison, James R.   17n30
Hartog, Pieter B.   4, 80, 80n36, 80n37,
   80n38, 82n47, 98n113, 233, 233n131,
   267n4, 268n7, 269n12, 270n18, 272n34,
   273n38, 274n40, 274n42, 275n46,
   277n53, 280n61, 280n65, 281n67,
   281n68, 282n71, 282n73, 285n83,
   375n52, 378n65, 455, 455n7, 457,
   457n15, 459, 459n20, 459n21, 465–466,
   466n55, 466n56, 480–482
Hauptman, Andreas   303n29
Haverlock, Eric A.   24n50, 475
Hayes, Christine   207n29
Haysom, M.   424n38
He, Sheng   90n80
Hearon, Holly E.   267n5, 379n66, 476m6
Hedner Zetterholm, Karin   180n103
Heilmann, Jan   30, 30n72, 30n74, 30n75,
   32n77
Hellholm, David   172n67
Hempel, Charlotte   4, 5, 76n18, 81n43, 84,
   84n57, 84n59, 89n79, 91n85, 95n100,
   101n120, 109n155, 114, 114n178, 115, 135n1,
   138, 138n13, 168n48, 170n58, 175n82,
   176n89, 177, 177n94, 178n95, 178n96,
   178n98, 179n100, 182n112, 182n113,
   183n114, 184n118, 199n1, 202n9, 203n10,
   205n21, 206–207, 206n29, 206n30,
   207n31, 215n72, 233n132, 237n148,
   238n150, 239n154, 240n156, 240n159,
   242n167, 242n168, 244n174, 244n180,
   245n181, 245n182, 246–247, 246n187,
   247n189, 247n190, 248n192, 248n194,
   249, 249n201, 250n203, 251n205,
   251n208, 252, 252n209, 253n209, 257,
   257n214, 276n49, 281n69, 283n76,

INDEX OF MODERN AUTHORS

Hempel, Charlotte (*cont.*)
284*n*77, 285*n*80, 317*n*94, 337*n*5,
337*n*9, 337*n*10, 338*n*11, 339*n*16,
340*n*21, 340*n*22, 340*n*23, 341*n*27,
342*n*33, 346*n*51, 346*n*52, 346*n*55,
347*n*56, 347*n*59, 348*n*64, 349*n*66,
350*n*72, 350*n*73, 351*n*74, 358*n*1,
392*n*24, 393*n*26, 394, 394*n*33, 394*n*34,
395*n*36, 395*n*37, 399*n*50, 417*n*5,
418*n*9, 421*n*24, 428, 429*n*56, 454*n*4,
456, 457*n*14, 459*n*23, 460, 460*n*26, 461,
461*n*32, 465–466, 466*n*54, 466*n*57, 468,
468*n*63, 468*n*64, 483–484, 483*n*36,
491*n*9, 497*n*25
Hendel, Ronald   18*n*32, 19*n*34, 37*n*98,
367–368, 367*n*23
Henrich, A.   83*n*55
Henten, Jan Willem van   105*n*139
Henze, Matthias   267*n*4
Hepp, Andreas   165*n*43
Hepworth, Thomas C.   73*n*4
Herdt, Gilbert   407*n*71
Hess, Richard S.   15*n*21
Hezser, Catherine   9*n*1, 12*n*10, 15*n*22, 77*n*20,
105*n*140, 111*n*165, 112*n*168, 137*n*11, 145*n*53,
270*n*17, 315*n*83, 326, 326*n*127
Hiebert, Theodore   15*n*21
Hill, Caroline E.   158*n*12
Hill, Charles E.   31*n*77
Hilton, Allen R.   29*n*66
Hirschfeld, Yizhar   94*n*96
Hjarvard, Stig   165*n*43
Hockey, Marilyn I.   306*n*41
Hoffmeier, James K.   37*n*98
Hofius, Otfried   474*n*8
Hogan, Bernie   348, 348*n*61
Høgenhaven, Jesper   300*n*13, 302, 302*n*24,
302*n*25, 303*n*27, 305, 305*n*37, 305*n*39,
309, 309*n*53, 310, 310*n*57, 312*n*72,
313*n*73, 324, 325*n*123
Hollander, August den   19*n*35, 21*n*42
Holmén, Tom   35*n*91
Holmes, Michael W.   19*n*35, 20*n*38, 478*n*26
Holm-Nielsen, Svend   340, 340*n*24
Horbury, William   87*n*66
Horrell, David G.   43*n*120
Horsley, Richard A.   26*n*57, 26*n*59, 27*n*59,
29*n*70, 476, 476*n*16, 479*n*28
Horst, Pieter W. van der   105*n*139
Houghton, Hugh A. G.   19*n*37

Hoyland, Robert G.   110*n*161
Huebner, Sabine R.   339*n*15
Humbert, Jean-Baptiste   105*n*137, 205*n*22,
321*n*105, 324*n*121, 415, 416*n*2, 439*n*94
Humphrey, Caroline   158, 159*n*16
Hunt, C. O.   303*n*29
Hunter, David G.   402*n*57
Hurtado, Larry W.   1*n*3, 2*n*3, 15*n*22, 30*n*71,
31, 31*n*77, 139*n*19, 377*n*61, 474*n*8,
476*n*18
Hüsken, Ute   43*n*121, 166*n*43
Hylen, Susan E.   44*n*124
Hymes, Dell   136*n*5

Iddeng, Jon   200, 200*n*4, 212*n*63
Imaeda, Yoshirō   491*n*8
Iverson, Kelly R.   26*n*57, 30*n*71

Jacobus, Helen R.   93*n*92
Jaffee, Martin S.   3, 145*n*53, 148, 148*n*67,
148*n*68, 151, 151*n*78, 362*n*15, 368,
368*n*26, 459*n*22, 479*n*28
Jain, Eva   98*n*111
Janzen, David   166*n*45
Jassen, Alex P.   111*n*166, 146, 146*n*58, 146*n*59,
147*n*60, 440–441, 440*n*97, 440*n*98,
440*n*99
Jefferson, Rebecca J. W.   336*n*3
Jellinek, Adolph   301*n*21, 308*n*49
Jense, Jeppe Sinding   386*n*5
Jerotijević, Danijela   398*n*47
Jeserich, Florian   158*n*11
Johnson, Luke Timothy   110*n*163
Johnson, Mark   386*n*6, 397*n*44, 397*n*45, 402,
402*n*58
Johnson, Michael Brooks   242*n*167
Johnson, William A.   1, 1*n*1, 2, 2*n*4, 4, 5, 6,
14*n*18, 29*n*69, 31, 31*n*76, 83*n*52, 84,
84*n*56, 137*n*11, 199*n*1, 200, 200*n*3,
200*n*5, 200*n*6, 212–213, 212*n*58, 212*n*63,
212*n*64, 213*n*65, 213*n*66, 213*n*67, 213*n*68,
214*n*71, 218, 218*n*87, 218*n*88, 218*n*90,
219, 219*n*94, 220, 220*n*96, 228, 229*n*119,
254–255, 269, 269*n*15, 269*n*16, 270*n*17,
270*n*18, 285*n*82, 303*n*26, 347*n*60,
349*n*65, 371*n*37, 395, 395*n*35, 395*n*36,
406*n*68, 472*n*3, 478, 478*n*27, 481–482,
491*n*9, 492, 492*n*11, 493, 494*n*16, 495*n*17,
495*n*18, 495*n*20, 496*n*21, 496*n*22,
499*n*33

Jokiranta, Jutta   3, 5, 100, 100n119, 101n121,
   101n122, 101n123, 105n141, 142, 142n37,
   171, 171n66, 171n67, 174, 174n81, 175n84,
   176, 176n89, 179n100, 180n103, 183n115,
   202n9, 240, 240n156, 242n167, 242n168,
   243n171, 250n203, 251n205, 278n54,
   279n58, 281n69, 370n31, 375n53,
   392n23, 393n25, 395n39, 399n50,
   416, 416n3, 417n5, 418n9, 461, 461n33,
   462–464, 463n38, 463n39, 463n40,
   463n41, 464n45, 467, 467n61, 468n67,
   469, 469n70, 469n71, 472n2, 482–483
Jones, Lindsay   161n26, 359n6
Joosten, Jan   18n34, 311n62, 312n72
Jost, Michael   442n105
Joyal, Mark   373n43
Jull, A. J. Timothy   245m81
Jürgens, Benedikt   45n128
Justnes, Årstein   88n73, 234n135, 336n3

Kafafi, Zeidan A.   303n29
Kampen, John   143–44, 143n40, 143n42,
   143n43, 144n46, 428n51
Kanngießer, Birgit   74n10, 75n13
Kapera, Zdzisław Jan   310n58
Kaše, Vojtěch   43n123
Katz, Steven T.   314n79
Kazen, Thomas   184, 184n119, 184n120
Keady, Jessica M.   408n76
Keegan, James G.   342n31
Keener, Craig   32n80
Keith, Chris   1n3, 2, 2n3, 5, 6, 10n2, 13n13,
   14n17, 15n22, 16n24, 23n47, 32, 32n78,
   33n83, 35n91, 35n92, 36n94, 36n95,
   36n96, 115m180, 137m10, 137m10, 138m12,
   139n19, 140n20, 140n21, 141n30, 149n72,
   164n41, 209n45, 228n118, 229n120,
   266m1, 286, 326m127, 349, 349n67,
   349n68, 359n7, 362n13, 386n3, 445, 472,
   472n1, 472n3, 474n8, 474n10, 475n12,
   477n19, 477n22, 478n24, 478n27,
   479n28, 483n35
Kelber, Werner H.   6, 23n47, 26, 26n57,
   26n58, 27n63, 141n30, 141n31, 142n32,
   363n16, 475–478, 475n13, 475n14,
   476n15, 477n23
Kelle, Brad E.   42n117
Kenyon, Frederic G.   77n19

Kertzer, David I.   41n114
Kessler, Nadine   95n99, 95m100
Kim, Dong-Hyuk   86n65
Kindzorra, Emanuel   74n10, 75n13
Kingsley, Sean   317n93
Kirk, Alan   35n89, 35n90, 35n91, 36n94,
   267n5, 477, 478n24
Kirk, Geoffrey S.   359n5
Kister, Menahem   233n130
Klawans, Jonathan   388m10, 489n3
Klein, Olivier   402n56
Klein-Franke, Felix   306n40
Klingbeil, Gerald A.   38n101, 39n102, 40,
   40n110, 40n111, 44n127, 166n45
Klinghardt, Matthias   415, 415n1, 420,
   420n17, 422n30, 430, 430n62, 430n63,
   431n66, 432, 432n68, 444
Kloner, Amos   314n81
Kloppenborg, John S.   1n3, 18n32, 19n35,
   31n77, 419, 420n13, 420n15, 424n37,
   426n44, 435n81
Klostergaard, Anders Peterson   82n48,
   386n5
Knibb, Michael A.   142n35
Knoppers, Gary   338m14
Knox, B. M.   30n73
Knust, Jennifer   474n9
Kobel, Esther   426n46
Koenen, L.   83n55
Kofoed, Jens Bruun   37n98
König, Jason   494n16, 500n35
Konstan, David   24n53, 142n36
Korner, Ralph   422n29
Kosmin, Paul J.   395n39
Kotansky, Roy D.   305n40
Kottsieper, Ingo   76m18, 77, 77n21, 77n23
Kövecses, Zoltán   402n58
Kraemer, Ross S.   12m12
Kraft, Robert A.   88n72, 208n36, 311n61,
   432n68
Krátý, Jan   398n47
Kratz, Reinhard G.   276n49, 281n66, 337n5,
   337n6, 340n23
Krause, Andrew R.   183n116
Krauß, Anna   30n75, 78n25, 81n40, 92n89,
   185n123, 215n72, 219n95, 478n27
Kreinath, Jens   39n103, 44n126, 156m1, 160,
   160n23, 160n24, 385n2

INDEX OF MODERN AUTHORS

Kruger, Michael J. 31n77
Kugel, James L. 274n41
Kugler, Robert A. 89n78, 110n164, 167n47, 168, 168n50, 168n51, 168n52, 168n53, 169, 171–72, 175, 175n84, 175n85, 463, 463n38
Kuhn, Karl G. 296n6, 300, 300n14, 301n17
Kundt, Radek 386n5

Lacoudre, Noël 300n11, 301n19
Laidlaw, James A. 158, 159n16
Lakoff, George 402, 402n58
Lama, Mariachiara 78n26
LaMantia, Anthony-Samuel 365n21
Lamoreaux, Jason T. 38n101, 43n120
Lang, Bernhard 11n4
Lang, Martin 398n47
Lang, T. J. 22n46
Lange, Armin 76n17, 87n67, 91n84, 114n176, 142n37, 167n47, 170n57, 338n12
Langlois, Michael 82n46
Lanzillotta, Lautaro Roig 227n117
Laperrousaz, Ernest-Marie 93n91, 313, 313n75, 319n102, 323n114, 325, 325n126
Lapham, Lewis H. 266n2
Lapierre, André 311n60
Lapin, Hayim 341n27
Larsen, Matthew D. C. 47n410
Larson, Erik 311n61
Lauwereyns, Jan 402n56
Law, Timothy Michael 338n13
Lawrence, Louis J. 43n120, 167n47
Lawson, E. Thomas 45, 45n130, 159, 159n17, 163, 163n33, 163n36, 389n15, 405n66
Leach, Edmund 39, 39n104
Le Donne, Anthony 33n82, 35n93, 36n95, 36n96, 267n5, 278, 278n55, 362n13, 483, 483n34
Lee, Sang-Il 13n15, 474n11
Lefkovits, Judah 304, 304n33, 324n120, 326n129
Legnaioli, Stefano 74n12
Lehmann, Manfred 313, 313n77, 313n78
Lieberman, Saul 351n74
Leibner, Uzi 305n40
Leipziger, Jonas 1n2, 30n75, 78n25, 81n40, 92n89, 185n123, 215n72, 219n95, 478n27
Lemaire, André 11n4, 11n7, 87n69, 93n91, 104, 104n135, 104n136, 105n137, 109n158, 110n159, 111n167, 112n171, 138n12, 205, 205n22, 205n23, 373, 373n44
Lembi, Gaia 211n51
Leonhard, Clemens 76n14, 209n42
Lethbridge, Emily 71n2
Leuchter, Mark 38n99
Levin, Christoph 34n87
Levin, Yigal 15n21
Levine, Amy-Jill 12n12
Levy, Thomas E. 36n97
Lewis, Naphtali 273n38
Lied, Liv Ingeborg 18n31, 20n40, 21n43, 45n131, 98n111, 267, 267n3, 267n4
Liénard, Pierre 45, 45n129, 162, 162n31, 163n34, 176n88, 398n47
Lietzmann, Hans 42n119
Lieu, Judith M. 91n85, 342, 342n32, 417n5
Lightstone, Jack N. 111n165
Liland, Fredrik 308n48
Lim, Timothy H. 142n33, 311n62, 337n8, 441n102
Lin, Yii-Jan 19n36
Lindbeck, Kristen H. 374n47
Lindsay, D. Stephen 33n84
Lindsay, R. C. L. 33n84
Löhr, Hermut 76n14, 209n42
Long, V. Philips 15n21
Longacre, Drew 76n18, 81n43, 89n79, 168n48, 175n82, 178n96, 179n100, 182n112, 184n118, 199n1, 203n10, 205n21, 215n74, 216, 216n79, 216n80, 217n84, 285n80, 337n5, 337n9, 337n10, 340n22, 341n27, 342n33, 421n24, 497n25
Longenecker, Bruce W. 17n30
Lord, Albert 23, 23n48, 364n17, 475
Lorenzetti, Giulia 74n12
Loubser, J. A. 10n3, 267n5
Louw, Theo A. W. van der 273n38
Lübee, J. C. 85n60
Lubetski, Meir 88n74, 268n10
Lühl, Lars 74n10, 75n13
Lundhaug, Hugo 18n31, 20n40, 98n111, 267n4
Luomanen, Petri 46n133, 469n70
Luria, Ben-Zion 313, 313n76
Luttikhuizen, Gerard P. 311n62
Lyons, William J. 205n21, 279n58, 338n12

MacDonald, Nathan   40n108, 167n45, 170n59
Macy, Michael   397n43
Maehler, Herwig   217n83, 217n86
Maeir, Aren M.   96n103, 316n90
Magary, Dennis R.   37n98
Magen, Yitzhak   94n96, 105n140
Magness, Jodi   89n77, 95n101, 96n103,
   203n10, 204n16, 206, 206n26, 316n90,
   347n58, 415, 416n2, 439n92, 439n93,
   459n23
Maiden, Brett E.   45
Malafouris, Lambros   406n67
Malik, Peter   21n42
Malzer, Wolfgang   74n10, 75n13
Mandel, Alice   214n69
Mandel, Paul D.   28n66, 372, 372n38
Manfredi, Manfredo   78n26
Maniaci, Marilena   21n43
Mantouvalou, Ioanna   74n10, 75n13
Marks, Susan   432n73, 436n83, 439, 439n95
Markschies, Christoph   474n8, 478n27
Marquis, Galen   82n47, 86n62, 111n166,
   301n18
Marrou, Henri I.   28n65
Martin, Luther H.   386n5
Martin, Malachi   85n60, 337n10
Martin Hogan, Karina   372n41
Martone, Corrado   93n93
Masic, Admir   74n10, 74n11
Mason, Eric F.   94n95, 233n131, 277n50,
   341n26
Mason, Steve   210–211, 210n51, 211n51, 211n52,
   211n53, 211n54, 211n55, 339, 339n15
Mastin, Brian A.   77n25
Mattingly, D. J.   303n29
Mauss, Marcel   172n70
Mavrogenes, Nancy A.   28n65
McCartney, Eugene S.   28n64
McCauley, Robert N.   45, 45n130, 159, 159n17,
   163, 163n33, 163n36, 171, 386n4, 389n15,
   405n66
McCorkle Jr., William W.   392n22, 398n47,
   398n48
McCutcheon, R. W.   30n72
McDonald, Lee M.   337n8
McDonnel, Myles   209n45
McDougall, Iain   373n43
McGann, Jerome J.   97n108

McIver, Robert K.   32n80, 33n81, 362n13
McKenzie, Steven L.   24n52
McLaren, S. J.   303n29
McLay, R. Timothy   139n17, 270n17, 371n35,
   394n32, 480n30
McLuhan, Marshall   266, 266n2, 385, 385n1
McNamee, Kathleen   277n52, 277n53
McVann, Mark   46n134
Mébarki, Farah   301n19
Mee, Christopher   108n153
Meeks, Wayne A.   42, 42n119, 43n120
Melzer, Gudrun   308n48
Menary, Richard   406n67
Mermelstein, Ari   170n59, 407n72, 469n69
Metso, Sarianna   80n36, 81n41, 86n65,
   95n100, 99n114, 100, 100n117, 100n118,
   149, 149n73, 150–151, 151n77, 180n105,
   202n9, 237n148, 238n150, 239n151,
   240n157, 241n164, 245n182, 245n185,
   248n192, 250n203, 251, 251n205, 267n4,
   268n6, 277n50, 338n11, 339, 339n17,
   339n19, 350n71, 416n4, 417n5, 432n68,
   456–457, 456n8
Metzger, Bruce M.   473n4, 473n5
Meyers, Eric M.   110n163
Mildenberg, Leo   315n84
Milgrom, Jacob   170, 170n60
Mili, M.   424n38
Milik, Józef T.   73n6, 80n39, 80n40, 81n40,
   106, 106n145, 203n14, 215, 219n92, 227,
   227n115, 227n116, 238n150, 243n172,
   244n181, 271, 271n28, 283, 283n74,
   296n3, 300n12, 301, 301n20, 303n28,
   304, 304n32, 309n50, 310, 310n58,
   319n99, 325, 325n125
Millar, Fergus   315n85
Millard, Alan   16n26
Miller, Marvin   375n50, 378, 378n64
Miller, Robert D.   24n52
Miller, Shem   1n2, 3, 278n56, 359, 359n8,
   362, 371, 371n33, 371n36, 374, 374n46,
   375n53, 377n62, 455–459, 456n8,
   456n10, 457n13, 459n25, 461, 468,
   468n65, 468n66, 479–480
Miller, Stuart   185n124, 406n70
Miller, Yonatan S.   185n122
Mimouni, Simon C.   104n136, 138n12,
   205n23, 373n44

INDEX OF MODERN AUTHORS

Mink, Gerd   19n35
Misgav, Haggai   105n140
Mitchell, Charles A.   73n4
Mitchell, T. Crichton   306n41
Mitkidis, Panagiotis   163n34
Mittmann-Richert, Ulrike   76n17
Mizzi, Dennis   203n10, 204n16, 233n132, 298, 346, 346n52, 347n58, 439, 439n93, 439n96
Młynarczyk, Jolanta   319, 319n100, 319n101
Modiano, Raimonda   97n109
Monger, Matthew P.   267n4
Montgomery, James A.   306n40
Mooney, Richard D.   365n21
Morales, Pablo A. Torijano   18n33, 99n114
Morenz, Ludwig   13n15
Morgan, G. C.   303n29
Morgan, Theresa   12n11
Mowinckel, Sigmund   301n20
Mroczek, Eva   97, 97n109, 98n110, 98n111, 337n8, 337n9, 406n68
Mueller, Martin   73n9
Mugridge, Alan   218n89
Muir, Steven C.   43n120
Mulder, M. J.   15n22
Mulken, Margot van   19n35
Müller, Darius   21n42
Müller, Reinhard   337n5
Müller-Kessler, Christa   306n41
Murphy, Bridget   73n9
Murphy, Catherine M.   81n41
Murphy-O'Connor, Jerome   338, 338n11, 349n66

Nadel, L.   405n66
Naeh, Shlomo   110n161
Najman, Hindy   80n36, 86n65, 100n119, 114n176, 147n61, 176n86, 202n9, 268n6, 277n50, 279, 279n59, 280n61, 280n62, 309n51, 337n8, 337n9, 358n3, 360n9, 392n23, 417n5
Nässelqvist, Dan   29n67, 209n45, 476n18
Nati, James   202n9, 237n148, 238n150, 242n167, 248n192, 248n194, 250–251, 250n204, 251n207
Naveh, Joseph   107–108, 107n149, 108n150, 108n151, 305n40
Nebe, G. Wilhelm   104n134

Nemeroff, Carol   407n71
Neubert, Frank   43n121
Neufeld, Dietmar   43n120
Newman, Judith H.   18n32, 19n35, 147, 147n61, 167n47, 175–176, 176n86, 177n92, 182n112, 184n121, 309n51, 360n9, 402, 402n57
Newsom, Carol A.   140, 140n23, 173, 173n72, 178n95, 182n112, 341n26, 349n66, 376, 376n59, 404n61, 441n101, 442, 442n104, 457, 457n16, 468, 468n68
Niccum, Curt   81n41
Nichols, Stephen   20n40
Nicklas, Tobias   282n69, 370n31
Niditch, Susan   24, 24n53, 25, 25n56, 26, 42n117, 42n118, 136n5, 149n71, 367–368, 368n24, 369n28
Nielbo, Kristoffer L.   163n34
Nielsen, Hanne Sigismund   430n61
Nielsen, Inge   430n61
Nir-El, Yoram   73n7
Nissinen, Martti   46n133, 89n78
Nitzan, Bilhah   102n125, 104n136, 183n115, 278n54, 372n39
Noam, Vered   170n58, 184n118, 396n41
Noegel, Scott B.   97n109
Nongbri, Brent   336n3
Norelli, Enrico   35n90
Norenzayan, Ara   386n5
Norton, Jonathan D. H.   92n89, 141, 141n28
Novick, Tzvi   207n30

Obbink, Dirk   277n51, 498n27
Oestreich, Bernard   29n70
Ogilvie, Elisabeth   462n35, 462n36
Oikonomopoulou, Katerina   494n16, 500n35
Olyan, Saul M.   41, 42n115, 42n116, 42n118, 167n45
Ong, Hughson T.   13n15
Ong, Walter J.   24n50, 27, 139, 139n18, 376, 376n58, 475
Orlinsky, Harry M.   136, 136n6
Orlov, Andrei A.   302n23
Otero, André Piquer   18n33, 99n114
Ott, Michael R.   112n170

Pagels, Marcel   74n10, 75n13
Paget, James Carleton   1n3, 15n22

Pajunen, Mika S.   98n111, 101n119, 174n81, 219n95, 362n14, 399n51
Pakkala, Juha   89n78, 337n5
Palleschi, Vincenzo   74n12
Panayotov, Alex   301n21
Papies, Esther K.   398n46, 401n55
Pardee, Dennis G.   89n76, 93n91, 318n96, 422n30
Parker, David C.   19n35, 19n37, 476n15
Parker, Holt N.   14n18, 29n69, 31n76, 395n36
Parker, Stephen   180n105
Parry, Adam   23n48
Parry, Donald W.   75n13, 85n61, 95n100, 149n73, 150n75, 180n105, 234n133, 339n17, 391n20, 456n8
Parry, Milman   23, 23n48, 364n17, 475
Parsons, Peter   498n27, 499n31
Parvis, Paul M.   44n125
Patrich, Joseph   105n139, 318n96, 319, 323–324, 323n115, 323n116
Paul, Shalom M.   88n72, 208n35, 311n61, 432n68
Peerbolte, Bert Jan Lietaert   402n57
Peleg, Yuval   94n96, 105n140
Penn, Michael P.   44, 44n125
Penner, Jeremy   172n68, 174n81, 181n111, 362n14, 389n13, 405n65, 407n73
Penner, Ken M.   172n68, 389n13, 405n65, 407n73
Perdue, Leo G.   114n176, 140n23
Perfect, Timothy J.   33n84
Perrin, Andrew B.   99n114, 202n9, 267n4
Perrot, Antony   77n25
Perry, Peter S.   29n70
Person, Raymond F.   10n2, 23n47, 24n52, 25n56, 101n120, 137n10, 138n12, 140n20, 140n21, 141n30, 149n72, 164n41, 209n45, 266n1, 349, 349n67, 349n68, 358n4, 359n7, 369–370, 369n27, 369n29, 386n3, 472, 472n1
Peters, Dorothy   98n113, 169n56
Peursen, Wido T. van   78n29, 216n75, 272n30
Pfann, Stephen J.   76n16, 80n39, 82n47, 94, 94n97, 95, 95n98, 97n107, 105n137, 107n149, 112n169
Phelps, E. A.   405n66
Piasetzky, Eli   14n20
Pichon, Cora-Lise   402n56

Pietersen, Lloyd K.   205n21, 279n58, 338n12
Pinnick, Avital   75n13, 182n113
Pioske, Daniel D.   37, 37n99
Pixner, Bargil   304n31, 311, 312n66, 321, 321n108, 322n112, 323n117
Platt, Michael L.   365n21
Plenderleith, Harold J.   73n6
Pleše, Zlatko   275n45, 370n31
Plicht, Johannes van der   74n12
Poirier, John C.   13n14, 106n143
Poorthuis, Marcel   184n119
Popović, Mladen   1, 1n2, 4, 78n27, 90, 90n80, 92–93, 93n90, 94n94, 95n99, 114n179, 138, 138n12, 138n14, 142n34, 199n1, 205n22, 206n28, 212n58, 227n117, 230n124, 234n134, 247n188, 248n194, 253n211, 270n17, 273n38, 276n49, 342n33, 347n57, 374n48, 395n35, 417n5, 438, 438n88, 438n89, 438n90, 438n91, 461, 461n33, 462n33, 462n37, 465, 481–482, 491–492, 491n10, 492n12, 492n13, 494, 494n15, 495n19, 497n23, 501n35, 503n45
Porter, Stanley E.   13n13, 35n91
Porubanova, Michaela   405n64
Porzig, Peter   393n28
Pouchelle, Patrick   102n127
Pouilly, Jean   338n11
Price, Jonathan J.   110n161
Propp, William H. C.   36n97
Puech, Émile   105n137, 108, 108n152, 205n24, 215, 245n181, 245n182, 252n209, 299, 300n11, 301, 301n18, 301n19, 304, 304n30, 304n34, 305n35, 317
Purves, Dale   365n21
Pyysiäinen, Ilkka   46n133, 160n24, 469n70

Qimron, Elisha   280n63, 428n52
Quack, Johannes   163n33
Quick, Laura   1n2, 11n6, 81n40, 215n72
Quine, Cat   167n45
Quinn, Judy   71n1

Raaflaub, Kurt A.   24n53, 142n36
Rabin, Chaim   110n160, 312n69
Rabin, Ira   74n10, 74n11, 75n13
Radovan, Zev   294n2
Ralls Baun, Jane   21n44

INDEX OF MODERN AUTHORS

Ramble, Charles   405n62
Rao, Ursula   157n6
Rappaport, Roy A.   158, 158n15, 159n15, 163n33, 168n51, 174n78, 175, 389n12, 390n16
Rappaport, Uriel   87n67, 89n77, 206n27
Rasmussen, Kaare Lund   74n12
Ratajczak, Henryk   93n91
Read, J. Don   33n84
Redman, Judith C. S.   33n81
Reed, Ronald   77n19
Reed, Stephen   110, 110n161, 110n162
Reed, William   296, 296n4, 318n97, 321, 321n105, 321n109
Reenen, Pieter van   19n35
Regev, Eyal   184n119, 205n21, 359n6, 418n9, 468n67
Rengstorf, Karl H.   94n96
Rey, Jean-Sébastien   246n187
Reynolds, Bennie   359, 359n7
Rezetko, Robert   101n120, 358n4
Rhoads, David   29n70, 476, 476n17
Riaud, Jean   104n136
Richey, Matthew   310n60, 312n67
Ricks, Stephen D.   75n13, 85n61
Robson, Eleanor   500–501, 500n35, 501n36
Rodenbiker, Kelsie G.   22n45
Röder, Jörg   282n69
Rodgers, Zuleika   315n86
Rodríguez, Rafael   24n52, 27, 27n61, 27n63, 36n95, 136n4, 140n26, 149, 149n72, 473n6, 477, 477n21, 480, 481n31
Rogers, Zuleika   339n15
Rohrhirsch, Ferdinand   90n81, 91n81
Roitman, Adolfo D.   442n103
Roitto, Rikard   40n110, 43n120, 43n123, 44n124, 46n131, 167n45
Rollston, Christopher A.   11n7, 14n19
Römer, Thomas   373n42
Roskovec, Jan   202n9
Ross, David F.   33n84
Roth, Dieter T.   1n3, 32n78
Rothenberg, Beno   304n29
Rothenbuhler, Eric W.   39n103
Royle, Anthony   22n46
Rozin, Paul   407n71
Rubin, Rechav   105n139
Rück, Peter   77n23
Ruge-Jones, Philip   267n5, 379n66

Runesson, Anders   180n103, 423–424, 423n30, 423n34, 423n35, 424n36
Ryder, Michael L.   77n23

Saenger, Paul   28n65
Safrai, Shmuel   12n8, 110n160, 312n69
Saley, Richard J.   234n133
Sander, Lore   308n48
Sanders, E. P.   476n14
Sanders, James A.   88n73, 230n123, 337n8
Sanderson, Judith E.   73n8, 220n97
Sandoval, Timothy J.   182n113
Sänger, Dieter   172n67
Santos, Ava   400n53, 402n56, 403n60
Sarri, Antonia   83n50, 83n51
Saukkonen, Juhana M.   89n78, 105n141, 114, 114n177
Sax, William S.   163n33
Schade, Ulrich   74n10
Schäfer, Peter   314n81
Schaper, Joachim   1n3, 15n22
Schechner, Richard   173n73
Schellenberg, Ryan S.   16n24
Scherbenske, Eric   21n44
Schiffman, Lawrence H.   3, 76n16, 77n18, 82n47, 86n62, 88n72, 93n91, 96n103, 102n125, 104n134, 111n166, 143n44, 144, 144n47, 144n48, 144n49, 145n50, 145n51, 145n54, 146, 146n55, 146n57, 147, 147n62, 147n63, 147n64, 148, 148n65, 148n66, 149, 151, 178n96, 180n103, 202n8, 208n36, 271n23, 274n41, 301n18, 311n61, 316n90, 351n74, 431, 431n67, 432n68, 442n103
Schmid, Ulrich   21n42
Schmidt, Brian B.   25n56, 369n27, 369n29
Schneider, Thomas   36n97
Schnelle, Udo   16n27
Schniedewind, William M.   24n51, 149n71
Schnocks, Johannes   87n69
Schoenfeld, Stuart   15n23
Schofield, Alison   91–92, 92n86, 92n87, 92n88, 92n89, 98n113, 101n120, 148n69, 148n70, 150, 150n74, 150n76, 205n21, 206n29, 207n34, 208, 208n36, 208n37, 208n38, 233n131, 267n4, 277n50, 283–284, 283n75, 284n77, 338n11, 339, 340n20, 341n26, 349n64, 416, 416n3, 418, 460n29

Schomaker, Lambert 90n80, 230, 230n124, 234n134
Schoonover, Myles 78n27, 248n194, 273n38
Schorch, Stefan 13n15
Schröter, Bernd 340n23
Schröter, Jens 33n85, 36n96, 474n8
Schücking-Jungblut, Friederike 30n75, 78n25, 81n40, 92n89, 185n123, 215n72, 219n95, 478n27
Schuller, Eileen 80n36, 86n65, 89n78, 167n47, 181n109, 181n111, 248n196, 249, 249n202, 268n6, 277n50, 404n61, 434n77, 441n101
Schürer, Emil 12n8, 315n85
Schwab, Moïse 306n40
Schwartz, Barry 34, 36n94
Schwartz, Daniel R. 75n13
Schwartz, Joshua J. 184n119
Schwartz, Seth 312n71
Schwiebert, Jonathan 43n123
Scodel, Ruth 375n54
Searle, John R. 159n18, 372n40
Searle, Leroy F. 97n109
Sedgwick, W. B. 28n65
Segal, Michael 18n33, 99n114, 99n115, 280n60
Segal, Moses H. 312n70
Segal, Robert A. 157n3
Sevenster, Jan N. 312n68
Shaked, Saul 305n40
Shamir, Orit 324n122
Shanks, Hershel 315n87
Shantz, Colleen 468n68
Sharbach Wollenberg, Rebecca 480n29
Shaus, Arie 14n20
Shaver, John 398n47
Shavit, Yaacov 93n91
Sherzer, Joel 136n5
Shiell, William D. 29n68
Shillingsburg, Peter L. 97n109, 364n19
Shils, David L. 39n104
Shiner, Whitney T. 29n69, 476
Shor, Pnina 72n3
Shurgaia, Gaga 22n45
Shweder, Richard A. 407n71
Siegel, Jonathan P. 85n60
Siegismund, Kasper 336n3
Sievers, Joseph 211n51

Signer, Michael A. 37n98
Siker, Jeffrey S. 76n16
Silberman, L. H. 301n20
Silverman, Jason M. 25n54, 361n11, 368n25, 373n45
Simmons, W. Kyle 400n53, 402n56, 403n60
Simon, Udo 166n43
Sinnott-Armstrong, E. A. 405n66
Sirinian, Anna 22n45
Skeat, T. C. 77n22
Skehan, Patrick W. 73n8, 81n41, 106n146, 220n97
Slater, Elizabeth 108m153
Slone, D. Jason 392n22, 398n47, 398n48
Sluiter, Ineke 277n51
Smelik, Willem 13n15, 21n42
Smith, Dennis E. 425n44, 426n46, 432, 432n71, 432n72, 432n73, 434, 434n79, 434n80, 436n82
Smith, Grant 311n60
Smith, Mark S. 37n98
Smith, Patricia 75n13
Smithuis, Renate 104n133, 115n180, 372n41
Smoak, Jeremy D. 306n40
Snoek, Jan 39n103, 44n126, 156n1, 160, 160n23, 160n24, 385n2
Snyder, H. Gregory 28n66, 82n47, 282, 282n70, 282n71
Sober, Barak 14n20
Sørensen, Jesper 163n33, 163n34, 174, 386n5
Sørensen, Jørgen Podemann 424n39
Sosis, Richard 163n34, 392n22, 398, 398n48
Sperber, Daniel 40n107, 311n65
Spolsky, Bernard 110n160
Staal, Frits 39n106, 40n106, 158, 158n14, 172, 172n68
Stacey, David 94n96, 97n107
Starr, Raymond 73n3, 200, 200n4, 209–210, 209n43, 209n44, 210n46, 210n47, 210n49, 212, 212n63, 229n119
Staszak, Martin 246n187
Stausberg, Michael 39n103, 44n126, 156n1, 160, 160n23, 160n24, 385n2
Stavrianopoulou, Eftychia 40n108
Steckoll, Solomon H. 73n6
Stegemann, Hartmut 87n67, 90n81, 204, 204n15, 204n17, 271n23
Stephenson, Barry 38n100

INDEX OF MODERN AUTHORS

Sterling, Gregory E. 233*n*130
Stern, Elsie R. 10*n*2, 23*n*47, 137*n*10, 140*n*20, 140*n*21, 141*n*30, 149*n*72, 164*n*41, 209*n*45, 266*n*1, 349*n*67, 359*n*7, 386*n*3, 472, 472*n*1
Stern, Menahem 312*n*69
Steudel, Annette 275*n*44, 281*n*66
Stigler, James W. 407*n*71
Still, Todd D. 43*n*120
Stock, Brian 115, 139–140, 140*n*22, 140*n*24, 140*n*25, 168*n*52, 347*n*57, 461, 491, 491*n*10
Stökl Ben Ezra, Daniel 95–96, 95*n*100, 96*n*102, 106*n*144, 112*n*170, 171, 171*n*63, 171*n*64, 171*n*65
Stone, Michael 313*n*74
Strange, James R. 106*n*143
Strawn, Brent A. 82*n*47
Stroker, William D. 474*n*8
Strugnell, John 215, 268–269, 268*n*7, 268*n*8, 268*n*9, 269*n*14, 274
Stuckenbruck, Loren T. 35*n*90, 102*n*124, 276*n*49, 286, 362*n*14
Sukenik, Eleazar L. 96*n*107, 335–336, 340
Sumiala, Johanna 165*n*43
Sunderland, Kathryn 97*n*108
Sysling, Harry 15*n*22

Tal, Oren 170*n*59
Talmon, Shemaryahu 85*n*61, 135, 135*n*2, 136, 137*n*7, 146, 146*n*55, 146*n*56, 245*n*185, 363*n*16, 374–376, 374*n*49, 376*n*56, 376*n*57, 378, 378*n*63, 468, 468*n*65
Taussig, Hal 43*n*123, 425*n*44, 426, 426*n*45, 432*n*69, 432*n*73, 432*n*74, 436*n*83, 463, 463*n*42
Taylor, Joan E. 4, 74*n*12, 96, 96*n*103, 96*n*104, 96*n*105, 96*n*106, 96*n*107, 108–109, 109*n*155, 109*n*156, 233*n*132, 273*n*36, 296, 315*n*87, 316*n*90, 316*n*91, 317*n*93, 317*n*95, 322*n*113, 324*n*118, 324*n*119, 339*n*15, 464–465, 464*n*47, 482, 482*n*32, 488*n*2, 489*n*3, 490*n*7, 494*n*15
Taylor, Sophia 12*n*8
Tenorio, Anna Lluveras 74*n*12
Tervanotko, Hanna 101*n*119, 399*n*51
Teske, John A. 406*n*67
Testa, Emmanuele 306*n*40
Thatcher, Tom 10*n*2, 16*n*24, 23*n*47, 24*n*51, 26*n*57, 35*n*89, 35*n*90, 35*n*93, 36*n*94,

137*n*10, 139*n*19, 140*n*20, 140*n*21, 141*n*30, 149*n*72, 164*n*41, 209*n*45, 266*n*1, 267*n*5, 278, 278*n*55, 349*n*67, 359*n*7, 362*n*12, 386*n*3, 472, 472*n*1, 477, 478*n*24
Thomas, D. C. 303*n*29
Thomas, Günter 39*n*103, 158*n*10, 385*n*2, 394*n*29
Thomas, Rosalind 14*n*18, 24*n*51, 359*n*5
Thomas, Samuel I. 98*n*113, 143*n*39, 144*n*45, 233*n*131, 267*n*4, 277*n*50, 341*n*26
Tiemeyer, Lena-Sofia 201*n*8
Tigchelaar, Eibert J. C. 18*n*32, 71*n*2, 78, 79, 79*n*30, 79*n*31, 79*n*32, 86*n*65, 88*n*70, 88*n*72, 89*n*79, 90*n*80, 95*n*100, 100*n*119, 113*n*175, 114*n*176, 147*n*61, 176*n*86, 180*n*105, 199*n*1, 202*n*9, 205, 205*n*25, 207, 207*n*32, 208*n*35, 208*n*40, 215*n*74, 216*n*81, 217, 217*n*82, 217*n*84, 217*n*85, 220*n*98, 223, 223*n*108, 235*n*141, 236*n*145, 236*n*146, 236*n*147, 241*n*161, 242*n*168, 244, 244*n*173, 244*n*174, 244*n*176, 244*n*177, 244*n*178, 246*n*186, 253*n*210, 253*n*212, 257, 257*n*213, 272*n*31, 272*n*32, 281*n*69, 285*n*80, 305*n*36, 337*n*10, 344, 344*n*43, 344*n*44, 392*n*23, 417*n*5, 497*n*25
Toglia, Michael P. 33*n*84
Tooman, William A. 365*n*20
Toorn, Karel van der 77*n*23, 337*n*7
Tov, Emanuel 76*n*15, 76*n*18, 77*n*24, 77*n*25, 79, 79*n*33, 79*n*34, 79*n*35, 80*n*39, 81*n*41, 81*n*41, 81*n*42, 81*n*46, 82*n*47, 85–87, 85*n*61, 85*n*62, 86*n*62, 86*n*63, 87*n*68, 87*n*69, 88*n*70, 88*n*71, 99*n*115, 104*n*136, 107, 107*n*146, 107*n*147, 111*n*166, 113*n*173, 137, 137*n*8, 150*n*75, 167*n*47, 185*n*123, 214, 214*n*70, 219*n*95, 220*n*97, 221*n*100, 222, 222*n*104, 222*n*105, 223*n*110, 227*n*116, 229*n*121, 236*n*143, 241*n*165, 245*n*181, 248*n*194, 269, 269*n*11, 270–271, 270*n*18, 270*n*19, 270*n*20, 270*n*21, 271*n*23, 271*n*24, 271*n*29, 273*n*35, 273*n*37, 284, 284*n*79, 301*n*18, 337*n*10, 338*n*12, 338*n*13, 343, 343*n*37, 343*n*38, 346, 346*n*54, 361*n*10, 370*n*30, 370*n*32, 391*n*20, 464*n*46, 502, 502*n*43, 503*n*45
Trebilco, Paul R. 228*n*118
Trebolle Barrera, Julio 81*n*41

Trever, John C.   88*n*73, 230*n*122, 230*n*123, 231, 231*n*126, 232*n*129

Tropper, Amram   459*n*24

Tucker, James M.   99*n*114, 202*n*9, 251, 251*n*205, 267*n*4

Turley, Stephen R.   46*n*134

Turner, John D.   45*n*131

Turner, Victor   41, 41*n*113, 157, 157*n*6, 158, 158*n*12, 159*n*19, 173*n*73

Tzoref, Shani Berrin   268*n*6, 274–275, 274*n*41, 275*n*43, 442*n*103

Ulrich, Eugene   18*n*34, 73*n*8, 81*n*41, 85*n*61, 88*n*71, 88*n*72, 99*n*115, 149*n*73, 201*n*8, 202*n*8, 207*n*30, 208, 208*n*39, 219*n*92, 220*n*96, 220*n*97, 221*n*101, 221*n*102, 222*n*103, 222*n*106, 222*n*107, 223*n*109, 224*n*111, 224*n*112, 226*n*113, 230*n*123, 230*n*125, 231, 231*n*128, 233*n*131, 234*n*133, 235*n*142, 236*n*143, 242*n*168, 243*n*169, 243*n*170, 277*n*50, 337*n*7, 338*n*13, 338*n*14, 339*n*17, 341*n*26, 456*n*8

Uro, Risto   32*n*79, 40*n*110, 42*n*120, 43*n*123, 44*n*124, 45, 45*n*131, 46*n*131, 46*n*133, 46*n*133, 160*n*21, 167*n*45, 171*n*66, 390, 390*n*18, 469*n*70

Valette-Cagnac, Emmanuelle   30*n*72

Vandenberghe, Marijn   78*n*27, 248*n*194, 273*n*38

Vandendorpe, Christian   97*n*108

VanderKam, James C.   76*n*16, 82*n*47, 85*n*61, 86*n*62, 87*n*70, 93*n*91, 104*n*134, 111*n*166, 182*n*112, 183*n*115, 202*n*8, 301*n*18, 310*n*56, 337*n*7, 337*n*8, 360*n*9

Vanonen, Hanna   101*n*119

Vaux, Roland de   91*n*82, 105*n*137, 203, 203*n*10, 203*n*11, 203*n*14, 204, 206, 206*n*26, 219*n*92, 227*n*115, 296*n*3, 300*n*12, 303*n*28, 306, 306*n*44, 310*n*59, 318–319, 318*n*98, 319*n*99, 319*n*103, 320*n*104, 321*n*107, 322*n*110, 322*n*112, 324, 324*n*120, 325, 325*n*123, 325*n*124, 438–439, 439*n*92, 439*n*93

Vegge, Tor   16*n*28

Venbrux, Eric   166*n*43

Vermès, Géza   100*n*117, 207*n*30, 221*n*100, 237*n*148, 237*n*149, 238*n*150, 239–240, 239*n*151, 239*n*154, 240*n*155, 240*n*157,

240*n*158, 240*n*159, 241*n*160, 241*n*163, 241*n*164, 244*n*175, 245*n*182, 245*n*183, 245*n*184, 247*n*190, 248, 248*n*194, 249*n*200, 251*n*208, 315*n*85, 338*n*11, 371, 371*n*34, 428*n*51

Vincent, Louis-Hugues   306*n*40

Viviano, Benedict T.   93*n*91

Vleeming, Sven P.   309*n*55

Voitila, Anssi   105*n*141

Voorst, Robert E. Van   474*n*8

Vroom, Jonathan   408*n*75

Wachtel, Klaus   19*n*35, 19*n*37

Walfish, Barry   137*n*7

Walker-Ramisch, Sandra   420–421, 420*n*15, 421*n*22

Wallensten, J.   424*n*39

Wallraff, Martin   21*n*42, 22*n*46

Walton, Steve   228*n*118

Wansbrough, Henry   135*n*2, 363*n*16, 468*n*65

Warner, Daniel A.   423*n*34

Warni, Randi R.   159*n*20

Wassén, Cecilia   5, 82*n*48, 91*n*84, 93*n*90, 93*n*92, 93*n*93, 94*n*93, 94*n*97, 102*n*125, 103, 103*n*128, 103*n*129, 103*n*130, 110*n*161, 171*n*67, 172*n*67, 172*n*68, 179*n*100, 179*n*101, 180*n*103, 205*n*22, 342*n*33, 347*n*57, 375*n*51, 389*n*13, 405*n*65, 407*n*73, 418*n*9, 427*n*49, 431*n*65, 441*n*100, 442*n*105, 460, 460*n*29, 460*n*30, 463*n*42, 464*n*43, 464*n*44, 482–483

Wasserman, Emma   372*n*41

Wasserman, Tommy   20*n*39, 474*n*9

Wasserstein, David J.   110*n*161

Watts, James W.   42*n*115, 166*n*45, 176, 176*n*90, 177*n*91

Weeden, Theodore J.   26*n*59

Weigold, Matthias   167*n*47

Weinberg, Gisela   74*n*10, 74*n*11

Weinfeld, Moshe   420–421, 420*n*16

Weinhold, Jan   163*n*33

Weiss, Zeev   170*n*59

Weissenberg, Hanne von   82*n*48, 317, 317*n*94

Weissenrieder, Annette   24*n*53, 145*n*53

Weitzman, Steven   167*n*47, 181*n*108, 302, 302*n*24, 309, 309*n*51, 309*n*52, 309*n*54, 313*n*74

Wenham, Gordon J.   15*n*21

INDEX OF MODERN AUTHORS

Werline, Rodney A.   166n45, 167n45, 167n47, 468n68
Werrett, Ian   94n93, 169n57, 170n59, 180n105, 342n33, 408n75
White, Benjamin L.   35n90
White, Claire   163n32, 163n36
White, Hayden   278, 279n57
White, Leonard E.   365n21
White Crawford, Sidnie   18n34, 91n84, 93n90, 93n92, 93n93, 94n93, 94n95, 94n97, 99n115, 106n144, 107n147, 108n150, 110n161, 204, 204n18, 204n19, 205n22, 205n24, 206–207, 206n27, 207n33, 257, 257n215, 337n7, 342n33, 347n57, 361n10, 418, 418n10, 418n11, 419n12
Whitehouse, Harvey   46, 46n32, 157, 158n8, 163n33, 171, 389n15, 405n66
Wilde, Clare   227n117
Wiley, Henrietta L.   170n59
Williams, Alex   348, 348n63
Williams Jr., Prescott H.   15n21
Williams, Travis B.   1n2, 2, 3, 276n49, 286, 362n14, 372n41, 406n68, 445, 453, 453n2, 453n3, 455n5, 455n6, 460, 460n28, 461, 461n31, 462n33, 479, 483n33, 495n18, 503n45
Williamson, Hugh G. M.   11n7, 18n32
Wills, Lawrence M.   80n40
Wilmot, David   300
Wilson, Brian   420n15
Wilson, Ian D.   35n88, 38n99
Winninge, Mikael   82n48
Wise, Michael O.   14n18, 15n22, 77n24, 89n75, 89n76, 93n91, 111n165, 138, 138n15, 199n2, 203n12, 208, 208n41, 211–212, 211n56, 211n57, 212n58, 212n60, 212n61, 212n62, 215, 216n75, 216n76, 227n117, 228, 256, 300, 300n13, 301n22, 309, 309n54, 309n55, 318n96, 326, 326n128, 422n30, 503, 503n46
Wohleb, Leo   28n64

Wold, Benjamin G.   35n90, 276n49, 362n14
Wolff, Timo   74n10, 74n11, 75n13
Wolmarans, J. L. P.   43n123
Wolters, Al   310n56, 310n58, 310n59
Woodward, Scott R.   75n13
Woolf, Greg   494n16, 500n35
Woude, Adam S. van der   237n147
Wright, Benjamin G.   77n25
Wright, Brian J.   29n67
Wright, David P.   38n102, 39n102, 40, 41n112, 167n45
Wright, G. Ernest   203n11
Wright, Jacob L.   42n117
Wright Baker, Henry   219n92, 303, 303n28, 306, 306n43, 306n45, 306n46, 322, 322n111

Xygalatas, Dimitry   398n47, 401n54

Yadin, Yigael   180, 180n104, 335, 336n2, 340n25
Yardeni, Ada   88, 88n74, 215, 268, 268n10
Yardley, John C.   373n43
Yogev, Johnathan   214n69
Yona, Shamir   214n69
Young, Frances M.   44n125
Young, Ian M.   14n19, 98n112
Youtie, H. C.   498n29
Yuh, Jason N.   46n134

Zahn, Molly M.   272n32, 337n9, 393n25
Zangenberg, Jürgen   344, 344n39, 344n40, 344n41, 344n42
Zetterholm, Magnus   180n103
Zias, Joe   75n13
Zimmerman, Reuben   36n96, 484, 484n37
Zissu, Boaz   314n81
Zsellengér, József   362n14
Zumthor, Paul   18n31
Zurawski, Jason M.   102n126, 103n127, 112n169

Index of Ancient Sources

Jewish Scriptures

Genesis

1:1–2:4a	366
1:5	366–367, 371
1:8	366
1:13	366
1:14	366–367
1:16	366–367
1:18	366–367
1:19	366
1:23	366
1:31	366
2:2	366
2:3	366
27:19–21	107
48:1–11	107n146

Exodus 301

13:9	185
16	400
19:10–11	443n108

Leviticus

12–15	185
15	408

Numbers

6	372

Deuteronomy

6:6–9	11, 395
14:22–26	313
27	178
27–30	409
29:17–20	178
33:9	235

Joshua

1:8	395

Ruth 8n46

1 Kings 301

2 Kings 301

1 Chronicles 301

15:16	403
15:28	403

2 Chronicles 301

Nehemiah

12:17	403

Psalms 98, 296, 340

81:10	403
147:9	403

Qohelet 8n46

Canticles 8n46

Isaiah 201, 213, 215, 224, 228, 243

1:10–28:22	223
1:10–29:8	223
2:1–14:24	224
7:14–15	226
8:11–14	226
10:14	403
13:18	233
14:28–15:2	225
23:12	223
28:26–29:9	224
33:16–17	223
40:3	440
42:4–11	226
42:14–25	223
43:1–4	223
43:16–24	223
45:20–58:7	223
56:7–57:8	224
58:13–14	226
59:15–16	224n111
61:3–6	226

Lamentations 8n46, 296

Ezekiel 296

Daniel 311

3:5	311n63
3:7	311n63
3:10	311n63
3:15	311n63
7	442

Nahum

1:4	274

Habakkuk 370

1:13	142n38
2:4b	142n38

Jewish Apocrypha

Ben Sira

Prol. 30	210n50

Tobit

1:8	379n67

INDEX OF ANCIENT SOURCES

Jewish Pseudepigrapha

1 Enoch

1–36	442

Jubilees 79, 184, 279–280, 296

12.25–27	313

Testament of Judah

25.1–3	313

Treatise of the Vessels 301, 308, 309n50

Dead Sea Scrolls and Judaean Desert Discoveries

1QHᵃ	74, 143n39, 173, 231n126, 442
4:36	441
5:12–14	176
5:35–36	441
6:23–24	441
10	403
10:12	403n59
10:22–32	403–404
11:22–23	443n106
11:22–24	443
13:11	441n101
13:28	441n101
1QIsaᵃ	88, 218, 219n92, 220n96, 221, 223, 230–236, 230n123, 234n133, 242, 254, 256, 369, 482
10:15	232
11:25–26	233
28:18–19	231
28:19a–19b	232
28:19–20	231
28:25	231
30:10–11b	231
30:10–12	231
32:12–14	232
32:14	231, 231n126, 232
33:7	231–232, 232n129, 234–236, 235n136, 235n137, 235n138
33:14–16	231–232
33:19	231–232
35:15	236n143
40:13	231
40:21	231
40:29	231
44:15	231
49:26	231–232
54:15	231
54:16	231

1QpHab (Pesher Habakkuk) 142, 233, 256, 268n7, 271–272, 276, 281–282, 286n84, 370

2:2–3	441
2:5–10	280, 282
2:7–10	441
2:8–9	280
2:13–14	282
4:5	282
4:10–12	282
5:10	142n38
6:11–12	233
6:12–7:18	282
7:1	281
7:1–5	441
1QS	3, 84, 84n58, 88, 99–100, 143n39, 175, 178, 201–202, 204, 206, 207n30, 208, 215n72, 231–238, 231n126, 236n146, 237n147, 237n149, 240–246, 242n167, 242n168, 245n181, 249, 251–252, 253n209, 254–255, 285, 286n84, 338, 375n55, 401, 409, 415–416, 417n5, 428, 434, 441, 466, 482
1:1–5	247
1:16–2:18	178
1:16–3:12	172, 178, 178n97
1:17–18	399
1:24–26	138n16
1–4	241
2	183
2:5–6	183n114
2:8–9	183n114
2:12–14	376
2:14	235n140
2:19–23	391, 401
2:19–25a	178
2:21	235n139
2:22	180
2:24	235n137, 235n140

1QpHab (Pesher Habakkuk) (*cont.*)

2:25b–3:12	178
2:26	235*n*140
3:1	235*n*137
3:1–12	409
3:2	235*n*140
3:4	235*n*137
3:4–6	250
3:6	235*n*140
3:7–12	247
3:9	235*n*138
3:12–4:26	399
3:15	235*n*137
3:16	235*n*137
3:17–18	393
3–4	392
4	409
4:2	403*n*59
4:21	235*n*138
4:22	441–442
4:23c–26	393
4:24–26	393
5	479
5:1–22	394
5:2	149
5:7c–9a	138*n*16
5:11	235*n*140
5:13	170, 429
5:14	235, 235*n*140
5:17	235*n*136
5:26–6:5	244
5–7	250, 349, 417*n*5
6	179, 431, 433, 479
6:1–2	204
6:1–4	417
6:1b–7a	138*n*16
6:1–8	417*n*5
6:2–3	394, 415, 430–431
6:2–5	433
6:2b–8	433–434
6:3	434
6:3b	179
6:3–4	427
6:3–7	434
6:4	235*n*137, 235*n*140, 431, 433*n*76
6:4c–5	179
6:6–7	395

6:6–7a	395*n*34
6:6–8	111, 371, 394, 434, 438
6:6b–13a	138*n*16, 149–150
6:7	479
6:7–8	363, 438–439, 444
6:7b–8a	138, 138*n*15
6:8	235*n*137
6:8–11	430, 435
6:8–13	150, 434
6:9	235*n*137, 235*n*139
6:9–11a	150
6:9–13	431
6:12	427*n*50
6:13–23	427, 427*n*50
6:13b–23	138*n*16
6:16–21	428
6:20–21	170
6:22	419
6:24–7:25	428
6:25	235*n*136, 428
7:2	235*n*136
7:3	235*n*136
7:4	235*n*136
7:5	235*n*136
7:6	235*n*136
7:6–8	419
7:8	235*n*136
7:8–9:24	244
7:8–9:26	244
7:9	460
7:12	235*n*136
7:13	235*n*136
7:14	235*n*136
7:15	235*n*136
7:16	235*n*136
7:18	235*n*136
7:18–20	170
7:19	235*n*136
7:19–20	430
7:20–21	431
7:21	430
8:14–16	440–441
8:17–19	440–441
9:1	235*n*140
9:3	149
9:4	235*n*138
9:7	151
9:9–10	347*n*56

INDEX OF ANCIENT SOURCES

1QpHab (Pesher Habakkuk) (*cont.*)

9–10	240
10:2	235n140
10:16	235n140
10–11	394
11	242n167
11:7	235n138
11:9	235n138
11:12	235n138
11:14–22	239
11:17	235n140
1Q8 (1QIsa[b])	218, 219n92, 220n96, 221, 223, 223n110, 229, 238–239, 257
1Q11 (1QPs[b])	88n71, 208, 223n109
1Q26 (1QInstruction)	143, 143n39
1Q27 (1QMysteries)	143
1Q28a (1QSa)	84, 88, 102, 215n72, 242, 242n167, 372, 415–416, 434, 443
1:1	433
1:4–5	102
1:6	102
1:7–8	102
1:10	235
1:25–26	443
2:2–9	443
2:10–22	434n77
2:11–22	179
2:17–22	430, 433, 443
2:18–19	242n167
2:22	427, 431, 443
6–8	138n15
1Q28b (1QSb)	84, 88, 215n72, 242, 242n167, 434n77
1Q29a (1QTwo Spirits Treatise?)	236n147
1Q33 (1QM)	99, 143n39, 178, 180, 223n110, 285, 286n84, 466
1:6	282
2:1–6	181
7:3–6	443n107
8	180n104
9:17–14:15	180n104
10:8b–11	442
10:8b–16	442

10–14	180
13:4–6	183
17:8	442
1Q34 (1QPrFetes)	174, 182
3Q1 (3QEzek)	318
3Q2 (3QPs)	318
3Q3 (3QLam)	318
3Q4 (3QpIsa)	284, 318
3Q5 (3QJub)	318
3Q6 (3QHymn)	318
3Q7 (3QTJud?)	318
3Q14 (3QUnidentified)	318
3Q15 (Copper Scroll)	4, 293–328, 482
1:1–2	304, 326
1:9	313, 326
1:9–10	313
3:2–3	313
11:4	313
11:10	313
11:14	313
12:6–7	313
12:10	326
4Q6 (4QGen[f])	106n146, 207
4Q7 (4QGen[g])	366–367, 371
4Q11 (4QpaleoGenesis–Exodus[l])	73n8
4Q16 (4QExod[e])	81n44
4Q30 (4QDeut[c])	218, 230n123
4Q41 (4QDeut[n])	81n44
4Q44 (4QDeut[q])	81n44
4Q51 (4QSam[a])	223n110
4Q53 (4QSam[c])	88, 207n30, 235, 237n149
4Q55 (4QIsa[a])	218, 221, 223, 229, 238–239, 257
4Q56 (4QIsa[b])	218, 221–223, 228–229, 238–239, 243, 255–256
4Q57 (4QIsa[c])	88n71, 208, 218, 221–223, 223n109, 229, 257
4Q58 (4QIsa[d])	218, 221, 223, 229, 238–239, 257
4Q59 (4QIsa[e])	218, 221, 224

4Q60 (4QIsa^f)	218, 221, 223
4Q61 (4QIsa^g)	218, 221, 223, 229, 255, 257
4Q62 (4QIsa^h)	218, 221, 224–226, 244, 244*n*179, 255
4Q62a (4QIsa^i)	219, 221, 227, 240, 255
4Q63 (4QIsa^j)	219, 221, 225, 255
4Q64 (4QIsa^k)	219, 221, 224–226, 244*n*179, 255
4Q65 (4QIsa^l)	219, 221, 225–226, 255
4Q66 (4QIsa^m)	219, 221, 225–226, 244*n*179, 255
4Q67 (4QIsa^n)	219, 221, 225–226, 244*n*179, 255
4Q68 (4QIsa^o)	219, 221, 225–226, 243, 244*n*179, 255
4Q69 (4QpapIsa^p)	76, 219, 220*n*97, 221–222
4Q69a (4QIsa^q)	219, 220*n*96
4Q69b (4QIsa^r)	219, 220*n*96
4Q83 (4QPs^a)	81, 87
4Q85 (4QPs^c)	81
4Q87 (4QPs^e)	81
4Q89 (4QPs^g)	81*n*44
4Q98 (4QPs^q)	81
4Q98g (4QPs^x)	106
4Q109 (4QQoh^a)	82*n*46, 87, 242*n*168
4Q161 (4QpIsa^a)	268, 268*n*7
8–10 8	282
4Q162 (4QpIsa^b)	233*n*131, 268*n*7
1:4	281
4Q163 (4QpappIsa^c)	268*n*7, 272, 275, 282
4Q165 (4QpIsa^e)	268*n*7, 270*n*18
4Q166 (4QpHos^a)	268, 268*n*7
4Q167 (4QpHos^b)	268, 268*n*7, 272
4Q168 (4QpMic)	268, 268*n*7
4Q169 (4QpNah)	4, 142, 266–287, 268*n*7, 466, 480–482
1–2 3–5	274–275, 282
1–2 7	282
3–4 i 3	282
3–4 i 6–8	275
3–4 iii–iv	268
3–4 iv 2	282
4Q170 (4QpZeph)	268*n*7

4Q171 (4QpPs^a)	268, 268*n*7, 281–282
4Q172 (4QpUnid)	268
4Q174 (4QFlorilegium)	379
1–2 i 15	360
4Q175 (4QTestimonia)	81, 88, 175
17	235
4Q186 (4QHoroscope)	313
4Q201 (4QEn^a ar)	106, 207
4Q217 (4QpapJub?)	78
4Q223 (4QpapJub^h)	76, 78
4Q224 (4QpapJub^h)	76, 78
4Q234 (4QExercitium Calami A)	107, 207
4Q242 (4QPrNab)	215*n*72
4Q246 (4QapocrDan ar)	81*n*44
4Q249 (4QpapCryptic Rule of the Congregation)	245*n*181
4Q251 (4QHalakhah A)	184
4Q255 (4QpapS^a)	76, 207*n*30, 236–238, 247–249, 248*n*194, 252, 253*n*109, 255
2:1–9	178*n*97
4Q256 (4QS^b)	81*n*44, 100, 236–241, 238*n*150, 241*n*160, 244–245, 252, 257, 284
2:1–6	178*n*97
2:12–13	178*n*97
3:1–4	178*n*97
23:2	239
4Q257 (4QpapS^c)	76, 236–239, 241, 245–247, 247*n*191, 252
2:1–8	178*n*97
3:1–14	178*n*97
4Q258 (4QS^d)	81*n*44, 100, 236–241, 238*n*150, 241*n*160, 244, 251–252, 257, 284, 338, 417*n*5
2:5–9	244
2:6	204
2:9–10a	179
7:9	347*n*56
8:9	238*n*150
9:8	238*n*150

INDEX OF ANCIENT SOURCES

4Q259 (4QSᵉ)	100, 175, 236–238, 244–246, 244n181, 252, 252n209, 253n209, 255
2:12	245
3:3–4	245, 247
4Q260 (4QSᶠ)	81n44, 236–238, 240–241, 241n160, 243–244, 245n181, 251, 284
4Q261 (4QSᵍ)	236–238, 249
2a–c	179
4b–5	179
4Q262 (4QSʰ)	236–238, 249–250, 253n210, 255
1:1–4	178n97
4Q263 (4QSⁱ)	236–237, 237n149, 243–244, 253n210, 255
4Q264 (4QSʲ)	81n44, 236–241, 251–252, 255, 257, 284, 285n79
4Q264a (4QHalakah B)	81n44
4Q265 (4QMiscellaneous Rules)	184, 415–416, 416n4, 427, 428, 428n54
4 i 2–ii 2	428
4 i 8	428
4 ii 1–9	427n50
4 ii 6	427n50
4Q266 (4QDᵃ)	
5 ii	438
8 i	427
8 i 6b–9	443n107
8 xiii 11–13	427
9 iii 5–7	103
10 i 5–10	350
10 i 9	350n72
10 i 14–ii 15	428
10 ii 1	428
4Q267 (4QDᵇ)	277n50
3:7	277n50
4Q270 (4QDᵉ)	
2 i 2	277n50
6 ii 8–9	443n107
4Q273 (4QpapDʰ)	76
4Q274 (4QTohorot A)	184, 415, 427n49, 431
4Q274a (4QHarvesting)	184

4Q275 (4QCommunal Ceremony)	183, 416n4
4Q279 (4QFour Lots)	183, 416n4
4Q280 (4QCurses)	183, 243n172
2:2–3	183n114
2:3–4	183n114
4Q284 (4QPurification Liturgy)	183
4Q286 (4QBerᵃ)	176, 183, 399
7 ii 1	183
7 ii 1–5	183
4Q287 (4QBerᵇ)	183
4Q288 (4QBerᶜ)	183
4Q289 (4QBerᵈ)	183
4Q290 (4QBerᵉ)	183
4Q298 (4QcryptA Words of the Maskil)	81n44, 112n169, 245n181
4Q299 (4QMystᵃ)	143, 143n39
4Q300 (4QMystᵇ)	143, 143n39
4Q317 (4Qcryptic A Lunisolar Calendar)	245n181
4Q319 (4QOtot)	175, 244–246, 249, 255
4	247
5	245
4Q321 (4QCal Doc/ Mish B)	81n44
4Q338 (4QGenealogical List?)	107n147
4Q339 (4QList of False Prophets ar)	81n44, 207
4Q340 (4QList of Netinim)	207
4Q341 (4QExercitium Calami C)	107–109, 207
4Q350 (4QAccount)	311
4Q360 (4QExercitium Calami B)	107, 207
4Q365 (4QReworked Pentateuchᶜ)	361, 361n10
4Q375 (4QapocrMosᵃ)	81n44
4Q393 (4QCommunal Confession)	183
4Q396 (4QMMTᶜ)	81n44
4Q398 (4QpapMMTᵉ)	76, 244n181
4Q399 (4QMMTᶠ)	81n44
4Q400 (4QShirShabbᵃ)	173, 181, 216n78, 399
1 i 17	442

INDEX OF ANCIENT SOURCES

4Q400 (4QShirShabb^a) (*cont.*)

1 17	442*n*104
2 1	442*n*104
2 3	442*n*104
2 7	442*n*104
4Q401 (4QShirShabb^b)	173, 181, 399
4Q402 (4QShirShabb^c)	173, 181, 399
4Q403 (4QShirShabb^d)	81, 173, 181, 399
1 14	442*n*104
1 24	442*n*104
4Q404 (4QShirShabb^e)	173, 181, 399
4Q405 (4QShirShabb^f)	173, 181, 399
23 ii 12	442*n*104
4Q406 (4QShirShabb^g)	173, 181, 399
4Q407 (4QShirShabb^h)	173, 181, 399
4Q414 (4QRitual Purification A)	183, 407
4Q415 (4QInstruction^a)	143, 143*n*39
4Q416 (4QInstruction^b)	143, 143*n*39
4Q417 (4QInstruction^c)	143, 143*n*39
4Q418 (4QInstruction^d)	143, 143*n*39
4Q433a (4QpapHodayot-like Text B)	247–249, 248*n*194, 255
4Q444 (4QIncantation)	182
4Q448 (4QApocryphal Psalm and Prayer)	81*n*44
4Q460 (4QNarrative Work and Prayer)	311
4Q464 (4QMultiple Compositions)	
8	313
9	313
4Q471 (4QWar Scroll-like Text B)	181
4Q477 (4QRebukes Reported by the Overseer)	113, 183, 207, 346, 416*n*4
4Q494 (4QM^d)	181
4Q496 (4QpapM^f)	180*n*107, 181
3 i 6	282
4Q497 (4QpapWar Scroll-like Text A)	180*n*107
4Q499 (4QpapHymns/Prayers)	180*n*107
4Q501 (4QapocrLam B)	81*n*44
4Q502 (4QpapRitMar)	183, 241
4Q503 (4QpapDaily Prayers)	174, 181

4Q504 (4QDibHam^a)	87, 173, 181, 242*n*168
4Q505 (4QpapDibHam^b)	173, 174, 180*n*107, 181, 182
4Q506 (4QpapDibHam^c)	173, 180*n*107, 181
4Q507 (4QPrFetes^a)	174, 182
4Q508 (4QPrFetes^b)	174, 182
4Q509 (4QpapPrFetes^c)	174, 180*n*107, 182
4Q510 (4QShir^a)	182, 399–400
1 4–8	400
4Q511 (4QShir^b)	182, 399–400
10 3	400
10 7–9	400, 403
4Q512 (4QRitual Purification B)	183
4Q514 (4QOrdinances^c)	415, 427*n*49, 431
4Q550 (4QprEsth^a ar)	81*n*44, 215*n*72
4Q550a (4QprEsth^b ar)	81*n*44
4Q550c (4QprEsth^d ar)	81*n*44
4Q551 (4QDanSuz? ar)	81*n*44, 106*n*145
4Q560 (4QMagical Booklet)	182
4QMMT	184, 312, 317, 340
4Q(?)Ruth (MS 5441)	82*n*46
5Q3 (5QIsa)	219, 219*n*92, 220*n*96
5Q11	236–237, 237*n*147, 243, 243*n*172
1 i	178*n*97
5Q13 (5QRule)	243*n*172, 416*n*4
5Q14 (5QCurses)	183
6Q18 (6QpapHymn)	182
8Q5 (8QHymn)	182
11Q5 (11QPs^a)	81
11Q11 (11QapocrPs)	182, 216*n*78, 272*n*31, 372, 399
11Q14 (11QM)	88*n*71, 208, 223*n*109
11Q17 (11QShirShabb)	173, 181
11Q19 (11QT^a)	184
11Q29 (11QSerek ha-Yaḥad Fragment?)	236*n*147
CD (Cairo Damascus Document)	99, 415
1:1	378
2:2	378
2:14	378
10–11	397
14:3–6	151
14:3b–12a	138*n*16

INDEX OF ANCIENT SOURCES

531

CD (Cairo Damascus Document) (*cont.*)

14:12–13	419
14:12–17	350
14:20–22	428
15	427n50
15:5b–10a	138n16
15:5–16:5	427
15:15–17	443n107
20:27–30	138n16
20:28	277n50
20:28–30	392
20:32	277n50
KhQ 161	104–105, 205
KhQ 1313	205
Kh 2207	106n144, 205
KhQ 2289	105
KhQOstracon 3	105n137
Masık (Songs of the Sabbath Sacrifice)	173, 181
Mur3 (MurIsa)	219, 220n96, 221, 227–228, 227n116, 256

Philo

Contempl.

40	436
40–63	436
75	437
79	437

Hypoth.

11	489
11.5	435

Legat.

16.115–116	12
31.210	12

Prob.

75–88	489
81–82	437n87
82	438
85–86	435

New Testament

Matthew

20:28	474n9
23:5	467n60

Mark | | 480 |

Luke

1:26–38	442
4:16–17	16

John

7:53–8:11	474n9
21:25	474

Acts

6:9	424
16:1	379n67

Romans

5:1	473

1 Corinthians

8:10	425
11:20–21	436
13:3	473
15:54	473

2 Timothy

1:5	379n67

Josephus

Against Apion

1.1	312
1.60	12
2.193–198	315
2.204	12

Jewish War | 211 |

2.120–161	489
2.129	429, 435
2.136	490
2.138–139	429
2.139	429
2.142	490
2.145	490
2.151	489
2.159	489–490
4.443–50	316
6.282	317
6.390–391	317
7.114–115	317
7.148	317

Jewish Antiquities

15.368–371	317
18.11	489
18.18–22	316, 489
20.262–264	312

Rabbinic

b. 'Abod. Zar.

13a	313

b. B.Bat.

21a	12

b. Bek.

53a	313

b. Šeqal.	
22a	313
b. Yoma	
66a	313
m. 'Abot	
5.21	12
m. Ber.	
6.1	432
m. Ma'aś. Š.	
5.7	313
m. Meg.	
2.2	76
m. Ter.	
9.5	313
Pirkei Avot	
1.1	459
1.1–18	459
Sof.	
1.1–4	76
t. Ma'aś. Š.	
5.1	313
y. Kethub.	
8.32a	12
y. Meg.	
1.71d	76

Early Christian Writings

Acts of Peter	83n55
Augustine	
Conf. 6.3	28
Epistle of Barnabas	
16.4	314n80
Eusebius	
Hist. eccl.	
2.15.1	474n10
4.6.1	314n80
4.6.3	314n80
John Moschus	
Pratum spiritual	
31	82n49
Regular Magistri	
57.4	82n49

Other Greek and Roman Texts and Artefacts

Athenaeus	
Deipn.	
182a	436n83

Cyranides	
First Book	108
Dio Cassius	
Roman History	
69.12–14	314
69.12.1	314n80
69.12.2	314n82
Diodorus Siculus	
4.21.4	494
Galen	
Commentary on Hippocrates, Epidemics III	
17A.576K	496
On My Own Books	496
10	496
11–12	496
42–43	497
Gellius	
Attic Nights	
17.7.5	495
Lindian Chronicle	302
Pausanias	
Description of Greece	
4.26.8	309
Plato	
Phaedrus	373, 377
Pliny the Elder	
Natural History	
4–6	488
5	488
5.45	488
5.73	488
6	488n1
P.Lond.Lit.	
96	83
P.Oxy.	
IV 724	500n34
VI 849	83n55
XVIII 2192	211, 232
XLI 2988	500n34
P.Petaus	
2	498n29
P.Yadin	
52	315
54	311
57	311